Macroeconomic Principles and Problems

Macroeconomic Principles and Problems: A Pluralist Introduction offers a comprehensive overview of the major topics in modern macroeconomics, from mainstream and heterodox perspectives.

This textbook examines the key macroeconomic problems and policy debates facing contemporary society, including economic crises, sustainability, fiscal and monetary policy, government debt, state-led vs. market-led approaches for growth, and unregulated trade vs. protectionism.

Written in an engaging style and focused on real-world examples, this textbook brings macroeconomics to life. Multiple examples of how each economic model works, coupled with critical analysis of the assumptions behind them, enable students to develop a sophisticated understanding of the material. Digital supplements are also available for students and instructors.

Macroeconomic Principles and Problems offers the most contemporary and complete package for any pluralist macroeconomics principles class.

Geoffrey Schneider is Presidential Professor of Economics at Bucknell University, Pennsylvania, U.S.A. He is an award-winning teacher, author or co-author of seven books and numerous scholarly articles, and executive director of the International Confederation of Associations for Pluralism in Economics.

Macroeconomic Principles and Problems
A Pluralist Introduction

Geoffrey Schneider

LONDON AND NEW YORK

Cover image: © Getty Images

First published 2023

by Routledge
4 Park Square, Milton Park, Abingdon, Oxon OX14 4RN

and by Routledge
605 Third Avenue, New York, NY 10158

Routledge is an imprint of the Taylor & Francis Group, an informa business

© 2023 Geoffrey Schneider

The right of Geoffrey Schneider to be identified as author of this work has been asserted in accordance with sections 77 and 78 of the Copyright, Designs and Patents Act 1988.

All rights reserved. No part of this book may be reprinted or reproduced or utilised in any form or by any electronic, mechanical, or other means, now known or hereafter invented, including photocopying and recording, or in any information storage or retrieval system, without permission in writing from the publishers.

Trademark notice: Product or corporate names may be trademarks or registered trademarks, and are used only for identification and explanation without intent to infringe.

British Library Cataloguing-in-Publication Data
A catalogue record for this book is available from the British Library

Library of Congress Cataloging-in-Publication Data
Names: Schneider, Geoffrey Eugene, author.
Title: Macroeconomic principles and problems: a pluralist introduction/Geoffrey Schneider.
Description: Abingdon, Oxon; New York, NY: Routledge, 2022. | Series: Routledge pluralist introductions to economics | Includes bibliographical references and index. |
Identifiers: LCCN 2022015459 (print) | LCCN 2022015460 (ebook) | ISBN 9780367024819 (hardback) | ISBN 9780367024826 (paperback) | ISBN 9780429399350 (ebook)
Subjects: LCSH: Macroeconomics.
Classification: LCC HB172.5 .S36 2022 (print) | LCC HB172.5 (ebook) | DDC 339–dc23/eng/20220406
LC record available at https://lccn.loc.gov/2022015459
LC ebook record available at https://lccn.loc.gov/2022015460

ISBN: 978-0-367-02481-9 (hbk)
ISBN: 978-0-367-02482-6 (pbk)
ISBN: 978-0-429-39935-0 (ebk)

DOI: 10.4324/9780429399350

Typeset in Bembo
by Deanta Global Publishing Services, Chennai, India

I dedicate this book to my pluralist colleagues in economics, who exposed me to the sophisticated ideas embodied in the various approaches to the discipline. In particular, my colleagues at Bucknell University and in the Association for Evolutionary Economics, the Association for Institutional Thought, the Association for Social Economics, the International Association for Feminist Economics, the International Confederation of Associations for Pluralism in Economics, and the Union for Radical Political Economics have been invaluable in my intellectual development and in the development of the ideas that form the core of this book.

Contents

List of figures   *x*
Preface   *xv*
Acknowledgments   *xvii*

PART I
Economics: A pluralist definition   1

1. What is economics? The answer depends on who you ask   3

2. Scarcity, choice, and opportunity cost: The mainstream approach, the PPC model, the limits of this approach, and the importance of institutions   21

PART II
The evolution of economic ideas and systems   41

3. The evolution of economic systems and the ideas of Adam Smith: From communal societies to early capitalism   43

4. Marx, Veblen, and the dark ages of capitalism: Historical materialism, the exploitation of labor, and monopoly capitalism   68

5. Keynes and mixed market capitalism: How to save capitalism from itself   97

6. Modern economic systems: Market-dominated, social market, and state-dominated economies   122

7 Markets and how they work: The institutional foundations of markets and the supply and demand model   144

PART III
Macroeconomic issues and problems   175

8 Modern macroeconomics: The evolution of macroeconomic theory and the macroeconomy in the modern era   177

9 Macroeconomic well-being: Measuring and describing the macroeconomy   204

10 Unemployment and price instability: The major macroeconomic market failures   229

PART IV
Macroeconomic models   259

11 Aggregate demand and aggregate supply: A mainstream economics model of the macroeconomy   261

12 The Keynesian aggregate expenditure–income model: The foundation of modern macroeconomics   287

PART V
Stabilization policy   311

13 Fiscal policy, debt, and deficits: Fiscal activism vs. austerity and the macroeconomic role of government   313

14 Money, banking, and the financial sector: How money markets make the world go around   348

15 Monetary policy: The role of central banks in stabilizing economies and regulating financial markets   375

16 Crises, financial and otherwise: On the causes and consequences of economic crises and how they can be averted   394

PART VI
Growth and global interconnectedness — 419

17 The sources of economic growth — 421

18 International trade and integration: How unregulated trade, protectionism, and trade agreements affect economies — 447

19 International finance and open economy macroeconomics: Exchange rates, financial flows, and the balance of payments — 475

20 Economic development: The barriers facing less developed countries and how they can be overcome — 501

Glossary of key terms and concepts — *525*
Index — *537*

Figures

1.1	U.S. real gross domestic product growth (%) in the modern era (1971–2021)	5
1.2	A typical demand curve	10
1.3	The ten major schools of thought in economics	16
1.4	Different kinds of economics	16
1.5	The size of government in select economies	18
2.1	Production possibilities curve for the U.S. government	25
2.2	Table showing the production possibilities combinations in Figure 2.1	26
2.3	Table showing changes in opportunity cost due to the specialization of resources	28
2.4	A PPC without specialized resources	29
2.5	Shifts in the PPC from changes in resources or technology	30
2.6	Growth in the PPC from additional capital goods	32
2.7	The ten largest military spenders in 2019, plus Iran and North Korea	32
2.8	PPC for problem 3	38
2.9	PPC for problem 4	39
3.1	The first moving assembly line for 1913 Ford cars	57
3.2	Oliver Asking for More, by George Cruikshank	61
3.3	The simple circular flow model of the economy	62
4.1	Addie Card in 1910	71
4.2	Karl Marx (1818–1883)	72
5.1	The circular flow model of the economy, with savings and investment	101
5.2	John Maynard Keynes	102
5.3	Economic instability in the U.S. economy: Real GDP growth per capita, 1890–2021	119
6.1	Table showing key data on selected MDEs and SMEs	126
6.2	OECD Better Life and UN Human Development rankings, 2019	126
6.3	Table showing hourly compensation costs in manufacturing, 2017	134
7.1	The price of a barrel of crude oil ($), 2000–2021	145
7.2	The ten largest pizza companies in 2019	154

7.3	A graph of the supply and demand model for pizzas	155
7.4	Prices adjust to eliminate surpluses or shortages	156
7.5	The quantity of pizza demanded per month at each price	158
7.6	Demand curves for Kate, Juan, Bo, and the market	159
7.7	A shift in demand to the right (increase in demand). (a) Shift in demand to the right. (b) Change in equilibrium from a rightward shift	160
7.8	A shift in demand to the left (decrease in demand). (a) Shift in demand to the left. (b) Change in equilibrium from a leftward shift in D	162
7.9	A decrease in the price of a substitute good (gas) causes a decrease in demand (oil). (a) Increase in supply & decrease in the prices of gas. (b) Decrease in D for heating oil when the price of a substitute decreases.	163
7.10	Table showing the quantity of pizza supplied per month at each price	166
7.11	Supply curves for Pizza Hut, Domino's, and the market for pizzas	166
7.12	Equilibrium where $Q_S = Q_D$	167
7.13	A shift in supply to the left (decrease in supply). (a) Shift in supply to the left. (b) Change in equilibrium from a leftward shift in S	169
7.14	A shift in supply to the right (increase in supply). (a) Shift in supply to the right. (b) Change in equilibrium from a rightward shift in S	169
8.1	Table showing average annual growth rates of key U.S. macroeconomic variables	183
8.2	Table showing average annual growth of real GDP per capita in regions, 1961–2018	189
8.3	Annual U.S. real GDP growth, 1970–2020	194
8.4	U.S. real GDP and potential real GDP (billions of $), 1979–2019	195
8.5	U.S. unemployment rate (%) and rate of inflation (CPI_U, %), 1979–2020	196
9.1	Table showing U.S. nominal GDP, real GDP, and the GDP deflator, 2000–2020	208
9.2	U.S. nominal GDP and real GDP, 2000–2020 (billions of $)	208
9.3	The circular flow model of the economy	210
9.4	Table of U.S. nominal GDP, by component of aggregate demand, 2020	212
9.5	(a) National income by type of income. (b) Gross value added by sector	212
9.6	Various measures of U.S. national income and national product	213
9.7	Completion of paid and unpaid work by men and women	216
9.8	OECD Better Life Index	220
9.9	Better Life Index for the United States and Norway	221
9.10	Table showing the U.S. real genuine progress indicator	224
9.11	Table showing the top 15 OECD countries, GDP vs. GPI, 2013	224
9.12	Table showing World Happiness Index rankings	225
9.13	Table for problem 7	227
10.1	Civilian unemployment rate (%), various groupings, 1950–2021	233
10.2	United States cyclical and natural rates of unemployment (%), 1948–2021	235

FIGURES

10.3	Labor force participation rates, select OECD countries, 2018	239
10.4	Monthly rate of inflation and deflation, 2000–2021	244
10.5	Median usual weekly earnings for wage and salary workers, 1979–2020	245
10.6	Nominal and real return on 10-year Treasury Bills, 1989–2020	246
10.7	A one hundred trillion dollar bank note from Zimbabwe in 2008	250
10.8	The money supply and inflation, 2000–2020	253
10.9	The U.S. Phillips curve, 1960–1969 and 2000–2020	255
11.1	A typical aggregate demand and aggregate supply graph	263
11.2	The slope of the aggregate supply curve	265
11.3	An increase in aggregate demand	267
11.4	Table showing the determinants of shifts in aggregate demand	268
11.5	An increase in aggregate supply	269
11.6	Table showing the determinants of shifts in aggregate supply	269
11.7	The impact of an appreciation of the dollar on U.S. prices and real GDP	270
11.8	A shift in aggregate demand with the multiplier	274
11.9	(a) AD shift when AS is flat and (b) AD shift when AS is upward-sloping	274
11.10	The long-run equilibrium at LRAS (PRGDP)	276
11.11	(a) A recessionary gap and (b) An inflationary gap	276
11.12	(a) Recessionary gap elimination (classical model) and (b) Inflationary gap elimination (classical model)	278
11.13	A political economy aggregate demand and aggregate supply graph	282
11.14	AD–AS graph	285
12.1	U.S. real disposable income and real consumer spending, 2002–2020	289
12.2	(a) DI, C, and S (billions of $), (b) Consumption ($C$) and savings ($S$) functions	290
12.3	The components of aggregate expenditure at each level of real GDP (billions of $)	292
12.4	Construction of the aggregate expenditure curve, $AE = C + I + G + X - IM$	294
12.5	Keynesian equilibrium: Aggregate expenditure = Real GDP	296
12.6	Injections ($I + G + X$) and leakages ($S + T + IM$)	298
12.7	The determinants of shifts in the aggregate expenditure curve	299
12.8	Shifts in the aggregate expenditure curve from autonomous changes in AE	300
12.9	Shifts in the aggregate expenditure curve from a change in MRR	301
12.10	A recessionary gap (equilibrium real GDP < potential real GDP)	302
12.11	An inflationary gap (equilibrium real GDP > potential real GDP)	304
12.12	The correspondence between aggregate expenditure and aggregate demand	305
12.13	Y, DI, and C	308
12.14	Table of AE and its components for problem 2	308
12.15	Graph of AE and Y for problems 3 and 5	309

FIGURES

13.1	Table of U.S. federal government spending, 2019	316
13.2	Table showing U.S. state and local government spending, 2017	318
13.3	Total U.S. government spending as a percentage of GDP, 1948–2020 (Q1)	319
13.4	U.S. government employment as a percentage of total employment, 1939–2020	319
13.5	Table of general government expenditures as a percentage of GDP, 2018	320
13.6	Sources of tax revenue as a percentage of total U.S. government revenue, 1940–2019	320
13.7	U.S. average tax rates by income group in 2018 (% of pretax income)	322
13.8	Automatic stabilization of shocks to household income by country, 2019	323
13.9	Fixing a recessionary or inflationary gap with fiscal policy	326
13.10	Federal budget deficit or surplus, 1970–2020	332
13.11	Total U.S. national debt held by the public, 1970–2020	333
13.12	U.S. public debt as a percentage of GDP, 1970–2020	334
13.13	Table showing national debt as a percentage of GDP, various developed countries, 2020	334
13.14	U.S. net national saving, personal saving, and budget deficit as a percentage of GDP (1950–2019)	338
13.15	U.S. Treasury debt held by other countries in 2019	338
13.16	CARES Act of 2020 major spending categories	343
13.17	Fiscal and monetary responses to the COVID-19 recession as a percentage of GDP	343
13.18	Aggregate demand and supply problem	345
14.1	An ancient French tally stick and ancient Chinese coins	350
14.2	M1 and M2 (billions of $)	355
14.3	(a) Table of a bank T-account and (b) Table of the effect of a deposit on reserves	356
14.4	The mainstream model of the money market	360
14.5	(a) An increase in money demand and (b) An increase in money supply	362
14.6	The political economy model of an increase in the money supply (M1)	364
14.7	A hybrid model of the money market	366
14.8	Shiller CAPE price/E10 ratio, 1881–2020	369
15.1	Effective federal funds rate and primary credit (discount) rate (%), 2004–2020	381
15.2	Total assets held by the Fed (millions of $), 2003–2020	382
15.3	(a) An increase in money supply and (b) The goal of expansionary monetary policy	384
15.4	Velocity of money in the United States, 2000–2021	390
15.5	An inflationary gap at point **a** and its elimination	392
16.1	Profit rate and capital accumulation (Bakir), 1960–2018	399

16.2	Stagflation from a supply shock	400
16.3	Asset bubbles (% of peak value)	408
16.4	Flow of private MBSs and CMOs	410
16.5	Ten-year minus two-year Treasury spread, 1987–2020	414
17.1	Average annual growth of real GDP per capita, 1980–2019	425
17.2	Change in a country's production function from an increase in capital ($K_2 > K_1$)	427
17.3	Table showing the Global Innovation Index rankings, 2020	432
17.4	Educational spending as a percentage of GDP, various countries	433
17.5	The U.S. environmental Kuznets curve for CO_2, 1800–2016	440
17.6	Real GDP per capita and CO_2 emissions per capita, 2019	442
17.7	Production function for the United States	445
18.1	Production possibilities curves for the United States and Mexico	451
18.2	Consumption possibilities curves for the United States and Mexico	452
18.3	The effect of a 100% tariff	460
18.4	Table showing the top U.S. trading partners, 2017 and 2019	461
18.5	Table of largest value export and import products for the United States, 2019	462
18.6	PPCs for the United States and Kuwait	473
18.7	PPCs for Japan and the United States	473
19.1	(a) The foreign exchange market for U.S. dollars and (b) U.S. assets become more attractive	478
19.2	(a) Increase in incomes in Europe and (b) Interest rates in euro area increase	481
19.3	Table showing the two sides of the balance of payments	485
19.4	U.S. current account	485
19.5	Largest U.S. trade deficits, 2019	486
19.6	U.S. financial account	486
19.7	U.S. financial account and current account, 1960–2020 (millions of $)	487
19.8	Savings rates of U.S. trading partners	489
19.9	U.S. dollars per euro, 2016–2021	493
19.10	(a) Actions to increase the value of the yen, (b) Increase in interest rates in Japan, (c) Actions to decrease the value of the yen, and (d) Decrease in interest rates in Japan	494
20.1	Table of the Human Development Index (HDI), select countries, 2019	504
20.2	Table showing the human development of various regions of the world in 2019	505
20.3	Table showing goods and services with high and low income elasticities	509
20.4	Percentage change in commodity prices from 1900 to 2015	510

Preface

In 2008, the housing bubble and financial crisis confounded mainstream economists. Only a few of them predicted the meltdown was coming, and most were caught completely surprised.

Interestingly, large numbers of political economists who were not part of the mainstream, including this author, spotted the real estate bubble, anticipated the financial crisis, and advised their friends and colleagues to pull their money out of financial markets prior to the collapse. What did political economists know that mainstream economists did not?

First, political economists drew on the lessons of economic history. There are numerous examples demonstrating that the deregulation of financial markets encourages speculative behavior, which can lead to spectacular booms and equally spectacular busts. The Great Depression of the 1930s, the Savings and Loan Crisis of the 1980s, and the Asian Financial Crisis of the 1990s all featured deregulated lenders taking incredible risks with other people's money. Similarly, the deregulation of financial markets in the 1980s and 1990s paved the way for the Great Financial Crises of 2008–2010, which sparked the Great Recession. Studying the evolution of economic systems is particularly helpful in predicting when conditions are ripe for the next crisis.

Second, political economists drew on the economic ideas of Keynes, Marx, and Veblen, among others—economists who studied the roots of economic crises carefully and had much to say on the topic. Meanwhile, most mainstream economists were utilizing mathematical models that assumed that markets would always be rational and efficient and could never experience a crisis.

Thus, the analysis of the evolution of economic systems and a broader knowledge of economic ideas could have saved the profession from the embarrassment it suffered in 2008. Even more surprising, perhaps, is the fact that most mainstream principles of economics texts still ignore economic history and some of the major economists whose ideas were most useful in predicting the housing bubble and the financial crisis. This book seeks to remedy those omissions.

More specifically, most current principles of macro economics textbooks cover only mainstream economics, ignoring the rich ideas of the heterodox schools of thought. They also tend to lack material on the great economists, so readers usually leave the introductory course without learning in depth about who Adam Smith, Karl Marx, Thorstein Veblen, Joseph Schumpeter, John Maynard Keynes, and Friedrich Hayek were and why their ideas and philosophies are important to the modern world.

Mainstream books are also missing the kind of historical analysis that is crucial to understanding trends and patterns that can help us predict the future. In addition, they tend to focus more on abstract models rather than on existing economic realities.

This book attempts to addresses these inadequacies. The book includes explicit coverage of the major heterodox schools of thought, and the book includes the mainstream economics models that form the core of the discipline. This allows the reader to choose which ideas they find most compelling in explaining modern economic realities.

This book is intended to give you a broader background that will help save you from the tunnel vision that infected mainstream economics in recent decades. By understanding the evolution of economic systems and the ideas of the great economists, you will be better prepared to confront the complex realities of the modern world. By understanding multiple views of markets and how they work, you will gain a more sophisticated understanding of the functioning of a market economy. This will help you better understand the behavior of firms, consumers, and government officials.

As you approach this material, it is important to keep an open mind. All of the major economists you will read about in this book were brilliant, and their ideas are worth studying. Each of them has devoted followers among modern economists. Your task is to consider all of these ideas and then, observing the world around you, decide which ideas make the most sense in understanding our modern economic system.

Acknowledgments

I would like to thank all of the research assistants who helped with the writing of this book. Those research assistants include Spandan Marasini, James Weissenborn, Marissa DiPalo, Kailyn Angelo, Nghia (TN) Doan, James Elmendorf, Colin Randles, Kathryn Tomasi, Katelyn Schneider, Jingyi Zhou and many others.

I would also like to thank my mentors who stimulated my interest in a broad-based, pluralistic approach to economics. In graduate school, William (Sandy) Darity and Vincent Tarascio taught pluralistically, embodying the values that I came to embrace. My colleagues at Bucknell University also provided a rich, engaging environment where our regular discussions of how to develop a pluralistic course and curriculum were invigorating. My regular collaborators on writing projects were particularly instrumental in developing a pluralistic approach, including Charles Sackrey, Janet Knoedler, Jean Shackelford, Berhanu Nega, Erdogan Bakir, Nina Banks, Paul Susman, and Steve Stamos. I am also deeply indebted to a number of economists whose ideas I draw on heavily in this book. In particular, Karl Polanyi's masterwork *The Great Transformation* looms large, as do the ideas of the great economists Adam Smith, Karl Marx, Thorstein Veblen, and John Maynard Keynes.

A thanks is also due to the staff at Routledge and to Editor Andy Humphries, who made this project possible. And thanks to the many colleagues who offered feedback on the book at various stages, including Nathan Sivers Boyce, Barbara Hopkins, Paula Cole, Zdrvaka Todorova, and Xiao Jiang. James Cypher, Shahram Azhar and Matias Vernengo offered suggestions on the chapter on economic development.

The material in Chapters 1 to 19 was previously published in the book *Economic Principles and Problems: A Pluralist Introduction* (London: Routledge, 2022), by Geoffrey Schneider. That material has been edited and updated for this book and is reused with permission. *Economic Principles and Problems: A Pluralist Introduction* brings together the author's work on principles and problems in both macroeconomics and microeconomics.

PART I
Economics
A pluralist definition

Part I explores several different definitions of what economics is and the different ways in which economists practice the social science of economics (economic methodology).

Chapter 1, What Is Economics?, begins by describing why economic policy matters to the country and to every person. It begins by describing the debate over whether or not politicians should balance their budgets every year given the regular occurrence of **recessions** in the economy (downturns in which unemployment increases and business activity decreases). The chapter then offers four different definitions of economics: one offered by mainstream economists (who tend to advocate a capitalist market system with limited government intervention), one preferred by economists practicing progressive political economics (PPE, which includes institutionalist, social, post-Keynesian, and feminist economists who believe that capitalism can and should be reformed), another from economists who engage in radical political economics (RPE—Marxists and others who believe that **capitalism** is fatally flawed and should be replaced), and a broad definition of pluralistic economics that synthesizes the other definitions.

Chapter 1 then takes up methodology, or how economists attempt to "do" economics. This will give you an idea of what it means to be an economist from the various perspectives—the kind of things you study, what you look for, and how you construct knowledge about the economy. The chapter then goes through a series of short examples so you can see different types of economic analysis in action when economists study consumer behavior, labor markets, and the business cycle. The chapter concludes by briefly laying out the ten different schools of economics that will be discussed in the book.

Chapter 2, Scarcity, Choice, and Opportunity Cost, takes up a simple mainstream economics concept, opportunity costs, and a simple economic model, the production possibilities curve (PPC). The PPC model is applied to several economic issues, including a treatment of defense spending and its impact on economic growth. The chapter concludes with a section on the potential limitations of economic models in capturing economic reality, building on the work of PPE and RPE economists.

What is economics?

The answer depends on who you ask

In his famous book, *The General Theory of Employment, Interest and Money*, John Maynard Keynes said, "The ideas of economists and political philosophers, both when they are right and when they are wrong, are more powerful than is commonly understood. Indeed the world is ruled by little else." This quote highlights the extent to which economic policy is a major determinant of what our lives are like. Economic ideas led the followers of Adam Smith to demand an end to mercantilism and ushered in the beginnings of capitalism in the late 1700s. Karl Marx provoked the masses to strike and revolt against the oppressions of unregulated capitalism in the 1800s. Thorstein Veblen and Keynes provided a vision of regulated, mixed market capitalism that proved compelling in the Great Depression of the 1930s and Friedrich Hayek's critique of bloated bureaucracy helped persuade Ronald Reagan and Margaret Thatcher to reduce the size of government in the 1980s. Economic ideas play a significant role in shaping the type of economic system you live in, which has a major impact on the opportunities you have and the challenges you face.

This is why everyone needs to have a solid understanding of economics. To help you grasp the material, each chapter in this book will begin with a list of learning goals. These goals will help you to focus on the key themes.

1.0 CHAPTER 1 LEARNING GOALS

After reading this chapter you should be able to:

■ Explain in your own words the importance of economics for you and for society as a whole.

■ Briefly contrast unregulated market capitalism with mixed market capitalism.

DOI: 10.4324/9780429399350-2

- Describe the difference between mainstream economics, progressive political economy (PPE), and radical political economy (RPE), using their different definitions of economics and their different methods.

- Explain and begin to apply the methods of mainstream, PPE, and RPE economists to economic issues.

- Understand how the ten different schools of economics match up with conservative, moderate, liberal, and radical political approaches to the economy.

Note that there are a lot of new ideas in this chapter. However, the topics in this chapter will become clearer as the book progresses, so do not feel like you need to get all of the details down now. Instead, work to grasp the basic ideas and gain a general understanding of the material.

1.1 WHY ECONOMICS MATTERS: ECONOMIC POLICY

Economics is a crucial subject that every educated voter and politician should understand. To show this, we begin with a brief example of how economic debates and a government's economic policy can matter to us all. As we go through this book, it is especially important for you to try to understand all of the different views of the various schools of economic thought that we will be studying. Understanding their differences teaches us more about this subject than any other way we might study it. As you read through this first example, and as a general rule while going through this book, take the time to try to figure out the meaning of each part of each section, including the key terms that are used, what they mean, and how they work.

Let's begin by taking a look at a government policy called **austerity**, **where governments reduce or eliminate social programs like food stamps, unemployment insurance, and education in order to balance the government budget** (they try to balance the incoming tax revenues with the spending amounts going out). Political leaders around the world regularly make the argument that the government should balance its budget each year, spending no more than it takes in via tax revenue. Such a policy is frequently justified by folksy expressions such as, "if households balance their checkbooks, then the government should balance its budget." And this policy is sometimes supported by a few "crank" economists who are, in general, opposed to any type of government intervention. (These economists can be labeled "cranks" because their views have been dismissed by the vast majority of the economics profession.) The problem is that an obsession with balancing the government budget each and every year could cause an economic disaster. Here is a brief explanation for why it is a bad idea to try and balance the government budget when a recession hits.

In the modern United States, the economy tends to hit a major crisis, called a recession, every 8 to 12 years. As you can see in Figure 1.1, the United States experienced recessions beginning in 1980, 1990, 2000, 2008, and 2020, when the U.S. real gross domestic product, which is the total output of goods and services, declined.[1] A recession is usually sparked by a major panic of some sort, such as the financial crisis of 2007–2008 when stock markets plunged, banks failed, and the global economy shrank considerably. After a financial market collapse, businesses and consumers become pessimistic. Businesses lay off workers and consumers stop spending. This reduces overall spending in the economy, which reduces the incomes of both workers and business owners.

Reduced incomes in the economy mean that governments take in less tax revenue from income and sales taxes and that the government will start running a large budget deficit because tax revenues will have fallen below the level of government spending. How should the government respond to the fact that a recession caused a decline in incomes, which caused a decline in tax revenues and an increase in the government deficit? If the government decides to balance the government budget right away, then it must either raise taxes or cut spending, an economic policy called **austerity**. But—and here is where the crucial knowledge of economics comes in—*austerity will not succeed in balancing the budget in a recession!*

Here is why: If a nation's economy is in a recession, and if its government responds by raising taxes and cutting government spending, then the result will be that consumers and businesses have even *less* money to spend than before.

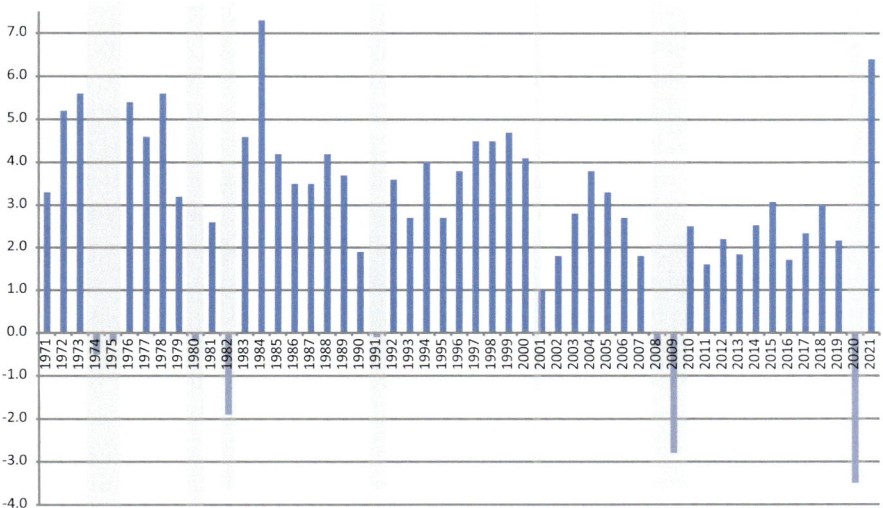

FIGURE 1.1 U.S. real gross domestic product growth (%) in the modern era (1971–2021).

Raising taxes directly reduces the money consumers and businesses have to spend. Reducing government spending directly reduces incomes: Teachers and other government personnel are laid off, construction firms see less revenue from building fewer roads and bridges, and so on. Therefore, cutting government spending and raising taxes directly reduce income and spending. Also, the decline in incomes and spending means additional reductions in tax revenues from income and sales taxes, making the government deficit *worse*! Thus, as any student of economics should know, trying to balance a government budget in a recession via austerity makes the recession worse, which usually makes the government deficit worse, not better.

Furthermore, even though it seems counterintuitive, governments can actually improve the deficit situation over the long term by spending more in a recession and running larger deficits! If the government cuts taxes and increases spending when a recession hits, which means running a larger budget deficit, it directly increases the incomes of consumers and the revenues of businesses. This leads consumers to spend more money and businesses to hire more people, raising incomes further and increasing tax revenues in the process. By stimulating economic growth, government spending and tax cuts can help to pay for themselves. After the COVID-19 recession hit in March 2020, the U.S. government spent more than $5 trillion on various types of stimulus programs, as we will study later. The result was a dramatic rebounding of the economy in late 2020 and 2021. By 2022 the U.S. economy was growing so quickly it was considered to be overheated! (Before you go on, try reading back through the last two paragraphs until you understand the material. They contain a number of terms that we will deal with all semester.)

There are some major lessons to be learned from these examples. First, what seems to be logical to most people (balancing one's budget every year) can fly in the face of what economists have learned. For example, the best way to combat a recession is for the government to increase spending, cut taxes, and inject money into the banking system to promote lending. Even though this will increase government deficits in the short term, it will likely stimulate economic growth, which will actually reduce deficits over the long term once economic growth is restored. However, efforts to balance the government budget in a recession via austerity will not work. When a recession hits, incomes and spending fall, and that reduces tax revenues, leading to substantial government deficits. If the government responds by raising taxes and cutting spending (austerity), this makes a fragile economy even worse, slowing economic growth, reducing incomes and tax revenues further, resulting in even more deficits.

Second, our example demonstrates that economics is an uncertain field, and there is much disagreement between economists from the different economic schools of thought. This means that it is usually possible for politicians to find support for their ideas, no matter how bad those ideas are. Politicians frequently seize on bad ideas from crank economists because those ideas support their political perspective, even though most of the economics profession would consider those ideas to be ridiculous. This was certainly true of austerity policies, which have been promoted recently by a few crank economists but opposed by most economists.

Your job, as you read through this book, is to understand and evaluate the best ideas that economists have about how the economy works and what economic policies should be used in certain situations. However, we need to avoid making the mistake that some politicians do when they listen only to the economists who say what they want to hear. Instead, critically evaluate the ideas of all the economists you study, assess the available evidence, and develop your own perspective regarding which economic ideas best explain the world you see around you. The world is desperately in need of economically literate people who will call politicians on their craziest economic ideas. You will find that a solid understanding of the economy will help you in your personal life as well.

1.2 HOW DOES THE ECONOMY AFFECT YOUR LIFE?

The economy is vitally important to each of us. Consider for a minute the following factors that affect what your life and your community are like:

- An austerity program could slash government funding for financial aid and other programs at your college, resulting in huge increases in tuition and layoffs (possibly of a family member).
- The economic system largely determines whether you get enough food to eat, the various kinds of opportunities for work that are available to you, what your workday is like, and whether or not our society is equal or unequal.
- Major economic events, such as financial crises, economic booms, and shifts in major industries, can have a huge influence on your life and your community.
- The functioning of the global economy determines what the planet is like, including how much pollution there is and whether beautiful coastlines are owned by particular people or whether they are public parks.
- In the modern economy, businesses produce an ever-changing, ever-expanding quantity of goods and services for sale to people, often using extensive advertising to increase sales.
- Large corporations play a particularly important role in today's global economy, determining what goods are sold, where they are produced, and what future endeavors they think are worth investing in.
- Governments play a major role in establishing the rules of the economic system, shaping what types of economic activities are undertaken—often regulating the behaviors of companies and individuals—and sometimes developing or promoting key industrial sectors.
- Global trade has a significant impact on jobs and communities, promoting growth in some places while undermining it in others.

To study such important topics, the social science of economics developed. Economists seek to understand the above factors and many more. If they can successfully determine how the economy works, economists can then make useful recommendations regarding how the economy can be improved.

The study of the economy can be quite difficult, however. The world economy is extremely complex, involving almost 200 countries, about 8 billion people from culturally diverse backgrounds, and millions of organizations interacting in a variety of situations. Economists are often able to recognize trends and patterns, which can allow us to make accurate predictions. Yet, as is commonly known, economists are frequently wrong in their predictions due to the complex nature of the economy. In other words, economics is an inexact social science. Furthermore, the fact that the study of the economy is uncertain and inexact means that at any given time economists will often disagree with each other over what is happening in the economy and what should be done in order to improve its outcomes.

Economists also disagree over what type of economy we should have. As we will see below, some advocate an economy based on unregulated markets in which private individuals and corporations make most of the economic decisions without the interference of government (unregulated market capitalism). Others tend to see markets as bad for people and the environment, preferring to have workers and a democratically elected government in control of the major economic decisions (democratic socialism). Most economists advocate a middle path between these two perspectives: Mixed market capitalism.

1.3 WHY TAKE A PLURALISTIC APPROACH TO THE STUDY OF ECONOMICS?

Because there are debates and divisions among economists regarding the nature of the economy and the role of public policy in it, this book takes a *pluralistic* approach. **Pluralistic economics** seeks to include the best ideas from all major economic perspectives, while also highlighting the important areas of agreement and disagreement. This book will share the best ideas from a wide variety of economists, and you are tasked with the job of deciding which ideas are most relevant to the world you see around you. For instance, do you think markets are usually efficient and effective, as Adam Smith believed, or do they tend to be ruthless and exploitative as Karl Marx argued? Is government intervention in markets inherently inefficient, as Friedrich Hayek believed, or is government intervention essential to the healthy functioning of markets, as John Maynard Keynes maintained?

One clear way to differentiate between some of the different schools of thought is to consider their definitions of the study of economics.

Mainstream economics (ME) is **the study of how society manages its scarce resources to satisfy individuals' unlimited wants**. To mainstream economists, economics involves studying the costs and benefits of the decisions facing consumers, producers, and governments and making rational choices between alternatives using society's limited resources. Mainstream economists are particularly good at establishing the consistent statistical relationships between economic variables. These ideas can be used to predict, for example, how an increase in the price of gasoline is likely to affect the demand for gasoline or how an increase in consumer spending will affect a country's total income and its unemployment rate and inflation rate. Mainstream economics includes both conservative economists who prefer little government intervention in markets and liberal economists who see government intervention in markets as essential.

Progressive political economics (PPE) is **the study of social provisioning—the economic processes that provide the goods and services required by society to meet the needs of its members**. These economists study culture, history, and **technology** to understand how the economy is evolving over time and how different societies function in distinct ways. Progressive political economists are particularly good at analyzing matters such as how consumers in Germany behave differently than consumers in the United States or how the legal and political systems in a particular country affect their economic system.

Radical political economics (RPE) is **the study of power relations in society, especially conflicts over the allocation of a society's resources by various social classes and how those conflicts cause society to evolve**. Radical political economists see power, conflict, and technology as the major drivers of changes in economic systems. They are particularly good at analyzing how **class** relations affect the economic system and the dynamics of how economic crises form.

If we combine definitions, a pluralist definition of economics would be as follows: **Pluralist economics** is **a social science whose practitioners, from a variety of distinct schools of thought, study economies, how they grow and change, and how they produce and distribute the goods that societies need and want**.

Another important topic is the different ways to study the economy. Next, we turn to the different *methods* that economists use in economics.

1.4 ECONOMIC METHODOLOGY: HOW TO "DO" ECONOMICS

Given the vast complexity of the global economy, it is impossible for economists to study everything. Thus, they choose to narrow their focus on the variables that they see as most important.

Mainstream economists attempt to be as scientific as possible. The mainstream economics methodology can be summarized as follows:

1. **Mainstream economists make simplifying assumptions about the economy so that they can focus on what they determine to be the most important economic variables.**

For example, mainstream economists typically believe that consumers are rational, calculating, fully informed, and self-interested most of the time. In theory, this allows mainstream economists to assume that all consumers behave in a consistent manner, which should allow mainstream economists to make reasonable predictions about consumers' economic behaviors. Thus, mainstream economic models are based on a hypothetical "**economic man**" who behaves quite predictably.

2. **Mainstream economists construct mathematical models of the economy so that they can make predictions about how it will behave.**

   Mainstream economists make logical deductions based on their assumptions and construct a hypothesis about how the economy should work if their assumptions hold. For example, if we assume that consumers are rational, well-informed, and self-interested, then we can construct a model of consumer demand demonstrating that when the price of a product increases, consumers will buy less of that good for themselves. This is known as the **law of demand**, and it can be expressed as a mathematical equation or as a graph, such as Figure 1.2.

3. **Mainstream economists test their models using statistical analysis and observations of whether or not the real world conforms to their predictions.**

   If the assumptions are reasonably accurate and the models are good, then the predictions of mainstream economic models should match what we see in the real world. For example, historically, a 10% increase in the price of gasoline caused a 2% decrease in the quantity of gasoline purchased by consumers. Thus, assuming no changes in the assumptions behind the model, and holding all other economic variables constant, we could predict that a gasoline tax that raised the price of gasoline by 100% would cause consumers to purchase 20% less gasoline than usual.

Political economists—those from the PPE and RPE groups—believe that the methods adopted by mainstream economists are often flawed and thus approach

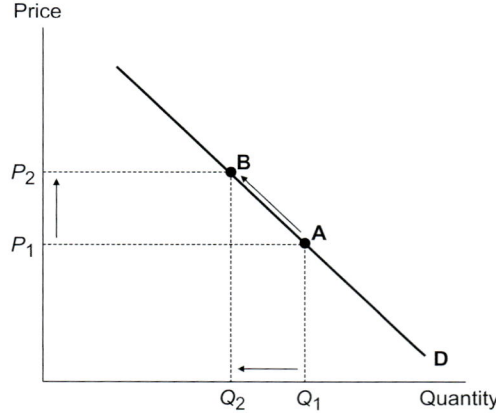

FIGURE 1.2 A typical demand curve.

the study of economics quite differently. Indeed, they see each of the assumptions behind "economic man" as flawed in key ways. From the political economy perspective, consumers can be irrational and ill-informed much of the time. And whereas a fully informed, calculating, and rational individual would never be convinced to buy something he or she doesn't need, we know that most of us are affected by advertising in key ways, such as making impulsive purchases or buying products we do not really need at prices that we know are too high for our budgets.

More interesting and more important, from the political economy perspective, are the social factors that shape consumers and their decisions. How does culture (peer pressure, social groups, etc.) shape consumers' tastes and purchases? How do companies manipulate consumers via advertising and attempting to control the market? How does one's gender, race, and social class affect one's purchases? Is it truly rational to buy consumer goods that are not necessary for survival when those goods use resources that contribute to global warming? Or is such consumerist behavior the unique product of a particular culture in a particular place at a specific time?

In order to differentiate between the two approaches to economics highlighted above, the next section uses the ideas of both mainstream and political economists to analyze consumer shopping behavior on Amazon.com. Notice that *both* perspectives contribute something valuable to our understanding of consumer behavior, which is why a pluralistic approach to economics is likely to leave you with a better understanding of the economy!

1.5 METHODOLOGY IN MICROECONOMICS: AMAZON.COM AND CONSUMER BEHAVIOR

Economics is traditionally broken up into the study of microeconomics and macroeconomics. Microeconomics is the study of how individual **markets** work, such as the market for labor, cell phones, or other specific goods and services. Macroeconomics is the study of the dynamics of national and international economies, including the factors affecting recessions and booms, economic growth, and financial markets.

To explore microeconomic analysis from a mainstream and a political economy (PPE/RPE) perspective, we turn to an analysis of the shopping behavior of consumers with the online retailing giant Amazon.com. Amazon.com is the world's largest online retailer, and it analyzes consumer behavior relentlessly in the pursuit of higher sales. Thus, we learn a lot about consumers from the various strategies that Amazon.com uses successfully.

To improve sales, mainstream economists would emphasize the importance of providing rational, calculating, fully informed, and self-interested consumers with the best product at the best price. This is, indeed, one of Amazon.com's signature strengths. For books, music, and electronics, Amazon.com is consistently cheaper than its competitors. For other goods, such as groceries or household appliances, Amazon.com tends to be slightly more expensive than Walmart or local grocery stores. However, many consumers continue to shop for these goods at Amazon.com for the convenience (consumers' time is also a "cost"). Amazon.com provides a lot of information for consumers about their products, including customer reviews, so that consumers can make an informed decision. Thus, much consumer behavior on Amazon.com confirms the mainstream view.

However, PPE and RPE economists look at additional factors. First, consumers on Amazon.com are often impulsive. This is why Amazon.com often gives you suggestions when you shop, telling you what other consumers bought who purchased the same items you did and giving you personalized recommendations. As we know, for many consumers, the suggestions have a significant impact on their buying behavior. Thus, from a PPE or RPE perspective, we must also study consumers' impulsive side, especially the ways in which sellers work on us, even to the point of hiring psychologists to study how best we can be tricked and fooled.

Second, consumers are affected by culture, and especially the behavior of their peers. This is one of the reasons why customer reviews are so successful. People feel much more secure in making a purchase if their peers approve of the item. For this and many other reasons, PPE and RPE economists view culture as an essential subject of study.

Third, Amazon.com exercises its market power to compete unfairly. The company demands that publishers discount books and other sellers discount items that are provided to Amazon.com or it will refuse to offer those entities' items for sale. This is a strategy also pursued by Walmart. By demanding and getting lower prices from their suppliers, the big retailers get a cost advantage over smaller competitors, allowing them to sell goods for lower prices and to reap higher profits because they are bigger and more powerful, not because they provide better goods or services. Analyzing the main institutions in a society, and the power and control exercised by those institutions, is another important topic to PPE and RPE economists and surely among the most important differences between the methodology of political economists and that of mainstream economists.

Fourth, some retailers whose products are sold on Amazon.com try to cheat the system by paying people to review their products favorably. Consumers who are taken in by these reviews will not be purchasing an item based on valid information. Understanding a country's legal system and how the profit motive can lead to unsavory behavior is another topic of focus for PPE and RPE economists.

What we can see is that mainstream economics focuses on certain aspects of consumer behavior and PPE and RPE economists broaden that focus considerably. We see similar divisions in the area of macroeconomics, as will be found below. But first, it is worth considering the scientific approach to economics more carefully.

1.6 THE SCIENTIFIC METHOD IN ECONOMICS: HOW SCIENTIFIC CAN ECONOMICS BE?

The scientific approach to economics, in which economists make simplifying assumptions to construct models and then test those models against the real world, is often called positive economics. This is named after the economic philosophy of positivism, which seeks to determine definitive, "positive" facts about how the economy works, without the influence of political biases. This approach has yielded some very useful information about the economy, but there are limits to how scientific economics can be.

For example, for many years economists using a model of the labor market believed that there was an inverse relationship between wages and employment: It seemed logical that if wages were increased, businesses would hire fewer workers due to the increase in costs (assuming there were no other major changes in the economy happening at the time that might alter that basic relationship). However, in a groundbreaking study in the 1990s, economists David Card and Alan Krueger proved that a higher minimum wage had no effect on employment; businesses needed a certain minimum number of employees to serve their customers and did not lay off workers after the minimum wage went up. Following the work of Card and Krueger, many other studies of the minimum wage were undertaken, with most supporting their work (some contradicted the findings, though). Overall, the studies seem to indicate that raising the minimum wage by a modest amount usually has little or no effect on employment, although sometimes a higher minimum wage may reduce employment very slightly.

We learn several important things from this example. First, scientific economics can be extremely useful if it can successfully determine how the economy works, which can then inform governments of the best economic policies to use. Second, it is very difficult to establish "positive" and conclusive economic facts. Due to the conflicting findings of numerous studies, economists still disagree on whether or not we should raise the minimum wage. Third, the uncertain nature of the "science" of economics means that economists usually disagree about the way the world works and what policies should be adopted. There are limits to how scientific the study of economics can be. Fourth, logical analysis, though useful, can have serious pitfalls. The logic of the model of the labor market implies that any increase in the wage rate will lead to a decrease in employment, but real-world data indicate that this logic seems to be flawed much of the time.

We see similar disagreements in macroeconomics, especially in the study of economic crises.

1.7 MACROECONOMIC ANALYSIS OF ECONOMIC CRISES

One of the most striking differences between mainstream economics and political economics became apparent in the lead up to the financial crisis of 2007–2008. Prior to the crisis, most mainstream economists held the view that the macroeconomy tended to be stable. They believed the macroeconomy tended to reach a stable equilibrium from which there would only be small, unimportant deviations. Mainstream economists, using sophisticated mathematical and statistical techniques, were able to develop elaborate general equilibrium models to analyze the interaction between key macroeconomic variables. These models helped the Federal Reserve Bank of the United States and other national banks tweak interest rates in order to keep economies growing and relatively stable. These models, however, did not account for the possibility of an economic crisis occurring.

Meanwhile, political economists, especially those who study economic crises and how they form, began to be concerned with the housing bubble forming in the United States that was causing an exceptionally rapid increase in the value of financial assets associated with housing markets. To political economists, economic crises are frequent occurrences, due to the fundamental instability in businesses' investment decisions and the potential for a shortfall in consumer and investor spending once confidence is eroded by some sort of economic shock.

From the political economy perspective, economies typically follow a business cycle of about ten years in length. After a recession starts, businesses are very pessimistic and investment spending on factories and equipment declines. Households are pessimistic and millions of people have lost jobs, so consumer spending also declines. After a few years of sluggish growth, the economy usually starts to pick up. Businesses need to replace outdated and worn-out equipment, and new, profitable opportunities emerge, so business investment rises. This puts more people to work, improving consumer confidence, and consumer spending also increases, raising businesses' profits. This, in turn, stimulates more business investment and hiring. The economy begins to boom and businesses' profits grow rapidly. Businesses have substantial profits, and they invest heavily to take advantage of new opportunities. But eventually, after the economy has boomed for several years, the most secure business opportunities are already taken, and businesses invest their profits in increasingly risky ventures. Eventually, these risky ventures crash and the economy falls into another recession.

For example, in the early 2000s, businesses in the United States invested in extremely risky financial securities tied to real estate markets, which tend to be quite volatile. The value of these risky securities increased incredibly rapidly as more and more money poured in. But eventually investors realized that the real estate market was overvalued, and they sold the risky securities in a panic. The result was a crash in the financial markets, which eliminated billions of dollars in investor wealth, undermined consumer confidence, and threw the economy into the Great Recession of 2008. Prior to the Great Recession, a number of political economists (and one mainstream economist!) published material predicting the financial crisis, and a number of political economists (including the author of this book) quietly began advising their friends that a crisis was coming.

In the wake of the Great Recession, most mainstream economists returned to the work of the great economist John Maynard Keynes, whose analysis of recessions formed the basis of the ideas political economists used to anticipate the recession. During the coronavirus recession of 2020, both mainstream and political economists called for a dramatic increase in government spending, a cornerstone of Keynesian idea. There is now more similarity between mainstream economics and political economics in macroeconomics, although mainstream economists still see the macroeconomy as fundamentally stable, whereas political economists see it as volatile and unstable. It would be wise for an economics student to understand both views! This is a topic we will take up at length in later chapters.

1.8 THE RICH SOCIAL SCIENCE OF ECONOMICS

Previous sections of this chapter explored microeconomic and macroeconomic examples of how different economists view important economic issues. You should now have some idea of the richness of the field of economics and the insights you can gain from some of the schools of thought. Each school of thought has crucial ideas that you will find useful in understanding certain aspects of the economy you see around you.

Note that, at times, we will broaden our definition of economics to cover ten different schools of economic thought. Each of these schools of thought uses a particular method of analysis and has areas in which their analysis is particularly insightful. Those schools of thought are listed in Figure 1.3 on the next page.

There is often much overlap between various groups, so do not view the schools of thought as rigid. Conservative mainstream economists, including monetarist, new classical, and supply-side economists, share much with Austrian economists, preferring a mostly unregulated capitalist market system in which private firms own and control the major economic resources of society and allocate those resources based on the activities that earn the most profit. This approach is known as *laissez-faire* economics, after the French phrase meaning "let it be." Moderate mainstream economists, also known as New Keynesians, believe that markets must be regulated by the government in order to reduce the negative side of markets, such as economic crises, pollution, and inequality. Progressive political economists, including institutional, social, feminist, and post-Keynesian economists, along with the most liberal mainstream economists, want the government to play a larger role in society, managing and guiding markets rather than letting markets dictate the direction of the economy. Finally, radical political economists, drawing on the ideas of Karl Marx, see markets as ruthless and exploitative, and they would rather replace capitalist markets with some variety of socialism or communism.

The ten schools of economic thought are laid out in Figure 1.4 on the next page, based on how much or how little government the economists from each school tend to prefer, which is perhaps the central issue that creates the different approaches to each school of thought.

Fortunately, there is enough overlap between various schools of thought that we will often simplify our discussion to a few major perspectives on key topics. With respect to policy issues, it is often possible to break economists down into conservative (laissez-faire), moderate (New Keynesian), liberal (progressive political economy), and radical (radical political economy) groups.

Economic School of Thought	Methodology	Key Areas of Strength	Some Major Thinker(s)
Austrian	Focus on individual choices and their impact on the economy; tend to avoid the use of models and statistics and the analysis of group behavior	Efficiency of markets and how public policy can be stifling, corrupted, and inefficient	Friedrich Hayek, Ludwig von Mises
Monetarist	Mainstream economics: Make simplifying assumptions about economic actors, construct economic models to make predictions and (to the extent possible) test those predictions using statistical analysis	Importance of the money supply in affecting inflation, gross domestic product	Milton Friedman
New Classical (Rational Expectations)		How individuals' rational decisions can anticipate market changes and affect the economy	Robert Lucas, Eugene Fama
Supply Side		How tax rates and regulations affect individuals and businesses and economic activity in general	Martin Feldstein
Moderate (New Keynesian)		Where markets are effective but where they need appropriate regulation to fix market failures and operate more efficiently	Paul Krugman, Joseph Stiglitz, Gregory Mankiw
Institutional	Focus on the evolution of key human institutions and group behaviors, including technology and culture	How an economy is fundamentally shaped by its institutions, including culture, social norms, companies, the legal system, and government	Thorstein Veblen, John Kenneth Galbraith
Social	Focus on the ethics and social impact of economic activities and policies, along with social (as well as self-interested) behavior	The ethical and social causes and consequences of economic behavior, institutions, organizations, theory, and policy	E. K. Hunt, John B. Davis
Feminist	Attempt to overcome male, patriarchal biases by analyzing social constructs, discrimination, and inequities	Economics of households and the impact of gender on economic outcomes	Marilyn Waring, Nancy Folbre
Post-Keynesian	Focus on effective demand (spending), investment instability, and money creation of banks as major economic factors	How demand affects the macroeconomy and how instability and uncertainty affect investment	Hyman Minksy, Paul Davidson
Marxist	Focus on class conflict over the wealth (surplus product) produced by workers and the dynamics produced by this conflict	Exploitative and unstable nature of markets and the effect of capitalism on workers and communities	Karl Marx, Friedrich Engels

FIGURE 1.3 The ten major schools of thought in economics.

More Markets, Less Government ←		The major economic schools of thought in the modern era					Less Markets, More Government →
		Mainstream			PPE	RPE	
Economic School of Thought	Austrian	Monetarist, New Classical	Supply Side	Moderate (New Keynesian)	Institutional, Social, Feminist, Post-Keynesian	Marxist	Economic School of Thought
Preferred economic system	Unregulated Market Capitalism	Unregulated Market Capitalism	Pro-Business Capitalism	Regulated Market Capitalism	Managed Market Capitalism	Socialism, Communism	Preferred economic system
Political views	Conservative			Moderate	Liberal	Socialist	Political views

FIGURE 1.4 Different kinds of economics.

Conservative economists generally favor unregulated market capitalism with less government intervention. **Unregulated market capitalism (laissez-faire)** is **an economic system in which the main productive resources of society—the labor, land, machinery, equipment, and natural resources—are owned by private individuals who use those resources to produce goods and services that are bought and sold in markets for profit**.

Moderate economists believe in regulated or "mixed" market capitalism. **Mixed market capitalism** is **an economic system in which private sector firms and individuals produce goods and services for markets for profit and a public sector established by the government regulates those markets and provides public goods such as schools, roads, airports, health care, and other goods and services that are usually provided inadequately by private markets**. Most of the economies in the world have chosen this type of economic system because it has the benefits of a market system, including innovations, competition, and economic growth, without the worst problems you tend to see in unregulated market capitalism, such as exploitation of workers or the environment.

Liberal economists are highly suspicious of markets, seeing them as dominated by a handful of wealthy corporations and rich individuals. They prefer **strictly regulated capitalism**. Radical economists go even further, preferring **democratic socialism**, **an economic system in which the most important resources of society are controlled democratically by all citizens, including workers, who usually have little say in how market capitalist economies are run**. From this perspective, markets are not particularly efficient, because they produce wasteful and unnecessary goods while neglecting other, more important things such as public health, leisure time with one's family, workers' quality of life, and the environment.

Depending on which economists have the most influence and the economic views of politicians, the economic systems of countries around the globe exhibit substantial variations. Almost all modern economies can be classified as mixed market capitalist, in that they depend on markets for the production and distribution of most goods and services but they also utilize a substantial degree of government intervention.

As you can see from Figure 1.5 on the next page, which depicts the size of the government sector in selected economies around the world, the United States has the smallest government of any developed economy, coming the closest to unregulated market capitalism. One of the reasons for this is that the United States is the only developed economy without a national health care system. Even very market-oriented countries like the United Kingdom and Australia provide national health care to all citizens. Economies such as Sweden's and Norway's, though still predominantly market based, come closer to democratic socialism in that they have very large state sectors that provide important goods and services such as college education, childcare, dental care, and housing for any citizen who needs them.

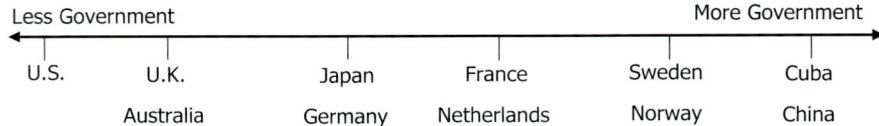

FIGURE 1.5 The size of government in select economies.

As communist countries, Cuba and China have the most government intervention. **Communism** is **an economic system in which the government controls society's productive resources and makes the major economic decisions**. However, both Cuba and China utilize markets to some degree, so even their economies are "mixed."

1.9 CONCLUSION

This chapter described why economics is an important subject to study. It also detailed various definitions of what economics is. The differences between mainstream economics and political economics (PPE and RPE) were covered, along with how the conservative, moderate, liberal, and radical political approaches to economics affect the size of government in various economies. Remember that each school of economic thought has something useful to add to our understanding of the economy, so it is important to study each approach. In the areas where economic approaches disagree, your job is to critically analyze the different perspectives and to decide for yourself which ideas best capture the world you see around you. This should leave you with a sophisticated and useful understanding of the world.

Also, the economic views that a society chooses to adopt determine the type of economic system that a society develops. Conservative economic views result in an economy closer to unregulated market capitalism. Moderate economic views result in a mixed market capitalist economic system that is mostly market oriented but that includes government intervention to fix the worst problems in markets. If liberal economic views are adopted, the result is a mixed market capitalist economic system with a larger role for government in directing and guiding markets. Finally, a radical economic view would result in a democratic socialist or communist economic system, in which the role of markets is very small and where most economic decisions are made by citizens or by the government.

To clarify the different types of economics, Chapter 2 goes through a mainstream economic model, the production possibilities curve, and contrasts this approach with the views of political economists.

QUESTIONS FOR REVIEW

1. What is **austerity**? Why do most economists think it is a bad economic policy to pursue in a recession?
2. Read about what is happening in the nation or around the globe in a reputable magazine or newspaper, such as the *New York Times*, *Wall Street Journal*, *The Economist*, *The Financial Times*, or *The Guardian*. Which events would be considered relevant to the study of *economics*, given the definitions of economics in this chapter? How are these events important to people and their communities? Explain briefly.
3. What are the primary differences between mainstream economics and political economics (PPE and RPE)? Explain briefly in your own words.
4. Consider the description of "economic man" above and the description of positive, scientific economics. Also consider how political economists (PPE and RPE) study human behavior. Then reflect carefully on your own shopping habits. Do you usually make rational, calculated, fully informed purchases (like "economic man"), or do you tend to buy on impulse for a variety of reasons, or do you do both? Analyze how much of your purchasing behavior can be captured by "positive economics" and when the methods used by political economists would better reflect your behavior. How much of your shopping behavior could be predicted scientifically? How much of it would be hard to predict?
5. Briefly explain the main differences between the economic systems of unregulated market capitalism, mixed market capitalism, and democratic socialism. Using a recent issue of *The Economist* or another reputable publication that features significant international economic news, find examples that show how two countries exhibit characteristics of one or more of these types of economic systems.
6. One of the main economic problems in the modern world is climate change. Scientists have concluded that the world is likely to experience a major ecological crisis unless we reduce the amount of greenhouse gases (especially carbon) that we produce. Greenhouse gases are generated by economic activity. Almost all economists acknowledge the problem but disagree vehemently on how to solve it. Given the definitions of radical, moderate, and conservative economists in the reading, identify which group would be most likely to support each set of policies listed below. Explain your answer briefly.
    a. Establish a carbon tax (on fossil fuels) to give businesses and consumers incentives to change their behavior.
    b. Subsidize the development of solar and wind power industries while taxing carbon to push the economy toward more sustainable practices.
    c. Close down the most harmful industries (coal, shale gas), tax carbon, and mandate the comprehensive use of renewable energies in the very near future; create jobs for any displaced workers.

7. Which of the ten schools of economic thought listed in Figure 1.3 do you find most interesting? Which do you find least interesting? What does this indicate about your own background and approach to economics at this point?

NOTE

1 Source: Federal Reserve Economic Data (FRED). Note: Data for 2021 are for the first quarter only.

Scarcity, choice, and opportunity cost

The mainstream approach, the PPC model, the limits of this approach, and the importance of institutions

In this chapter we will examine some mainstream economic concepts, including scarcity, opportunity cost, efficiency, cost–benefit analysis, and how those concepts frame the **choices** faced by a society. We will also use a simple mainstream economic model, the production possibilities curve (PPC), to capture some of these concepts and to display a variety of choices that a society might face. We will apply these concepts and the PPC model to several economic issues, including an analysis of defense spending and its impact on economic growth. The chapter concludes by drawing on the work of political economists to show the limitations of these mainstream economic concepts and the PPC model in capturing economic reality. Rather than focusing on scarcity and choice, political economists tend to focus on the institutions that shape a society and its choices.

2.0 CHAPTER 2 LEARNING GOALS

After reading this chapter you should be able to:

- Define and apply the concepts of scarcity, opportunity cost, efficiency, and cost–benefit analysis.
- Use a production possibilities curve to analyze the opportunity cost of allocating resources in a particular way.

DOI: 10.4324/9780429399350-3

- Identify and explain the difference between capital goods and consumer goods and analyze their impact on economic growth using a PPC.

- Explain why political economists find the mainstream approach to scarcity and cost–benefit analysis limited and how political economists would approach these topics differently using an analysis of the institutional factors that shape a society's choices.

- Critically analyze the strengths and limitations of the production possibilities curve model and the political economy approach to choices regarding the allocation of resources.

Work on understanding each new concept in this chapter carefully. Also, spend some time working with the production possibilities curve to make sure you understand how it works and what it can be used for. Finally, the chapter is primarily concerned with how mainstream economists and political economists study the choices a society makes to allocate its resources. As always, critically analyze the different approaches and develop your own ideas on the topic.

2.1 SCARCITY, CHOICE, AND OPPORTUNITY COST

The problem of scarcity is absolutely central to mainstream and Austrian economics (this is one of several areas in which mainstream economics and Austrian economics overlap). **Scarcity** exists **when a society's seemingly unlimited desire for goods and services exceeds the resources available to produce and provide those goods and services**. From this perspective, scarcity exists everywhere because there are never enough resources to produce everything society wants, and much of human life is a struggle to overcome scarcity. Consumers always want more than they have—bigger houses, better cars, faster smart phones, trendier clothes, more new stuff of all kinds—but they have limited budgets. Companies want to produce more goods so they can generate higher profits, but they have limited inputs (labor, machinery, technology, buildings, raw materials). Governments would like to build more roads, improve the environment, spend more on social programs, and expand their militaries, but they have limited tax revenues to spend. Thus, society as a whole wants more of everything it values. However, because of limited resources, people cannot have everything they want, which necessitates making difficult choices. **Choice** involves **consumers, producers, and governments selecting from among the limited options that are available to them due to scarcity**.

Mainstream economists like to frame making choices in terms of cost–benefit analysis: Good decisions depend on carefully weighing the costs and benefits involved in a decision. In order to undertake such analysis, economists use the concept of **opportunity cost**: **What is given up when a choice is made to allocate resources in a particular way.** When a consumer is considering the purchase a $40,000 car, what is the **next best alternative** for which they could use that money? They could put an addition on their home, work 2000 fewer hours at their job, buy 4000 cases of cheap beer, among many other things. A rational decision would weigh the benefits of the new car against the value of what is perceived as the next best alternative to that car, which would be considered the car's opportunity cost.

The concept of opportunity cost can be a powerful tool in improving decision making, because it forces us to consider not just the benefit of what we are choosing to devote resources to but all alternative uses of those resources as well. Consider the following examples.

2.1.1 The opportunity cost of attending college

The average cost of four years of tuition and room and board in 2020–2021 was $103,000 at a public university and $216,000 at a private university in the United States. But one must consider more than just the financial cost. Instead of going to college, a person with a high school degree could go to work full-time and earn, on average, $30,000 per year. So the financial opportunity cost of attending college for four years is about $223,000 at a public university, including $120,000 in foregone salary and $103,000 in tuition and room and board. Similarly, the opportunity cost of attending a private college would be $336,000, on average. Is this a good investment? Fortunately for college students, the lifetime earnings of a typical U.S. college graduate—about $1,200,000—are more than double the $580,000 that a typical high school graduate would earn in their lifetime, so a college education clearly has a substantial financial benefit. Also, college education provides opportunities to cultivate one's passions, become an informed voter, learn to work with diverse people, and much, much more.

2.1.2 The opportunity cost of Sony devoting resources to its computer division

The Japanese company Sony once had a very large computer division. However, personal computer sales began to drop, whereas mobile device (smart phones and tablets) sales surged after 2010, so Sony decided to sell off its computer division. Given the poor prospects for personal computers, it made little sense to continue to devote so many resources to that area. For Sony, the opportunity cost of running its computer division was the resources and staff that it could instead devote to the rapidly growing market for mobile devices.

2.1.3 The opportunity cost of the U.S. government spending $55 billion on B-2 stealth bombers

The stealth bomber was designed during the Cold War to evade Soviet radar systems and empower the United States to drop nuclear bombs on them. The Soviet Union collapsed in 1990, and most modern conflicts utilize drones much more than old-fashioned bombers. Nonetheless, the U.S. Air Force recently asked for $55 billion for a fleet of new B-2 bombers. What is the opportunity cost of this purchase? In other words, what else could the government do with $55 billion? They could provide 533,980 people with a free education at a public university. They could give every taxpayer a $450 tax cut. These are just two of many worthwhile options.

As you can see from the above examples, the concept of opportunity cost can be applied to almost any decision facing consumers, companies, or governments. An analysis of opportunity cost can help people make a carefully considered choice between two viable alternatives.

Note that the idea of opportunity cost only makes sense if resources are being used efficiently. **Efficiency** in mainstream economics refers to a situation in which **all resources are employed as productively as possible**. No resources are being wasted or used inefficiently. Efficiency matters because if there are unused resources or if resources are being used inefficiently, then more goods can be produced by putting all resources into use or by using resources more efficiently. There is *no opportunity cost* when production is increased by employing unused or inefficiently used resources. Nothing has to be given up.

For example, if everyone in a country is employed, then producing more of one good necessarily means producing less of other goods. Producing more bombers for national defense means producing fewer cars for consumers. However, the average U.S. unemployment rate from 2005 to 2015 was 6.8%. If all of the unemployed were put to work, a huge amount of additional goods and services could be provided for no opportunity cost (without sacrificing the production of any other good or service).

Mainstream economists have developed a simple economic model to display the choices that societies, especially individuals, companies, and governments, face when allocating scarce resources: The production possibilities curve.

2.2 THE PRODUCTION POSSIBILITIES CURVE: A SIMPLE, MAINSTREAM MODEL

An **economic model** is **a theoretical, simplified construct designed to focus on a key set of economic relationships**. Economists use models because they cannot conduct real-world experiments that isolate key factors, like scientists do, to determine how the real world functions. The best they can do is to construct a theoretical picture of how they think the economy works—a model—and then see whether their model fits with what they observe happening around them. For example, as we saw in Chapter 1, economists have created a model of the demand curve that suggests that when the price of a good goes up, consumers buy less of it. This model is reasonably accurate much of the time, as we will see later.

However, models are only as good as the simplifying assumptions upon which they are based. Any failing in the underlying assumptions will render the model inaccurate. Additionally, all models are based on a major, additional **ceteris paribus assumption** that **all other relevant factors do not change**. When economists draw a demand curve showing that higher prices cause people to purchase less of a good, they have to assume, *ceteris paribus*, that consumer confidence remains unchanged (improved consumer confidence would likely mean additional consumer spending on all goods even if prices were higher) and that the product did not become a hot item (which would also increase consumer demand even if prices were higher).

To demonstrate the usefulness and limitations of economic models, we will use a **production possibilities curve (PPC)**, which is **a model that shows all combinations of two goods that can be produced, holding the amount of resources and the level of technology fixed**. The PPC model is designed to show the trade-offs (opportunity costs) that occur when more of a single good is produced.

Consider the production possibilities curve in Figure 2.1, which shows all possible combinations of two services, defense and education, that the U.S. government can provide using all of its available resources and current technology. If the U.S. government decides to devote all of its available resources to defense, it would select option A, with 40 units of defense and 0 units of education. Or the U.S. government could produce 100 units of education, but this would leave no resources left to use for defense, reducing defense production to 0. Thus, the opportunity cost of increasing the production of education from 0 units to 100 units, moving from point **A** to point **D**, is 40 units of defense (what is sacrificed when the government chooses to switch all of its available resources from defense to education). The government can also choose to produce at any point between point **A** and point **D**

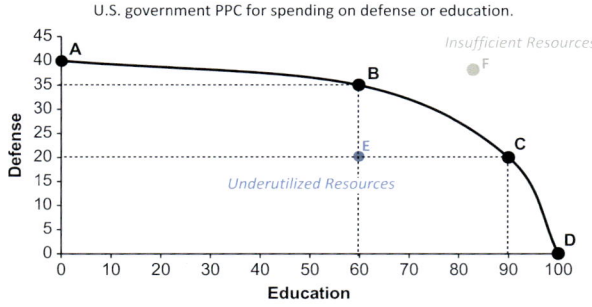

FIGURE 2.1 Production possibilities curve for the U.S. government.

Choice	Education	Defense
A	0	40
B	60	35
C	90	20
D	100	0

FIGURE 2.2 Table showing the production possibilities combinations in Figure 2.1.

on the production possibilities curve. Figure 2.2 displays the combinations of defense and education that the U.S. government can choose in table form, matching the options that are graphed in Figure 2.1.

Suppose that the government is currently at point **B**, producing 35 units of defense and 60 units of education. Now suppose the government decides to increase the production of education to 90 units, moving from point **B** to point **C**. The only way they can increase the production of education, given that they are stuck with existing resources and technology, is by reducing the production of defense from 35 units to 20 units. The opportunity cost of moving from point **B** to point **C** would be 15 units of defense, which is what is given up in exchange for 30 additional units of education.

The assumptions behind the PPC model include the following: (1) There are only two relevant goods, (2) any point on the PPC curve involves the full employment of available resources, (3) resources are fixed, (4) technology is fixed, and (5) any other factors that might affect the production of the two goods in question will remain unchanged (the *ceteris paribus* assumption).

Note that any point on the PPC, including points **A**, **B**, **C**, and **D**, involves utilizing *all* of the government's available resources efficiently. If some resources were not being used, or if resources were being used inefficiently, then the U.S. government would be at a point *inside* the production possibilities curve, such as point **E**.

Also note that, although the U.S. government would like to be able to provide more defense and more education for its citizens, it cannot choose a point outside the PPC because it does not have sufficient resources or effective enough technology (scarcity). The only way for the U.S. government to reach point **F**, which is beyond the PPC, would be if it had additional resources or if there were an improvement in technology that allowed more production of both education and defense than is currently possible. Any change in the availability of resources or technology, however, would be a change in the assumptions behind the model, and we would have to draw a new PPC reflecting the new assumptions.

2.3 THE SPECIALIZATION OF RESOURCES

The shape of the production possibilities curve is also important. The PPC above has a downward (negative) slope that becomes steeper and steeper (it is concave to

SCARCITY, CHOICE, AND OPPORTUNITY COST

the origin). This occurs whenever a PPC reflects the **specialization of resources**: **When some resources cannot be easily adapted from one use to another**. For example, some resources that are used to produce defense, such as tanks and bombers, are not well-suited for producing education. Similarly, some resources that are used to produce education, such as schools and school buses, are poorly suited for producing defense.

We can see the specialization of resources in the PPC in Figure 2.1 and in the table in Figure 2.2 when the amounts of education exchanged for defense vary. If we begin at point **A**, the government is producing all defense and no education. Even schools, buses, and teachers are being used for national defense! Now suppose that the government decides to shift some resources out of defense and into education, moving from point **A** to point **B**. They will, of course, shift the resources most specialized for education first. By shifting the schools, buses, and teachers from producing defense to producing education, the result is very little loss in defense (5 units) for a very large gain in education (60 units). Between point **A** and point **B**, 5 units of defense (D) use the same resources that could produce 60 units of education (E). To put this in mathematical terms:

$$\text{From A to B}, 5D = 60E.$$

Dividing both sides by 5 to find the opportunity cost of one unit of defense, we get:

$$\text{From A to B}, \left(\frac{5}{5}\right)D = \left(\frac{60}{5}\right)E; \text{ and } 1D = 12E.$$

From **A** to **B**, each unit of defense sacrificed results in 12 units of education being produced.

Now suppose that the government wants to devote even more resources to education. Moving from **B** to **C** involves producing 30 additional units of education while giving up 15 units of defense. The resources that were best suited for education were already shifted into education when the government moved from **A** to **B**. Now the government is shifting resources that are well suited for either defense or education. This would include soldiers who could also be teachers, computers, and equipment that could be used for education or for defense, and so on. Now the opportunity cost of each unit is different. From point **B** to point **C**, 15 units of defense (D) are given up for 30 units of education (E). In mathematical terms,

$$\text{From B to C}, 15D = 30E; \text{ and if we divide both sides by } 15, 1D = 2E.$$

Similarly, if the government moves from point **C** to point **D**, 20 units of defense are given up in exchange for only 10 units of education. Now the government is shifting all of their resources into education, even those that are well suited for defense but very poorly suited for education, such as bombs, bombers, tanks, and guns.

$$\text{From point C to point D}, 10E = 20D; \text{ and } 1D = \frac{1}{2}E.$$

Choice	Education	Defense	Opportunity Cost	Opportunity Cost of 1 Unit of Education	Opportunity Cost of 1 Unit of Defense
A	0	40			
A-B			60E = 5D	1E = (1/12)D	1D = 12E
B	60	35			
B-C			30E = 15D	1E = (1/2)D	1D = 2E
C	90	20			
C-D			10E = 20D	1E = 2D	1D = (1/2)E
D	100	0			

FIGURE 2.3 Table showing changes in opportunity cost due to the specialization of resources.

From **C** to **D**, each unit of defense that is given up only results in half of a unit of education (½E) being produced.

The last column in Figure 2.3 shows how the opportunity cost of one unit of defense changes as the government moves from point **A** to point **D**.

Similarly, we can compute the opportunity cost of one unit of education in each region of the PPC, which you can see in the fifth column of the table in Figure 2.3.

The change in the opportunity cost of one unit of each good on a curved production possibilities curve displays something mainstream economists refer to as the **law of increasing opportunity cost**: **If resources are specialized and if all resources are being used efficiently, then, as more and more of a particular good is produced, the opportunity cost of producing each additional unit of that good will increase.** In other words, as we produce more and more units of education, moving from point **A** to point **D** on the PPC in Figure 2.1 (page 25), each unit of education will have a higher opportunity cost. This occurs because we have to give up more and more units of defense to get one unit of education as we shift resources that are better suited to defense into the production of education. This situation also works in reverse: As we produce more and more units of defense, moving from point **D** to point **A** on the PPC in Figure 2.1, each unit of defense has a higher opportunity cost because we are shifting resources into defense that are better suited to education as we get closer to point **A**.

There are some important real-world examples of the law of increasing opportunity cost at work. For instance, in the 1980s, the Soviet Union devoted about 17% of its economy to national defense. The Soviet Union collapsed in 1990, ending the Cold War in which the United States and the Soviet Union built up huge military arsenals. The Soviet Union became Russia and a group of independent countries. Russian officials decided to reduce the size of their military to 3% of the economy and shift from the production of defense into the production of consumer goods, energy, health care, and other non-defense items that Russia needed. They hoped to see a huge boom in other sectors as they shifted resources out of defense. But the boom was much smaller than they anticipated. Why? One of the biggest reasons was the specialization of resources: All of the huge defense factories

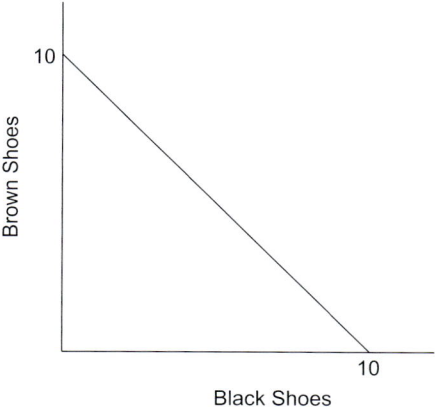

FIGURE 2.4 A PPC without specialized resources.

and specialized defense workers who built tanks and served as soldiers were not very productive when it came to producing non-defense goods. After 1990, Russia sacrificed a vast amount of defense in exchange for a much smaller increase in the production of non-defense goods.

American business magnate T. Boone Pickens once proposed that the United States should stop using so much imported oil by converting automobiles to use U.S.-produced compressed natural gas. It was an interesting proposal, but due to the specialization of resources, the opportunity cost of doing so would have been prohibitive. The transportation infrastructure in the United States is built around using gasoline made from oil; converting all of the cars, gas stations, and refineries to produce compressed natural gas would be difficult and expensive—and would come with a significant opportunity cost.

The above examples all refer to cases in which resources are specialized. However, if resources are not specialized, then opportunity costs would be constant along a PPC rather than increasing and the PPC would be a straight line. For example, Figure 2.4 shows a production possibilities curve for a company producing black shoes and brown shoes. Because the only difference between the shoes is the color of the dye used, resources (labor, machinery, etc.) can be shifted easily from the production of black shoes to the production of brown shoes.

2.4 SHIFTS IN THE PRODUCTION POSSIBILITIES CURVE

A production possibilities curve is drawn based on the assumption that resources and technology are fixed. But what would happen if more resources or better technology were made available? We would need to draw a new PPC that is shifted outward. The type of shift would depend on whether or not the resources or technology were better suited for the production of one good or both goods.

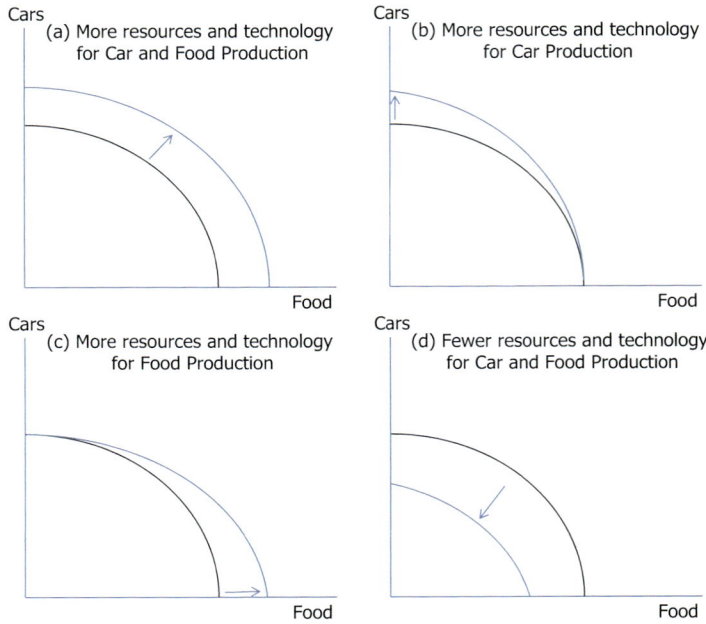

FIGURE 2.5 Shifts in the PPC from changes in resources or technology.

For example, consider an economy producing cars and food. If better robots were invented that can produce either item, then the PPC would shift out, showing that society can now have more of both goods. This is shown in example (a) in Figure 2.5. What if the newly invented robots can only be used to produce cars? Then the PPC shifts out on the "cars" axis but not on the "food" axis, as shown in Figure 2.5, example (b). If the robots could only be used for producing food, the PPC would shift out only on the "food" axis, as shown in Figure 2.5, example (c). Finally, suppose that a natural disaster reduced the resources available for food and car production. The result would be a PPC that has shifted in on both axes, as shown in Figure 2.5, example (d).

2.5 CAPITAL GOODS, CONSUMER GOODS, AND ECONOMIC GROWTH

One of the key issues in determining whether or not an economy (and its PPC) grows is the priority that the people in an economy give to generating productive resources. **Capital goods** are **the machinery, equipment, buildings, and productive resources (other than labor) used to produce goods and services**. When an economy produces capital goods, it becomes more productive, shifting out its PPC. A PPC could also shift out from an improvement in **technology**, which would make capital goods more productive. **Labor** is another productive resource. When an economy has more laborers, it can produce more goods and services, shifting out its PPC. Economists also consider **human capital** to be a capital good: Education and training make our labor force more productive, which also shifts out the PPC. **Consumer goods**, on the other hand, are **goods that are purchased and used by consumers but that do not contribute to future productivity**. Consumer goods include such items as beer, clothing, and food. The addition of labor, human capital, or capital goods increases an economy's productivity and shifts out its PPC, but producing additional consumer goods does not shift the PPC.

Mainstream economic theory suggests that, in general, economic growth (growth in the PPC) is a result of increases in labor, increases in capital goods, and increases in productivity (from better technology or greater human capital):

$$\text{Economic growth} = \Delta L + \Delta K + \Delta \text{Productivity},$$

where Δ = change, L = labor, and K = capital.

An economy that draws more of its population into the labor force, devotes more of its resources to capital goods than to consumer goods, and improves its education and technology will experience more rapid economic growth.

Much of China's recent growth can be explained by these factors: For the last 35 years, China drew millions of relatively unproductive rural workers into its highly productive urban factories, and it invested heavily in capital goods, technology development, education, and infrastructure (roads, bridges, ports, and airports, also considered capital goods), which in turn increased productivity. The result was an astounding economic boom and economic growth averaging 9.8% a year from 1979 to 2013. For comparison, the average annual U.S. economic growth rate during the same period was 2.7%.

2.5.1 Defense spending and growth

Interestingly, government spending on national defense is considered to be a consumer good. Defense spending protects people within a country, but it does not increase the economy's productive capacity. Thus, we "consume" defense much like we do other services that we value but that do not contribute to economic growth.

Consider Figure 2.6, which shows a PPC for capital goods and consumer goods. If the society depicted in Figure 2.6 (on the next page) chooses point **A**, with more capital goods and fewer consumer goods like national defense, it will experience greater economic growth, its PPC will shift out further, and it will have a higher standard of living in the future (a larger PPC, which allows it to consume more of both goods). If the society chooses point **B**, with fewer capital goods and more consumer goods, the PPC will shift out less in the future.

The facts that economic growth is generated in part by capital goods and that defense spending is a consumer good make the choice of whether or not to devote

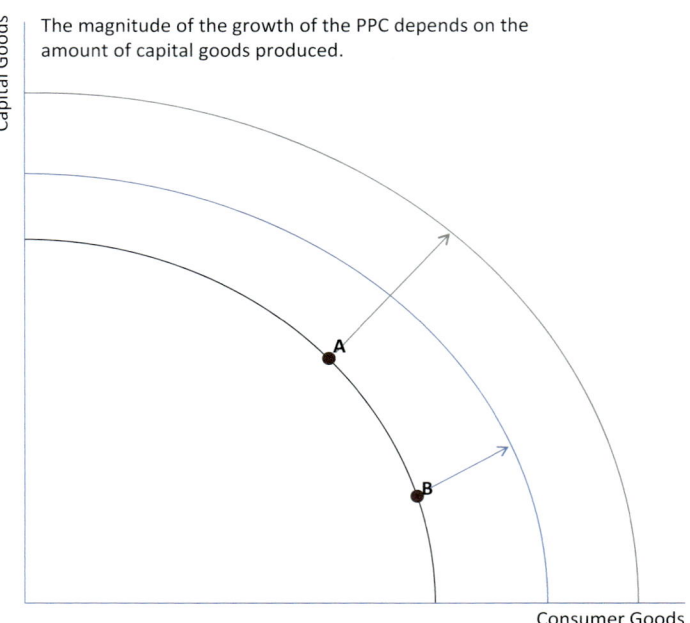

FIGURE 2.6 Growth in the PPC from additional capital goods.

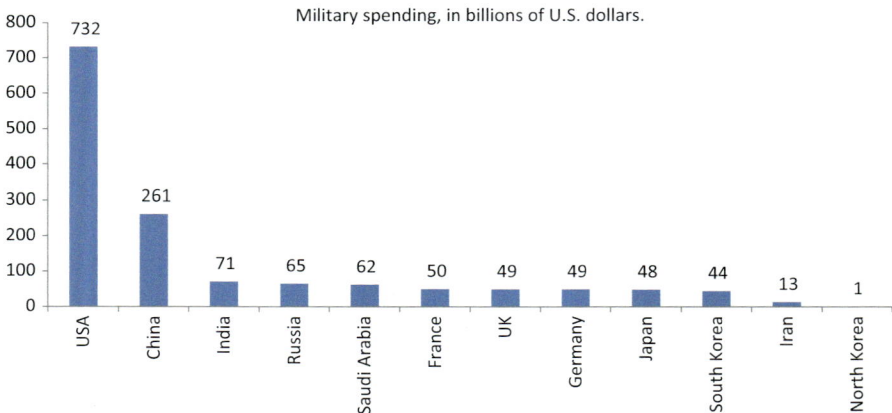

FIGURE 2.7 The ten largest military spenders in 2019, plus Iran and North Korea.

significant resources to national defense a very important one for a society. As you can see in Figure 2.7, the United States devotes more of its resources to military spending than any other country in the world.[1] In fact, the United States devotes more money to defense than the next nine countries combined! The United States spends more than twice as much on defense as the countries the United States sees as major security risks: China, Russia, Iran, and North Korea. The opportunity cost of spending so much on defense is both the current goods that are given up *and* the future goods that are sacrificed due to lower economic growth.

Thus, the mainstream PPC model focuses on how society chooses to allocate its scarce resources. In doing so, the model encourages society to consider carefully the opportunity costs of making choices. However, as we will see in the next section, political economists extend their analysis of scarcity and choice into additional areas.

2.6 A POLITICAL ECONOMY CRITIQUE OF SCARCITY AND CHOICE IN MAINSTREAM ECONOMICS

The economies of the modern developed world produce enough goods and services for everyone to have a standard of living that would have been unthinkable a century ago. Thus, to characterize economics as the study of scarcity rather than abundance is a reflection of a particular set of assumptions and value choices. To mainstream economists, an efficient allocation of resources occurs when no one can be made better off without making someone else worse off. The idea of redistributing goods and services from one person to another is considered outside the realm of analysis. This is a reflection of the mainstream's attempt to practice value-free, "positive" analysis rather than taking into consideration values and other normative elements of economic issues. Political economists of various types find the mainstream analysis of scarcity and choice overly limiting, and they extend their analysis into a number of areas, including ethics, culture, underemployment of resources, inequality, and gender empowerment. A brief analysis of each of these areas will provide an excellent introduction to the crucial differences between mainstream analysis and that of different schools of political economy.

2.6.1 Ethical considerations

Social economists urge us to consider the ethical considerations of our decisions regarding resource allocation. Is it ethical to devote additional resources to B-2 bombers and other defense goods when many children do not have enough food to eat? One of the most important economic decisions a society can make is how it chooses to allocate its resources, and such ethical considerations play a crucial part in that choice.

2.6.2 Culture and conspicuous consumption

The fact that rich consumers in wealthy countries want to buy more and more lavish goods can be seen as an indication not of scarcity but of what the **institutionalist** economist Thorstein Veblen called **conspicuous consumption**: **Purchasing goods in order to display social status**. To Veblen and other institutionalists, a crucial aspect of an economic system is the cultural forces that encourage conspicuous consumption at the expense of other worthwhile societal goals. Why do human beings seem bent on showing off their wealth to achieve social status? From this perspective, understanding consumer choices is less about scarcity than the fact that consumers with an unprecedented level of material well-being, drowning in high-tech gadgets and luxury goods, think that they need to buy even more goods than they already have. Determining the cultural processes that drive consumerist attitudes is therefore important to our understanding of resource allocation in the economy.

2.6.3 Underemployed resources

Another issue concerns whether or not resources are ever fully employed and how easily they can be switched to new uses. The production possibilities curve model implies that resources are usually fully employed and that resources can always be shifted to another use, although there may be increasing opportunity costs when that is done. Does this match the real-world experiences we see around us? As U.S. manufacturers have increasingly moved their factories to foreign sites in China, Mexico, and elsewhere, there has been a significant increase in availability of resources. Buildings, factories, machines, and manufacturing workers in the United States are now available to produce different goods instead of the steel, cars, and other manufactured goods that they used to produce. However, instead of shifting easily and quickly into other productive activities, most of the old factories sit unused, and many manufacturing workers remain unemployed. The "rust belt" of the United States, with depressed cities like Detroit, Youngstown, and Allentown, shows us that the shift of resources to new uses has not happened effectively. In reality, given chronic unemployment and underutilized resources, the United States may never have been on its PPC. From a **post-Keynesian** perspective, the key economic problem is not scarcity but how society can put all of its productive resources to their best possible use. In every society, there are people who need work and work that needs to be done. The key economic issue is not so much scarcity as the underemployment of resources, something that can be addressed by good government policies.

2.6.4 Inequality

It is also worth pointing out that abundance for the few is accompanied in wealthy countries by vast poverty. At the same time that the rich are consuming ever more luxury goods, more than 1.5 million people experience homelessness in a single year in the United States. To a **Marxist** (radical political) economist, the key issue is not scarcity but the structure of the class system and power structures of society that result in abundance for a few and poverty and homelessness for millions. Why are the lower classes in the United States, and especially citizens from Black and Latino backgrounds, so poor while others are so rich? Scarcity, from a Marxist perspective, is a condition imposed on the **working class** by greedy capitalists who want more for themselves while denying workers a decent standard of living. Only in countries where strong labor movements have reduced the power of corporate interests do we see workers earning a decent share of what is produced. Marxists focus on the analysis of social classes to understand resource allocation in societies, a topic that is omitted from mainstream analysis.

2.6.5 Gender empowerment

Another key issue, from the perspective of **feminist** economists, involves who is making the decisions and what priorities their decisions reflect. If women had greater political and economic power, would the decisions of society reflect different priorities? The Northern European countries that lead the world in gender empowerment tend to have much more generous family leave policies and welfare states. They provide new parents with up to a year of paid leave to care for a child (compared with six weeks of unpaid leave in the United States), and they provide all citizens with high-quality health care and education (including college), paid for by taxes on income and consumption. These countries have decided to devote more resources to family time, health, and education, while devoting fewer resources to consumer goods. There is a gendered component to decision making that reflects crucial aspects of an economic system, so any analysis of resource allocation must include an analysis of gender.

The above examples of how various groups of political economists view scarcity and choice illustrate the fundamental difference between mainstream economics and political economy: Mainstream economists prefer focusing on specific decisions using the concepts of scarcity and opportunity cost, whereas political economists prefer a **much broader approach** that emphasizes various crucial **institutions** in the economy. That approach is described in more detail in the next section.

2.7 INSTITUTIONAL ANALYSIS: A POLITICAL ECONOMY APPROACH TO THE STUDY OF RESOURCE ALLOCATION

When political economists study resource allocation, they focus on institutions. **Institutions** are **the organizations, social structures, rules, and habits that structure human interactions and the economy**. Formal institutions include laws, regulations, firms, government bodies, and the political system. Informal institutions include culture, social classes, habits, and other patterns of behavior that shape how people act and interact. Institutions are specific to a particular time and place. From this perspective, the opportunity cost of producing bombers is less informative than the factors that shape the actual choice of bombers and national defense over education in the modern United States.

In analyzing why the United States has chosen to devote vast resources to B-2 bombers and other defense goods over education, political economists focus on power structures, class, politics, culture, and other key institutions. The economic system in the modern United States is dominated by huge corporations. Similarly, the political system is dominated to a large degree by those corporations and the wealthy individuals who own them and who give vast sums of money to politicians. Some of the most powerful corporations and wealthy individuals have financial interests in the defense industry, and via political donations they encourage politicians to keep building B-2 bombers. U.S. corporate interests in foreign countries sometimes need the U.S. military to intervene on their behalf, which requires a U.S. military presence around the globe. In general, political economists see the U.S. military as supporting the dominant class of corporate leaders, wealthy owners, and politicians.

The U.S. military is itself a powerful institution that has been very successful in persuading Congress to continue funding defense expenditures at an extremely high level, even in times of peace. Furthermore, Congress can safely spend huge sums of money on defense due in part to U.S. cultural attitudes. The United States is known to be much more patriotic than other countries, as measured in the World Values Surveys. This contributes to a willingness of citizens to devote more resources to the military than other countries do and the ability of politicians to appeal to patriotism when they increase funding for national defense.

These factors led President Dwight D. Eisenhower, a five-star general during World War II, to warn against the powerful alliance of the corporate defense industry and the military. In a famous speech in 1961, he warned, "In the councils of government, we must guard against the acquisition of unwarranted influence, whether sought or unsought, by the military–industrial complex. The potential for the disastrous rise of misplaced power exists, and will persist." The fact that defense spending in the United States continues to be at a level much higher than that of other countries indicates the ongoing vitality of the military–industrial complex.

From a political economy perspective, the decision of the United States to place a very high priority on national defense and a lower priority on education in comparison to most developed countries is a product of a variety of institutional factors. Scarcity is one of the important issues that affects how many resources can be devoted to defense and education. Nonetheless, political economists prefer a much broader focus for economics than scarcity. Economic models can be useful in helping us to focus on a few key economic relationships, but they can ignore many other important factors that come into play. The question of which relationships to focus on deeply divides mainstream and political economists.

2.8 CONCLUSION

To mainstream economists, economics is about the difficult choices an individual, firm, or society must make when resources are scarce. By carefully considering the opportunity cost as well as the benefits of choosing to devote resources in a particular way, decision making can be improved. A simple mainstream model, the production possibilities curve, can be used to analyze the opportunity cost of a particular allocation of resources, including the relationship between capital goods, consumer goods, and economic growth. This is a flexible approach that can be applied to numerous situations.

Political economists acknowledge the usefulness of cost–benefit analysis, while also stressing the need to broaden this approach. From a political economy perspective, economists must go beyond scarcity to study the institutions that shape choices in a society. By combining the focused cost–benefit analysis of mainstream economics with the breadth of political economy, you are likely to get a very clear picture of the trade-offs facing society and how those trade-offs are shaped by key institutional factors.

To be sure, the analysis above is but a quick glance at a set of different approaches taken by mainstream and political economists. As we continue, these differences will become more apparent. Also, it is important to recognize that the example of the mainstream PPC model suggests a fundamental focus by the mainstream on mathematical approaches and an attempt to make their analysis as scientific as possible. Political economists, on the other hand, prefer to bring in additional factors that cannot always be measured precisely but that nevertheless can have an important influence on the economy.

Now that you are familiar with some of the fundamental premises and applications of mainstream economics and political economy, the next crucial topic to explore is the evolution of the global economy over time. The institutions of society were developed in the past and shape the future in key ways. The best way to understand where the economic system is going is to understand where it has been. Analyzing economic history can help you anticipate the likely trends in the future, and such economic forecasting is an invaluable economic skill.

QUESTIONS FOR REVIEW

1. Explain how each of the following events would affect scarcity.
   a. Consumers' desire for goods and services decreases.
   b. Resources become less plentiful.
   c. The government discovers a large amount of unused resources.
2. Use the concept of opportunity cost to analyze the decision of whether or not you should study economics tonight.
3. The graph in Figure 2.8 displays a production possibilities curve for the world in choosing between allocating resources to food or machinery.
   a. What is the opportunity cost of moving from point **B** to point **D**?
   b. What is the opportunity cost of one unit of machinery between point **D** and point **C**?

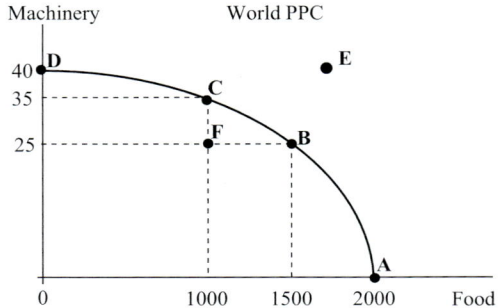

FIGURE 2.8 PPC for problem 3.

    c. Which points on the graph are considered to be efficient and feasible? Explain briefly.

    d. The reason for the curved shape of the PPC above is that (choose the best answer):

       (i) Resources are scarce.
       (ii) Increasing food production causes a decrease in machinery production.
       (iii) There are opportunity costs for producing more of either good.
       (iv) Some inputs are better at producing food than machinery.
       (v) None of the above.

    e. Scientists estimate that global climate change will destroy 10% of land that is current used to produce food. Show on a graph how this will affect the PPC.

    f. Assuming that the world is at point **B** on the PPC, producing and consuming 1500 units of food, and that the world will need to continue consuming the same amount after global climate change destroys 10% of land, how will the destruction of land affect the production of machinery? Will economic growth in the future be affected by these changes? Why or why not?

    g. How would political economists broaden the analysis in parts e and f of this question? What institutions would they think are most relevant to the issues being raised?

4. The graph in Figure 2.9 displays a production possibilities curve for the United States in choosing between allocating resources to transportation or beer.

    a. What is the opportunity cost of one unit of beer between point **A** and point **B**?

    b. What is the opportunity cost of moving from point **A** to point **C**?

    c. Show what would happen to the graph if the government fails to maintain their transportation infrastructure.

    d. The president of the United States recently proposed that the United States should dramatically increase its transportation spending. Assume

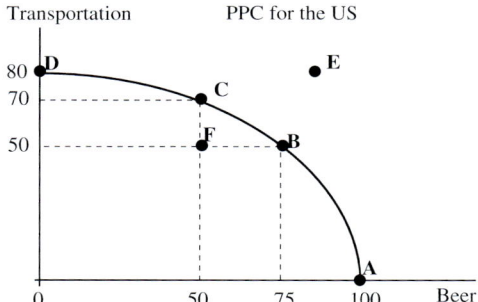

FIGURE 2.9 PPC for problem 4.

      that the economy is currently at point **B** in Figure 2.9. If we follow the president's plan and increase transportation spending dramatically, what would be the immediate, short-term effect?
   e. Economic data indicate that transportation spending by the government improves businesses' productivity. Using the PPC model, analyze what the president's proposal to increase transportation spending will do in the long run to the U.S. economy.
   f. How would political economists respond to the analysis in parts d and e?
5. Given the factors that mainstream economists believe contribute to economic growth, what would happen to economic growth and to the production possibilities curve for the United States if it halts all immigration into the country and the U.S. population actually declines?
6. Scientists are convinced that the burning of fossil fuels is contributing to global climate change, which will harm future economic growth.
   a. Construct a PPC showing the trade-off between fossil fuels and renewable energy. Explain how different points on the PPC will affect future growth in the PPC.
   b. Undertake an analysis from a political economy perspective about the choice of whether or not to devote resources to renewable energy. Why do you think the United States devotes fewer resources to renewable energy than many other developed countries?

NOTE

1 Source: SIPRI (Stockholm International Peace Research Institute).

PART II
The evolution of economic ideas and systems

The economic systems of the world have changed dramatically over the course of human history. The only certainty about economic systems appears to be that they will continue to change as they are forced to confront inherent contradictions and new problems. Human economic systems evolved from cooperative hunting and gathering communities to kingdoms that exploited slaves to variations of market capitalism in which privately owned firms controlled the bulk of society's resources. The fact that no economic system has lasted forever leads to an interesting question: *What type of economic system might replace contemporary market capitalism?*

As economic systems evolved, so did economic thought. All economic thinkers reflect the society and the economic problems of their era. Some of the earliest authors who took up economic topics, including Plato and Aristotle, justified slavery on the grounds that some people were naturally inferior. Adam Smith lived toward the end of the mercantilist era, when giant monopolies working with autocratic governments dominated global trade and extracted resources from the rest of society. He believed that unregulated market capitalism would be preferable to mercantilism because competition would limit the power of monopolistic firms and enhance the well-being of workers. Karl Marx wrote during the dark ages of capitalism, when it was not uncommon for children to be shackled to machines for up to 78 hours a week. Marx hoped that a socialist or communist system would solve the worst excesses of capitalism. In the early 1900s, Thorstein Veblen saw that small U.S. firms were being displaced by vast corporations run by the robber barons, who ruthlessly extracted profits from their workers and from society. Like Smith, Veblen believed that only by reining in large corporations would market capitalism be able to function for the well-being of all people. John Maynard Keynes wrote his masterwork, *The General Theory of Employment, Interest and Money*, during the Great Depression, a crisis that convinced him and many others that unregulated market capitalism could not work. Keynes advocated a regulated form of capitalism, which is the economic system that came to dominate the modern

DOI: 10.4324/9780429399350-4

world. But, as Keynes was advocating the development of a government-regulated market capitalist economy, the rise of Hitler in Germany and Stalin in the Soviet Union caused Friedrich Hayek to question whether or not we should put our trust in government.

Part II describes the evolution of economic systems from ancient times to the present. In the process, we will take up the best ideas of the most influential economists in the context in which they wrote their ideas. As we study the different forms that economic systems have taken, think carefully about what lessons emerge regarding human nature from the many ways in which human beings have organized themselves to produce the goods and services necessary for survival. And, as we study the theories of the great economists, critically evaluate their ideas against the economy you see around you to decide for yourself which theories are still relevant to the modern world.

Chapter 3 briefly describes the evolution of economic systems from communal, tribal societies to slave-based empires, followed by feudalism and mercantilism. The chapter then turns to the establishment of capitalism and the ideas of Adam Smith. Chapter 4 goes through the labor unrest and economic crises that were a product of the dark ages of capitalism in the 1800s and early 1900s and the ideas that Karl Marx and Thorstein Veblen developed in this era. Chapter 5 describes the rise of mixed market capitalism in the wake of the Great Depression based on the ideas of John Maynard Keynes. Chapter 6 examines the market-dominated, social market, and state-dominated economies we see in the modern world. Part II concludes with Chapter 7 covering how markets function in modern economies.

3 The evolution of economic systems and the ideas of Adam Smith

From communal societies to early capitalism

Every society needs an economic system of some sort to provide the goods and services its people need to survive and thrive. But only in modern times, under capitalism, has that economy been controlled by markets and the pursuit of private profit. Early human societies did make use of markets, but their use was extremely limited and markets were almost never entrusted with the provision of the main goods a society needed for its survival.

The harsh conditions of the ancient world required people to band together for survival. The survival of individuals required doing everything necessary for the group to ensure its survival, and the largest, most closely knit groups were the ones that triumphed over smaller, less cohesive ones. Thus, due to our evolutionary history, individual motivations seem to be group oriented rather than completely self-interested. This is one of the biggest reasons why political economists dispute the mainstream economics portrayal of economic man as primarily individualistic and self-interested: throughout human history, people have cared deeply about their place in their social group. In fact, their survival depended on it.

Human beings have lived and worked in a wide variety of economic systems that they have designed over the centuries. As we will see below, early human societies were usually characterized by reciprocity, redistribution, sharing, and trust. They also engaged in some specialization of tasks and a simple division of labor to facilitate their survival.

Once societies began to produce enough surplus food that everyone did not have to work, hierarchical class systems began to develop. These grew in size and

DOI: 10.4324/9780429399350-5

complexity as the surplus expanded, accompanied by a gradual increase in the use of trade and markets to provide goods for the elites. In slave societies, a small minority controlled the resources and most of the population barely earned enough to survive. However, slave societies proved to be unstable, and they were followed by the static, hierarchical system of feudalism, where lords controlled the labor of serfs. Feudalism lasted for 1000 years, but it, too, eventually became untenable, and it was replaced by mercantilism in the 1500s. Markets began to take on an important role when kings and merchants constructed and expanded markets for their own benefit. But even under mercantilism, markets did not control the allocation of a majority of society's resources. It was only with the advent of full-fledged capitalism in the 1800s that market capitalism became the dominant economic system and society's productive resources, land, labor, and capital came to be allocated by markets.

This chapter will briefly describe the evolution of human economic systems from communal, tribal societies to the more hierarchical systems of slave-based empires, feudalism and mercantilism, and eventually to the beginnings of capitalism. It draws on the classic work by Karl Polanyi, *The Great Transformation*, along with recent discoveries in economic anthropology, psychology, and evolutionary biology that address the evolution of human societies over time. Subsequently, the chapter describes the ideas of Adam Smith and the argument for laissez-faire capitalism, along with the problems that developed under this economic system.

3.0 CHAPTER 3 LEARNING GOALS

After reading this chapter you should be able to:

- Describe the evolution of economic systems.
- List and analyze the major forces that eroded each economic system and paved the way for the next economic system.
- Explain the ideas of Adam Smith and his argument that laissez-faire capitalism was preferable to mercantilism.
- Describe some of the major problems that emerged during early capitalism.

We begin by considering what we know about the earliest human societies that existed.

3.1 TRADITIONAL ECONOMIES: ANCIENT HUNTER-GATHERER SOCIETIES

Human beings are inherently group-oriented, social creatures. The earliest tool-using human ancestors of 2 million years ago were nomadic hunter-gatherers living in groups of around 70 members, usually comprising large kinship groups (extended families). The earliest human societies lived at the edge of survival. They did not have the ability to store food for long periods, so obtaining a steady supply of food every day was the primary human activity. Any shortfall for a sustained period of time meant starvation. In this environment, cooperative, communal groups had an advantage.

Cooperation was useful in protecting the community from predators, including animals as well as other human groups. A larger community could also engage in larger scale, risky activities. While some community members were devoted to the regular hunting and gathering activities, some high-risk endeavors with potentially large payoffs, such as hunting large game, would be undertaken by a small portion of the community. This allowed for a degree of **specialization** and innovation in performing tasks and resulted in a more secure food supply.

Redistribution (sharing) and **reciprocity** within the group were defining characteristics of these early societies. Producers shared with their community because they could expect reciprocity: When another member of the community found food, they, too, would share it. Redistribution was crucial to survival, in that a family without the support of a larger group was at high risk of starvation. One bout of serious illness or a run of bad luck in hunting and gathering and the family could starve. But, with the support of the community, they could survive the lean times. Thus, although independent families did sometimes live on their own (householding), larger groups were more successful. This type of system has sometimes been labeled **primitive communism** because of the emphasis on common production and the relatively egalitarian sharing of the collectively produced goods.

To effectively allocate tasks and goods, our human ancestors developed customs or traditions. A traditional economy is one in which **resources are allocated based on communal patterns of reciprocity and redistribution and in which tasks are allocated and knowledge and skills are preserved through established social relationships**. A traditional economy is dominated by the cultural forces that shape the allocation of resources, goods, and tasks. In such societies, culture and tradition were crucial in making sure that society's knowledge was passed down to the next generation, guaranteeing that a community had enough people with the appropriate skill set allocated to each task (hunting, tracking, gathering, tool making, etc.) and in uniting society in the face of external threats.

In the harsh hunter-gatherer environment, the highest social status was allotted to those who were the most productive members of society. One of the characteristics of people in all human societies seems to be the desire to achieve social status. The desire for status is probably hard-wired into us by the evolutionary process: Those who achieved a higher social status were more likely to survive and procreate. Historical evidence indicates that human beings are inherently status-seeking, which is **the human propensity to strive to achieve the highest social status possible, given the values of the community in which they live**.

The criteria for achieving a high social status vary substantially based on the society and its priorities. Traditional economies valued the production of food and held the most productive hunters and gatherers in high esteem. To political economists, one of the keys to analyzing the economy of a particular place is understanding how its culture shapes the **status-seeking** of its members. Human beings work to succeed in their particular community, which means they try to **act rationally within a cultural context** to achieve social status.

In addition to valuing productivity above other activities, most traditional communities tended to practice a form of direct democracy. Each adult had a say in major decisions, so the power of the chief was quite limited.

In such communities, there was limited specialization of tasks. Everyone needed to perform a large number of tasks every day just to stay alive. The most significant division of tasks was along gender lines, with men performing the hunting and women focused on gathering, child-rearing, and cooking. Mothers would teach their daughters the knowledge and skills associated with their specialized tasks, and their daughters would follow in their footsteps. Fathers and sons followed the same pattern.

The development of technology was severely limited because traditional economies produced barely enough food to survive and because of the limited amount of specialization. **Technology** refers to **the tools, skills, and scientific knowledge that society develops in the use of resources to produce goods and services**. Technology, along with cultural factors, plays a crucial role in structuring what an economic system is like. Societies that face a constant threat of starvation tend to be deeply risk averse, and they are rarely willing to expend the labor and resources needed to develop new technologies. Nor do they have enough surplus labor or resources to undertake substantial investments in new technologies due to their low level of productivity.

Human groups steadily increased in size over time, indicating that larger groups had an evolutionary advantage over smaller groups, likely due to a greater degree of specialization of labor. **Specialization of labor** is a fundamental characteristic of all human societies in which **particular tasks are performed by specific individuals, rather than everyone performing all tasks**. Specialization tends to improve productivity because people develop **skills**, getting really good at the tasks they specialize in (tracking game, finding roots and berries, etc.). Via their expertise, they can develop simple **tools** (technology) for their work. The larger the group and the more specialized the tasks, the more productive that society is likely to be. Furthermore, larger groups have greater **military power** and are better able to dominate smaller groups. Correspondingly, those humans who could successfully function in large groups were more likely to survive. Our evolutionary past indicates that we evolved to function effectively in a large group setting.

3.2 AGRICULTURE AND THE ESTABLISHMENT OF CITIES, SOCIAL CLASSES, AND EMPIRES

About 12,000 years ago, the invention of agriculture (farming and herding), sharper tools, and new materials, especially pottery for food storage, caused a dramatic increase in the ability of communities to support a larger population due to the larger supply of food. Instead of each person providing subsistence just for oneself and one's family, farmers were able to produce enough food to provide for more people.

As groups grew larger, it became important to develop institutions, including codes of behavior and other rules, to develop the high degree of trust that is crucial to the functioning of a larger society. The development of a strong group identity, with cultural or religious bonds and a prevailing ideology, took on increased significance.

Group identification was now even more crucial because the production and storage of surplus food made warfare increasingly important. In agricultural societies, the rewards of military aggression were substantial. A powerful army could seize the stored food and the most productive land of other groups. Then they could force the conquered people to work for them as slaves and seize any surplus that was produced. This highlights a key aspect of all economic systems: the production and allocation of **surplus product**.

Surplus product is **the amount that is produced over and above what is needed for the community's survival**. The **necessary product**—**what is necessary for a community's survival—includes food and shelter for everyone, plus the replacement of tools and materials used up in production**.

The generation of a surplus product caused dramatic changes in society. In addition to being a cause of warfare, surpluses were a source of economic growth when they were used to augment the productive resources of society (investment). For example, excess grain that was used to feed horses or oxen that could be used as draft animals made farms more productive. Labor could be used to build irrigation canals and aqueducts to increase crop yields. In these cases, sacrificing current resources (grain, labor) in the short term to invest in the development of capital goods caused increased output in the future.

The surplus product was also necessary for cities to develop, because larger population centers relied on the surplus food produced by the agricultural areas for their sustenance. In those cities, artisans specialized in the development of more sophisticated tools, which increased productivity further. Human civilization as we know it grew out of the production of surplus food.

Control of surpluses proved to be a major source of power. The surplus of food allowed a more elaborate social hierarchy to develop in which some members of society no longer had to work at food production. Kings, emperors, chiefs, and priests seized and controlled the land and resources, sitting atop the hierarchy and avoiding manual labor while slaves or peasants did the most productive tasks of society. With the advent of agriculture in 10,000 BCE, for the first time in human history, property rights came into existence. **Property rights** exist when **a productive resource such as land or slave labor belongs to a particular person or group instead of to society as a whole**. The production of surplus is therefore also associated with the rise of private property and the establishment of social classes in human society. In economics, **class** refers to **a group of people that has a specific relationship with the production process**.

In order to protect property rights, stave off slave revolts, fend off invaders, provide public goods (irrigation, flood control, roads, etc.), and organize larger and more complex societies, it was necessary to develop a system of government for the first time. The role of a **government** is to **provide the institutions that develop and implement policies for the state**. The state could be a kingdom, a democratic republic, or something in between, but every state needs a government to undertake key tasks and to maintain the functioning of the economic system.

Closely related to the system of government was the **ideological system that justified the existing class structure**. Religions developed that supported the status quo, preaching, for example, the divinity of the Pharaohs and erecting the Great Pyramids to cement those views. Along with the rise of class interests, we also see the values of the community change. Instead of the solidarity and equality of hunter-gatherer communities, societies divided by classes tended to be much **more individualistic**, with people working more for themselves.

Despite the rise of an unproductive, elite class and the creation of occupations in government, the army, and the priesthood, the major work of society was still agricultural, and this work was done by peasants or slaves. The **peasants** of antiquity did not own their land; land was owned or controlled by a great lord. But peasants did tend to have rights to farm certain land, and that right was usually passed down to their children. Peasants produced for their own family and handed over a portion of their output (the surplus) to their lord. Peasants produced barely enough food to survive, so they tended to stick with well-known methods and avoid any risky undertaking that could result in starvation. Thus, peasants represented a particular class of people in agricultural systems, with some rights of access to land but with obligations to their lord. Their behavior was governed by **tradition**, including the established social relations; the basic, almost unchanging level of technology; and the **authority** of the lord.

In addition to peasants, the largest ancient human societies relied extensively on slave labor. A **slave** had no control over the resources used to produce goods and services, received only enough food to survive on, and was completely subject to the **authority** of the merchant or lord who owned them. In the city-state of ancient Athens in Greece as well as in the Roman Empire, between 30% and 80% of the people were slaves at various times. Slave economies required large governments and military operations to maintain power and control in the face of regular slave rebellions.

In the great cities of ancient Egypt, Greece, or Italy, one could find goods from all over the known world sold in markets. However, most of these goods were luxuries intended for the upper classes and food for the elites and their slaves and servants. The markets of this era fulfilled a limited role compared to their function in modern capitalism. Status (and wealth) was a product of political, military, or religious power more than one's productivity for the community.

Societies of this era did not develop at an equal rate, as Jared Diamond lays out in his book *Guns, Germs and Steel*. Groups living in the Middle East, Europe, and Asia had the great luck to have access to the most nutritious grains and the most easily domesticated animals (beasts of burden and animals for food). Greater food production led to higher population densities, and in those densely populated cities, people developed resistance to germs. Larger populations also meant more specialization and development of better technology, especially weapons and ships, and more elaborate political and military organizations.

Because of these advantages, the peoples living in the Fertile Crescent area of the Middle East were the first to develop large states, making this region the "cradle of civilization." A series of large empires developed in and around the Fertile Crescent, beginning with Mesopotamia around 2300 BCE, Egypt around 1500 BCE, the Hittites around 1300 BCE, the Assyrians around 715 BCE, the Persians in 539 BCE, Macedonia in 334 BCE, and eventually Rome from 50 BCE to 456 CE.

At the height of the Roman Empire, 1 million residents of the city of Rome were supported by 80 to 100 million subjects. Impressive military power, effective communication, and efficient transportation networks (roads and ships) allowed Rome to control a huge land area and to generate a steady inflow of goods and wealth. Rome was able to demand rents, taxes, tributes, and gifts from citizens and conquered provinces because of their military control of the region. Imported products included food (fruits, grains, honey, wine, olive oil, meats), metals (gold and silver to make coins, copper, tin, iron, and lead), materials (marble, ivory, pottery, cloth), and slaves. These resources were used to maintain the army, administer the government, support the city, and allow the elite to live in luxury.

Eventually Rome began to stagnate as its slave-based economy became less productive and as the power of the army declined. Slavery was initially very productive as free farmers developed new farming techniques (especially irrigation) and brought new land into cultivation using slave labor. However, over time, economic growth stagnated. Free farmers, who were driven to increase their status by increasing their wealth, were displaced by the vast slave estates of the elite. The elite looked down on work and technology and made no effort to develop new farming techniques. Slaves themselves had little interest in innovation because they had to work all day, every day no matter how innovative they were. Slaves also required intensive supervision and could not be trusted with complex independent tasks or tools that could be used as weapons. Also, the Roman Empire began to run short of slaves because so many died young or were killed (in revolts or in sport) and because of a decline in conquests as the army's power decreased. The army shrank as the supply of free farmers and peasants dwindled due to war and economic stagnation. After many years of decline, Rome fell in 456 CE to Germanic invaders and the era of empires in the Fertile Crescent came to an end. What followed in Europe was the era of feudalism, which lasted for the next 1000 years.

3.3 FEUDALISM AND THE MANOR ECONOMY IN WESTERN EUROPE

As the Roman Empire collapsed, chaos spread across Europe and the Middle East. Amidst the chaos, security and survival became the highest priority. In response, the Roman elite, and later the chiefs of Germanic tribes and other European leaders, turned to a new economic system: Feudalism. Feudalism was organized around independent **manors**, which consisted of large tracts of land controlled by a lord. Slaves were granted greater freedom and became serfs. **Serfs** were obligated to work for their lord on his land a certain number of days each year, in exchange for protection as well as the right to farm a small amount of land for themselves using the lord's tools (ploughs) and draft animals (oxen and horses). Serfs also had access to common lands where they could farm, graze animals, and collect wood. Thus, there was a degree of reciprocity to the relationship between serfs and lords, even though the relations were highly slanted in favor of the lord.

The serf system was more productive and sustainable than slavery. Serfs had more of an incentive than slaves to work hard for the lord thanks to the protection, stability, and small amounts of property and independence they were granted. Eventually, all of Western Europe came to be divided into independent, self-sufficient, isolated manors. On the manor, the lord was the master of all who lived there, serving as judge, general, and governor. Serfs were tied to the land and to the lord, but they had a measure of security because they could not be removed from their land or their family. The most powerful lords gained control over the most land, becoming kings and demanding loyalty and military support from lesser lords. However, the kings of the feudal era were not very powerful, and most of the wealth and control of the economy rested with the lords.

Like the agriculture-based empires of the Fertile Crescent, feudalism was a system in which resources were allocated by **authority** and **tradition**. The authority of the feudal lord was paramount, and one's station in life was determined traditionally by one's birth. The eldest son of the lord became the next lord. The son of a serf was also a serf. The son of a blacksmith would also become a blacksmith. Serf women worked for lords as servants or makers of clothing, and at home they prepared food, raised the children, and maintained the household. Many serf women were sexually exploited by their lords, however, and women could not own property, so women still occupied an inferior position in society.

Because most feudal manors were self-sufficient, there was very little trade other than a few luxury goods for the lords. However, there were small cities that depended on trade and that hosted traveling fairs of merchants and entertainers, so a small amount commerce did occur in exchange for money.

The towns did have some tradespeople, such as armorers, blacksmiths, shipwrights, potters, weavers, and dyers, indicating that some specialization of labor did exist. But anyone who wanted to produce and sell such goods and services had to join a guild. Guilds were a type of union governing a particular trade or profession. Independent manufacturers, known as guildmasters, banded together to set quality standards and wages, limit competition by dividing up territory, and establish rules and codes of conduct. Working for the guildmasters were adult journeymen who hoped to be guildmasters someday and apprentices (usually children aged 10–12).

The guilds were incredibly detailed in the prescriptions governing their members, and innovation was strongly discouraged. Any new type of product or new process for making a product had to be approved by the guild, and such innovations were usually rejected as a threat to other producers. If one craftsman developed a superior technique, he might displace other craftsmen and upset the accepted order of things. In a society that prized safety and stability above all else, this was unacceptable, so any deviation from approved procedures could result in imprisonment, torture, or even death! Unsurprising, given that the utilization of new techniques could lead to dire outcomes, very little innovation occurred during feudalism.

In this system of decentralized manors, the Catholic Church was the largest owner of land, and the Catholic religion played a huge role in shaping society and its values. A tour of the cathedrals of Europe built during the feudal era demonstrates that much of the little surplus that was produced went to the church. In addition, religious prescriptions played a prominent role in the economy. For example, merchants were expected to charge a "just price," selling items for what they were worth and no more. Greed was considered to be a sin, a corrupting influence to be scorned and even punished. The notion of profit or personal gain was largely condemned until very recently in human history.

Moneylending was considered sinful under Catholicism. However, the Old Testament of the Bible allowed Jews to lend to non-Jews. As a result, many European Jews, barred from most professions by guilds and prohibited from owning land, turned to moneylending to Christians in order to make a living. The Jewish monopoly on moneylending meant that they could make a lot of money, but Christians resented the success of Jewish moneylenders based on biblical condemnations of usury. There was much Christian hostility toward Jews stemming from this strained relationship. The roots of much anti-Semitism in Europe can be traced to the feudal era and the differing views of Christians and Jews on the acceptability of moneylending.

The characteristics of feudal society help us to understand why life in Europe went largely unchanged for 1000 years. The small amount of surplus that was produced went to provide military protection or was squandered on luxuries for the lords and the church. Without any substantial investment, and with substantial resistance to technological change, there was very little economic growth. However, over time, a series of changes undermined feudalism.

An increase in the surplus of food occurred when **better agricultural technology**—a three-field crop rotation system—was developed. The additional food could support more people and surplus grains could support more horses and other farm animals. Europe's population doubled between 1000 and 1300 and, as a consequence, there was a significant increase in **urbanization and specialization**, which prompted additional development of skills and technology. With the increase in surpluses and development of more specialized products, as well as the crusades that brought Europe in contact with the Middle East and Asia, **long-distance trade** developed.

As trade increased in importance, merchants chafed under the stifling commercial system of feudalism in which each lord demanded a tax and restricted passage on their lands. They found an ally in the kings, who were looking to expand their influence over the largely independent feudal lords. Kings, with the financial support of merchants, began to expand their power and influence and develop larger and larger kingdoms. They amassed armies and built navies using the revenues from trade, stimulating manufacturing in the process. By the 1500s, Europe was a collection of nation-states with growing economic and military power under the control of kings and merchants. Kings and merchants relied on trade to generate gold and silver, which were needed to hire mercenaries and maintain an army and navy. One of the ways they could do this was by finding new places to trade with and new sources of raw materials and gold. Kings outfitted fleets for **exploration and colonization**, seeking gold, silver, exotic goods, and slaves to pay off the high costs of these ventures and to support the empire.

Europe's advanced weaponry and resistance to disease, a product of a longer history of living in close quarters, allowed them to dominate and decimate large areas of the world as they roamed the planet in search of riches. Eventually, the European countries set up colonial empires in the Americas, Africa, and Asia designed to funnel resources and gold to Europe, often using slave labor. Greed had displaced the feudal prohibitions on such behavior, marking a major **shift in ideology and religion**.

Calvinists (early Protestants) saw hard work and professional activity as one's calling and a sign of godliness. Individual wealth accumulation from hard work was considered evidence of doing God's work. Additionally, wealth was to be invested in further productive endeavors rather than wasted on luxuries. Even earning income from interest on loans was acceptable as a sign of engaging in a productive, profitable venture.

Calvinism and later variations of Protestantism provided the ideal ideological support for a market capitalist economic system based on self-interest, greed, hard work, and reinvestment. The idea of improving one's standing in society and celebrating the riches earned through hard work fostered economic growth. Not surprising, it was the nations in which Protestantism took the greatest hold that developed the earliest and most robust market systems. England, in particular, had the strongest departure from Catholicism and embracement of Protestantism when King Henry VIII and the Church of England broke with the papacy in the 1530s. Meanwhile, the earliest forms of **capitalist manufacturing** were also getting started.

Merchants began to set up entire buildings with tools and equipment and hired journeymen and apprentices with the requisite skills, bypassing independent craftsmen entirely. Merchant-capitalists began developing markets for buying and selling inputs, including labor, to use in their new factories. For the first time in human history, labor and significant amounts of resources started to be allocated based on **money** in **markets** and not by tradition or authority.

To generate cash income, lords began seizing the common lands for their own use. In England, lords fenced off (enclosed) common lands to raise sheep for the booming textile industry. Similar patterns followed in continental Europe. By the 1700s, 75% to 90% of peasants had been forced off of farms all over Europe and into urban slums. This, coupled with a rising population and rising rural rents, meant that cities had huge, desperate populations of former peasants with no means of subsistence. They had no land or tools and only their labor power to sell.

At the same time, the **enclosure movement** established the legal right of lords to the land they seized. The lords began to use the land as productively as possible to generate the income they needed, and the use of land came to be associated with the amount of revenue or rent it could bring. Thus, the enclosure movement created a market for labor power (former serfs and peasants who had to sell their labor to survive) and a market for land (which now could be sold or rented).

We also see how private property can be both constructive and destructive. If a property owner is secure in their ownership of the land, they are willing to invest in the productivity of the land by adding irrigation, breeding draft animals, fertilizing, and so on. On the other hand, privatizing the common lands cast millions of peasants into desperate, landless poverty. The culmination of all of these changes in feudalism was the establishment of the first market-based economic system: Mercantilism.

3.4 MERCANTILISM AND THE UNEASY BEGINNINGS OF CAPITALISM

National, market-based economic systems did not evolve naturally during mercantilism. They were created by the merchant-capitalists and monarchs of Europe for their own benefit. A national market system was resisted vigorously by the smaller towns and rural areas, which fought to maintain their tight regulation of local trade and preserve existing jobs. It took deliberate actions by the state in the 1400s and 1500s to break down the fiercely protectionist policies of the towns. Once local resistance was broken, the state replaced local rules on trading and manufacturing with national rules. Mercantilist economies were a tightly controlled form of national capitalism run by and for the merchant-capitalists and monarchs, grounded in the social hierarchies of the period.

The early mercantilist countries tried to maximize the inflow of gold, an approach known as **bullionism**, to cement their power and wealth. To do this, they tried to maintain a trade surplus by subsidizing and encouraging exports while taxing and discouraging imports. Particular merchants were granted monopolies on segments of the market to generate maximum profits.

Colonial empires also improved the profits from trading. Resources, especially raw materials and slave labor, could be had cheaply from the colonies. The British dismantled the thriving textile industry in India and forced the colony to export raw cotton to England, where it could be used by British industries to manufacture textiles. Similar stories occurred in Africa, Asia, and the Americas, as industries in the colonies were displaced in favor of the production of raw materials for export to the colonial power.

The transatlantic slave trade was a particularly horrific example of mercantilist trading patterns. Slave ships left England for West Africa carrying cloth, guns, alcohol, iron wares, and other manufactured goods. These were traded in West Africa for slaves who were captured by African chiefs collaborating with the English traders. The ships then traveled to the West Indies in the Caribbean and the colonial United States, where the slaves were sold at auctions to plantation owners. The ships were then loaded with the produce from the plantations, especially commodities like sugar, coffee, tobacco, and cotton, which were brought back to England. Merchants profited from each stage of the trade, while extracting resources from Africa and the Americas.

Initially, countries experienced economic growth under tightly controlled mercantilism. The expansion of markets internally in countries and externally to colonies enhanced profits and stimulated the development of new industries. But the control of the economy by the monarch and a handful of huge firms began to stifle the development of new firms and industries. An emerging group of capitalists working in mining, manufacturing, and other industries that were stimulated by the growth of trade chafed at the restricted, monopolized markets. They wanted more trade, greater access to domestic and foreign markets, and fewer government restrictions on their behavior. At the same time, mercantilism experienced some major economic problems: The enclosure of the common lands had created large pools of desperately poor workers without sufficient jobs or opportunities, and fluctuations in the supply of gold caused large swings in prices. Such a system, which worked well only for a small part of the population, ultimately proved to be unstable.

3.5 THE INDUSTRIAL REVOLUTION AND CAPITALISM IN ENGLAND

Human economies from the earliest systems through mercantilism revolved around labor and agriculture. The industrial revolution changed everything. The creation of the industrial factory signaled the rise in importance of **capital**, or the machinery, equipment, buildings, and other technological resources used to produce factory goods. First in England then across Europe and around the globe, the industrial revolution made ownership of capital the major power in the economy. Capitalism is **an economic system in which the capital goods and other productive resources (land, natural resources) are privately owned and are bought and sold in markets based on the pursuit of profits**. Under a capitalist economic system, workers, instead of laboring for themselves and keeping the proceeds, sell their labor power to the capitalist in exchange for wages. The capitalist, as the owner, gets to keep any surplus that is produced.

Under capitalism, the primary focus of all economic activity is profit. An owner takes a large sum of money and invests it in setting up a factory and hiring workers. Those workers produce a commodity of some kind. That commodity is (hopefully) sold for a greater value than the initial investment:

$$\text{Money}(M) \rightarrow \text{Commodities}(C) \rightarrow \text{More money}(M').$$

Early entrepreneurs had to advance a considerable sum of money ahead of time to cover costs, with no assurance that they would get a substantial return once a commodity was produced. This uncertain situation made them, as described by economic historian Paul Mantoux, "tyrannical, hard, sometimes cruel."

The Industrial Revolution began around 1760 in England with just such a group of "hard" entrepreneurs. England was **ideologically** better suited to a money-oriented, invention-driven capitalist economy, due to the dominance of Protestantism and its long interest in science and engineering. Second, England was the site of the most comprehensive enclosure movement and destruction of feudal society, which resulted in the most secure system of **property rights** and the largest pool of landless laborers. Third, England was wealthy, and this created a **large market** for manufactured products. England was also lucky to have large deposits of coal and iron ore, which were crucial in early manufacturing. Luck plus the vast colonial empire meant plenty of **cheap inputs** and **captive markets** for English manufacturers. The result was a system in which immense profits could be earned if entrepreneurs were willing to invest sufficient sums of money. Many were willing to do so, and their successes encouraged other entrepreneurs to follow.

Capitalists, who had to advance a considerable amount of money without the guarantee of a return on their investment, worked to drive very hard bargains with workers and land owners. Thus, with the rise of capitalism in the mid-1700s, we see for the first time in human history the notion of individual gain—the profit motive—becoming an all-pervasive force in society driving the behavior of workers, landowners, and capitalists.

3.6 ADAM SMITH, LAISSEZ-FAIRE CAPITALISM, AND SMITH'S CRITIQUE OF MERCANTILISM

In the budding capitalism taking place around him, Adam Smith saw the possibilities for an economic system that he hoped could solve the major problems of mercantilism. That system was limited laissez-faire (lightly regulated) capitalism. *Laissez-faire* is a French phrase for "let it be." When applied to the economy, a laissez-faire approach means letting the market run without significant interference from government.

Adam Smith (1723–1790) lived most of his life in Scotland, where he was surrounded by dynamic entrepreneurs such as his friend James Watt. Watt invented a revolutionary steam engine that was an essential part of the industrial revolution. These entrepreneurs needed access to new markets for inputs and goods so they could produce on a larger scale. The only way to recoup the large investment needed to set up a factory was to get inputs at low prices and to sell large quantities of the product the factory was producing. But mercantilist monopolies dominated trade, charging high prices for the commodities that entrepreneurs needed as inputs and limiting entrepreneurs' access to foreign markets. Smith argued that mercantilist policies were limiting economic growth and preventing the alleviation of poverty for three main reasons.

First, with every European country strictly regulating trade and preventing imports of manufactured goods, manufacturing firms could only produce for the domestic market. With free trade, firms would be able to sell their products to multiple countries, and that would allow them to produce more goods on a larger scale, which would be more efficient. Factories could be larger, which would promote the development of additional machinery and workers with more specialized skills.

Second, mercantilist policies reduced competition, allowing monopolies to form in key sectors. Without competition, monopoly firms did not have to be efficient or innovative to make a profit, keeping prices high and growth low.

Third, Smith objected to mercantilist policies to suppress wages. Mercantilist policies encouraged employers in a particular trade or geographical area to form a trade association, which could then meet to set wages at the lowest possible level. If employers were instead forced to compete with each other for workers, they would tend to bid up wages as they sought to hire the best people away from other firms. Agreeing to a fixed wage rate for the area eliminated such competition and kept wages low.

In Smith's view, the two great evils of his era were the **government** and the **monopolies** that set up the mercantilist system for their own benefit. The way to solve the poverty problem was, he thought, to stop the government from interfering with markets and to let competition force firms to be efficient and innovative. This, he hoped, would raise the standard of living of all citizens, and especially the poor.

3.7 SMITH'S IDEALIZED PICTURE OF A CAPITALIST SYSTEM

Smith believed that lightly regulated capitalism was preferable to mercantilism due to a number of key features of how he envisioned a competitive market capitalist system working. The key difference between this system and mercantilism would be its effect on economic growth. Smith's economics book was titled *The Wealth of Nations* in large part because he sought to analyze the determinants of wealth.

Smith's first important insight was that **wealth comes from productivity**, not from money (gold). Money is only useful if it can lead to a high standard of living, but a country's standard of living is determined by how productive it is—how many goods and services it can produce and consume—not how much money it has. A country that has lots of gold but produces very few goods will quickly find that the prices of those few goods are very high. But a country that is very productive will be able to consume lots of goods and services, no matter how much money they have. The fact that countries today use gross domestic product, which is the total production of goods and services in an economy, to measure the standard of living of people in an economy is a testament to Smith's enduring insight.

Second, Smith identified **the importance of the specialization of labor in enhancing productivity** (and wealth). As noted before, the specialization of labor occurs when particular tasks are performed by specific individuals, rather than everyone performing all tasks. This enhances productivity for three reasons, according to Smith. First, workers get better at their job, improving their skill and dexterity, when they specialize in one task instead of many tasks. Second, less time is spent moving from one job to another. Third, specialization leads to the invention of machines that facilitate and replace labor. The last of these tends to be the most important driver of productivity increases.

A good example of the importance of specialization comes from the car industry. The first cars were produced by teams of skilled craftsmen and entrepreneurs. But once entrepreneurs broke the manufacturing process down into discrete tasks and developed specialized machinery, the manufacturing process became much more productive. Each car part could be manufactured using a specialized process, which was subdivided into a series of even more specialized tasks. Figure 3.1 shows workers in 1913 on the first moving assembly line assembling magnetos and flywheels, which comprised one part of a Ford car.

Another crucial insight in Smith's analysis was the importance of **competition** in making markets work efficiently and fostering growth. In the absence of

FIGURE 3.1 The first moving assembly line for 1913 Ford cars.

competition, monopolistic companies could produce shoddy products and charge high prices because consumers had no other options. They also had no incentive to invest in new technology or new products because they could continue to make profits indefinitely without fear of new competition. These dominant companies could also pay workers very little because other companies were not competing to hire workers. Competition changes all of this. Competitive markets tend to generate better quality, lower prices, more innovations, and higher wages.

Ideally, Smith hoped, **competition would** even **regulate incomes and benefit the poor**, solving the huge poverty problem of the day. Smith envisioned the pattern unfolding as follows: (1) Bold entrepreneurs trying to get ahead of their competition engage in risky innovations, such as creating a new product or designing a more cost-effective method of production (technology). (2) If effective, the new product or technology yields substantial economic (above-normal) profits and the business expands. (3) Timid entrepreneurs, once they see the innovation is effective, copy the new product or imitate the new technology, causing new firms to enter the market to compete with the bold entrepreneur. (4) The entrance of more competition increases the supply of the product, lowering the price and eliminating the excess profits earned by the bold entrepreneur. (5) The industry as a whole experiences economic growth as multiple businesses expand operations building the new product or utilizing the new technology. (6) This process tends to limit the incomes of the rich via competition and raise the standard of living of the poor because goods prices are kept low and demand for workers increases as industries expand. The result, according to Smith, is that a much more equal distribution of income would result in a capitalist economic system than was the case under mercantilism!

In highlighting the importance of competition, Smith also identified **self-interest** as a useful component of a market capitalist economy. The dynamic entrepreneurs of his era were providing essential goods and services to society, but they were doing so for selfish reasons—to make a profit: "It is not from the benevolence of the butcher, the brewer, or the baker, that we expect our dinner, but from their regard to their own interest. We address ourselves, not to their humanity but to their self-love, and never talk to them of our own necessities but of their advantages." To Smith, the profit motive, in the presence of sufficient competition, was a positive force providing the essential goods that society wanted and leading to economic growth in the process.

Along with competition, Smith believed that **moral sentiments** and a **system of justice** were key regulators of the competitive process. In his first important book, *The Theory of Moral Sentiments*, Smith stated, "How selfish soever man may be supposed, there are evidently some principles in his nature, which interest him in the fortune of others, and render their happiness necessary to him." Smith evidently saw people as both self-interested *and* interested in the welfare of others. Along with moral sentiments, Smith envisioned a government that had "the duty of protecting, as far as possible, every member of the society from the injustice and oppression of every other member of it, or the duty of establishing an exact administration of justice."

Combining these crucial ideas, to Smith, *a self-interested entrepreneur who (a) operates in a competitive market, (b) cares about the welfare of others, and (c) is prevented by law from exploiting others would tend to serve the public interest by producing good products at low prices, innovating regularly, fostering economic growth, and benefiting the poor*. This led Smith to his famous analogy of the **invisible hand** of the market:

> As every individual … endeavours as much as he can both to employ his capital in the support of domestic industry, and so to direct that industry that its produce may be of the greatest value; every individual necessarily labours to render the annual revenue of the society as great as he can. He generally, indeed, neither intends to promote the public interest, nor knows how much he is promoting it. By preferring the support of domestic to that of foreign industry, he intends only his own security; and by directing that industry in such a manner as its produce may be of the greatest value, he intends only his own gain, and he is in this, as in many other cases, led by an **invisible hand** to promote an end which was no part of his intention. Nor is it always the worse for the society that it was no part of it. By pursuing his own interest he frequently promotes that of the society more effectually than when he really intends to promote it.[1]

This was a powerful and counterintuitive claim. Self-interest, via the competitive market system, can end up benefiting society more effectively than intentionally benevolent acts! Consider this idea carefully and evaluate whether or not you think it holds true in our world.

Given what Smith actually said about capitalism, as described above, it is interesting how many commentators cite the portion of Smith's work on self-interest without acknowledging the other crucial components of the system that Smith discussed. Smith only mentioned the invisible hand once in *The Wealth of Nations*, so selecting this metaphor as the key to understanding Smith's work is questionable.

Smith was also a strong advocate of reducing regulations on imports and exports. He thought that with less regulated trade, companies could sell goods to a larger market (foreign as well as domestic consumers). This in turn would allow companies to increase the size of their factories, leading to greater specialization, the development of new machines, and ultimately greater productivity and economic growth. Smith thought that the result would be an improvement in everyone's standard of living as productivity increases resulted in lower prices and greater quantities of goods.

Despite Smith's distrust of government, which in his day acted on behalf of monopolistic interests rather than promoting the public welfare, Smith still saw a limited role for government policy. Smith's approach to government regulation is termed "limited laissez-faire" because he did envision a few limits being placed on market capitalism. First, as noted earlier, Smith wanted the government to establish a strong system of justice to protect every member of society from injustice and oppression. Second, the government needed to maintain order and provide for national defense. Third, the government needed to provide public goods, including roads, harbors, and education, all of which contribute to commerce and the functioning of the market.

Smith wanted greater investment in human capital via education. Without such efforts, Smith feared that most people would be poor and would have mindless jobs. Also, he hoped that education would lead to more innovations, possibly generated by workers themselves, and increase productivity.

Smith believed firmly that limited laissez-faire capitalism would be a better, more egalitarian system than mercantilism. Smith's goal was to create a society that was so productive that there would be enough for the "slothful and oppressive profusion of the great, and at the same time abundantly to supply the wants of the artisan, the laborer, and the peasant." In these words we see Smith's disdain for the rich and powerful of his era and his hope that capitalism would lead to a better world.

Such an idealistic vision was very powerful, especially in the face of ongoing problems of the mercantilist economies. The mercantilist governments in England had attempted to alleviate the plight of the poor with a series of welfare programs and wage subsidies beginning around 1600, but these programs came under attack in the early 1800s with the rise of the philosophy of laissez-faire.

3.8 FROM SUPPORTING THE POOR TO LAISSEZ-FAIRE CAPITALISM

3.8.1 Poor Laws

The expansion of markets under mercantilism was accompanied by major economic problems. Most important was the vast amount of poverty created when the peasants were thrown off their land by the enclosure movement. The poverty often provoked crime, food riots, and other desperate acts by the poor. To reduce some of the negative consequences, England established poor laws beginning around 1600 to ensure that the poor had enough food to survive. These laws were continued in various forms until 1834.

The Speenhamland system, for example, was established in 1795 to reduce rural poverty at a time when high grain prices were making the lot of the poor even worse than usual. Speenhamland subsidized wages based on the price of bread in order to guarantee a minimum income—a "living wage"—to the poor irrespective of their earnings. In essence, any worker who received less than a living wage would receive a subsidy from the government up to a minimum level necessary to support a family. The problem with the Speenhamland system was that it eroded incentives. Workers had no reason to work hard: If their pay was slashed because they slacked off on the job, they would then receive a higher subsidy from the government to make up for their lower wages. Employers had an incentive to pay workers less than a living wage because the government would subsidize low wages until they reached a living wage. The result was that productivity declined and the cost to taxpayers of the Speenhamland system became higher and higher.

In addition to the lower productivity and increasing cost of the Speenhamland system, Thomas Malthus, a minister and influential writer on economics, helped erode support for poor relief with his theory of population. Malthus argued that the population would expand as long as there was sufficient food available. Furthermore, he argued that the limited amount of land available could only produce enough food for a certain number of people. With a limited supply of food and an ever-increasing population, Malthus thought famine was inevitable.

Many members of the British Parliament used the population theory of Malthus to argue that giving money to the poor would only lead them to have more children and cause a famine. To eliminate this possibility, Parliament passed the Poor Law Reform Act of 1834, which eliminated poor relief except for those who were disabled and created an unregulated market for labor. Subsidies for the poor were replaced by a competitive labor market, and anyone who could not find a job was thrown into a workhouse. No longer was there a commitment to help those who fell upon hard times. Instead, the poor and the unemployed, and often their children, were subject to the brutal treatment of the workhouse. These were the conditions described by Charles Dickens in *Oliver Twist* after visiting a series of workhouses (see Figure 3.2). Even those who worked in factories faced a harsh environment, as we will see in the next chapter.

It is unfortunate that the hardships of the poor after 1834 in England were a product of bad economic theory. Modern economic research has proven that when the poor have higher incomes and more opportunities, they tend to have fewer (not more) children. Families that have lower incomes and are less secure tend to have more children because the extra labor is helpful and the children might earn

FIGURE 3.2 Oliver Asking for More, by George Cruikshank.

enough money to support their parents once they reach old age. For poor families in countries without secure retirement benefits, children are the primary provider of security for the elderly. Thus, the removal of support for the poor was based on faulty perceptions of the relationship between incomes for the poor and population growth.

3.8.2 Say's law and macroeconomic intervention

Laissez-faire policies were also promoted in England in another key area in the early 1800s: Macroeconomic policy. Malthus and a few other economists were worried about the instability of the macroeconomy, which was experiencing frequent recessions when spending and investment fell, products piled up on store shelves (gluts of goods), and unemployment increased as businesses laid off workers due to slack demand for their products. Despite the problem of frequent recessions, most politicians and economists were convinced by the arguments of Jean-Baptiste Say, who popularized and extended Smith's argument that a capitalist economy was fundamentally stable over the long term.

The key theory in Say's "law of markets" (Say's law) was that **supply creates its own demand**. When an entrepreneur makes a product, they hire workers, rent land, and buy raw materials, putting money into the hands of workers, landowners, and input suppliers. The money they pay for raw materials becomes income for those businesses, which goes to pay their wages, rent, and materials costs. Businesses also generate profits, which become the owners' income. Thus, the act of producing and supplying goods and services generates wages for laborers, rent for landowners, and profits for owners. What do people do with this income? They buy the goods and services that are produced. This is the famous circular flow of economic activity depicted in Figure 3.3.

According to Say's law, the income from producing goods and services generates exactly enough money to buy those goods and services.

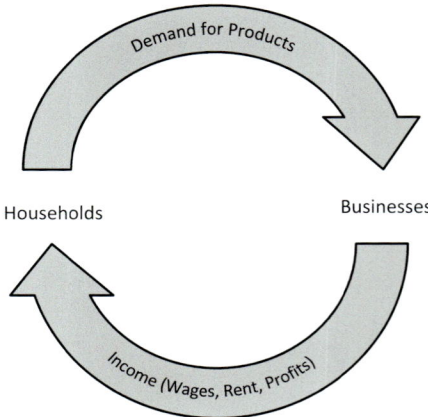

FIGURE 3.3 The simple circular flow model of the economy.

Say's law is based on a number of crucial assumptions about how the economy works. Recall from Chapter 2 that a model is only as good as its underlying assumptions, and when the assumptions fail, the model is usually inaccurate. The **assumptions behind Say's law** are the following:

1. Consumers' demand for goods and services is unlimited because they get satisfaction from consumption, so they always tend to spend most of their incomes.
2. An unregulated capitalist system will generate enough income for consumers to buy everything that is produced.
3. All money that is saved or earned as profits will be invested by entrepreneurs due to the (almost unlimited) profitable opportunities provided by capitalism.
4. Wages, prices, and interest rates will adjust very rapidly so that supply will equal demand.
5. The (standard) ceteris paribus assumption: All other relevant factors do not change.

If all of these assumptions hold, then it is likely that enough income will be generated to produce enough demand to buy all of the goods that are supplied. There may be temporary downturns in the economy, but these should be short-lived. Therefore, economists following Say's law believed that no government intervention was necessary in recessions because they thought that the market would fix itself soon.

As we will see in more detail later, there are several fundamental flaws in Say's law. For now, we will focus on one crucial problem: The view that there will always be enough demand for products. This flaw was pointed out by Malthus, Marx, and Keynes but ignored by most economists until the Great Depression of the 1930s. What economists now know is that in recessions consumers are reluctant to spend because they are worried about keeping their jobs, and businesses are reluctant to invest when they are pessimistic about future sales. In a recession, consumer demand and businesses' investment purchases both fall, and they tend to stay low until confidence returns. Pessimistic consumers reduce spending and save more. If the extra money that consumers saved in banks was then spent by businesses on investment goods, the economy would not experience a prolonged recession. However, economic research indicates that *the most important determinant of business investment is expected sales*: Businesses are only willing to buy new machinery and equipment to expand the size of their operations if they think they will be able to sell more goods in the future. Certainly this is not the case if consumers are buying less goods than normal. Say and most economists of his era assumed there would always be enough opportunities that businesses would want to invest all the money available in the banking system. But, in reality, when the business environment is poor and expected sales are low, businesses tend to reduce their investment spending. Money piles up in banks, which are then unable to loan out all the money in their vaults. Even if banks lower their interest rates on loans, businesses are reluctant to borrow money to invest as long as they believe they will not be able to sell all of the products they produce. One of the key implications is that if businesses expect a bad economy in the future, they reduce investment right away, which then helps to create the bad economy that they expected! Hence, we see that recessions occur regularly due to shortages in demand.

Despite the major flaw in Say's law, most economists of the early 1800s subscribed to this theory and believed that the market would always fix itself very rapidly. They believed that no government intervention was necessary to alleviate unemployment and stimulate a stagnant economy because those problems would always be fixed rapidly by the market system. Another economic dogma of the economists of this era was the belief in unregulated ("free") trade, based on the theory of comparative advantage developed by David Ricardo.

3.8.3 Free trade and comparative advantage

Under the mercantilist system, trade was heavily protected and imported goods faced stiff tariffs. Given the importance of agriculture to mercantilist economies, agriculture was one of the most protected sectors. In England, the Corn Laws established a high domestic price of grains (corn, wheat) to generate wealth for landlords. However, entrepreneurs and workers objected to the high cost of food, which had the effect of raising wages because workers had to be paid more in order to survive.

David Ricardo argued that England should deregulate trade. That would allow entrepreneurs to earn greater profits, which would be reinvested as purchases of capital goods, which would stimulate economic growth and make everyone better off. According to Ricardo's (1817) theory of comparative advantage, which we will study in more detail later in Chapter 18, if all countries engaged in unregulated trade, each country would end up producing the goods that it was relatively best at producing. The competition of the market once tariff protections were eliminated would lead to the most efficient firms surviving and would decrease the costs of all goods, which would raise everyone's standard of living. Also, if firms could sell to a larger market, including domestic and foreign consumers, they could increase their level of specialization, which would then increase productivity, as Smith argued. The result would (in theory) be an economy with more rapid economic growth and a higher standard of living than under regulated (mercantilist) trade.

The Corn Laws were repealed in 1846 based on Ricardo's arguments, marking the completion of England's transition to a grand experiment: Laissez-faire capitalism. Under this economic system, the economic power no longer resided with the merchants and the king. Instead, the most powerful individuals were the entrepreneurial factory owners, and the factory became the center of economic life.

3.9 THE RISE OF THE FACTORY AND THE DOUBLE MOVEMENT

Once the Industrial Revolution was underway, it fed on itself and became self-sustaining. The earliest entrepreneurs made huge sums of money, which they invested in new ventures. Many of these new ventures were successful, generating additional profits to be reinvested. As this process continued, the factory came to be the center of the economy, transforming the commercial, agricultural mercantilist system into a more urban, industrial capitalist system. The pace of change was breathtaking. In 40 years, Glasgow was transformed from a sleepy farming center to an industrial powerhouse with 100 mills producing manufactured goods, iron, leather, chemicals, and more.

By the mid-1800s, many factory owners were wealthy and politically powerful. The factory was the most important institution in the community, determining what life was like for much of the population. Unfortunately for many workers, the transition to factory life was a difficult one. Agrarian peasants did not have an easy life, but they worked at their own pace, and there were times of the year when they did not have to work much, especially in the winter. In the unregulated factories of early capitalism, the pace of work was dictated by the machine, and the work hours pushed people to the brink of human endurance.

So horrific were the conditions that in the late 1700s and early 1800s, workers regularly smashed machines and burned factories as part of the Luddite movement. However, the Luddites were arrested and many were hanged in 1813. In essence, the factory system was imposed on a resisting population by force and by the lack of viable alternatives for a poor and desperate population.

If we reflect on the major trends in the development of the market system, we see that national markets were initially created by mercantilist firms and monarchs in pursuit of gold and power. However, the expansion of markets was resisted actively by guilds and workers who sought to maintain their standard of living in any way they could, often using violence. Similarly, as England moved to manufacturing factories and laissez-faire capitalism in the 1800s, workers resisted the horrific conditions, as we will see in Chapter 4. Along with the workers' movements, laws regulating factories and various forms of social legislation began to be introduced to mitigate the worst effects of industrial capitalism.

This process of the relentless expansion of markets into new areas at the behest of the most powerful economic interests, coupled with the resistance of workers and communities to market expansion that threatened their livelihood, was termed the double movement by Karl Polanyi. More specifically, the **double movement** describes how **the push for the development of markets by businesses** (first mercantilists and then capitalists) **was met by a counter movement by workers and communities to regulate markets** to prevent them from doing too much destruction to society.

In many ways, early capitalism was, indeed, an ugly thing, and it provoked strong reactions from those it victimized. This is the form of capitalism that Karl Marx described when he wrote, "Capital comes [into the world] dripping from head to foot, from every pore, with blood and dirt." We turn to Marx, Thorstein Veblen, and workers' resistance to the dark ages of capitalism in Chapter 4.

3.10 CONCLUSION

The earliest human societies began as primitive communism, sharing resources in order to survive in a harsh environment. With the development of agriculture, food storage, and an economic surplus, the focus of economic systems shifted to empires where the maintenance of the status and lifestyle of the elites was paramount, while slaves and peasants did the work. Inefficiencies of slave-based systems and constant attacks of rival groups eroded empires, and feudal systems developed in much of the world, where lords provided protection in exchange for the labor and fealty of peasants. Feudalism was eventually eroded by trade, increased productivity, changes in ideology, and other factors that put a premium on trade and the enclosure of common lands to produce goods to trade, leading to mercantilism. The mercantilist system was run by merchants and kings, who maintained monopolies to extract as much gold as possible from domestic and colonial economies. But the monopolistic mercantilist system eventually stagnated, generating too much poverty and too little demand to satisfy workers and early capitalist businesses.

The capitalist economic system began in England based on set of unique institutions that help us to understand the crucial ingredients in a such a system. The key institutions include a money-driven, scientifically oriented culture; secure property rights; and a large domestic and colonial market. The successes of the early capitalists prompted Adam Smith to write *The Wealth of Nations*, in which he proposed that lightly regulated market capitalism would improve the well-being of all people. To Smith, the great evils of mercantilism, monopolies, and government manipulation of markets for the elites would be eliminated via the installation of a competitive capitalist system. Competition, moral sentiments, and a sound legal system would, he thought, harness the power of self-interest to generate rapid economic growth that would raise the standard of living for all.

Smith was followed by Say, who argued against the need for government to intervene in recessions, and Ricardo, who argued in favor of unregulated trade with other countries. These powerful ideas, coupled with the elimination of the Poor Laws, resulted in the installation of the world's first laissez-faire capitalist economic system in England between 1834 and 1846. Yet, as England was moving toward laissez-faire capitalism, a countermovement grew in opposition to capitalism, a phenomenon that Karl Polanyi described as the double movement.

QUESTIONS FOR REVIEW

1. Political economists argue that human beings are inherently social beings with strong levels of group identity. Is there evidence from economic history to support this view? Why or why not?
2. Describe the role played by (a) tradition, (b) authority, and (c) markets in traditional, slave, feudal, and mercantilist economic systems.

3. How is the generation and utilization of the surplus product important to understanding economic development?
4. What were the major institutional factors that spurred the development of capitalism in England? Which of these factors do you think was most important? Why?
5. Given the institutional factors that provided the foundation for capitalism in England, do you think capitalism would work as effectively in other countries with different institutions? Why or why not?
6. Why was Adam Smith critical of mercantilism? Why did he think capitalism was preferable to mercantilism?
7. Smith argued that unregulated (laissez-faire) capitalism would lead to substantial increases in income for all, and especially for workers. Carefully explain how Smith thought this would come about. Critically evaluate his analysis.
8. Smith believed that laissez-faire capitalism would be almost completely self-regulating via the invisible hand, as long as moral sentiments and an effective legal system were in place. Evaluate his argument, and use examples from current events in the newspaper to support your analysis.
9. Smith was an opponent of mercantilist governments. What role (if any) did Adam Smith envision for government in a capitalist economy?
10. Why did Malthus (and others) oppose the Poor Laws such as the Speenhamland system? What parts of their arguments were valid and what parts would modern economists consider invalid?
11. Describe Say's law and why it is important. Also explain the major criticism of Say's law.
12. Why did Smith and Ricardo advocate unregulated trade? What problems might occur when a country moves to unregulated trade? Do we see any such problems in the modern world?
13. Define Karl Polanyi's concept of the double movement, and apply this concept to the modern world. Do we see businesses pushing for fewer regulations and access to more markets today? Is there opposition to these business initiatives from people and communities? Give specific examples.

NOTE

1 Adam Smith, *The Wealth of Nations*, bk. 4, ed. Edwin Cannan (London: Methuen and Co., Ltd., 1904), ch. 2.

4

Marx, Veblen, and the dark ages of capitalism

Historical materialism, the exploitation of labor, and monopoly capitalism

By the mid-1800s, unregulated capitalism dominated economic systems in Europe and the United States. Adam Smith had hoped that unregulated capitalism would benefit workers, but this was not the case. Instead, this was the dark ages of capitalism: Children were sometimes shackled to machines to keep them at their jobs; workers regularly lost limbs on the job, at which point they were fired because they were no longer productive; work hours were pushed to the brink of human endurance so that laborers spent almost every waking minute working; and work was mind-numbingly dull and repetitive for most industrial laborers.

In this context, Karl Marx wrote his famous critique of capitalism. Although Marx is often thought of as the father of communism, he actually had very little to say about communism and how it might work. As we will see, Marx was able to anticipate many of the characteristics of modern capitalism. His analysis predicted, among other things, globalization, the rise of huge corporations, the influence of money in democratic political systems, the abiding alienation of wage workers, and much more. The power of the analytical framework he developed accounts for why many of his ideas still remain relevant today.

As capitalism developed in the late 1800s and early 1900s, huge, monopolistic conglomerates developed in the United States under the direction of ruthless robber barons. **Monopoly capitalism** of this era was a far cry from the competitive capitalism of Smith's era. Like mercantilism, monopoly capitalism generated fabulous wealth for the dominant firms but left most people desperately poor. It was into this environment that Thorstein Veblen developed his important ideas. Like Marx, Veblen saw capitalism as a vehicle for those on top—the vested interests—to

DOI: 10.4324/9780429399350-6

promote their interests at the expense of everyone else. Veblen also noted how capitalism was evolving and pioneered the study of evolutionary economics and the institutions that cause or resist change.

This chapter begins by describing the spread of capitalism from England to the United States and Europe and the horrible conditions that characterized capitalism of the mid-1800s. We then turn to Marx's ideas regarding the evolution of economic systems and his analysis of capitalism. Subsequently, we discuss the rise of monopoly capitalism and the ideas of Thorstein Veblen.

4.0 CHAPTER 4 LEARNING GOALS

After reading this chapter you should be able to:

- Describe the conditions of workers in the 1800s, assess the implications of these conditions for the functioning of laissez-faire capitalism, and determine whether or not you think laissez-faire capitalism inevitably results in exploitation.

- Explain the components of Marx's method of analysis, historical materialism, and apply this method to the evolution of economic systems.

- Use the concept of surplus value to analyze the functioning of a capitalist economic system.

- Evaluate Marx's views on competition and commodification using specific examples from history and from modern capitalism.

- Describe the rise of U.S. monopoly capitalism and how this system was structured relative to owners, workers, and the government, as well as race, gender, and ethnicity.

- Define and apply the major concepts developed by Thorstein Veblen, including evolution, institutions, culture, pecuniary emulation, conspicuous consumption, making money vs. making goods, and the vested interests.

4.1 INFANT INDUSTRY PROTECTION AND THE SPREAD OF CAPITALISM

Beginning in the 1300s, England enacted policies to develop the wool industry. They used measures such as protective tariffs, subsidies, and the poaching of skilled workers from foreign manufacturers to give their industry an advantage. This classic approach to economic development is known as an **infant industry promotion strategy**, where **a country protects and subsidizes a new industry until it can be globally competitive.** In the 1700s, England used similar policies to promote additional industries. By the 1800s, England was the world technological and industrial leader, and its shift to free trade policies in 1846 was designed to cement the advantages of British industries and undermine the development of competing industries among its European rivals. When you are the global leader with the most efficient industries, free trade benefits your economy while undercutting the industries of other countries.

Most other countries followed England's example, protecting new industries until they could compete with the established industries of other countries. The United States used infant industry promotion strategies once it was independent from England in 1780. Alexander Hamilton, a founding father and the country's first secretary of the Treasury, successfully persuaded the U.S. Congress to install protective tariffs to allow U.S. industries to develop and compete with British industries. In Germany, the state provided subsidies and established a number of factories. The French hired British skilled workers and engaged in industrial espionage to close the technological gap with Britain. In country after country, governments protected and encouraged industrial development to stimulate the economy and to catch up with the technological leaders. Only small countries such as Switzerland that were already technologically developed and that needed to sell to larger markets in other countries pursued free trade policies as they were industrializing.

But as capitalist industries spread to Europe and across the globe, they were accompanied by horrific working conditions. The rosy scenario that Adam Smith anticipated, where the growth of competitive capitalism would dramatically improve the welfare of workers and the poor, did not play out as he had hoped.

4.2 THE CONDITIONS OF WORKERS UNDER CAPITALISM IN THE 1800s

The vast mass of impoverished people created by the enclosure movement meant that many people were desperate for work. Due to the large surplus of laborers, workers had no bargaining power with employers because they could be easily replaced. Consequently, workers had to accept whatever wages and working conditions were offered. As noted previously, the earliest entrepreneurs were hard men, uncertain in their ability to make a profit and driven to squeeze every drop of profit out of their operations. The result was that working and living conditions for the average person were usually terrible.

Consider some of the following characteristics of work in England, the wealthiest country in the world in the mid-1800s:

FIGURE 4.1 Addie Card in 1910.

- Employers often preferred women and children for manufacturing work because they were more submissive. Children began to work as early as age 4. They worked for 14 to 18 hours every day or until they dropped from exhaustion. Sometimes they were chained to machines and beaten to keep them working. Figure 4.1 depicts Addie Card, a 12-year-old cotton mill worker in 1910.[1]
- There were few safety precautions, and workers regularly lost fingers, hands, arms, and legs in industrial accidents. Upon experiencing a debilitating injury, workers were usually fired and received no compensation or medical care from their employer.
- Once at the factory, workers had no control over their lives. Breaks were limited to a few minutes each day, despite the incredibly long workdays. Factory owners and managers regularly took sexual advantage of female employees.

As businesses sought to expand markets and gain access to additional resources, there was a countermovement to regulate the worst excesses of markets, which economist Karl Polanyi labeled the **double movement**. But the reforms themselves were modest, and they confirm the overall ugly state of affairs. Consider some of the following child labor "reforms" in England:

- 1819: The employment of children under the age of 9 was prohibited in cotton mills.
- 1833: The work week for children under the age of 18 was limited to 69 hours.
- 1842: Children under the age of 10 were prohibited from working in coal mines.
- 1847: The workday for women and children was limited to 10.5 hours.

The low wages paid by the factories also meant squalid conditions for working-class families. Most families lived in one-room apartments. They often could not afford clothes, furniture, or even food, and they lived in squalid, unhealthy conditions that led to regular outbreaks of cholera, typhoid, and other diseases. Many people died from disease or malnutrition. The life expectancy in the manufacturing city of Manchester, England, in the mid-1800s was only 17 years.[2]

Not surprising, the dreadful working and living conditions prompted regular uprisings. Various types of riots and rebellions occurred in England in most years between 1811 and 1850. Yet employers saw no need to address the desperate conditions of their workers. Their belief was that once an employer had paid employees their wages, he had no further obligation to them. This was the embodiment of the laissez-faire, every-man-for-himself philosophy that dominated the business community in the early stages of capitalism. It was in response to this world that Karl Marx wrote his critique of capitalism.

4.3 KARL MARX, HISTORICAL MATERIALISM, AND CLASS CONFLICT

Karl Marx, pictured in Figure 4.1, was born in 1818 into a German economy that was structured to funnel resources to the rich. As in England, German factories were organized in a brutal, militaristic structure designed to discipline and exploit desperate workers. Employers could do so with impunity due to the support of the government. Outraged by this society, Marx gravitated to radical politics. He was thrown out of Germany, France, and Brussels for his activism on behalf of workers. He eventually settled in England, where he collaborated with Friedrich Engels (1820–1895).

In 1848, Marx and Engels wrote one of their most powerful documents, *The Communist Manifesto*. In it, they encouraged workers to rise up against their exploitative employers. They also developed a powerful theory of historical change

FIGURE 4.2 Karl Marx (1818–1883).

featuring class conflict and technology as the driving factors behind the major shifts in society.

Marx was interested in understanding and analyzing historical change. Adam Smith wrote about capitalism as if it would always operate in a particular way, with small, competitive firms acting to enhance the well-being of society. Marx, however, observed that no economic system was permanent. Within each economic system were forces that threatened to break it apart, sometimes resulting in a new economic system. Marx cited historical evidence indicating that the driving force of the major changes in economic systems was **class conflict**. Marx and Engels began *The Communist Manifesto* with a famous statement regarding the importance of class conflict to historical change:

> The history of all hitherto existing society is the history of class struggles. Freeman and slave, patrician and plebeian, lord and serf, guild-master and journeyman, in a word, oppressor and oppressed, stood in constant opposition to one another, carried on an uninterrupted, now hidden, now open fight, a fight that each time ended, either in a revolutionary reconstitution of society at large, or in the common ruin of the contending classes. … Our epoch, the epoch of the bourgeoisie [capitalists], … has simplified class antagonisms. Society as a whole is more and more splitting up into two great hostile camps, into two great classes directly facing each other — Bourgeoisie and Proletariat [workers].

Marx focused on the contradictions within each economic system that would eventually force the system to change. This **method of analysis, focusing on contradictions and the struggle of opposing forces**, is known as *dialectics*.

Consider for a moment how powerful Marx's observation on class conflict is in helping us to understand the major shifts in economic systems. In each major shift in economic systems—Roman Empire to feudalism, feudalism to mercantilism, and mercantilism to capitalism—class antagonisms featured prominently. For example, the clash of the feudal elites (lords and church officials) with kings and merchants destroyed feudalism and ushered in mercantilism, as kings and merchants reshaped society based on their interests in extending markets. With their rise in power and importance, capitalists were able to prevail against the interests of merchants and kings and replace mercantilism with laissez-faire capitalism. And, as we shall see later, the conflict between capitalists and workers under laissez-faire capitalism produced the mixed market capitalist economies of the modern world. In each case, an economic system was unable to resolve major conflicts over resources in society, resulting in conflicts between key classes and leading to a new type of economic system.

Technology also plays an important role in reshaping economic systems. The development of agriculture prompted the change from hunter-gatherer societies to agriculture-based empires. The rise in agricultural productivity during feudalism promoted urbanization and trade and established conditions that were ripe for mercantilism. The development of shipping, guns, and steel in Europe made mercantilism and colonial empires possible. The steam engine stimulated the development of factories in early capitalism. In all of these examples, technological changes prompted changes in class structures that helped to undermine existing class relations. *Given that no economic system has lasted forever and that there are many conflicts and technological changes occurring in contemporary society, how might the next economic system arise and what might it look like?*

Marx focused on the fight over economic resources as the primary source of conflict because historically it has been the most important factor in changes in economic systems. Also, the **material conditions** of society are the primary influence on what our lives are like, determining whom we interact with during most of the day, how hard we have to work, our status in society, whom we are likely to marry, and so on.

For example, the social class you are born into has a huge influence on what your life will be like, affecting whether or not you are likely to go to an elite college, whether you are more likely to end up working on Wall Street or at Wal-Mart, and whether you are likely to be a manager or a laborer. The **relations of production** are the relationships between people in the workplace, and they are primarily determined by your social class.

Also important in shaping the conditions of society are technological factors, including tools, machinery, infrastructure, resources, labor power, and knowledge. Marx called these the **forces of production**. The physical, non-human parts of the forces of production, including machinery, tools, buildings, infrastructure, and natural resources, are called the **means of production**. In a capitalist economic system, capitalists own and control the means of production, whereas workers have to sell their labor to capitalists in order to survive. Together, the forces of production (technology, knowledge) and the (class) relations of production are the driving forces behind the changes in society. **Marx's approach to the study of economics, focusing on the class conflicts and technological changes that provoke changes in the material conditions of society over time**, is called historical materialism.

Marx turned his sophisticated analytical method to the study of the laissez-faire capitalist system of the mid-1800s. Where Smith saw profit-seeking as a positive force, Marx saw a system that brutalized workers and turned everything—people, love, religion, democracy, justice—into a commodity to be bought and sold. The key to understanding how exploitation and commodification come about is Marx's concept of surplus value.

4.4 SURPLUS VALUE AND THE EXPLOITATION OF LABOR

In the capitalist system of the mid-1800s there were two main social classes, the capitalists who owned the means of production and the workers who were forced to sell their labor to survive. During Marx's era, the small **middle class** that existed, consisting of skilled craftspeople and owners of small shops, was being rapidly displaced by the ever-growing capitalist firms. Thus, Marx concentrated on the two main social classes of his day: Capitalists and workers.

The main dynamic between capitalists and workers is shaped by the pursuit of profit by the capitalist. In a competitive capitalist system, owners are forced to be "hard men" who extract the most they can from their business. In the cutthroat capitalist world, if you can't produce the best product for the lowest possible price, you will likely get displaced by a competitor who is better or more efficient, and you must constantly reinvest your profits in new ventures and new technology to stay one step ahead of your competitors. Indeed, the reinvestment of profits into new production techniques and products is usually the key to long-term survival. Thus, in order to survive, firms must keep costs as low as possible and accumulate sufficient profits for reinvestment. These profits are invested in capital goods (machinery, equipment, research and development, etc.), resulting in **capital accumulation** (a larger and larger capital stock). Marx saw capital accumulation as one of the key forces in capitalism, driving the development of new products, the search for new markets, and the exploitation of labor.

In their relentless pursuit of profit (and capital accumulation), firms have to extract as much effort as possible at as low a wage as possible from their workers. In other words, firms seek the maximum production from workers for the least cost.

To demonstrate this fundamental aspect of capitalism, Marx developed a simple model of the workday based on the concept of **surplus value**. During the first part of the workday, the worker produces goods or services to generate enough profits to pay for their wages (and benefits) for the day. Once a worker has paid for his or her wages, the rest of the work for the day generates profits for the owner. Thus, the workday can be broken down into the following:

$$A – – – – – – – – – – – – B – – – – – – – – – – – C,$$

where A–B pays for the wage and B–C is profit (surplus value).

Surplus value is defined as **the amount of value produced by workers over and above the cost of their wages and benefit costs**.

In this relationship, a firm that is pursuing maximum profits must increase the B–C part of the workday as much as possible. That can be done in two different ways:

1. Increasing the length of the workday (moving C to the right).
2. Reducing the amount of time necessary to pay for a laborer's wage (moving B to the left). This can be done by (a) reducing wages, (b) replacing workers with more cost-effective machinery, or (c) increasing the productivity of workers by speeding up the pace of work or other measures that target productivity.

This is where the fight over the workday in capitalism comes in. Clearly, employers want to maximize profits, and that means getting the most surplus value possible from their workers. Once they have paid a worker's daily salary, the employer's incentive is to work them as many hours as possible. In addition, employers always want to pay the lowest wages possible. But what do workers want? Mostly, they prefer just the opposite: Workers want higher pay and shorter hours.

During the years of unregulated capitalism, factory owners went to great lengths to increase their profits and undercut their competitors. With daily wages fixed, employers engaged in relentless efforts to expand work hours, as documented in Juliet Schor's (1991) book, *The Overworked American*:

- The invention of artificial lighting was used to increase work from daylight hours (about 12 hours a day) to as many as 16 hours a day.
- Mealtimes and breaks were shortened to only a few minutes each day.
- Holidays and days off were eliminated.
- Clocks at factories were set ahead in the morning and turned back at night to manipulate laborers into working more hours. Workers, who usually did not own watches and who lived in fear of beatings or being fired, could only accept these manipulations.

Factory work hours reached between 75 and 90 hours a week in England and the United States in the mid-1800s. Employers pushed working hours to the brink of human endurance, indicating how much power they had over workers.

In addition to extending work hours, employers sought to increase surplus value in other ways. They tried to reduce wages by employing children and women instead of men, using slave labor if it was allowed, and moving operations to locations where wages were lower. They replaced workers with machinery that was less costly. In particular, they replaced highly paid skilled laborers with less skilled workers using machines, which resulted in considerable cost savings, and they increased the pace of work by speeding up assembly lines and closely supervising workers. For example, Frederick Taylor (1856–1915) developed factory systems in which every motion of every worker was monitored and controlled for optimum efficiency.

Marx saw the relationship between capitalists and workers as fundamentally exploitative. First, employers have more power than workers in the market for labor. Employers control the number of jobs, and they are able to select from an abundant supply of workers. As long as there are surplus workers around, workers have to take whatever the employer wants to offer. Marx called the chronic surplus of workers the **reserve army of the unemployed**, and he noted that having a ready supply of disciplined, desperate, unemployed laborers was very useful to capitalists. Unemployment helps to push wages down and to keep workers in line due to their fears of being replaced by an unemployed person. Also, the unemployed provide a ready pool of labor if a firm needs to expand the size of its operations.

Second, surplus value is exploitative because if a worker owned the business, the worker would get to keep the surplus value instead of having it seized by the capitalist. Surplus value goes to whoever owns the business (the means of production). But, why do capitalists own the factory instead of workers? In the 1800s, most wealth could be traced back to the era when resources (especially land) were seized in the enclosure movement, establishing a wealthy class that in turn became factory owners. To Marx, ownership of factories and businesses was usually a product of the theft of public resources or luck of birth, so he saw the seizure of surplus value as an exploitative and unjustified act. It was this idea that private property was born out of theft and exploitation that led Marx to advocate a socialist or communist system where workers would own and control the factories.

Workers, of course, resisted the extension of work hours, intensification of work, and efforts to reduce wages in any way they could. When workers functioned as individuals, they were expendable and had little power. But when they joined together to form **labor unions**, they were able to demand changes. Their major weapon was the strike: When all workers refused to work at the same time, they could bring production to a halt. When workers were united and when employment conditions were favorable (a high demand for labor to produce goods during an economic boom), workers were able to demand shorter hours, better conditions, and higher pay. This is exactly what Marx and Engels were arguing when they ended *The Communist Manifesto* with their famous call-to-arms: "Workers of the world, unite! You have nothing to lose but your chains!"

Marx was describing capitalism of the mid-1800s, but it is worth noting the extent to which the processes he described are still visible in modern capitalism. Every year firms such as Wal-Mart are convicted of forcing laborers to work off the clock (work for no pay). Employers increasingly demand that workers be available evenings and weekends for work. Firms still shift their operations around the globe in search of cheaper, more vulnerable workers. They continue to replace skilled labor with mechanization and less-skilled workers, and they monitor workers to keep them on task and working efficiently.

Nothing indicates the enduring importance of the idea of surplus value more strongly than the modern employment relationship. Ask yourself, "When you graduate from college, why will a company want to hire you?" The answer, as Marx noted so many years ago, is, "Because you will make the company more money than you will cost them." In other words, you will produce profit (surplus value), which your employer gets to keep. If you ever find yourself in a situation where you cost your employer more money than you make them, you can expect to be cast into the reserve army of the unemployed.

The power of Marx's concept of surplus value can also be seen in the major trends in modern capitalism that Marx predicted. These include Marx's view of competition as a race to the bottom and his predictions of globalization, the concentration of capital, and the commodification of most aspects of life.

4.5 MARX ON COMPETITION, GLOBALIZATION, CONCENTRATION, AND COMMODIFICATION

As noted above, Adam Smith saw competition as a positive force in the economy, keeping firms innovative, prices low, and demand for workers high. Marx, however, saw a darker side to capitalist competition. Marx acknowledged that the Industrial Revolution and the capitalist economic system that sparked it had generated impressive amounts of new products and worthwhile inventions. But the effect on workers had not been the rosy scenario Smith laid out, with upstanding, moral employers creating better and better conditions for workers. Instead, many workers were worse off under capitalism than they had been under feudalism.

The problem was that competition also put pressures on firms to engage in the most ruthless, cutthroat practices possible. If one employer found it cheaper to use child laborers than adults, other firms would have to follow suit or be competed out of business. If one employer spent less money on worker safety and extracted more work out of each worker, that employer could undercut the competition. In essence, competition served as a **race to the bottom**, with each firm forced to sink to the level of the least scrupulous firm in the market.

In a competitive, laissez-faire market economy, employers could not adhere to their moral beliefs as Smith had hoped. Instead, they were forced to adopt the morals of their least ethical, most ruthless competitor in order to survive.

This is another of Marx's insights that still has relevance. To give a modern example of the race to the bottom, for most of its history Levi Strauss prided itself on being a socially responsible company that manufactured jeans in the United States and paid its workers well. But in 1999 they began closing their U.S. factories and using sweatshop labor overseas to manufacture their products. As Levi's CEO Robert Haas stated, despite investing tens of millions of dollars to keep U.S. plants competitive, "We can't swim against the tide." In a throwback to the dark ages of capitalism, Levi's factories abroad were accused of exploiting Chinese prison labor, firing workers who tried to unionize, and forcing laborers to work more than 12 hours per day while withholding overtime pay. Levi's factories in Saipan paid workers $3 an hour, much less than the $18 an hour that U.S. workers earned. Although Levi's was one of the last holdouts against using sweatshop labor abroad, they eventually succumbed to the race to the bottom provoked by competitive pressures. They joined the company of firms like Nike, who boasted in the late 1990s that workers in their factories were required to be at least 16 years old and to work no more than 60 hours a week. Evidently, they considered these employment rules to be a form of progress!

We see many other examples of the race to the bottom in contemporary capitalism. Firms sometimes move operations overseas to escape taxes, labor laws, or environmental regulations. There have been numerous attempts by companies around the globe to bribe government officials so they do not enforce laws and regulations. The fact that we have had to outlaw child labor, deceptive advertising, unsafe working conditions, hazardous waste dumping, and other unsavory business activities indicates the powerful drive toward the bottom produced by competitive capitalism.

The drive to increase profits is at the root of **globalization**. As Marx and Engels observed in *The Communist Manifesto*, "The need of a constantly expanding market for its products chases the bourgeoisie over the whole surface of the globe. It must nestle everywhere, settle everywhere, establish connections everywhere." The efforts of large multinational firms to establish operations to open markets in China and to gain access to raw materials and labor in Africa, South Asia, and South America demonstrate the ongoing relevance of this part of Marx's analysis.

Another characteristic of capitalist markets that Marx anticipated was the **increasing concentration of capital** into fewer and fewer hands. Marx predicted the domination of markets by huge companies that would, if allowed, monopolize markets. Whereas Smith hoped that there would always be a sufficient amount of competition, Marx noted that in competition there were winners and losers, and the winning firms would get larger and larger as they swallowed up competitors and used their size as an advantage. One look around the landscape of modern capitalism reveals the accuracy of Marx's prediction. In each major industry we see a handful of huge companies dominating: Internet searches and ads (Google), smart phones (Apple, Samsung), breakfast cereals (General Mills, Kellogg, Post), soft drinks (Coke, Pepsi), fast food (McDonald's, Subway, Burger King, Wendy's), pizza (Pizza Hut, Domino's), beer (Budweiser, Miller), social media (Meta), and so on. Some industries are moderately competitive, such as cars (Toyota, General Motors, VW, Hyundai, Ford, Nissan, Fiat Chrysler, Honda) and small retail businesses, but most manufacturing industries are dominated by a few huge firms. If not for antitrust laws that limit the ability of huge firms to get even larger, it appears that most markets would end up being monopolized because of the advantages that huge firms have. Not only can large firms achieve greater efficiency (greater size leads to greater degrees of specialization and lower costs) but they can use their financial resources to buy up competitors or to snap up the latest innovations, thereby staying atop the heap.

Marx also observed how economic systems tended to shape the values of society. In capitalism, the emphasis on making money affects everything; or, as Marx put it in 1846, "Money abases all the gods of mankind and changes them into commodities." This is the process of **commodification.** Christianity had been transformed from a religion in which greed was considered to be a sin during feudalism to a religion that celebrated greed and wealth during mercantilism and even more so during capitalism.

Even more destructive was the commodification of labor under capitalism. Instead of seeing workers as human beings, capitalists were forced by competitive pressures to view workers as tools to be used up and then cast aside. The brutal conditions of laissez-faire capitalism were evidence of the dehumanizing effect capitalism had on the relationship between workers and owners.

Marx developed the term **alienation** to describe how work under capitalism tended to be unnatural and isolating. In previous human societies, people were usually connected to their work as a farmer or skilled craftsperson. They were connected to nature and to work that was usually social, involved a variety of tasks, and could even be interesting and creative at times. Under capitalism, however, work became isolated, repetitive drudgery. **Deskilling** took place, where skilled craftspeople were replaced by unskilled workers using a machine. These unskilled workers toiled by themselves at a machine for 16 hours a day in a dreary, unsafe factory.

Even in modern, regulated capitalism, most workers find their jobs to be alienating. A 2014 Gallup survey asked more than 5 million workers whether they found their jobs to be "engaging," by which they meant "involved in, enthusiastic about and committed to their work and workplace." Only 31.5% of employees in the survey reported being engaged at work, whereas 51% were not engaged and 17.5% were actively discouraged. Drudgery, it seems, is a defining characteristic of work in a capitalist system for most people.

In addition to the commodification of labor, another particularly glaring example is the commodification of holidays and major societal events. If you are the CEO of a company that must generate the maximum amount of profits possible to survive, you have to push for new sales in every way possible. One of the best ways to do this is to connect your product to deep human emotions, such as those associated with love or a religious holiday.

The diamond engagement ring exemplifies the commodification of love under modern capitalism. Human beings have used rings as a symbol of unity for thousands of years. But the widespread use of the diamond engagement ring was a product of a particularly effective marketing campaign by the De Beers Corporation, a South African mining company that controls most of the world's supply of diamonds. In the 1930s, only 10% of engagement rings contained diamonds. De Beers began featuring glamourous movie stars adorned in diamonds in movies and magazines. They emphasized the purity, sparkle, and durability of the diamond as a symbol of a man's love for a woman and suggested that men spend one month of their salary on an engagement ring, putting a very specific price on love! They later raised their definition of the appropriate amount of salary to spend to two months in the 1980s. The idea that love and engagement to be married have come to be associated with a specific value and a specific commodity is a classic example of commodification.

Another classic example is the commodification of Christmas. The modern messages are very explicit about what you should do for your loved ones at Christmas: Buy them expensive commodities.

It is also worth noting the extent to which capitalism commodifies public services such as the administration of justice. In the United States, those who can afford better lawyers are more likely to get better legal outcomes. Even democracy has been commodified to a significant degree in the United States, where it takes millions of dollars to mount a political campaign for congress and a trillion dollars to compete in a presidential election. More than half of the members of congress are millionaires. In another perceptive prediction, Marx argued that politicians in a capitalist system would become beholden to the capitalists and that this would limit the ability of democracy to work on behalf of workers.

The commodification and exploitation of labor led Marx to believe that capitalism was irredeemable. Ultimately, given the corrupt nature of political systems and the brutal conditions of workers, Marx predicted that a workers' revolution was inevitable. He thought that a revolution would likely occur during one of the prolonged economic crises that plagued laissez-faire capitalism.

4.6 CRISIS AND REVOLUTION

Capitalism of the mid-1800s was prone to regular economic crises. To Marx, this was a product of the inherent contradictions in capitalism. On the one hand, capitalists are driven to invest in new machinery and new markets, relentlessly increasing the amount of goods they produce. At the same time, they work as hard as possible to suppress wages and minimize costs. But if output is constantly expanding while wages are stagnant or falling, the economy will eventually reach a point where a large supply of goods exists but workers have limited incomes to buy those goods. The result of too much supply and too little demand is a crisis of underconsumption. As goods sit unsold on store shelves, businesses are forced to cut back on production, resulting in layoffs of workers and increasing poverty, which further undermines spending and ultimately results in a crisis (recession).

Along with the regular crises, capitalism was getting more unequal during Marx's day as firms grew larger and larger and as more independent craftspeople were displaced by capitalist firms. The combination of regular crises and increasing inequality led Marx to believe that some sort of major change was inevitable. He hoped that a revolt of the working class would replace capitalism with socialism, a system in which the means of production would be used for the benefit of all instead of to generate profits for the elites. He also hoped that once people became more publicly minded and less selfish, they might we willing to replace socialism with an even more egalitarian system, communism, in which all of society's resources are shared equally. In a communist system, people would work "each according to their ability" and they would be provided for "each according to their needs."

This is, without question, an idealistic vision. Like Smith, Marx truly wished for an economic system that would create a better life for all, and especially for those who were most exploited under capitalism.

As workers increasingly joined unions and became more powerful, there was talk of revolution, especially in the most unequal societies. However, as we will see later, pressure from labor unions and reformers and the severity of the worst crisis in capitalist history, the Great Depression, undermined the credibility of laissez-faire capitalism and ushered in the modern era of regulated capitalism.

Marx said very little about communism and how it might work. Given that he was throughout his life a tireless advocate of workers' power and well-being, it is unlikely that he would have approved of dictatorial communism. In Soviet Russia under Stalin, workers were exploited and had very little power and control over their work and their lives, much as was the case under unregulated capitalism. In the ultimate irony, the fall of the Soviet Union and the Eastern Block was sparked by a workers' revolt in Poland led by the Solidarity movement, an independent, self-governing trade union! Thus, it is most correct to consider Marx an astute analyst of laissez-faire capitalism rather than as the architect of totalitarian communism.

Despite the accuracy of many of his predictions, Marx's ideas were ignored by mainstream economists, who continued to see the market as efficient and effective. However, changes in the structure of capitalism made such views increasingly difficult to maintain. With the rise of the robber barons and huge corporations in the United States, the era of competitive capitalism was replaced by a new era of monopoly capitalism in the late 1800s and early 1900s. It was in that period that Thorstein Veblen wrote his famous critique of the leisure class and the monopolistic forces that had come to dominate laissez-faire capitalism. In the process, Veblen developed a very sophisticated and useful economic methodology known as institutionalism.

4.7 THE DEVELOPMENT OF MONOPOLY CAPITALISM IN THE UNITED STATES

When Adam Smith first wrote about capitalism, firms were small and markets were primarily local. High transportation costs and the limited size of local markets created conditions favorable for small firms manufacturing and selling goods locally.

A series of factors changed the structure of capitalism in the late 1800s:

1. Changes in technology in transportation (canals and trains, followed by automobiles) and communication (the telegraph, then the telephone) made it possible to travel and communicate across large distances, creating a national, interconnected market.
2. New manufacturing technologies (steel, chemicals, engines, electricity) allowed large firms that made substantial investments to dominate smaller firms.
3. Laws establishing **limited liability corporations** promoted investment by ensuring that stockholders would receive a share of profits but the most they could lose would be the amount of their investment, and they would not be liable for any debts incurred by the company.

4. The development of the banking sector provided financing for large firms to expand, and larger firms were able to borrow at lower interest rates than smaller firms.
5. Large firms had more influence over the government and were able to obtain government contracts, subsidies, and protection from foreign competition more easily than small firms.
6. Once a large firm came to dominate an industry, it could raise prices and increase profits, which gave the owners even more money with which to make investments and buy out competition.

The **ability to control prices** is defined as monopoly power, and the amount of monopoly power a firm has is directly proportional to its market share.

Industry after industry came to be dominated by a few huge firms. In the early 1800s, no company controlled more than 10% of the output in a manufacturing industry. By the early 1900s, most industries were dominated by a few large firms, and in more than 160 industries one firm produced more than half of the output. U.S. Steel controlled 85% of steel production and Standard Oil owned 95% of the oil industry. Companies used size, collusion (forming secret trusts), mergers (buying out competitors), bribes (to get favorable treatment from the government or shipping companies), and other illegal means to dominate their industry.

The story of how Standard Oil came to dominate the oil industry is emblematic of the robber baron era. John D. Rockefeller purchased an oil refinery in Cleveland in 1862. He then merged with and purchased other competitors, forming Standard Oil as a limited liability corporation in 1870. Now that Standard Oil had a degree of monopoly power, Rockefeller began to collude and combine secretly with other large refineries to raise prices and profits, forming the Standard Oil Trust in 1882. Standard Oil used its large size to demand lower shipping costs from the railroads, and the lower costs allowed them to double the size of their company by undercutting competitors. Once it was the dominant company, Rockefeller demanded that railroads pay Standard Oil rebates whenever they shipped competitors' oil, and he required that the railroads share all data from competitors' shipments, including the buyer and price of the shipment. This gave Rockefeller immense advantages. Rockefeller was also known for bribing and threatening competitors, and Standard Oil officials even arranged for an explosion to occur at a rival refinery. Other robber barons such as Andrew Carnegie and J.P. Morgan engaged in similar manipulations.

The robber barons made a special point of crushing any attempt by workers to form unions and to get higher pay and better conditions. As in England, work hours were long and working conditions harsh. Workers responded the only way they could, by forming labor unions and going on strike. However, the police, at the urging of employers, responded brutally, and striking men, women, and children were shot with disturbing frequency.

The ruthless behavior of the robber barons provoked resistance from farmers and workers, who increasingly demanded laws to reign in the power of corporations. Also, government officials became worried about the increasing power of corporations as the size of the largest firms became larger than entire states. The Sherman Antitrust Act, passed in 1889, outlawed trusts and conspiracies that would lead to monopolies or otherwise restrain trade. However, the law was twisted by pro-corporation courts from an antitrust law to a measure to prevent labor unions from striking, and numerous labor leaders were arrested based on the new law. In a similar fashion, many federal regulatory agencies such as the Interstate Commerce Commission that were originally charged with regulating industries eventually were manipulated into helping industries make excess profits at the expense of the public. At this point in U.S. history, the duly elected government was operating almost entirely on the side of business, just as Marx predicted.

Despite these problems, under monopoly capitalism, the U.S. economy became the largest and most advanced in the world. Meanwhile, the working class was not able to counter the power of the robber barons. Divisions that existed with respect to race, ethnicity, and gender made it difficult for the working class in the United States to unite.

4.8 RACE, ETHNICITY, CLASS, AND GENDER IN THE UNITED STATES

Slaves were introduced into the American colonies in 1619, establishing racist exploitation as one of the foundations of the early economic system. Slavery was immensely profitable for plantation owners until the end of the Civil War. James Madison, instrumental in writing the U.S. Constitution, once boasted to "a British visitor shortly after the American Revolution that he could make $257 on every Negro in a year, and spend only $12 or $13 on his keep."[3] However, wealthy landowners feared a revolt by Black slaves allied with poor white indentured servants. They gave whites who completed their indentured servitude land, money, and greater status to separate their interests from those of Black slaves.

In the early United States, wealthy white landowners sat atop the class structure. Below them were a small number of free white merchants and small farmers. Next were white sharecroppers and indentured servants. At the bottom were Black slaves. Native Americans were excluded from white society for the most part and were thus outside the class system.

Even after the end of slavery after the Civil War, the Black population of the United States remained at the bottom rung of society. Although African Americans were no longer slaves, they had no land and no money, so they had little choice other than to work for landowners as sharecroppers: They farmed the owner's land and gave the owner half of what was produced, similar to the feudal system. But the value of the crops they produced was not enough to live on most years, so sharecroppers fell increasingly into debt. In addition to their desperate economic situation, African Americans faced the terroristic violence of the Klu Klux Klan, which tortured, raped, and murdered Blacks in the Southern United States. Furthermore, legal racial segregation established by the "Jim Crow laws" made it difficult for Blacks to vote and established segregated schools, transportation, bathrooms, restaurants, drinking fountains, and so on. With such a deep history of racial discrimination, most labor unions actively discriminated against Black workers, refusing to let them join white unions.

Ethnic differences also splintered the white working class. White immigrants to U.S. cities from Ireland, Italy, and other countries faced discrimination and stereotyping, making it difficult for workers to unite. Gender divisions were also intractable.

Many women worked in factories, but they were paid lower salaries than men. Almost all labor unions excluded women. Women were barred from many professions, especially the highest paid jobs in law and medicine, and women were still not allowed to vote. As a consequence, an increasingly powerful women's movement lobbied for greater rights and especially the right to vote, which was finally achieved in 1920.

If we fast forward to today, although there is a lot more class mobility now, the descendants of slaves and indentured servants are more likely to be members of the lower classes than descendants of the wealthy landowners. Many Native Americans are still separated from white society. Women today are on average paid significantly less than men and are less likely to be selected for top positions in corporations and government. The social classes and race and gender structures at the beginning of our history evidently had a significant impact on our current class structure. This is partly because the social classes on top have numerous advantages, including better education, health, wealth, and connections, which they use to stay on top. Also, as we will study later, discrimination with respect to race and gender has proven very difficult to root out. As Thorstein Veblen pointed out in his work, the cultural patterns of a society—its institutions—are very difficult to change.

4.9 VEBLEN ON EVOLUTION AND INSTITUTIONS

One of the most important aspects of Veblen's analysis was his methodology—his approach to the study of economics. Veblen saw an economic system that was dynamic and constantly changing. Where Smith and Marx saw certain "laws" governing how a capitalist economy worked, Veblen saw a world in which the patterns were constantly shifting. To Veblen, anyone who adopted a rigid view of the economy and assumed the future would always work the same as the past was doomed to failure. Instead, Veblen adopted an **evolutionary** approach, studying the forces causing the economy to change (or resist change) over time. Veblen believed that economists should analyze the key processes that shape the economy and economic behavior. For example, consumers' behaviors are shaped by biological needs (for food and shelter, procreation, etc.), cultural factors (the need to fit in and succeed in a particular society), industrial factors (competition or the lack of it in various industries, advertising and other media, etc.), government structures (the system of law, regulation, and taxation), and more.

But if the economy is constantly changing and if consumers and firms are constantly buffeted by a variety of factors that affect their behavior, what should economists focus on? To Veblen, the answer was to study **institutions**, which are **the organizations, social structures, rules, and habits that structure human interactions and the economy**. Once we understand the major institutions in a society, we should have a good grasp of the forces that promote and resist change, which allows us to analyze the evolution of the economy. The result of Veblen's unique approach was the founding of **institutional economics**, based on the following core ideas:

1. Institutions are the key factors shaping an economy and should be the primary focus of economists.
2. The economy is constantly changing, and studying how those changes are shaped by technology and key institutions (culture, power structures, and so on) gives us the best possible understanding of the structure of the economic system, how it is evolving, and how it might be improved with effective government policy.
3. Humans are social beings whose behavior is shaped fundamentally by the institutions of society and who seek status and power based on their cultural values.

Implicit in this approach is a critique of mainstream economics. To Veblen, individual behavior is much less important than studying culture and other institutions that shape human behavior.[4] Utilizing this approach, Veblen made a series of penetrating observations about capitalism, culture, and the "leisure class" that still are relevant today.

4.10 VEBLEN ON CULTURE, EMULATION, AND CONSPICUOUS CONSUMPTION

In his studies of human societies throughout history, Veblen saw a pattern. In each human society the members strove to fit in and succeed within the existing cultural norms. Human beings tend to be status-seeking and to act rationally within a cultural context. If, due to a harsh climate or difficult conditions, a society prioritized the sharing of food and resources, people would tend to work cooperatively within that society, seeking status by becoming the most prolific producers of food to share. In a cooperative society, those who were selfish were a threat to the community's survival, and they would be ostracized and shunned, making it less likely that they would survive and reproduce. Survival meant succeeding within the cultural norms of that particular society.

Meanwhile, if a society was more hierarchical, with those on top living ostentatiously and eschewing work while the masses did all of the productive tasks, a different set of cultural values would develop. Overt displays of wealth and leisure came to be valued because they demonstrated that a person was important and of high status in that society. Veblen observed that over time, societies with emperors, kings, and nobility came to value outward displays of wealth, such as jewelry, fine clothes, fancy vehicles, and vast estates. Elites tended to avoid the type of productive work associated with the common laborers. The elites formed a "leisure class" that sought to develop knowledge of fine wines, food, music, sports, and other cultural markers that showed they had the leisure time to spend on developing these skills instead of work skills. Thus, the leisure class worked very hard at displaying that they did not need to engage in productive work by cultivating useless skills and hobbies!

Veblen saw in all people an **instinct of workmanship**—a desire to work at productive tasks and to achieve something in the process. This, too, was probably a product of our evolutionary history: Lazy, unmotivated people most likely did not survive. However, in hierarchical societies, the fundamentally productive instinct of workmanship in all people became perverted into a vehicle for conspicuous leisure and conspicuous consumption. People worked very hard at acquiring useless goods or skills.

These values of the leisure class were then imitated by the classes below, who sought to move up in society, and thus became the values of society as a whole. This is the Veblenian concept of *pecuniary emulation*, where **people from the lower classes imitate the culture, habits, and spending of the upper classes to achieve status for themselves**. This helps us a great deal in understanding how consumption habits in particular societies get established.

Consider some specific examples of how human behavior is shaped directly by the culture of the leisure class and how culture evolves over time. Europeans wore cloth around their necks for centuries to use as napkins or to keep shirts closed in cold weather. However, when King Louis XIV of France began wearing a fancy lace necktie, or cravat, the necktie became a hot fashion accessory and, eventually, a symbol of status and respect among European nobility. Once the necktie became a symbol of status, it was adopted by businessmen who wanted to improve their social standing. Eventually, wearing a necktie came to symbolize one's seriousness in business and it became a required article of clothing for men at formal occasions in Western societies, even when it no longer fulfilled its once-practical purpose as a napkin or neck warmer. This convention spread to other societies around the globe as European countries dominated the global economy during the colonial era. One can find businessmen and government officials wearing neckties in the summer in tropical Africa! Thus, the best way to understand why men in modern societies still purchase and wear neckties is to grasp how the necktie came to symbolize status and respect in the European leisure class in a particular era.

We see another example in the origins of certain fashion trends for women that developed in the late 1800s when women of status wanted to differentiate themselves from women who worked in factories. Veblen discusses this in his famous book, *The Theory of the Leisure Class*:

> The woman's shoe adds the so-called French heel to the evidence of enforced leisure afforded by its polish; because this high heel obviously makes any, even the simplest and most necessary manual work extremely difficult. The like is true even in a higher degree of the skirt and the rest of the drapery which characterizes woman's dress. The substantial reason for our tenacious attachment to the skirt is just this; it is expensive and it hampers the wearer at every turn and incapacitates her for all useful exertion.[5]

High heels, polished shoes, long hair, long nails, and skirts became signs of status in distinguishing upper-class women from working-class women in the United States and other industrial societies in the late 1800s. No one could possibly engage in productive work in a factory or on a farm when dressed in this way. Ironically, women's fashions still reflect these trends to a certain degree: Business environments and formal occasions usually are associated with women wearing a skirt and polished shoes with high heels.

Thus, in Veblen's era, those at the top of the pecking order, the "leisure class," displayed that they were too important to work via their "conspicuous consumption" and "conspicuous leisure" patterns. Others then emulated the leisure class, wearing skirts and high heels to work and to important events. This tradition became institutionalized, and it persists to some extent even today, more than a century after it became a cultural norm.

The concept of conspicuous consumption is emblematic of Veblen's sophisticated analysis of how culture and human institutions shape purchasing patterns. **Conspicuous consumption** refers to **the practice of consumers purchasing and using goods for the purposes of displaying their status and importance to others**. All goods have a "use value" or "utility," meaning that they are useful to us and improve our well-being. But conspicuous consumption goods also have a "display" or "honorific" value. A good example can be found in the difference between a normal watch such as a Timex and a luxury watch such as a Rolex. Both watches have "use value": They tell us what time it is. But luxury watches also have "display" value. Wearing a Rolex sends a signal to others from our culture that the wearer is a wealthy, important individual. Another obvious example would be the difference between an economy car and a luxury car. Both cars will get the riders to their destination. But only the luxury car will get the rider to their destination in style, impressing others on the way. Luxury items send a signal to others from that particular culture that the person who possesses them is important and of high status.

As noted above, the definition of what signifies status varies widely by culture. In ancient human tribal societies, everyone knew who the chief was, so it was not as important for the chief to consume conspicuously. But in modern, large-scale societies, people tend to try to impress others by wearing expensive clothes, jewelry, and watches and driving expensive cars. A fashionably dressed person driving up in a limousine or an expensive car signals to modern society that an important person has arrived. Social media today involves substantial conspicuous displays. People attend a concert to listen to the music. But now that social media is a powerful cultural force, some people spend large amounts of time at concerts taking and posting pictures and videos to their social media accounts. The use value of the event—listening to music—is only part of the experience. The conspicuous display value of proving that you were at a particularly coveted event is just as important for many people.

Cultural values and consumption patterns do shift over time. In Veblen's era, the elites demonstrated their status via displays of leisure, proving to the world that they were not engaged in productive work via their impractical and impeccable clothing and their knowledge of fine wine and high culture. In the modern United States, a different value set seems to be emerging. New studies by Neeru Paharia, Silvia Bellezza, and Anat Keinan indicate that in the modern knowledge economy of the United States where hard work is prized, people associate busyness with high status.[6] People go out of their way to show and discuss their busy schedules, and this is taken as a sign of how important they are in the knowledge sector. Interestingly, when the same studies were conducted in Italy, the researchers got the opposite results: Participants tended to think those with leisure time were of higher status and those who were busy were of lower status. Thus, the aspiration to be part of the leisure class is still alive and well in Italy!

Human institutions such as culture have a past-binding, ceremonial aspect that holds onto traditions. However, institutions also have an industrial, technological aspect that promotes change. This dualistic character is readily apparent in the fundamental contrast that often manifests in capitalism between making money and making a useful product that enhances human well-being.

4.11 MAKING MONEY VS. MAKING GOODS

Veblen observed a conflict that often existed in capitalist businesses between making money and making goods. The productive aspect of capitalist businesses occurred when they provided high-quality products that consumers needed at the best possible price. The pursuit of newer technologies to reduce costs and the invention of new, useful products also stemmed from this productive impulse. This side of capitalism is beneficial. Businesses' investments in new technologies after the Civil War ushered in the U.S. Industrial Revolution, developing entirely new industries such as automobiles, telephones, photography, and electricity. These products were often invented by individuals, but it was large-scale businesses engaging in mass production that made these products affordable to the common people.

However, the useful, industrial side of capitalism is often countered by the focus on making money. Businesses could increase profits by eliminating competition or by manipulating consumers via questionable marketing and advertising practices. In the robber baron era, Veblen thought that too much business activity was devoted to wasteful and destructive activities, which he called **industrial sabotage**, and too little was spent on productive efforts. Businesses during the monopoly capitalism era were relentless in colluding (forming "trusts" to fix prices and reduce competition), merging, or using other means to stomp out competition. They bribed or manipulated politicians to get subsidies, prevented foreign competition from entering the market, and kept wages low. In addition to the focus on keeping prices high by reducing competition and wages low by clamping down on workers, companies engaged in deceptive advertising.

Prior to government regulations, advertising was often misleading or dishonest. Post Foods Company advertised that Grape-Nuts cereal would cure malaria, heart disease, appendicitis, and other maladies and that it would straighten teeth. Early pharmaceutical companies sold cocaine and opium as elixirs that could cure cancer or as cough remedies, fostering drug addiction in the process. Coca-Cola was developed originally as a "medicine" containing cocaine and caffeine (from kola nuts) that, according to its creator, would cure indigestion, headaches, impotence, and other health problems. These efforts highlight a significant flaw in capitalism: Firms may be able to increase their profits more via manipulative advertising than they can by producing a good product at a low price. This encourages firms to focus on advertising and marketing more than on the product they are producing.

A quick look around the U.S. economy indicates that these opposing forces—making a good product vs. making money—are still a feature. Each year firms improve old products and invent useful new products or new methods for producing existing products for a lower cost. From 2000 to 2021, firms invented or refined numerous products, including the smart phone and mobile broadband, social media websites, tablets (iPads, Kindles), electric and hybrid cars, GPS navigation systems, robots for surgery and manufacturing, smart devices of all types controlled via voice commands, artificial limbs and medical devices, life-saving drugs, and many more. The ability of capitalist firms to innovate continues unabated.

Unfortunately, there are also many examples of firms prioritizing making money over making a good product. Firms change the styles, colors, packaging, or outward design of their products to manipulate consumers into thinking they should purchase the latest versions instead of living with the ones they have. For example, some clothing firms including Zara and Forever 21 are now churning out new styles every week ("fast fashion") so that consumers keep purchasing new clothes that they do not need to stay up with the latest trends. Car companies change models almost every year so consumers keep buying new models instead of keeping their cars for the normal life span of more than 10 years.

Companies still engage in deceptive or manipulative advertising. Kellogg advertised that Rice Krispies could boost your immune system and Mini-Wheats could make you smarter, making unsubstantiated claims that harken back to the snake oil salesmen of old. Fortunately, we now have laws, enforced by the Federal Trade Commission, that prevent such distortions, and Kellogg was forced to pay fines and compensate consumers for making unsubstantiated health claims.

As a result, most modern advertising is much more subtle, and companies concentrate on manipulating cultural norms and pecuniary emulation to increase sales. Companies sell an image of their product that connects with our cultural values rather than emphasizing the product's practical, useful characteristics. SUV companies show their cars driving up mountains and across rugged terrain, cultivating an image of freedom and adventure even though most SUV owners will never drive their vehicle off-road. Marketing to teenagers shows people having fun, fitting in, and being "cool" when they buy certain products.

In all of these cases, advertisers are playing on the basic human tendency to engage in pecuniary emulation of those who are successful. It is no accident that celebrities are featured prominently in most ads or that the message of many commercials is that you will appear to be more successful if you buy a particular item.

Similar to the monopoly capitalism era, we also see regular mergers and acquisitions as large firms preserve their dominance of industries by reducing competitive pressures. Apple, Facebook, Amazon, and Google are famous for buying up patents and small companies with new ideas that operate in their markets, in the process ensuring their continued market dominance.

In addition, firms continue to curry favor with the government. In the United States, firms and their executives donate vast sums of money to the campaigns of candidates *from both political parties* to ensure that they will receive favorable treatment no matter who wins. If any candidate seems likely to question the status quo, businesses donate huge amounts of money to the competitor. In this way, firms can continue to dominate the economy even if they are not efficiently producing good products. To Veblen, the ability of the dominant powers in a society to resist productive change was one of the worst characteristics of a society.

Veblen objected to the domination of the economy by a small group of political and economic elites. Veblen called this group the **vested interests**, because **their goal as the group dominating society is to preserve the status quo that they benefit from**. Their focus is to resist any changes that would displace them from their privileged position atop the social structure. This means preventing new competition in the markets that they dominate via mergers, collusion, and threats and using their power and influence to manipulate the government to do what they want. In Veblen's view, the vested interests tend to impede progress and distort the allocation of resources, preventing the economy from functioning as efficiently as it might otherwise.

Veblen's core ideas—that the economy is structured primarily for the benefit of the few rather than the many and that monopoly capitalism is deeply inefficient due to industrial sabotage, conspicuous consumption, and other wasteful activities—had little influence on the economics profession of his era. Veblen's call to rein in the powers of the vested interests on behalf of the common people went unheeded. As the monopoly capitalist era proceeded, it was subject to vast economic fluctuations, and inequality exploded to levels never before seen in the United States.

4.12 THE MANUFACTURING BOOM AND THE ROARING TWENTIES

From 1900 to 1929, the U.S. economy grew rapidly alongside the rising power and influence of large corporations. The development of electric power drove a huge expansion in manufacturing, which also fed on the large influx of immigrants from Europe and resulted in a significant increase in urbanization. Dramatic increases in production occurred in various manufacturing industries, such as transportation, energy, printing, chemicals, paper, and steel. Manufacturing output nearly tripled during this period.

Some of these increases in production were driven by new inventions in manufacturing, in particular, the assembly line. Henry Ford pioneered the assembly line and began making large numbers of the Model T car in 1908. Despite the difficult working conditions, Ford was able to keep his workers by paying them $5 a day, more than twice the going wage rate of $2.25. Also, with the higher wages, his workers were better able to afford the cars they were producing.

The advent of World War I further stimulated production in the United States and cemented the role of the United States as the dominant manufacturing power. Following a short recession after the war, the economy boomed with an explosion in mass-produced consumer goods such as cars and appliances. However, the economic growth was extremely uneven and unequal. From 1900 to 1929, the United States experienced eight recessions, although they were usual short in duration. (The modern U.S. economy usually experiences one recession every 10 years.) During the extremely rapid growth of the Roaring Twenties (1920s), inequality exploded to unprecedented levels. One useful way to measure inequality is to look at the share of national income that goes to the richest 1% of the population. In 1920, the richest 1% of the U.S. population made 14.8% of the country's income. By 1928 that amount had grown to 23.9%.

Inequality can be a major problem for an economy in that it can result in macroeconomic instability. On average, rich people save much more than poor people. When more income goes to those at the top rather than those at the bottom, the result is more savings and less spending on goods. Unless the increase in savings is invested (spent on investment goods such as machines and factories), there will be a shortage of demand (purchases of goods), and the economy will spiral into a recession. Businesses that aren't selling all of their goods lay off workers, which reduces incomes further, causing spending to decline even more. What we know from economic history is that the savings of the richest 1% is usually invested in sufficient quantities when investors are confident about that future of the economy, but when investors get spooked for some reason, investment falls below the amount of savings and the economy enters a recession.

In general, the government of the day took a pro-business, laissez-faire approach. In many locations, the Progressive Movement during this era succeeded in making small changes to the economy for the benefit of workers, such as factory inspections to improve worker treatment and safety; public utilities commissions to limit the pricing of train travel, streetcars, water, and gas; and public health bureaus to address issues of housing, food safety, and disease. At the national level, repeated crises, and especially the Panic of 1907, led to the creation of the Federal Reserve, the U.S. national bank, to control the money and banking system. But the economy remained mostly unregulated until the Great Depression.

4.13 THE GREAT DEPRESSION AND THE FALL OF LAISSEZ-FAIRE

As the U.S. economy boomed during the 1920s, few people saw the increasingly fragile nature of the economic system. The 1920s saw a doubling of consumer debt, including mortgages for houses as well as installment debt for purchases of cars and appliances. At the same time, investors increasingly bought stocks with borrowed money, called "buying on the margin." Investors were only required to put a 10% down payment on their stock purchases. The increased demand for stocks and the boom of the 1920s caused stock markets to soar. The stock market doubled in 1928 alone! But a bubble based on debt can pop at any time when investors realize that their investments are not safe.

On October 23, 1929, the stock market started to fall toward the end of the day, especially in automobile stocks. As one investor after another panicked, it fell faster and faster, dropping 13% on October 28 and 12% more on October 29. Though there were some temporary recoveries, stock prices continued declining for 3 years, falling a total of 73.4% by 1932.

As the stock prices fell, banks started failing. People who borrowed money to invest in the stock market could not pay back their loans, and banks started to run out of money. When a few banks had lost so much that they were unable to give depositors their money when depositors wanted to withdraw it, depositors panicked. Even those depositors whose money was in stable banks decided to withdraw all of their deposits rather than worry that they might lose their money like other depositors at other banks. The result was a "run on the bank," where banks, which had loaned out most of the money of their depositors, could not meet the demands for cash withdrawals. By 1933, 11,000 of the country's 25,000 banks had failed. There was no federal deposit insurance yet, so when banks failed the depositors lost their money. This resulted in a significant decline in the U.S. money supply and an increase in the real interest rate of more than 10% as money became scarce.

These events were devastating to the economy. As people saw their life savings evaporate in the stock market or in failed banks, they cut back on spending. Businesses saw their sales plummet, so they laid off workers and cut investment. This reduced incomes, causing even more decreases in spending and more layoffs and declines in investment. The decline in consumer demand caused prices for farmers to plunge, driving thousands into bankruptcy. More than 85,000 businesses closed, and unemployment reached 25%. Unemployment insurance and welfare programs did not exist at the time, so people became desperate. Some starved, and others depended on charities, begging, or picking through garbage dumps for food. U.S. national income fell from $87 billion in 1929 to $42 billion in 1932 and kept falling. The contagion quickly spread, and soon the entire world was in a depression.

U.S. President Herbert Hoover, and most economists of the day, thought the Depression would pass quickly as others had. Hoover refused to take dramatic action, arguing that involving the government in the economy would be akin to socialism. Meanwhile, the mainstream economists of the day kept arguing that the economy would return to equilibrium in the "**long run**," which would happen very soon. Hoover and his economic advisors also pushed austerity (see Chapter 1). Believing that a balanced government budget was necessary, they slashed spending and enacted the largest tax increase in history (for that time) in 1932, throwing even more people out of work, all in the belief that the Depression would soon disappear. The response of the great macroeconomist John Maynard Keynes to this type of argument was a devastating critique. Keynes said, "The long run is a misleading guide to current affairs. *In the long run we are all dead*. Economists set themselves too easy, too useless a task if in tempestuous seasons they can only tell us that when the storm is past the ocean is flat again."[7] To Keynes it was ridiculous to wait for the long-run equilibrium, which might take years to come, when we had the tools to end the Depression much sooner.

Franklin Delano Roosevelt was elected president in 1932 by promising a "New Deal" for Americans in which the government would get much more directly involved in the economy, regulating huge firms, creating jobs, and providing a safety net for workers. Drawing on the ideas of Thorstein Veblen's students, and especially John Maynard Keynes, Roosevelt ushered in the modern era of the mixed economy in which the core economic system is still capitalist but the government takes on a significant role in regulating and stabilizing the economy. The era of laissez-faire capitalism had come to an end, destroyed by the Great Depression and the Keynesian revolution.

4.14 CONCLUSION

Capitalism spread across Europe and the United States in the mid-1800s as countries used infant industry promotion strategies to develop their economies. However, the conditions for workers under laissez-faire capitalism were abhorrent, sparking strikes and other forms of resistance. It was in this world that Karl Marx developed his analysis of capitalism, exposing the contradictory forces that led to rapid growth and development on the one hand and utter desperation and poverty for most workers on the other. His method of analysis, historical materialism, and his key analytical concept, surplus value, help us to understand how unregulated capitalism tends to work. In particular, Marx emphasized how competitive pressures all too often produced a race to the bottom and how the commodification of labor and other key aspects of society would demean and distort labor, culture, justice, and democracy.

The period from the mid-1800s to 1932 was a tumultuous one for the United States. After the Civil War, the manufacturing sector exploded, driven first by government-led investment in railroads and later by huge, monopolistic corporations and trusts. The first attempts to regulate corporations were undertaken as the Progressive Movement grew, but in general the government took a pro-business, laissez-faire approach to regulation. Despite the rapid rate of growth, there were warning signs in the frequent crises and rising inequality of the period.

Beginning in 1899, Thorstein Veblen developed the evolutionary, institutionalist approach to economics. He observed the status-seeking behavior common to human societies and noted how conspicuous consumption and conspicuous leisure had become the markers of respectability in the United States, demonstrating to the outside world the status and importance of a person.

Recent trends in economics demonstrate the ongoing importance of Veblen's methodology. Mainstream economists have increasingly been incorporating institutions into their analysis. Marxian economists have moved away from deterministic attitudes toward capitalism to a more evolutionary perspective. Thus, Veblen's contributions to the field are significant and enduring, as are those of John Maynard Keynes, whose ideas we take up next.

QUESTIONS FOR REVIEW

1. Given the experiences of workers under laissez-faire capitalism, analyze Smith's argument that laissez-faire capitalism would benefit workers. Which of Smith's ideas hold up? Which do not?
2. What are the key components of Marx's method, historical materialism? Explain briefly. Use historical materialism to explain the transition from one specific economic system to another.
3. Describe what you see as the major contradictions, technological changes, and class conflicts in our current society. What factors do you think are most likely to provoke a crisis? What type of economic system might evolve out of the crisis to resolve the existing contradictions?

4. Find three examples of commodification that you see around you. Choose different examples than those given in this chapter.
5. Contrast Marx's view of competition with that of Adam Smith. Analyze which aspects of their views of competition you think are most accurate, and support your answer with specific examples.
6. How was the era of monopoly capitalism different from the competitive capitalism of Adam Smith's era? Does Smith's argument that unregulated capitalism will tend to benefit the workers hold up under monopoly capitalism?
7. How do race and gender interact with social class to affect opportunities?
8. Describe the role of the leisure class, conspicuous consumption, and pecuniary emulation in the economy. Apply the concepts of conspicuous consumption and pecuniary emulation to the modern world, including examples from your community or university.
9. Define what Veblen means by conspicuous consumption. Make a list of at least three items that people in your community or university seem to purchase more for the purposes of conspicuous consumption than for the usefulness of the item. Briefly explain why you chose these particular items. Do not use examples already given in this book.
10. Why does Veblen distinguish between making money (via industrial sabotage) vs. making goods? Explain briefly.
11. Why does Veblen think that culture is important in understanding human behavior? Explain.
12. Veblen focused on institutions and how those institutions tend to persist over time, largely due to the forces of culture and the power of the vested interests to resist change. But these institutions also evolve. Using Veblen's approach, analyze the persistence and evolution of one of the following factors over time: (a) Racial inequality, (b) gender inequality, (c) class inequality, (d) domination of the economy by large corporations, or (e) domination of the global economy by the former imperial powers.

NOTES

1 Source: https://commons.wikimedia.org/wiki/File%3AAddieCard05282vLewisHine.jpg.
2 See Friedrich Engels, *The Condition of the Working Class in England* (1845).
3 Ibid., p. 33.
4 See Geoffrey M. Hodgson, "What Is the Essence of Institutional Economics," *Journal of Economic Issues* 34, no. 2 (June 2000): 317–329, for a broader description of institutional economics.
5 Thorstein Veblen, *The Theory of the Leisure Class* (Dover, reprinted 1994), p. 105.
6 Bellezza, Silvia, Neeru Paharia, and Anat Keinan, "Research: Why Americans Are So Impressed by Busyness," *Harvard Business Review*, December 15, 2016, https://hbr.org/2016/12/research-why-americans-are-so-impressed-by-busyness, accessed July 29, 2017.
7 John Maynard Keynes, *A Tract on Monetary Reform* (1923), ch. 3, p. 80.

5

Keynes and mixed market capitalism

How to save capitalism from itself

In the United States and Europe, a new role for government inspired by the ideas of Thorstein Veblen and John Maynard Keynes emerged, aiming to reduce the worst excesses of markets while still preserving the best aspects of market capitalism—competition, innovation, and economic growth. Followers of Veblen and Keynes worked in the U.S. government to establish stabilization policies, Unemployment Insurance, Social Security, and other programs to create a safety net for all citizens and to legalize labor unions.

Keynes revolutionized economic thinking by establishing the field of **macroeconomics**, which is **the study of the aggregate forces that shape national economies**. Macroeconomics studies large-scale, aggregate patterns in spending, saving, and investment and how these patterns create the **business cycle**—**the pattern of booms and busts created by economic fluctuations in market capitalist economies**. Keynes demonstrated that aggregate forces at the national and international levels have fundamentally different dynamics than microeconomic markets. National economies, and especially financial markets, are subject to "animal spirits" that spark booms and busts, rendering the economy unstable at times. Keynes advocated stabilization policy, to smooth out the business cycle, reduce the severity of recessions, and create a more sound economic system. In this way, Keynes sought to save capitalism from the destructive forces within it.

As governments began implementing Keynesian policies and regulating markets, the result was the modern mixed economy with some government and some markets. Mixed market capitalism proved to be a relatively stable and robust system, generating rapid economic growth and a much less unequal distribution of the gains from capitalism.

Friedrich Hayek criticized this growth of government's role, worrying that it would lead to totalitarianism of the kind seen in Nazi Germany and the Soviet Union. Despite Hayek's cautions, most Western democracies adopted mixed market

DOI: 10.4324/9780429399350-7

capitalism, with varying degrees of government intervention and varying degrees of success. However, the oil shocks of the 1970s, and the era of globalization and environmental crisis that followed, exposed some of the main contradictions in mixed market capitalism.

This chapter begins by describing the economic theories that led neoclassical economists to advocate a laissez-faire, hands-off approach to the economy even in the depths of the Great Depression. Next, we take up the ideas of John Maynard Keynes in more detail, describing his critique of **neoclassical economics** of his day and his major ideas regarding the circular flow of the economy, leakages and injections, the multiplier, sticky wages, and other market rigidities. Subsequently, we discuss the New Deal and the government policies that were established in the United States and elsewhere to stabilize economies and end the Great Depression. We then turn briefly to the ideas of Friedrich Hayek and his critique of Keynesian policies and central planning. The chapter concludes by looking at the mixed market economy that developed in the United States after the New Deal and that still exists today.

5.0 CHAPTER 5 LEARNING GOALS

After reading this chapter you should be able to:

- List, explain, and evaluate the three core theoretical ideas that drove neoclassical economists of the early 1900s to advocate a hands-off, laissez-faire approach to the economy: The marginal productivity theory of distribution, the belief that markets always clear, and Say's law.

- Reproduce the circular flow model of the economy and use it to explain how neoclassical economists and Keynes differ in their analysis of savings and investment (leakages and injections).

- List, explain, and evaluate the major ideas of John Maynard Keynes, including the volatility of investment, sticky wages and prices, the macroeconomic problems created by wage and price deflation, the multiplier process, and stabilization policy.

- Compare and contrast the ideas of Hayek and Austrian economists with those of Keynes.

- Describe and analyze the economic interventions made by the U.S. government in the economy from the New Deal to the present.

- Define and evaluate the effectiveness of an economic system of "regulated" or "mixed" market capitalism.

5.1 NEOCLASSICAL ECONOMICS AND THE IDEOLOGY OF LAISSEZ-FAIRE

The neoclassical (mainstream) economists of the early 1900s held three theoretical beliefs that led most of them to conclude that a laissez-faire approach to economic regulation was always preferable to government intervention. These theories were the marginal productivity theory of distribution, markets always clear (supply equals demand and the invisible hand), and Say's law. We will take each of these up below.

1. The **marginal productivity theory of distribution**: **The neoclassical theory that people are paid exactly what they are worth based on their marginal productivity under a competitive, capitalist economic system**. This theory assumes that there are no power imbalances and so no exploitative relationships exist.

    The implications of this theory are important to understand. Because all markets are assumed to be fully competitive, workers should always have multiple employers trying to hire them, and employers should always have multiple workers to choose from. In essence, workers are assumed to have as much bargaining power as their bosses. Under such conditions, a worker will end up getting paid exactly what they are worth based on how productive they are. If a worker is particularly productive (a high marginal productivity), many employers will bid for her services and her wages will be high. If a worker is less productive (a low marginal productivity), she will be paid a lower wage in a competitive marketplace. Also, another assumption behind this theory is that everyone has equal access to education and opportunities, so it does not matter whether someone is well connected. If this theory holds true, then the government should never take steps to reduce inequality, because that would mean taking money from highly productive people and giving it to less productive people, reducing the efficiency of the economy. Thus, despite the exploding inequality of the 1920s, no efforts were made to equalize incomes.

2. **Markets always clear**: **The neoclassical theory that supply always equals demand in all markets, so the invisible hand of the market always allocates resources efficiently**.

    If all markets are competitive and there is easy entry and exit of firms, then prices will always adjust to eliminate any surplus or shortage. If there is a glut of goods that is produced, the prices of those goods will fall, causing consumers to buy more and eliminating the glut. Therefore, the surplus of goods in a depression will be eliminated once prices of goods fall and that causes consumers to buy more of them. If there is unemployment, otherwise known as a surplus of laborers, unemployment will disappear as soon as wages fall because then firms will hire more workers and the surplus will be eliminated. According to this theory, the only possible reason for unemployment is workers demanding higher wages than they are entitled to. Edwin Cannan, president of the Royal Economic Society in England, put it this way in 1932: "General unemployment appears when asking too much is a general phenomenon. ... [T]he world ... should learn to submit to declines of money-incomes without squealing."[1] Neoclassical economists saw no need to intervene in the economy to help the unemployed or to help producers. Any government intervention was seen as reducing the efficiency of the market mechanism: Capitalist markets were seen as the ideal, rational, and efficient way to allocate society's resources.

3. **Say's Law**: **Supply creates its own demand, and savings is always equal to investment**.

    As we saw in Chapter 4, Say's law posits that in the act of supplying products, firms generate income. Because every penny a firm earns in revenue is income for someone—either the workers, suppliers, or owners—there is always enough income generated to purchase all of the goods produced. Also, any amount of income that people save will automatically be invested. When people save money, they put it in banks. The banks need to loan that money out to make a profit, so they offer loans at favorable interest rates. Businesses looking to expand their operations and consumers desiring more goods borrow from banks, and when they spend the money they borrowed, the money in banks has been returned to the economy and the circular flow is complete. Any time there is a decline in spending and an increase in savings, perhaps because consumers are pessimistic after a stock market crash, there will be a larger amount of money in banks, which in turn causes the banks to reduce interest rates, which then stimulates investment and consumption spending, eliminating any problems created by the original decline in spending. There is always exactly enough demand to buy all of the goods that are supplied. This is the famous depiction of the circular flow model of the economy displayed in Figure 5.1.

    Recall that in the circular flow model, firms produce goods and services, which they sell to consumers and to other businesses (businesses purchase capital goods, such as machinery and equipment). Every dollar of income the producers generate when they sell goods and services becomes income for somebody: Firms pay wages to workers hired in labor markets, they pay rent on land to landowners in real estate markets, and they pay interest to banks, dividends to shareholders, and profits to owners in capital (financial) markets. What do households do with the income they earn? They either spend it, in the form of consumer spending on goods and services, or they save it, putting their money in banks. The money placed in banks is then loaned out to businesses for purchases of capital goods or to consumers for the purchase of consumer durables (houses, cars, and appliances), putting the money back into the economy. Note that businesses' purchases of capital goods and consumer purchases of durable goods are considered physical investment. According to Say's law, all of the money that is taken out of the economy in the form of savings is put back into the economy in the form of investment.

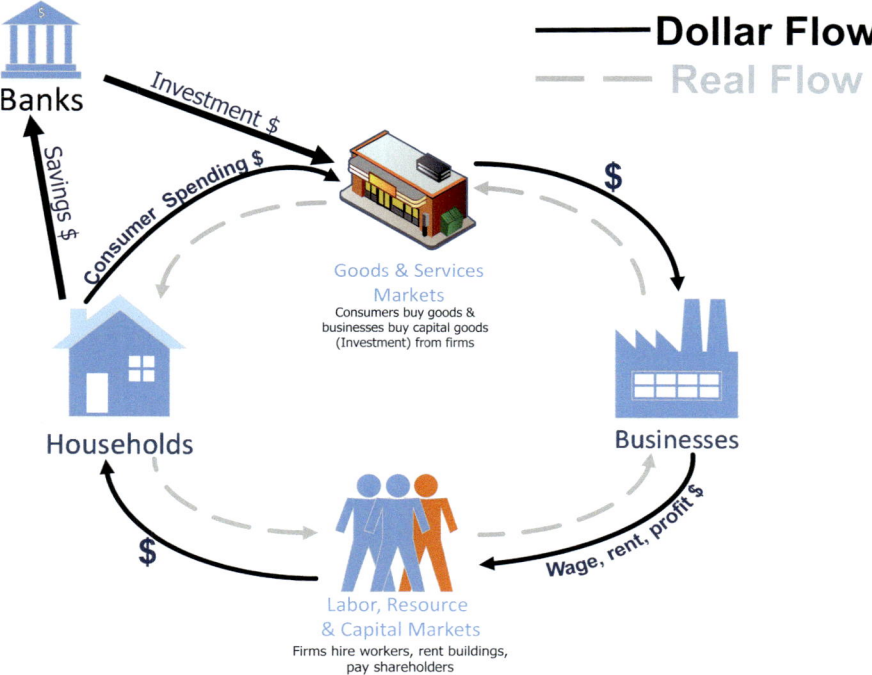

FIGURE 5.1 The circular flow model of the economy, with savings and investment.

If all three of these pillars of neoclassical theory hold, then markets are perfectly efficient, there is never an involuntary unemployment (the only unemployment that exists consists of those who demand wages that are too high), and there is never a lasting depression. In this way, neoclassical theory provided a theoretical basis for the laissez-faire approach taken by the government. Of course, the fact that the Great Depression grew longer and longer with no sign of ending completely undermined faith in the neoclassical, laissez-faire orthodoxy.

5.2 THE MACROECONOMIC REVOLUTION OF JOHN MAYNARD KEYNES

John Maynard Keynes (1883–1946), pictured in Figure 5.2 (next page), was born in Cambridge, England. His father was a well-known economist, and he studied with the famous neoclassical economist Alfred Marshall at Cambridge. Even early in his career, he demonstrated extraordinary sophistication and foresight in his analysis. In his famous book *The Economic Consequences of the Peace* (1919), he predicted that the harsh financial conditions imposed on Germany after World War I, requiring

FIGURE 5.2 John Maynard Keynes.

them to pay more than 80% of gross domestic product (GDP) in reparations, would cause impoverishment and starvation and would eventually lead to another war even worse than World War I. The German hyperinflation and crisis of the 1920s, followed by the rise of Adolf Hitler and Nazi Germany and the advent of World War II in 1939, showed just how accurate Keynes' predictions were. He was also able to use his knowledge of the economy to make a fortune for himself and for King's College in financial markets.

Rather than depending on abstract, deductive theory based on questionable assumptions, Keynes based his ideas on observations of actual investor and worker behavior. What he saw was a picture very different from the one described in the neoclassical theories of the day.

The first major flaw in neoclassical analysis, according to Keynes, was with Say's law. As you can see with the circular flow model in Figure 5.1, Say's law only holds if savings and other leakages out of the economy are equal to investment and other injections into the economy. (Later, we will include additional leakages such as export spending and taxes and additional injections such as import spending and government spending.) However, Keynes observed that when a crisis hits, savings increases but investment falls as businesses lose confidence; leakages then exceed injections, and the economy spirals into a recession. Thus, the first pillar of Keynesian analysis is the inherent volatility of investment.

1. **Volatility of investment**: **The Keynesian theory that business purchases of capital goods (investment) depend primarily on expected future profits, which is driven largely by expected sales, and expectations can vary dramatically**. When businesses' expectations change, we can anticipate large changes in investment, resulting in the booms and busts of the business cycle.

Say's law fails precisely because it does not incorporate this fundamental driver of investor behavior. When the stock market crashed in 1929 and banks failed, it undermined business confidence and reduced consumer spending as people saw their wealth decline. According to Say's law, the decrease in spending meant that people were saving more, and more money in banks should have led to lower interest rates, which should have prompted more investment. But few businesses were investing despite lower interest rates. Why? Because expected sales were very low. With consumer spending down and unemployment spiraling out of control, no sane businessperson would see 1932 as a good time to increase investment.

Recall that investment—the purchase of capital goods—usually increases the size and scale of business operations. Businesses will not invest unless they expect to sell more goods in the future. The main reason for this is that it can take a long time—often more than a year—for a business investment to start earning profits. A business that builds a new factory must lay out large sums of money now for a plant that could take two years before it has been built, staffed, and become operational. When it invests, the business is making a bet that it can sell more goods in two years than it does now. The only conditions under which the business will make the investment in the new factory is if they expect sales to be very good in two years. A pessimistic sales forecast would likely mean the business will not undertake the investment. This is why business expectations are such an important driver of investment, which is an important driver of the business cycle.

In the Great Depression, as unemployment increased and consumer spending fell, businesses cut their investment even though interest rates were low. Thus, there was no increase in investment forthcoming, as Say's law predicted, and the economy languished in the Great Depression for years. Savings continued to exceed investment. This problem was exacerbated when banks failed, reducing the money supply and causing interest rates to increase. Furthermore, the unemployment rate failed to decrease, as the neoclassical economists predicted. One of the main causes of this was sticky wages.

2. **Sticky wages and prices**: Keynes' observed that, **in a recession, wages and prices do not fall fast enough to encourage businesses to hire more workers and consumers to buy more goods**.

    What Keynes found was that it took a very long time after the start of a recession for wages to fall. Workers and their unions fought any wage cuts vigorously and angrily, so slashing wages often meant strikes and lower productivity, which was bad for profits. However, employers have found that if they keep wages the same and lay off some of their workforce, the results are different. Workers who keep their jobs in the face of layoffs are very happy to have them. They will work harder and more productively to keep their jobs so they do not get laid off in the future. In this sense, wages are "sticky downward": They tend to increase in booms when the unemployment rate falls and workers are in demand, but wages tend to stay the same for a long time in recessions before eventually falling if the recession persists for several years.

For example, Leo Wolman of the National Bureau of Economic Research reported that after the stock market crash in 1929, real wages fell very little in 1930 and 1931 and only fell in 1932 in non-union and non-utilities industries.[2] Meanwhile, unemployment surged. So three years after the crash, the Great Depression saw a huge increase in layoffs but only small declines in wages in some sectors. Wages did not fall far enough and fast enough to spark a rise in employment that would help to end the Great Depression, as neoclassical economic theory implied. But even where wages did fall, there was not the hoped-for increase in employment that neoclassical economic theory predicted, as we will see below.

The story with prices is a bit different. Prices of goods did not fall significantly for the first six months after the stock market crash, but then they began to fall quickly. As the economy crashed, surpluses of goods began to pile up because no one was buying them, and that caused prices to fall in one market after another. Prices fell by more than 20% from 1930 to 1933. According to the neoclassical theory of the day, that decline in prices should have sparked an increase in consumer purchases, helping to end the Depression. Instead, deflation and declines in wages proved to be ruinous.

3. **Macroeconomic problems created by wage and price deflation: Declines in wages undermine aggregate demand and declines in goods prices undermine business profitability, both of which harm the economy in particular ways.**

    One of the important economic facts that Keynes established was that, in general, wage declines are bad for economic growth. Neoclassical economic theory of the time predicted that a decline in wages, by reducing the cost of hiring, would cause employers to hire more workers and boost the economy. However, neoclassical economists were only focusing on the cost, or supply, side of the wage issue, ignoring the demand side. When wages fall, that means workers have less money to spend. When workers spend less, sales fall, and businesses then lay off workers because of poor sales. Thus, when wages decline, the total demand for goods and services (aggregate demand) falls, which prevents employment from increasing (despite the decrease in wage costs) and harms real GDP growth.

    Declines in prices are also destructive to economic growth. In fact, deflation is one of the worst things that can happen to a business. Imagine Henry Ford producing 1 million basic Model A cars for an average cost of $450 in 1930 and being able to sell them for $500 to make a reasonable profit. But with deflation, if the price at which he can sell the Model A car falls 11%, to $445, then he makes a loss on every car he sells. Losses, if they continue, will eventually result in bankruptcy. When deflation reduces goods prices to below businesses' costs of production, deflation is ruinous to producers.

    As a classic example from the Depression, the price of milk fell so low that farmers lost money on each gallon they sold. In desperation, the farmers went on strike, dumping their milk and blocking milk shipments of nonstriking farmers to try to boost prices and call attention to their plight. Similar dumping and destruction of food happened with oranges, potatoes, pigs, and other farm products. It is remarkable to think of children dying of malnutrition at the same time food was being destroyed due to low prices, something John Steinbeck called "a crime … that goes beyond denunciation" in his famous novel about the Depression, *The Grapes of Wrath*. Deflation was one of the most devastating aspects of the Depression, and it remains a significant problem for economies in recessions. It is also important to understand how the contagion of a downturn spreads from one sector to another via the multiplier process.

4. **Multiplier process: A respending process whereby a dollar in spending becomes income for someone else, which they then spend, which becomes additional income, and so on, so that a dollar of spending is respent multiple times.** Similarly, when a firm lays off workers and incomes decline, those workers spend less, which reduces incomes at the businesses they usually patronize, which lowers revenues of those businesses, which causes them to lay off workers, who then spend less, which lowers incomes more, which lowers spending more, and so on.

The stock market crash of 1929 caused businesses to cancel investment projects such as the building of new factories, and it caused consumers to cut their spending on expensive durable goods such as houses, cars, and appliances. These declines in spending reduced the incomes of firms in the construction and durable goods sectors. Those firms, in turn, laid off workers and cut their investment spending. When the workers in construction and durable goods lost their jobs, they, too, cut their spending, buying fewer goods of all types, which hurt those businesses that they usually patronized. And on and on it went. Thus, one major macroeconomic event, like a stock market crash, can spread like a contagion to other parts of the economy. Fortunately, Keynes observed, crashes can be reversed if the government engages in appropriate stabilization policy.

Taken together, these key Keynesian insights tell us that there is no reason to expect recessions to fix themselves. Given that the economy can linger in a recession for long periods of time, as it did in the Great Depression, Keynes argued that in recessions the government should use all of the tools at their disposal to stimulate the economy. This "stabilization policy" meant abandoning the laissez-faire approach and actively using government policy to improve the economy.

5.3 MACROECONOMIC STABILIZATION POLICY

As we noted in the previous chapter, Keynes thought it was ridiculous to wait for the economy to improve eventually, stating sarcastically that "in the long run we are all dead." Instead, he advocated taking concrete, immediate government action to stimulate the economy. He thought the government should engage in macroeconomic **stabilization policy**: **(1) increasing government spending, (2) reducing taxes, and (3) reducing interest rates in recessions, while doing the opposite when the economy is growing too quickly**.

Increasing government spending was the surest way to improve economic conditions in a recession. The biggest problem in a recession was that there was too little spending (a shortage of aggregate demand): Investors and consumers weren't buying enough goods to keep the economy going at its normal rate. Therefore, the best way to correct the economy was for the government to increase spending, because this would directly increase incomes and then, via the multiplier, spark additional rounds of spending. If the government were to spend billions of dollars building roads, bridges, parks, and schools, it would create jobs and income for millions of workers necessary to build those things. Those workers would then spend the income they received, further stimulating the economy.

The government could also cut taxes, giving consumers and businesses more money to spend. As they spend more, this will stimulate income and job growth. Tax cuts should be targeted at poor and middle-class families, who will spend the largest percentage of their tax cut and therefore stimulate spending the most. However, tax cuts tend to be less effective than government spending in recessions because of poor consumer and business confidence. If consumers are pessimistic about the future, worrying that they might lose their job or fall on hard times, they will likely save the tax cut instead of spending it. Similarly, businesses that get a tax cut in a recession might use that money to invest in new plants and equipment, but if they expect slow sales to continue, they also might save the money from the tax cut instead of spending it. Tax cuts tend to be less effective than government spending in a recession because some (and possibly a lot) of the tax cut will be saved, whereas all of the government project money is spent.

The government should also increase the money supply in order to reduce interest rates in a recession. As the government floods the banking system with money, banks will seek to loan out the new money to new borrowers, which will require them to lower interest rates to entice new borrowers. One of the major problems in the Great Depression was that as banks failed, this reduced the money supply significantly and increased real interest rates, which made businesses and consumers reluctant to borrow for spending on investment and consumer durable goods. Increasing the money supply would help to reverse that problem.

Unfortunately, like tax cuts, declines in interest rates can have limited effectiveness in a recession due to pessimism. Consumers might not be willing to borrow more money for new houses and cars if they are worried about keeping their job in the future. And employers might not be willing to borrow money to finance new investments in plants and equipment if they expected slow sales to continue in the future. There is no guarantee that lowering interest rates will spark significant increases in investment and consumer spending.

The best possible way to combat a recession would be to enact all three policies, increasing spending, reducing taxes, and reducing interest rates so that every possible lever is used to stimulate the economy. In fact, the government did all of these things to combat the Great Recession of 2008–2009. Note that enacting stabilization policy not only requires the government to intervene in the economy but also requires that the government must run a deficit and borrow money in a recession. Running deficits, however, was the opposite of the policy of austerity recommended by most neoclassical economists of the day.

As we noted in Chapter 1, government deficits tend to increase automatically in recessions, and they increased a lot in the Great Depression. As incomes and spending fell after the stock market crash, tax revenues fell as well, creating budget deficits for the government once tax revenues were below spending. Neoclassical economists argued that the government should increase taxes and cut government spending to balance the budget. But in cases where the government did this, the recession worsened. Increases in taxes reduced spending, as did cuts in government programs. Keynes suggested the opposite. Even though the budget deficit increases in a recession, the government should run even larger deficits by cutting taxes and increasing spending. Those policies will increase income and stimulate economic growth, which will then increase tax revenues in the future. In essence, running government deficits in recessions pays for itself eventually once economic growth returns.

Here, Keynes argued for a revolution in thinking about government intervention and government budgets. Instead of running a balanced budget each and every year, governments should run deficits in recessions, which could then be paid off by surpluses that are run during expansions when economic growth is more rapid and incomes (and tax revenues) are higher. The government budget should be balanced over the entire business cycle, not each year. Governments must have the flexibility to run deficits when conditions are bad and to slow down the economy by running a surplus when they see the economy growing too quickly—an overheated economy—which can lead to a bubble and a crash.

5.4 THE NEW DEAL AND THE RISE OF THE MIXED ECONOMY

In the 1932 campaign for president, Franklin Delano Roosevelt promised to stop following a laissez-faire approach and to take direct government action to end the Great Depression, adopting a philosophy similar to Keynes' that he called the "New Deal." He won the election in a landslide over Herbert Hoover, winning by 18 percentage points and bringing a Democratic Congress into office with him. After inauguration in 1933, Roosevelt and Congress enacted 15 major bills in the first 100 days to begin to transform the United States into a mixed market economy. Over the next two years, even more changes were made. The major areas of reform were (1) regulation of banking, financial markets, and the money supply; (2) the creation of a safety net for people who had fallen on hard times; (3) the direct provision of jobs for the unemployed; (4) the establishment of the Social Security retirement program for the elderly; and (5) the creation of an agricultural price support system.

5.4.1 Regulation of banking, money, and financial markets

One of the major problems after the stock market crash had been bank failures. Consumers and businesses lost their savings when the banks failed, which made everyone reluctant to put their money into banks once they had some. Many people hid cash under their mattresses rather than entrust their money to a bank! But the lack of savings in banks was very bad for the economy. There was little money for businesses and consumers to borrow, which stifled business investment and consumer purchases of houses, cars, and appliances.

To solve this problem, the Roosevelt administration created Federal Deposit Insurance, where the government would guarantee deposits of up to $5000 per individual in banks (that amount has grown to $250,000 per individual today). This means that if the bank failed, the government would reimburse depositors for any money the bank lost. In exchange for providing this insurance, the government imposed strict regulations on banks. Insured banks were prohibited from engaging in speculative investments in the stock market, they had to agree to keep a certain amount of cash on hand (reserves) to prevent runs on the bank, and they were required to submit to regular inspections from bank regulators. The government split the banking sector into safe, insured mortgage banks and riskier, noninsured investment banks. The government also established itself as the "lender of last resort," meaning that if a bank ran short of cash it could borrow from the Fed. In addition, it established the possibility of the federal government seizing insolvent banks and bailing out banks experiencing financial difficulty.

Investment banks and stock markets were now to be regulated by the newly created Securities and Exchange Commission (SEC). The SEC established rules and guidelines for financial markets, mandated transparency, and outlawed insider trading and other unethical market manipulations.

The government also took greater control of the money supply, which at the time meant controlling the supply of gold and the issuance of Federal Bank notes backed by gold. By devaluing the dollar relative to gold (and also relative to other currencies backed by gold), this had the effect of increasing the money supply. By flooding banks with money, this reduced real interest rates as banks sought to find new borrowers, stimulating investment and consumer spending. Devaluing the dollar relative to other currencies also increased U.S. exports because it made U.S. goods cheaper to foreign consumers.

Together, the banking, financial market, and money supply reforms restored faith in the financial system. People began putting their savings in banks and stock markets once again, the money supply expanded significantly, real interest rates fell, and consumer spending and business investment started to increase. Ironically, although many of these reforms were looked at as "socialism" by those opposing government intervention, they were proposed and enacted by conservative bankers who saw these changes as the only way to save capitalism.

5.4.2 The safety net: Social Security, Unemployment Insurance, and Welfare

In addition to its path-breaking regulation of banks, financial markets, and the money supply, the New Deal established a "safety net" for those who fell on hard times with the Social Security Act. This, too, was a revolutionary change in philosophy, with the government for the first time taking on the role of ensuring that its citizens "fared well," in what came to be termed the "welfare state." The first key component of the new welfare state was the Social Security program.

In the 1930s, the elderly were among the poorest segments of the population. Most workers in that era did not receive pensions, there was no government-provided old-age insurance, the jobs that did exist in the Depression went to younger workers, and many of the elderly had lost their life savings in the bank failures of the early 1930s. To rectify this situation, the Roosevelt administration established the Social Security program as a national system of old-age insurance. Once workers reached age 65 they would receive a payment from the government based on the amount they had earned during their lifetime, up to some maximum limit. In order to start the program immediately to address the poverty of the elderly, the Social Security program was established as a pay-as-you-go system: Workers and employers in the 1930s would pay a Social Security tax, which would go directly to existing retirees. When those workers and employers retired, say, in the 1950s, their Social Security benefits would be paid out of taxes paid by a new group of workers and employers. There are no retirement accounts within the U.S. Social Security system. Rather, by working in the United States you acquire the right to a certain amount of Social Security retirement benefits, which will be paid as long as there are enough workers and employers paying Social Security taxes to support you and other retirees.

Another major innovation of the Social Security Act was the establishment of Unemployment Insurance. This program provides temporary assistance to workers, usually for up to six months, after a job loss. (In recent recessions the government has regularly extended unemployment benefits beyond six months when conditions are such that unemployed workers have little chance of finding a job.)

Workers who were unable to find jobs or generate income for prolonged periods of time and who became destitute would qualify for welfare programs, designed to help the poorest, most desperate people in society. These programs also helped to support single mothers and their children and the disabled. In the Depression, because many families were no longer able to support their relatives who had fallen on hard times, the government increasingly took on this role.

5.4.3 Intervention in the labor market: Job creation and labor laws

Due to the massive nature of the unemployment problem, Roosevelt also created new programs to put people back to work directly. The Civilian Conservation Corp employed hundreds of thousands of unemployed, unmarried men between the ages of 17 and 27. They planted more than 3 billion trees to stop land erosion and beautify towns. The Civil Works Administration, the National Industrial Recovery Act, and the Works Progress Administration employed people to build roads, schools, national parks, and airports or to serve as teachers. Until the United States entered World War II, these programs employed more than 15 million people at various times on a variety of public works projects. The efforts were so successful at job creation and achieved so many useful things in communities that some reformers began to consider the idea that the government should be the "employer of last resort" in recessions, employing people who wanted to work but could not find a job.

Other dramatic actions were taken in labor markets as well. The government legalized the right of workers to unionize and the right of unions to collectively bargain with employers. **Collective bargaining** occurs **when workers bargain as a group (union) with employers instead of each worker bargaining separately with an employer**. This significantly strengthens the bargaining power of employees, allowing them to get better wages and benefits and greater job security. When employees bargain on their own with their employer they have little power in negotiations. When workers bargain as a group, they can threaten to go on strike and shut down the entire company if their demands are not met, giving them much more say in pay and working conditions. The government also established minimum wages in many industries, reduced the standard work week to 40 hours, and abolished child labor. In addition to these interventions in labor markets, the government began regulating agricultural markets.

5.4.4 Agricultural price supports

Farmers were among the groups hardest hit by the Depression when agricultural prices plummeted in the early 1930s. To alleviate farmers' plight, Roosevelt paid farmers to produce less, reducing the supply of agricultural products so that prices would increase and farmers would make more money. Although this policy was condemned by many given that there were many hungry people in the United States at the time, it succeeded in stabilizing agricultural markets.

5.4.5 The success of the New Deal

The New Deal reforms had a very positive effect on the economy, finally ending the freefall that began in 1929. Financial markets and banks were stabilized by the reforms. Unemployment Insurance, Welfare, job creation, and Social Security programs directly put money into the hands of poor households, and they spent it, stimulating aggregate demand, increasing businesses' sales and sparking even more hiring. From 1933 to 1937, business investment increased by more than 1200%, consumer spending increased by more than 46%, and real GDP had returned to its 1929 level.

In general, the New Deal was pragmatic and modest in scope, intending to stabilize markets and to correct **market failures** where they were most glaring—especially labor, finance, banking, and agriculture. Despite these modest goals, it ushered in a new era of government intervention in the economy, with the state assuming the role of stabilizer of markets and insurer of the welfare of its citizens. Nonetheless, many people were worried about this unprecedented increase in the government's role and especially the 83% increase in government spending.

5.4.6 The Recession of 1937–1938

Despite all of the successes of the New Deal and the positive growth that had been achieved, the Roosevelt administration still had not completely embraced Keynesian economics and the need to run substantial deficits and engage in expansionary monetary policy until the economy had fully recovered. Business investment in 1937 was still 27% lower in 1937 than it had been in 1929, despite Roosevelt's efforts. Even with the fragility of the recovery, in 1937 the Roosevelt administration decided to raise taxes, slash spending by $1 billion, and reduce the money supply. This produced another devastating recession, with real GDP falling by $5 billion (another example of the multiplier in action). This experience produced an important lesson for economists: When the economy is still in fragile condition from a major recession, it is a mistake to cut spending, raise taxes, or raise interest rates, because this can derail the expansion by undermining business and consumer confidence just as it is beginning to rebound. Fortunately, after the financial crisis of 2008–2009, the government heeded that lesson and continued to stimulate the economy until 2017, when the economy had returned to full strength.

5.4.7 World War II proves Keynes right

After 1938, the economy made a sluggish recovery, and it was not until the United States entered World War II and engaged in a massive increase in military spending that the Great Depression finally ended. But World War II did demonstrate conclusively that the government can end any recession, no matter how severe, if it is willing to spend enough money. The war spending also proved another of Keynes' ideas true: Running budget deficits for short periods of time does not necessarily create macroeconomic problems. The U.S. government ran huge deficits to finance war spending, but rather than constrain economic development, business investment surged along with government spending. The U.S. public national debt reached 106% of GDP in 1946—the government owed more money than the value of all goods and services produced in a year! Yet not only did the economy remain strong but the stage was set for one of the most rapid periods of economic growth the U.S. economy has seen.

5.5 HAYEK'S CRITIQUE OF GOVERNMENT INTERVENTION

Following the success of Keynesian policy in the United States and other countries where it was used, economists became more and more comfortable with the idea of government intervention in the economy to fix market failures. However, one group of economists, the **Austrian** school led by Ludwig von Mises and Friedrich Hayek, found this approach to be deeply problematic.[3]

The Austrian economists had much in common with neoclassical economic theory, believing that the individual (not groups or institutions) should be the focus of economic analysis. However, they tended to avoid the use of the mathematical models that neoclassical economists favored. Austrian economists also harbored a deep suspicion of government intervention. With the rise of authoritarian regimes on either side of Austria—Nazi Germany and the Soviet Union—this revulsion of government grew even stronger with time.

Hayek was an insightful economist in several key areas, and his ideas had substantial influence on conservative politicians in the United States and England. Both Ronald Reagan and Margaret Thatcher cited him as a major influence and inspiration. His often controversial ideas on the business cycle, central planning, freedom, and the efficiency and effectiveness of markets provide an important potential counterargument to Keynesian approaches.

5.5.1 The business cycle

One of Hayek's major disagreements with Keynes was on the business cycle. Hayek believed that periods of overinvestment create a boom and an imbalance between savings and investment. A shortage of savings causes interest rates to rise, which halts investment and leads to a crash. He thought that after a crash, financial markets would return to equilibrium and that there were no major consequences to recessions. In fact, recessions could be useful in his view by weeding out inefficient firms, so recessions should not necessarily be avoided. However, most economists today reject the idea that the government should do nothing to alleviate extraordinarily high levels of bank and business failures and unemployment, believing that the costs of recessions are too high.

5.5.2 Central planning and freedom

Hayek also disagreed with the idea that government should become a welfare state or intervene extensively in industrial development. He saw the New Deal moving the United States closer to command communism, and he believed that this increased level of government intervention was a threat to freedom, which he defined as freedom from government interference. He argued in *The Road to Serfdom* that "planning leads to dictatorship because dictatorship is the most effective instrument of coercion and the enforcement of ideals and, as such, essential if central planning on a large scale is to be possible." He worried that any government venture into planning would ultimately lead to dictatorships, so he resisted public health care, public education, and government economic development programs.

In contrast, Karl Polanyi, whose book *The Great Transformation* was written during the same time when Hayek was active, thought that Hayek's definition of freedom would result in freedom being available only for the rich and powerful. Polanyi believed that workers and the non-elites needed government intervention to protect them from market outcomes, arguing that unemployment and destitution are "brutal restrictions of freedom." To Polanyi, true freedom—the freedom to live a good life and make choices—comes from having security, a decent income, and job opportunities. He saw government intervention as a crucial part of creating an economy in which everyone, including working people, has significant freedoms.

In Hayek and Polanyi we see two sides to economic freedom. In philosophy, negative freedom is the absence of barriers or constraints, whereas positive freedom is the ability to have opportunities and to control one's life. Hayek's (negative) definition of freedom emphasizes the right of individuals to do as they will with their person and their property, free from government interference. This view supports a laissez-faire approach in which government plays as little a role as possible. Polanyi's (positive) definition of freedom focuses on the factors that enable most people to live a good life free from the threat of starvation, poverty, and exploitation. This view supports the use of government intervention to regulate the functioning of the economy so that all citizens can live a good life. When we study modern economic systems, we will see this ongoing tension between "freedom from" government, which is the hallmark of the most market-dominated (laissez-faire) economies, and "freedom to" have a good life, which is the hallmark of most government-centered economies.

5.5.3 Markets and information

One of Hayek's most important insights was his understanding of markets as superb gatherers and disseminators of information. Hayek pointed out that markets and prices are perfect vehicles for transmitting massive amounts of information to coordinate an economic system. Consumers transmit exactly how much they value goods and how many they want via their purchases. Manufacturers respond to consumer demand by making goods consumers want in the right quantities. In the process, manufacturers send signals to input markets about what materials they need—how much machinery, raw materials, and labor is required to build their goods. The suppliers of inputs then know how many people they need to hire and can figure out what materials they need to obtain for their production. And so on.

In one of Hayek's most astute insights, he predicted that the central planning of the Soviet Union could never compete with the efficiency of markets. Planners, he thought, could never duplicate the sophisticated signaling inherent to markets in order to coordinate an entire economy and were doomed to produce inefficiently. Certainly, the Soviet Union did run into numerous problems deriving from central planning. Despite developing sophisticated measures of the input requirements for each industry, they regularly experienced gluts or shortages of a huge magnitude that resulted in delays and inefficiencies.

5.5.4 Joseph Schumpeter and creative destruction

In addition to production inefficiencies, the Soviet Union lagged behind the United States in innovation. A key reason was what another Austrian economist, Joseph Schumpeter, called the "creative destruction" of capitalism. Building on Marx's ideas but coming from a very different perspective, Schumpeter noted that one of the keys to understanding capitalism was the constant innovation and remaking of industries. As he put it in his 1942 book, *Capitalism, Socialism and Democracy*, "The opening up of new markets, foreign or domestic, and the organizational development from the craft shop and factory to such concerns as U.S. Steel illustrate the same process of industrial mutation … that incessantly revolutionizes the economic structure from within, incessantly destroying the old one, incessantly creating a new one. This process of Creative Destruction is the essential fact about capitalism." **Creative destruction** is **the process by which businesses are forced to invent constantly to stay one step ahead of the competition and where creative, new industries inevitably destroy and replace older ones**. Certainly, capitalism in the United States was much more innovative than the command economy of the Soviet Union. Whereas Russia faced a stifling bureaucracy, firms in competitive U.S. capitalist markets were constantly investing and innovating, although this was less true during the Depression than it had been previously.

Schumpeter thought that the process of creative destruction would be too destabilizing for markets, as was the case when entire communities were devastated by the loss of an outmoded industry. Ironically, an adequate safety net can help communities recover from creative destruction and prevent the destabilizing properties of markets from manifesting. So, although Hayek and Schumpeter might not approve given their preference for laissez-faire approaches, modern economies have found a certain amount of government intervention crucial to stabilizing markets, thereby reducing the pressures to rein in markets when communities are suffering from creative destruction, which in turn allows the process of creative destruction to continue.

5.5.5 Market institutions

Hayek also understood that capitalism depends on an important set of supporting institutions in order to function properly. These include the sanctity of private property so businesses would invest in their enterprises. There also need to be social norms of trust facilitated by systematic and fair laws so that people freely and willingly enter into exchanges and bargains. No one will invest and start a business if they think it will be seized by others once it is successful. Markets also must be contestable—open to the entry of new firms. The government's role, to Hayek, was to enforce contracts and laws fairly rather than discriminating arbitrarily among individuals. Where market-supporting institutions are absent, markets will not perform effectively, as we see in many cases in less developed countries.

Hayek has had an important influence on economic systems, especially in the United States and the United Kingdom where conservative politicians regularly cite him as a major influence. Even though most economies today utilize more government intervention than Hayek preferred, his cautions about the need to avoid authoritarianism and the inefficiencies of central planning have played a major role in spurring most democracies to impose checks on government behavior.

Next we turn to the U.S. economy in the post–World War II era. We will only cover this period briefly to give you a flavor of the broad sweep of U.S. history and the most important trends.

5.6 THE MIXED ECONOMY AND THE GOLDEN AGE OF U.S. CAPITALISM, 1945–1973

The establishment of a mixed economy in the United States after the Great Depression and the global dominance of U.S. manufacturing created the perfect combination for a period of unprecedented growth and stability. By the early 1950s, the United States was producing 80% of the world's manufacturing output due to its advanced technology and the devastation that other manufacturing industries in Europe and Japan had experienced during World War II.

This era is sometimes termed the "capital–labor accord" in that workers and management got along very well for the most part. Manufacturers could afford to pay their workers well due to their domination of industries, and they had to pay their workers well because unions had become quite powerful now that they were legal. The unionization rate peaked in 1954 with 35% of the workforce being represented by a union, and unions were heavily concentrated in manufacturing. Workers experienced rising wages and were able to afford a middle-class lifestyle, with a car, a house, and all the appliances and accoutrements that go with a home purchase. The creation of a large middle class in the United States stems from this era, and the spending by the middle class proved to be very good for businesses, sparking growth in one consumer industry after another.

The economy grew rapidly and experienced only short recessions in this era, with per capita real GDP growth averaging 2.49% per year from 1948 to 1973. This was much faster than the per capita real GDP growth rate during the monopoly capitalism era of 1890–1929, when growth averaged 1.92%. It was also faster than growth during the global capitalism era of 1974–2015, which averaged 1.65%. The increase in incomes during the "golden age" was also very equally distributed. Rich, middle-class, and poor citizens all experienced significant increases in income. Rapid economic growth and strong unions meant that workers received a substantial share of the wealth that was being generated. But firms still benefited significantly as record consumer spending expanded sales and profits. The wealth injected at the bottom to workers trickled up to the owners of businesses.

Despite the rapid growth of the era, African Americans and women were still excluded from the best positions. Overt racial discrimination, separate but unequal education and facilities, and lynchings combined to provoke the civil rights movement, led by Martin Luther King. It achieved some major victories, with new laws enacted in the 1960s prohibiting discrimination in employment and preserving voting rights.

Women and minorities were assisted by affirmative action laws, which mandated that in cases where two applicants for a position had equal qualifications but differed by race or gender, the job should go to the person from the underrepresented group (women or minorities). This helped pry open jobs in law and business that had previously been the purview of white males.

The government also began intervening more directly in helping the poor. As part of the "War on Poverty," President Lyndon Johnson and Congress established Medicare and Medicaid to provide health care for the poor and the elderly. The Food Stamps program was established, as well as the Head Start program to provide subsidized preschool for poor children. The government also made its first major attempts to regulate environmental damage. By the end of the 1960s, the government was firmly established in the United States as a major factor in markets. However, the stagflation of the 1970s and the deindustrialization associated with globalization that began at the same time would set the stage for a new effort to bring back rapid growth by deregulating the economy.

5.7 THE ERA OF NEOLIBERALISM AND GLOBALIZATION, 1974–2018

In 1973, the Organization of the Petroleum Exporting Countries (OPEC) cut production and imposed an embargo on selling oil to the United States due to U.S. support for Israel. Oil prices surged from $3 per barrel to $12 a barrel internationally (a 300% increase!), and prices were even higher in the United States because of the embargo. This devastated the U.S. economy, which had become completely dependent on oil to run its cars and factories. The explosion in the price of energy caused businesses' costs to rise and profits to fall, so they laid off workers. The result was stagflation—**stagnation and inflation at the same time**—as businesses laid off workers to cut costs and raised prices to try to recoup the higher cost of energy. A major recession resulted. A second oil crisis occurred in 1979 when oil supplies were disrupted by the Iranian Revolution. This time oil prices doubled, once again spurring a major recession in the United States and other oil-dependent economies.

Meanwhile, in a decade that saw two major recessions, there was also a steady erosion in manufacturing jobs due to mechanization and overseas competition from Japan and Europe. Wages for workers stagnated while unemployment and inflation stayed disturbingly high.

Ronald Reagan was elected president in 1980 on a platform of reducing the size of government and the scope of government intervention in the economy—a return to laissez-faire principles. This was known as the era of **neoliberalism**, in that it sought a return to the liberalism of Adam Smith. Many countries followed the lead of Reagan in the United States and Thatcher in England and began moving toward a more laissez-faire economic system.

Reagan was able to enact large tax cuts for businesses and the wealthy, known as supply-side tax cuts because the money went to suppliers (firms and entrepreneurs) rather than demanders (consumers). The Reagan administration also reduced spending on social programs while increasing spending on the military. The U.S. economy did recover by 1984; however, growth in the 1980s was less robust than in previous decades, and the federal deficit quadrupled in size from 1980 to 1990. The tax cuts did not generate sufficient growth to pay for themselves, as supply-side supporters had hoped. Similar policies emphasizing deregulation and scaling back of government programs were pursued by subsequent presidents George Bush, Bill Clinton, and George W. Bush. Nonetheless, these administrations did follow basic Keynesian stabilization policy, stimulating the economy whenever it hit a recession, so this was not a complete reversal of Keynesian policy.

A recession in 1991 was followed by the tech boom of the 1990s under President Clinton. However, a stock market bubble formed toward the end of the 1990s as investors clamored for the latest internet stock offerings even from companies that had never made a profit. That bubble burst in 2000, with tech stocks falling by 78% and the economy falling into a recession. After a period of modest growth, another bubble formed in the mid-2000s, this time in real estate.

From 2004 to 2007, a huge speculative bubble fueled by massive debt and unsound loans in the sub-prime housing market formed. Deregulation of financial markets pursued by Reagan, Bush, Clinton, and G. W. Bush allowed banks to invest in very risky and volatile financial instruments. When these investments crashed, they brought the stock market and the entire banking system with them, sparking the worst recession since the Great Depression. Fortunately, the G. W. Bush administration and, after 2008, the Obama administration engaged in a massive bailout of the banking system and a significant increase in government spending. Rather than repeat the errors of 1937 in the Great Depression, the Fed kept stimulating the economy by injecting money into financial markets for years after the worst part of the recession was over. Obama also signed the Affordable Care Act, making the United States the last developed country to install a national health care system of some kind. Keynesian policy had returned to the United States, and it reduced the length of the recession significantly. As conclusive evidence of how useful Keynesian policy is, the European Union, which imposed austerity programs on the economies of Greece, Spain, and other poorly performing economies, fared very poorly compared to the United States, which instead injected large amounts of money into the economy.

The recovery from the Great Recession was slow, as is often the case after a major financial crisis. Hoping for a change in policies that would reinvigorate economic growth, U.S. voters elected Donald Trump president in 2016. Trump promised to bring back jobs to the United States from abroad by renegotiating trade deals to be more favorable and by cutting taxes and regulations on businesses. In essence, Trump was promising more government intervention in some areas (trade) and less in others (regulation). The unrest that propelled Trump to the presidency was also present in other developed economies where workers' wages stagnated and communities experienced deindustrialization as jobs shifted to China and other inexpensive manufacturing locations. In 2020, the COVID-19 pandemic struck, throwing the global economy into a sharp recession as businesses were forced to close. In response, the U.S. government, first under Trump and then under President Joseph Biden (elected in part due to Trump's uneven management of the pandemic), engaged in the largest government stimulus in history while undertaking a major public health effort to develop vaccines and treatments. By 2022, the recession was over and the economy was growing quickly, once again demonstrating the effectiveness of Keynesian stabilization policies.

5.8 CONCLUSION: THE MIXED ECONOMY OF THE UNITED STATES

In general, there has been a trend toward greater deregulation in the United States since 1980, but the country continues to use government policy and programs to fix market failures. The United States is a laissez-faire-leaning mixed economy, with less government intervention than most other developed countries but much more government intervention than was the case in the United States prior to the Great Depression. Keynesian economic policy has been very good for the U.S. economy in general. As you can see from Figure 5.3, prior to 1950 the U.S. economy experienced dramatic fluctuations in economic growth.[4] After 1950, the U.S. experienced more rapid and steady growth, which was achieved with the help of government efforts to stabilize the economy. A stable business environment makes firms more likely to invest, which drives growth and prosperity.

This type of economic system is called "regulated capitalism" or a **mixed economy: Where markets are seen as worth preserving due to the efficiency and innovation they promote but sound government policy can improve the functioning of the capitalist market system by reducing or**

KEYNES AND MIXED MARKET CAPITALISM 119

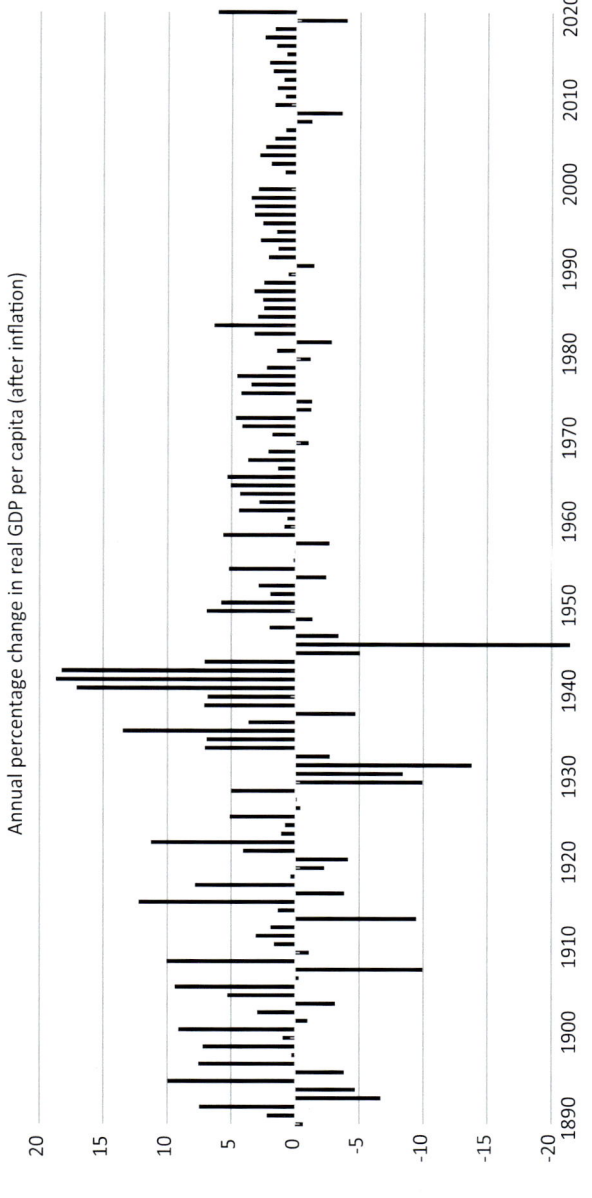

FIGURE 5.3 Economic instability in the U.S. economy: Real GDP growth per capita, 1890–2021.

eliminating market failures such as recessions. A mixed economy relying on markets and government is seen by most economists as preferable to a laissez-faire or a state-dominated economy.

Keynes can be thought of as wanting to save capitalism from itself. In its unregulated state, capitalism can result in lengthy recessions, as well as bad outcomes for workers and the environment. Appropriate government policy can solve those problems. In a recession, the government can spend money, cut taxes, and increase the money supply to pump money back into the economy and, via the multiplier, increase spending significantly to end the recession. If banks are prone to speculative bubbles and risky behavior, the government can regulate them to make sure they behave in a financially sound manner. Where markets fail to safeguard workers or the environment, the government can impose laws or regulations to force markets to address these shortcomings.

As we will see in the next chapter, which looks at modern economic systems, other economies strive for a different balance of state and markets than the United States. The U.S. is a **market-dominated economy**, striving for the least amount of government intervention possible to keep markets functioning effectively. Even though our government is large, it controls only about 30% of the economy, while the rest of the economy is controlled by private sector firms. In other countries such as most of Europe and Japan, we find **social market economies** where the government controls a much larger share (sometimes over 50%) and strives to manage the economy in accordance with domestic social values. Meanwhile, in **state-dominated economies** like China, the government plays an even larger role in controlling the economic system. All of these economic systems use some degree of markets and some amount of government intervention, so they are all considered mixed market economies, but the mix of market and government can be quite different.

QUESTIONS FOR REVIEW

1. Explain how the neoclassical concepts (a) marginal productivity theory of distribution, (b) markets always clear, and (c) Say's law combine to result in a conclusion that no government intervention is necessary in a capitalist market system.
2. Describe the nature of the Keynesian "revolution" in economics. How did Keynes reshape the way economists thought about the economy? How did he address the major flaws in the neoclassical economics of his time?
3. Why do many economists see the volatility of investment along with the multiplier as the key to understanding the business cycle (the cycle of booms and busts that characterize our economic system)?

4. How do sticky wages and prices prevent the economy from adjusting in a recession?
5. In what areas of the economy do we tend to see the market fail to work well? What government programs have been designed to address those market failures?
6. How would you explain to someone with no economics background why deflation can be a major macroeconomic problem?
7. How do Keynes' ideas relate to those of Smith and Marx?
8. Which of Keynes' ideas do you find most compelling in capturing the realities of the modern world? Explain and give examples.
9. Which of Hayek's ideas do you find most compelling? Which are least compelling? Support your answer with examples and analysis.
10. Compare and contrast Keynes' ideas with those of Hayek.
11. Explain the concept of creative destruction and give examples from the world around us.
12. Describe the evolution of the U.S. economic system from 1920 to the present. How has our approach to regulating the economy shifted over time?

NOTES

1 Edwin Cannan, "The Demand for Labour," *The Economic Journal* (September 1932): 357–370.
2 Leo Wolman, "Wages During the Depression," National Bureau of Economic Research Bulletin, Number 46, May 1, 1933, pp. 1–5. http://www.nber.org/chapters/c2256.pdf.
3 The founder of the Austrian school is considered to be Carl Menger, who taught at the University of Vienna in Austria in the late 1800s. Although later scholars from this tradition worked and lived outside of Austria, the original label stuck.
4 Our World in Data, https://ourworldindata.org/grapher/gdp-per-capita-over-the-long-run-Maddison, World Bank and Federal Reserve Economic Data (FRED). 2021 data are for the first quarter only.

Modern economic systems

Market-dominated, social market, and state-dominated economies

The economic systems of the modern world draw extensively on the ideas and philosophies of the great economists. From Smith, we see the widespread use of markets and the tendency to allow firms to compete and to make major economic decisions for society based on the profit motive. From Marx and Veblen, we see the need to check the unfettered power of large firms and to safeguard workers and communities from exploitation. From Hayek and Smith, we see the need to check the coercive power of the state to prevent it from becoming too powerful and bureaucratic. From Keynes, we see the approach that dominates modern economic systems: The construction of a mixed economy that builds on the best aspects of market capitalism while regulating market failures is likely to deliver the best outcomes.

All modern economies combine a mix of markets and government to some degree. Even market-dominated economies, such as the U.S. economy, have a substantial amount of government (state) intervention. And even state-dominated economies, such as China, Cuba, and North Korea, use markets, often extensively. The key to understanding modern economic systems is therefore to grasp the mix of state and market in a particular economy.

In general, we can group economies into three broad categories.

1. **Market-dominated economies (MDEs)**, also called liberal market economies, are **economic systems in which the primary economic decisions are made by private actors (businesses, individuals) in the market.** Government and social values play a secondary role.
2. **Social market economies (SMEs)**, also called coordinated market economies, are **economic systems in which social values take a leading role in directing the economy, usually through the actions of a government which manages the economy in accordance with social values**.

DOI: 10.4324/9780429399350-8

3. **State-dominated economies (SDEs)** are **economic systems in which the government is the main economic actor in most major industries or economic decisions, owning or controlling most of the economy**.

This chapter will briefly survey the different types of successfully developed economic systems in the world and offer some case studies of each type. (We consider developing countries later.) We begin by describing the key factors that shape economic systems. We then contrast MDEs and SMEs, followed by a case study of the U.S. MDE and the Nordic SME. Next, we take up socialism and communism, which culminates in a case study of China's SDE.

6.0 CHAPTER 6 LEARNING GOALS

After reading this chapter you should be able to:

- Define and describe the characteristics of market-dominated economies, social market economies, and state-dominated economies.

- Analyze, compare, and contrast the characteristics and functioning of an MDE such as the United States, an SME such as the Nordic countries, and an SDE such as China.

- Explain the difference between socialism, communism, and capitalism.

- Evaluate the strengths and weaknesses of a market capitalist approach (U.S.), a guided market approach (Nordic model), and a central planning approach (U.S.S.R.) to economic development.

6.1 FACTORS SHAPING ECONOMIC SYSTEMS

Economists have identified a number of factors that are important in shaping the type of economic system that emerges in a particular place. Rosser and Rosser, along with political economists utilizing a Veblenian approach, emphasized the importance of culture in shaping an economic system. Individualistic cultures tend toward market-dominated economies, whereas more cooperative cultures or strongly religious cultures lean more toward social market or state-dominated economies.[1] History also plays a crucial role, shaping how economies evolve over time and the institutions that structure them, such as the type of legal system, political system, and property rights that establish the "rules of the game" in a particular economic system.

Geography is another important factor determining the opportunities available to countries for trade and cooperation and the regional threats presented by conflict and instability. The availability of natural resources also influences the priorities of an economic system, with most resource-rich countries focused on resource extraction rather than industrialization. Economies focused on resource extraction tend to lag behind those focusing on industrialization with respect to long-term economic growth, which is why resource-rich economies are said to experience a "resource curse."

Acemoglu and Robinson argued that the key to economic success is whether or not an economic system features *inclusive institutions*, where the entire population benefits from economic activity, or *extractive institutions*, where the elites are the primary beneficiaries.[2] When elites hold most of the power, they can ruin a market-dominated system by seizing monopoly power and rigging markets for their own benefit. Similarly, elites can ruin a state-dominated economy by structuring the government to funnel money into their personal accounts. Therefore, a key determinant of the effectiveness of an economic system is the extent to which an economy encourages inclusive growth and avoids becoming a vehicle for the enrichment of the elites.

As you can see, a variety of cultural, institutional, geographic, and economic factors affect the type of economic system that evolves in a particular place. The type of economic system, in turn, shapes the outcomes of the economy. It is to this topic that we turn next, by contrasting modern market-dominated economies and social market economies.

6.2 COMPARING MARKET-DOMINATED ECONOMIES AND SOCIAL MARKET ECONOMIES

Most of the world's wealthy (developed) economies are either market-dominated economies or social market economies. In this section, we describe and compare these economies and look at their effectiveness as economic systems in delivering economic growth and human well-being.

In market-dominated economies, most major economic decisions are made by corporations and other private sector businesses. These businesses determine what society produces and how it is produced. The private sector dictates how a society's scarce resources are allocated based on the profit motive and businesses' desire to persuade consumers to buy more of their products.

The government's major role in MDEs is to support the market system by building and maintaining infrastructure (roads, airports, ports, a postal system), providing a fair and effective judicial system that enforces contracts, and fixing market failures when they threaten the functioning of the market system. The major market failures that are usually addressed by government include macroeconomic instability (especially major recessions), poverty and inequality, the exploitation of laborers and the environment, and the lack of sufficient private health care or education.

Interestingly, when we look at wealthy countries in the world that have adopted a market-dominated economic system (the United States, Canada, Ireland, Australia, New Zealand, and the United Kingdom), we see that they were all part of the British Empire at one point. The culture and values of that empire, emphasizing Protestantism, self-interest, hard work, and material rewards, fits well with a market economy. In this sense, MDEs reflect a particular set of cultural values.

In SMEs the role of social interests is more balanced compared to the role of the market. Social values often take precedence over market outcomes in SMEs. Some economic decisions are made by markets, especially those related to consumer goods. Many, and sometimes most, decisions are made by society, acting through government. Many services are considered to be human rights, including health care, childcare, dental care, housing, education (including college)—and even a job. The government is charged with providing all citizens with these services, sometimes through government agencies and sometimes by working with and through the private sector. In SMEs, the state can also play a role in preserving domestic culture, such as the French government's efforts to protect traditional agriculture, food, and wine.

Although the SMEs represent a variety of very different cultures, they do have some commonalities. Though England was the first country to industrialize, countries that industrialized later usually utilized government intervention to spur industrialization and to catch up with England. SMEs therefore are accustomed to a larger degree of government intervention in determining the direction of the economy. Most SMEs have industrial policies that they use to stimulate economic development in key sectors in order to gain advantages in these industries relative to other countries.

Lest you be tempted to think that one of these models is superior to the other, consider carefully the data in Figure 6.1, which compares key economic indicators of the largest and wealthiest MDEs and SMEs in the world. First, a good indicator of whether or not a country is an MDE or an SME is the amount of its gross domestic product (GDP) devoted by the public sector to social expenditures, such as health, welfare, unemployment, job assistance, and childcare. Social expenditures also go along with a high tax rate: If you spend a lot on social services for your citizens, you have to raise a lot of tax revenue. As you can see from the first two columns of Figure 6.1 on the next page, MDEs tend to spend less on social expenditures and have lower taxes than SMEs.

One of the key issues for economists when evaluating an economic system is how well it performs. Column 3 displays real GDP per capita in MDEs and SMEs, and column 4 looks at the rate of growth in GDP per capita over the last 48 years. Interestingly, there is no clear pattern. Both MDEs and SMEs are rich, and both have experienced substantial economic growth (1.69% per year in MDEs and 1.86% per year in SMEs). There is no reason to prefer one system over another based on growth performance: An effective MDE can perform just as well as an effective SME. Where we do see significant differences are in terms of inequality. Because

Market-Dominated Economies	GDP Devoted to Social Expenditures, 2019 (%)	Tax Revenue % of GDP, 2019	Real GDP per Capita, 2019	Growth in Real GDP per Capita, 1971-2019 (%)	Poverty Rate, % 2017
Australia	16.7	28.7	$57,071	112%	12.4
Canada	18.0	33.5	$51,589	113%	12.1
United States	18.7	24.5	$55,670	141%	17.8
New Zealand	19.4	32.3	$38,993	93%	10.9
United Kingdom	20.6	33.0	$43,688	144%	11.7
MDE Average	**18.7**	**30.4**	**$49,402**	**120%**	**13.0**
Social Market Economies					
Japan	22.3	32.0	$49,188	162%	15.7
Norway	25.3	39.9	$92,556	186%	8.4
Sweden	25.5	42.9	$57,975	118%	8.9
Germany	25.9	38.8	$47,628	140%	10.4
Denmark	28.3	46.3	$65,147	116%	5.8
Belgium	28.9	42.9	$47,541	139%	10.1
France	31.0	45.4	$44,317	120%	8.1
SME Average	**26.7**	**41.2**	**$57,765**	**140%**	**9.6**

FIGURE 6.1 Table showing key data on selected MDEs and SMEs. Source: OECD, http://stats.oecd.org, accessed January 30, 2021.

Country (MDE or SME)	OECD Better Life Index Rank	UN Human Development Index Rank
Norway (SME)	1	1
Australia (MDE)	2	6
Iceland (SME)	3	6
Canda (MDE)	4	13
Denmark (SME)	5	11
Switzerland (SME)	6	2
Netherlands (SME)	7	10
Sweden (SME)	8	8
Finland (SME)	9	12
United States (MDE)	10	15
New Zealand (MDE)	12	14
Belgium (SME)	13	17
United Kingdom (MDE)	14	15
Germany (SME)	15	4
Ireland (MDE)	16	3
Austria (SME)	17	20
France (SME)	18	26
Spain (SME)	19	25
Japan (SME)	25	19

FIGURE 6.2 OECD Better Life and UN Human Development rankings, 2019.

of the substantial amount of money devoted to social expenditures, SMEs tend to have very low levels of poverty and inequality. MDEs that spend less on these programs have much higher levels of poverty and inequality.

Another way to look at the success of economic systems is to consider a broad range of indicators. For example, the Organisation for Economic Cooperation and Development (OECD) Better Life Index ranks OECD countries according to the following factors: Housing, income, jobs, community, education, environment, civic engagement, health, life satisfaction, safety, and work–life balance (Figure 6.2). The United Nations (UN) Human Development Index focuses on a subset of the OECD measures: Life expectancy, education, and income per capita indicators. Notice that the Scandinavian countries (Norway, Iceland, Denmark, Sweden, and Finland) do particularly well on these broader measures of welfare, something we will discuss below when we take up the Nordic model. Nonetheless, both MDEs and SMEs perform well for the most part, providing another indication that there are different paths to wealth and well-being.

Next, we take up case studies of each type of economic system. We begin by describing the unique characteristics of the modern U.S. MDE relative to other economics systems. We follow that with a case study of the Nordic model of SMEs. Then we take up state-dominated economies, focusing primarily on China.

6.3 THE U.S. MODEL OF A MARKET-DOMINATED ECONOMY

Having traced the evolution of the U.S. economy in previous chapters, here we only describe the key aspects of the U.S. system as they compare to other economies. The major characteristics of the U.S. economic system include ready access to productive resources, a Protestant work ethic and melting pot of immigrants, early protectionism followed by later globalization, a business-friendly legal system, massive multinational corporations, an innovation system promoting revolutionary innovations, a small welfare state and few regulations, and macroeconomic stabilization policies.

6.3.1 Ready access to productive resources

One of the important reasons for U.S. economic success was its access to human and natural resources. The United States has historically had a large pool of mobile and highly motivated immigrant labor. Immigrant groups included religious dissidents, people pursuing commercial enterprises, convicts, indentured servants, slaves, and waves of migrants from Europe. The United States also had rich land and abundant natural resources, acquired via war, negotiation, or purchase, that were crucial in agricultural and industrial development. This ready supply of labor and resources provided fuel for economic growth.

6.3.2 Protestant work ethic and the melting pot

The United States has a culture that is very hardworking and individualistic. This is often attributed to that fact that many of the early settlers were Protestants who valued personal independence and material success. Later immigrants from Europe, Mexico, India, China, and many other countries also tended to be extremely hardworking and willing to take the least desirable jobs so that they or their children would have a chance to move up in the future. Hard work is so ingrained into the U.S. culture that American workers put in more hours than most other developed countries, and surveys indicate that social status is strongly associated with hard work. Highly motivated labor facilitates production and growth.

6.3.3 Early protectionism, later globalization

The split with Great Britain in the Revolutionary War prompted the United States to protect its market from British competitors, which allowed domestic industries to develop and sell to the large internal U.S. market. This allowed infant industries that would not have been able to survive otherwise to grow and develop. However, after World War II, the United States increasingly embraced globalization and free trade because its industries dominated international manufacturing. U.S. corporations moved their operations all over the globe in search of new markets and cheap labor and resources.

6.3.4 Business-friendly legal system

The stable U.S. Constitution and a pro-business legal system provided solid grounding for market exchange. Checks and balances with an independent judiciary tended to keep corruption to an acceptable level and to safeguard contracts and property rights. Civil liberties and democratic rule meant that many citizens had opportunities to succeed and to change the system, although this was mitigated by systemic racism and sexism. Corporations were given substantial power in the U.S. system, including legal standing as a person with all the rights that citizens have, along with low taxes and other forms of government support. As we saw earlier, the U.S. government sided with corporations and against workers throughout much of its history.

6.3.5 Massive multinational corporations

U.S. corporations were allowed to grow into vast, market-dominating enterprises that controlled entire global industries. The typical U.S. multinational corporation (MNC) is huge and very hierarchical, with power and decision making resting in the hands of the chief executive officer (CEO) and upper administration. Workers tend to have very little power and control, given the low unionization rates in the modern United States and in the countries in which MNCs operate. These huge companies are almost all owned by shareholders, and their shares are traded publicly in stock markets, so their primary goal is to maximize short-term profits to please shareholders. Massive MNCs dominate the United States and much of the world economy.

6.3.6 Innovation system promoting revolutionary innovation

The U.S. government has always invested substantially in public goods, especially infrastructure, building canals, railroads, roads, ports, and airports to stimulate economic development. Free public education and the vast public university system helped to develop a skilled workforce and to stimulate scientific research, which fostered numerous inventions. A 2017 study published in *Science* found that 80% of high-impact scientific papers (those cited frequently by other scientists) can be traced forward to some future marketplace invention, demonstrating how crucial basic scientific research is for innovation.[3] The strong patent system in the United States, which gives inventors a monopoly over their new product for 20 years, also provides a strong incentive for investment and innovation. The combination of low taxes on corporations and wealthy individuals, along with strong higher education and patent systems, and a hardworking, individualistic culture provides excellent conditions to prompt people to come up with the next big product. The United States is one of the world leaders in revolutionary innovation (inventing brand-new products and industries) due to these conditions.

6.3.7 Small welfare state and few regulations

In general, the United States has the least generous welfare state of any developed country. The most glaring difference is in the area of health care: The United States is the only developed country without a national health care system. Even other MDEs consider basic health care a human right that should not be left up to the market to provide, meaning that millions who cannot afford health care will have to do without it or depend on charity. The Affordable Care Act (ACA) enacted by President Obama caused the number of uninsured in the United States to decline from a high of 18% in 2013, just before the ACA went into effect, to 11% in 2017. However, there remain political pressures to repeal or replace the ACA from conservative politicians who preferred to leave health care in the hands of individuals and markets.

The United States also does less to address inequality and poverty than any other developed country. Taxes on the wealthy are relatively low, while financial assistance for the poor for housing, food, childcare, dental care, and higher education is also low. Welfare and unemployment benefits are also less generous, and the United States provides very little in the way of job training. This explains why the United States has the highest poverty rate of any developed country.

The United States tends to have fewer regulations on business behavior than other countries, with relatively lax approaches to regulating the environment, labor markets, and food and product safety. The United States has the highest per person carbon emissions in the world, but it has yet to take significant steps to address climate change, unlike most other developed countries.

Note that we are discussing the United States in comparison to other countries. Despite the tendency to have fewer regulations than other countries, the United States still regulates food and drug safety, water and air quality, traffic safety, agricultural safety, workplace safety, and consumer product safety.

6.3.8 Macroeconomic stabilization policy

Though the United States does not intervene much in specific (microeconomic) markets, it does take an activist role in stabilizing the macroeconomy to reduce the severity of recessions and to stave off inflation. The U.S. government spends more, taxes less, and injects more money into financial markets in most recessions. This is very distinct from the European Union (E.U.), which adopted austerity policies that slashed spending and raised taxes while keeping interest rates stable after the 2008 financial crisis. Ironically, though the E.U. intervenes less in the macroeconomy, most corporations and markets in the E.U. are tightly regulated, with strict laws regarding environment, workers, and product safety.

In general, the United States is the quintessential model of a market-dominated, mixed economy. Most decisions are made by private sector firms and individuals, and the government corrects the most egregious forms of market failure but does not take more proactive steps. The model has worked well in terms of generating economic growth and a steady stream of innovations. Those successes are marred somewhat by the inequality, poverty, and environmental degradation that are generated in the process. Interestingly, the Nordic countries are also wealthy and innovative, but their success is achieved in a more government-centered economic system.

6.4 THE NORDIC MODEL OF A SOCIAL MARKET ECONOMY

The Nordic model is often referred to as the "middle way" between the two extremes of an MDE and an SDE. The Nordic countries—Sweden, Norway, Denmark, Iceland, and Finland—are considered SMEs because of the manner in which their egalitarian social values inform government intervention in their economies. They are ultimately still capitalist economies utilizing markets for many economic decisions, but their governments play a much larger role than is the case in MDEs. One of the interesting questions for economists is why this region of the world evolved more cooperative, egalitarian systems than most other regions.

6.4.1 Cooperative culture and homogeneous population

Driven by the harsh climate of northern Europe, Scandinavians were forced to work hard and to cooperate in order to survive. The cooperative culture has persisted into the modern era in part due to its success—all of the Nordic countries are wealthy. In addition, the homogeneity and small size of the population tends to foster empathy. When someone in a Nordic country is destitute, it is easy for their neighbors to imagine that they, too, might experience the same fate. Note, however, that the Nordic countries were not particularly equal 100 years ago. It took powerful, well-organized labor movements to create the Nordic model over the last century. This, of course, implies that any country in which workers have strong solidarity and organization might be able to emulate the Nordic model.

6.4.2 Gender equity

Another area in which we see the Nordic culture at work in affecting market outcomes is gender equity. A Norwegian law requires 40% of corporate boards of directors to be women so that it is more likely that larger numbers of women will be selected for upper management. Norway's parental leave policies are quite generous, as are those of other Nordic countries. Together, Norwegian parents are allowed to take 46 weeks off at 100% pay or 56 weeks off at 80% pay. Employers are required to allow workers to return to their old jobs at the end of parental leave, which means that there is little or no detriment to your career if you choose to have children. The employment guarantee, along with free childcare, results in 75% of Norwegian women working outside the home, as opposed to 68% in the United States. There are also payments for parents who choose to be stay-at-home parents.

With similarly generous policies, in 2015, the five Nordic countries ranked at the very top of the world in terms of best places to be a mother, while the United States ranked 33rd. The United States only requires employers to grant new mothers four weeks of unpaid maternity leave. The intentional efforts by Nordic countries to create greater gender equity have spilled over into the political realm: 40% of representatives in Parliament in Nordic countries are women, compared with 19.4% in the United States.

6.4.3 Dramatic expansion of human rights

The egalitarian culture led Nordic countries to expand the definition of human rights well beyond what we find in MDEs. All Nordic citizens have the right to childcare, health care, dental care, free education (through college), housing, and food. These essentials are either provided by government agencies or the government subsidizes the private sector to provide them. The government invests substantially in all of these services so that they are of very high quality. As one might expect, the provision of such extensive services comes with a hefty price tag, which requires high tax rates in order to pay for them.

6.4.4 Government-guided development

Rather than letting market forces determine the direction of the economy, the state in Nordic countries guides and facilitates economic development with a sophisticated set of policies. Sweden, for example, is famous for its "triple helix" economic development approach utilizing government, universities, and the private sector. In the 1970s and 1980s, Sweden began experiencing deindustrialization in the face of increased global competition, just as the United States did. Rather than trying to save dying industries, Sweden implemented an initiative to attract new high-wage industries based on government, university, and private sector partnerships. The government would identify new, key industries that were likely to generate high-wage jobs and that were suitable for the local economy. These industries included biotechnology, research and development, computer programming, and information technology. After consulting with private sector firms, the government would provide state-of-the-art infrastructure and universities would provide training and education to make sure that the workforce had exactly the right set of skills. This made Sweden an ideal location for industries in the targeted sectors, attracting a huge influx of foreign investment and leading to the creation of new jobs in each of the above industries. This focus on cutting-edge industries, education, and research and development has resulted in Sweden generating more patent filings per resident than the United States.

Note that other countries, including Japan and South Korea, have also been very successful in targeting cutting-edge industries and developing them via substantial state support. Many economists see such industrial policies as a key step in developing an industrial sector in an underdeveloped region. However, such policies require an efficient, noncorrupt government sector. In countries with poor quality state institutions, industrial policies have not worked well.

Another interesting example of state-guided development is Norway's state oil company, Statoil. This public company was created to manage North Sea oil drilling to ensure that all Norwegian citizens benefited from the oil discoveries. The government places all profits from Statoil into an Oil Fund, which is used to pay for much of the Norwegian welfare state and to provide Norway with economic security in the future, even after the oil runs out. The government treats the Oil Fund like an endowment, spending only the interest and 4% of the principal in any year. In 2022, the Oil Fund was valued at $1.3 trillion, which was 1.4% of global stock markets!

We also see substantial government intervention in Sweden's ultra-Keynesian macroeconomic policies. Sweden was the first country to use Keynesian stabilization policies extensively, beginning in the early years of the Great Depression. In addition to generous unemployment and welfare benefits, Sweden provides public employment for many of those who cannot find jobs otherwise. The idea is that in each community there are plenty of tasks that need to be done. The government should hire those willing and able to work but unable to find a private sector job to complete useful tasks, in the process pumping money into the economy. Businesses are also allowed to make tax-free investments if they do so in a recession, which stimulates investment when it is needed most. Sweden recovered very rapidly from the 2008 financial crisis thanks to these stabilization policies.

6.4.5 Active labor market policies (flexicurity)

When workers in Sweden lose their job, they are given generous benefits with a time limit and provided with free education, training, and money for relocation costs so that they can find a new job. If they are still unable to find a job at that point, they can get a job on a public works project. This makes Sweden's labor market flexible in that workers are regularly moving from one job to another, but it also offers workers significant job security, because they will almost always have a job or state support. Note that this is not a "soft" system—everyone is expected to work. These flexicurity programs resulted in Sweden having the highest rate of labor market participation in the world (the highest percentage of the population working).

It is also interesting that, like the United States, Nordic countries are hotbeds for entrepreneurship and innovation. Start-up rates in Norway are among the highest in the developed world, and Norway has more entrepreneurs per capita than the United States. This can be traced to state support for entrepreneurs in Norway. First, the security of the welfare state means that you have little to lose if your business fails. If it does fail, you will still get guaranteed retirement and health benefits, along with education and training for a new job. Free college education means that you have no student loan debt that has to be paid off if your business fails, so you can start a business right out of college. There are free courses on starting a business, you can get a state-sponsored three-month internship in a start-up company, and it is easy to start a company, taking only seven days.

6.4.6 Inequality and poverty

As Figure 6.1 shows (on page 126), the poverty rate in the Nordic countries is half that of the United States. This reflects the disparate levels of government spending to fight poverty and create opportunities for the poor. Similarly, the United States is the most unequal developed country, whereas the Nordic countries are the most equal in terms of income and wealth, which is reflected in the differences in tax policies. Sweden imposes a 1.5% annual wealth tax on rich individuals, whereas the United States has no wealth tax, and the richest people in Sweden pay 60% of their income in taxes, whereas the tax rate for the richest Americans is 39.6%. The 400 richest families in the United States only paid 20% of their income in taxes thanks to a plethora of tax deductions and low taxes on investment income.

Greater equality is also associated with a greater likelihood of moving up in the world. There is significantly greater class mobility in Nordic countries than in the United States. Statistically, a poor child in Denmark has a 22% chance of becoming rich, whereas a poor child in the United States has only a 1% chance. This disparity is a product of the greater resources available to poor children in Denmark, especially high-quality education and health care, which give them a better chance to succeed.

In general, we see in the Nordic model a set of countries that is globally competitive because of their effective use of the state to facilitate economic development. They also have exceptionally high measures of human development because of their use of heavily progressive taxes to provide high-quality services and support for all citizens.

6.5 OTHER VARIETIES OF SOCIAL MARKET ECONOMIES

Because there is so much variety in social market economies, it is worthwhile documenting some of the ways in which other SMEs differ from the Nordic model and reflect unique sets of cultural and institutional factors. Below, we briefly describe some of the unique characteristics of the largest SMEs, Germany, France, and Japan.

6.5.1 Germany, co-determination, and precision manufacturing

Germany is a world leader in producing high-value manufactured goods such as robotics, cars, and electronics. The German emphasis on technology is reflected in the fact that most CEOs of manufacturing firms are engineers, whereas in the United States it is more common to find CEOs with finance or marketing backgrounds. German education has two tracks, one targeting college and the other the development of sophisticated vocational skills that will culminate in an internship and a skilled job. Workers in Germany are extremely well paid, as you can see in Figure 6.3, whereas U.S. workers make $6 less per hour. German workers also have substantial input into how work is done, and at large firms workers elect members to the supervisory boards of corporations that appoint the members

Country	Hourly Compensation in Manufacturing (wages and benefits)
Belgium	$45.62
Norway	$43.32
Switzerland (2016)	$43.08
Germany	$42.00
France	$41.34
Netherlands	$40.37
Denmark	$39.85
Sweden	$39.21
Austria	$39.17
United States	$35.87
Italy	$35.62
Finland	$35.06
Iceland	$33.09
Ireland	$31.72
United Kingdom	$29.78
Spain	$29.64
Canada	$26.27
Australia (2011)	$20.12
New Zealand	$19.15

FIGURE 6.3 Table showing hourly compensation costs in manufacturing, 2017. Source: ILOStat, https://ilostat.ilo.org/, accessed January 31, 2021.

of the board of directors. This system is called co-determination because both workers and firms together make major decisions regarding the future of the company.[4] Thus, German workers have much more input into how corporations are run than American workers do. This has translated into an empowered workforce that displays some of the highest productivity and greatest skill levels in the world. Interestingly, although Germany is a highly regulated economy, it tends to avoid substantial macroeconomic intervention, a philosophy that it has carried over into the European Union.

6.5.2 France, culture, fashion, and leisure

France is another large, wealthy country in which cultural considerations play a large role in structuring the economy. The French work very hard to preserve their culture and way of life. This includes strict rules designed to preserve local food sources and cuisine. Correspondingly, France has very strong culturally based industries, including tourism (France is the most visited destination in the world) and fashion. France is home to the world's two largest luxury products companies, LVMH (Moët Hennessy Louis Vuitton) and Kering (Gucci, Yves San Laurent, etc.).

The French government also works as a member of the European Union to guide and protect established industries such as clothing and steel. It is well known for utilizing expert government planners to work with industry to construct economic development programs. In addition to guiding the economy, the government imposes strict regulations on businesses, including laws that make it difficult for firms to fire workers or to close an unprofitable manufacturing plant.

After it experienced the same forces of deindustrialization that hit other developed countries, France decided to deal with its high unemployment rate by reducing work hours for existing laborers and increasing leisure time. The maximum work week was reduced to 35 hours or 39 hours for CEOs and upper management. (This did reduce the unemployment rate, although France still has chronically high unemployment.) To enforce the law, the government hired inspectors to count cars in parking lots after business hours, scrutinize office entry and computer records, grill employees about their schedules, and make sure no one was bringing work home with them! (Isn't there something appealing about a government inspector telling you to go home because you are working too hard?)

With the short work week, five weeks of paid vacation, and 11 paid holidays, the French work fewer hours than most other countries. France and the United States both generate about $60 in GDP per hour worked, so the main reason GDP per capita in the United States is higher than in France is because people in the United States work 19% more hours than the French do. Essentially, the French work four days a week, whereas Americans work five days a week, on average. This brings up an interesting question: Would you rather have more money or more leisure time? The French have chosen the latter.

6.5.3 Japan, keiretsu, and lifetime employment

Japan has the third-largest economy in the world, behind the United States and China and just ahead of Germany, the United Kingdom, and France. As with other SMEs, Japan's unique culture shapes its economy in significant ways. Like France, Japan's government uses highly skilled planners to work with industry to determine the direction of the economy. Top university graduates often go into government work and then move from government to industry leadership positions, which is a sign of how highly valued public service is.

As a deeply Confucian society featuring an emphasis on respect for elders, loyalty, and harmony, Japan has evolved unique organizational structures. The Japanese economy is dominated by six huge conglomerates, known as keiretsu. Each keiretsu is owned primarily by a bank, and these banks tend to prefer long-term growth and steady returns over short-term profits. This gives Japanese corporations a much longer focus than we tend to see in U.S. corporations. Within each keiretsu one finds networks of companies working together for a common goal. For example, Toyota works closely with all of its suppliers so that production changes can be made swiftly and seamlessly with minimal disruptions. This close integration of Toyota with all of its suppliers within the same keiretsu reduces costs, fosters innovation, and allows Toyota to respond more rapidly to changes in consumer preferences.

Within each large corporation, employees tend to act like an extended family. It is common for employees at the top Japanese firms to stay at the same firm for their entire career—lifetime employment! Workers socialize together, and promotions often come from within the company. This family-like atmosphere fosters cooperation and loyalty, leading to high levels of productivity and trust and a flat organizational structure in which workers need little supervision.

In all of the SMEs, we see much larger government involvement in the strategic direction of the economy, with government planners working with industry officials to determine what industries to focus on and where to invest. Government regulation of the economy is more in line with local social values than it is with the market. Some commentators call such economies "socialist," but private sector firms still dominate most industries, so SMEs are actually still mixed market capitalist systems. True socialism or communism is a very different system, as we will discuss in the next section.

6.6 SOCIALISM AND COMMUNISM

Anyone who has experienced the dark side of capitalism—especially poorly paid workers abused by powerful, uncaring bosses—has likely longed for an alternative economic system. Since the very beginnings of capitalism more than 200 years ago, the downtrodden have turned to socialism and communism as a possible solution to the problems with capitalism.

A **socialist economic system** is one in which the means of production and distribution are either owned or regulated by society. Note that in most SMEs, only 40% to 60% of the economy is controlled or regulated by the state, whereas a fully socialist system would mean control or regulation of almost all industries. A communist economic system is one in which the means of production and distribution are publicly owned and each person works according to their abilities and is paid according to their needs. Socialism can be considered the first step of an economy on the way toward communism. In general, communist systems involve central planning, with the government determining what is produced, how it is produced, who does what job, and how goods and services are distributed. State ownership and control of the economy is nearly absolute.

Beginning with the Russian Revolution of 1917, numerous countries experienced communist uprisings in the 20th century. Just before the fall of the Union of Soviet Socialist Republics (U.S.S.R.) in 1989, a third of the world's population lived in a communist country. However, although Marx proposed communism as a solution to the problems of capitalism, he never laid out how a communist system would work in practice. Countries attempting to implement communism had no blueprint to follow, so they had no choice but to try various methods and hope that they worked.

The U.S.S.R. developed a system of central planning where the state made all major economic decisions. Fearing invasion by the United States and other hostile capitalist countries, the U.S.S.R. undertook an effort to industrialize a previously rural and backward economic system. Planners instructed every industry on what to produce, along with when and how to produce it. They set up elaborate input–output tables for the entire economy detailing every input needed for every product so that they could allocate the correct resources in the right quantities to each manufacturer. They focused on manufacturing and especially on defense, given the external threats they faced.

Initially, this system was remarkably successful. While most of the world was experiencing the Great Depression, the economy of the U.S.S.R. grew rapidly, between 4% and 13% per year. The Soviet Union succeeded in industrializing a previously rural, agrarian economy with remarkable speed. This success prompted worries in Western capitalist countries, where it appeared that the communist system was more successful than capitalism.

But it was not to last. The centralization of control allowed ruthless dictators like Joseph Stalin to seize power in the U.S.S.R. Stalin killed more than a million people during his time as Soviet general secretary and premier. As the bureaucracy became more entrenched, efficiency declined, and the U.S.S.R. began to experience regular shortages of inputs and even basic consumer goods.

Most other communist countries who imitated the Soviet central planning model experienced similar problems. In places where control was more decentralized, however, more positive results were achieved. In addition, in places in which local culture was already communal in nature, the system worked reasonably well.

In Cuba, though political power was controlled by the communist party under Fidel Castro and subsequent leaders, workers had substantial power and control over the workplace. This is an ironic reversal of the United States, where workers have the political power that comes with voting but lack power in the workplace. Cuba was able to achieve impressive results in education, literacy, and health, reaching levels of developed countries. Cuba's economic growth averaged 2% from 1990 to 2016, which is impressive given that it faced a huge cut in subsidies when the U.S.S.R. collapsed in 1990 and that it has continually faced U.S. economic sanctions during that period.

Yugoslavia, like Cuba, gave workers substantial control over workplaces, developing a series of worker-owned cooperatives as the basic organizational unit. They experienced some substantial successes before being derailed by regional and ethnic differences.

After a century of efforts by various countries to construct communist economic systems, the following lessons have emerged:

- Central planning can be a good way to organize and mobilize resources to industrialize in societies that were previously underdeveloped.
- Central planning does not tend to be as dynamic, efficient, or inventive as capitalism over the long term.
- Communist systems can result in better economic outcomes than exploitative capitalist systems—most Cuban citizens were better off after their communist revolution than they were under colonial capitalism; most Russian citizens were better off economically under the U.S.S.R. than they are now under oligarchic capitalism.
- When it builds on a culture of communal values and production and when it empowers workers, communism can work reasonably well.
- External pressures can derail any inclination toward democracy in state-dominated systems.
- Central control can and frequently does devolve into bureaucracy and dictatorship, which tends to undermine the effectiveness of communist systems and results in human rights abuses.

When the U.S.S.R. collapsed in 1990, most communist countries began a transition from communism to capitalism. The transition went very poorly in most cases. It proved much more difficult for communist countries that had little experience with markets to develop market-based economies than economists thought. Too little attention was paid to the need to develop all of the detailed legal and institutional structures and even the cultural characteristics that drive markets. Economists had evidently forgotten the lessons of history highlighted by Polanyi that the market system is complex and needs to be constructed carefully by the state. The biggest success story in the transition from a centrally planned economy to a market-based one was the case of China, which we turn to next.

services, and generate funds for reinvestment. This gave TVEs an incentive to be successful, proving to be a source of entrepreneurship as the TVEs sought out niches in the newly created markets. By this point, China had moved away from a centrally planned, communist economy toward a market socialist economy.

The creation of markets also involved the use of special economic zones (SEZs) in China. SEZs were free trade zones within which firms could function in a market-based, capitalist manner while the rest of the economy was separate and protected. China attracted foreign investors to SEZs by offering low wages and taxes, few rules or regulations governing treatment of workers or the environment, a highly disciplined and skilled workforce, and a devalued currency that made exporting from China extraordinarily profitable. In exchange for such attractive conditions, China mandated that foreign investors work with local partner firms and share their technology so that Chinese firms would gain experience with international manufacturing. Foreign firms were only too happy to comply with these conditions in order to gain access to the vast Chinese market.

Foreign investment poured in beginning in the 1980s. The SEZs coupled with the rural market reforms caused an astounding economic boom in China. From 1978 to 2019, China's per capita economic growth averaged 8.5% while most other countries were experiencing average growth rates of less than 2%! With this rate of growth, the Chinese economy has been doubling in size every 8.2 years. China is now the world's second largest economy and will likely pass the United States as the largest economy in 2029. China is now the world's largest exporting country, the largest manufacturer of automobiles, and the largest manufacturing country in general.

Although there is much economic independence of firms in China, the government still maintains a significant degree of control. The communist party preserves close ties to all large firms, and the Red Army even runs a lot of firms. The government determines the main direction of investment, and new ventures cannot take place without government approval. Some economists have actually referred to modern China as a form of state capitalism, given that the state is so closely involved in profit-making activities.

China is frequently criticized by other countries for its human rights violations and poor environmental record. Media and internet searches are still censored, and dissidents are regularly arrested and imprisoned. The student-led Tiananmen Square protests of 1989 were met with brutal repression, and between 200 and 1000 people were killed.[5] Since that crackdown, protests have been more muted. China is facing numerous ecological disasters thanks to its rapid growth without substantial environmental regulation. Its largest cities are choked with smog, and it also faces water and soil problems, as well as habitat destruction and biodiversity loss.

It is not clear at this point whether China will move in a more democratic direction or whether it will continue to be led by a one-party communist state. A 2014 Pew Research Global Attitudes survey indicated that Chinese citizens are more satisfied with the direction their country is heading than any other country in the world, with 87% of citizens satisfied (compared with 33% in the United States). There appear to be no major pressures for change coming from within China.

Other Asian countries have also been successful in adopting a state-led approach to development, including South Korea, Malaysia, Taiwan, and Vietnam. It is interesting that so many emerging markets are successfully adopting this approach. This seems to support the idea that utilizing an SDE approach in an underdeveloped country can be effective.

However, many other SDEs have been dismal failures when it comes to economic development. In countries where the state is kleptocratic—stealing resources for itself at the expense of the rest of society—or where the state bureaucracy is overly controlling and inefficient, SDEs tend to work very poorly. Dozens of countries have failed at utilizing a state-centered approach to development. There are actually more failures than success stories at this point, which you will study if you take a course on developing countries. Interestingly, it does not seem to matter whether an abusive SDE adopts a capitalistic or a socialistic approach: Its stranglehold over the economy will stifle development either way. However, where SDEs work in the public interest and offer a more flexible, pragmatic approach, as is the case in China, the results can be quite positive.

6.8 CONCLUSION

This chapter has briefly sketched out the types of economic systems that we see in the modern world. Modern economic systems can be grouped into three broad categories: Market-dominated economies, social market economies, and state-dominated economies. We have focused on successful, developed economies in this chapter as a guide to the possible recipes for economic prosperity.

The United States is the dominant MDE, generating high levels of income and wealth and spawning a noteworthy amount of innovation and entrepreneurship while struggling with inequality and poverty. The Nordic model of an SME combines substantial government intervention with private sector development to achieve a similar level of income and innovation to the United States with fewer social problems. China's SDE has produced the most rapid rate of growth in the world for 40 years, a remarkable, sustained success story marred by human rights abuses and significant environmental problems.

In the modern economic systems, we see reflections of the ideas of the great economists that we studied earlier. In a nod to Adam Smith, all modern economies use market capitalism substantially. Fueled by competition, markets produce the products that consumers want while keeping prices low and fostering innovations. In a nod to Karl Marx, all economic systems work to safeguard the rights and safety of laborers and use the state to make peoples' lives better than the market would on its own. Two countries, Cuba and North Korea, still reject capitalism and espouse a communist philosophy. Reflecting Veblen's ideas, modern economies work to promote the productive side of markets, striving to develop new, productive industries via public–private partnerships. But, responding to Hayek's cautions, most economic systems are wary of having too much state interference in the economy. Ultimately, all modern economic systems reflect the ideas of John Maynard Keynes, having developed mixed economic systems that rely on market capitalism for some economic decisions while using the state for others. What is interesting is the variation one finds in modern economic systems, with MDEs leaning more toward Smith, SDEs leaning more toward Marx, and SMEs in the middle.

QUESTIONS FOR REVIEW

1. Explain the key differences between market-dominated economies, social market economies, and state-dominated economies. Use specific examples to support your answer.
2. What are the key elements of the U.S. MDE? What factors do you think are essential contributors to U.S. economic success? What are the major problems with the U.S. MDE?
3. What are the key elements of the Nordic SME? What factors do you think are essential contributors to its economic success? What problems do you see with the SME approach?
4. How do socialism and communism differ from capitalism?
5. What are the strengths and weaknesses of a market capitalist approach (U.S.), a guided market approach (Nordic model), and a central planning approach (U.S.S.R.) to economic development?
6. The most successful countries in the last 50 years have used the government extensively in economic development efforts. However, many developing countries in sub-Saharan Africa, Latin America, and Southeast Asia have adopted similar approaches with little success. Why might a government-centered approach to development have such an uneven track record?
7. What are the key ingredients in China's economic success? Why was China's transition from a centrally planned system to a market-oriented system more successful than the transition in Russia?
8. Innovation is a key ingredient in economic success over time. What are the lessons regarding innovation that emerge from the experiences of the countries described in this chapter?
9. Compare and contrast the U.S. economic system with the Nordic model. In your answer, take up the following issues: (a) What role does government play in each economy? (b) How does each economy reflect the ideas of Adam Smith, Karl Marx, Thorstein Veblen, John Maynard Keynes, and Friedrich Hayek? (c) What are the strengths and weaknesses of each economic system?

10. What role does culture seem to play in structuring economic systems? Explain using specific examples.
11. Would it be possible to implement a social market economy in the United States? Why or why not?

NOTES

1 J. Barkley Rosser and Marina V. Rosser, *Comparative Economics in a Transforming World Economy*, 3rd ed. (Cambridge, MA: MIT Press, 2018).

2 Daron Acemoglu and James A. Robinson, *Why Nations Fail: The Origins of Power, Prosperity, and Poverty* (New York: Crown, 2012).

3 Satyam Mukherjee, Daniel Romero, Benjamin F. Jones, and Brian Uzzi, "The Nearly Universal Link Between the Age of Past Knowledge and Tomorrow's Breakthroughs in Science and Technology," *Science Advances* 3, no. 4 (April 19, 2017).

4 Note that the co-determination system has been weakened in recent years in the face of global competition. It will be interesting to see how much of this system is maintained in the future. Given that it is credited with Germany's much-vaunted labor skill and productivity, it is difficult to imagine the system going away altogether.

5 Official Chinese government estimates range from 200 to 300, whereas journalists put the number of deaths between 300 and 1000.

Markets and how they work

The institutional foundations of markets and the supply and demand model

Markets have existed in one form or another for much of human history, but their forms have often been very different, and it is only since the advent of capitalism that we have depended on markets to provide the goods and services we need for our survival. Even in the modern world in which markets are dominant, markets vary widely in how they work.

As a brief case study of markets, let's consider what has happened to the price of oil over the last two decades years. As Figure 7.1 shows, there has been a huge variation in the price of oil. Understanding the oil market involves knowledge of the factors that affect the supply and demand for oil, as well as geopolitical affairs and other political and industrial factors. The dramatic increase in the price of oil from a low of $17.50 per barrel in 2001 to a high of $145.16 in 2008 was a product of several factors. Rapid economic growth in China and other emerging market economies led to a huge increase in the demand for oil. There were also changes on the supply side of the market. About 40% of crude oil is produced by a group of countries that form a cartel, the Organization of the Petroleum Exporting Countries (OPEC). As such a large player in the oil market, OPEC plays a major role in oil supply. OPEC countries agreed to reduce their production in the early 2000s in order to increase the price of oil. The combination of an increase in demand and a decrease in supply sent crude oil prices soaring.

Then the Great Recession hit in late 2008. The demand for crude oil decreased dramatically as economic growth slowed and companies cut back significantly on their production, using less energy in the process. As the economy recovered from the Great Recession, demand increased again and crude oil prices rose until 2014. But in 2014, economic growth in China and emerging markets fell, once again reducing the demand for oil. Alternative energies such as solar and wind

DOI: 10.4324/9780429399350-9

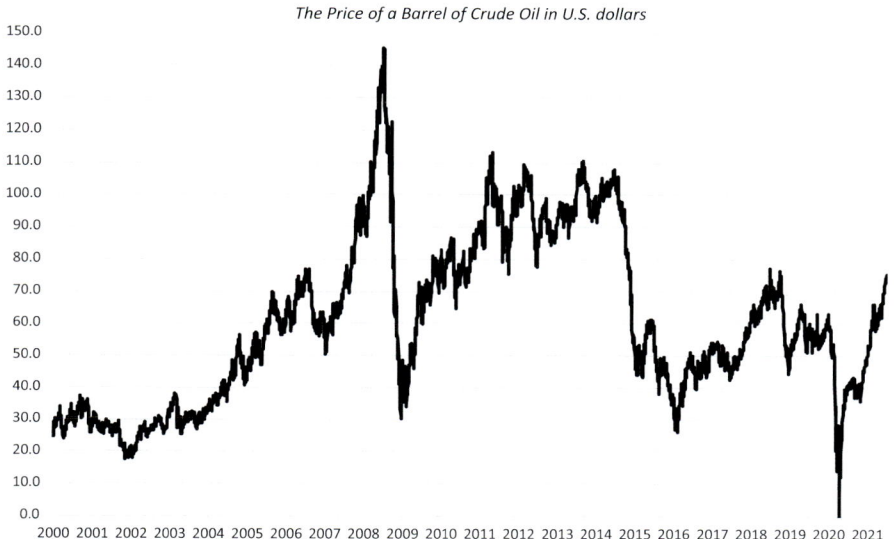

FIGURE 7.1 The price of a barrel of crude oil ($), 2000–2021.

power also led to some decreases in the demand for oil. At the same time, new hydraulic fracturing (fracking) techniques increased the supply of oil, especially in the United States and Canada. This combination of a decrease in demand and an increase in supply caused oil prices to drop dramatically in 2014 and then to stay low for the next several years. The COVID-19 pandemic recession of 2020 caused another crash in oil prices as factories closed and people stopped traveling, decreasing demand for oil sharply. The price of oil briefly fell into negative territory on April 20, 2020! There was such a large surplus that oil suppliers were willing to pay people to take it off their hands rather than make costly storage arrangements for surplus oil. Then, in 2022, a surging global economy sparked large increases in the demand for energy, including oil, as businesses expanded production, at the same time that the Russian invasion of Ukraine reduced oil supplies, causing the price of a barrel of oil to surge to over $120 per barrel.

What we learn from this example is that most of the price of oil can be explained by straightforward supply and demand factors. But we also need to be aware of OPEC's strategies to manipulate the price of oil and the likely impact of new technologies in renewable energies and oil extraction. Governments around the world are pushing for more sustainable sources of power that contribute less to global warming than the burning of fossil fuels, which will probably have an increasing impact on the oil market in coming years. In short, market analysis involves understanding supply and demand along with the major institutional and technological structures that affect market behavior. That is the topic of this chapter.

7.0 CHAPTER 7 LEARNING GOALS

After reading this chapter you should be able to:

- Define and give examples of a market and a market transaction.
- Describe the key institutions that make markets work and analyze how those institutions support markets.
- List and critically evaluate the assumptions upon which the supply and demand model rests.
- Using supply and demand curves, explain the concept of equilibrium and why markets tend toward an equilibrium price and quantity.
- Explain the theory of demand and the theory of supply.
- Analyze how changes in the determinants of demand and the determinants of supply shift demand and supply curves and affect equilibrium price and equilibrium quantity.

7.1 MARKETS AND MARKET TRANSACTIONS

Markets are a central part of our lives, but they can be difficult to understand fully, because so much of what makes markets work is hidden from plain sight. In simple terms, a **market** is **an institution that organizes and facilitates transactions between buyers and sellers**. A **transaction** is **an agreement between economic agents—buyers and sellers—to exchange goods, services, or assets**. Each market has a set of formal and informal **rules** that govern the behavior of economic agents. Economic agents can be individuals or groups such as corporations or government agencies.

There are many different types of markets in a capitalist economic system, each with its own characteristics. The market for food or clothing includes all of the stores and vendors in your area and online that you could patronize to buy the food or clothes that you need or want. We can analyze the market for food at a local, national, or even global level. Each level would have its own characteristics and dynamics. The market for stocks includes all of the companies with publicly issued stocks and the investors and brokers who are interested in buying those stocks. The local market for labor includes all of the businesses in your area that are looking for employees and all of the people who want to find jobs. We usually subdivide the labor market into the market for particular skills, because not everyone is qualified for every job. As you can see from the examples above, when analyzing a market, it is very important to specify the scope of the market you are describing so you can determine which factors are most important to incorporate into your analysis.

The most common markets in capitalist economies are structured as follows:

- **Retail markets** are **firms such as Walmart and Amazon (suppliers) that sell directly to consumers (demanders)**.
- **Wholesale markets** are **retailers like Walmart and Amazon (demanders) that purchase the goods they sell from the companies that produce them (suppliers)**. For example, Walmart buys food containers from Rubbermaid, which it then resells directly to consumers.
- **Resource markets** are **the markets for labor, land, capital, and natural resources where producers purchase the inputs they need (producers are the demanders) from the owners of those resources (suppliers)**.
- **Financial markets** are where **those wishing to borrow money (demanders) are matched with those with money to lend (suppliers)**.

We also see informal markets and markets for illegal drugs and other illicit products in all economies. Informal markets have a different dynamic because most transactions take place in cash and are based on trust rather than established rules and laws.

In each of these markets, the interaction of suppliers (sellers) and demanders (purchasers) will determine the market price, as we will study in some detail. In competitive markets the conditions affecting supply and demand are the primary determinant of prices. In less competitive markets, issues of monopoly power and bargaining power come into play. Government intervention can also play a role in determining prices.

Markets are actually quite complicated in that they require a host of formal and informal institutions to make them work. The key institutions that make markets and market transactions work effectively are described in the next section.

7.2 THE INSTITUTIONS THAT MAKE MARKETS WORK

Economists have identified a **set of market-supporting institutions that must exist in order for markets to function effectively**. Understanding these institutions and how they work will give you a deeper understanding of markets. If you go to work for a private sector business, you will need to gain an intimate understanding of the institutions that affect the market in which your business operates. The key market-supporting institutions include **property rights, laws to facilitate the aggregation of capital, trust, contract laws, competition, a lack of coercion, and infrastructure to lower transactions costs**. The most important market institution, according to mainstream economists, is that of property rights.

7.2.1 Property rights

In order to sell something to someone else, you must own it. Technically, this means you have been granted a property right to that thing by society. Property rights in a capitalist economic system stem from ownership of productive resources, and property can be owned by individuals, businesses, or governments. Most mainstream economists see property rights as the essential characteristic of capitalist markets. Property rights give the owners of resources the incentive to be as productive as possible with their property so they can make as much money as possible.

Where property rights are unstable, such as places where property can be seized at any time, people are reluctant to make investments. In his classic book *Tropical Gangsters*, Robert Klitgaard described how businesses in Equatorial Guinea would not invest anything in their businesses because as soon as their business became profitable, it would be seized by corrupt government officials. When cocoa was profitable, the government nationalized cocoa farms. Government food inspectors stole chickens from the farms they inspected. And so on. These efforts completely undermined investment in the country. But where property rights are stable, owners are willing to build factories and invest in productivity enhancements because they are confident that they will reap the benefits of their investments.

One fact noted particularly by progressive and radical political economists is that property rights confer power upon property owners. Owners of the means of production have the right to hire and fire workers, which gives them power and control over the lives of laborers, and their wealth gives them immense power over governments.

Most property rights are inherited in capitalist countries (children inherit the businesses and properties owned by their parents), but there is no particular reason that property rights need to be associated so strongly with inheritance. Norway, France, Switzerland, and Spain have a wealth tax in order to reduce the amount of inequality that is caused by unequal property rights. Socialists argue that if property rights to society's productive resources were granted to workers, the result would be a much more equitable economic system. In a typical capitalist firm, workers do not own what they produce, so they cannot sell it—that right goes to the owner of the firm, and the owner gets to keep all of the profits from sales. But in a worker-owned firm, the people who do the work also get to sell the product because they collectively own the resources. As the worker-owned Mondragon Cooperative Corporation in Spain has demonstrated, workers running firms can make them efficient, productive, and profitable.

Feminist economists note that property rights in most societies are distributed unequally by gender. Around the world, men are more likely to own property and assets, which means that governments that strictly protect property rights and refuse to redistribute property cement existing gender inequality. The same is also true of the racial distribution of property. African Americans and Latino Americans are much less likely to own property and businesses than whites.

Given that property rights are the cornerstone of markets, the World Bank has made the establishment of clear property rights a key component of many of its development programs in poor countries. However, due to gender inequities, this has had some significantly negative consequences. In several countries in Africa, efforts to establish secure property rights led to land ownership being granted almost exclusively to men, taking the land away from women who had farmed it for decades under traditional land rights allocated by tribal elders. Sadly, taking access to the land from productive women and giving it to men with no farming experience led to declines in agricultural production.

Property rights are therefore both the cornerstone of economic markets and a source of much dissatisfaction with markets on the part of those who have been historically excluded from having property rights. Laws facilitating the aggregation of capital are similarly divisive.

7.2.2 Laws to facilitate the aggregation of capital

In the modern world, firms in many industries need to be large in order to achieve **economies of scale** to compete with other huge firms. Correspondingly, every country has laws that allow individuals or groups to pool their resources in order to form large businesses. Many economists see the law that established the limited liability corporation as an essential component of U.S. economic success, because it facilitated the pooling of capital into huge trusts that became the first large manufacturing companies. Other countries such as Japan and Germany allow banks to own a controlling interest in companies so that banks can directly use their vast financial resources for producing goods and services.

As with property rights, laws that foster huge corporations are controversial. By facilitating the pooling of financial resources, corporations grow larger and more powerful than they might otherwise, augmenting and centralizing the power of property rights significantly. Economist E.F. Schumacher argued in his book *Small Is Beautiful* that once corporations became huge and impersonal, it was easier for them to exploit workers they did not know and ruin the environment in locations the owners did not live in. The solution to problems of exploitation and environmental degradation was, to him, a return to local, small-scale production. The power of huge multinational corporations over workers, resources, and governments is an issue we return to throughout the book as one of the defining issues in modern capitalism.

7.2.3 Trust and contract laws that foster trust

Most transactions in markets are based on trust. Buyers have to trust that the seller will deliver a product of the expected quality at the expected time. Sellers have to trust that the buyer's payment will be made in the appropriate amount in the correct currency at the required time. Both agents have to trust that the other party will not try to steal or cheat during the transaction. Because trust is so essential to transactions, personal relationships are a major facilitator of exchange.

Another way to get people to trust you is to establish a solid reputation. Indeed, one of the reasons why marketers work so hard to establish a brand's reputation is because when people trust a particular brand, they are often willing to pay more for it and to purchase that brand over similar products that do not have as solid a reputation. It is hard to overstate how valuable reputation is. A survey by the World Economic Forum and Fleishman-Hillard, a public relations firm, found that "corporate reputation is a more important measure of success than stock market performance, profitability and return on investment, according to a survey of some the world's leading CEOs and organization leaders. Only the quality of products and services edged out reputation as the leading measure of corporate success."[1] Most CEOs think that a corporation's brand and reputation are worth *more than 40% of their company's value.*

Cultural norms can also facilitate or inhibit trust and particular types of transactions. For example, in countries adhering to strict Islamic law, religious beliefs prohibit charging interest. This makes banking very complex and inhibits numerous types of banking transactions. Instead of making traditional loans, Islamic banks have to engage in joint ventures and share in the profits of the ventures instead of charging interest. This requires a higher degree of trust on the part of the bank, and that makes it quite difficult for businesses to obtain funding. In countries that value honesty and transparency, such as Denmark and New Zealand, which rank as the least corrupt countries in Transparency International's Corruption Perceptions Index, market transactions are safer to engage in because it is less likely that someone will try to cheat or steal.

One of the ways in which large, impersonal, capitalistic markets achieve trust is via a system of contract laws. Contract laws specify the terms of a transaction. They are legally binding, so if one party violates the conditions of the contract, the other party has a legal right to seek compensation. Similarly, the Universal Commercial Code in the United States specifies the general rules governing transactions. With these laws in place, it is safe to assume that most transactions can be trusted. This makes people much more confident when engaging in market transactions.

There are other government functions that also facilitate trust. One of the main reasons that people are willing to entrust their food supply and health to private firms operating in a market is because of laws, regulations, and regular inspections by government regulators. Regulations protecting worker safety and the right to unionize ensure that workers participate in fair transactions with employers.

Interestingly, macroeconomic stability also encourages market transactions. If consumers are secure in their jobs, they tend to spend more, and if businesses are secure in their sales expectations, they tend to invest more. Therefore, successful government stabilization policies also facilitate transactions by instilling trust in the future of markets. Laws and regulations to reduce monopoly power and ensure competition also make markets work more effectively.

7.2.4 Competition and a lack of coercion

Markets tend to work well when all of their components are competitive. In product markets, prices stay low and firms remain innovative when they face the threat of significant competition. In labor markets, workers get paid and treated well when they have many employers bidding for series. In market systems dominated by huge firms with monopoly power, the result is usually extreme inequality, which causes people to lose faith in the market system and demand an alternative. Similarly, in markets with rampant discrimination with respect to gender, race, and ethnicity, excluded groups will see the market as illegitimate and seek changes, potentially destabilizing markets.

7.2.5 Infrastructure to lower transactions costs

One of the biggest impediments to markets is the cost of engaging in a transaction. If transaction costs are too high—for example, if it costs too much to transport goods to where consumers are—no seller will participate in a market. There are many different types of transactions costs. These include **transportation costs, information costs that are incurred when actors identify and evaluate different opportunities, bargaining, monitoring and enforcement costs, and other costs associated with engaging in a transaction**.

The government plays a primary role in reducing transactions costs. An effective transportation infrastructure of roads, rails, ports, and airports is crucial, as is a fast, efficient, and safe internet service. Establishing the market infrastructure itself is another key role of government. The government can create a local farmers market by providing a place, parking, and information to buyers and sellers. It can create a stock market by creating rules, laws, and regulations governing transactions. By providing a stable currency, economic actors are more willing to engage in all types of transactions. An efficient postal service that can deliver bills and goods to any address is also essential. The government needs to provide **physical infrastructure (roads, buildings, ports, airports, etc.), market infrastructure (information, rules, regulations, laws, and internet services),** and **financial infrastructure (a stable currency and banking system) to make markets work effectively**.

An understanding of market institutions is crucial for a business owner. It is very difficult to operate a business successfully unless you fully understand all of the key aspects of the markets in which you operate. You need to know the laws and regulations that affect all aspects of your operations, the competitive landscape, financial options for raising capital, the characteristics of consumers and consumer financing, and so much more.

If we assume that the government has put all of the necessary characteristics of markets in place, we can use the supply and demand model to analyze how prices and quantities of various goods are likely to change in response to shifts in consumer, producer, and government regulatory behavior. The supply and demand model is the cornerstone of mainstream economics.

7.3 THE ASSUMPTIONS OF THE SUPPLY AND DEMAND MODEL OF MAINSTREAM ECONOMICS

Analysis of changes in prices and quantities is at the center of much mainstream economic analysis. Together, prices and quantities are the main mechanism by which resources are allocated in market capitalist economies. In markets that pursue maximum profits, prices provide crucial information, signaling whether companies should allocate more or less resources to the production of a particular product and causing firms to change the quantity of the product they supply. Similarly, prices signal to consumers that an item is more or less expensive relative to other commodities, which affects their purchasing decisions. Quantity is another crucial variable, indicating how many goods or services businesses produce, something that affects how many resources they need to purchase and how many workers they need to hire in order to produce those goods and services. Their demand for workers in turn affects workers, households, and communities.

To analyze the forces that cause prices and quantities to change, economists developed the model of supply and demand. Like all economic models, the supply and demand model rests on a series of assumptions. Understanding these assumptions helps you determine when the model is useful in understanding economic phenomena and when it is less likely to apply.

The supply and demand model makes assumptions about what markets are like, as well as assumptions about suppliers and demanders. Making these assumptions is what allows us to make systematic predictions about how supply and demand will change in response to a variety of factors, and how these changes will likely affect prices and quantities. The supply and demand model is a simplified approximation of how markets work that focuses on a key set of characteristics present in most markets.

This chapter focuses on markets for commodities like pizza, beer, gas, wheat, and clothing operating in the short run. Markets for inputs such as labor and markets for financial assets work on slightly different principles. We will examine these markets later in the book. Also, different dynamics play out in the long run that cannot be captured by the supply and demand model alone.

The supply and demand model of commodities markets is based on ten major assumptions.

1. **Transactions take place in a capitalist market system with privately owned firms and individual consumers**.
2. **Markets are perfectly competitive or at least competitive enough to mirror the behavior of perfectly competitive markets**. In perfectly competitive markets, (a) suppliers sell an identical good or service and (b) no individual buyer or seller can influence the market price by themselves.

3. **Suppliers and demanders engage in optimizing behavior, with suppliers maximizing profits and demanders maximizing the satisfaction, or "utility," they get from purchases.**
4. **Markets tend toward a stable equilibrium, settling on an equilibrium price and quantity.**

The specific *assumptions about demanders (consumers)* are as follows:

5. **Consumers are rational, calculating, fully informed, and self-interested about their purchasing options.** They engage in optimizing behavior, carefully weighing their options. Note that this assumption eliminates purchases driven by impulse buying and by emulating one's peers.
6. **Consumers prefer having more to having less, but they have a limited budget so they cannot buy all that they want, and they get less and less satisfaction from having more and more of the same good.** This assumption implies that consumers have an insatiable demand for goods and services in general but they don't want too much of any one item.
7. **There are substitutes for each good, and consumers can rank goods according to how much of each good they want at various prices. This leads them to want more of a good at lower prices and less of a good at higher prices.** Consumers have a good idea about the quality of substitute goods and how much satisfaction they will get from each type of good. Consumers behave like mini-computers, tabulating how much satisfaction they will get from each dollar of spending on each good, choosing to purchase the items that give them the most satisfaction per dollar until they exhaust their budget. The result is that rational, fully informed consumers desire to purchase smaller quantities of a good at high prices and larger quantities of a good at low prices.

The specific *assumptions about suppliers* are the following:

8. **Firms pursue as much short-term profit as possible and, in doing so, decide what to produce, how much to produce, and how to produce it.**
9. **Capital and technology are fixed in the short run.** The short run is a period in which firms are stuck with the existing size of operations, usually a period of 1 to 12 months during which firms do not have time to dramatically expand the size of their business or develop new technologies. This means they cannot produce beyond their maximum capacity in the short run.
10. **Firms are encouraged to increase the quantity of a good supplied when the price increases.** With a fixed size of operations in the short run, it usually costs firms more in order to supply more. Thus, the only way to encourage firms to supply more is to offer them a higher price.

Pizza Restaurant Name	Market Share
Domino's	30.10%
Pizza Hut	27.14%
Little Caesars Pizza	10.60%
Papa John's	7.78%
Papa Murphy's	1.80%
California Pizza Kitchen	1.74%
Marco's Pizza	1.42%
Chuck E. Cheese/Peter Piper Pizza	1.11%
Sbarro	1.07%
Round Table Pizza	1.04%

FIGURE 7.2 The ten largest pizza companies in 2019.

If these assumptions hold reasonably well, then the supply and demand model can be a powerful tool to analyze markets.

Let's consider the local market for pizza in the United States as it compares to the assumptions above. Most of the assumptions hold reasonably well: The pizza market in the United States is operated by private firms in a market capitalist system. Consumers are generally well informed about the quality of pizzas from different pizzerias in their town, along with other options for quick food (substitutes) such as sandwich shops and Chinese restaurants. However, pizza is not a completely homogeneous product: There are quality and location differences. Nonetheless, most economists think that pizzas are close enough substitutes for each other that we can still talk about a local market for pizza. Pizza firms are not all small operations, either. As Figure 7.2 shows, Dominos and Pizza Hut both have very large shares of the market.[2] On the other hand, even small towns have lots of local competitors in addition to the national chains, so the pizza market is reasonably close to being a competitive market.

The prices that different restaurants charge for a similar size and type of pizza in a particular location cluster together, varying only slightly. This makes sense, because no restaurant wants to charge significantly more than its competitors for fear of losing business. The price of a large cheese pizza in the Theater District in Manhattan was $13.50 in 2014, and there was remarkably little variation among various restaurants. In Lewisburg, Pennsylvania, a 14-inch cheese pizza went for $10 in 2018. Gourmet pizzerias can charge more, and some discount pizzerias charge less, but most pizzerias charge a price within $1 of each other. To mainstream economists, this means that the market for pizza has settled on an equilibrium price, and we can safely analyze a market for a commodity like pizza using the supply and demand model, even though there are some slight variations in the product and the price.

7.4 OVERVIEW OF THE SUPPLY AND DEMAND MODEL AND EQUILIBRIUM

According to the supply and demand model, in competitive markets, supply and demand interact to determine the equilibrium price and equilibrium quantity in the market. In this section we will briefly describe the model and how it works at a general level. In subsequent sections, we go through each part of the model in detail.

In studying the relationship between price and quantity, economists have identified two major tendencies that dominate markets: (1) Firms tend to increase the amount of a good they want to sell as the price rises because it gets more and more profitable for the firm to supply a good as the price increases and (2) consumers tend to decrease the amount of a good they want to purchase as the price increases, switching instead to lower priced goods or doing without the good altogether.

If we plot out the positive relationship between price and the quantity firms want to supply, we get the positively sloped supply curve in Figure 7.3. The supply curve has a positive slope because the higher the price, the larger the amount of the good firms want to supply. Similarly, if we plot out the inverse relationship between price and quantity demanded, we get the negatively sloped demand curve in Figure 7.3. The demand curve has a negative slope because the higher the price of the good, the smaller the quantity of the good consumers want to purchase. Where the supply and demand curves intersect, we find the equilibrium point, where the quantity supplied is exactly equal to the quantity demanded, which determines the equilibrium price and equilibrium quantity.

Competitive markets always tend to move toward an equilibrium price and quantity due to the innate characteristics of markets—the invisible hand of the market that Adam Smith identified. In fact, markets abhor surpluses and shortages and, unless prevented by law, prices in markets will adjust to eliminate any surplus or shortage and move the market into equilibrium.

Consider graph (a) in Figure 7.4 on the next page. We know that the equilibrium price (P_e) of a large cheese pizza in Lewisburg, Pennsylvania, is $10. Now suppose that pizza restaurants in town try to charge a higher price than that, (P_H), of $14. What will happen? Pizza restaurants want to sell more pizzas at a price of $14 than they do at $10. Making pizzas would be so profitable at that price that they

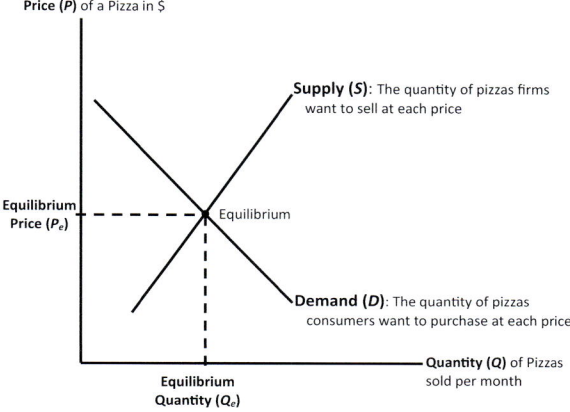

FIGURE 7.3 A graph of the supply and demand model for pizzas.

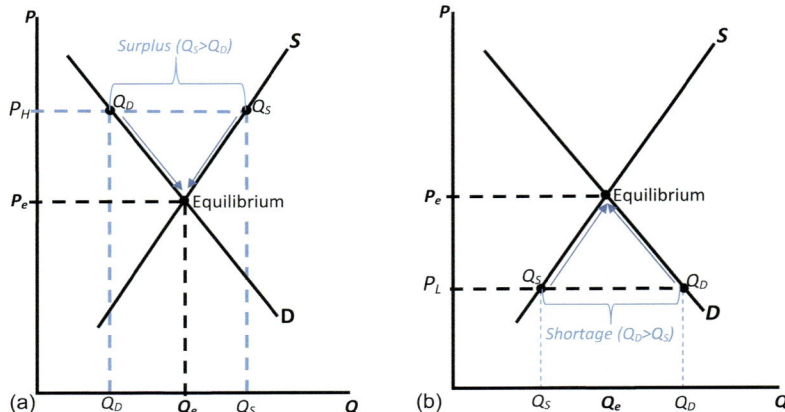

FIGURE 7.4 Prices adjust to eliminate surpluses or shortages. (a) High price (P_H) above P_e. (b) Low price (P_L) below P_e.

could afford to hire more workers, buy more pizza delivery vehicles, and increase the quantity of pizzas they supply. The quantity they want to produce increases substantially. However, consumers have the opposite reaction. At $14 pizzas are too expensive for many people, who will cook for themselves or buy other types of fast food instead of buying a pizza. When the price increases from $10 ($P_e$) to $14 ($P_H$), the quantity demanded decreases.

The result in Figure 7.4(a) is that at the high price, (P_H), the quantity of pizzas supplied is much greater than the quantity of pizzas demanded ($Q_S > Q_D$). This results in a surplus of pizzas: More pizzas are produced than are purchased. But for pizza producers, this is an unsustainable situation. As pizzas pile up, businesses cut back on production and lower prices to get rid of the surplus. As prices fall, consumers buy more pizzas. This process continues until we return back to equilibrium at P_e, where there is no longer any pressure for restaurants to cut prices and production.

Similarly, suppose pizza restaurants were to cut their prices below the equilibrium price of $P_e = \$10$ to a price of $P_L = \$6$ per pizza, which is depicted in Figure 7.4(b). That price is so low that many pizza restaurants would go out of business, and all firms would produce fewer pizzas because it is less profitable to do so. (They would probably start selling other types of food such as pasta and wings that were more profitable.) The quantity of pizzas supplied, (Q_S), declines as the price falls. Consumers, on the other hand, want to purchase a lot more pizzas at the new, lower price P_L. Quantity demanded, (Q_D), increases as the price falls. The result is a large shortage: Consumers want a lot more pizzas than restaurants are willing to supply: $Q_D > Q_S$. How will the market respond to this shortage? Once businesses realize there is a shortage, they know they can increase prices and sell more pizzas. As they increase the price of pizza more and more in response to the shortage, the quantity of pizzas demanded falls steadily. Eventually, we once again reach equilibrium at P_e and Q_e.

Next, we turn to how the supply and demand model works in more detail, analyzing the key factors that affect each curve. We can use this model to analyze how supply and demand interact to determine the price and quantity of goods and services and how price and quantity change in response to variations in key determinants of supply and demand.

7.5 THE THEORY OF DEMAND

To use the supply and demand model, you need to understand each of its components and the major factors that affect them. We will start with the **theory of demand** and the **demand curve**.

According to the **theory of demand** in mainstream economics, **consumers' willingness to pay for a product (demand) depends on the benefit (marginal utility) they expect to get from consuming the product, the price of the product, disposable income and wealth, tastes and preferences, the prices of substitute and complementary goods, the number and size of buyers, expectations about the future, and the availability and cost of consumer credit**.

In order to determine the relationship between the factors that affect consumer demand and the prices and quantities of goods, economists developed the demand curve, which shows the precise relationship between the price of a good and the quantity of the good demanded at each price. Marginal utility and price determine the slope of the demand curve (whether it is steep or flat), and the other factors, known as the determinants of demand, affect the location of the demand curve (whether it shifts to the left or to the right).

To begin, we will focus on the relationship between price and the quantity demand. **Quantity demanded** is **the amount of a good or service that buyers are willing to purchase at each price in a particular time period**. Neoclassical economist Alfred Marshall's **law of demand** states that, **other things being equal, the quantity of a good demanded is inversely related to its price. When price increases quantity demand decreases. When price decreases quantity demanded increases.** The law of demand focuses exclusively on the relationship between price and quantity demanded, whereas the theory of demand includes the effect of price and other factors on demand.

Consider your own purchases of a product like a pizza. If pizza is extremely expensive—perhaps if it sells for a price of $30 per pizza—you would probably only purchase it on rare occasions as a treat. If pizza is really cheap—if the price is only $4 a pizza—you might buy it much more regularly. Note, however, that consumers tend to be less and less willing to purchase an item the more they have of it. If you have had pizza three nights in a row, on the fourth night you are much less likely to want pizza again. This means, in economic terms, that you are less willing to pay as much for pizza that night.

Economists use the concept of utility to explain this phenomenon. **Utility** is **the amount of satisfaction a person gains from consuming a product**.

Price	Kate's Quantity of Pizza Demanded	Juan's Quantity of Pizza Demanded	Bo's Quantity of Pizza Demanded	Market Quantity of Pizza Demanded (sum of all 3)
$ 14.00	0	0	0	0
$ 12.00	1	2	3	6
$ 10.00	2	4	6	12
$ 8.00	3	6	9	18
$ 6.00	4	8	12	24
$ 4.00	5	10	15	30
$ 2.00	6	12	18	36
$ 0	7	14	21	42

FIGURE 7.5 The quantity of pizza demanded per month at each price.

The **law of diminishing marginal utility** reflects the fact that **as a person consumes more and more of one product, while holding consumption of other products constant, that person experiences a decline in the additional (marginal) utility from each additional unit of that product consumed**. The law of diminishing marginal utility is the source of the negative relationship between price and willingness to pay (quantity demanded). Consumers are willing to pay a lot for something that is scarce and that they want very badly. They are much less willing to pay for something that they have had a lot of and are sick of having.

Economists construct a model of the demand curve based on such behavior. Figure 7.5 shows the quantity of large cheese pizzas demanded at each price every month by three consumers, Kate, Juan, and Bo. At a price of $14 per pizza, none of them want to buy any. At that price, they prefer to buy less expensive alternative forms of fast food. If the price falls to $12 per pizza, Kate will buy one pizza per month, Juan will buy two, and Bo will buy three. At a prize of $10 per pizza, Kate will buy two pizzas per month, Juan will buy four, and Bo will buy six. And so on.

To construct a market quantity demanded, we simply add up the quantity demanded for all economic actors in the market. If we assume that Kate, Juan, and Bo are the only consumers, the market quantity demanded is found by adding up all of the individual quantities demanded at each price. The result is the market quantity demanded in Figure 7.5.

We can use the information in Figure 7.5 to construct a graph of the demand curves for Kate, Juan, Bo, and the market. A **demand curve shows the quantity of a good buyers would like to purchase at each price within a particular period of time**. Figure 7.6 plots out the demand curves for Kate, Juan, Bo, and the market (if Kate, Juan, and Bo make up the entire market) using the data from Figure 7.5. As you can see, all of the demand curves have a negative slope, in keeping with the law of demand.

We can also use an equation to express a demand curve. In general, quantity demanded depends on price. In mathematical terms, $Q_d = f(P)$. Linear demand curves take the form

$$Q_d = a + bP.$$

6.7 THE CHINESE STATE-DOMINATED ECONOMY

Under Mao Zedong, China's centrally planned economy emphasized rural industrialization, regional self-reliance, and decentralization. This differed dramatically from the centralized approach of the U.S.S.R. The Chinese government confiscated the lands of feudal lords and developed rural markets, giving farmers and workers more freedom and control over their work. This worked well initially, boosting productivity and rural incomes.

However, when the state tried to force farmers and workers into collectives, a more Soviet-style approach, the results were disastrous, with production declines, shortages, and extremely unhappy workers. In response, Mao implemented the "Hundred Flowers Campaign" and the "Great Leap Forward" to prompt creative thinking and solutions to the problems that China was experiencing. Efforts to develop the countryside utilizing traditional technology rather than cutting-edge methods did prompt the creation of numerous collective firms in rural China, which would later prove useful. However, the strategy was not effective in producing goods efficiently, and China again faced repeated shortages and crises. These crises led to the re-imposition of central planning, as China returned to a more traditional communist economy.

With Mao's death in 1976, the way was opened for a new approach led by Deng Xiaoping. Deng gradually incorporated market reforms into the centrally planned system. Government officials were selected and promoted based on their ability to foster economic growth in the region they governed. Incentivizing government officials in this manner refocused regions of the Chinese economy on growth-stimulating policies.

Communes were eliminated and rural farmers were granted property rights and the right to farm small private plots for their own benefit. The household once again became the main agricultural unit, and rural markets were created so that farmers could sell their goods.

In a particularly adept policy, farmers and privatized small firms were required to sell a certain amount of produce to the state at a low price so that the state could preserve the central planning system. Any goods produced over the state quota could be sold in the newly created markets. This allowed enterprises to adapt to markets and market prices over time while preserving the stability of the economic system. Rather than experiencing a collapse as most communist countries did when markets were introduced, the gradual introduction of markets to China resulted in a huge economic boom.

Locally owned Township and Village Enterprises (TVEs), started under Mao's earlier efforts at rural industrialization, began to serve as a dynamic component of new markets. TVEs were owned by a village or town, and the manager was selected by local government officials, freeing them from centralized control. Profits from a TVE went to the community that owned it to pay wages, provide local public

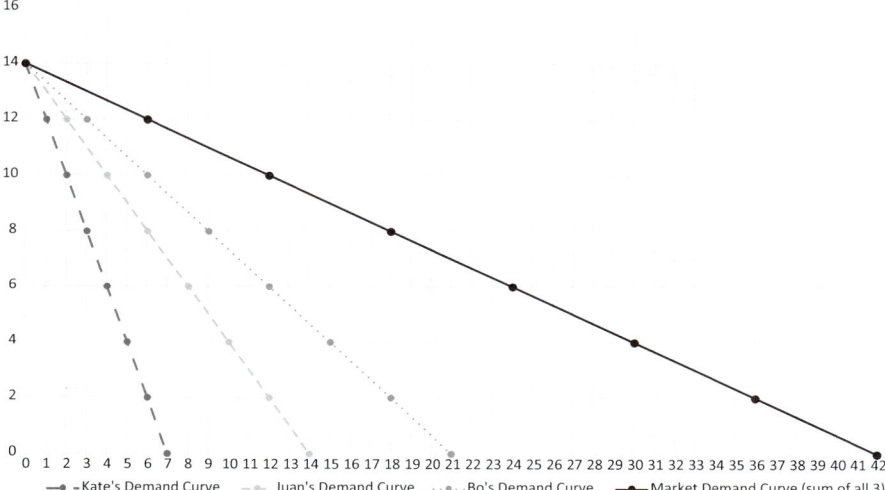

FIGURE 7.6 Demand curves for Kate, Juan, Bo, and the market.

a is the quantity demanded when $P=0$ and b is the inverse of the slope. The slope of the demand curve is the rise over the run. Slope $= (\Delta P / \Delta Q_d) = (1 / b)$.

b is always a negative number because when price increases, quantity demanded decreases and vice versa.

In Figure 7.6, the equation for Kate's demand curve is $Q_d = 7 - (0.5)P$. The equation for the market demand curve is $Q_d = 42 - 3P$.

The slope of the demand curve shows how quantity demanded changes whenever price changes. The location of the demand curve, whether it shifts to the left or to the right, depends on the **determinants of demand**.

7.6 THE DETERMINANTS OF DEMAND THAT CAUSE SHIFTS IN THE DEMAND CURVE

The demand curve is designed to show the direct relationship between price and the quantity demanded for a particular product (the law of demand). A change in price produces a change in the quantity demanded and causes a movement along the demand curve. For example, in Figure 7.6, if the price of a pizza falls from $12 to $10, the quantity of pizzas demanded in the market will increase from 6 to 12 (the second and third points on the market demand curve).

There are six factors that cause a shift in the entire demand curve. These are known as the **determinants of demand**: **the six factors that determine the location of the demand curve and whether or not it shifts to the left or to the right.** The determinants of demand are (1) disposable income and wealth, (2) tastes and preferences, (3) the prices of substitute and complementary goods, (4) the number and size (buying power) of buyers,

(5) buyers' expectations about the future, and (6) the availability and cost of consumer credit. The determinants of demand are held constant (the ceteris paribus conditions) when we draw a particular demand curve. This also means that when the determinants of demand change, we have to draw an entirely new demand curve reflecting the new information—the demand curve will have shifted.

Before we proceed, we need to highlight some very specific and precise language economists use when they talk about changes in demand. A **change in the quantity demanded** is **a movement along the demand curve caused by a change in the price of the good being demanded**. A **change in demand** refers to **a shift in the demand curve to the left or to the right due to a change in one of the determinants of demand**. We go through each of the determinants of demand below, starting with the most important one: Disposable income and wealth.

7.6.1 Disposable income and wealth

Disposable income is **the income people have to spend after the government has taken out taxes (after tax income)**. **Household wealth** is **the value of the assets held by individuals and households**.

In general, for all normal goods an increase in income or wealth will lead to consumers wanting to buy more of a good at each price than they used to. The entire demand curve shifts to the right. Suppose that incomes in Lewisburg, Pennsylvania, double because of a huge natural gas boom in the area that creates a lot of jobs and income. When people have more money, they tend to buy more goods in general, and they definitely tend to buy more pizzas. As you can see in Figure 7.7(a), when income or wealth increases, the demand curve moves further to the right at each price. For example, at a price of $10, consumers in Lewisburg

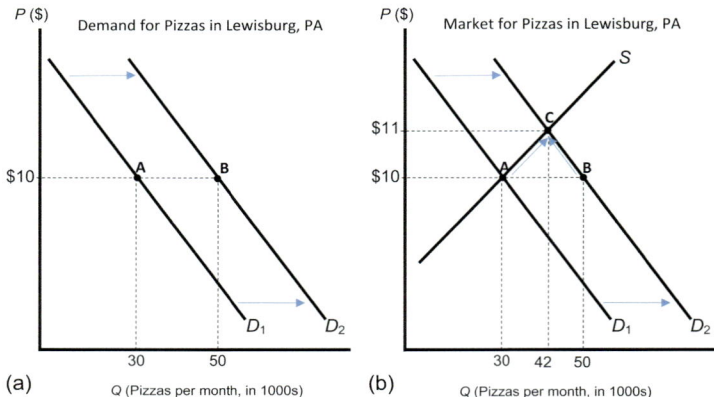

FIGURE 7.7 A shift in demand to the right (increase in demand). (a) Shift in demand to the right. (b) Change in equilibrium from a rightward shift.

wanted 30,000 pizzas per month before the increase in income (point **A**), but they want 50,000 pizzas per month after the increase in income. The entire curve has shifted to the right by 20,000 pizzas: At each price, people want 20,000 more pizzas than they used to as a result of the increase in income. (Note that we are depicting the full market for pizzas, rather than the market of three people we used earlier as an example. Now we have thousands of consumers in the market.)

If we put the demand curve from Figure 7.7(a) together with a supply curve, we can see how a rightward shift in demand affects the equilibrium price and quantity of pizzas. The rightward increase in demand creates a shortage of pizzas at a price of $10: 50,000 people want pizzas (point **B** in Figure 7.7[b]), but suppliers only want to supply 30,000 pizzas (point **A**) at that price. Once pizza producers see that more people want their pizzas than pizzerias can provide, they will take advantage of the increase in demand to raise their prices and hire more workers so they can increase pizza production, moving from point **A** to point **C** along the supply curve. As the price of pizzas increases, consumers purchase fewer of them, reducing their quantity demanded from 50 to 42 and moving from point **B** to point **C**, which is the new equilibrium.

A decrease in income or wealth would do the opposite. When the stock market crashed in 2008 and people saw the value of their assets decline by 60%, they purchased fewer goods of all types, and the demand curves for most goods, including pizza, shifted to the left (decreased).

The examples given above describe **normal goods**, which are defined as **goods that consumers want to buy more of when their income or wealth increases and that they want to buy less of when their income or wealth decreases**. But we do sometimes find **inferior goods**, which are **goods that consumers want to buy less of as their income or wealth increases, or more of as their income or wealth decreases**. Examples of inferior goods include used clothing, used cars, inexpensive brands of all types, less desirable types of foods, and other goods that people would choose not to buy if they had more money. If people have more money, they tend to increase their demand for higher quality items and decrease their demand for lower quality items. For example, during economic booms when incomes and wealth increase, people buy more expensive brands of beer, including imported brands (Heineken, Stella Artois) and microbrews (Samuel Adams, Victory, Dogfish Head), while buying less of bargain brands (Pabst Blue Ribbon, Natural Light, Old Milwaukee). The demand for premium beers *increases* when income increases but the demand for bargain beers (inferior goods) *decreases*.

7.6.2 Tastes and preferences

Consumers' tastes and preferences can have a significant influence on the demand for a product when large numbers of consumers shift their buying habits. For example, as health concerns about obesity, diabetes, and artificial sweeteners grew and as anti-carbohydrate diets became prominent, demand for sodas (soft drinks) plummeted. From 2004 to 2017, U.S. consumers decreased their purchases of sodas

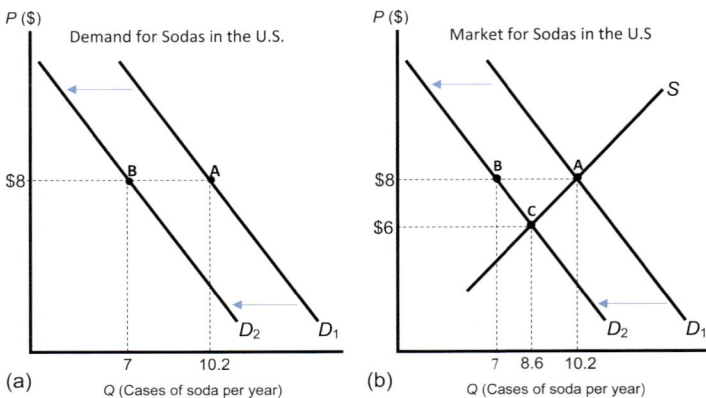

FIGURE 7.8 A shift in demand to the left (decrease in demand). (a) Shift in demand to the left. (b) Change in equilibrium from a leftward shift in D.

from 10.2 billion cases to 8.6 billion cases, a drop of 15%. In Figure 7.8(a) you can see that the demand curve for sodas shifts to the left by 3.2 billion cases due to the decrease in consumers' interest in soda. Figure 7.8(b) shows how the leftward shift in demand creates a surplus of soda (the line between point **A** and point **B**). As surplus soda builds up in inventories, soda companies like Coca-Cola and Pepsi cut back production and lower prices, moving the quantity supplied from point **A** to point **C**, the new equilibrium. As firms drop their prices, consumer demand moves from point **B** to point **C**.

7.6.3 The prices of substitute and complementary goods

Demand curves also shift when the prices of closely related goods change. A **substitute good** is **a product that consumers are willing to purchase instead of another good; when the price of one good increases, many consumers will switch to buying the substitute good, increasing the demand for the substitute**. A substitute for Coca-Cola is Pepsi. A substitute for beef is chicken. A **complementary good** is **a product that consumers tend to purchase along with another good; when the price of one good increases and consumers buy less of it, there will also be a decrease in the demand for any complementary goods**. Complements for peanut butter are bread and jelly. A complement for a cell phone is a case for the phone.

As an example of substitute goods, when deciding how to heat their homes, households choose between electric, coal, wood, oil, and natural gas—these goods are substitutes for each other. As you can see in Figure 7.9, the increase in the supply of natural gas from fracking has led to a dramatic drop in natural gas prices during the last decade, which has caused households to increase the quantity of natural gas demanded (moving along the natural gas demand curve down and to the right from point **A** to point **B**). There is a movement along the demand curve for natural gas because of the decrease in the price of natural gas. In the heating oil

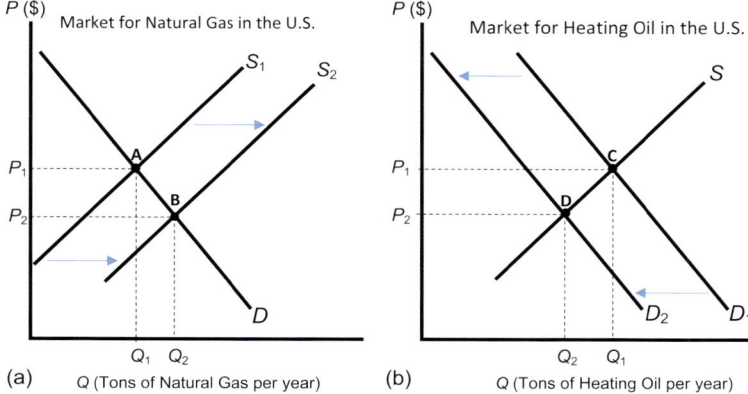

FIGURE 7.9 A decrease in the price of a substitute good (gas) causes a decrease in demand (oil). (a) Increase in supply & decrease in the prices of gas. (b) Decrease in D for heating oil when the price of a substitute decreases.

market, however, there is a shift in the demand curve for heating oil to the left as households buy more gas and less heating oil. Equilibrium in the heating oil market moves from point **C** to point **D**, with a lower equilibrium price and quantity. Note that in these graphs we use P_1, P_2, Q_1, and Q_2 instead of putting in specific numbers. Economists are often interested in general trends in markets. In this case, economists were able to predict that the decrease in the price of natural gas and the increase in the quantity of natural gas demanded in Figure 7.9(a) would be matched by a decrease in demand (leftward shift) for heating oil that we see in Figure 7.9(b).

There are also numerous examples of complementary goods. When someone buys a laptop computer, they also tend to buy a laptop bag, an external mouse and monitor, and a printer. When you buy a printer, you will eventually need more ink for it. When you buy a car, you will also need to buy gas, tires, and car insurance.

For another concrete example, there was a large increase in the market supply of gasoline from 2014 to 2015, which caused gas prices to fall by more than 50%. Gasoline is a strong complement for large trucks like sport utility vehicles (SUVs). SUV sales increased by 16% as gas prices fell, a significant increase in demand (rightward shift). However, sales of passenger cars fell by 2%—passenger cars are substitutes for SUVs. When consumers shift their tastes toward SUVs because of low gas prices, this causes a decrease (leftward shift) in the demand for passenger cars. (See if you can draw this situation on a set of three graphs of the gasoline market, the SUV market, and the passenger car market.)

7.6.4 The number or size of buyers

The number of buyers, and especially the number of larger buyers, has a big influence over the demand for a product. If there is an increase in the number or size of buyers, the demand for a product will increase (shift to the right). If there is a decrease in the number or size of buyers, the demand for a product will decrease (shift to the left). For example, when the government raised the national drinking age to 21 in 1984, this meant fewer consumers could legally drink in bars. Many bars started losing money due to the *decrease in demand* for drinks at bars, causing some bars to close. Interestingly, most data indicate that the increase in the drinking age had no significant impact on alcohol consumption—there was just less alcohol consumption in public settings such as bars.

The size of buyers also impacts demand significantly. If you manufacture a product and Walmart, the largest retailer in the United States, decides to stock your product to sell to consumers, you will experience a significant *increase in demand* because you have attracted a huge buyer.

7.6.5 Buyers' expectations about the future

Expectations can affect the demand for a product in several ways. If consumers expect their incomes or wealth to increase, or if they are confident about the future, they tend to *increase their demand* for goods. If consumers worry that they might lose their job or that the value of their stock market portfolio might drop significantly, they will *decrease their demand* for goods. Ironically, if consumers expect a recession, they can help to cause one by reducing their purchases due to pessimism! Consumers might also change their demand for a particular good if they expect its price to change: If people expect home prices to drop, they often wait to purchase a home. People also shift their demand for a product if they think they might lose access to it. A mass shooting in San Bernardino in 2015 led President Obama to call for stricter background checks and gun regulations. This caused a significant *increase in demand* for guns by consumers who were worried that they might not be able to buy guns in the future. Thus, consumer expectations of all types affect the demand for products.

7.6.6 The availability and cost of consumer credit

The more access consumers have to borrowing and the lower the interest payments they have to make on their debt, the more purchases they can make. In 2017 consumer credit card debt reached $784 billion—that means consumers were able to buy over $700 billion more goods than they could have if they just relied on their income and wealth to make purchases. That amounts to a huge *increase in demand* for many products. Low interest rates on car loans and easier access to those loans increased the demand for cars in the 2010s.

Now that we have discussed the factors that drive the behavior of the demand curve, it is time to turn to the supply curve and the behavior of sellers in more detail.

7.7 THE THEORY OF SUPPLY

According to the **theory of supply** in mainstream economics, **sellers' willingness to offer a product for sale (supply) in a perfectly competitive market** depends on the price they expect to get from selling the product, the cost, productivity and availability of inputs, the technology available to make the product, sellers' expectations about the future, changes in the profitability of other markets the seller can supply, and the number and size of suppliers.

In order to determine the relationship between the factors that affect suppliers and the prices and quantities of goods, economists developed the supply curve that shows the precise relationship between the price of a good and the quantity of the good supplied at each price. The **marginal cost** of producing a product, which is driven by the cost and marginal productivity of inputs, determines the slope of the supply curve (whether it is steep or flat), and the other factors affect the location of the supply curve (whether it is shifted to the left or to the right).

First, we will focus on the relationship between price and the quantity supplied. **Quantity supplied** is **the amount of a good or service that sellers are willing to offer for sale in a particular time period at each price**. The **law of supply** states that, **other things being equal, the quantity of a good supplied is directly related to its price. When price increases, quantity supplied increases. When price decreases, quantity supplied decreases.** This means the supply curve is upward sloping in the short run.

The **short run** is **the period of time in which one or more inputs are fixed and cannot be changed, so only variable inputs can be adjusted**. For a pizzeria, in the short run they are stuck with the size of their restaurant and kitchen—their capital stock is fixed. If they experience an increase in demand for pizzas, they can supply pizzas quickly and easily until all of the specialized jobs in the pizzeria are taken. But, once all of the ovens are baking and all the waiters, cooks, delivery persons, and cashiers are working at capacity, it is extremely difficult to increase pizza production any further. And it would be less efficient to do so, involving people crowding in each other's way to do their work, waiting for a pizza oven to become free, and so on. The cost of each additional pizza would rise as more are produced under these conditions. Thus, the only way the pizzeria will continue to increase production when the restaurant is running out of capacity and costs per pizza are increasing is if the price of pizza is high enough to offset the increasing costs. In other words, the only way to entice a pizzeria to produce more pizza is for consumers to offer a higher price: An upward-sloping supply curve.

Economists construct a model of the supply curve based on these characteristics of small firms in competitive markets. Figure 7.10 on the next page shows the quantity of large cheese pizzas supplied every month at each price by two firms, Pizza Hut and Dominos. At a price of $4 per pizza, neither pizzeria wants to sell any pizzas: That price isn't high enough to cover their costs, and they would have to close down. If the price increases to $6, Pizza Hut will offer 1000 pizzas for sale and Dominos will offer 2000 pizzas for sale. If the price increases to $8, Pizza Hut will offer 2000 pizzas for sale and Dominos will offer 4000. And so on. Notice that as the prize of a pizza rises and selling pizzas becomes more profitable, the quantity of pizzas supplied per month increases.

THE EVOLUTION OF ECONOMIC IDEAS AND SYSTEMS

Price	Pizza Hut's Quantity Supplied	Domino's Quantity Supplied	Market Supply (sum of both)
$14.00	5000	10000	15000
$12.00	4000	8000	12000
$10.00	3000	6000	9000
$ 8.00	2000	4000	6000
$ 6.00	1000	2000	3000
$ 4.00	0	0	0

FIGURE 7.10 Table showing the quantity of pizza supplied per month at each price.

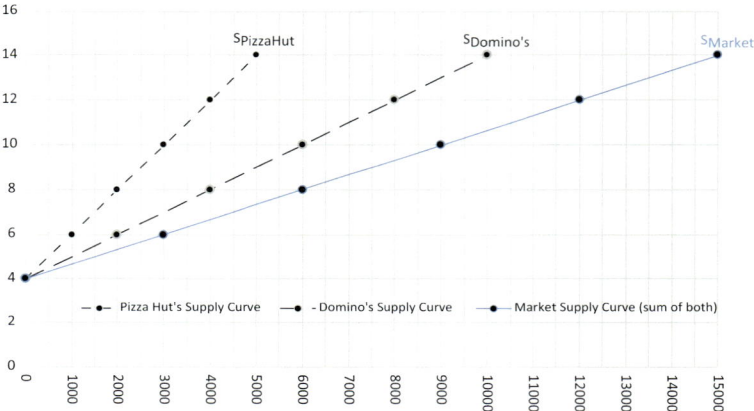

FIGURE 7.11 Supply curves for Pizza Hut, Domino's, and the market for pizzas.

To construct a market quantity supplied, we add up the quantity supplied for all sellers in the market. If we assume that Pizza Hut and Dominos are the only sellers, the market quantity supplied is found by adding up all of the individual quantities supplied at each price. The result is the "quantity supplied" column in Figure 7.10.

We can use the information in Figure 7.10 to construct a graph of the supply curves for Pizza Hut, Domino's Pizza, and the pizza market. A **supply curve shows the quantity of a good that a seller will offer for sale at each price within a particular period of time**. Figure 7.11 plots out the supply curves for Pizza Hut, Dominos, and the pizza market (if Pizza Hut and Dominos make up the entire sellers' side of the market). All of the supply curves have a positive slope, in keeping with the law of supply.

We can also use an equation to express a supply curve. Quantity supplied depends on price. In mathematical terms, $Q_s = f(P)$. Linear demand curves take the form

$$Q_s = a + bP.$$

$-a/b$ is the intercept on the price axis when $Q=0$ and b is the inverse of the slope. The slope of the supply curve is the rise over the run. Slope = $(\Delta P / \Delta Q_s) = (1/b)$.

b is always a positive number in the equation for a supply curve, because when price increases, quantity supplied increases, and when price decreases, quantity supplied decreases.

In Figure 7.11, the equation for Pizza Hut's supply curve is $Q_s = -2000 + (500)P$. The equation for the market supply curve is $Q_s = -6000 + 1500P$.

We can use equations for supply and demand to solve for equilibrium price and quantity. Suppose that the equation for the market demand curve is $Q_d = 12,000 - 300P$.

In equilibrium, we know that $Q_S = Q_D$. Setting the equations for Q_S and Q_D equal to each other, we get the following:

$$Q_s = -6000 + 1500P; Q_d = 12,000 - 300P;$$
$$Q_s = Q_d; (-6000 + 1500P) = (12,000 - 300P)$$

Solving for P we get, 1800P=18,000. The equilibrium price $P_e = 10$. If we plug $P = 10$ into the equations for Q_S and Q_D, we find that the equilibrium quantity $Q_e = 9000$.

If we plot out the equations for the demand curve and the supply curve, we get Figure 7.12. The supply (S) and demand (D) curves intersect at the equilibrium price of $10 and the equilibrium quantity of 9000 pizzas per month. Therefore, we can use either an equation or a graph to show the relationship between supply and demand and to find equilibrium price and quantity.

The slope of the supply curve shows how the quantity supplied changes whenever price changes. The location of the supply curve, and whether it shifts to the left or to the right, depends on the **determinants of supply**.

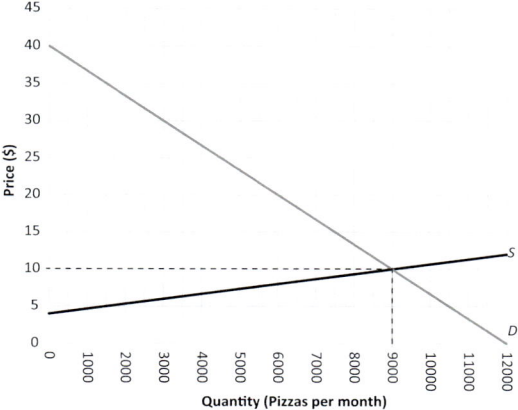

FIGURE 7.12 Equilibrium where $Q_S = Q_D$.

7.8 THE DETERMINANTS OF SUPPLY

The **determinants of supply** are **the five factors that determine the location of the supply curve and whether or not it shifts to the left or to the right. The determinants of supply are (1) the cost, productivity, and availability of inputs; (2) the technology available to make the product; (3) sellers' expectations about the future; (4) changes in the profitability of other markets the seller can supply; and (5) the number and size of sellers**. The determinants of supply are held constant (the ceteris paribus conditions) when we draw a particular supply curve. When the determinants of supply change, we draw an entirely new supply curve reflecting the new information that caused the supply curve to shift.

7.8.1 The cost, productivity, and availability of inputs

Inputs are **the factors of production—labor, capital, land, and natural resources—used to produce goods and services**. Let's focus on labor for now, because it is the most important input for most firms, making up about 61% of the costs of production on average. Suppose that the president of the United States suggests a complete ban on the use of illegal immigrant labor and threatens to impose huge fines on any companies that are caught employing illegal immigrants. Businesses that slaughter and process chickens depend on illegal immigrant labor to do much of the work in their industry—they find that legal U.S. citizens do not want to do this kind of work at the wages businesses want to pay. The result of a crackdown on illegal immigration would be a reduction in the availability of laborers for chicken processing firms. Suppliers of chicken would not be able to supply as much chicken at each price as they used to, so the entire supply curve for chicken would shift to the left, as we see in Figure 7.13(a).

When we put the shift in supply on a graph with the demand curve for chicken, we see that when the supply curve shifts to the left, this creates a shortage (the distance from point **A** to point **B**). This causes the equilibrium price to rise from $1.50 per pound of chicken to $1.75 per pound, and the equilibrium quantity falls from 39 billion pounds per year to 32 billion.

Anything that raises the cost, reduces the productivity, or reduces the availability of inputs will cause the supply curve to decrease (shift to the left). Anything that lowers the cost, increases the productivity, or increases the availability of inputs will cause the supply curve to increase (shift to the right).

7.8.2 The technology available to make the product

Technology can be a major driver of the costs of production and therefore a major determinant of the location of the supply curve. Improvements in technology increase productivity and reduce the cost of producing each unit of output, reducing a supplier's costs of production.

MARKETS AND HOW THEY WORK   169

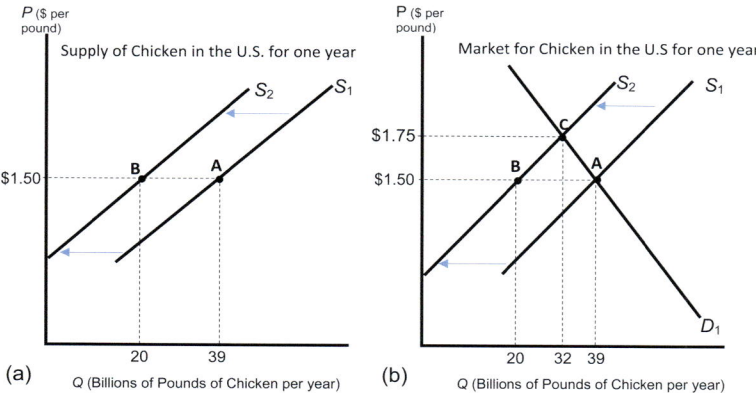

FIGURE 7.13 A shift in supply to the left (decrease in supply). (a) Shift in supply to the left. (b) Change in equilibrium from a leftward shift in S.

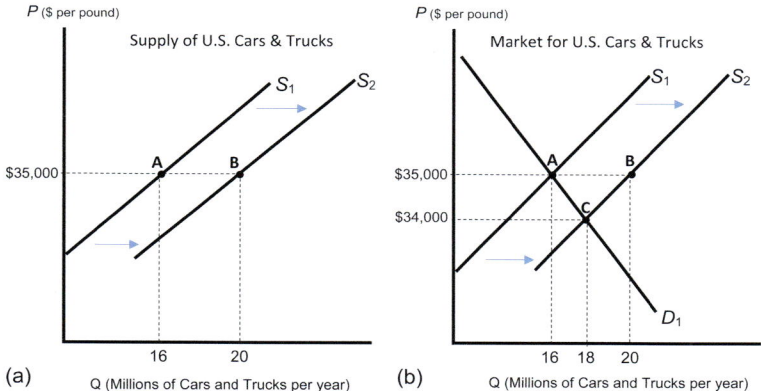

FIGURE 7.14 A shift in supply to the right (increase in supply). (a) Shift in supply to the right. (b) Change in equilibrium from a rightward shift in S.

The invention of robots to produce cars and trucks dramatically increased productivity and reduced the cost of producing cars. This caused the supply curve for cars to shift to the right: At each price, car suppliers were willing to offer more cars and trucks for sale than before. This is shown in Figure 7.14(a) with the shift in the supply curve for cars and trucks to the right. In Figure 7.14(b) we see that when we include the demand curve in the market for U.S. cars and trucks, the increase in supply from point **A** to point **B** creates a surplus of cars and trucks: At a price of $35,000, suppliers offer 20 million new cars and trucks for sale (point **B**) but consumers only want to purchase 16 million cars and trucks. The surplus causes suppliers to drop prices and reduce the number of cars and trucks they offer for sale (the quantity supplied), and they move from point **B** to point **C**. As producers of cars and trucks drop prices, the quantity demanded increases, moving from point **A** to point **C**. Notice that, compared with the original equilibrium at point **A**, the increase in supply causes the equilibrium to move to point **C**. The equilibrium price falls from $35,000 to $34,000 and the equilibrium quantity increases from 16 million to 18 million cars and trucks sold per year.

7.8.3 Sellers' expectations about the future

Sellers change the amount of goods and services they offer for sale based on **expected profitability**. If firms expect an increase in price or profitability in their market in the future, they will often decide to increase production and offer more goods for sale (an increase in supply) immediately to take advantage of the expected opportunity. This is partly because it can take a significant amount of time between the decision to increase production and the actual sale of a product to consumers. For complex manufactured goods, it can take more than six months. Correspondingly, if firms expect a recession in the near future, they may well curtail production right away, reducing their supply of goods and laying off workers. This can, of course, help to bring about the recession that firms anticipated.

7.8.4 Changes in the profitability of other markets the seller can supply

Changes in profitability in other markets a firm operates in can also cause a shift in the supply curve. For example, IBM was once a big player in the personal computer and laptop market. But in the early 2000s it was losing money on personal computers, whereas its business consulting division was highly profitable. The logical decision was for them to reduce their supply of computers, which they did by selling off their computer division to Lenovo, who now produces the (originally IBM-designed) ThinkPad. IBM poured the resources they garnered from selling their personal computer division into business consulting and other ventures, increasing their supply of services in these markets.

As another example, milk prices fell by 34% from 2014 to 2015 due to a decline in demand from foreign buyers. Faced with low prices and poor profitability in milk markets, farmers reduced their supply and turned to other products, increasing their supply of beef and soybeans. Because farmers can use their land to produce a variety of products, when one good is less profitable, they will reduce their production of that good and increase their supply of the other goods they can produce. In terms of supply and demand, with the recent milk example we saw the following: In the milk market, the demand curve shifted to the left as foreign buyers purchased less U.S. milk. This caused the price of milk to fall, which in turn resulted in a decrease in the quantity of milk supplied (a movement along the supply curve). In the soybean market, farmers decided to raise fewer cattle on their land and to grow soybeans instead, increasing the supply (rightward shift) of soybeans. This caused the equilibrium price of soybeans to fall while the equilibrium price declined as well. (Exercise: See if you can draw this chain of events on your own.)

7.8.5 The number and size of suppliers

If more suppliers enter a market, and especially if more large suppliers enter a market, the market supply curve will increase (shift to the right). The early smartphone market was dominated by Ericsson, Palm, and Blackberry. In 2007, Apple changed the market significantly with the iPhone, which was the first commercial smartphone to use touchscreen input instead of relying primarily on a stylus or keyboard. Apple completely dominated the smartphone market and charged very high prices until 2010, when Samsung released the Galaxy and began making larger, slimmer, and cheaper touchscreen smartphones. With the increase in the supply of smartphones in 2010 as the huge firm Samsung entered the market, the market supply of smartphones shifted to the right and the market price of smartphones fell. Even Apple was compelled to lower its prices to compete.

7.9 CONCLUSION

In this chapter, we began by defining what a market is and giving examples of the different kinds of market transactions we see in modern capitalism. We also described the major institutions that make markets work and how those institutions support markets. In a market capitalist economy, creating and safeguarding the institutions that make markets work is a major role for government.

We then turned to the supply and demand model and the assumptions upon which that model rests. When these assumptions are violated, the supply and demand model may not apply accurately to the real world, something that is very important to understand.

Subsequently, we used supply and demand curves to explain why markets tend toward an equilibrium price and quantity and why markets inevitably work to eliminate surpluses and shortages via changes in prices. Then we went through the supply and demand model in greater detail, working through what moves the market along a curve and what shifts a curve. The basics of the supply and demand model are as follows:

- A **movement along the demand curve** (an increase or decrease in the quantity demanded) is caused by a shift in the supply curve or, as we will see in the next chapter, a government law mandating a legally set minimum or maximum price.
- A **shift in the demand curve** (increase or decrease in demand) is caused by a change in one of the six determinants of demand.
- A **movement along the supply curve** (an increase or decrease in the quantity supplied) is caused by a shift in the demand curve or, as we will see, a government law mandating a legally set minimum or maximum price.
- A **shift in the supply curve** is caused by a change in one of the five determinants of supply.

In almost all cases, a change in a determinant will cause a shift in either the demand curve or the supply curve. Only one curve will shift. However, as we will see in more detail in the next chapter, there are two exceptions to this rule: wages and advertising. **Wages affect consumers' incomes, which shifts the demand curve, but wages also affect suppliers' costs of production, which shifts the supply curve.** Similarly, **advertising affects consumers' tastes and preferences, which shifts the demand curve, but advertising is very costly and any change in costs shifts the supply curve**.

This chapter focused primarily on microeconomic markets and the supply and demand model. As we will see later, macroeconomic markets work on somewhat different principles. Nonetheless, it is important for macroeconomists to be able to anticipate the likely impact of macroeconomic events on microeconomic markets.

QUESTIONS FOR REVIEW

1. Carefully explain what a market is and give *specific* examples of two different kinds of markets.
2. Which of the institutions that make markets work do you think is most important? Why? Explain carefully.
3. Cuba has little history of using markets over the last half century. Suppose that the Cuban government wants to develop a robust market system while still preserving the equality and high level of human development they have achieved via a communist approach. What should they do? Explain in terms of the institutions necessary to support markets.
4. Suppose that the cost of engaging in internet transactions increases substantially due to cybercrime. What are the likely consequences? What markets would be affected, and what types of impacts would you expect to see?
5. Which of the assumptions of the supply and demand model are most likely to cause the model to lead to inaccurate results? Explain carefully. Give specific examples to support your argument.
6. Using a graph of the U.S. market for wheat, show how the supply and demand curves for **wheat** will be affected by specific events, and show what happens to equilibrium price and quantity. (Note: Make sure to identify whether or not the demand and supply curves shift, or whether you are moving along the demand and supply curves.) Draw a new graph for each part (a to d).
    a. Wealth increases due to a boom in the stock market.
    b. Lower oil prices cause the price of fertilizer used in growing wheat to decrease.
    c. Consumers' preferences change toward buying more gluten-free products, so they reduce the amount of products they buy that contain wheat (which contains gluten).

d. Corn prices increase. (Note: Most farmers grow both corn and wheat on their farms. Consumers do not consider wheat and corn to be substitutes or complements.)
7. Using a graph of the U.S. market for Uber rides, show how the supply and demand curves for Uber rides will be affected by specific events, and show what happens to equilibrium price and quantity. (Note: Make sure to identify whether or not the demand and supply curves shift or whether you are moving along the demand and supply curves.) Draw a new graph for each part (a to d).
   a. New, inexpensive technology allows all Uber vehicles to become driverless, replacing existing drivers without compromising service.
   b. The price of Lyft, another type of taxi/ride-sharing service, increases significantly.
   c. An Uber self-driving vehicle has a major accident in which several people die due to a software glitch. Consumers start to prefer rides with non-Uber companies.
   d. Wages increase for workers around the country (including Uber drivers and others) due to an economic boom.
8. Find an article in a major newspaper that describes a change in the price of some type of good or service. Use a graph of supply and demand to explain the forces that caused the price of the good or service to change.

NOTES

1 World Economic Forum, "Corporate Brand Reputation Outranks Financial Performance as Most Important Measure of Success," January 22, 2004. https://www.csrwire.com/press_releases/21696-corporate-brand-reputation-outranks-financial-preformance-as-most-important-measure-of-success, accessed July 26, 2021.

2 Source: Pizza Today, "2019 Top 100 Pizza Companies," November 1, 2019. https://pizzatoday.com/pizzeria-rankings/2019-top-100-pizza-companies/, accessed May 8, 2022.

PART III
Macroeconomic issues and problems

This section provides a broad overview of the current state of macroeconomics and the key issues that macroeconomists are studying.

Chapter 8 introduces modern macroeconomics and the importance of understanding aggregate economics as a different way of thinking than microeconomics. The chapter also describes the evolution of macroeconomic policy, beginning with the Keynesian consensus of the 1950s and 1960s, the return of laissez-faire approaches from 1980 to 2007, and the switch back to Keynesian economics after the financial crisis of 2008-2010 and the coronavirus recession of 2020. Key macroeconomic topics are discussed, including the business cycle, stabilization policy, economic growth, and financial markets.

Chapter 9 discusses economic well-being. There are debates over the most important goals for an economic system and what data we should use to measure, describe, and analyze the macroeconomy. Traditionally, economists used real gross domestic product (real GDP) to measure the health of the economy. However, political economists and some mainstream economists argue that other measures, such as the OECD Better Life Index, the genuine progress indicator, and the United Nations Human Development Index are better measures of welfare due to the limitations of GDP. Some prefer to use measures of happiness.

Subsequently, in Chapter 10, we turn to the major macroeconomic market failures: Unemployment and price instability. The chapter describes the different types of unemployment and the problems that occur due to unemployment. Then, the chapter discusses inflation and deflation and the problems they can cause for the macroeconomy. The chapter includes both mainstream and political economics perspectives on these topics and a case study of unemployment during the Great Recession in the United States and Europe.

We begin the section by describing the evolution of macroeconomic theory and macroeconomic trends in the modern era. The perspectives of economists on macroeconomics changed dramatically over the last century.

Modern macroeconomics

The evolution of macroeconomic theory and the macroeconomy in the modern era

There is a crucial distinction in economics between microeconomics and macroeconomics. **Microeconomics** is **the study of how distinct economic actors, such as consumers, workers, and firms, interact in the economic system**. In a market system, microeconomists study the interactions between buyers and sellers of goods, services, resources, and inputs. Many people have a good, intuitive grasp of how microeconomic markets work, based on their personal experiences and observations operating in markets.

Macroeconomics, however, is much harder to grasp, because many of its inner workings are difficult to discern. **Macroeconomics** is **the study of the aggregate forces that shape national and global economies**. To aggregate means to add up all of the components. When studying the macroeconomy, economists look for trends that are affecting large numbers of consumers, producers, or investors. For example, instead of focusing on consumer demand for one particular product, macroeconomists study **aggregate demand**, which is **the sum of the demands for all goods and services by all economic actors, including households, businesses, banks, and government agencies**.

Macroeconomics focuses on **short-term** and **long-term** issues. A key short-term issue in macroeconomics is the **business cycle**—the patterns of booms and busts created by economic fluctuations in market capitalist economies. Short-term macroeconomic policy focuses on stabilization policies designed to avoid booms and busts and policies to alleviate the worst problems created by the business cycle, especially policies to reduce unemployment and restore economic confidence when the economy falls into a recession. A **recession** is **a generalized slowdown of economic activity where reductions in production result in an increase in unemployment. A decline in production (real gross domestic product, GDP) for six months or more** (at least two quarters) **is considered to be a recession**.

DOI: 10.4324/9780429399350-11

A key long-term macroeconomic issue is how to best generate **economic growth**. Economists try to determine what set of policies will result in the highest rate of economic growth and thereby raise the standard of living of the population. However, economic growth can have a very negative impact on the environment, and it can benefit some groups at the expense of others. Therefore, the details regarding the impact of economic growth on people and the environment are extremely important.

In studying short-term and long-term issues, macroeconomists focus on key macroeconomic goals. The most important goal of a macroeconomy is to provide for the **well-being** of the entire population. The main barriers to human well-being are the intertwined problems of unemployment and poverty, market failures that create widespread deprivation and undermine the stability of an economic system. This is why many countries established full employment as an important goal and why all developed countries have established a safety net to support the most vulnerable in society. Well-being typically includes access to opportunities, meaningful work, leisure time, civic engagement, and the necessities of life.

Improvements in well-being usually depend to a significant degree on economic growth, another important macroeconomic goal. As far back as Adam Smith, some economists have focused on economic growth as the crucial economic topic of study. However, with the steady drumbeat of negative news about the climate and the environment, some economists such as Herman Daly now advocate zero growth and promote the macroeconomic goal of **sustainability**. Policies that promote sustainability without overly compromising economic growth are crucial in the modern era. Typically, economic growth has been accompanied by increased environmental destruction, but this does not have to be the case if appropriate environmental rules and regulations control environmental damage while also promoting the development of new industries.

Another macroeconomic goal is **stability**. Stability fosters investment and growth, whereas uncertainty undermines them. In fostering stability, governments work to avoid severe economic crises, including financial crises. This necessitates careful management of the money supply and monitoring of price levels, because deflation and inflation can both be destructive. Similarly, the financial system, and especially asset markets (such as markets for stocks, bonds, and derivatives), must be monitored and regulated, because financial crises can be particularly debilitating to the macroeconomy. Governments must also work to maintain sufficient aggregate demand in crises, when declines in consumer and investor confidence cause spending to drop.

Macroeconomics is extremely complex. In 2018, the U.S. macroeconomy involved more than 329 million people, 27.9 million businesses, and 22 million government officials interacting in a $21 trillion economy. The global macroeconomy is, of course, even larger, with 7.7 billion people living in 195 countries that utilize many different approaches to economic development and produce more than $80 trillion worth of goods and services. As a result of this complexity, it is difficult to make precise predictions about the macroeconomy, and there is much room for debate about what policies work best. Economists disagree on macroeconomic policy substantially, with a wide variety of approaches.

Broadly speaking, we can characterize four different approaches to structuring a macroeconomy. The **laissez-faire, market-dominated approach** utilizes as little government intervention as possible, even in recessions, preferring unfettered market forces. The **supply-side approach** believes in deregulating markets, while using government intervention on behalf of business. The **New Keynesian, mixed approach** combines markets and the state. New Keynesians see market forces as the primary driver in the economic system but recognize the need for sound regulations, extensive stabilization policies, and a strong safety net to support those who fall upon hard times. In contrast, the **political economy, state-centered approach** sees the need for extensive government guidance of the economic system, with the state restricting or directing many market activities, guiding investment decisions, and providing significant employment via state-owned industries and services. One can also find many economists who fall in between these categories.

In addition, a country's macroeconomic approach does not always reflect the same philosophy as its microeconomic approach to regulation. The United States is considered a market-dominated economic system due to its largely deregulated markets, but its macroeconomic approach involves substantial government intervention in recessions, a mixed market–state approach. Germany is considered to be a social market economy with substantial government intervention in microeconomic markets, but its macroeconomic policy leans toward the laissez-faire approach. Sweden is more consistent, with a highly interventionist approach to both microeconomic and macroeconomic problems reflective of the political economy approach.

This chapter begins by describing the evolution of U.S. macroeconomic history from the Great Depression to the present, along with the changes in macroeconomic theory that have accompanied the changes in the U.S. economic system. The chapter also briefly surveys the economic growth performance of the United States and other economic systems in the modern era.

Subsequently, the chapter discusses the modern business cycle and the different perspectives economists have regarding how the government should respond to recessions.

8.0 CHAPTER 8 LEARNING GOALS

After reading this chapter you should be able to:

- Compare and contrast Say's law with a Keynesian understanding of macroeconomics.

- Define real GDP, unemployment, inflation, and labor force participation and explain how they illustrate an economy's macroeconomic performance.
- Describe the evolution of the U.S. macroeconomy and the global macroeconomy since the Great Depression.
- Analyze how macroeconomic theory has changed in the United States since the Great Depression in response to macroeconomic changes.
- Contrast the views of New Keynesian economists with the views of supply-side, laissez-faire, and political economists.
- Explain the characteristics of the typical modern business cycle in the United States, along with the three major perspectives of economists regarding how the government should respond to recessions.

8.1 KEYNES AND THE BIRTH OF MACROECONOMICS

We begin with a brief overview of modern macroeconomic theory, which will be developed in greater detail in subsequent chapters. As we saw earlier, classical economists such as Adam Smith and David Ricardo did not develop a workable theory to explain the regular business cycles that occur in capitalist economic systems. They focused more on the factors that caused long-term economic growth, such as technological change and the specialization of labor. The neoclassical economists such as Leon Walras and Alfred Marshall who followed Smith and Ricardo emphasized marginal analysis, developing a theory based on the assumption that individual consumers and firms optimized behavior by comparing marginal costs and marginal benefits. According to mainstream, neoclassical theory of the late 1800s and early 1900s, unregulated markets generated the optimal allocation of resources.

Specifically, according to Say's law, supply creates demand: When goods are produced and supplied, this generates an equivalent amount of income, which is then used to purchase (demand) all of the goods produced. Therefore, Say's law implies that there is always enough demand to purchase all products that are produced and overproduction or underconsumption of goods can only be a temporary phenomenon. There can be no involuntary unemployment from this perspective: All workers who desire a job can find one as long as they are willing to accept lower wages when the demand for labor falls. Capital markets efficiently allocate all savings to investment. If consumers spend less and save more, the increase in savings causes an increase in the amount of money in banks, prompting banks to lower interest rates. Lower interest rates can spur investment and offset any decrease in consumer spending. From this rosy perspective, recessions will be solved very quickly by the automatic adjustment mechanisms of the market, and no government intervention is necessary.

However, the Great Depression undermined this perspective thoroughly. By 1940, the idea that the macroeconomy was self-adjusting was no longer widely accepted. The economist who most clearly and successfully explained why neoclassical theory of the time failed was John Maynard Keynes.

Keynes' research demonstrated that (1) **business investment is extremely volatile** and subject to "animal spirits." When businesses lose confidence, investment will plunge and the economy will fall into a recession. Due to the (2) **multiplier process**, once investment or consumer spending falls, this causes declines in income and businesses' sales, causing additional rounds of investment and spending cuts, multiplying the initial change many times over. Keynes also established that (3) **wages and prices are sticky** and do not fall quickly in recessions. Therefore, the economy does not experience increases in the demand for labor or goods that might accompany such price drops. Furthermore, if wages and prices do eventually fall, (4) **deflation can be ruinous for the economy**. Lower wages erode consumer demand for products, which in turn prompts businesses to reduce production and investment. Lower goods prices cause businesses to go bankrupt once the price for which they could sell products falls below the cost of producing goods. The implications are that markets are inherently unstable, they do not correct themselves quickly, and they may linger in recessions indefinitely.

Keynes ushered in the era of the mixed market economy. In microeconomic markets, governments operating capitalist economic systems allowed private firms to produce most goods and services, while regulating firms to prevent the worst excesses of markets. In macroeconomic markets, governments actively engaged in stabilization policies to offset recessions and encouraged economic growth via a variety of economic policies. In the United States, growth-stimulating policies included substantial provision of infrastructure and high-quality education for workers, subsidies for research and development in key industries, and support for technology industries related to national defense. Stabilization policies included the establishment of safety nets such as unemployment insurance and welfare programs, along with increased spending, lower taxes, and lower interest rates in recessions to stimulate aggregate demand.

Meanwhile, European countries and Japan adopted an even more interventionist approach, engaging in substantial government planning to stimulate industrial development in fast-growing sectors. Many of these countries developed extensive safety nets and stabilization policies. The result in the United States, Western Europe, and Japan was rapid economic growth.

8.2 ECONOMIC GROWTH AND PAX AMERICANA, 1945–1973

After the Great Depression, almost all economies experienced economic growth, driven by technological advances and increases in labor productivity. However, the rate of economic growth in a country can vary widely from one decade to the next. Furthermore, some countries may experience robust economic growth while others stagnate. As we will see, market-dominated, social market, and state-dominated economies experienced periods of economic growth during various time periods, with varying degrees of success.

Recall that market-dominated economies (MDEs) are economic systems in which the primary economic decisions are made by private actors (businesses, individuals) operating in market, while the government plays a secondary role. Social market economies (SMEs) are economic systems where social values take a leading role in directing the economy through the actions of a government. State-dominated economies (SDEs) are economic systems in which the government is the main economic actor in most major industries or economic decisions, owning or controlling most of the economy.

From 1945 to 1973, MDEs such as the United States and the United Kingdom and SMEs such as Sweden, Germany, and Japan saw rapid economic growth. SDEs such as the U.S.S.R. and China saw less economic growth during this period. However, as we will see below, since 1973, some SDEs such as China and Vietnam have had better growth performances, as have some SMEs that feature significant government intervention, such as South Korea and Taiwan. The major causes of economic growth are thus complex, with a variety of economic systems experiencing success in different eras utilizing an assortment of approaches.

The United States emerged from World War II in a very favorable economic position. The world's other huge industrial powers, especially in Europe, were devastated by the war. The United States was the dominant economic power, producing 80% of the world's manufactured products, including cars, steel, and high technology goods. U.S. industrial dominance allowed it to pursue a policy of tariff reductions with trading partners to promote unregulated trade flows. This benefited dominant U.S. industries significantly during this era by opening up foreign markets, and it gradually drew more and more countries into the U.S. trading orbit.

The post–World War II boom also proved to be very good for U.S. manufacturing workers, who joined unions in record numbers and experienced rapidly increasing wages. Workers used their higher wages to buy homes, cars, televisions, and other goods. When a country has a large middle class with significant spending power, the demand for products is substantial. The establishment of a basic safety net and the war on poverty under President Lyndon Johnson also supported consumer spending by those at the bottom of the income distribution. The growing consumer demand for products, coupled with Keynesian stabilization policy,

MODERN MACROECONOMICS

Variable	Average Annual Rate of Growth by Decade (%)							
Decade	1950s	1960s	1970s	1980s	1990s	2000s	2010s	2020
Real GDP Growth	4.0	4.1	2.8	2.7	5.4	4.1	2.3	-3.5
Per Capita GDP Growth	5.0	3.2	2.1	2.4	2.2	0.7	1.5	-4.0
Unemployment	4.4	4.8	6.2	7.3	5.8	5.5	6.2	8.1
Labor Force Participation	59.3	59.2	61.5	64.8	66.7	66.2	63.3	61.7
Inflation	2.4	2.0	7.1	6.7	2.9	2.6	1.8	1.3

FIGURE 8.1 Table showing average annual growth rates of key U.S. macroeconomic variables.

provided a very profitable environment for business investment, fostering rapid economic growth.

Figure 8.1 shows how key macroeconomic variables changed since World War II in the United States. The 1950s and 1960s were the golden age of U.S. capitalism, with rapid growth in real GDP, low rates of unemployment, and low rates of inflation.[1]

Real gross domestic product (real GDP) is **the total output of goods and services produced within an area in a given time period, corrected for changes in prices so that real GDP only measures actual changes in the amounts of goods and services produced**. Real GDP *growth* measures the percentage change in real GDP from one year to the next. **Real GDP per capita** is equal to **real GDP divided by the number of people in a country**. Real GDP per capita is one of the best measures of the standard of living for people in a particular country. Growth in real GDP per capita measures how much the standard of living of people in country increased per year, on average. The 1950s and 1960s were the decades in which the United States experienced the most rapid growth in real GDP per capita.

The **unemployment rate** is **the number of people actively seeking work but without a job divided by the labor force**. The **labor force** is a measure of all people available for work, including all people working and all people who are unemployed and are actively seeking work. The **labor force participation rate** measures **the percentage of the population working, self-employed, or unemployed divided by the number of people of working age who are eligible to work in a country**. As such, the labor force participation rate is a good measure of how many people are productively engaged in the economy, especially when combined with the unemployment rate. The unemployment rate stayed at relatively low levels and the labor force participation rate stayed high during the boom times of the 1950s and 1960s. Meanwhile, the inflation rate stayed quite low despite the booming economy.

The **inflation rate** is **the percentage increase in the average level of prices, such as the Consumer Price Index for urban consumers (CPI-U)**. Deflation can be destabilizing, as it was in the Great Depression, so it is to be avoided. However, high levels of inflation can also be problematic, undermining banks and those on fixed incomes. Thus, governments usually pursue price stability, shooting for steady but low levels of inflation such as an inflation rate of 2% per year. The 1950s and 1960s were a wonderful time for the U.S. macroeconomy, with high levels of growth and labor force participation accompanied by low levels of unemployment and inflation. Of course, one of the problems with macroeconomic measures is that they obscure other issues. For example, the 1950s and 1960s were a sign of significant social unrest, featuring the civil rights movement, the Vietnam War protests, and the women's liberation movement, factors not captured by macroeconomic measures.

The period of Pax Americana was also very good for Western Europe, which rebuilt with assistance from the United States via the Marshall Plan. The United States gave $12 billion (an amount that worth $100 billion in 2018 dollars) for reconstruction efforts. The United States also aided Japan and other Asian countries with reconstruction. This investment, along with the peace of the post–World War II era, the stability provided by Keynesian economic policy, and the increase in consumer spending from unionized workers, ushered in an era of rapid growth and prosperity for the United States, Europe, and Japan. Europe and Japan succeeded with social market economies that featured generous social welfare states, substantial investment in education and training, strong unions, and industrial policies designed to stimulate development in key sectors. Japan was particularly successful, with their real GDP per capita increasing by an astounding 9.11% per year in the 1960s.

Meanwhile, beginning in 1945, countries in Africa, Asia, and Latin America gained their independence from colonial powers, allowing them to control their own economic systems. Some were particularly successful, such as Botswana, a country that achieved rapid, sustained economic growth after it achieved independence from Great Britain. Botswana utilized newly discovered diamond deposits to invest in social welfare programs and economic development. Other countries were less successful, with the corrupting, extractive institutions of colonialism proving too tempting for new regimes to ignore. In many countries, new exploiters slipped into place following the exit of colonial exploiters. During the same period, the Soviet Union, Eastern European countries, China, and several smaller countries maintained centrally planned, state-dominated economic systems, many of which became increasingly rigid and dysfunctional over time.

Economic theory of this era was dominated by a moderate form of Keynesian economics, in which most governments undertook modest efforts to stabilize the economy. Meanwhile, a vibrant group of political economists advocated more extensive government ownership and control over markets, to better address problems such as poverty, inequality, and environmental devastation. In addition, a growing group of Austrian and conservative mainstream economists began to challenge the Keynesian consensus. The idea that markets benefited from regulation, stabilization, and guidance was challenged with the advent of two global recessions from oil price shocks in the 1970s and the resulting stagflation, a problem that caused a major rethinking of economic theory and policy.

8.3 OPEC'S OIL SHOCKS AND THE BEGINNINGS OF NEOLIBERAL GLOBALIZATION, 1974–2000

Oil prices quadrupled in 1973 as the Organization of the Petroleum Exporting Countries (OPEC) slashed production and placed an embargo on selling oil to the United States due to U.S. support of Israel during the Arab–Israeli conflict. This exposed the Achilles heel of the U.S. economy: It was extremely dependent on imported oil to run factories and transport goods. The dramatic increase in oil prices caused businesses' costs to rise dramatically, undercutting their profitability and forcing them to lay off workers and raise prices at the same time. This generated stagflation, which occurs **when economic stagnation (declining production and worker layoffs) accompanies inflation**. As you can see in Figure 8.1 (page 183), both unemployment and inflation jumped in the United States in the 1970s compared with previous decades.

Unfortunately, most mainstream Keynesian economists were confounded by how to address stagflation. Mainstream Keynesian policy of the time emphasized stimulating aggregate demand in recessions, via increased government spending, lower interest rates, or lower taxes. However, increased spending in an inflationary environment caused additional inflationary pressures. On the other hand, if policymakers targeted inflation, they could slash government spending, raise interest rates, or raise taxes, reducing spending and reducing inflationary pressures, but this would make stagnation worse, increasing unemployment. Thus, standard Keynesian economics could solve the stagnation problem or the inflation problem, but it could not solve both problems simultaneously. When oil prices doubled again at the end of the 1970s and sparked another bout of stagflation, the circumstances were ripe for a radical rethinking of economic policy.

The stagflation of the 1970s prompted a resurgence in laissez-faire ideas. Austrian and conservative mainstream economists proposed that the main problem in Western economies was too much government regulation, interference, and taxation. Three strains of conservative economics surged to the forefront of mainstream economics. Monetarists, under the guidance of Milton Friedman, suggested that government intervention was hopelessly inefficient and that economies would thrive under a minimum of regulation and intervention. New classical economists, including Robert Lucas Jr. and Eugene Fama, argued that markets were inherently efficient due to the rational, optimizing behavior driving firms and individual actors, reaching a conclusion similar to that of monetarists that government regulation and intervention were intrusive and unnecessary.

Perhaps most important in terms of its influence on policymakers in the United States and the United Kingdom, Arthur Laffer and a group of extremely conservative economists developed the approach labeled supply-side economics. Supply-side economics refers to the belief that **the primary determinant of economic growth is the profitability of suppliers, including corporations** and wealthy business owners. **The best way to achieve profitability is therefore to eliminate regulations and to reduce taxes on corporations and the wealthy.** In theory, such efforts would prompt corporations and the wealthy to invest additional funds in their businesses or to start new ones, stimulating economic growth and reversing the stagflation of the 1970s. This approach is often labeled "**trickle-down economics,**" because tax cuts for the rich are supposed to lead to economic growth, which will (hopefully) create jobs and raise incomes for the poor, so tax cuts for the rich eventually trickle down to help the poor. Furthermore, Laffer argued that, in a high tax environment, cutting taxes would actually stimulate so much growth that *the tax cuts would pay for themselves.* Conservative politicians seized on this approach, which was extremely appealing, because it implied that huge tax cuts for the rich would stoke economic growth but would not result in large government budget deficits.

Conservative economists also promoted the expansion of unregulated trade at the urging of certain U.S. corporations, so firms could obtain resources and labor at lower costs in other countries. In theory, this could also assist corporations by lowering their costs and restoring profitability while opening up new markets abroad. Supply-side economists' faith in the efficiency and rapid adjustment of all markets meant they believed that workers who lost their jobs when some companies moved abroad would be quickly absorbed in growing sectors of the economy.

Another basic tenet of the supply-side approach was a reduction of the social safety net and attacks on labor unions. Supply-side economists believed that generous government benefits and labor unions undermined work efforts, productivity, and profitability.

Collectively, the package of policies was labeled neoliberalism. **Neoliberalism** refers to **contemporary ideas grounded in the classic, laissez-faire liberalism of Adam Smith. Market-oriented policy prescriptions include reducing trade barriers, deregulating financial markets, austerity (especially reductions in spending on the welfare state), deregulation, reduced taxation on the rich, and the privatization of government assets and functions.**

The United States and the United Kingdom entered another recession at the end of the 1970s driven by a second oil price shock generated by the Iranian Revolution of 1979, another event that disrupted oil supplies. This resulted in stagnation along with a high inflation rate that reached 14.8% in the United States. In response, Paul Volcker, the chairman of the Federal Reserve (the Fed), increased interest rates to 20%, causing the economy to experience a steep decline. The Fed is the U.S. national bank, and it has the power to set interest rates, manipulate the money supply, and serve as the lender of last resort to failing banks. When the Fed increased interest rates to 20%, very few consumers were willing to buy houses and cars on credit, and very few businesses were willing to borrow to invest in new or expanded business ventures. Consumer spending and business investment spending plunged. Unemployment increased to over 10% as the economy entered a deep recession, but inflation finally began to fall. This series of events proved that *the*

Fed can eliminate substantial inflationary pressures but only by incurring a steep increase in unemployment. This was a high price to pay, as millions lost jobs, devastating families and communities.

In this fraught environment, a message of tax cuts, deregulation, and unregulated trade was espoused by President Ronald Reagan in the United States and Prime Minister Margaret Thatcher in England, both of whom were elected as their countries faced a serious economic crisis. Beginning in 1979, Thatcher embarked on a radical restructuring of the U.K. economy. More than 80% of state-owned firms were privatized (sold to the private sector), including the national train system. The top tax rate on the wealthy was slashed from 83% to 40%, social programs were cut, and labor unions were attacked. The U.K. economy recovered from the recession, but inequality exploded and conditions for many workers deteriorated in the face of job and program cuts.

President Reagan undertook similar policies, cutting the tax rate on the richest individuals in the United States from 70% to 28% and working to undermine labor unions. Reagan also increased defense spending significantly as part of the cold war with the U.S.S.R., while cutting some social programs. The tax cuts and increased defense spending helped to end the deep recession of 1981–1982, along with lower interest rates and the rebounding of markets. As with Thatcher's approach, Reagan's policies affected people differently. The rich benefited significantly, but wages stayed stagnant for workers. U.S. economic growth in the 1980s was better than in the 1970s but worse than the U.S. growth performance in the 1950s, 1960s, or 1990s. In addition, the national debt of the U.S. government quadrupled in the 1980s with the combination of increased defense spending and lower taxes. The supply-side tax cuts failed to pay for themselves.

The experience of high inflation during the 1970s made central banks such as the Fed wary of any signs of inflation. When inflation reached 6% at the end of the 1980s, the Fed once again increased interest rates dramatically, this time to 10%, to squeeze the economy and wring out inflation. High interest rates, slowing growth, and a crisis in the Middle East that led to the first Iraq war led to the recession of 1990–1991. It is important to note that both the recession of the early 1980s and the recession of 1990 were driven largely by tight monetary policy of the Fed in which they restricted the money supply to raise interest rates.

After a sluggish recovery, the rise of the internet and information technology in the late 1990s caused the U.S. economy to enter another boom. The rapid development of the internet caused companies to invest vast amounts of money in new technologies, including computing, fiber-optic cables, social media, and more. Huge numbers of startups grew rapidly as e-commerce and social media platforms developed for the first time.

Meanwhile, Presidents George H. W. Bush (a Republican) and Bill Clinton (a Democrat) continued to enact policies to deregulate markets, especially financial markets, and to reduce social programs. Bush negotiated the initial outlines of the North American Free Trade Agreement with Canada and Mexico to reduce dramatically the tariffs between the neighboring countries, and Clinton signed the agreement into law. Clinton also signed a welfare reform bill that significantly slashed federal funding for the poorest Americans. Thus, Bush and Clinton largely continued Reagan's approach of deregulation, cuts to social programs, and the pursuit of unregulated trade. The U.S. economy in the 1980s and 1990s had been restructured so that the gains went to the richest Americans, whereas workers experienced stagnant wages.

The pursuit of unregulated trade and changes in the global economy began to devastate manufacturing communities in the United States and Western Europe in the 1970s. Manufacturing employment in the United States fell from 19 million in the 1970s to less than 13 million in the 2010s, driven by international competition, the movement of U.S. manufacturing jobs overseas, and the rise of increasingly sophisticated robotic technology that could replace workers. The U.S. Midwest suffered, including Detroit, Cleveland, Youngstown, Pittsburgh, Milwaukee, and Allentown, becoming the core of the "rust belt" of declining industrial cities. Poverty and unemployment in these communities increased. Fueled by worsening economic conditions and cuts to social programs, homelessness became a national disgrace beginning in the 1980s. The U.S. technology sector boomed with the growth of the internet and new information technologies, but manufacturing workers were unprepared for jobs in those sectors, and most were unable to benefit from the tech boom. Some of these problems were tied to the rise of global competition in manufacturing.

8.4 THE RISE OF GLOBAL COMPETITORS TO THE UNITED STATES

Beginning in the 1970s, U.S. corporations faced increasing competition from international firms. By this time, Europe had recovered from World War II and European firms were globally competitive, especially in high-end manufacturing and luxury goods. Japan, South Korea, Taiwan, and Malaysia developed into industrial powerhouses, using protectionism and government support to develop from light industry (such as textiles) to heavy industry (steel, shipbuilding) to refined manufactured goods (computers, electronics, cars). Their rapid growth was facilitated by the U.S. push for less regulated trade, lower tariffs, and increasingly unregulated and open financial markets, policies that allowed financiers from all over the world to invest in emerging markets.

Figure 8.2 shows that average annual growth of real GDP per capita for a variety of regions and countries.[2] If a country experiences rapid and sustained growth in real GDP per capita, the economy is undergoing a tremendous economic transformation. An annual growth rate of 3% in real GDP per capita would mean that the average person is 34% better off after a decade. Japan's annual growth rate of 9.11% in the 1960s meant that Japanese incomes increased by 239%, more than

Region	Average Annual Growth Rate of Real GDP (%) by Decade					
	1960s	1970s	1980s	1990s	2000s	2010s
European Union	4.21	3.07	2.04	1.94	1.29	1.37
East Asia and Pacific	6.27	2.73	3.42	2.44	3.45	3.99
Sub-Saharan Africa	1.59	1.57	-1.29	-0.77	2.47	0.87
Latin America and Caribbean	2.71	3.61	0.02	1.01	1.68	1.12
Central Europe and the Baltics				1.47	4.30	3.13
Middle East and North Africa	8.54	5.49	-3.00	2.1	2.27	1.32
South Asia (IDA and IBRD)	1.87	0.65	3.18	3.3	4.24	5.34
World	3.52	2.07	1.24	1.12	1.56	1.81
Country						
Japan	9.11	3.06	3.70	1.23	0.41	1.52
Korea, Republic of (South)	6.71	8.55	7.46	6.13	4.09	2.82
Botswana	5.41	11.77	7.48	2.72	1.56	3.30
China	1.23	5.27	8.17	8.76	9.68	7.25
Malaysia	3.55	5.55	3.11	4.53	2.69	3.93
India	1.77	0.59	3.34	3.74	4.6	5.79
Vietnam			2.23	5.59	5.62	5.15

FIGURE 8.2 Table showing average annual growth of real GDP per capita in regions, 1961–2018.

doubling in a decade! Notice that East Asia and the Pacific, including Japan, South Korea, and Malaysia, experienced extraordinary growth in real per capita GDP in the 1960s, 1970s, and 1980s, with South Korea and Malaysia continuing to grow rapidly after that, while Japan's growth slowed.

China also began to grow quickly after the death of Mao in 1976, when they began a series of dramatic reforms to move from command communism to a form of state capitalism. China began by building incentives into their central planning system, encouraging farmers and firms to increase productivity. Under Mao, farmers and firms were required to meet a production quota established by the state. They did not benefit from producing above their quota and could even end up worse off. Producing in excess of one's quota was dangerous, because the state might increase your quota the next year once you demonstrated the ability to produce a larger amount. After 1978, the Chinese state began to allow farmers and firms to sell goods they produced in excess of their state-mandated quota in newly created markets for a profit. This caused a dramatic increase in production because farms and firms had incentives to increase production above their government quota.

China also created special economic zones (SEZs) where firms could operate in an unregulated trade environment, sparking the development of a robust private sector. China then enticed foreign companies to these SEZs, offering them access to the vast and growing Chinese market along with low wages and government support, in exchange for a commitment from foreign firms to work with a Chinese partner and to transfer the latest technology to Chinese operations. Seeing vast potential in China, U.S. and European companies were happy to participate.

Another change in incentives came when the Chinese government began to be reward officials with bonuses and promotions when their regions experienced rapid economic growth, prompting a national focus on state-led economic development. As Figure 8.2 shows, China experienced the most rapid structural transformation in modern history, with unparalleled economic growth rates from the 1980s through the 2010s.

India followed China in becoming a rapidly growing emerging market after 1991. India was the most protected economy in the world in 1991, with an inefficient and intrusive bureaucracy. They embarked on a series of reforms to reduce tariffs, open markets, and improve government efficiency, just as the internet revolution was occurring. The combination of India's superb education system, excellent English language skills, and the new information technology revolution allowed India to become a global hub for call centers and computer services.

However, other countries were largely excluded from these shifts. Latin America and sub-Saharan Africa experienced growth in the 1960s and 1970s, but their growth in real GDP per capita was lower in the 1980s and 1990s. Most countries in these regions still depended on the export of primary products such as cocoa, coffee, copper, and other agricultural and mining products, and they were not able to move successfully into new industries. The commodity boom of the 2000s temporary sparked growth, but the 2010s saw Latin America and sub-Saharan Africa falling further behind the rest of the world as commodity prices declined.

With the opening of financial markets and the explosion of growth in Asia in the 1990s, vast sums of international money began to flow into Asia. Investors in developed countries wanted to cash in on the rapid growth that was generating huge returns in many Asian markets. Investors acted as if the good times could never end, funneling vast sums into increasingly questionable ventures. Banks loaned money to companies that were not performing well in Asian markets, and defaults began to pile up. Government support for banks and industries in many Asian countries masked growing problems. Eventually, investors realized their folly and started to pull their money out of Asian investments and markets. Panic ensued, causing bank failures and currency crashes in Thailand, Malaysia, Indonesia, South Korea, Singapore, Hong Kong, and Japan, and neighboring countries experienced smaller problems. This was the first warning sign that the deregulation of financial markets was resulting in unsustainable and destructive speculative behavior.

8.5 FINANCIALIZATION AND NEOLIBERAL GLOBALIZATION, 2000–2022

The tech boom of the 1990s prompted an internet stock bubble, called the dot-com bubble, to form late in the decade in the United States. As it became increasingly clear that the internet was the hot new business opportunity, money poured into new internet companies, and their stock prices exploded. From 1995 and 2000, the NASDAQ Composite Index of technology stocks rose 400%. Many companies saw their stock prices increase by 1000% to 2000%. However, most of the companies that people were investing in were not profitable. Sparked by a recession in Japan and an increasing realization that many internet companies would never become profitable, a mass sell-off began in March 2000. The huge loss of paper wealth caused consumers to panic, cutting spending on houses, cars, and other consumer goods. Business investment also plummeted, and the economy entered a recession. Further pessimism followed the terrorist attacks of September 11, 2001. By October 2002, the 100 biggest companies on the NASDAQ stock index had lost 78% of their value. Numerous companies went bankrupt, and others laid off workers.

President George W. Bush, a Republican and the son of President George H. W. Bush, used the recession of 2000–2001 to call for another round of tax cuts targeting investors and the wealthy. This indicated the ongoing influence of supply-side economic policy in the Republican Party. Stimulated by tax cuts, low interest rates, and the normal economic recovery process, the U.S. economy entered another period of economic growth beginning in 2003. However, the boom was to be short-lived.

As was noted above, beginning in the 1970s, the macroeconomics discipline shifted rapidly away from Keynesian economics. Supply-side economics, monetarism, and new classical economics, all strains of laissez-faire macroeconomics, gained traction. The election of conservative presidents elevated the ideas of laissez-faire economists so that they came to influence government policy. One of the ideas used to drive policy changes was the efficient market hypothesis.

Developed by Eugene Fama, the **efficient market hypothesis** posited that **financial markets always incorporate all available information and function in an efficient manner, so asset prices (the prices of stocks, bonds, and derivatives) are always accurate and cannot form irrational bubbles**. Fama believed that the hypercompetitive nature of financial markets forced firms to be rational, calculating, and ruthlessly efficient.

Based on this theory, Republican and Democratic presidents and congresses systematically deregulated financial markets from the 1980s to the 2000s. What government officials and laissez-faire economists forgot were the lessons of history regarding the herd-like "animal spirits" of investors.

In the early 2000s, banks began making increasingly risky investments in derivatives. In financial markets, a **derivative** is **a financial security whose value is derived from an underlying asset or group of assets**. Derivatives involve a contract between two or more economic actors, and the value of the derivative varies with the fluctuations in the value of the asset(s) underlying the derivative. In many cases, a derivative is a bet between two parties, with one party betting that the value of the asset will fall and the other betting that the value of the asset will rise.

As we will see in more detail later, in the 2000s, banks began issuing vast quantities of increasingly complex derivatives. For example, banks began giving large mortgages to increasingly risky "sub-prime" borrowers with bad credit ratings, including first-time homeowners and speculators lured by rapidly rising real estate prices in urban areas. Then, banks bundled millions of dollars of these risky mortgages into derivatives called collateralized mortgage obligations (CMOs), which they then sold to investors. Mortgages had historically been a very safe investment, and the derivatives were so complex that it was difficult to determine that they were risky, so investors snapped them up because of the high expected returns and their belief that mortgages would have low default rates. So much money was being made on sub-prime loans that by 2006 over 20% of all mortgages were being given to sub-prime borrowers, amounting to more than $600 billion in 2006 alone. This helped spark a large, rapid increase in the demand for homes and in home prices.

However, as one might expect, many of the high-risk, sub-prime borrowers began to default on their loans after a few years. Housing prices peaked and began to fall, causing housing speculators to default in increasing numbers. As mortgage defaults increased in number and magnitude, the derivatives on which those mortgages were based became worthless, causing the investors who purchased them to lose their investment. The crisis spun out of control, with homeowner defaults and a crash in the real estate market, followed by bankruptcies in large banks and insurance companies that had invested in housing market derivatives.

The result was the worst financial crisis since 1929. Once again, deregulated financial markets led to a speculative bubble and subsequent crash. The bank failures and the resulting crash in property values were devastating. The economy experienced the Great Recession from 2008 to 2010, which was the worst recession since the Great Depression of the 1930s.

Under President Barack Obama and a Democratic congress, a new set of financial regulations was passed to reign in banks' speculative behavior, and the government resumed Keynesian economic policy, spending large amounts to reduce the severity of the Great Recession and bail out failing banks. However, the financial crisis was so severe that economic growth remained sluggish for years after the official end of the recession. Slow growth and ongoing depressions in rust belt cities created conditions that Donald Trump was able to exploit to win the 2016 election, promising to return jobs to the United States from China, Mexico, and other countries. Trump engaged in a series of trade wars to attempt to promote U.S. exports, although these did not achieve a significant impact. Trump's other policies included traditional supply-side measures, such as huge tax cuts aimed at the very rich and corporations, and deregulation related to the environment, food, health, and safety. After a botched response to the COVID-19 pandemic of 2020, Trump was replaced by President Joe Biden, who reintroduced Keynesian stimulus policies and regulations. Thus, the period from 2000 to 2022 found the United States lurching from supply-side tax cuts and deregulation under Bush to Keynesian-style regulation under Obama, back to supply-side policies under Trump, and returning to Keynesian policies under Biden.

Looking back at the changes in economic policy since the Great Depression, we see Keynesian economic policy dominant until the 1970s. After that, supply-side economics became dominant in the United States and the United Kingdom, where its adherents focused on reducing businesses' costs by attacking unions, reducing regulations, and facilitating global trade, while cutting taxes for the wealthy and for businesses. Unfortunately, supply-side policies were not successful in rejuvenating economic growth in the United States. After rapid growth in the 1950s and 1960s, the United States experienced steadily declining growth in real GDP after 1970, as shown in Figure 8.3 on the next page.

We will return to the debate over why economic growth in the United States slowed later in the book.

The previous several sections focused on the long-term issue of economic growth, sketching out the gradual evolution of the U.S. macroeconomy and macroeconomic policy since the Great Depression. Another key issue in macroeconomics is the business cycle and what economic policies (if any) should be used to stabilize the business cycle.

8.6 MACROECONOMIC PATTERNS OF THE MODERN BUSINESS CYCLE

Economists have identified a set of macroeconomic patterns that characterize the business cycles of the mixed market economies of the world since the Great Depression. The patterns include the following key characteristics:

- The macroeconomy experiences regular business cycles, with strong growth periods followed by recessions (crises). The cycles occur approximately every 8 to 12 years. Economists often disagree on the causes of these regular crises and the actions that governments should take to stabilize economic systems in the face of a crisis.
- Most governments use expansionary fiscal policy (increasing government spending or decreasing taxes) and expansionary monetary policy (increasing the money supply and reducing interest rates) in recessions to stabilize the economy. This is a New Keynesian approach.
- Prices and wages tend to increase slightly during economic booms but stop increasing during recessions. However, in recent decades, increases in prices and wages have been quite limited in most developed economies even during economic booms.
- Unemployment increases dramatically in recessions and decreases during booms.

Figure 8.4 (page 195) displays U.S. real GDP and potential real GDP, which is **the output of goods and services that would be produced if the economy were utilizing all of its productive resources, including all of its**

194 MACROECONOMIC ISSUES AND PROBLEMS

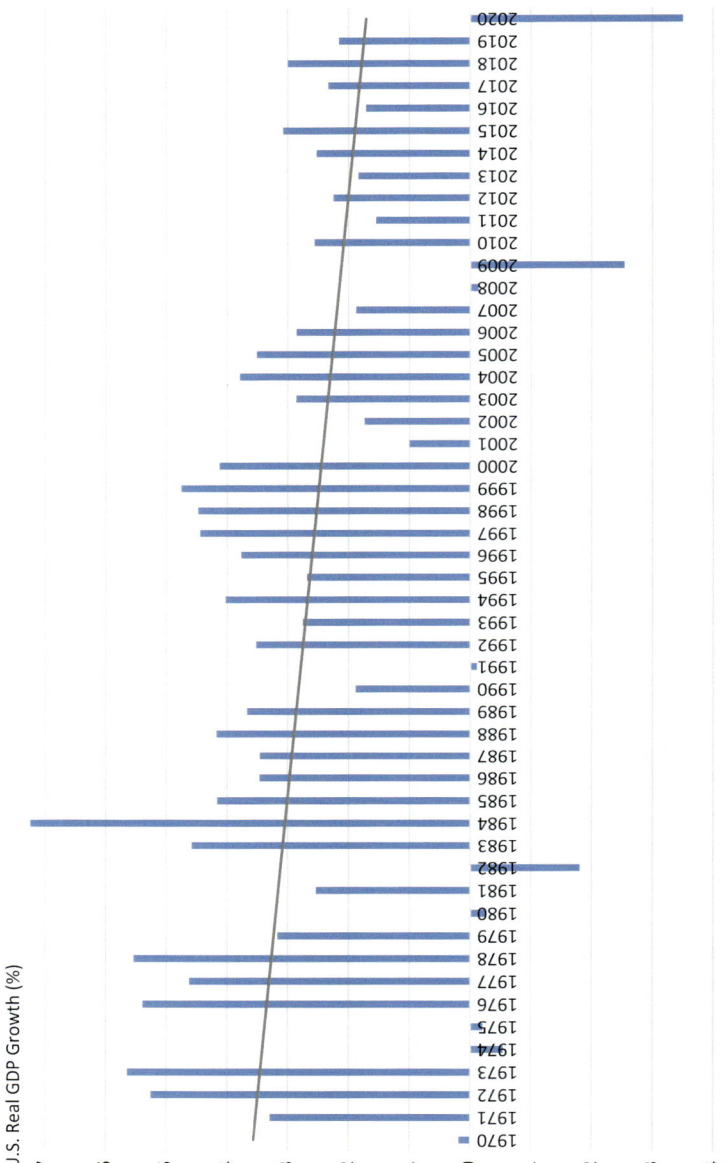

FIGURE 8.3 Annual U.S. real GDP growth, 1970–2020.

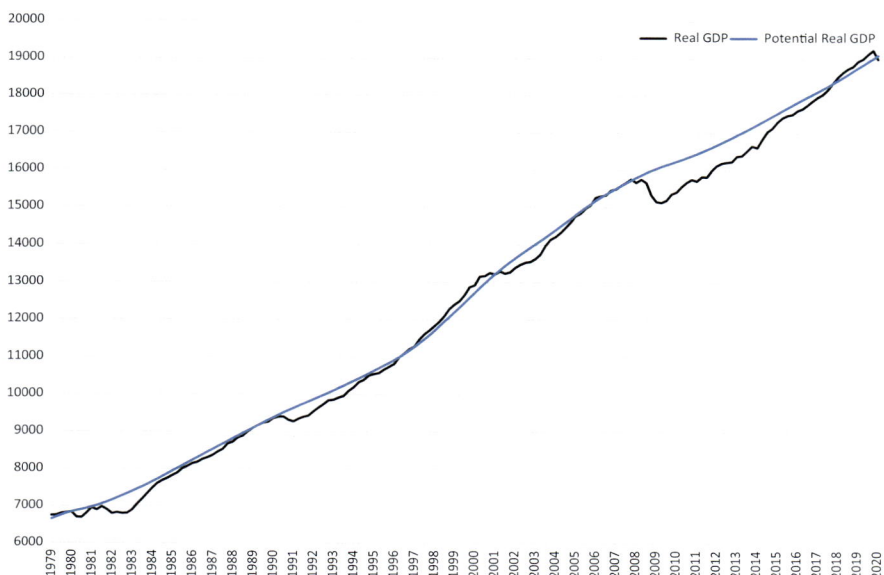

FIGURE 8.4 U.S. real GDP and potential real GDP (billions of $), 1979–2019.

employable workers and all of its capital stock. To measure potential real GDP, economists estimate the general trend in real GDP, while smoothing out business cycle fluctuations. This allows economists to estimate how far above or below normal capacity the economy is at any given time. The gap between potential and real GDP can serve as a guide to macroeconomic policy.

If real GDP is below potential real GDP, the economy is operating at below capacity (a recession or a slowdown). In such cases, most economists believe that the government should undertake efforts to stimulate economic growth, including increased government spending, decreased taxes, or decreased interest rates. If real GDP is above potential real GDP, the economy is overheated, which is likely to result in inflation and/or a bubble that could lead to a crash in asset values. In an overheated economy, most economists believe that the government should attempt to slow down economic growth and reduce asset prices, which it can achieve by reducing government spending, increasing taxes, or increasing interest rates. The goal in an overheated economy is to achieve a "soft landing," gently slowing down the economy to eliminate inflationary pressures and asset bubbles to avoid a recession.

Figure 8.4 shows us that the U.S. economy grew significantly in recent decades, from a real GDP of $6742 billion in 1979 to $19,254 billion in 2019. However, it also shows that the U.S. economy regularly falls into recessions, when real GDP falls below potential real GDP, indicating that a significant number of workers are unemployed and capital resources lie idle. The United States experienced recessions in 1980 and 1982 (a double-dip recession), 1990, 2000, 2008, and 2020. After each of these recessions, the U.S. economy stayed well below its capacity, potential real GDP, for several years before finally recovering. Thus, Figure 8.4 depicts two essential characteristics of a modern, mixed market economic system: Steady growth over time, with regular recessions every 8 to 12 years.

Figure 8.5 shows the unemployment rate and the inflation rate in the United States from 1979 to 2020. Notice that when a recession hits, we tend to see a decrease in the rate of inflation and a sharp increase in the rate of unemployment. Unemployment then falls as the economy grows out of the recession and starts to boom, while inflation increases. The pattern repeats itself with the next recession.

A key question that emerges from these patterns is whether or not the government should take action to address the fluctuations in the business cycle. There are four primary approaches to macroeconomic policy with respect to business cycles: Laissez-faire (noninterventionist), supply-side (trickle-down), New Keynesian (moderate intervention), and political economy (intensely interventionist, especially in recessions).

According to the **laissez–faire approach**, advocated by most monetarist, new classical, and Austrian economists, the government should not intervene significantly in the macroeconomy, even in recessions. To these economists, government intervention is too cumbersome and inept to successfully manage the economy. Furthermore, they oppose increased government borrowing to finance spending projects in recessions, worrying that government borrowing will displace or "crowd out" private sector investment, taking money from banks that would normally be used by the private sector.

The laissez-faire approach has had limited impact on policies in recessions in the United States. However, the European Union government and central bank

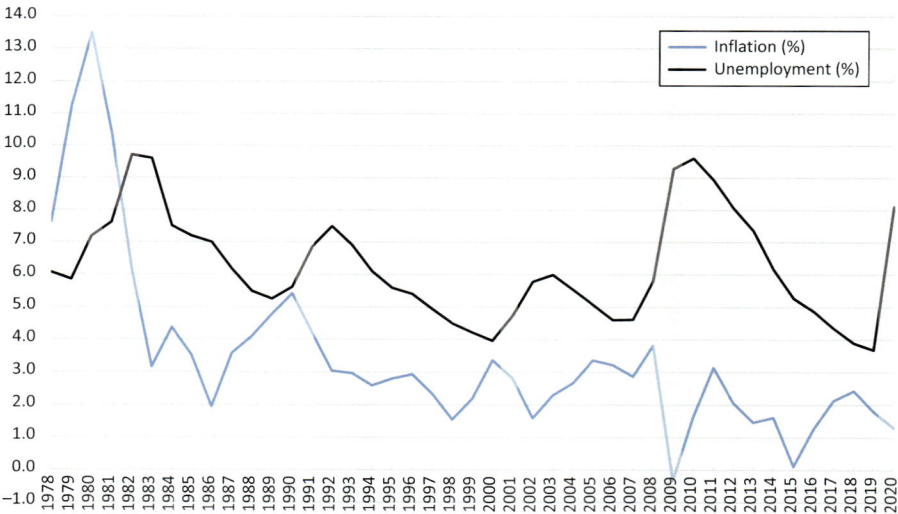

FIGURE 8.5 U.S. unemployment rate (%) and rate of inflation (CPI_u, %), 1979–2020.

subscribed to a laissez-faire approach early on in the Great Recession. They refused to take substantial steps to reduce the severity of the downturn by spending additional money and injecting new money into the financial sector. In contrast, from 2008 to 2010, the United States spent additional money on government projects, lowered interest rates, and purchased bad debts from banks in order to stimulate the economy. As a result, the U.S. economy recovered much more quickly from the Great Recession than the European Union's economy.

The **supply-side approach** advocates government policies to benefit suppliers in recessions to stabilize the economy. In particular, bailouts for failing businesses, low interest rates, and tax cuts for corporations and wealthy business owners are favored policies from this conservative perspective. Such policies were proposed by the George W. Bush administration in 2001 and 2008 and by the Trump administration in 2020.

The **New Keynesian approach** is advocated by most mainstream economists.[3] In recessions, these economists advocate increasing government spending and lowering taxes, both of which will increase government deficits but also stimulate economic growth. Ideally, the economic growth will spark a boom during which deficits can be repaid. New Keynesians also advocate cutting interest rates and injecting financial capital into the banking system during recessions to stimulate lending and borrowing. Meanwhile, during economic booms, New Keynesians advocate reductions in government spending, higher taxes, and higher interest rates if the economy starts to grow too quickly (e.g., if it becomes overheated and starts to form a bubble that might burst). *The U.S. government has followed a moderate Keynesian approach in every recent recession*, working to enact modest stimulus programs such as lower taxes, increased spending, extended unemployment benefits, and decreased interest rates whenever the economy experienced a recession. The main difference between the New Keynesian approach and the supply-side approach is the focus of the programs. New Keynesians prefer policies and tax cuts to benefit workers and communities and to stimulate aggregate demand, whereas supply-side economists target the wealthy, corporations, and aggregate supply. The Biden administration took a New Keynesian approach in the United States in 2021 to cope with the lingering effects of the coronavirus recession.

Some economists think that the U.S. government usually does not go far enough in recessions. The **political economy approach** includes progressive and radical political economists (and a few liberal mainstream economists) who want the government to intervene more extensively. From this perspective, the capitalist economic system is inherently unstable and structured to benefit capitalists over workers. Only via active, widespread stabilization policy on behalf of workers can unemployment be minimized and growth stimulated. From this perspective, substantial government investment in infrastructure, employment, and new industrial development, such as the Green New Deal proposal to create new, environmentally friendly technologies and industries, is required to create a stable macroeconomy that benefits workers.

What we find, therefore, is that most economists agree on the necessity for Keynesian intervention in recessions, with the exception of a few far-right, laissez-faire economists. What economists usually debate is the extent of the Keynesian intervention that should take place, with conservative mainstream economists preferring the smallest possible intervention; supply-side and New Keynesian (moderate) economists preferring more interventionist actions, albeit with a different focus; and political economists preferring extensive government action on behalf of workers and the poor. We see similar divisions in the area of sustainability.

8.7 SUSTAINABILITY AND MACROECONOMICS

Sustainability refers to **the ability of an economic system to sustain itself over time by meeting its current needs without compromising its future. Sustainability has three primary dimensions: Environmental, social, and financial.**

Environmental sustainability refers to the need for an economic system to preserve its environmental services, including sources and sinks, sufficiently for future generations. If an economy grows rapidly but destroys its environmental services in the process, future growth will be more difficult. The economic system will need to devote increasing amounts of investment toward correcting environmental devastation and finding alternatives to spent resources.

With climate change and an increasingly interlocked global economy, environmental sustainability has a global character. If one country reduces its carbon emissions but other countries increase theirs, the country reducing its carbon emissions will still experience the problems associated with increasing carbon emissions globally, including global warming, ocean acidification, heat waves, and more. It is crucial in the modern world for environmental sustainability to be attacked globally rather than nationally, making global climate agreements extremely important in the current era.

A small number of far-right economists oppose efforts to reduce carbon emissions and to establish environmental regulations. Most conservative economists (laissez-faire and supply-side) believe the government should make modest efforts to promote environmental sustainability utilizing market-based methods such as carbon taxes and subsidies for alternative energy. New Keynesian economists advocate more extensive regulations and a more elaborate system of taxes and subsidies to promote sustainability, in keeping with the mixed market–state approach. Political economists argue that capitalism is inherently unsustainable because it promotes profit accumulation and economic growth to the exclusion of environmental preservation. From this state-centered perspective, extensive government intervention is warranted to severely constrain market activity or to promote public enterprises with a goal of sustainability.

Social sustainability refers to the importance of an economic system providing an acceptable standard of living to its entire population. Extremely unequal economic systems are prone to instability, and even revolution. Two of the market failures most commonly associated with unregulated capitalism are inequality and poverty. Therefore, most countries devote substantial resources to a safety net that protects the most vulnerable members of society to ensure that people do not become desperate. Similarly, economic systems need to be fair and provide everyone with sufficient opportunities. Otherwise, resentment and desperation can lead to a social breakdown, with crime, homelessness, and pressures for radical change becoming more prevalent.

Laissez-faire and supply-side economists tend to believe that unregulated markets generate the most opportunities and the most robust economic growth and that most inequality is a product of poor choices of individuals. Therefore, they tend to oppose extensive safety nets, other than a modest minimum income guarantee, suggested by Friedrich Hayek to make sure that poverty and deprivation do not become too extreme. New Keynesian economists believe a safety net is extremely important and that the government should work actively to reduce inequality and poverty. From their perspective, markets tend to be biased toward those with wealth and connections, and such imperfections need to be corrected by government policy. Political economists want to go much further, arguing that capitalist economies systematically exploit workers and leave many destitute, requiring extensive government intervention and job creation to create social stability.

Lastly, financial sustainability is important to an economic system. Financial sustainability requires an economic system to maintain manageable levels of debt in the public sector and the private sector. Growing public sector debt can become a drag on an economic system, with payments on the debt consuming an ever-increasing portion of real GDP. Growing private sector debt can make companies and individuals prone to bankruptcy, exacerbating economic crises. In addition, debt to foreign countries can be particularly problematic if a country encounters an economic crisis.

For example, Turkey borrowed extensively from foreign banks in foreign currencies to fund construction projects under the rule of Recep Tayyip Erdoğan. Many of these were excessive and wasteful, such as the 1150-room Presidential Palace, so the economic impact was short-lived. Turkey's steadily increasing foreign debts caused the Turkish lira to lose significant amounts of value. In 2005, one U.S. dollar exchanged for 1.34 Turkish lira in international currency markets. In 2021, one U.S. dollar exchanged for 7.33 Turkish lira. By 2021 the Turkish lira was worth only 18% of what it was in 2005. This meant that money Turkey borrowed in 2005 from U.S. banks required 547% more Turkish lira to repay, placing a huge burden on the Turkish economy and contributing to the formation of a recession.

Note, however, that debt can facilitate economic growth if the money is invested wisely. If governments invest funds in growth-generating projects, such as education, infrastructure, and research and development, this sparks economic growth in the future and pays for itself over time. Governments that use their own currency to make wise investments, without incurring foreign debt, often generate better economic growth than governments that do not do so.

As with other areas, economists differ in how they approach financial sustainability. Laissez-faire conservatives tend to oppose government deficit spending, preferring to leave investment to the private sector. Supply-side conservatives do not mind government deficits for tax cuts for the wealthy, believing this will generate enough growth to offset the tax cuts. New Keynesians tend to believe that the government is safe engaging in deficit spending in recessions and investing in growth-generating projects, as long as the budget deficit remains a steady proportion of real GDP. They do not want the debt burden to increase over time. Political economists, on the other hand, are less concerned with government deficits and more concerned with the welfare of workers. They believe that spending money on those at the bottom stimulates aggregate demand, which stimulates economic growth. Therefore, political economists see deficit spending as one of the major sources of economic growth and prosperity. We will investigate all of these perspectives in more detail later.

8.8 CONCLUSION: THE STATE OF MODERN MACROECONOMICS

This chapter introduced the issues that are the primary focus of study for macroeconomists: Economic growth, well-being, stability, and sustainability. Economists studying these issues tend to fall into four perspectives: Laissez-faire, supply-side, New Keynesian, and political economy. Laissez-faire economists prefer the least possible government intervention in the macroeconomy. Supply-side economists also prefer deregulation of markets, but they are comfortable utilizing government on behalf of business and the wealthy. New Keynesian economists believe that markets usually function efficiently but that they need some government intervention when markets fail, such as in recessions. Political economists argue that markets are inherently unstable and unequal and can only function on behalf of all citizens with substantial state guidance, regulation, and direction.

Macroeconomic theory changed substantially during the last century. Prior to the Great Depression, most mainstream economists believed that capitalist economic systems were inherently efficient and would eliminate any downturn in short order, based on their belief in Say's law, an economic theory that supply creates demand. The Great Depression ushered in the ideas of John Maynard Keynes, whose research demonstrated that business investment and consumer spending are extremely volatile and cause large swings in economic output. At the same time, wages and prices are sticky and do not adjust quickly in recessions, and lower wages and prices (deflation) turn out to be very bad for the economy, undermining consumer spending and business profits. Thus, to Keynes, economies tend to be unstable and prone to regular recessions, but the government can end recessions with appropriate macroeconomic policy, including increases in government spending, decreased taxes, decreased interest rates, and injecting liquidity into the banking system.

Keynesian views dominated the economics profession from the 1940s until the 1970s, the period during which the United States dominated the global economy. However, stagflation in the 1970s caused a rethinking of economic views and prompted the ascendency of laissez-faire and supply-side views. Supply-side economics became particularly powerful due to its links with conservative republican politicians beginning with Ronald Reagan. The United States and other countries such as the United Kingdom embarked on a macroeconomic approach that emphasized lowering tariffs, deregulating trade and industrial development, and cutting taxes for the wealthy and for large corporations. Meanwhile, the U.S. Federal Reserve raised interest rates dramatically in the early and late 1980s, successfully reducing inflationary pressures but causing recessions and high unemployment in the process.

Global competition to U.S. manufacturing increased substantially beginning in the 1970s, especially from Japan, followed by South Korea and the Asian tigers and, more recently, by China and India. Deregulation of trade allowed U.S. corporations to move abroad, and many did so to take advantage of low wages and lax regulations. Deregulation of financial markets allowed banks and individuals to invest in increasingly risky and obtuse assets, such as derivatives, sparking a series of speculative bubbles resulting in the Asian Financial Crisis, the dot-com bubble, and the sub-prime mortgage bubble. Supply-side economic policies were reversed somewhat under President Obama in the United States, were reinstated under President Trump, and then reversed again under President Biden.

Throughout the recent history of the United States, its economy experienced regular recessions, usually ever 8 to 12 years. Most economists advocate government intervention to reduce the severity of recessions, a New Keynesian approach. Some conservative economists prefer a laissez-faire approach with limited or no government intervention in recessions. In contrast, conservative, supply-side economists advocate bailouts of businesses and tax cuts in recessions, an approach that results in large government budget deficits. Meanwhile, political economists prefer extensive government intervention to benefit workers and the poor during recessions and are comfortable with large government budget deficits from such programs.

There are similar divisions with respect to how economists view sustainability. Political economists see the need for substantial government efforts to address sustainability, New Keynesian economists want some intervention, and conservative laissez-faire and supply-side economists prefer less intervention.

Interestingly, one of the topics economists debate extensively is how we should measure the health of the macroeconomy. Since the Great Depression, most economists tended to focus on the growth of real GDP as the best measure of the health of an economic system. However, as we will see in the next chapter, real GDP does not adequately capture many aspects of well-being, so modern economists are developing a new set of measures to reflect more accurately how the macroeconomy functions in all of its multifaceted elements.

QUESTIONS FOR REVIEW

1. List the key goals economists have identified for a macroeconomic system. Which do you think is most important? Why?
2. How did Keynes demonstrate that Say's law would not hold in recessions and that the market would not self-correct itself?
3. Describe the evolution of post–World War II macroeconomic thinking as it relates to changes in global economies. What ideas dominated during Pax Americana? How did these ideas change with the advent of stagflation and the beginnings of neoliberal globalization? What did economists learn from the Asian financial crisis, the dot-com bubble, and the sub-prime housing bubble?
4. Define each of the following economic concepts in your own words, and briefly explain why the concept is important.
    a. Real GDP.
    b. Real GDP per capita.
    c. Unemployment rate.
    d. Labor force participation rate.
    e. Inflation rate.
5. What is stagflation, and why did it prove to be difficult for mainstream Keynesian economists to cope with in the 1970s?
6. Describe the efficient market hypothesis in your own words. How did this hypothesis contribute to policies to deregulate financial markets? What were some of the results of the deregulation of financial markets?
7. What are the major patterns economists have identified in the modern business cycle?
8. Describe the different approaches to macroeconomic policy with respect to business cycles. Which approach do you find most compelling? Why?
9. Describe the different dimensions of sustainability and explain why each dimension is important.

NOTES

1. Source: FRED (Federal Reserve Economic Data).
2. Source: World Bank, World Development Indicators.
3. There is a debate among economists over the ideas of John Maynard Keynes. Mainstream economists who combine the ideas of Keynes with the marginal analysis of neoclassical economic theory call themselves "New Keynesians." This reflects the fact that they use some Keynesian ideas, especially stabilization policy, while using different economic methods than those that Keynes used. Meanwhile, political economists, especially those from the post-Keynesian perspective, believe themselves to be the true intellectual heirs to Keynes, utilizing his ideas on macroeconomics using different models and methods. Instead of seeing investors as rational and financial markets as efficient, as implied by neoclassical models, political economists argue that investors are affected by animal spirits and financial markets are subject to wild speculative swings.

Macroeconomic well-being

Measuring and describing the macroeconomy

This chapter addresses a fundamental economic question: What should the goals of an economic system be? Following immediately upon that topic, economists want to know: How can we best determine whether we are successfully meeting our goals?

Establishing the goals of an economic system involves ethical considerations. For example, is a successful economic system one that maximizes the production of goods and services or one that makes sure every person has the necessities of life and opportunities for meaningful work? Should a country maximize income, or should it pursue sustainable growth, even if that means sacrificing some income? Should citizens work long hours to maximize production, or should the government ensure that everyone has ample vacation time and a reasonable work–life balance? All of these issues come into play when an economic system establishes the goals it will pursue and the measures it will use to determine the successes or failures of that economic system.

A country's response to such ethical considerations tends to be influenced substantially by culture and values. Countries with cooperative cultures, such as the Nordic countries of Europe, tend to emphasize work–life balance as well as providing meaningful work and necessities to all citizens. Individualistic cultures such as those in the United States and the United Kingdom tend to prioritize the option of individuals to use their money as they see fit over the provision of necessities to all citizens.

In addition, there are political considerations in determining the range of feasible alternatives. Groups wielding the most political and economic power are often able to determine the goals of an economic system even when those goals diverge from the interests of the broader population. Economic systems display **hegemony when a particular group exerts undue influence within a society**. Such systems are called a **plutocracy** if **the group that dominates the economic**

system comprises the wealthiest members of society. Such systems contrast with well-functioning democracies where each citizen plays a role in determining the priorities of the economic system.

This chapter lays out the different goals that a variety of economists have put forward as their definition of what economic well-being looks like. We begin defining real gross domestic product (GDP), how it is computed based on its components, and its relationship with nominal GDP and the GDP deflator. We take up some definitions of national income accounting, so you can better understand how national income (real GDP) is determined and what it shows us. We also note that, although real GDP was used historically as the standard barometer of economic success, it has some substantial deficiencies as a measure of economic welfare.

Next, we discuss alternative measures that economists use to determine economic well-being. Some economists and politicians favor a focus on happiness, life satisfaction, environmental sustainability, human development, income, or a combination of all these factors. Economists developed a variety of measures to reflect these different values, including the genuine progress indicator, the Human Development Index, and the World Happiness Index. The most comprehensive measure, the OECD Better Life index, incorporates real GDP, environmental quality, human development, *and* life satisfaction.

9.0 CHAPTER 9 LEARNING GOALS

After reading this chapter, you should be able to:

■ Explain and demonstrate how real GDP is constructed and how it is related to nominal GDP and the price index (GDP deflator).

■ Describe the circular flow model of the economy, including the expenditure side and the income side as well as all of the leakages and injections in the model.

■ Relate the three different ways in which GDP can be computed using the expenditure, value added, or income approach and how GDP is related to other measures of national income such as gross national product.

■ Analyze the limitations of real GDP as a measure of well-being.

■ Explain how the Better Life Index, the genuine progress indicator, and the World Happiness Index are constructed and evaluate their effectiveness relative to real GDP in measuring human economic well-being.

9.1 NOMINAL GDP, REAL GDP, AND THE GDP DEFLATOR

To understand what real GDP actually measures, we need start by discussing how real GDP is constructed. The determination of real GDP begins by first measuring nominal GDP.

Nominal GDP is **the value of all final goods and services produced in a particular place at current prices**. Nominal GDP measures the **total revenue of an entire country or region**. In mathematical terms, nominal GDP is computed by multiplying the price and the quantity sold of every *final* good or service produced in a particular time period.

Final goods are those products sold directly to consumers, whereas *intermediate* goods are the inputs that go into making final goods. The value of intermediate goods is already included in the price of final goods, so we do not include intermediate goods in GDP to avoid double counting. For example, the price of a car, a final good, already includes the value of the steel, aluminum, and other intermediate goods used as inputs in the car manufacturing process. Therefore, when computing total production in an economy, we use the prices and quantities of the cars sold but not the prices and quantities of the steel and other inputs that go into the car.

The nominal GDP of the United States in 2019 was determined by multiplying the price of every final good or service in 2019 by the quantity of that good or service sold in 2019:

$$\text{Nominal GDP}^{2019} = P_a^{19} Q_a^{19} + P_b^{19} Q_b^{19} + P_c^{19} Q_c^{19} + \ldots + P_z^{19} Q_z^{19}.$$

The price of good *a* in 2019 (P_a^{19}) is multiplied by the quantity of good *a* produced in 2019 (Q_a^{19}) and so on. In 2019, nominal GDP for the United States was $21,428 billion.

Nominal GDP has limitations when it comes to measuring the productivity of an economy because it includes both prices and quantities. If prices increase by 10% but quantities stay the same, nominal GDP increases by 10% even though quantities have not changed. Thus, nominal GDP can increase when prices go up or when quantities go up.

To correct for this, economists compute **real GDP**, which is **the total output of final goods and services holding prices constant**. Economists pick a stable base year, such as 2012, when the economy was not experiencing a boom or a recession. To find the real GDP in 2019, economists multiply *prices* of goods and services in the base year (2012) by the *quantities* of goods and services produced in the year we are studying (2019).

$$\text{Real GDP}^{2019} = P_a^{12} Q_a^{19} + P_b^{12} Q_b^{19} + P_c^{12} Q_c^{19} + \ldots + P_z^{12} Q_z^{19}.$$

The price of good a in 2012 (P_a^{12}) is multiplied by the quantity of good a produced in 2019 (Q_a^{19}) and so on. In 2019, real GDP for the United States was $19,073 billion.

Nominal GDP and real GDP use the same quantities of goods and services sold but different prices. Therefore, if we divide nominal GDP by real GDP, we get a ratio of prices:

$$\frac{\text{Nominal GDP}^{2019}}{\text{Real GDP}^{2019}} = \frac{\$21,428\,b.}{\$19,073\,b.} = 112.3(\%) = \frac{\text{Prices in 2019}}{\text{Prices in 2012}}$$

$$= \text{GDP Deflator}(P_{GDPD}).$$

The **ratio of prices in the particular year to prices in the base year** is called the **GDP deflator** (P_{GDPD}). The GDP deflator is the price index for all final goods in the economy. The GDP deflator for 2019 was 112.3 in percentage terms, indicating that prices in 2019 were 12.3% higher than they were in 2012 (the base year when the GDP deflator is 100).

P_{GDPD} is called a "deflator" because it can be used to deflate the value of nominal GDP to get real GDP. If we take nominal GDP and divide by the GDP deflator, we get real GDP, which is GDP without inflation.

$$\frac{\text{Nominal GDP}^{2019}}{P_{GDPD}^{2019}} = \text{Real GDP}^{2019}.$$

Figure 9.1 on the next page shows nominal GDP, real GDP, and the GDP deflator for the United States from 2000 to 2019.[1] There are several important things to notice about this table. First, the GDP deflator increases steadily over time, which shows that the U.S. economy experiences inflation. Second, notice that nominal GDP increases more rapidly than real GDP over time. This is because in most years, both prices and quantities increase in the United States, and nominal GDP goes up by the amount prices *and* quantities increase. Real GDP only goes up by the amount quantities increase, thereby concentrating on how much actual production of goods and services is increasing. Third, the GDP deflator is equal to 100% in the base year. In earlier years when prices are lower, the GDP deflator is below 100%. After the base year, the GDP deflator is above 100% because prices were higher in subsequent years. Fourth, nominal GDP is always equal to real GDP in the base year, because we are using the same prices and the same quantities for both measures.

Figure 9.2 on the next page plots out U.S. nominal and real GDP on a graph so you can see these relationships clearly. Real GDP increases only when the production of goods and services increases, whereas nominal GDP increases whenever prices or the production of goods and services increase. Therefore, real GDP increases more slowly than nominal GDP.

Real GDP measures national production of goods and services at constant prices and, as such, it is a good indicator of a nation's standard of living as a whole.

Year	Nominal GDP	Real GDP	GDP Deflator (PGDPD, %)
2000	10252	13131	78.1
2001	10582	13262	79.8
2002	10936	13493	81.1
2003	11458	13879	82.6
2004	12214	14406	84.8
2005	13037	14913	87.4
2006	13815	15338	90.1
2007	14452	15626	92.5
2008	14713	15605	94.3
2009	14449	15209	95.0
2010	14992	15599	96.1
2011	15543	15841	98.1
2012	16197	16197	100.0
2013	16785	16495	101.8
2014	17527	16912	103.6
2015	18225	17404	104.7
2016	18715	17689	105.8
2017	19519	18108	107.8
2018	20580	18638	110.4
2019	21428	19073	112.3
2020	20933	18423	113.6

FIGURE 9.1 Table showing U.S. nominal GDP, real GDP, and the GDP deflator, 2000–2020.

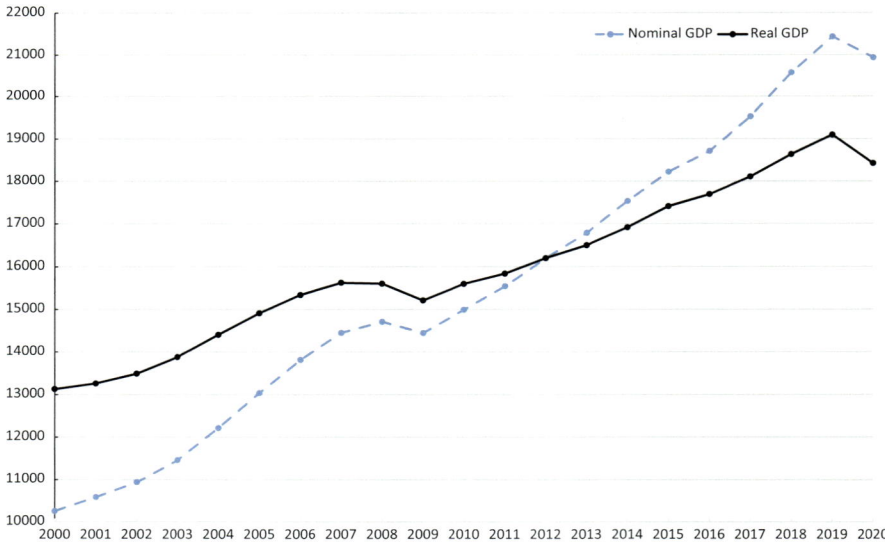

FIGURE 9.2 U.S. nominal GDP and real GDP, 2000–2020 (billions of $).

Increases in real GDP generated by economic growth improve the standard of living of a nation. Interestingly, real GDP is equal to national income as well as national expenditure, as we can see in the circular flow model.

9.2 THE CIRCULAR FLOW MODEL OF THE MACROECONOMY

Figure 9.3 on the next page displays the circular flow model of the macroeconomy, which explains why total income for an economy is the same as total expenditure. Let's begin with the business sector. In a capitalist economic system, businesses produce goods and services, which they sell in goods markets. The sell consumer goods to households, which is classified as consumer purchases (C). Businesses sell machinery, equipment, and other capital goods to other businesses, which is called investment purchases (I). Businesses sell goods and services to the government (G), which purchases military services, buildings and building materials, and much more. Businesses also sell goods to citizens in foreign countries, which is defined as export purchases (X). Domestic businesses lose out on sales when consumers engage in import purchases (IM), buying goods from businesses located in foreign countries. **Adding up all purchases of goods and services in an economy**, we get **aggregate demand (AD)**. In mathematical terms,

$$AD = C + I + G + X - IM.$$

Recall that real GDP is the total revenue (all prices multiplied by all quantities) for all final goods and services in the entire economy, holding prices constant. Real GDP can be found by adding up all of the different categories of spending. In other words, real GDP is equal to aggregate demand.

Another important insight from the circular flow model is that *every dollar of income a business receives becomes income for someone*. Workers receive wages for their labor. Landowners receive rent for the property they lease to businesses. Owners and stockholders receive profits or dividends from the corporations they own. Therefore, aggregate demand is also equal to income (Y).

What, then, happens to the income generated by corporate activity? First, the government takes some of it out of the economy in taxes. A significant portion of tax revenues is paid back to taxpayers in the form of transfer payments, such as Social Security and unemployment benefits that transfer money from some taxpayers to others. Net taxes (T) is the amount of money the government keeps from taxpayers in order to fund other government programs, such as national defense and building roads.

If we take income, Y, and subtract the amount of net taxes that the government takes, T, we are left with **disposable income (DI)**, which is **the amount of after-tax income households have at their disposal to spend on consumer**

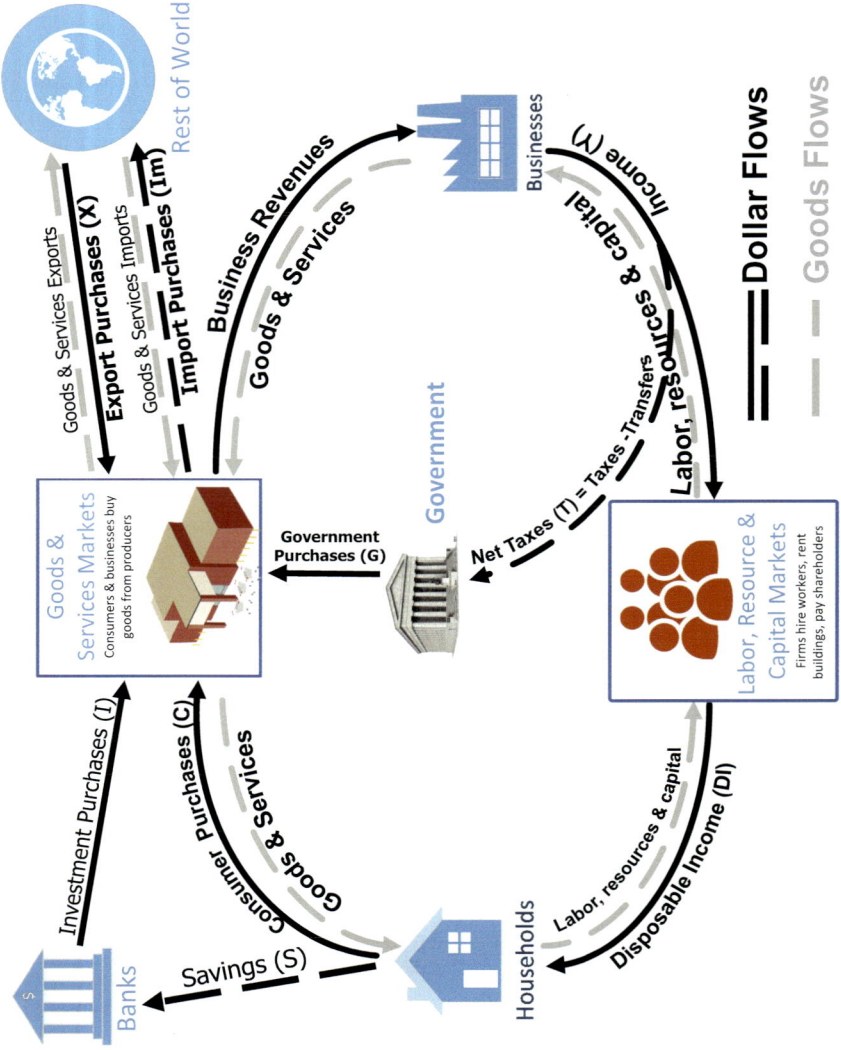

FIGURE 9.3 The circular flow model of the economy.

goods (*C*) or to save for retirement or a rainy day (*S*). $DI = C + S$. Therefore, $Y = DI + T = C + S + T$.

The money that households save ends up in banks or other parts of the financial system. Financial intermediaries like banks make their money by loaning savings out to businesses for investment purchases or to consumers for purchases of homes, cars, and other household durable goods, which is also considered a form of investment. Thus, money saved goes into the banking system, from whence it is loaned out for investment purchases.

Using the circular flow model, you can see the following:

$$\text{Real GDP} = \text{Income}(Y) = C + I + G + X - IM = DI + T.$$

Real GDP is equal to total income for the entire economy, and it is equal to aggregate demand for the entire economy.

If we substitute $DI = C + S$ into the above equation, we get

$$C + I + G + X - IM = C + S + T.$$

Rearranging that equation by subtracting C and adding IM to both sides, we get the important equation:

$$I + G + X = S + T + IM.$$

$$\text{Injections} = \text{Leakages}.$$

Injections are purchases other than consumption that inject money into the economy. Leakages are flows of money that leak out of the economy, heading to banks, government, and other countries. When the economy is operating normally, all money that leaks out of the economy in the form of savings, taxes, and imports in injected back into the economy in the form of investment purchases, government purchases, and export purchases. As we will see later, when injections fall below leakages, the economy may be headed for a recession.

9.3 MEASURES OF NATIONAL INCOME

As noted above, national income can be measured either by total expenditures on goods and services (aggregate demand) or by total income. Figure 9.4 on the next page shows the values of consumption, investment, government spending, exports, and imports in early 2020 (before the recession hit).[2]

Recalling that each dollar that businesses receive from expenditures becomes income for someone, we can also look at the income/cost side of U.S. nominal GDP. The costs businesses incur include compensation for employees (wages, salaries, and benefits), profits (which go to owners of corporations and small businesses),

Component of Aggregate Demand	Billions of $
Personal consumption expenditures (C)	14584.9
Gross private domestic investment (I)	3626.3
Government expenditures (G)	3850.7
Exports (X)	2421.7
Imports (IM)	2947.8
Nominal gross domestic product (NGDP)	21534.9

FIGURE 9.4 Table of U.S. nominal GDP, by component of aggregate demand, 2020.

(a)

Types of Income (billions of $)	
Employee compensation	11,586.9
Proprietors' income	1,702.1
Rental income	797.7
Corporate profits	1,835.6
Net interest and dividends	642.7
Production and import taxes	1,612.7
Depreciation	2,220.4
Statistical discrepancy and miscellaneous	1,136.8
Gross domestic product	21,534.9

(b)

Gross Value Added (billions of $)	
Business	16325.9
Households and nonprofits	2743.4
General government	2465.6
Gross domestic product	21534.9

FIGURE 9.5 (a) National income by type of income. (b) Gross value added by sector.

rent, interest and dividend payments, depreciation (wearing out of capital stock), production taxes, and other miscellaneous costs.[3]

Figure 9.5(a) shows how national income in the United States is divided between wages, small business owners' income (proprietors), corporate profits, income for lenders and investors in the form of interest and dividends, the amount of business income taken directly by government taxes, and depreciation (the amount of business income lost due to the depreciation of capital stock). There is also a category for miscellaneous income and statistical discrepancies.

Last, we can also determine the income of each business by computing its value added, which is the value of what the business sells minus the value of all the intermediate goods (inputs) it buys from other businesses. For example, in 2016, the parts in an Apple iPhone 7 cost $219.80. These intermediate goods included the display, transmitter, processor, glue, batteries, etc. The iPhone 7 sold for $649; thus, the value added was $429.20. This is the amount of money generated in the production of the iPhone. Of the value added, $5 went to compensate the workers who built the iPhone 7, leaving the remainder for Apple's profits.[4]

Thus, a business' value added is equal to the wages and profits generated by its productive activities. In addition to value added by businesses, households, nonprofits, and governments generate value added when they provide goods and services and sell them for more than the cost of intermediate goods. Figure 9.5(b) shows value added by businesses, households, nonprofits, and government.

MACROECONOMIC WELL-BEING

One important insight to take away from this analysis is that *GDP can be measured in three ways*. GDP = Total value added = Total income = Total expenditure (AD). All three methods give us the total economic output of the economy.

Up to this point, we have focused on GDP as the most important measure of an economy's production. We can also look at other aggregate measures to gather data on a variety of macroeconomic topics. Figure 9.6 shows other breakdowns of national income.

For example, **gross national product (GNP)** is **the total market value of goods and services produced by a country's citizens and companies during one year, and it is equal to gross domestic product plus the net income from foreign investments**. Gross *national* product includes production by U.S. corporations in the United States *and* in other countries, whereas gross *domestic* product includes production within the borders of the United States, whether or not that production is done by U.S. or foreign companies. GDP is a better indicator of a country's productive capacity, whereas GNP is a better measure of value added generated by a country's companies wherever they might be.

Computation of GDP, GNP, NNP, NI, PI, and DPI (Billions of $)

Domestic product and income	2019	2020*
Gross domestic product (*GDP*)	21,427.69	21,534.91
PLUS: Income receipts from the rest of the world	1,158.83	1,063.50
LESS: Income payments to the rest of the world	863.3	811.33
EQUALS: Gross national product (*GNP*)	21,723.21	21,787.08
LESS: Consumption of fixed capital	3,462.96	3,551.95
EQUALS: Net national product (*NNP*)	18,260.26	18,235.13
Statistical discrepancy	98.22	52.12
EQUALS: National Income (*NI*)	18,162.04	18,183.01
LESS: Corporate profits with inventory valuation and capital consumption adjustments	2,074.64	1,835.61
Taxes on production and imports less subsides	1,420.06	1,460.85
Contributions for government social insurance, domestic	1,420.37	1,449.33
Net interest and misc. payments on assets (dividends)	644.95	642.72
Business current transfer payments (net)	170.73	175.71
Current surplus of government enterprises	-12.18	-18.57
PLUS: Personal income receipts on assets	2,992.89	3,013.94
Personal current transfer receipts	3,171.94	3,298.47
EQUALS: Personal income (*PI*)	18,608.31	18,949.78
LESS: Personal tax payments	2,183.16	2,214.08
EQUALS: Disposable personal income (*DPI*)	16,425.15	16,735.70
LESS: Personal consumption expenditures (C)	14,562.66	14,584.06
Personal interest payments by consumers	359.92	343.41
Personal transfer payments	199.76	198.44
EQUALS: Personal savings (*S*)	1,302.81	1,609.79

FIGURE 9.6 Various measures of U.S. national income and national product.

Net national product (NNP) is the net creation of new wealth (value added) resulting from the productive activity of the economy during the accounting period (usually one year). NNP is computed by taking GNP and subtracting the decline in the current value of the stock of fixed assets (capital) owned and used by producers as a result of physical deterioration, normal obsolescence, or normal accidental damage. By subtracting depreciation of capital that takes place during production, NNP measures the actual wealth created in a given time period.

National income (NI) measures the total monetary value of the flow of output of goods and services produced in an economy. NI is found by taking NNP and subtracting indirect business taxes and transfer payments. Indirect business taxes are primarily sales and excise taxes, customs duties on imported goods, and business property taxes. Transfer payments occur when governments redistribute income via social welfare programs such as Social Security, old age or disability pensions, student grants, unemployment compensation, etc. By eliminating indirect business taxes and transfer payments, we are left with the national income generated by productive market activities.

Personal income (PI) measures national income going to persons and nonprofit corporations. This includes wages and net transfer payments. To compute PI, the government begins with NI and subtracts income earned by corporate sector (depreciation, undistributed profits), payments to the government (taxes), and adjustments such as subsidies, government and consumer interest, and any statistical discrepancy.

Disposable personal income (DPI) is the income remaining to households after the deduction of personal tax and nontax payments to the general government. After-tax income (DPI) is computed by taking PI and subtracting personal taxes, which include income and property taxes that are not deductible.

If we take DPI and subtract household interest and transfer payments, the remaining amount of money is devoted to consumption and savings. Consumption expenditures (C) are the market value of purchases of goods and services by individuals and nonprofit institutions. Savings (S) is the money that households keep in cash, banks deposits, security holdings, and private pension, health, welfare, and trust funds.

9.4 THE LIMITATIONS OF REAL GDP AS A MEASURE OF ECONOMIC WELFARE

Real GDP measures the entire country's standard of living and, as such, is a reasonable measure of economic activity and the country's total standard of living. To some economists, this makes real GDP a very good measure of the effectiveness of an economic system and a good proxy for the economic welfare of a nation. However, real GDP incorporates only measurable, market-based economic activity, and it can increase for reasons that are not associated with an improvement in people's welfare. More specifically, there are four main problems that render real GDP an inaccurate measure of well-being: excluded production, inaccurate measurement of the quality of life, the inclusion of economic "bads" in real GDP calculations, and the fact that real GDP tends to be correlated with unsustainable practices.

1. **Excluded production**: Real GDP only includes official, market activity, neglecting unpaid household work, informal sector work, much work done for cash payments, and illegal activities.

   By ignoring unpaid household work, real GDP significantly underestimates the amount of productive activity taking place in an economy. Unpaid household work includes housework, home maintenance, shopping, caring for household members (including adults and children), volunteer work in the community, and travel related to household activities. Figure 9.7 on the next page displays the typical amount of time per day devoted to paid and unpaid work by men and women from a variety of countries.[5]

   The data indicate several important trends:

   - Women do more unpaid work than men in *all* countries, and they do a lot more unpaid work in particular countries.
   - Women spend a larger percentage of their days working on paid and unpaid work than men in almost all countries, with Denmark as one of the few exceptions.
   - On average, women spend 21% more of their time on unpaid work than they do on paid work. On the other hand, men spend 145% more of their time on paid work than on unpaid work.
   - On average, unpaid work takes up a huge amount of time, averaging 74% of paid work. Therefore, *real GDP excludes 74% of economic activity*.

   Clearly, the amount of productive household work not included in real GDP is substantial. Economists estimate it would cost between 12% and 24% of real GDP to hire workers to do the amount of household work that is undertaken in most countries (the replacement cost of household labor). However, this number is a low estimate, because the wages paid for most household work are low. If we consider the opportunity cost of workers—what they could earn in other professions if they did paid work instead of unpaid work—the increase in real GDP from including unpaid work would range from 41% to 66%.

   As one example of the skewed priorities implied by real GDP, if a family places its children in daycare or hires a nanny, they increase real GDP, whereas if they spend quality time with their children every day in their home but spend fewer hours in the workplace, real GDP will decline.

   Furthermore, household work is only one important area of excluded production. In many countries, especially those in the developing world, much work is done in the informal sector by individuals and small businesses that

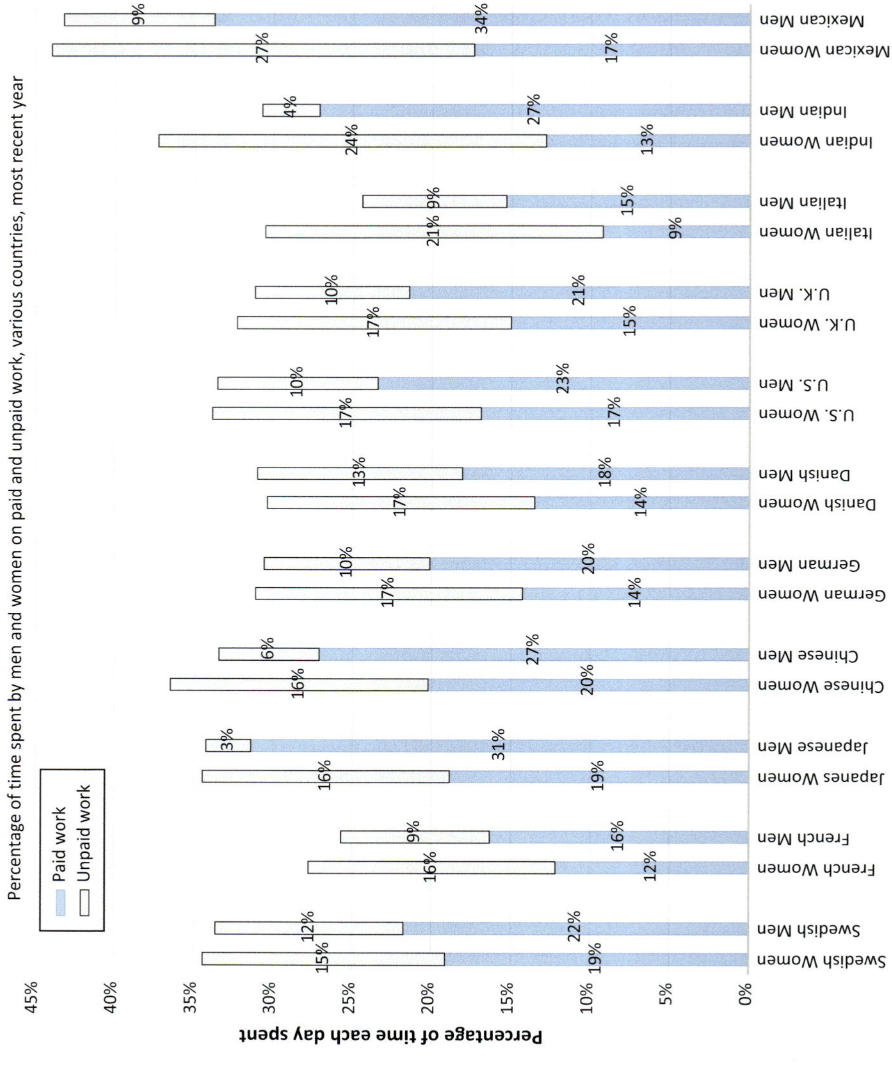

FIGURE 9.7 Completion of paid and unpaid work by men and women.

engage in cash transactions and do not report their activities to the government. Even in developed countries, many people do work for cash and do not report these payments to the government. In 2018, the consulting firm Kearney estimated that 23% of economic activity is done "off the books."

Lastly, illegal activities are not included in real GDP. (Drug dealers do not report their income to the government!) According to the U.S. Bureau of Economic Analysis, in 2017 including illegal drugs in measures of GDP adds $111 billion, illegal prostitution adds $10 billion, illegal gambling adds $4 billion, and theft from businesses adds $109 billion. All illegal activities together add up to about 1% of U.S. real GDP.

2. **Real GDP is an inaccurate measure of human quality of life.**

    Income is certainly an important determinant of quality of life. However, real GDP, in measuring national income, does not necessarily capture the experiences of most individuals, especially in a very unequal nation like the United States. Given the high poverty rate in the United States and the high rate of homelessness (554,000 people were homeless in 2017, a year during an economic boom), many people's experiences are not reflected in the high level of U.S. real GDP. Even though real GDP in the United States increased in recent decades, all or almost all of the benefit went to the richest 20% of the population, obscuring the fact that well-being is stagnant for most citizens.

    In addition to income, well-being includes citizens' levels of health, happiness, security, material comfort, and leisure, categories that are not reflected by real GDP. France has a lower GDP than the United States, but French laborers work on average 19% less than American workers. It is hard to argue that French workers are worse off than U.S. workers because they prefer more leisure time to a higher income.

3. **Real GDP includes many economic "bads."**

    Real GDP increases whenever manmade or natural disasters occur. Buildings that are destroyed by hurricanes have to be rebuilt, which increases real GDP, but homeowners are no better off. The Deepwater Horizon oil spill in the Gulf of Mexico required a massive cleanup effort, increasing GDP, but people and the environment in the Gulf region suffered significantly. Having to spend increasing amounts of money on health or car insurance may safeguard against calamity, but it does not improve our well-being directly. Similarly, spending money on elaborate alarm and security systems due to high crime rates may make keep us from harm, but it is difficult to see such expenditures as an indication of increased well-being. The fact that real GDP increases whenever calamities occur or whenever households have to make defensive expenditures to ward of calamities indicates that many expenditures within real GDP do not reflect well-being.

4. **Real GDP ignores and often directly undermines sustainability.**

    Real GDP usually increases when companies exploit the environment more intensively. Fracking led to a huge boom in Pennsylvania, North Dakota, and

Texas as new natural gas fields were discovered, leading to substantial increases in real GDP. However, fracking processes spoiled water sources and natural beauty, and they contributed substantially to climate change. Cutting down rainforests and intensifying fishing efforts can increase real GDP in the short term, but the long-term costs can be devastating and will likely require huge corrective expenditures in the future to solve the environmental problems that are being created. In general, in our current capitalist system, exploiting the environment tends to result in increased short-term profits and real GDP, but no adjustment is made to account for the long-term environmental costs.

Thus, to most economists, real GDP is at best an imperfect measure of welfare. However, measures of economic progress are crucial to determine the direction of an economy and to measure whether it is functioning effectively. Therefore, the key question is: How should we measure the well-being of society? In many ways, the measures we choose are a reflection of a society's priorities. The selection of real GDP as the primary criterion for economic success prioritizes market-based income growth, while ineffectively addressing household work, life satisfaction, leisure, calamities, environmental concerns, and many other important factors. A much more comprehensive measure than real GDP is the OECD Better Life Index.

9.5 THE OECD BETTER LIFE INDEX

We started off this chapter by asking some fundamental economic questions: What should the goals of an economic system be? How can we determine whether we are successful in meeting those goals? Unlike real GDP, the OECD's Better Life Index was designed to answer those questions directly.

Developed in 2011 by three eminent mainstream economists, Joseph Stiglitz, Amartya Sen, and Jean-Paul Fitoussi, the Better Life Index compares well-being across OECD countries in 11 different sectors determined as essential to human well-being. These sectors are (1) housing, (2) income, (3) jobs, (4) community, (5) education, (6) environment, (7) civic engagement, (8) health, (9) life satisfaction, (10) safety, and (11) work–life balance. Each sector is measured using a set of indicators and is than ranked on a scale from 0 to 10, with 0 being the worst possible score and 10 being the best. Below we briefly describe the determinants of the Better Life Index (BLI).

1. **Housing**: Shelter is one of our most important necessities. In addition, people desire a comfortable, safe space to raise families and spend time with friends. The Better Life Index measures housing from three vantage points: Housing affordability, dwellings with basic facilities (access to sanitation), and rooms per person (to determine whether housing is overcrowded).

2. **Income**: Higher income levels often mean that households have greater access to high-quality education, health care, and an overall better standard of living. In the Better Life Index, income is measured in terms of household net wealth (household assets such as housing equity, ownership of stocks, etc.) and net disposable (after-tax) income. These figures are adjusted for inflation and exchange rates so that they reflect purchasing power parity, making it possible to compare accurately the income and wealth of different countries. This part of the BLI is similar to GDP per capita but is broader because it includes measures of wealth.
3. **Jobs**: One of the most important characteristics of well-being is having a meaningful, fulfilling job that provides a decent standard of living. Jobs connect us to society, providing self-confidence and access to personal growth. The Better Life Index measures jobs in terms of job security, personal earnings, the long-term unemployment rate, and the employment rate.
4. **Community**: Our communities are the backbones of our personal and social lives. We rely on them for friendship, civic engagement, and help when we are in distress. In the Better life Index, community is measured through the quality of the community support network, which is determined by surveys.
5. **Education**: A good education system creates a knowledgeable, skilled labor force, as well as a more engaged, healthier, and politically conscious citizenry. Therefore, education is important for essential employment skills and for the cultivation of an informed worldview. The Better Life Index measures education on the basis of years in education, student skills, and educational attainment.
6. **Environment**: The environment directly impacts health and well-being. Green spaces let us partake in physical activities and reduce stress. The environment is a vital source of natural resources (environmental services), and a key issue is how best to preserve these resources while reaping their current benefits. Water quality and air pollution are the two indicators that serve as proxies for the quality of the environment in the Better Life Index.
7. **Civic Engagement**: Regardless of ideology, a government and a political system that is responsive to and trusted by the electorate is very important to well-being. We need to be able to trust those making consequential policy decisions, which requires transparent governance. The ability of the public to engage with government and affect policy, along with the level of voter turnout, are used to measure civic engagement in the BLI.
8. **Health**: Being healthy brings so many benefits, from living a longer, more fulfilling life to spending less on health care services. Health is one of the central factors determining our success and overall quality of life. In the Better Life Index, health is measured by life expectancy as well as surveys of the levels of health self-reported by the population.
9. **Life satisfaction**: Although this is one of the most subjective factors in the index, some people consider it the most important because it directly reflects

people's general satisfaction with life. To determine this measure, people are given a survey that asks them to rate their general satisfaction with life on a scale from 0 to 10.

10. **Safety**: Feeling safe in our own community is very important. Living in areas with more crime poses a higher risk of becoming a victim of violence, increases stress, and destroys community. The Better Life Index measures safety in terms of the homicide rate and how safe individuals feel while walking alone at night.

11. **Work–Life Balance**: Another meaningful measure to many people is the ability to strike a balance between work and home life. Working longer hours may increase income and opportunities, but this comes at the expense of leisure, family time, and personal care. The BLI uses time devoted to leisure and personal care and the percentage of employees working very long hours (50 or more per week) as indicators for work–life balance.

Figure 9.8 shows the Better Life Index in 2019 for 27 OECD countries as well as Brazil and South Africa. Each of the 11 determinants is given equal weight in this figure.

The broadened definition of well-being in the BLI shows the strength of the Nordic model in delivering an extremely high quality of life, with Norway, Iceland, Denmark, Sweden, and Finland all in the top ten and all ahead of the United States. Nonetheless, market-dominated economies such as Australia, Canada, the United States, New Zealand, and the United Kingdom still fare well.

Figure 9.9 shows a direct comparison between the United States and Norway in each category of the Better Life Index. Norway fares particularly well with respect to environment, life satisfaction, safety, work–life balance, and community. The United States is particularly strong in one area: Income. Thus, the BLI

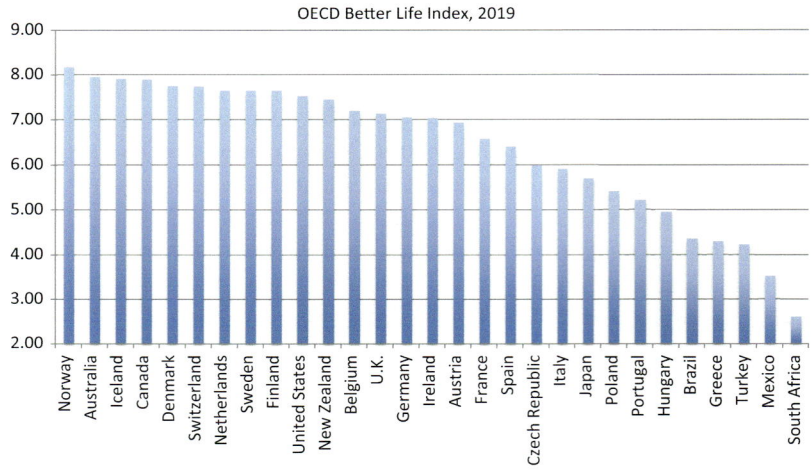

FIGURE 9.8 OECD Better Life Index.

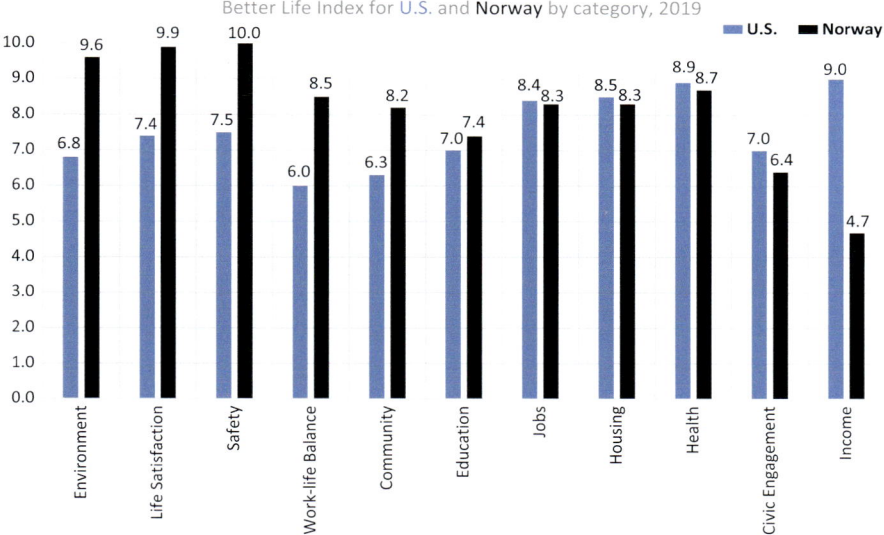

FIGURE 9.9 Better Life Index for the United States and Norway.

indicates that high incomes in the United States, achieved via long work hours and the market-dominated system, come at the expense of other important life indicators.

One of the unique aspects of the Better Life Index is that it is an interactive tool that lets you determine what matters most *to you* across the 11 sectors. This allows countries to make their own value judgments regarding the aspects of well-being that should prioritized.

The Better Life Index is a much more sophisticated measure of the well-being of citizens in a particular location. Another effective measure that attempts to correct the flaws in real GDP is the genuine progress indicator.

9.6 THE GENUINE PROGRESS INDICATOR AND THE WORLD HAPPINESS INDEX

The **genuine progress indicator (GPI)** is **a monetary measure of economic welfare that accounts for benefits and costs experienced by a particularly population from investment, production, trade, and consumption of goods and services**.[6] GPI was created by ecological economists Herman Daly and John Cobb as an alternative measure of the standard of living of a country or region.[7] GPI attempts to measure economic welfare by accounting for the benefits of market *and nonmarket* goods and services and by estimating the economic, social, and environmental costs of economic activity.[8] Thus, GPI attempts to add in positive economic activities that real GDP omits and subtract negative economic activities that detract from our well-being to come up with a more accurate measure of well-being.

Although there are several different variations, there is a general consensus of what the GPI should incorporate. In this section, we will be using the GPI originally developed by Daly and Cobb and updated by contemporary researchers John Talberth and Michael Weisdorf.[9] This GPI (also called the Index of Sustainable Economic Welfare) contains 27 different indicators that add to or detract from well-being. However, we can group these into five broad categories for the following calculation:

$$GPI = C_{adj} + W + G_{nd} - D - E - N.$$

C_{adj} is personal consumption adjusted for inequality. W is nonmonetary contributions to welfare. G_{nd} is nondefensive government expenditures (public goods). D is defensive and rehabilitative household expenditures, investments, and social costs. E is the costs of environmental degradation, and N is net depreciation of natural capital stocks. Each of these categories is explained more fully below.

C_{adj} = **Personal consumption, adjusted for income inequality (+).** Personal consumption captures purchases of essential goods, such as food, water, and shelter, as well as things that might not be essential but that give us some amount of happiness, like watching a movie or going to a concert. Personal consumption must be adjusted for income inequality. If per capita consumption increases, but if all of the increase goes to the richest 20% of the population, as has been the case in recent decades in the United States, then per capita consumption does not accurately capture the well-being of the entire population.

W = **Nonmonetary contributions to welfare (+).** As noted above, real GDP only accounts for acts that involve the exchange of money. Real GDP excludes all unpaid work done in the home, including the time and skills it takes to raise children, cook food, and clean the house. Real GDP ignores the value of leisure time and ignores any services in the community provided by volunteers. In addition, real GDP misses external benefits from higher education and green jobs and the value contributed by infrastructure and other forms of built capital. GPI calculates and includes the value of each of these contributions to well-being.

G_{nd} = **Nondefensive government expenditures (+).** The government plays an important role in funding public goods. From public education to the maintenance of roads, a large part of government expenditure is used for the well-being of the country. The GPI does not include defensive expenditures, which are those made to offset declining levels of well-being in human, social, and environmental capital. For example, spending to clean up oil spills or toxic waste sites is crucial, but it does not lead to an improvement in human welfare. Instead, it is correcting a past problem and should not be considered genuine progress. Therefore, defensive or corrective government expenditures are not included in GPI.

D = **Defensive and rehabilitative household expenditures, investments, and social costs (−).** We all have an incentive to invest in defensive measures to minimize harm when things go wrong and to protect our future. Health insurance, car insurance, or legal services protect us from potential harm. However, these expenditures do not increase our well-being when we make them. Instead, they act as defenses when we are at risk of experiencing a decrease in well-being. Household investments in durable goods (cars, appliances) cost large amounts up front (increasing C) but provide much more limited benefits each year, so the value of future benefits is subtracted and only the current benefit is included. Other household investments that generate future benefit streams, such as home improvements and retirement savings, are discounted in a similar manner. In addition, there are significant social costs that accompany economic activity, including crime, underemployment, homelessness, time wasted commuting, and the cost of vehicle accidents. All of these items detract from well-being and are subtracted from the GPI.

E = **Costs of environmental degradation (−).** Industrialization and urbanization over the past several centuries have taken a huge toll on the environment. Climate change is but one example of the negative effects of human practices. Many economic activities that contribute to GDP, such as the burning of fossil fuels and deforestation, create costly environment problems that will impact human society negatively in the near future but that are not accounted for. GPI includes indicators like the costs of water, land, and air pollution to calculate the impact of environmental degradation.

N = **Net depreciation of natural capital stocks (−).** Similarly, production of goods and services depletes our natural capital stocks. Many natural resources are nonrenewable, and heavy present-day consumption takes its toll on the availability of resources for future generations. Renewable resources, such as fish stocks, are often overused so much that it jeopardizes future reproduction. Therefore, GPI includes indicators like long-term nonrenewable resource depletion and long-term environmental damage. If we take the depreciation of natural capital stocks and subtract the value of services from protected natural capital from conservation efforts (a positive long-term impact), we get a measure for the net depreciation of natural capitals stocks.

Figure 9.10 on the next page tells us that U.S. real GPI per capita in 2014 was $28,459.35, which is 53.6% of real GDP per capita in the same year. The GPI tells us a number of important facts about our well-being: Almost half of our well-being comes from nonmonetary factors, demonstrating how much is missed by real GDP. In addition, the costs of environmental damage and depreciation, coupled with defensive household expenditures that do not enhance welfare, demonstrate the extent to which well-being is mismeasured by real GDP.

Computation of the U.S. Real Genuine Progress Indicator, 2014 (in 2012 dollars)	
Indicator	Contribution to GPI
Gross Household Consumption	$25,529.42
Costs of income inequality	-3,121.57
Adjusted household consumption (C_{adj})	22,407.85
Non-monetary contributions to welfare (W)	24,122.18
Nondefensive government expenditures (G_{nd})	7,025.32
Defensive household expenditures, investments, and social costs (D)	-16,440.40
Costs of environmental degradation (E)	-3,714.65
Net depreciation of natural capital stocks (N)	-4,940.95
U.S. real GPI per capita (2014)	28,459.35
U.S. real GDP per capita (2014)	53,076.00

FIGURE 9.10 Table showing the U.S. real genuine progress indicator.

Country Position	GDP per Capita	GPI per Capita
1	Luxembourg	Norway
2	Norway	Denmark
3	Denmark	Sweden
4	Sweden	Luxembourg
5	United States	Finland
6	Netherlands	Japan
7	Ireland	Austria
8	Austria	Netherlands
9	Japan	France
10	Finland	Belgium
11	Belgium	Ireland
12	Germany	United Kingdom
13	France	Germany
14	United Kingdom	Italy
15	Italy	United States

FIGURE 9.11 Table showing the top 15 OECD countries, GDP vs. GPI, 2013.

Interestingly, in some countries, GPI and GDP correspond much more closely than they do in the United States. Figure 9.11 displays the 15 OECD countries with the highest real GDP per capita and the highest real GPI per capita in 2013.[10] Countries with strong social and environmental programs fared extremely well in both categories. For example, Norway, Denmark, and Sweden maintained a very high real GDP per capita without compromising the well-being of citizens and the environment, resulting in a similarly high real GPI per capita. The United States, however, slips from 5th in real GDP per capita to 15th in real GPI per capita, by far the largest drop of any OECD country.

In addition to the OECD Better Life Index and the genuine progress indicator, there are several other important measures of well-being. The United Nations Human Development Index focuses on three essential components of the development of human capabilities: Life expectancy at birth, years of formal education, and real GDP per capita. The Happy Planet Index looks at average life expectancy, average subjective well-being, and the ecological impact of a society.

Rank	Country	Score	GDP per Capita	Social Support	Healthy Life Expectancy	Freedom for Life Choices	Generosity	Perceptions of Corruption
	World Happiness Index rankings by country and category, most recent year (2017-2019)							
1	Finland	7.77	1.34	1.59	0.99	0.60	0.15	0.39
2	Denmark	7.60	1.38	1.57	1.00	0.59	0.25	0.41
3	Norway	7.55	1.49	1.58	1.03	0.60	0.27	0.34
4	Iceland	7.49	1.38	1.62	1.03	0.59	0.35	0.12
5	Netherlands	7.49	1.40	1.52	1.00	0.56	0.32	0.30
6	Switzerland	7.48	1.45	1.53	1.05	0.57	0.26	0.34
7	Sweden	7.34	1.39	1.49	1.01	0.57	0.27	0.37
8	New Zealand	7.31	1.30	1.56	1.03	0.59	0.33	0.38
9	Canada	7.28	1.37	1.51	1.04	0.58	0.29	0.31
10	Austria	7.25	1.38	1.48	1.02	0.53	0.24	0.23
11	Australia	7.23	1.37	1.55	1.04	0.56	0.33	0.29
12	Costa Rica	7.17	1.03	1.44	0.96	0.56	0.14	0.09
13	Israel	7.14	1.28	1.46	1.03	0.37	0.26	0.08
14	Luxembourg	7.09	1.61	1.48	1.01	0.53	0.19	0.32
15	United Kingdom	7.05	1.33	1.54	1.00	0.45	0.35	0.28
16	Ireland	7.02	1.50	1.55	1.00	0.52	0.30	0.31
17	Germany	6.99	1.37	1.45	0.99	0.50	0.26	0.27
18	Belgium	6.92	1.36	1.50	0.99	0.47	0.16	0.21
19	United States	6.89	1.43	1.46	0.87	0.45	0.28	0.13
20	Czech Republic	6.85	1.27	1.49	0.92	0.46	0.05	0.04

FIGURE 9.12 Table showing World Happiness Index rankings.

Lastly, the United Nations World Happiness Index incorporates real GDP per capita, healthy life expectancy at birth, social support (of relatives and friends), freedom to make life choices, generosity, and perceptions of corruption. Though the last four categories are subjective measures determined by surveys, they get at aspects of well-being that are extremely important to most people and that cannot be measured in other ways.

We can see in Figure 9.12 that the Nordic countries are at the top of the World Happiness Index, making up the first four countries and five out of the top seven. They perform particularly well on social support and freedom to make life choices. The United States does well in per capita income but poorly in healthy life expectancy, freedom to make life choices, and perceptions of corruption.

As the last two sections have shown, broader measures of well-being tend to favor economic systems that emphasize broad-based prosperity, significant social welfare programs, public goods, work–life balance, and sustainable economic practices. Economic systems like the United States that focus primarily on economic growth do well in terms of real GDP but fare poorly according to the Better Life Index, the genuine progress indicator, and the World Happiness Index.

9.7 CONCLUSION

This chapter began by defining and discussing the relationship between nominal GDP, real GDP, and the GDP deflator. Nominal GDP is total revenue generated by the production and sale of all final goods and services at current prices. Real GDP is equal to nominal GDP divided by the GDP deflator and represents the total revenue from sales of all final goods and services at constant prices.

We went on to discuss the circular flow model. The expenditure side of the model is composed of the components of aggregate demand: Consumption, investment, government, export, and import **purchases** of goods and services. The income side of the circular flow can be broken down into the categories of taxes and disposable income. Disposable income includes wages, rent, interest, profits, and all other sources of income generated in the production of goods and services.

The circular flow model shows that GDP is equal to aggregate demand as well as national income. National income can also be computed by measuring value added for all industries, because value added is the income generated in all productive activities. Sometimes economists look at other measures of income, such as gross national product, to analyze different variations in how income is generated.

Determining what measure we use to determine well-being is one of the most important aspects of macroeconomics, because it determines a society's economic goals. A society focused on real GDP may well generate high levels of income, but this may not be a good indicator of how well people are doing. This is because there are four main limitations of real GDP as a measure of well-being. (1) Real GDP excludes important types of production, especially by households. (2) Real GDP is an inaccurate measure of human quality of life, ignoring key elements such as health, leisure, and the welfare of *all* citizens. (3) Real GDP includes many economic "bads," such as rebuilding from disasters or defensive expenditures. (4) Real GDP in our current capitalist economic system tends to be inversely correlated with sustainability, jeopardizing our long-term well-being.

In contrast to real GDP, the Better Life Index, the genuine progress indicator, and the World Happiness Index are constructed to generate a much more comprehensive measure of human well-being. They attempt to correct the limitations of real GDP by including excluded production, subjective measures of well-being, the costs of economic calamities, and the costs of environmental destruction. The Nordic countries fare particularly well in rankings utilizing these more comprehensive measures of well-being, whereas the United States fares poorly due to its high levels of inequality and environmental destruction and its low levels of social welfare support.

In the next chapter, we turn to two additional macroeconomic variables that are crucial to well-being: unemployment and inflation. As we will see, both of these macroeconomic market failures can be extremely harmful to a country's citizens, so government policies to limit their impact are very important.

QUESTIONS FOR REVIEW

1. In 2017, U.S. nominal GDP was $19,519 billion and U.S. real GDP (measured in 2012 dollars) was $18,108 billion. Explain the difference between these two measures of 2017 GDP, and use these numbers to determine how much inflation there was from 2012 to 2017.
2. Using the circular flow model, explain why total spending (aggregate demand) tends to be equal to total income.
3. List and explain the main limitations of real GDP as a measure of well-being.
4. Do you think the Better Life Index is a better measure of economic well-being than real GDP? Why or why not? What are the strengths and weaknesses of the Better Life Index?
5. Explain how the genuine progress indicator is constructed and how it differs from real GDP and the Better Life Index.
6. How is the World Happiness Index constructed, and how does it compare to real GDP, the Better Life Index, and the genuine progress indicator?
7. Determine which indexes are most closely associated with each characteristic listed in Figure 9.13.

Characteristic	Index(es) with this characteristic (real GDP, BLI, GPI, and/or WHI)
An exclusive focus on income	
Contains no subjective measures	
Ranks countries based on a set of key indicators	
Subtracts economic "bads"	
Includes education and housing as key categories	
Includes "perceptions of corruption" as a key category	

FIGURE 9.13 Table for problem 7.

8. Why does the United States perform relatively well when it comes to real GDP per capita but relatively poorly when it comes to the other measures discussed in this chapter? If the United States wanted to change its performance with respect to the Better Life Index and the genuine progress indicator, what would it need to do?
9. Write an essay in which you compare, contrast, and critically evaluate real GDP, the Better Life Index, and the genuine progress indicator. Make an argument for which measure should be used as the best barometer of a country's well-being.
10. What do you think is most important to the well-being of most people? Explain, and support your position. Which measure of economic welfare would best capture well-being as you have defined it? Do you think others would agree with your determination of well-being?

NOTES

1. Source: Federal Reserve Economic Data (FRED).
2. Source: Federal Reserve Economic Data, Table 1.15.
3. A good way to think about the actual profit rate is to take profits and subtract depreciation. Depreciation of capital means that machinery and equipment must be replaced and that replacement cost comes out of profits.
4. Rakesh Sharma, "What It Costs Apple to Make an iPhone 7: $219 Parts, $5 Labor," Investopedia, Company News (2016). https://www.investopedia.com/news/what-it-costs-apple-make-iphone-7-219-parts-5-labor-aapl-snssf/. Accessed May 28, 2020.
5. Source: OECD.Stat, accessed January 17, 2020.
6. John Talberth and Michael Weisdorf, "Genuine Progress Indicator 2.0: Pilot Accounts for the U.S., Maryland, and City of Baltimore 2012–2014," *Ecological Economics* 142 (December 2017): 1–11. https://doi.org/10.1016/J.ECOLECON.2017.06.012.
7. Herman Daly and John Cobb, *For the Common Good. Redirecting the Economy Toward Community, the Environment and a Sustainable Future* (Boston: Beacon Press, 1994).
8. Talberth and Weisdorf, supra note 6.
9. Ibid.
10. Source: D.F. Pais, T.L. Afonso, A.C. Marques, and J.A. Fuinhas. "Are Economic Growth and Sustainable Development Converging?" *International Journal of Energy Economics and Policy* 9, no. 4 (2019): 202–213.

10 Unemployment and price instability

The major macroeconomic market failures

In the last chapter, we described various measures of economic well-being. Any discussion of macroeconomic well-being would be incomplete if it did not address the two major macroeconomic market failures: Unemployment and inflation.

Unemployment can be devastating for individuals, families, and communities. Households in which the main breadwinner loses their job have a much higher likelihood of poverty, hunger, and homelessness. Communities where large numbers of people become unemployed for a significant length of time deteriorate into poverty, crime, abandoned buildings, and outmigration of those with the means to leave. The broader macroeconomy also suffers, as unemployment results in declines in aggregate demand, reduced business sales, and, subsequently, additional rounds of layoffs due to the multiplier effect. The end result is reductions in economic growth. The costs of unemployment can be mitigated by a generous and effective social safety net, but many countries such as the United States provide only a minimal safety net. This renders the economic impact of unemployment very high.

Price instability is the other major macroeconomic market failure. Economic systems need a degree of price stability to function effectively. Deflation is devastating, causing a rash of business failures and, as in the case of the Great Depression, contributing to an economic collapse. Rapid bouts of inflation or hyperinflation can also be destabilizing, undermining the health of the financial sector and causing the banking system to collapse. Thus, deflation or rapid inflation can both result in economic crises, demonstrating the importance of maintaining stable prices.

This chapter begins by discussing systematically the problems that occur due to unemployment and why economists consider it to be a market failure. We then describe the different types of unemployment and the potential policy solutions to solve the unemployment problem. This includes a brief discussion of some of the unemployment mitigation programs we see in economic systems around the world.

Subsequently, the chapter turns to how we measure inflation and deflation and how we use this measure to compute real wages and real interest rates. Next, we take up the causes of and problems created by deflation, along with the policies that

DOI: 10.4324/9780429399350-13

can reduce its impact. We also discuss the problems created by inflation and the forces that cause inflation.

We close the chapter by discussing two important but controversial economic theories regarding the main causes of inflation. The quantity theory of money, put forth by laissez-faire economists, proposes that the major cause of inflation is increases in the money supply. The Phillips curve posits that inflation is caused by rapid economic growth and low unemployment. Adherents of these policies prefer to use austerity policies to keep inflation under control, albeit at the cost of slower growth and higher unemployment. Political economists and liberal New Keynesian economists dispute the empirical validity of these theories and argue for policies to promote economic growth and low unemployment while worrying less about inflation.

10.0 CHAPTER 10 LEARNING GOALS

After reading this chapter, you should be able to:

- Describe the costs of unemployment, how the unemployment rate is computed, and the types of unemployment.
- Evaluate the effectiveness of the unemployment rate and the labor force participation rate in reflecting the unemployment situation in a country.
- Critically analyze the possible solutions to the problems of unemployment and underemployment.
- Compute the rate of inflation, the real wage, and the real interest rate.
- Explain the causes and costs of deflation and inflation and critically evaluate potential policy solutions to these market failures.
- Compare and contrast perspectives on the quantity theory of money and the Phillips curve.

10.1 THE ECONOMIC COSTS OF UNEMPLOYMENT

Finding meaningful work is one of the most important determinants of economic well-being. People want a job that pays well enough so that they can live a good life. This includes earning enough to support their family and to provide their children with education and opportunities to succeed. People also want a job where the work that they do is important and interesting.

Unemployment, on the other hand, is devastating. In a capitalist system with no safety net, such as the laissez-faire systems in England in 1850 or the United States in 1900, unemployment means no income and brings with it the threat of poverty, homelessness, and starvation. Unemployment renders people helpless and dependent on others for their survival, something that people find deeply humiliating, according to survey data. Unemployment is so devastating that having a bad job is better than having no job at all, something the famous Cambridge economist Joan Robinson alluded to when she said, "The misery of being exploited by capitalists is nothing compared to the misery of not being exploited at all."[1]

Unfortunately, unemployment is an ever-present part of a capitalist economic system. There has almost never been a time when everyone who wanted to work could find a job. The lowest unemployment rate in U.S. history was 1.2% in 1944, when the mobilization of millions of soldiers and workers for the World War II war effort employed almost everyone. Therefore, economists consider unemployment to be a market failure because it is a chronic plague in capitalist systems: Markets are not able to eliminate unemployment on their own, and unemployment imposes devastating costs on individuals, families, communities, and the macroeconomy.

First, consider the **costs of unemployment to the individual**. Unemployed individuals do not have access to the latest workplace technology, and they are excluded from opportunities for training and advancement in the workplace. This results in the loss of skills and significant, long-term reductions in income for workers who experience unemployment. Similarly, numerous studies indicate that college graduates who begin work during a recession when levels of unemployment are high earn less for at least 10 to 15 years than students who graduate when economic growth is strong.[2] In addition to lost income and opportunity, unemployed individuals are more likely to experience stress, ill health, reduced life expectancy, depression, loss of motivation and self-worth, and even suicide. Unemployment also leads to social exclusion—one's social circles are often tied to employment—and the loss of various enabling freedoms, especially the freedom to have a good life free from stress and deprivation.

The costs of unemployment invariably spill over from the individual to the family. **The costs of unemployment to the family** include increased stress; the undermining of relationships and family life; increased rates of spousal abuse, child abuse, and divorce; higher rates of hunger, poverty, and homelessness; poorer health for all family members; and harm to children's development, their performance in school, and their employment futures.

Meanwhile, communities that experience high levels of unemployment are also devastated. The **costs of unemployment to the community** include increased levels of crime; a greater need for defensive expenditures on policing and security; increased poverty, hunger, and homelessness; business failures as a result of lower levels of spending; an increase in racial inequality (unemployment rates are much higher for people of color); and the loss of social cohesion.

Lastly, we need to consider how the entire economy is affected. The **macroeconomic costs of unemployment** include the loss of current output due to idled workers; the cost of government programs to support the unemployed, including unemployment insurance and welfare programs; as well as the residual costs of all of the problems to individuals, families, and communities that impact government budgets and the country as a whole. Arthur Okun attempted to estimate the relationship between unemployment and GDP, coming up with **Okun's law**, which states that **a 1% increase in the rate of unemployment is associated with a 2% decrease in the growth of real GDP**. Thus, unemployment has huge macroeconomic costs. Spending plummets and businesses' sales decline, which leads to even more layoffs of workers, and so on. Economist Bill Mitchell estimated that, at the height of the Great Recession in the United States from September 2009 through December 2010, the United States was *losing more than $10 billion in output per day due to unemployment*, for an annual loss of more than $3 trillion![3] When this macroeconomic cost is added to the costs to individuals, families, and communities, it becomes clear how devastating a market failure unemployment can be.

10.2 THE UNEMPLOYMENT RATE AND THE TYPES OF UNEMPLOYMENT

Most people think of a person who is unemployed as someone who does not have a job but wants one. However, there are some nuances to how the official unemployment rate is calculated. In the United States, the **unemployment rate** is computed as follows:

$$\text{Unemployment rate} = \frac{\text{\# of Unemployed}}{\text{Labor force}} \times 100\%.$$

The complexities arise in the definition of the **labor force**, which **includes all people working or actively looking for work**. Anyone who is under 16, living in prison or another type of institution, or on active duty in the military is not included in the labor force. In recent years, about 31% of the U.S. population has fallen outside of the definition of the labor force.

However, millions of former workers have dropped out of the U.S. workforce as deindustrialization eliminated good-paying manufacturing jobs. Many searched for jobs for years but finally gave up. U.S. unemployment benefits usually run out after six months (unless extended by government mandate, which happens only in major recessions). Some former workers qualify for government disability payments due to chronic conditions from manufacturing work, such as bad backs or carpal tunnel syndrome. Others live with their family and depend on other earners for their survival. And some are in prison, after desperation from chronic unemployment caused them to resort to crime. *There are millions of people who are no longer employed but who are not counted as unemployed.*

In May 2020, the U.S. civilian labor force was 158.23 million people, the number of employed people was 137.24 million, and the number of unemployed was 20.99 million. $20.99/158.23 \times 100\% = 13.3\%$. Thus, the unemployment rate in the United States in May of 2020 was 13.3%.

However, the labor force was higher, 164.55 million, in February 2020. Therefore, 6.32 million people left the labor force from February to May 2020. This likely includes workers who were furloughed (temporarily laid off), discouraged workers who gave up looking for work, and more. Economists estimate that the actual unemployment rate was at least 5% higher.

Figure 10.1 shows the unemployment rate in the United States from 1950 to 2021.[4] Notice how much higher the unemployment rate is for blacks—usually about twice as much as the unemployment rate for whites. Latinos also have higher than average unemployment rates, as do women who are the head of the household and teens. However, these official unemployment rates significantly understate the amount of unemployment due to discouraged and underemployed workers.

To understand unemployment in more detail, we need to delve into the different types of unemployment. There are *three major types of unemployment*: frictional, structural, and cyclical.

1. **Frictional unemployment** is **unemployment resulting from normal turnover in the labor market**.

    Workers who have decided to change jobs or occupations and college graduates looking for their first job are considered to be examples of frictional unemployment. At any given time, about 2% of the labor force is likely to fall into this category of unemployment. People in this category are fully expected to find a job in the near future, so frictional unemployment is not usually considered a major problem. Nonetheless, due to the huge costs associated with unemployment, governments try to reduce the amount and duration of

Year	Unemployment Rate for All Workers (%)	Unempoyment by Sex and Age			Unemployment by Race/Ethnicity			Unemployment by Marital Status	
		Teens (Both Sexes, 16-19)	Male Adults (20 & over)	Female Adults (20 & over)	White	Black or African American	Hispanic or Latino Ethnicity	Married Men (Spouse Present)	Women Who Maintain Families
1950	5.3	12.2	4.7	5.1	4.9	-	-	4.6	-
1960	5.5	14.7	4.7	5.1	4.9	-	-	3.7	-
1970	4.9	15.3	3.5	4.8	4.5	8.2	-	2.6	5.4
1975	8.5	19.9	6.7	8.0	7.8	14.8	12.2	5.1	10.0
1980	7.1	17.8	5.9	6.4	6.3	14.3	10.1	4.2	9.2
1985	7.2	18.6	6.2	6.6	6.2	15.1	10.5	4.3	10.4
1990	5.6	15.5	5.0	4.9	4.8	11.4	8.2	3.4	8.2
1995	5.6	17.3	4.8	4.9	4.9	10.4	9.3	3.3	8.0
2000	4.0	13.0	4.1	3.6	3.5	7.6	5.7	2.0	5.9
2005	5.1	16.6	4.4	4.6	4.4	10.0	6.0	2.8	7.8
2010	9.6	25.9	9.8	8.0	8.7	16.0	12.5	6.7	12.3
2015	5.3	16.9	4.9	4.8	4.6	9.6	6.6	2.8	7.4
2016	4.9	15.7	4.5	4.4	4.3	8.4	5.8	2.7	6.8
2017	4.4	14.0	4.0	4.0	3.8	7.5	5.1	2.4	6.0
2018	3.9	12.9	3.6	3.5	3.5	6.5	4.7	2.0	5.4
2019	3.7	12.7	3.3	3.2	3.3	6.1	4.3	1.8	5.0
2020	8.1	18.2	7.5	8.0	7.3	11.5	10.5	4.9	9.7
2021*	6.1	12.3	6.0	5.7	5.4	9.5	7.9	3.7	7.7

FIGURE 10.1 Civilian unemployment rate (%), various groupings, 1950–2021.

frictional unemployment by offering free job search assistance and employment listings.

2. **Structural unemployment** is **unemployment resulting from the permanent displacement of workers due to automation, globalization, shifting demand for products, and other forces that eliminate the need for certain skills in the workplace**.

   Examples of structural unemployment include U.S. steel and textile workers who lost jobs to cheaper foreign competition from China and India, retail service workers replaced by Amazon workers selling goods online, and automobile workers replaced by sophisticated robots. Structural unemployment represents a serious problem because workers' jobs are not expected to return. Structurally unemployed workers will need comprehensive re-education and retraining to develop new skills to qualify for new occupations, or they will be forced to accept unskilled work for low wages. The United States offers subsidized community college tuition and training programs for structurally displaced workers. Many countries in Europe, especially the Nordic countries, offer workers stipends along with comprehensive retraining and free education so they can develop a new skill set for a new, in-demand occupation. Many countries, including Sweden and Japan, also utilize industrial policies to try to create new industries to replace dying ones.

3. **Cyclical unemployment** is **unemployment caused by the decreased demand for labor in a recession** (due to the business cycle). This stems from the decrease in the demand for goods and services that occurs in recessions, which sparks repeated rounds of layoffs and large declines in the demand for labor. Cyclical unemployment can be very large and quite devastating to the entire economic system. Therefore, governments attempt to reduce cyclical unemployment via stabilization policies to stimulate aggregate demand, especially increases in government spending, reductions in taxes, and increases in the money supply. Some governments also provide subsidies or tax cuts to businesses to stimulate hiring.

   To measure cyclical unemployment, mainstream economists use a concept called the **natural rate of unemployment**, which is **the normal rate of unemployment when the economy is not in a recession**. The natural rate of unemployment is also sometimes called **full employment**. The natural rate of unemployment is found by adding together frictional and structural unemployment. Figure 10.2 (next page) displays the U.S. unemployment rate (in black) as well as the natural rate of unemployment (in blue). The difference between the unemployment rate and the natural rate of unemployment is equal to cyclical unemployment, which are the black peaks in Figure 10.2 that occur during and after recessions. Recessions are marked by the grey sections on the figure. Note that in recessions, the unemployment rate shoots up, and then it usually takes years for the unemployment rate to fall back to the natural rate.

UNEMPLOYMENT AND PRICE INSTABILITY 235

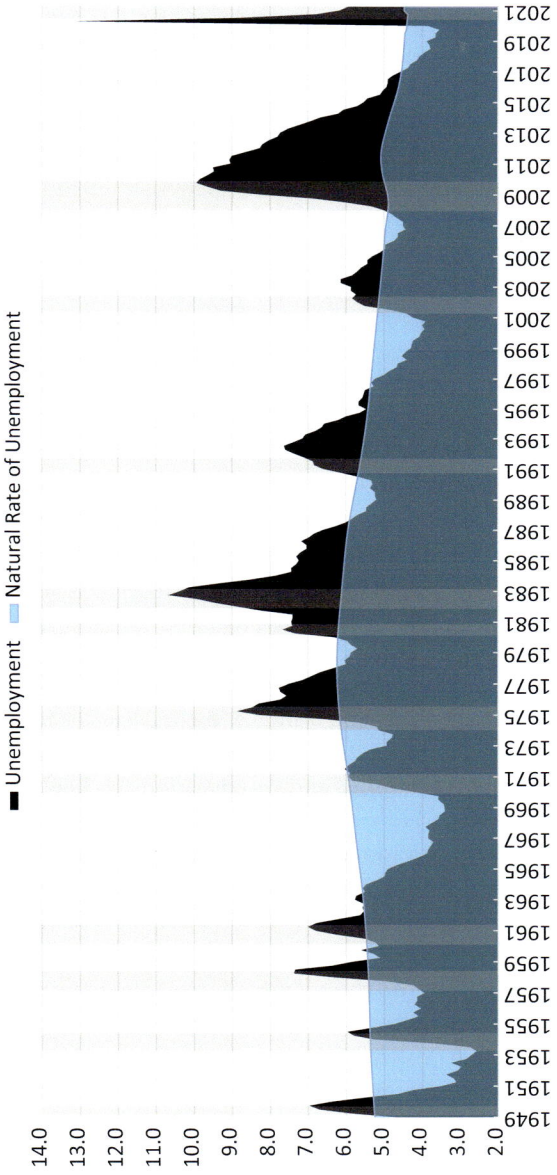

FIGURE 10.2 United States cyclical and natural rates of unemployment (%), 1948–2021.

According to mainstream economists, **the determinants of the natural rate of unemployment are (1) labor force characteristics and demographics, (2) labor market institutions, and (3) government policies**. In terms of (1) labor force characteristics and demographics, older workers with better skills tend to have a lower rate of unemployment, whereas younger, less experienced workers have higher rates of unemployment.

Determining the impact of (2) labor market institutions on the natural rate of unemployment is more complex. For example, the presence of labor unions can impact the natural rate of unemployment but sometimes in surprising ways. In some countries such as France, labor unions that can command high wages and iron-clad job security may cause employers to hire fewer employees than they would otherwise, increasing the natural rate of unemployment. In an uncertain business environment, French employers report that they are unwilling to hire new workers because they cannot fire workers easily if the business situation changes. However, in the Nordic countries, labor unions are often more prevalent than in France, but this has not increased the natural rate of unemployment. Unions in Nordic countries are associated with higher levels of productivity, which more than offsets higher union wages. Meanwhile, the Nordic flexicurity model developed by politicians associated with labor unions ensures that unemployed workers get retrained and/or re-educated for new jobs in growing industries, reducing the structural unemployment component of the natural rate of unemployment. This is where (3) government policies become a key determinant of the natural rate of unemployment.

In general, a government unemployment system that pays workers who lose jobs but does not provide them with the skills they need for a changing workplace will tend to be ineffective, generating a higher natural rate of unemployment as well as high levels of underemployment. In contrast, an unemployment system that provides sophisticated retraining and re-education for unemployed workers coupled with policies designed to cultivate the development of new industries can work very well. We find the lowest natural rate of unemployment in countries such as Norway, the Netherlands, and Japan that utilize these policies effectively.

To political economists, the high degree of variability of the natural rate of unemployment is an indication that the concept is fundamentally flawed. From the political economy perspective, the natural rate of unemployment is the unemployment rate a country chooses to live with given its unique economic structure, and there is nothing particularly "natural" about it. From 1989 to 2019, the unemployment rate in Japan and Norway averaged about 4%, the United States averaged about 6%, France averaged 10%, and Spain had an average unemployment rate of over 16%!

Countries that want a low unemployment rate must pursue policies to achieve that goal, along with policies to limit inflation if economic activity becomes overheated. The experiences of countries who have done this successfully seem to indicate that no country needs to live with high levels of structural unemployment.

Workers can be put to work doing useful tasks in the community or retrained for new occupations in growing industries.

A less important form of unemployment is **seasonal unemployment, which results from changes in the seasonal demand for labor**. Examples include farmworkers and landscapers laid off in the winter and ski instructors and snowplow operators laid off in the summer. Seasonal unemployment can be solved by setting up year-round employment systems that provide alternative jobs for workers in other seasons.

The unemployment rate is one of the most important measures of the health of the macroeconomy. Unfortunately, the unemployment rate tends to understate the degree of unemployment that actually exists.

10.3 HOW THE UNEMPLOYMENT RATE UNDERSTATES EMPLOYMENT INSECURITY

There are two major flaws with the unemployment rate that cause it to understate the level of unemployment and employment insecurity: (1) Hidden unemployment and (2) underemployment.

1. **Hidden unemployment** includes people who are unemployed and would like to work but are unable to find a job. They have looked for work in the last year but not in the last month. Once they quit actively looking for work, these former workers are no longer considered to be part of the labor force, and they are not counted as unemployed even though most people would consider them to be examples of unemployment. There are three categories of hidden unemployment: Discouraged workers, other marginalized workers, and workers forced into retirement.

    Discouraged workers would take a job if one were available, but they have given up looking for work after repeated failures. Many structurally unemployed workers end up in this category. **Other marginalized workers** are those who would like to work but are prevented from doing so by illness, school, family responsibilities, transportation issues, or other reasons. For example, many poor people do not have access to adequate transportation or childcare, which makes it very difficult to get to work even if you want to. The final category of hidden unemployment includes those in **forced retirement** who wanted to keep working but were forced to retire by their employers. Employers often use forced retirement as a cost cutting measure during tough times.

2. **Underemployment** includes involuntary part-time workers who work fewer hours than they want to or underemployed workers confined to jobs that do not utilize their skills.

    Involuntary part–time workers are forced to work less than they want to due to labor market conditions or the actions of employers. Sometimes, only part-time jobs are available due to poor economic conditions. In addition, it is common in the United States for some employers to prevent an employee from working more than 35 hours so they do not have to pay for the employee's health care benefits. To eliminate this problem, the Netherlands passed a law requiring part-time work to come with partial benefits that were equivalent to the benefits per hour that full-time workers were getting.

Underemployed laborers are working in a job that does not utilize the skills they developed. For example, after the collapse of investment banks in the Great Recession of 2008–2010, some people who had worked in investment banking took jobs in the fast food sector because there were no jobs available that utilized their skills and education. As automobile plants replaced skilled blue-collar workers with robots, many autoworkers turned to unskilled work in warehouses or fast food. Involuntary part-time workers and underemployed workers are employed, so they do not count in unemployment statistics. But these laborers are not working the number of hours or the type of employment that they desire.

The Bureau of Labor Statistics tracks discouraged workers, other marginalized ("marginally attached") workers, and involuntary part-time workers. On average from 1994 to 2020, the official unemployment rate averaged 5.79% and hidden unemployment and involuntary part-time employment averaged 4.64%. Thus, a more realistic measure of the unemployment rate that included hidden unemployment and involuntary part-time employment would have averaged 10.43%, *80% higher than the official unemployment rate*. In 2010 in the deepest part of the Great Recession, the official unemployment rate was 9.6%, and hidden unemployment and involuntary part-time employment totaled 7.13% of the labor force. Thus, the official unemployment rate significantly understates the level of employment insecurity (unemployment and underemployment) that is actually occurring.

Due to the prevalence of hidden unemployment, the labor force participation rate is often a much better indicator of actual employment and unemployment. The labor force participation rate measures the percentage of people of working age (ages 16–64) who are employed. A high labor force participation rate means that almost all workers who want to work are able to find a job. A low labor force participation rate indicates that many workers are unable to find work or have chosen not to work. Figure 10.3 displays labor force participation rates for selected countries in 2018. The countries to the left have the highest labor force participation rate for all persons, and those to the right have the lowest.

We see the highest labor force participation rates in European social democracies such as Iceland, Switzerland, and Sweden that feature sophisticated employment creation strategies (industrial policies), active labor market policies, and generous family benefits that encourage women to work, especially generous parental leave and the provision of free childcare. In countries that are very patriarchal and/or that have poor employment creation policies and family benefits, such as Spain and

UNEMPLOYMENT AND PRICE INSTABILITY 239

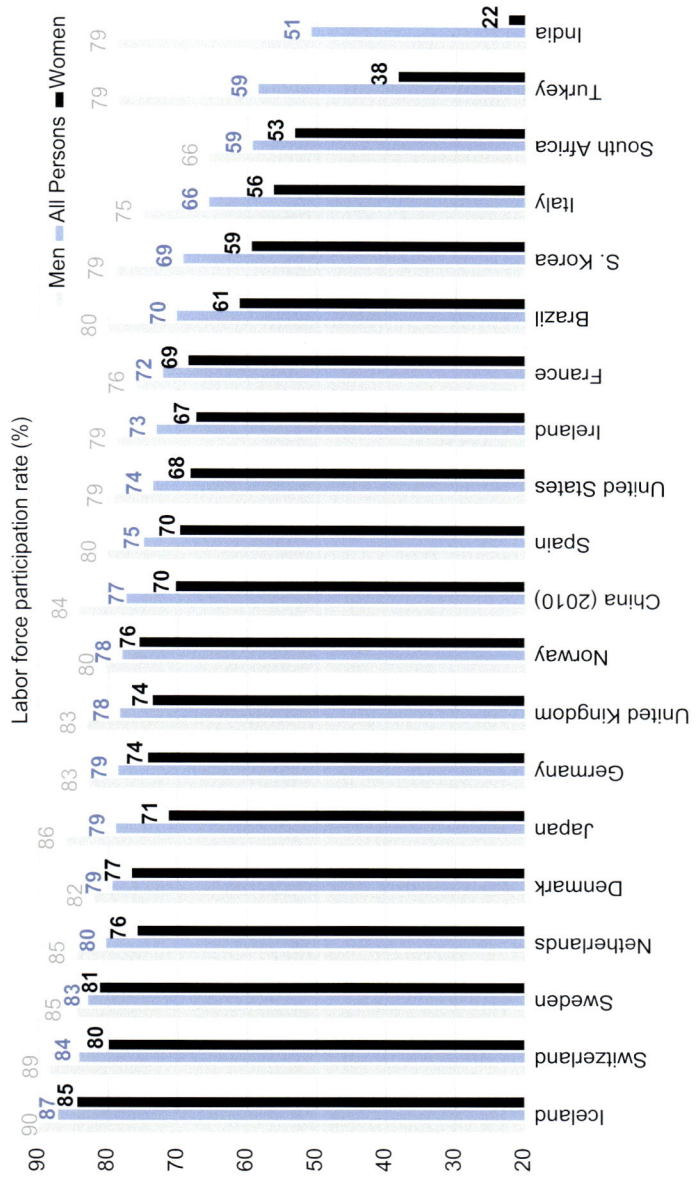

FIGURE 10.3 Labor force participation rates, select OECD countries, 2018.

the United States, we see a much lower labor force participation rate, especially for women. Countries that have chronic structural unemployment, such as South Africa, Turkey, and India, have the lowest labor force participation rates.

Notice also that the gap between male and female labor force participation is lowest in the Nordic countries that have the most generous family leave and child support policies, whereas developed countries with poor family benefits, such as the United States and the United Kingdom, have a much larger gap. The largest gender gaps in labor force participation occur in patriarchal developing countries such as Turkey and India.

A few economists argue that the unemployment rate may be overstated. In surveys, it is possible for a person to claim falsely that they are actively searching for work, or people might be working illegally off the books while reporting that they are unemployed. Most economists believe these problems to be very small and are more concerned with underestimates of the unemployment rate.

10.4 SOLUTIONS TO THE UNEMPLOYMENT MARKET FAILURE

The impact of unemployment, as the major macroeconomic market failure, is so devastating to so many people that all governments enact policies to reduce unemployment. Those policies vary widely, but there are some common patterns. The most widely used policies to reduce the levels and impact of unemployment are the following:

1. **Income replacement**, via some type of unemployment insurance, minimum income guarantee, or other safety net type of program.

    This helps unemployed workers to afford food and shelter while they search for a new job and also serves to maintain the aggregate level of spending in the community if there are many job losses. In most countries, unemployment insurance is paid for by some combination of employed workers and employers via payroll taxes or general tax revenues. Unemployment benefits are usually time limited to discourage workers from staying unemployed for long periods.
2. **Job search assistance**, including employment listings and job counseling, is also provided by virtually all governments.

    Job search assistance reduces the length of time workers are unemployed and improves the efficiency of labor markets.
3. **Stabilization policies** in recessions to eliminate or reduce cyclical unemployment.

    In recessions, increases in government spending, tax cuts, and increases in the money supply can stimulate aggregate demand, returning many businesses to profitability and reducing unemployment. All countries use stabilization policies, although the degree of intervention varies.

4. **Retraining and reeducation** to develop new skills.

    This is one of the preferred methods to deal with structural unemployment. The most sophisticated of these programs are the active labor market policies in Northern Europe, where unemployed workers are given a stipend and enrolled in a training and education program that is tied directly to employment at a particular business in a growing sector. These policies are often tied with industrial policies.

5. **Industrial policies** to promote regional and national economic development.

    An **industrial policy** is **a strategic initiative coordinated by the government to create favorable conditions for particular industry**. Key aspects usually include the provision of infrastructure, workforce training and education tailored to the industry, technological assistance via university and government research labs, tariff protection, various types of subsidies, and other methods to foster employment in a high-growth, high-wage industry. The United States shies away from industrial policies, preferring to let industries develop on their own. However, Northern European and newly industrialized Asian economies use industrial policies extensively and quite successfully.

6. **Private sector incentives**, such as tax cuts and hiring bonuses.

    Some countries, such as the United States, give employers tax credits or subsidies for creating jobs.

7. **Employer of last resort** (ELR) programs.

    ELR programs involve the government providing a job to anyone who wants one but does not have one at a living wage. This is also called a "job guarantee." ELR programs ensure that the economy is always at the lowest possible level of full employment and that workers always have a job if they want one. It would also mean that, instead of paying unemployment benefits to people who are not working, the government would be paying people without jobs to do work that needed to be done in the community. Argentina experimented with such a program in the 2000s, and during the Great Depression the Work Progress Administration (WPA) in the United States also took similar steps to put unemployed people to work doing useful jobs in their communities. The Nordic countries have a job guarantee for workers under age 25, who traditionally have had much higher unemployment rates. Although ELR programs are not widespread, their impacts have been quite positive where implemented.

As is usually the case, economists differ in the types of policies they advocate and the degree of government intervention they prefer. Political economists see unemployment as the most devastating macroeconomic market failure and, correspondingly, they advocate dramatic actions such as ELR programs, active labor market policies, and industrial policies, in addition to the other policies listed above. Most New Keynesian U.S. economists support moderate efforts to reduce the costs of unemployment, such as unemployment insurance and stabilization policies, but not the other policies advocated by political economists. Supply-side economists prefer to alleviate unemployment via private sector incentives, especially tax cuts for businesses. Such incentives can be effective if the business climate is improving. However, business tax cuts do not tend to have much impact on employment if business confidence is low.

Laissez-faire advocates do not approve of dramatic government intervention to alleviate unemployment. Ludwig von Mises, one of the founders of Austrian economics, argued that "Unemployment in the unhampered market is always voluntary. … [T]here is always for each type of labor a rate at which all those eager to work can get a job."[5] From this perspective, if unemployed workers would simply lower the wage that they would accept, they would find work.

The laissez-faire perspective is in direct opposition to Keynes' arguments and the data cited above, showing that there are times in which there are simply not enough jobs available for everyone who wants to work. Furthermore, when recessions are so bad and so long that wages do fall, that erodes aggregate demand and keeps the economy in a recession. Therefore, only a small number of modern economists adopt the laissez-faire view of unemployment.

The coronavirus recession of 2020 provides an interesting case study of how different economic systems approached the economic crisis that resulted from the massive economic shutdowns required to stop the spread of the virus.[6] Only by sending most workers home and preserving social distancing were countries able to stop the spread of the virus and the accompanying deaths. But the decline in economic activity was devastating, businesses' sales dropped precipitously, and firms began to contemplate mass layoffs.

Instead of waiting for workers to lose jobs, the German government decided to pay employers a share of workers' wages. Workers were also required to share tasks, reduce their hours, and take pay cuts of about 10%. Nonetheless, almost all German workers remained employed.

Meanwhile, the United States government expanded unemployment benefits, increasing the benefit amount and the length of time that people could collect benefits. In addition to these measures, workers were given tax rebates of up to $1200, and mortgage, rent, and student loan payments were delayed for almost a year. The United States spent more per person on unemployment benefits than Germany.

The differential impact of these programs on the unemployment rate was massive. In Germany, the unemployment rate increased only slightly from 5.0% in March 2020 to 5.8% in April 2020. In the United States, unemployment more than tripled from 4.4% to 14.7% over the same time period. Almost all German workers kept their jobs, whereas many U.S. workers lost jobs permanently as employers went bankrupt.

The contrast between the German and the U.S. approach reflects different priorities. The German government sees maintaining employment as one of its main priorities. The U.S. government helps out unemployed workers and businesses, but it is up to the private sector to create and maintain employment.

Along with unemployment, another important macroeconomic market failure is price instability. We turn to this in the next section.

10.5 PRICE INSTABILITY: INFLATION, DEFLATION, REAL WAGES, AND REAL INTEREST RATES

The **price level** is the general level of prices of goods in a country or region compared to base year prices. The price level is measured via the construction of a **price index**, a specific measure used to compute the cost of a particular, weighted combination of goods. For example, the most widely used price index is the Consumer Price Index (CPI), which is constructed by calculating the average cost over time of purchasing a basket of consumer goods, weighted by the importance of those goods in a typical consumer's budget. The CPI includes the prices of housing (the largest item in consumers' budgets), transportation, food and beverages, apparel, medical care, recreation, education, communication, and other goods and services.

$$\text{CPI} = \frac{\text{Current cost of consumer goods}}{\text{Base year cost of consumer goods}} \times 100.$$

Once we have the CPI, we can use it to compute the rate of change in prices, which tells us whether there is inflation (an increase in CPI) or deflation (a decrease in CPI) in a particular time period. **Inflation** is **an increase in the average level of prices in an economy**, and it is measured via the increase in a price index such as the CPI. Similarly, **deflation** is **a decrease in the average level of prices in an economy**. We take the CPI this year, CPI_2, subtract the CPI last year, CPI_1, and divide by the CPI last year to get the percentage change in CPI. The percentage change in the CPI is the rate of inflation if it is greater than zero or the rate of deflation if it is less than zero.

$$\text{Rate of Change in Prices} = \frac{\text{CPI}_2 - \text{CPI}_1}{\text{CPI}_1} \times 100\%.$$

Figure 10.4 on the next page shows the monthly rate of change in the CPI_U.[7] CPI_U is the consumer price index for urban consumers, and it is used most frequently to measure inflation. Shaded areas in Figure 10.4 represent recessions.

We can see that when the economy is experiencing booms, the rate of change in prices tends to be positive (inflation). However, in deep recessions, such as 2008 and 2020, we see deflation.

The Producer Price Index (PPI) measures the average change over time in the prices of a representative basket of goods and services sold by businesses in the wholesale market to the producers of goods and services. The PPI measures the prices paid for supplies and inputs by producers.

Another important topic related to inflation is the real wage rate. Here, economists use the same terminology as they do when they refer to GDP. Nominal GDP is GDP at current prices. Similarly, the nominal wage rate is the wage rate

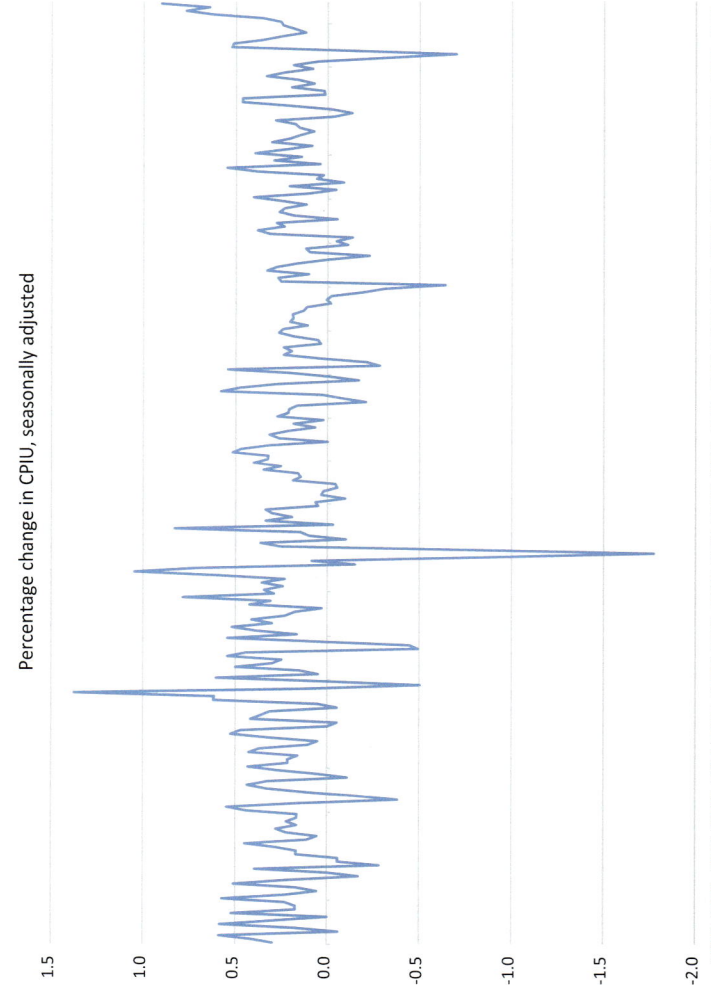

FIGURE 10.4 Monthly rate of inflation and deflation, 2000–2021.

at current prices. Real GDP is GDP at constant prices, which is found by dividing nominal GDP by the GDP deflator (a price index). The **real wage rate is equal to the nominal wage rate divided by the consumer price index** (CPI$_U$).

$$\text{Real wage rate} = \frac{\text{Nominal wage rate}}{\text{CPI}_U}.$$

The real wage rate is a much more accurate measure of workers' purchasing power than the nominal wage rate because it accounts for inflation. The real wage also yields another important insight: *Workers only receive a real wage increase if the increase in nominal wages exceeds the increase in prices.* If nominal wages and prices increase at the same rate, then real wages stay the same, and if nominal wages increase by less than prices increase, workers are experiencing a real wage cut. This is why many labor unions build a cost of living adjustment into their contracts, so that their nominal wages always go up at least as fast as inflation.

Figure 10.5 compares median weekly nominal wages and real wages in the United States from 1979 to 2020. Nominal wages increased dramatically over this period, from $344 per week in 1979 to $1421 per week in 2020, a 413% increase. However, wages and prices *both* increased dramatically over this time period. When we take into account increases in the price index, real wages changed very little, increasing from $322 in 1979 to $381 in 2020, an 18% increase. For 2020, if we take the nominal wage of $1421 and divide by the price index of 3.73, we get the real wage of $381. Thus, most of the increase in nominal wages over the last 41 years was a result of inflation.

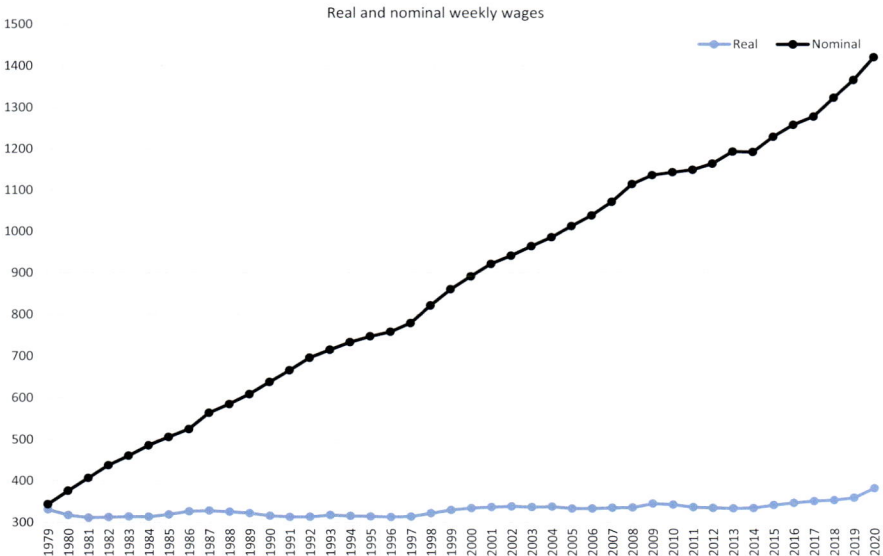

FIGURE 10.5 Median usual weekly earnings for wage and salary workers, 1979–2020.

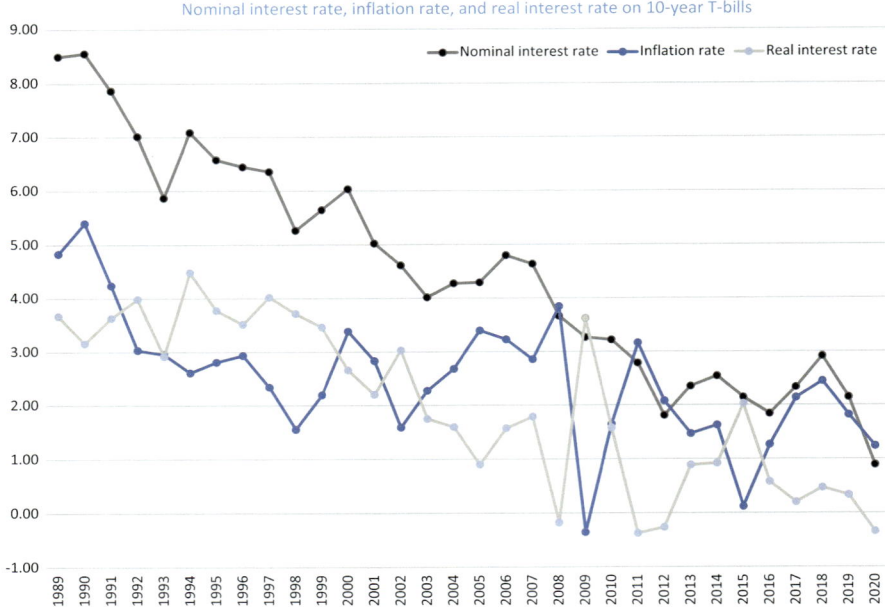

FIGURE 10.6 Nominal and real return on 10-year Treasury Bills, 1989–2020.

Similarly, economists prefer to use the real interest rate rather than the nominal interest rate to determine how much money banks are actually making on their loans. The real interest rate is computed by taking the nominal interest rate and subtracting the rate of inflation:

$$\text{Real interest rate} = \text{Nominal interest rate} - \text{inflation}.$$

Figure 10.6 shows the relationship between nominal interest rates, inflation rates, and real interest rates. In the 1990s, real interest rates usually fell between 3% and 4%, whereas nominal interest rates fluctuated depending on inflation. After the financial crisis in 2008 and 2011–2012, and after the COVID-19 crash of 2020, real interest rates were negative because inflation rates exceeded nominal interest rates. When negative real interest rates occur, this is very hard on banks, because they end up losing money on all of their loans. This is one of the potential problems that can occur from inflation.

10.6 PRICE INSTABILITY AS A MARKET FAILURE: THE PROBLEMS CREATED BY DEFLATION AND INFLATION

Economists consider price instability to be a market failure because unregulated markets regularly generate price instability, and when price instability occurs, it can have a detrimental impact on consumers, manufacturers, the financial sector, and the macroeconomy. Deflation and inflation have very different impacts. Deflation contributes directly to economic crises. Moderate levels of inflation are not problematic and economic actors can easily adjust. But higher levels of inflation, especially sudden increases and wage-price spirals, can be very problematic.

Deflation is usually a sign of an economy in distress, with prices falling due to gluts of goods. A glut of goods is usually a product of a decrease in aggregate demand and subsequent declines in consumer and investor confidence. The decline in aggregate demand can be caused by a stock market crash, government austerity programs, an increase in interest rates, a decrease in the money supply, an overvalued exchange rate, a political or economic crisis domestically or abroad, an increase in unemployment, and so on. Unfortunately, deflation that follows an aggregate demand shock tends to exacerbate the economic crises that caused the deflation.

The major problems created by deflation include the following:

1. **Falling output prices can bankrupt firms.**
    When the prices of goods that firms sell are falling but their costs remain the same (because they have already produced the goods they are trying to sell or because wages and input prices are sticky and do not fall quickly even in downturns), firms will lose money on goods they produce. These losses tend to result in layoffs and decreases in production, events that can be the first step toward a significant decline in economic growth.
2. **Deflation increases the real value of debt.**
    The revenues that a firm takes in tend to fall during deflation, but the firm's debts stay at the same level, making it harder to pay off loans. This, too, can bankrupt firms.
3. **Deflation makes credit more expensive.**
    Deflation causes real, inflation-adjusted interest rates to increase, potentially causing declines in business investment and consumer purchases of durable goods (houses, cars, and appliances) that tent to be purchased on credit. Declines in business investment and consumer purchases reduce aggregate demand, business production, and real GDP.
4. **Deflation can lead consumers to delay purchases**, postponing spending until the future.
    When car prices are falling, consumers will wait to purchase a new car until they think prices have gone as low as possible. Therefore, falling prices can cause immediate declines in aggregate demand, which can in turn lead to business production cuts, layoffs, and declines in real GDP.
5. **Deflation increases real wages, which can prompt layoffs.**
    As Keynes observed, nominal wages are sticky and do not fall quickly even in recessions. If workers' wages stay the same but the prices of goods fall, then workers' purchasing power—their real wage—increases. But this makes labor more costly for firms, further cutting into profits and making

layoffs increasingly likely. Layoffs reduce income and spending, decreasing the demand for products and prompting further layoffs.

Deflationary forces can also become entrenched, creating a deflationary spiral. Falling prices causes reduced spending and business failures, which prompts layoffs and more reduced spending, which causes further deflation and another bout of reduced spending and business failures, and so on.

Correcting deflation requires expansionary fiscal and monetary policies. Increased government spending and tax cuts can stimulate spending and reverse business contraction. Increasing the money supply and purchasing corporate debt can reduce interest rates and promote borrowing, which stimulates consumer spending and business investment. Governments can also prevent deflation by establishing price floors on goods and services to preserve businesses' profitability. During the Great Depression, the U.S. government placed price floors on agricultural products to prevent prices from going so low that farmers went out of business.

The opposite of deflation is **inflation**. In general, rates of inflation in the range of 0% to 5% are easy for businesses and consumers to cope with and do not create significant problems. If everyone expects a 3% rate of inflation, then workers ask for a 3% raise, businesses raise prices by 3%, banks raise interest rates by 3%, and the economy adjusts to a higher price level. Modest rates of inflation can create minor problems, as we will see below. However, rapid inflation, and especially hyperinflation, can create major economic problems, including a financial collapse.

The major problems created by inflation include the following:

1. **Perceptions**: People are misled when looking at wages and interest rates.

    Almost every worker can tell you a story of a boss that promised them a big raise of 2% in a year when inflation was 2.5%, meaning that the worker actually took a pay cut in real terms. "Raises" of less than the rate of inflation actually mean a decline in purchasing power, so these workers are getting a pay cut. Similarly, sometimes nominal interest rates increase, making it seem like it is more expensive to borrow, but real interest rates actually decrease due to the impact of inflation. From Figure 10.6 (page 246), we can see that in 2016 the nominal interest rate was 1.84% and the inflation rate was 1.26%, so the real interest rate was 0.58%. In 2017, the nominal interest rate was higher at 2.33%, but the inflation rate rose to 2.13%, making the real interest rate in 2017 0.20%. Even though the nominal interest rate was higher in 2017 than it was in 2016, the real cost of borrowing money had decreased slightly from 0.58% to 0.20%. Unfortunately, homeowners often focus on nominal interest rates instead of real interest rates.

2. **Lenders lose and borrowers gain from inflation.**

    Inflation somewhat arbitrarily redistributes income from one group to another. Inflation erodes the value of assets that pay fixed (not adjusted for inflation) rates of return, including many bonds, pensions, savings accounts, and other accounts of lenders. High rates of inflation can discourage saving due to this phenomenon, which can be bad for banks and business investment. More important, substantial amounts of inflation mean that borrowers pay back money that is worth less, and lenders end up receiving money that is worth less. With inflation, it becomes easier to earn the money to pay back a loan because wages tend to increase at or above the rate or inflation. In general, the more rapid the rate of inflation, the more wages will increase, while existing loan amounts stay the same. Interestingly, most college students with student loan debt would benefit from an inflationary environment: Wages and salaries when they graduate would be higher due to inflation but their student loan amounts would have stayed the same.

3. **Inflation leads banks to raise nominal interest rates.**

    Recall that banks try to earn a real interest rate of 2% to 4%, onto which they add the inflation rate to arrive at the nominal interest rate. Higher inflation leads directly to higher nominal interest rates, which can cause businesses and consumers to rethink or delay purchases that require borrowing. Thus, higher nominal interest rates can reduce business investment and consumer purchases of durable goods.

4. **Significant levels of unanticipated inflation can cause a financial crisis**.

    Banks take expected inflation into account by raising nominal interest rates, and workers take expected inflation into account by demanding wage increases. Therefore, predictable inflation is rarely a major problem. However, unexpected inflation at significant levels causes negative real interest rates to result (inflation exceeds the nominal rate of interest), which causes banks to lose money on all loans that are not indexed to inflation. High, unanticipated inflation in the 1970s caused large numbers of savings and loan banks to go bankrupt due to such losses. These problems can be especially problematic if interest rate ceilings are in effect. For example, some countries limit the interest rates that banks can charge on loans to poor farmers to prevent usury. However, if the inflation rate exceeds the interest rate ceiling, banks will experience negative real interest rates, which can cause them to go bankrupt.

5. **Inflation can cause the central bank (such as the Fed in the United States) to slow down the economy.**

    In order to eliminate inflationary pressures, central banks sometimes increase interest rates significantly. In the United States, contractionary monetary policy and higher interest rates created by Fed action caused recessions in 1980 and 1990. When inflation increased to over 8% in 2022 due to a booming economy coupled with supply shocks from the coronavirus pandemic, the Fed raised interest rates dramatically, prompting a significant decline in stock prices and fears of a recession. Fears of inflation in the 2010s led the European Central Bank to maintain high interest rates (relative to those in the United

States and the United Kingdom), which reduced Europe's economic growth significantly.

There are also some minor problems that inflation can cause. For example, in the United States, increases in nominal wages can put you in a higher tax bracket, which will result in your paying higher taxes even though your real wages may not have changed. This may be a disincentive to earn a higher income if the tax increase is significant enough.

Although inflation is a problem, **hyperinflation**, which is **rapidly accelerating inflation that is out of control**, can be devastating. During episodes of hyperinflation, prices change daily. The worst modern example of hyperinflation occurred in Zimbabwe in 2007–2008, when prices increased by 98% a day. This means prices were doubling every 24.5 hours! Zimbabwe's annual inflation rate reached 89.7 sextillion percent (89,700,000,000,000,000,000,000%) in 2009. The currency became worth so little that the government was issuing bank notes of $100 trillion, as shown in Figure 10.7.

The fact that prices change daily during hyperinflationary episodes causes people to go out and spend money as soon as they receive it, which causes prices to increase further. We also see a wage-price spiral form, where inflation causes workers to demand higher wages, which causes businesses to raise prices, which causes another round of inflation, which creates demands for more wage increases, and so on.

Eventually, hyperinflation causes people to lose faith in the currency. They buy gold and other nonmonetary assets or put their money in foreign currencies. The financial system ceases to function and people use foreign currencies or barter to make exchanges. Savings and investment collapse as a result. As we will see later, hyperinflationary episodes are usually caused by shortages of

FIGURE 10.7 A one hundred trillion dollar bank note from Zimbabwe in 2008.

essential goods, coupled with unsustainable increases in the money supply by the government.

Given that price inflation can create some serious economic problems, it is important to recognize the causes of inflation and the policies governments can use to correct it. **Cost-push inflation** occurs when a shock to input prices, such as dramatically higher oil prices, causes businesses' costs to increase, which causes them to increase output prices. Cost-push inflation can lead to problematic spikes in inflation due to **wage–price spirals**, as higher prices lead to demands for higher wages, which causes a secondary round of price increases, and so on. This is the most important driver of inflation in the modern economy. **Demand-pull inflation** occurs when increases in the demand for goods cause prices to increase, usually due to increasing wages and input prices in a rapidly growing, overheated economy.

Both of these types of inflation are driven by increases in businesses' costs of production. This can be solved via wages and price controls that limit how much prices can increase, policies to reduce businesses' costs in other ways, or austerity policies that reduce the demand for goods and services and throw the economy into recession.

Political economists argue that inflation is a result of a conflict over the distribution of income between or within classes, such as capital and labor, landowners and peasants; between different groups of workers; or between producers in different sectors. For example, workers often benefit from low levels of unemployment and moderately higher levels of inflation because their bargaining power improves when unemployment is low. However, employers' profits are usually higher when there is a higher degree of unemployment, which keeps wages low, and a lower degree of inflation, which keeps the real rate of profit high. Therefore, the pursuit of a low inflation policy by the government indicates greater support for employers than workers.

Investment banks also like austerity policies because they prefer low inflation and a strong U.S. dollar, which makes their investments more profitable. However, manufacturers benefit from higher demand for products, which is associated with more spending and inflation, and a weaker U.S. dollar that makes U.S. goods more competitive. So, a high-growth, higher inflation, devalued currency approach tends to favor manufacturers, whereas a lower growth, lower inflation, strong currency approach tends to favor financial interests.

Mainstream economists tend to see inflation as a result of exogenous supply shocks, such as an increase in input prices or an overheated economy that causes the cost of inputs to increase. Distributional issues associated with inflation are not a major focus of their work.

Inflation can also be driven by changes in the money supply, although there is substantial debate about this among economists. Furthermore, the austerity philosophy of conservative economists depends on an economic theory called the Phillips curve, which is also hotly debated.

10.7 ECONOMIC THEORY AND POLICY REGARDING INFLATION AND UNEMPLOYMENT

The relationship between the money supply and inflation is a contested one in economics. The **money supply** (abbreviated at M1) **is the total amount of currency and checkable deposits in an economic system**. Some economists think the money supply is directly tied to the rate of inflation, whereas others see the relationship as more tenuous.

As early as 1568, French economist Jean Bodin identified a relationship between the money supply and inflation. He observed that whenever there was an increase in the money supply while the quantity of goods produced remained the same, the result was inflation. This important observation was developed further in the 19th century by classical economists who developed the **quantity theory of money**, which posits that **the quantity of money in circulation (M1) is directly proportional to the price level of goods and services**. This theory was later reiterated by well-known laissez-faire economist Milton Friedman, who stated in 1970 that "inflation is always and everywhere a monetary phenomenon in the sense that it is and can be produced only by a more rapid increase in the quantity of money than in output."

The quantity theory of money is based on the **equation of exchange**:

$$\text{Money supply} \times \text{Velocity} = \text{Price level} \times \text{Real GDP}$$

$$M1 \times V = P \times \text{Real GDP}.$$

Velocity is **the number of times a unit of currency ($) changes hands in a year**.

P in this equation in the real GDP deflator, which is the price index for the whole economy.

The basic intuition of this model is straightforward and important. If we take the amount of money that is available and multiply by the number of times that money is spent in a year, we get total spending in the economy (nominal GDP, which is equal to P multiplied by real GDP). If an economy wants to have economic growth (an increase in real GDP), it also must have an increase in M1. However, if M1 increases faster than real GDP, and if velocity stays constant, then the economy will experience inflation.

This equation implies a direct, proportional relationship between the money supply and the price level. To connect the money supply and inflation, Milton Friedman made three important assumptions:

1. Velocity is constant.
2. Real GDP cannot be influenced by M1 and is driven instead by productivity and technology.
3. Money can influence prices but not vice versa.

If these assumptions hold, then any increase in the money supply will lead to a similar increase in the price level.

We will study the quantity theory of money in more detail later when we take up monetary policy. For now, if we observe the relationship between the money supply (M1) and the price level (CPI), we can see that in recent years they are not closely correlated. Figure 10.8 shows that we regularly see spikes in the money supply, M1, that are not matched by corresponding increases in prices (CPI_U). These spikes in M1 are examples of the Fed engaging in "expansionary monetary policy," dramatically increasing the money supply to combat a recession (recessions are the gray regions in Figure 10.8).

During the Great Recession and its aftermath from 2008 to 2012, laissez-faire economists following Milton Friedman's ideas predicted rampant inflation due to the increases in the money supply that were used to stimulate the economy to reduce the recession's severity. Instead, they recommended that money supply growth should be restricted, known as a "tight" or "contractionary" or "hawkish" monetary policy in the press. However, the inflation they predicted never materialized.

Interestingly, there was inflation of asset values when the money supply expanded. Some economists believe there is more of a connection in the modern world between the money supply and asset values than there is between the money supply and the prices of goods and services.

The fact that increases in M1 do not seem to cause inflation in the United States in the modern era made policymakers much more willing to use expansionary monetary policy to combat recessions. With the coronavirus recession of 2020, the Fed increased the U.S. money supply by an astounding 23%, a modern record. At the same time, prices fell, indicating that deflation was occurring, with all of its

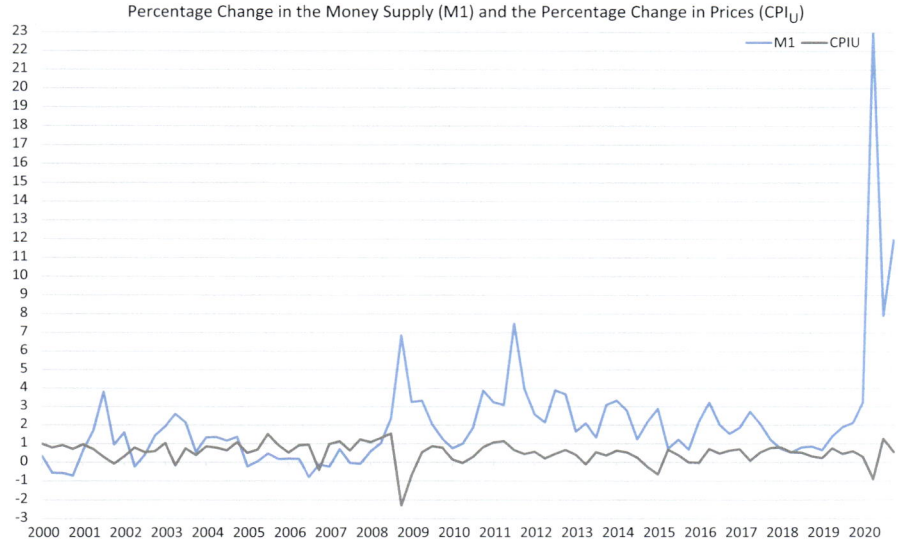

FIGURE 10.8 The money supply and inflation, 2000–2020.

accompanying problems. However, the increases in M1 did prop up asset values. After losing more than 33% of its value in March 2020, the Dow Jones Industrial Average of stocks regained most of its lost ground by June 2020 thanks largely due to the huge increase in M1. By early 2021, stock markets set new records thanks in part to the huge infusions of money from the Fed.

Another contested area of economic theory is the argument that there is an inherent trade-off between inflation and unemployment. Economist A.W. Phillips found that a stable, inverse relationship between inflation and unemployment existed in the British economy for more than a century. A similar relationship was found in the United States in the 1960s. The basic idea is that when an economy grows very quickly, unemployment tends to be very low. But rapid growth and low unemployment lead to increases in wages and input prices as the bargaining power of workers and input suppliers is improved, raising costs and causing businesses to raise prices. Strong demand for goods also allows firms to raise good prices more easily than when demand is low. The result is low unemployment and high inflation. But in a recession, unemployment increases dramatically, reducing the demand for labor and inputs. Costs and goods prices tend to fall in recessions, reducing inflation. Therefore, in recessions we would tend to see high unemployment and low prices, whereas in booms we would see low unemployment and high prices. Thus, the **Phillips curve posits an inverse relationship between inflation and unemployment based on the impact of booms and busts on businesses' costs of production**. The Phillips curve depends on flexible wages and input prices to achieve this result, a potentially problematic assumption.

The Phillips curve has very important policy implications. If the Phillips curve relationship holds, one of the main drivers of high inflation is low unemployment. The belief that this relationship was a strong one led central banks to increase interest rates whenever unemployment rates dipped below the natural rate of unemployment. The U.S. Fed raised interest rates in the boom phase of every recent business cycle in the 1980s, 1990s, 2000s, and 2010s. However, the Phillips curve relationship is no longer as clear as it used to be.

The Phillips curve is supposed to show an inverse relationship between the percentage change in prices (inflation) and the rate of unemployment. Figure 10.9(a) shows that in the 1960s, there was a clear, inverse relationship between inflation and unemployment in the United States consistent with Phillips' ideas. However, that relationship has gotten much more tenuous in recent decades. Figure 10.9(b) plots the Phillips curve in the United States from 2000 to 2020. As we can observe, the Phillips curve became much flatter, having only a slightly negative slope, as indicated by the blue logarithmic trend line.

The flattening of the Phillips curve has important implications. The latest data indicate that an economic system can now grow quickly and have a low unemployment rate without generating significant inflation. This further implies that the austerity policies pursued in the past to reduce inflationary pressures during booms may no longer be as necessary. Economists have theorized that in the

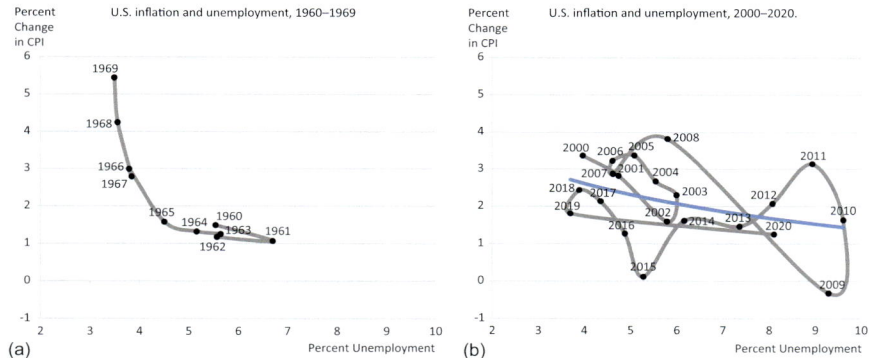

FIGURE 10.9 (a) The U.S. Phillips curve, 1960–1969 and (b) The U.S. Phillips curve, 2000–2020.

modern, globalized economy, firms are less able to raise prices and workers are less able to demand higher wages in booms due to extensive foreign competition. This keeps input prices and wages low even when economies boom, limiting inflationary pressures. Therefore, the Phillips curve likely varies with particular aspects of markets.

We will discuss the Phillips curve and how it has changed in more detail later in the book after we have covered economic theory in more detail. For now, the key thing to note is that in modern developed economies, there may be a weak inverse relationship between inflation and unemployment. This may cause central banks to implement tight money policies in booms. However, central banks may be pressured to keep interest rates low by those who see inflation as less of a problem. Both President Trump and political economists argued that the Fed should lower interest rates in the United States during the economic boom of the late 2010s. The Fed complied, indicating a significant shift in their approach.

10.8 CONCLUSION

Unemployment is the most serious macroeconomic market failure. Its costs to people, families, communities, and the macroeconomy are devastating. Therefore, all governments enact policies to extend safety nets to workers who become unemployed, to assist the unemployed in finding jobs, and to create jobs where possible.

There are three major types of unemployment: Frictional, structural, and cyclical. The frictionally unemployed are between jobs and are expected to be rehired quickly. Structurally unemployed workers present a thornier problem because their skills are no longer in demand in the labor market. Cyclical unemployment is unemployment in excess of the natural rate of unemployment, and it occurs during and following recessions.

The natural rate of unemployment is used as a guide by mainstream economists and policymakers to indicate whether the economy is overheated (when the unemployment rate falls below the natural rate of unemployment) or in a recession (when the unemployment rate is above the natural rate of unemployment). Overheated economies can result in inflation, so policymakers often raise interest rates to slow down overheated economies to reign in inflationary pressures. Recessionary economies require expansionary fiscal and monetary policies to eliminate cyclical unemployment. Political economists argue that the concept of the natural rate of unemployment is fundamentally flawed and that it is possible to have rapid growth, low unemployment, and low inflation simultaneously with the right set of policies. They argue that the government should always pursue maximum employment to benefit workers.

The unemployment rate tends to understate the actual level of unemployment due to hidden unemployment and underemployment. Discouraged workers and part-time workers who want to work full time are important categories of unemployment and underemployment that are not included in the official unemployment rate. Therefore, economists often use the labor force participation rate instead of the unemployment rate to indicate how many people are actually working in an economy.

Policies to reduce the costs or level of unemployment include income replacement (unemployment insurance), job search assistance, stabilization policies in recessions, retraining, and reeducation. Some countries, especially social market economies and state-dominated economies, use industrial policies to stimulate the development of new industries. Some of the world's most effective policies to address unemployment combine active labor market policies and industrial policies, where workers receive specific training and education to prepare for a particular job, at the same time the government creates conditions to stimulate development on an industry that will hire the workers being trained. Market-dominated economies tend to use private sector incentives instead of government-led industrial development efforts to stimulate employment creation.

A few countries have experimented with programs where the government serves as the employer of last resort, providing useful work in communities to any worker who wants a job but cannot find one. Successful examples of ELR programs included the Works Project Administration in the United States during the Great Depression and Argentina's Plan Jefes.

Price instability is another important macroeconomic market failure. Deflation can bankrupt businesses and deepen economic crises. Rapid inflation, especially hyperinflation, can destabilize the financial system and bankrupt banks. Moderate inflation, however, is straightforward for economic agents to incorporate into their expectations and causes only minor issues.

Because deflation is a major problem but low levels of inflation are not, most governments pursue economic policies designed to foster stable, moderate inflation. Both the United States and the European Union have selected 2% as their target inflation rate. If inflation falls below 2%, this may be a sign of an impending recession, so the money supply is increased and other efforts to stimulate the economy are enacted. If the inflation rate exceeds 2%, the central bank will likely increase interest rates to slow down the economy to reduce inflationary pressures and to prevent a wage–price spiral. This shows the broad adherence among policymakers to the Phillips curve idea that there is an inherent trade-off between unemployment and inflation.

Inflation is primarily driven by factors that increase businesses' costs of production. This includes higher input prices driven by supply shortages or by increased demand for inputs during expansions. According to the quantity theory of money, inflation can also be generated by increases in the money supply; however, empirical evidence indicates that this relationship in the modern world in not as clear as it once was. Also less certain in the modern era is the Phillips curve relationship between inflation and unemployment. In the United States in the 1960s, there was a clear, inverse relationship between inflation and unemployment. In the 2000s and 2010s, there was a very small inverse relationship between inflation and unemployment.

The debates over the relationship between inflation and unemployment or the money supply and inflation are driven by economic theory. We turn next to economists' theories regarding how macroeconomies work in the next section to gain greater insights into these issues.

QUESTIONS FOR REVIEW

1. List the major costs that result from unemployment to individuals, families, communities, and the macroeconomy.
2. (a) Define each of the three major types of unemployment in your own works and come up with at least one specific example for each type. Do not use examples from the book. (b) Explain which type of unemployment you believe to be most harmful to the economy and why.
3. Why do many economists find the unemployment rate to be problematic in terms of representing how well workers are doing? Explain carefully.
4. List the major programs that are used to reduce the levels and impact of unemployment. Which policies do you think are most effective? Why?
5. Which of the following statements about inflation are true (select one or more). Explain each answer briefly.
    a. Inflation is worse than deflation because deflation is good for businesses.
    b. Inflation helps lenders because it leads to higher interest rates.
    c. Worries about inflation usually cause the Fed to raise interest rates.
    d. Inflation leads banks to increase nominal interest rates.
    e. Unanticipated inflation can cause a financial crisis.
    f. Inflation causes borrowers to lose and lenders to gain.
6. List the major problems created by deflation. Which of these do you think is most problematic? Why? How can deflation be solved?

7. List the major problems created by inflation. Which of these do you think is most problematic? Why? How can inflation be solved?
8. According to political economists, which groups benefit most from a low inflation, high unemployment economy, and which groups benefit from a high inflation, low unemployment economy?
9. According to the quantity theory of money and the equation of exchange, what will happen to the economy when the money supply is increased by 20% (as it was in 2020), assuming that the assumptions behind the theory hold? What are the potential problems with this approach?
10. According to the Phillips curve, if the economy experiences a rapid economic boom, what can we expect to happen? What are the potential problems with the analysis of the Phillips curve?

NOTES

1 Joan Robinson, *Economic Philosophy* (New York: Doubleday, 1965), 45.
2 Schwandt, Hannes, "Recession Graduates: The Long-lasting Effects of an Unlucky Draw," Stanford Institute for Economic Policy Research, April 2019.

https://siepr.stanford.edu/research/publications/recession-graduates-effects-unlucky#:~:text=Leaving%20school%20for%20work%20during,called%20%E2%80%9Cdeaths%20of%20despair.%E2%80%9D.

3 Bill Mitchell, "The Costs of Unemployment—Again," http://bilbo.economicoutlook.net/blog/?p=17740, accessed June 14, 2020.
4 Sources: *Economic Report of the President*, Federal Reserve Economic Data, and the U.S. Bureau of Labor Statistics.
5 Ludwig von Mises, Human Action: A Treatise on Economics (Auburn, AL: Ludwig von Mises Institute, 1998), 596–597.
6 My thanks to Spandan Marasini, who conducted the research and drafted the initial text for this section.
7 Source: FRED, CPIAUCSL, https://fred.stlouisfed.org/series/CPIAUCSL.

PART IV
Macroeconomic models

In this section, we take up the key models that economists use to analyze the macroeconomy and to determine the best policies to use to confront the major macroeconomic problems. The macroeconomy is so complex that an economist cannot possibly analyze every action of every individual or firm. In addition, microeconomic phenomena often have macroeconomic consequences that are counterintuitive. It seems rational for each individual firm to close its operations in expensive, developed countries and to reopen in cheaper, developing countries. However, as many companies moved operations overseas, wages in developed countries stagnated, growth rates slowed, and sales slowed, undermining profitability to some extent. Even though the microeconomic actions seemed rational, the macroeconomic consequences were destructive.

To analyze the macroeconomy effectively, macroeconomists rely on analysis of the broad patterns of human behavior that lead to large changes in economic outcomes. Instead of analyzing individual consumers, macroeconomists study the patterns affecting the consumption and savings habits of all consumers. Instead of analyzing the capital investment decisions of each firm, macroeconomists study the investment patterns of all firms. This requires the development of models to capture the patterns and relationships between macroeconomic variables.

Interestingly, the models of macroeconomics are not simply microeconomic models that are aggregated (added up). Sometimes, it is possible to intuit macroeconomic behavior from microeconomic models. For example, we know that when individual consumers have more money they tend to spend more, and that holds at the macroeconomic level as well. Increases in national income will lead to increases in national consumption levels. However, there are also macroeconomic foundations for microeconomic behavior. The general macroeconomic environment, including the availability of employment, the rate of economic growth, and the value of the stock market, all drive individual consumer behavior. In this sense, there are macroeconomic foundations for much

DOI: 10.4324/9780429399350-14

microeconomic behavior. Thus, macroeconomists must carefully observe what factors affect the macroeconomy writ large, to determine when microeconomic behavior results in macroeconomic outcomes, and vice versa.

Chapter 11 focuses on the aggregate demand and aggregate supply (AD–AS) model, which is the cornerstone of modern New Keynesian analysis. Unlike the demand curve model of microeconomics, which focuses on individual consumers, the macroeconomic aggregate demand curve incorporates purchases by consumers, purchases of capital goods (investment) by firms, government purchases, and net purchases of goods and services from the international sector. Aggregate demand is the demand curve for all sectors of the macroeconomy. Similarly, aggregate supply is the supply curve for the whole economy, reflecting the behavior of all suppliers in all industries. Due to the complexity of the macroeconomy, there is often disagreement about the structure of macroeconomic models. Political economists dispute certain aspects of the AD–AS model, as we will see in this section.

Chapter 12 lays out the Keynesian aggregate expenditure–income model, sometimes called the "Keynesian cross," with a number of examples and applications. For most of the 20th century, this model was considered the cornerstone of macroeconomics. The chapter goes through how each sector (consumption, investment, government spending, and net exports) fits into the Keynesian model and how changes in the components of aggregate expenditure work with the multiplier. The chapter also includes debates over the Keynesian model.

11 Aggregate demand and aggregate supply

A mainstream economics model of the macroeconomy

Aggregate demand and aggregate supply is one of the most important models in mainstream macroeconomics. This chapter will lay out the basic mechanics of how that model works in the short term and the long term.

As with the supply and demand model developed earlier in the book, the aggregate demand and aggregate supply model works on a consistent set of principles. In the short run, changes in the price level cause the economy to move along the aggregate demand curve and the aggregate supply curve, whereas changes in the determinants of aggregate demand shift the aggregate demand curve, and changes in the determinants of aggregate supply shift that aggregate supply curve. The aggregate demand and aggregate supply model can also be used to analyze the long-run adjustment of the economy. However, there are significant debates among economists regarding the long-term functioning of the economy, and it is important for you to understand the basic parameters of the debate.

This chapter begins by describing the short-run aggregate demand and aggregate supply (AD–AS) model. The chapter then takes up how the multiplier determines the magnitude of shifts in the aggregate demand curve. Subsequently, the chapter discusses the classical and Keynesian models of how the AD–AS model adjusts in the long run and the debate over how the government should intervene during recessions and expansions. The chapter finishes by discussing some of the problems with the AD–AS model according to political economists.

DOI: 10.4324/9780429399350-15

11.0 CHAPTER 11 LEARNING GOALS

After reading this chapter you should be able to:

- Use an aggregate demand and aggregate supply graph to determine how a variety of factors will affect the national price index and real gross domestic product (GDP).

- Define the marginal responding rate, list its components, and explain how the marginal responding rate and its components are related to the multiplier.

- Compute the multiplier using the marginal responding rate.

- Use the multiplier to determine exactly how much the aggregate demand curve will shift in response to specific changes in one of the components of aggregate demand.

- Use the classical model and the Keynesian model to analyze how the macroeconomy will respond to a temporary downturn, a recession, and an overheated economy.

- Critically evaluate the applicability of the classical model and the Keynesian model to the modern economy.

- Describe and analyze the critique of the AD–AS model by political economists.

11.1 THE SHORT-RUN AGGREGATE DEMAND AND AGGREGATE SUPPLY MODEL

Figure 11.1 depicts a typical aggregate demand and aggregate supply graph for the economy. We use the price index for the whole economy, the GDP deflator, on the price axis. On the quantity axis, we use real GDP, which is the total quantity of goods and services produced in a year. Recall that, unlike nominal GDP, real GDP is corrected for changes in prices and measures the total output of goods and services.

As with regular supply and demand graphs, the aggregate demand (AD) and aggregate supply (AS) model always moves toward the equilibrium price index (P_e) and equilibrium real GDP (Q_e). For any price above P_e in Figure 11.1, such as P_H, aggregate supply is greater than aggregate demand. At price index P_H, AS is equal to Q_2 and AD is equal to Q_3, which means that production (AS) is greater than purchases (AD). This causes businesses' inventories to increase because they are selling fewer goods than they produced. As goods pile up in firms' warehouses,

AGGREGATE DEMAND AND AGGREGATE SUPPLY

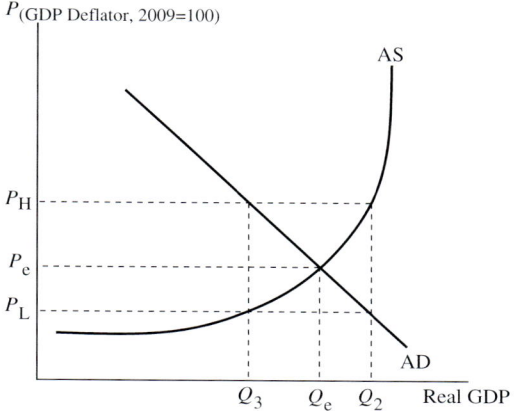

FIGURE 11.1 A typical aggregate demand and aggregate supply graph.

firms reduce production and lower prices, moving the economy toward equilibrium at P_e.

Similarly, for any price below equilibrium, such as P_L, aggregate demand is greater than aggregate supply. At P_L, AD is equal to Q_2 and AS is equal to Q_3. This would mean that at P_L purchases (AD) are greater than production (AS), which would cause inventories of goods decrease. As firms see goods flying out of their warehouses and their inventories of goods falling, firms will increase production and raise prices, moving the economy back toward equilibrium at P_e and Q_e. The economy always ends up at the equilibrium price level and real GDP where AD = AS.

Next, we turn to more details regarding the aggregate demand and aggregate supply curves.

Aggregate demand (AD) is **the total quantity of output (of goods and services) demanded by all sectors in the economy at various price levels**. Aggregate demand is made up of five components: Consumption (C), investment (I), government spending (G), exports (X), and imports (IM).

$$AD = C + I + G + X - IM.$$

Consumption refers to consumer purchases of goods and services. Investment refers to businesses' purchases of investment goods and services, such as machinery, equipment, and construction services, that expand the physical size of businesses' operations. Government spending includes all government purchases of goods and services, such as the services of soldiers and teachers, the construction of roads, and so on. Exports refers to foreign purchases of domestically produced goods and services, such as U.S. exports to Europe. Imports refers to domestic purchases of foreign-produced goods and services, such as U.S. imports of goods from Europe. Note that imports are subtracted from aggregate demand because increased spending on imports means that *less* money is spent in the domestic economy.

11.1.1 Slope of aggregate demand

The aggregate demand curve slopes downward because of three effects:

1. The **real balance effect**: Higher prices mean less real wealth for consumers, causing consumers to spend less. Similarly, lower prices increase consumers' purchasing power, leading to increases in consumer spending.
2. The **real interest rate effect**: Higher prices cause real interest rates to rise because firms and individuals need to borrow more money to pay for more expensive goods. This results in decreases in spending on goods purchased with borrowed funds, including consumers' purchases of houses and cars and businesses' purchases of investment goods.
3. The **foreign trade effect**: Higher prices on U.S. goods and services make U.S. goods less competitive, reducing exports (X), while making imports more attractive to U.S. citizens and thereby increasing imports (IM). The reduction in X and increase in IM decreases aggregate demand.

A shift in the aggregate supply curve will cause a change in the price index, which will then move the economy along the aggregate demand curve due to the three reasons listed above. It is important to note that the real balance effect, real interest rate effect, and foreign trade effect are very small according to economic research, so the real-world aggregate demand curve is much steeper than the one in Figure 11.1. In fact, as we will see later, some economists believe that the AD curve is perfectly inelastic or maybe even upward-sloping. Nevertheless, to make it easier to see how the graphs work, economists tend to draw the aggregate demand curve with a flatter slope than it has in reality.

As we will see later, the aggregate demand curve *shifts* whenever there is a change in one of its components (C, I, G, X, IM) from something other than a change in the price level. As we will also study later, the magnitude of the shift of the aggregate demand curve depends on the initial change in spending and the multiplier.

Aggregate supply (AS) is the **total quantity of output supplied by all producers at various price levels**. **Aggregate supply is equal to the total income of the economy.**

Recall that in the circular flow model, supplying goods and services generates income (GDP), which is paid to households in the form of wages, rent, interest, and profits. (Note that GDP is often abbreviated as Y in many economics texts.) The government takes a share of income in taxes (T), and the rest is left to households in the form of disposable (after-tax) income, which households use for consumption spending (C) or savings (S). Thus,

$$\mathbf{AS = Income = GDP} = C + S + T.$$

11.1.2 Slope of aggregate supply

The aggregate supply (AS) curve slopes upwards because higher prices encourage firms to increase production, increasing real GDP. The shape of the aggregate supply curve depends on where the economy is relative to its capacity.

Full employment, also called potential real GDP (PRGDP), is the economy's normal capacity. This reflects a sustainable level of production without too much or too little unemployment. When the economy is well below its normal capacity, the aggregate supply curve is flat because real GDP can increase without increasing prices. Unemployment and excess capacity keep wages and input prices low, so firms' costs do not increase as they produce more. This corresponds with region I in Figure 11.2, where the economy is deep in a recession and well below its normal capacity (PRGDP).

As the economy nears its normal capacity, increases in real GDP cause some increases in the price level: Prices start to increase as firms increase production as laborers become relatively scarce and as firms begin to reach their productive capacity. This corresponds with region II in Figure 11.2.

Past normal capacity, the economy becomes overheated and the costs of production increase rapidly as real GDP expands. Now, firms must expand plant size to meet demand, and they must train workers for new jobs or lure skilled workers from other jobs because there are not enough skilled laborers for the new positions. Costs increase rapidly as real GDP increases when the economy is beyond its normal capacity. This corresponds with region III in Figure 11.2.

In general, a shift in the aggregate demand curve will cause a change in prices, which will cause the economy to move along the aggregate supply curve.

As we still study in more detail later, the aggregate supply curve shifts when there are changes in costs or profitability that affect most businesses. Generally, if costs increase or profitability decreases, the aggregate supply curve will shift up and to the left; if costs of production decrease or profitability increases, the aggregate supply curve will shift down and to the right.

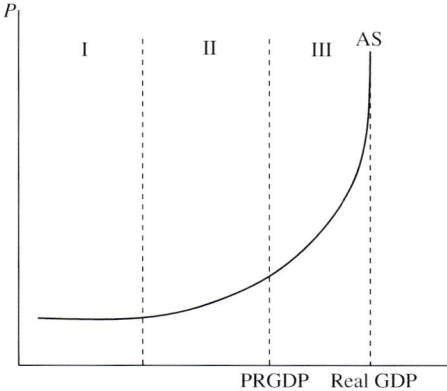

FIGURE 11.2 The slope of the aggregate supply curve.

11.2 SHIFTS IN AGGREGATE DEMAND AND AGGREGATE SUPPLY CURVES

When the aggregate demand curve shifts, this causes a change in the price index (P) and a movement along the aggregate supply curve. When the aggregate supply curve shifts, this causes a change in the price index and a movement along the aggregate demand curve. Shifts in aggregate demand and aggregate supply are a result of changes in the determinants of each curve.

11.2.1 Shifts in aggregate demand

Changes in any one of the components of aggregate demand (AD) will shift the AD curve, unless the change occurs as a result of a change in the price index. Price index changes are already built into the slope of the AD curve.

Consumption. The major factors that affect **consumption** (C) and, as a result, shift AD are changes in (1) income, (2) wealth (stocks, bonds, housing values), (3) expectations, (4) income taxes, and (5) demographic factors. The following changes would *increase* consumption and cause the aggregate demand curve to shift up and to the right:

- Higher incomes, which would give consumers more money to spend.
- More wealth, which gives consumers more assets (stocks and bonds, housing equity) that they can sell to increase spending.
- Positive expectations about the future, which encourage consumers to spend more than usual.
- Lower income taxes, which give consumers more disposable income to spend.
- More people having children and spending money on their children.

Figure 11.3 shows the impact of an increase in aggregate demand. The AD curve shifts to the right, which causes the price index to increase and real GDP to increase as the economy moves along the AS curve.

Aggregate demand would decrease if variables move in the opposite direction as those listed above. Lower incomes, reduced wealth, negative expectations, higher income taxes, and a reduction in the number of children would all result in a decrease in AD, which would in turn cause the price index and real GDP to decrease.

Investment. As noted above, investment is businesses' purchases of investment goods and services, which include machinery, equipment, construction services, and other factors that increase the physical size of businesses' operations. The major factors that affect **investment** (I) and result in a shift in aggregate demand are changes in (1) sales expectations, (2) interest rates, (3) expectations about input/output prices, (4) firms' need for production capacity, (5) technology purchases, and (6) taxes on corporate investment.

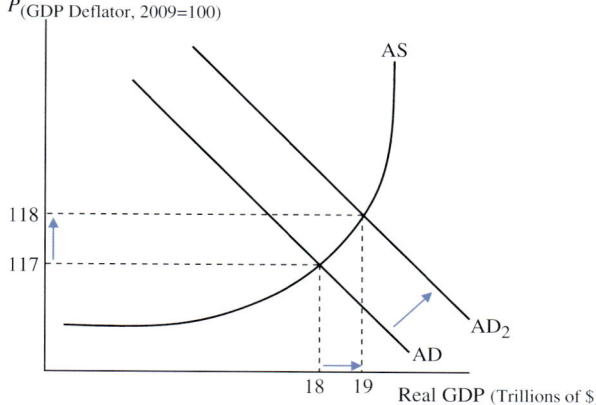

FIGURE 11.3 An increase in aggregate demand.

The following factors would increase investment and cause an increase in aggregate demand such as the one depicted in Figure 11.3:

- Improved sales forecasts would cause firms to want to increase their productive capacity, which would mean purchasing more machinery and equipment and undertaking construction and other types of investment spending.
- Lower interest rates make it cheaper to borrow money, which makes firms more willing to borrow to finance investment spending (investments often require borrowing vast amounts of money).
- Lower expected input prices would cause firms to expect profits to increase in the future, which would spur new investment spending.
- Firms running out of production capacity when they need to produce more would necessitate investment spending to increase capacity.
- Availability of a new technology that could lower costs if implemented would prompt firms to invest in new equipment.
- Lower taxes on business investment, such as investment tax credits, would encourage business to make more investment purchases.

The opposites of the above (e.g., poor sales forecasts, higher interest rates, higher expected input prices, excess capacity, a lack of new technology, and higher taxes on investment) would decrease investment and aggregate demand.

Note that when businesses invest in new equipment or technology, the immediate (short-run) impact is an increase in aggregate **demand** because purchases of investment goods and services have increased. Once that new equipment or technology is implemented effectively by the firm, perhaps a few months or even more than a year later, the firm might see a reduction in the costs of production, which might affect supply. But that is a long-term effect that is NOT reflected in short-term AD and AS analysis.

Government spending. The major factors that affect **government spending** (G) and shift AD are if congress and the president decide to spend more or less on government programs. For example, greater government spending on infrastructure, wars, or alternative energy research would increase government spending and thereby increase aggregate demand. Lower government spending would decrease G and AD.

Net exports. Net exports are exports minus imports. The major factors that affect **net exports** (Exports [X] − Imports [IM]) and shift aggregate demand are changes in (1) U.S. income (we buy more imports when our income is higher), (2) foreign income (foreign countries buy more of our exports when their income is higher), (3) the price of U.S. goods relative to foreign goods, (4) exchange rates, and (5) taxes and tariffs.

The following factors would increase net exports (X − IM) and thereby increase aggregate demand as depicted in Figure 11.3:

- Higher foreign incomes, which causes foreign countries to buy more U.S. exports.
- A decrease in the prices of U.S. goods relative to foreign goods, which would cause U.S. consumers to buy fewer foreign goods (a decrease in imports) and foreign consumers to buy more U.S. goods (an increase in exports).
- Devaluing the U.S. dollar, which makes U.S. goods less expensive (promoting exports) and foreign goods more expensive (decreasing imports).
- An increase in tariffs on foreign goods, which makes foreign goods more expensive for U.S. consumers and reduces spending on imports.

The opposites of the above (e.g., lower foreign incomes, higher prices of U.S. goods, appreciation of the U.S. dollar, and a decrease in tariffs on foreign goods) would decrease net exports and aggregate demand.

Putting all of this together, the determinants of aggregate demand—the factors that cause the aggregate demand curve to shift—are listed in Figure 11.4.

11.2.2 Shifts in aggregate supply

The aggregate supply curve shifts when major changes affecting costs and profitability affect most businesses in a country. Specifically, the **aggregate supply curve shifts** as a result of changes in (1) input prices (wages, oil prices, etc.), (2) the

The factors that cause changes in each component of aggregate demand, which causes the AD curve to shift.

Consumption (C)	Investment (I)	Government Spending (G)	Net Exports (X− IM)
1. Income	6. Sales expectations	12. Government decisions	13. U.S. income
2. Wealth	7. Interest rates		14. Foreign income
3. Expectations	8. Expectations about profits		15. Relative goods prices
4. Income taxes	9. Need for productive capacity		16. Exchange rates
5. Demographic factors	10. Technology		17. Tariffs
	11. Taxes on investment		

FIGURE 11.4 Table showing the determinants of shifts in aggregate demand.

availability of productive resources (land, labor, and capital), and (3) productivity improvements (technology implementation, worker skills, etc.). If costs increase or profitability decreases, the AS curve will shift up and to the left; if costs of production decrease or profitability increases, the AS curve will shift down and to the right.

The following factors would increase AS, shifting it down and to the right:

- Lower oil prices, which reduce energy costs and thereby reduce businesses' costs of production (all businesses use energy).
- Immigration that increases the availability of laborers, reducing costs and increasing productivity.
- The invention of new computer technology that decreases businesses' costs of production and improves efficiency and productivity.

Figure 11.5 shows the effect of an increase in aggregate supply on prices and real GDP. The price index falls from 117 to 116 and real GDP increases from $18 trillion to $19 trillion.

The following factors would cause a decrease AS (a shift up and to the left), an increase in the price index, and a decrease in real GDP: Higher oil prices, a reduction in immigration, and computer hacking, which increase businesses' costs and reduce their productivity. Figure 11.6 lists the major determinants of shifts in the aggregate supply curve.

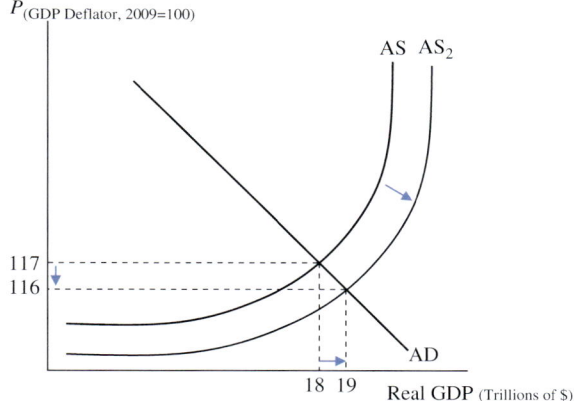

FIGURE 11.5 An increase in aggregate supply.

The major factors (determinants) that cause a shift in the aggregate supply curve are as follows:
1. Input prices
2. Availability of productive resources
3. Productivity changes

FIGURE 11.6 Table showing the determinants of shifts in aggregate supply.

11.2.3 The factors that shift *both* AD and AS: Wages and exchange rates

A change in wages shifts both AD and AS because wages affect consumers' incomes AND businesses' costs of production. Higher wages would increase consumers' incomes, causing an increase in consumption (C) and AD. But higher wages increase costs, causing a decrease in AS. The result would of an increase in AD and a decrease in AS would be no change in real GDP but a significant increase in the price index. (Try to draw a graph on your own to show this.)

A change in exchange rates causes a large shift in AD and a small shift in AS for the U.S. Exchange rates affect foreign purchases of U.S. goods and services (*X*) and U.S. purchases of foreign goods and services (*IM*), and they also affect the cost of imported inputs, affecting AS a small amount. Imported inputs make up a small but still significant share of U.S. businesses' costs, so a change in exchange rates causes a small shift in AS.

For example, an appreciation of the U.S. dollar makes foreign goods less expensive for U.S. consumers and it makes U.S. goods more expensive for foreign consumers. This would decrease U.S. net exports and decrease AD (fewer U.S. goods would be purchased). However, the decrease in the cost of foreign inputs would reduce businesses' costs of production slightly, causing a small increase in AS. Figure 11.7 shows that an appreciation of the U.S. dollar causes a large decrease in aggregate demand and a small increase in aggregate supply, resulting in a decrease in the price index and a decrease in real GDP.

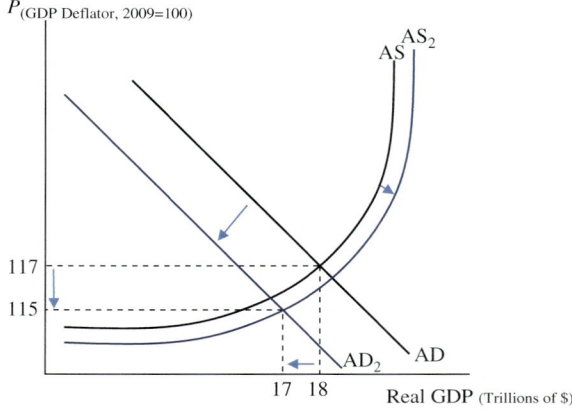

FIGURE 11.7 The impact of an appreciation of the dollar on U.S. prices and real GDP.

11.3 THE MULTIPLIER

One of the most important aspects of macroeconomics is how changes in the economy become amplified via the multiplier. The **multiplier** effect explains **how a $1 change in spending causes aggregate demand and real GDP to change by more than $1 due to a responding process**.

The responding process is driven by the **marginal propensity to consume (MPC)**, which is **the change in consumption (ΔC) that results from a change in disposable (after-tax) income (ΔDI)**. MPC = $\Delta C/\Delta DI$.

If we take national income (GDP) and subtract taxes, (T), we get disposable income (DI), which is the income consumers actually have at their disposal to spend. Disposable income is either spent by consumers (C) or saved (S):

$$DI = C + S.$$

Any change in income is therefore allocated by consumers to either consumption or savings:

$$\Delta DI = \Delta C + \Delta S.$$

If we divide both sides by ΔDI, this can be rewritten as

$$\Delta DI/\Delta DI = 1 = \Delta C/\Delta DI + \Delta S/\Delta DI.$$

Economists define the marginal propensity to save (MPS) as follows:

$$\text{MPS} = \Delta S/\Delta DI.$$

So our equation can be rewritten as MPC+MPS=1. This means that any change in disposable income is divided up between the amount that consumers spend, the MPC, and the amount that consumers save, the MPS.

The responding process plays out in the following way. Suppose that the marginal propensity to consume is 0.8 (MPC=0.8), which means the MPS is 0.2. This means consumers will spend 80% of any increase in income and save 20%. Suppose also that someone goes out and spends $100. From the circular flow model, we know that every dollar of spending becomes someone else's income. So, what will happen to the $100 in income that is generated by the $100 in spending? If the marginal propensity to consume is 0.8, we know that for each $1 in income, people will on average spend 80% of that, or $80. Thus, from $100 in income we would expect to see an additional $80 in consumer spending:

$$\text{MPC} \times \Delta DI = 0.8 \times \$100 = \$80.$$

But this $80 in spending becomes income for another group of people, who will then spend 80% of $80, which is $64. This $64 in spending is income for yet another group of people, who will spend 80% of $64 or $51.20, which is then income for someone else.

The total change in consumption from the initial change in consumer spending of $100 is

$$\$100 + \$80 + \$64 + \$51.20 + \ldots = \$100\left(1 + 0.8 + 0.8^2 + 0.8^3 + \ldots + 0.8^n\right).$$

This is an infinite series that has a solution of the following form:

$$\text{Total change in spending} = \$100 \times \frac{1}{1-0.8} = \$100 \times 5 = \$500.$$

In this case, the **simple multiplier** is 5, which **is equal to** $\frac{1}{(1-\textbf{MPC})}$. This means that each $1 change in spending ultimately generates $5 in total spending, after the money gets spent and respent over and over.

Note that this analysis excludes the presence of taxes and imports, so this is called the "simple multiplier" because it ignores some of the more complex aspects of real-world consumer spending. To develop a fully accurate multiplier, we need to build in two additional factors: Taxes and imports. Each time income is generated, the government taxes a certain percentage of that income in taxes, and that money is not able to be respent. Also, we need to factor in imports. When consumers spend money on imported goods, that money flows out of the country and is not available to be respent on domestic goods and services.

The **marginal responding rate (MRR)** is defined as **the additional spending that is generated from a change in income. MRR depends on the marginal propensity to consume, the net tax rate (t), and the marginal propensity to import (MPM)**:

$$\text{MRR} = \text{MPC}(1-t) - \text{MPM}.$$

The net tax rate (t) is the average amount that the government takes out of a change in income. To find the net tax rate, we add up all of the revenue the government takes in taxes, subtract the money the government gives back to households in the form of transfer payments (welfare payments and other income payments people get from the government), and then divide by total income. Thus, the net tax rate is the average percentage of income that the government takes in taxes. If t is the net tax rate, then $1 - t$ is the percentage of income households can actually spend—disposable income.

The **marginal propensity to import (MPM)** is **the increase in imports that results from an increase in disposable income**. Because this money flows out of the country and is not available to be respent in the domestic economy, we subtract MPM from the responding rate.

What we can glean from this is that some of each $1 of income will be respent, depending on the amount consumers save, the amount the government takes in taxes, and the amount that flows overseas to pay for imports.

For example, if marginal propensity to consume (MPC) is 0.9, the net tax rate (*t*) is 0.2, and the marginal propensity to import (MPM) is 0.12, then the marginal respending rate (MRR) can be computed as follows:

$$\text{MRR} = \text{MPC}(1-t) - \text{MPM} = (0.9)(0.8) - (0.12) = (0.72) - (0.12) = 0.6.$$

With an MRR of 0.6, the multiplier is equal to 2.5:

$$\text{Multiplier} = \frac{1}{1 - \text{MRR}} = \frac{1}{1 - 0.6} = \frac{1}{0.4} = 2.5.$$

11.4 AGGREGATE DEMAND AND THE MULTIPLIER

Because of the multiplier, an initial change in aggregate demand (AD) causes a total change in the aggregate demand curve to be larger than the initial amount. The total shift in the aggregate demand curve will be equal to the initial change multiplied by the multiplier:

$$\text{Total shift in AD} = (\Delta \text{AD}) * (\text{Multiplier}).$$

For example, suppose that consumers increase their spending by $100 billion due to an improvement in consumer confidence. With a multiplier of 2.5, a $100 initial increase in consumption will cause a total shift in aggregate demand of $250 billion:

$$(\Delta \text{AD}) * (\text{Multiplier}) = \text{Total shift in AD}$$

$$(\$100\text{b}) * 2.5 = \$250\text{b}.$$

The initial increase in consumption of $100 billion shifts the aggregate demand curve $250 billion dollars to the right. If aggregate demand equaled $14,000 billion before consumption changed, then it will now equal $14,250 (see Figure 11.8 on the next page), assuming that the price level does not change.

The next question is how much real GDP will increase from this increase in aggregate demand. If the aggregate supply curve is flat between $14,000 billion and $14,250 billion, then real GDP will increase by the same amount, as shown in Figure 11.9(a).

However, if any of the shift in aggregate demand occurs in the upward-sloping portion of the aggregate supply curve, then real GDP will change by *less than* the shift in aggregate demand. As Figure 11.9(b) shows, when the aggregate demand curve shifts by $250 billion, the increase in real GDP is only $200 billion. The

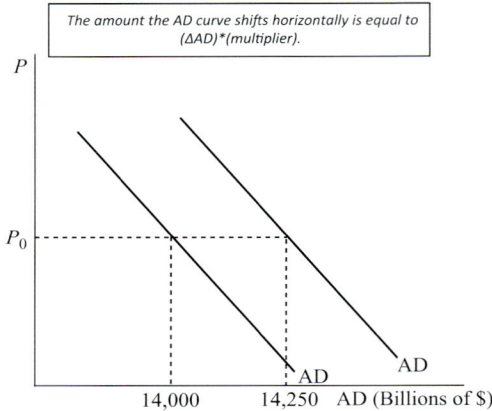

FIGURE 11.8 A shift in aggregate demand with the multiplier.

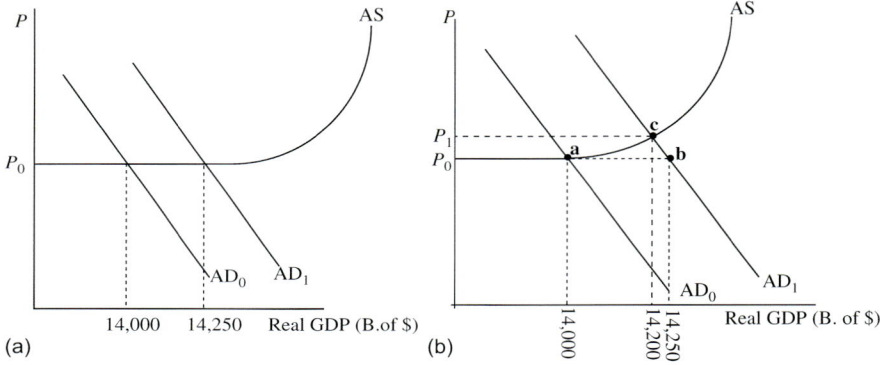

FIGURE 11.9 (a) AD shift when AS is flat and (b) AD shift when AS is upward-sloping.

increase in prices from P_0 to P_1 causes aggregate demand to decline by $50 billion (the movement along the AD curve from point **B** to point **C** as prices increase).

If the change in the aggregate demand shift occurred in a steeper portion of the aggregate supply curve, real GDP would increase by even less.

Note that the same process works in reverse. If there is a decrease in one of the components of aggregate demand, this will cause AD to shift to the left by a larger amount than the initial change due to the multiplier. Real GDP will change by less than the shift in AD (unless we are in the flat part of the AS curve), because prices will fall after the leftward shift in AD, and that will cause movement along the AD curve.

In addition to the five components that directly impact the aggregate demand curve, we need to analyze how tax increases or tax cuts affect AD via their impact on consumption. To compute the impact of tax changes, we use both the MPC and the MRR.

Suppose that the MPC is 0.8, the MRR is 0.5, and the government decides to cut taxes by $100 billion. The MPC tells us the percentage of disposable (after-tax) income that consumers will spend. Therefore, a $100 billion tax cut will mean that consumers have $100 billion *more* in after-tax income, and they will spend 80% of that (with an MPC of 0.8), for an increase in consumption of $80 billion. We would then compute the multiplier, which, using the MRR of 0.5 is equal to 2, to compute the change in aggregate demand of $160 billion.

The formula to compute the change in consumption from a change in taxes is the following:

$$\Delta C = -(\Delta T * \text{MPC}).$$

Note that the economic impact of tax cuts is always smaller than the economic impact of directly spending government money, because consumers save a portion of tax cuts instead of spending all of it. Furthermore, consumers often become pessimistic in deep recessions, which can lead to a reduction in the marginal propensity to consume, which makes the impact of tax cuts even smaller. This is why Keynes preferred government spending to tax cuts as a way to end recessions: Government spending has a larger, more direct impact on real GDP. Tax cuts have a smaller impact, and that impact shrinks further when expectations about the future are poor.

The impact of tax cuts on AD and real GDP also depends on whose taxes are cut. The marginal propensity to consume varies with income. Rich people save more and have a lower MPC than poor people. For example, in recent years the marginal propensity to consume of the richest 20% of the U.S. population has been 0.88, the middle 20% has had an MPC of 0.94, and the MPC of the poorest 20% has been 1.00. Unsurprisingly, the poorest portion of the population spends 100% of their income. This also means that *tax cuts for the poorest U.S. citizens have a 12% larger impact on aggregate demand than tax cuts for the rich.*

Now that we have described how the aggregate demand and aggregate supply model works in the short run, we next turn to long-run adjustment and the debate over whether or not the government should intervene in the business cycle.

11.5 THE CLASSICAL MODEL OF LONG-RUN ADJUSTMENT

In the long run in the classical model of aggregate demand and aggregate supply the economy tends toward a long-run equilibrium on the long-run aggregate supply (LRAS) curve. The LRAS curve is a straight line at full employment, or potential real GDP (PRGDP). **Long-run aggregate supply** represents **the economy at "full employment," when the economy is producing at its maximum normal capacity given existing resources and technology**. Potential real

GDP (PRGDP) reflects the idea that when the economy is in a recession, production (real GDP) is below potential. When real GDP is above PRGDP, the economy is beyond its maximum safe capacity and is overheated.

In Figure 11.10, the economy is in long-run equilibrium whenever the short-run AD and AS curves intersect on the LRAS curve directly above PRGDP.

In the short run, the economy is often in a short-run equilibrium that is above or below potential real GDP. For example, in Figure 11.11(a), the economy is in equilibrium below potential real GDP, which indicates that the economy is in a **recession**. There is a **recessionary gap**, which is equal to **the amount that real GDP is below potential real GDP**.

Figure 11.11(b) shows the economy in equilibrium above potential real GDP. This is called an **overheated economy**, and there is an **inflationary gap** that is equal to **the amount that real GDP is above potential real GDP**. This

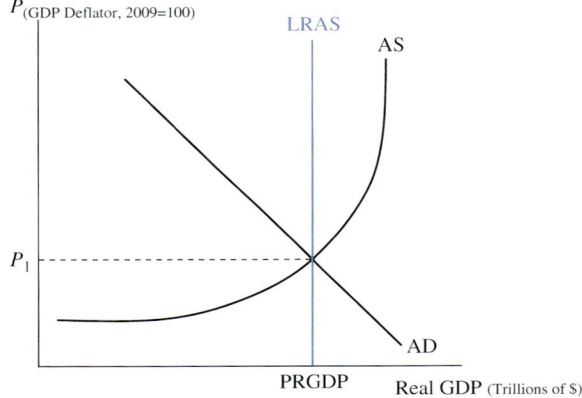

FIGURE 11.10 The long-run equilibrium at LRAS (PRGDP).

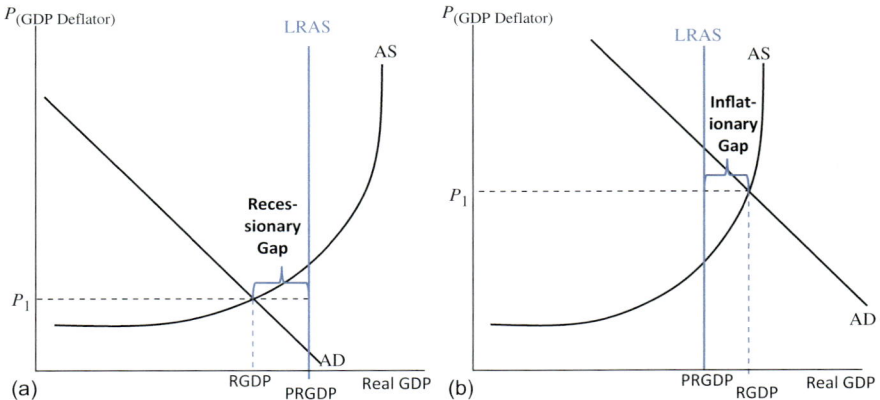

FIGURE 11.11 (a) A recessionary gap and (b) An inflationary gap.

is called an inflationary gap because inflation usually occurs when the economy enters an overheated state.

One of the questions that economists still debate today is whether or not the economy has a tendency to return automatically to potential real GDP in the long run. The two main perspectives on this topic are the classical model and the Keynesian model.

Adherents of the classical model believe that the economy always returns to the LRAS curve at potential real GDP in the long run and therefore the economy needs no government intervention. They are opposed by Keynesian economists, who believe that the economy does not tend toward a stable equilibrium at the LRAS curve and that the government should use stabilization policy to move the economy back to potential real GDP when it strays into a recessions or an overheated economy.

The classical model. According to classical economists such as J.B. Say, the economy always returns to equilibrium at potential real GDP on the long-run aggregate supply curve. Note that this perspective also has modern adherents. A small number of U.S. economists argued that the U.S. government should not intervene after the financial crisis of 2008. The European Central Bank, which is governed by modern-day adherents of the classical model, refused to intervene for many years after the financial crisis impacted Europe. The reasons for the belief that the economy is self-adjusting are outlined below with respect to three cases: Temporary downturns, recessions, and overheated economies.

Temporary downturns. Classical economists did not believe that decreases in spending would lead to recessions. Instead, they though that a decline in consumption would only lead to a temporary downturn. If people consume less ($\downarrow C$) and save more because of worries about the economy, then the decrease in spending will cause a temporary downturn as businesses' sales decline. However, the supply of savings has increased, which means there is more money in banks, and banks want to loan that money out in order to earn profits. This leads banks to lower interest rates, which in turn increases business investment. Thus, the increase in savings by consumers is automatically counteracted by an increase in business investment. The economy stabilizes, and the lower level of spending (and higher levels of savings) does not cause a recession thanks to the increase in investment (I).

Recession. In a full-fledged recession (as opposed to a temporary downturn), according to the classical model, wages and input prices tend to fall due to high levels of unemployment and slack demand. This decrease in the costs of production causes the aggregate supply curve to shift to the right, increasing real GDP until the economy reaches equilibrium at PRGDP on the LRAS curve at a lower price level. Figure 11.12(a) shows this happening.

Overheated economy. If the economy becomes overheated, according to the classical model, wages and input prices increase dramatically due to the economy operating beyond its normal capacity. Firms cannot find the skilled workers they need, and they must pay higher wages to attract new workers. Inputs become

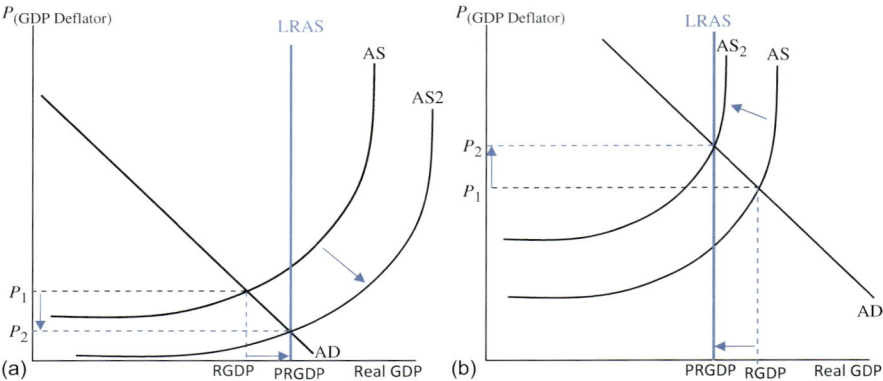

FIGURE 11.12 (a) Recessionary gap elimination (classical model) and (b) Inflationary gap elimination (classical model).

more expensive due to high demand. This dramatic increase in the costs of production causes the aggregate supply curve to shift to the left until the economy reaches equilibrium back at PRGDP at a higher price level. Figure 11.12(b) shows the aggregate supply curve shifting to the left, back to LRAS. Real GDP decreases to potential real GDP.

Therefore, according to the classical model, wages and input prices always adjust to return the economy to full employment at PRGDP on the LRAS curve. Note, however, the fact that the classical model completely ignores aggregate demand and the impact of economic fluctuations on consumer and investor behavior. These are omissions taken up in the Keynesian model.

11.6 THE KEYNESIAN MODEL OF LONG-RUN ADJUSTMENT

Keynes disputed the assertions by the adherents of the classical model that the economy would always adjust quickly and return to PRGDP. To Keynes, this rarely happened in the way the classical economists believed due to four concepts we first discussed in Chapter 5: The *volatility of investment, sticky wages and prices, macroeconomic problems created by wage and price deflation (especially their impact on aggregate demand),* and *the multiplier process.*

11.6.1 Temporary downturn that is not temporary

According to the classical model, if consumers become pessimistic and spend less on consumption (C) while saving more (S), an increase in investment will offset the decline in investment. But Keynes pointed out that this is not how investors actually behave. The primary determinant of business investments is expected sales.

Only if a business expects strong sales in the future will it be willing to invest (purchase machinery and equipment and expand the size of its operations). If sales to consumers decline, this makes businesses pessimistic and they *reduce* their investment. More and more savings piles up in banks, unused because businesses do not want to borrow money to invest when the economic outlook is poor. Indeed, in every period of economic pessimism (and every downturn), money pools in banks and interest rates fall, but investors usually refuse to invest because of their pessimistic outlook for the future. Leakages out of the economy exceed injections. Thus, the temporary downturn that classical economists thought would be self-correcting can spiral into a major recession.

11.6.2 Recessions without end

Keynes also disputed the assertion that the economy will adjust quickly out of a recession for two main reasons. First, his research indicated that wages and input prices are sticky. They do not fall quickly, if at all, even in a recession. Firms do not like to cut wages, because it erodes morale and productivity, so they lay off workers instead. Input producers often cannot cut prices because their costs have not changed and they need to sell goods for a certain price to stay in business. If there is no decrease in wages and input prices, there is no decrease in the costs of production in a recession, and the increase in aggregate supply expected by the classical economists will never happen. As we saw in Chapter 5, in the worst recession in the history of the United States, the Great Depression, prices did not fall significantly for three years despite the poor economic conditions.

Second, classical economists focused only on the supply side of the economy while ignoring the demand side. This was a fatal mistake. Investment depends on expected sales more than any other factor. Once wages and input prices do fall in a major recession, this reduces the incomes of workers and the profits of input suppliers, which reduces their spending. Wage and price deflation has a devastating effect on aggregate demand: When workers and input suppliers reduce spending, the multiplier effect results in that reduction being multiplied through the economy, causing a significant decrease in aggregate demand that is much larger than the initial decrease in spending. Other businesses, seeing this reduction in consumer spending, will invest *less* due to poor expected sales. Thus, even if wages and input prices do fall in a recession, reducing costs and increasing AS, there is a corresponding decrease in AD that keeps the economy in a recession. The economy can linger in a recession for many years.

Keynes also noted that when the economy does finally pull its way out of a recession, it will be led by aggregate demand, especially consumer and investment spending, not aggregate supply. Once consumers and investors become less pessimistic and begin spending, AD will increase, which will cause firms to begin to produce (and supply) more. The government can jump-start this process by engaging in stabilization policy: Increasing spending in the recession to spur consumer and investment spending. The government can increase aggregate demand through fiscal policy, by increasing government spending or cutting taxes, or through monetary policy, by reducing interest rates to stimulate borrowing so that consumers and firms can spend more. This way, the government can shorten the length and severity of recessions.

11.6.3 Overheated economies (booms) become busts

Keynes also disagreed with classical economists on the self-adjustment process out of an overheated economy. According to the classical model, an overheated economy causes wages and input prices to increase, which raises businesses' costs of production, causing AS to shift back to PRGDP. However, that happy story rarely ends the way that classical economists predicted. Instead, the boom sparked by an overheated economy usually turn into a full-fledged bust, causing the economy to spiral into a recession.

Keynes agreed with the classical economists that an overheated economy would cause increases in wages and input prices and that this would erode profitability for businesses. The problem according to Keynes is the behaviors that result when profitability starts to decline in an economic boom. What we know from recent booms that have turned into busts, including the dot-com bubble of 2000 and the real estate bubble of 2007, is that when the bubble bursts, the economy falls apart.

Once people realize that their financial investments in bubble assets are no longer safe, they panic and engage in a mass sell-off. The prices of assets crash. There is a huge decrease in wealth as people see the value of their stocks and homes plummet. In this environment of pessimism, consumers scale back on their purchases, and businesses reduce their investment spending. This decreases aggregate demand. Then, businesses that experience declining sales of goods and services lay off workers and reduce investment further, reducing incomes significantly. The decrease in incomes causes another round of declines in consumer and business investment spending, causing even larger decreases in incomes. Via the multiplier process and the volatility of investment, the economy enters a recession.

Keynes believed in avoiding an overheated economic state by reducing government spending, increasing taxes, or increasing interest rates to slow down the economy. Keeping the economy from growing too quickly can prevent booms from accelerating unsustainably and turning into busts.

Thus, according to Keynes, the economy rarely returns quickly and gently to the long-run aggregate supply curve and potential real GDP. To Keynes, careful macroeconomic policy can almost always improve on the outcomes of an unregulated macroeconomic market.

11.7 LIMITATIONS OF THE AGGREGATE DEMAND AND SUPPLY MODEL

One of the starkest areas of disagreement between mainstream economists and political economists has to do with macroeconomic modeling. Most mainstream economists see the macroeconomy as very stable, with prices adjusting to push aggregate demand and aggregate supply into equilibrium. Political economists see the macroeconomy as fundamentally unstable, and prices are largely unimportant in determining real GDP.

From the perspective of political economists, and some New Keynesian economists, the aggregate demand and aggregate supply model is fundamentally flawed. The main problems with the AD–AS framework include the slopes of the AD and AS curves, feedback effects between AD and AS, and the notion of a stable macroeconomic equilibrium.[1]

The slope of the aggregate demand curve is likely vertical or possibly upward-sloping, rather than downward-sloping. The downward slope of the aggregate demand curve depends on three key effects, each of which is undermined by recent empirical research. The **real balance effect** requires that lower prices increase the real value of wealth, causing consumers to spend more, thereby increasing the aggregate quantity demanded (moving the economy along the aggregate demand curve up and to the left). However, this analysis ignores the fact that most households are net debtors—they owe more money than they have in savings. This is especially true of lower and middle-income households. If you are a household that owes money, then a decrease in prices increases the real amount of the debt that you owe, making you poorer and causing you to spend less. Therefore, depending on the level of debt in an economy, it is quite possible for lower prices to decrease the spending by debtors as much or more than lower prices increase the spending of those with positive wealth balances.

The **foreign trade effect** requires that lower prices make one country's products cheaper than those produced by rival countries, increasing the exports of the country with lower prices and increasing the aggregate quantity demanded. However, in both the Great Depression of the 1930s and the Great Recession of 2007–2010, the fall in prices in the United States rapidly spread to other countries as they also experienced an economic crisis. *The foreign trade effect was thus very small and short-lived because of the rapidity with which deflation spread from one country to another.*

According to the **real interest rate effect**, lower prices lead consumers and businesses to borrow less money because the prices of durable goods and investment (capital) goods have declined. In essence, loan volumes decline as people borrow smaller amounts of money now that prices are lower. However, lower prices usually occur in the presence of economic stagnation, something that is often accompanied by declines in consumer and investor purchases. Similarly, in economic booms when prices are increasing, consumers and investors are confident about the economic situation and tend to increase purchases even though prices have gone up. A more realistic aggregate demand curve that incorporated expectations would therefore be upward sloping under many circumstances.

Taking all of these factors into consideration, if the aggregate demand curve is downward-sloping, it is very, very steep. Furthermore, it might be vertical or even upward-sloping depending on which effects are strongest.

Although political economists see the AD curve as very steep, **the slope of the aggregate supply curve is likely flat for almost the entire graph**. An upward slope to the aggregate supply curve depends on businesses' costs increasing as they produce more. This condition requires the existence of competitive markets where firms experience the law of **diminishing returns** (higher costs as they produce more) and/or where inputs are limited in supply. However, in the modern world, most firms have some market power in output markets, most experience economies of scale where it becomes less expensive to produce larger quantities, and most have multiple input sources from around the globe. This means that firms respond to changes in demand by increasing production but not necessarily by increasing prices. As long as this relationship holds true—as long as firms can increase production without experiencing higher costs—we will get a flat aggregate supply curve. The aggregate supply curve may increase in slope very slightly as the economy becomes very overheated, which is when the economy might actually see higher wages and input prices and scarcities of skilled workers. In recent decades in the United States, prices increased only during the most rapid portion of economic booms. Levels of markups are also difficult to determine. In theory, firms with monopoly power can increase prices when demand for their products increases. However, in the global era, firms have less monopoly power in output markets than they used to, even as **monopsony** power in input markets has increased. This, too, limits how much firms can increase prices and how much their costs increase as production increases.

Figure 11.13 shows what the AD–AS graph looks like from a political economy perspective. The AD curve is very steep, reflecting the ambiguous impact of prices on aggregate demand. The AS curve is very flat except at the very end, because prices are relatively stable as production increases until the economy becomes significantly overheated.

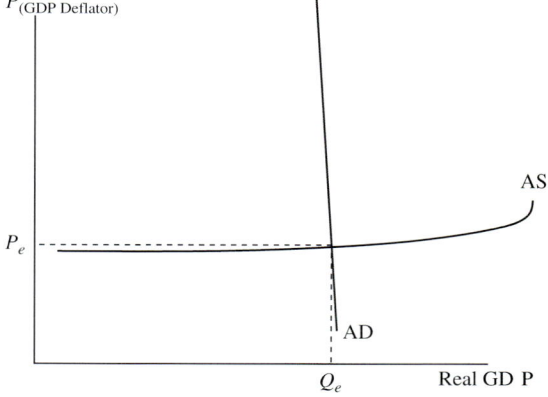

FIGURE 11.13 A political economy aggregate demand and aggregate supply graph.

The concepts of potential real GDP and full employment are also fundamentally flawed from a political economy perspective. The idea of an upper limit on production is reasonable in the short run because resources are limited. However, estimating an economy's maximum production based on the concept of full employment, which assumes stable levels of frictional and structural unemployment, is problematic. As we noted in the chapter on unemployment and price instability, countries can increase production and reduce the level of structural unemployment dramatically via employer of last resort programs or via active labor market policies combined with industrial policies. Therefore, the economy's capacity, its potential real GDP, is somewhat variable.

In the long run, the economy's capacity is even more variable. According to mainstream economists, potential real GDP shifts out in the long run based on investments in a country's capital stock and changes in technology. To political economists, there are many more variables. For example, political economists see potential real GDP varying significantly based on whether or not governments can successfully implement industrial policies to generate economic growth and environmental policies to avoid the destruction of natural resources and environmental services upon which production depends. The notion that there is one potential real GDP that the economy returns to in the long run is therefore disputed by political economists.

Lastly, movements along aggregate demand and aggregate supply curves cannot be easily separated from shifts in these curves due to the interdependence of demand and supply factors in the macroeconomy. Here, one of Keynes' main insights looms large: In the macroeconomy, demand fluctuations tend to cause supply fluctuations. The crash of real estate prices in 2007 caused consumers and investors to reduce spending dramatically, decreasing AD. Firms responded by reducing supply dramatically as their expected sales dropped, which stimulated job losses and further decreases in aggregate demand and aggregate supply. During a boom, demand increases create business optimism, which can cause supply increases, which creates more income and sparks additional aggregate demand increases. The macroeconomy involves complex interactions that are very difficult to boil down to a simple demand and supply model.

Instead of the mainstream economics focus on stability and equilibrium, political economists believe it is better to model the economy as an unstable, evolutionary process. Political economy analysis attempts to model the feedback loops that are an essential characteristic of the macroeconomy. From this perspective, if we focus on the shifts of the AD curve using the multiplier and ignore the effect of prices unless the economy is overheated, we would have a much more accurate model.

Despite the criticisms of political economists and some New Keynesian economists, the AD–AS model remains an important tool used by policymakers to determine how to respond to various macroeconomic situations. Therefore, it is a very important model to understand.

11.8 CONCLUSION

This chapter outlined the aggregate demand and aggregate supply model of the macroeconomy. In the basic aggregate demand and aggregate supply model, aggregate demand shifts whenever there are events that cause (a) consumers to change their spending patterns, (b) businesses to change their purchases of investment goods and services, (c) governments to change their spending patterns, and (d) international actors to shift their purchases of exports or imports. The aggregate supply curve shifts whenever businesses experience changes in profitability or the availability of productive recourses.

The multiplier helps us understand why changes to aggregate demand become magnified in the macroeconomy. Because of the respending process in macroeconomics, each dollar gets spent and respent multiple times, causing real GDP to change by more than any initial change in aggregate demand.

The chapter also laid out the debate over long-run adjustment by two schools of economic thought, classical economists and Keynesian economists. Classical economists believe the economy is self-adjusting and needs little or no economic interference by government. Keynesian economists believe the economy is rarely self-adjusting and usually benefits from appropriate macroeconomic stabilization policies.

Lastly, the chapter explored some of the main criticisms of the aggregate demand and aggregate supply model. Political economists argue that AD curves are very steep, AS curves are very flat, potential real GDP is quite variable, and equilibrium is a flawed concept.

QUESTIONS FOR REVIEW

1. (a) Briefly explain why the aggregate demand curve has a negative slope in the standard AD–AS model. (b) Briefly explain the shape of the aggregate supply curve.
2. In each of the examples below, indicate what happens to aggregate demand, aggregate supply, the price level, and real GDP in the short run.
    a. The government cuts income taxes.
    b. A new, sophisticated robot is invented that dramatically reduces businesses' costs of production but that also causes millions of workers to lose their jobs.
    c. Wages of domestic workers fall due to the coronavirus pandemic.
    d. Domestic interest rates increase.
3. In 2010, the economy was at a real GDP of $12,000 billion and a price index of 101 (2009 = 100). Potential real GDP was estimated to be $13,500 billion. Due to the difficulty in gaining bipartisan agreement on the fiscal budget, the

government shut down. As a result of the government shutdown, measures built into previous budgets triggered an automatic government spending cut of $200 billion. Note that the marginal respending rate (MRR) in 2010 was 0.6. Draw a graph of aggregate demand and aggregate supply displaying the U.S. economy before and after the decrease in government spending. Determine what effect these spending cuts would have on real GDP and the price index.

4. Use Figure 11.14 to answer the following questions.
   a. If the MRR = 0.6 and there is an increase in government spending of $1000 billion, then the aggregate demand curve will shift by $_____ billion. We can expect the new price index to be $_____ and the new real GDP to be $_____.
   b. If the MRR = 0.8 and there is a decrease in investment of $600 billion due to a financial market crash, then the aggregate demand curve will shift by $$_____ billion. We can expect the new price index to be $_____ and the new real GDP to be $$_____ billion.

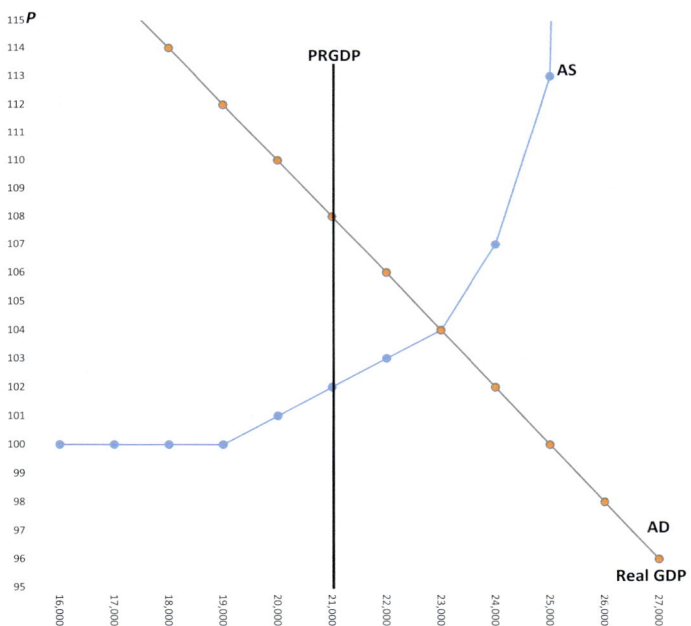

FIGURE 11.14 AD–AS graph.

5. If the MRR = 0.75 and the MPC = 0.9, a $1000 billion tax cut will cause a change in aggregate demand of $_____ billion. Explain, and show your work.

6. Suppose real GDP falls below potential real GDP *temporarily* due to a decline in consumer spending (C), which also has the effect of increasing the pool of savings in banks.

a. What does the **classical model** predict will happen to investment (purchases of capital goods) and aggregate demand in response to these events (a decrease in consumption and an increase in saving) in the **short term**?
   b. How does the Keynesian model differ in its predictions? Explain carefully.
7. Draw a **graph** showing an **overheated economy**. Include AD, AS, and potential real GDP on your graph.
   a. Show what will happen in the long run according to the classical model and explain your answer in words.
   b. What would Keynes like to see done in this case? **Explain** carefully.
8. (a) Draw a **graph** showing the **economy in a recession**. Include AD, AS, and potential real GDP on your graph. Show what will happen in the **long run** according to the classical model and **explain** your answer in words. (b) Discuss why Keynes disagrees with the assumptions of the classical model and what he would propose instead.
9. Explain the political economy critique of the aggregate demand–aggregate supply model.

NOTE

1 See Ron Baiman, *The Morality of Economics: Ghost Curve Ideology and the Value Neutral Aspect of Neoclassical Economics* (London: Palgrave Macmillan, 2016) for an excellent treatment of this topic.

12 The Keynesian aggregate expenditure–income model

The foundation of modern macroeconomics

In the previous chapter, we laid out the aggregate demand and aggregate supply model that is the cornerstone of modern mainstream economics. That model introduced you to a crucial aspect of macroeconomics: Sectoral analysis that details how the sectors of the macroeconomy—consisting of consumers, investors, government bodies, and foreign actors—affect aggregate demand. This chapter undertakes a more detailed sectoral analysis of the macroeconomy, based on the ideas of John Maynard Keynes as reinterpreted by Robert Samuelson and the mainstream economists who followed him.

More specifically, this chapter lays out the Keynesian aggregate expenditure–income model. It explains how each sector fits into the Keynesian model and how changes in the components of aggregate expenditure work with the multiplier. One of the key insights from the Keynesian model is that prices often play a relatively unimportant role in determining national income. Instead, the interplay between various components of aggregate expenditure is the primary determinant.

The chapter begins by describing the consumption and savings functions, which form the basis for the aggregate expenditure model. Then, we add in each additional sector of macroeconomic spending, including investment, government spending, and net exports (exports minus imports). In addition, we incorporate net taxes (taxes minus transfers) into the model. This gives us a comprehensive model of the macroeconomy that can help us to analyze how changes in any of the model's components will affect real GDP.

The chapter concludes with a brief discussion regarding economic debates over the Keynesian aggregate expenditure model and the mainstream aggregate demand and supply model. Both mainstream economists and political economists utilize the aggregate expenditure model, but political economists give it much more prominence in their analysis.

DOI: 10.4324/9780429399350-16

12.0 CHAPTER 12 LEARNING GOALS

After reading this chapter you should be able to:

- Describe the consumption function and its relation to the savings function.
- Explain how consumption, investment, government spending, and net exports interact to determine aggregate expenditure.
- Determine the equilibrium level of national income using an aggregate expenditure chart or graph.
- Analyze how changes in the components of aggregate expenditure or in the components of the marginal respending rate affect equilibrium national income.
- Explain how the aggregate expenditure model corresponds with the aggregate demand curve in mainstream economics.
- Compare and contrast mainstream and political economy approaches to the aggregate expenditure model and aggregate demand and supply model.

12.1 THE CONSUMPTION FUNCTION AND THE SAVINGS FUNCTION

As we saw in the previous chapter, consumers' after-tax, disposable income (DI) is either consumed (C) or saved (S): $DI = C + S$. The marginal propensity to consume (MPC) is the change in consumption (ΔC) that results from a change in disposable (after-tax) income (ΔDI). In mathematical terms, $\text{MPC} = \frac{\Delta C}{\Delta DI}$. Similarly, the marginal propensity to save (MPS) is the change in savings from a change in disposable income, which can be expressed mathematically as $\text{MPS} = \frac{\Delta S}{\Delta DI}$.

In recent decades, U.S. consumers spent about 90% of their disposable income and saved about 10%. Note, however, that consumption and savings rates vary with the confidence of consumers. Figure 12.1 displays U.S. real disposable income and real consumption from 2002 to 2020. The average level of consumer spending is 90% of real disposable income; however, the amount they spend varies significantly with the economic circumstances. In 2020, U.S. consumers received a large increase in disposable income due to significant lump sum tax cuts and stimulus spending that the government enacted to offset the COVID-19 recession. Despite the increase in disposable income, consumers spent *less* as the economy shuttered from lockdowns and as people worried about their futures in the face of mass layoffs and a stock market crash. U.S. consumers shifted from spending 89% of their

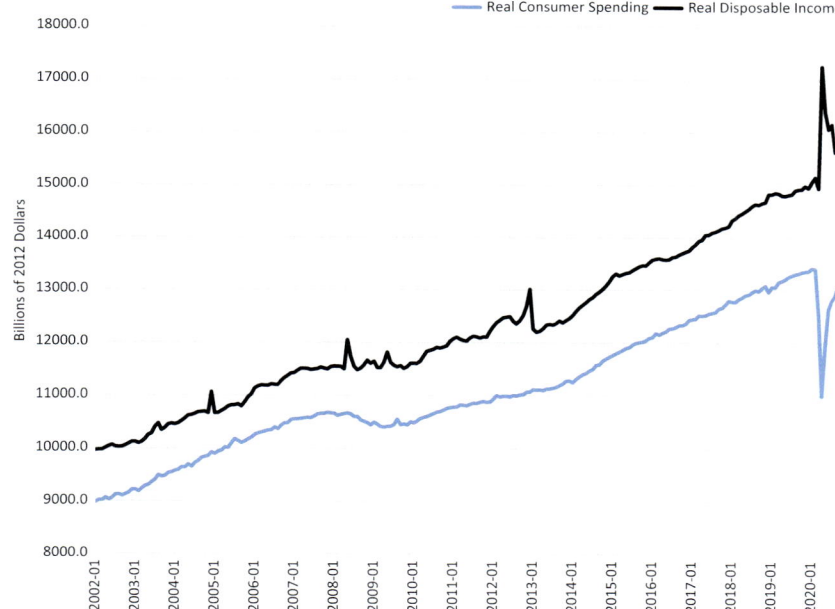

FIGURE 12.1 U.S. real disposable income and real consumer spending, 2002–2020.

disposable income on consumption goods in January of 2020 to spending only 64% in April of 2020. This is one of the reasons why tax cuts have limited effectiveness in recessions.

Due to the systematic relationship (in non-recession years) between disposable income and its two components, consumption and savings, we can model consumption and savings functions for the U.S. economy. Figure 12.2(a) shows a hypothetical relationship between real disposable income (DI), consumption (C), and savings (S). (Note that in this chapter we will use only real values that have been adjusted for inflation.) The table begins with real GDP, which is national income and which is abbreviated as Y. This table uses a tax rate (t) of 50%, which is the average level of taxation in many European countries, to compute real disposable (after-tax) income.

Note that whenever we talk about taxes in this chapter, we are actually talking about *net taxes*, which are taxes minus transfers. The tax rate is the percentage of income taken in by the government, not including money that is taken in and then immediately paid back out as transfer payments to the public. Transfer payments include Social Security, unemployment benefits, and other cash transfers the government pays directly to the public.

Disposable income is either consumed or saved, so at every level of disposable income, $DI = C + S$. Note that when $DI = \$0$, consumers still need to spend money to survive, so there is still $2000 of "autonomous" consumption spending (C_a)—consumption spending that does not depend on income. With $DI = \$0$ and

MACROECONOMIC MODELS

(a)

Real GDP (Y)	Real Disposable Income (DI)	Consumption (C)	Savings (S)
0	0	2,000	-2000
4,000	2,000	3,600	-1600
8,000	4,000	5,200	-1200
12,000	6,000	6,800	-800
16,000	8,000	8,400	-400
20,000	10,000	10,000	0
24,000	12,000	11,600	400
28,000	14,000	13,200	800
32,000	16,000	14,800	1200
36,000	18,000	16,400	1600

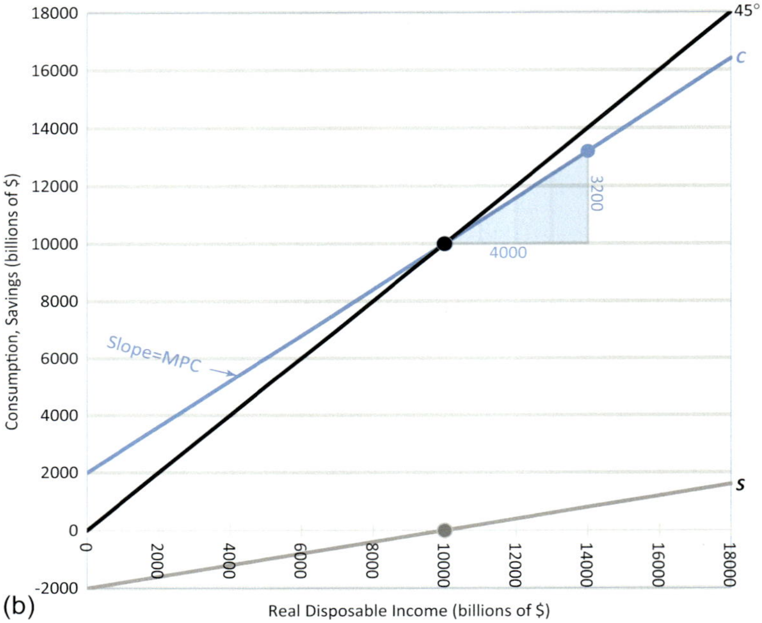

FIGURE 12.2 (a) DI, C, and S (billions of $), (b) Consumption (C) and savings (S) functions.

$C = \$2000$, Savings $(S) = DI - C = -\$2000$. In other words, when consumers have no money, they have to borrow money or spend their savings in order to purchase necessities.

In the table, every time disposable income increases by $2000 billion, consumption increases by $1600. Thus, in Figure 12.2(a), MPC $= \dfrac{\Delta C}{\Delta DI} = \dfrac{1600}{2000} = 0.8$. Similarly, MPC $= \dfrac{\Delta S}{\Delta DI} = \dfrac{400}{2000} = 0.2$.

Figure 12.2(b) plots out the information from Figure 12.2(a) to display a consumption function and a savings function. When disposable income is $0, $C_a = \$2000$ and $S = -\$2000$. When $DI = \$10,000$, $C = \$10,000$ and $S = \$0$. Note that this is where the consumption function, C, intersects the 45° line, which indicates all points where $C = DI$. Also note that the slope of the consumption function is equal to $\frac{\Delta C}{\Delta DI} = 0.8$, which is the marginal propensity to consume (MPC). The slope of the savings function, S, is equal to $\frac{\Delta S}{\Delta DI} = 0.2$, which is the marginal propensity to save (MPS).

As mentioned previously, **autonomous consumption**, C_a, is **the level of consumption that does not depend on disposable income**. Even with no income, consumers must borrow money or spend their savings in order to buy food and pay rent. **Induced consumption**, **consumption induced by changes in income**, is found by multiplying the MPC by disposable income. Therefore, the equation for the consumption function in Figure 12.2(b) is

$$C = \text{Autonomous consumption} + \text{Induced consumption}$$
$$= C_a + (\text{MPC})DI = 2000 + (0.8) \times DI.$$

See the endnote for the derivation of the general form of the consumption function.[1]

Consumption can also be affected by taxes, because taxes affect disposable income, and disposable income is the main determinant of consumption. Taxes affect consumption in two different ways, depending on the type of taxes levied on consumers. Lump sum (autonomous) taxes are one-time taxes (or tax cuts) that do not change as income changes. Lump sum taxes affect autonomous consumption. The tax rate (t) is the average percentage of income that households must pay as (net) taxes. Tax rates affect the amount of disposable income that is available and therefore the amount households can spend on induced consumption purchases.

Recall that Induced consumption (C_i) = MPC × Disposable income (DI).

This can be rewritten as $C_i = \text{MPC}(Y - T)$.

T, total taxes, is found by taking the net tax rate percentage (t) and multiplying by income: $T = tY$.

Substituting, $C_i = \text{MPC}(Y - tY) = \text{MPC}(1 - t)Y$.

Therefore, **induced consumption depends on income (Y), the marginal propensity to consume (MPC), and the tax rate (t)**.

The consumption function forms the basis for the aggregate expenditure model, which plots the total level of aggregate expenditure at each level of real gross domestic product (GDP; national income). We also need to incorporate investment, government spending, and net exports to get a more complete picture of the expenditure side of the economy.

12.2 THE COMPLETE AGGREGATE EXPENDITURE MODEL

Figure 12.3 (next page) contains a table that uses numbers that are typical for the United States to construct an aggregate expenditure model. The table begins with real GDP, which is defined as national income. Economists use Y to represent real GDP.

MACROECONOMIC MODELS

Real GDP Y	Taxes T=0.2Y	Real Disposable Income DI=Y-T	Consumption C=200+0.9DI C=200+0.72Y	Investment I I=3000	Government Spending G G=3600	Net Exports X-IM= 800-0.12Y	Aggregate Expenditure AE=C+I+G+X-IM AE=7600+0.6Y
0	0	0	200	3000	3600	800	7,600
1,000	200	800	920	3000	3600	680	8,200
2,000	400	1600	1640	3000	3600	560	8,800
3,000	600	2400	2360	3000	3600	440	9,400
4,000	800	3200	3080	3000	3600	320	10,000
5,000	1000	4000	3800	3000	3600	200	10,600
6,000	1200	4800	4520	3000	3600	80	11,200
7,000	1400	5600	5240	3000	3600	-40	11,800
8,000	1600	6400	5960	3000	3600	-160	12,400
9,000	1800	7200	6680	3000	3600	-280	13,000
10,000	2000	8000	7400	3000	3600	-400	13,600
11,000	2200	8800	8120	3000	3600	-520	14,200
12,000	2400	9600	8840	3000	3600	-640	14,800
13,000	2600	10,400	9560	3000	3600	-760	15,400
14,000	2800	11,200	10,280	3000	3600	-880	16,000
15,000	3000	12,000	11,000	3000	3600	-1000	16,600
16,000	3200	12,800	11,720	3000	3600	-1120	17,200
17,000	3400	13,600	12,440	3000	3600	-1240	17,800
18,000	3600	14,400	13,160	3000	3600	-1360	18,400
19,000	3800	15,200	13,880	3000	3600	-1480	19,000
20,000	4000	16,000	14,600	3000	3600	-1600	19,600
21,000	4200	16,800	15,320	3000	3600	-1720	20,200
22,000	4400	17,600	16,040	3000	3600	-1840	20,800
23,000	4600	18,400	16,760	3000	3600	-1960	21,400
24,000	4800	19,200	17,480	3000	3600	-2080	22,000

FIGURE 12.3 The components of aggregate expenditure at each level of real GDP (billions of $).

The next column of the table, taxes, is found by taking the average U.S. **tax rate** (t) of 20% ($t=0.2$) and multiplying by national income, Y, to get **total taxes**, T.

$$\text{Total taxes} = (\text{Tax rate}) \times (\text{National income}); \quad T = tY.$$

As before, real disposable income (DI) is found by subtracting total taxes (T) from national income (Y): $DI=Y-T$.

In the model depicted in Figure 12.3, the marginal propensity to consume is 0.9. Therefore, consumption (C) is equal to autonomous consumption (C when $Y=0$, which means that $C_a=\$200$) plus the marginal propensity to consume multiplied by disposable income: $C = 200+0.9(DI)$. Substituting $DI=Y-T$, we can rewrite the equation for consumption as $C=200+0.9(Y-T)$. But since $T=tY=0.2(Y)$, we can rewrite this further as

$$C = 200 + (0.9)(0.8)Y = 200 + (0.72)Y.$$

More generally, in aggregate expenditure models, consumption can be written as the equation

$$C = (C_a) + (\text{MPC})(1-t)Y.$$

Investment (I) and government spending (G) are autonomous in Figure 12.3: They do not vary with national income in this particular model. Economists often assume that investment depends on factors other than current income, such as expected sales and interest rates. Government spending often depends on political factors rather than real GDP. Therefore, under some circumstances, economists find it reasonable to assume in an aggregate expenditure model that I and G are autonomous.

We can construct an aggregate expenditure model in which investment does vary with real GDP because investment can be correlated with real GDP in some circumstances. This would mean we would add a marginal propensity to invest, $MPI = \frac{\Delta I}{\Delta Y}$, to the marginal responding rate. We could also construct a model in which government spending varies with real GDP. Governments with significant **automatic stabilizers** tend to increase government spending whenever income falls, resulting in a marginal propensity for government purchases that would be negative, $MPGP = \frac{\Delta G}{\Delta Y} < 0$. Or, we might have a government that spends money whenever it gets it, resulting in a marginal propensity for government purchases that is positive, $MPGP = \frac{\Delta G}{\Delta Y} > 0$. This would give us a much more complex marginal responding rate of

$$MRR = MPC(1-t) - MPM + MPI + MPGP.$$

However, for simplicity, we have ignored these special cases in this chapter.

Like consumption, net exports have an autonomous component and an induced component. Exports are usually considered to be autonomous because they depend primarily on foreign incomes and preferences, not on U.S. income. Therefore, in this model, exports are equal to $800 billion and they do not vary with real GDP (Y). Imports do vary with Y. The more income U.S. citizens have, the more they spend on purchases of imported goods and services. Because imports are subtracted from expenditure on U.S. goods and services, net exports decrease as U.S. income increases. Specifically, in Figure 12.4 (next page) imports increase (and net exports decrease) by an amount equal to the marginal propensity to import, $MPM = \frac{\Delta IM}{\Delta Y} = 0.12$, multiplied by Y. Therefore, the equation for net exports is

$$\text{Net exports} = (X_a - IM) = 800 - (MPM)Y = 800 - (0.12)Y.$$

If we add all of the components of aggregate expenditure together, $AE = C + I + G + (X - IM)$. Using the equations for each component,

$$AE = (200 + 0.72Y) + 3000 + 3600 + (800 - 0.12Y) = 7600 + (0.6)Y.$$

In this equation, 7600 would be autonomous aggregate expenditure, AE_a.

In the previous chapter, we defined the marginal responding rate (MRR) as the amount of each dollar of income that is respent on U.S. goods and services. Mathematically, $MRR = \frac{\Delta AE}{\Delta Y}$. In Figure 12.3, for each change in income of 1000, there is a change in aggregate expenditure of 600, so $MRR = \frac{600}{1000} = 0.6$.

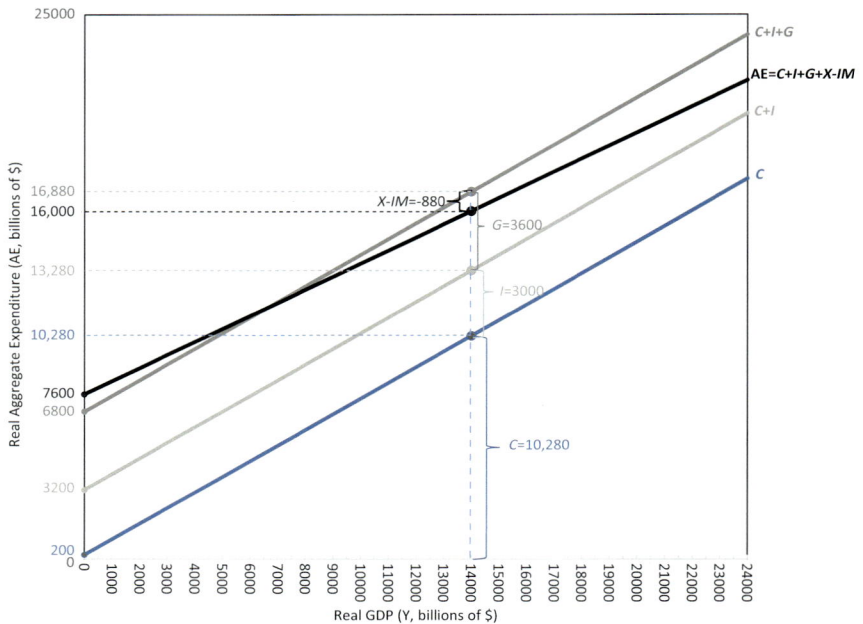

FIGURE 12.4 Construction of the aggregate expenditure curve, $AE = C + I + G + X - IM$.

Also, recall that the marginal respending rate can be expressed in terms of its components:

$$\text{MRR} = \text{MPC}(1-t) - \text{MPM} = (0.9)(0.8) - (0.12) = (0.72) - (0.12) = 0.6.$$

Therefore, the equation for aggregate expenditure (AE) in its general form is

$$AE = \text{Autonomous expenditure} + \text{Induced expenditure} = AE_a + \text{MRR}(Y).$$

Equilibrium in Figure 12.3 occurs where national income (real GDP) is equal to aggregate expenditure—when $Y = AE = \$19,000$ billion. In the Keynesian aggregate expenditure model, changes in business inventories push the economy toward equilibrium where $Y = AE$.

Business inventories are **the value of unsold goods held by retailers, wholesalers, and manufacturers**. Businesses hold inventories in anticipation of future sales, and inventories tend to be particularly large in the case of goods that take a long time to manufacture.

When aggregate expenditure is greater than real GDP, purchases are greater than the total production of goods and services. In this case, $AE > Y$, and businesses are selling more goods than they are producing. Their inventories fall. The decline in inventories below their normal level is a sign to businesses that they can sell more goods and make more money. Because the goal is to maximize profits, decreases in inventories are followed by increases in production and a corresponding increase in real GDP.

When aggregate expenditure is less than real GDP, AE < Y, just the opposite occurs. Businesses find that their inventories increase because total spending is less than total production. As goods pile up in businesses' warehouses, they scale back on production, which decreases real GDP. Therefore, equilibrium real GDP occurs where AE = Y, and there is no change in business inventories because total spending is exactly equal to total production.

Using the numbers in Figure 12.3, notice that when real GDP is $17,000 billion, aggregate expenditure is $17,800 billion. This means consumers, investors, government bodies, and foreign citizens purchased $800 billion more in goods than the economy produced. Businesses then see an $800 billion decline in their inventories. This encourages businesses to increase production, which increases real GDP above $17,000 billion. This process will continue until we reach equilibrium at $Y = AE = \$19,000$ billion.

Similarly, when real GDP is $24,000 billion in Figure 12.3, aggregate expenditure is only $22,000 billion. This would result in businesses experiencing a $2000 billion increase in inventories. They would respond by reducing production, which would reduce real GDP. This process will continue until real GDP has fallen to $Y = AE = \$19,000$ billion.

We also need to recall the importance of injections and leakages in the economy. When income is equal to expenditure, leakages are also equal to injections.

$$Y = DI + T = C + S + T$$

$$AE = C + I + G + X - IM.$$

When $Y = AE$,

$$C + S + T = C + I + G + X - IM, \text{ and}$$

$$S + T + IM = I + G + X$$

Leakages = Injections.

In Figure 12.3, when $Y = \$19,000$, $S = DI - C = 15{,}200 - 13{,}880 = 1320$. $T = 3800$. $X = 800$. Because net exports $(NE) = (X - IM)$, $IM = -NE + X = 1480 + 800 = 2280$.

Therefore, when $Y = \$19,000$, injections are equal to leakages:

$$S + T + IM = 1320 + 3800 + 2280 = 7400$$

$$I + G + X = 3000 + 3600 + 800 = 7400.$$

When $Y = \$15{,}000$, $S = 1000$, $T = 3000$, and $IM = 1800$, $S+T+IM=5800$ and $I + G + X$ is still 7400 (I, G, and X are all autonomous variables in this model).

Therefore, when $Y=\$15,000$, leakages are less than injections, and the extra money injected into the circular flow of the economy causes real GDP to increase. When $Y=\$24,000$, leakages are equal to $9400 while injections are still $7400, meaning that more money is leaking out of the circular flow than is flowing back in. In such circumstances, we can expect real GDP to decrease.

We can also display the aggregate expenditure model using a graph. Figure 12.4 plots out all of the components of aggregate expenditure. The consumption curve starts out where $Y=0$ and autonomous consumption is 200 and proceeds at a slope of $\frac{\Delta C}{\Delta Y}=0.72$. Adding autonomous investment of $3000 shifts the aggregate expenditure curve up by exactly that amount, resulting in the $C+I$ curve. Adding autonomous government spending of $3600 shifts the aggregate expenditure curve up by exactly that amount, resulting in the $C+I+G$ curve. Adding in the final component, net exports, shifts the curve up by $800 (autonomous exports) and then reduces the slope from 0.72 to 0.60 by incorporating the marginal propensity to import (0.12 in this example) into the MRR. The **aggregate expenditure curve** shows **the total level of real spending, including consumption, investment, government spending, and net exports, at each level of real GDP.**

Now that we have derived the aggregate expenditure curve graphically, we can use it to find the equilibrium level of real GDP. Figure 12.5 plots aggregate expenditure at each level of income. Real GDP is displayed in the graph by the 45° line labeled Y. The aggregate expenditure curve starts out at $Y=0$

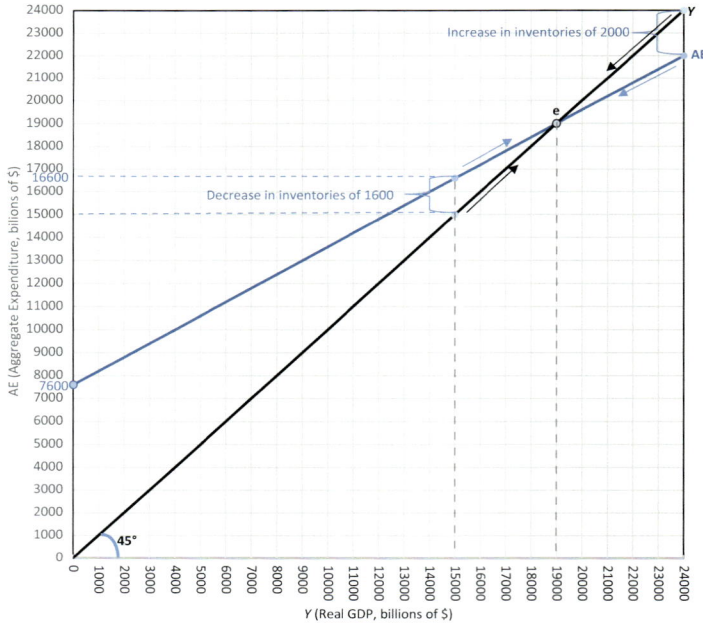

FIGURE 12.5 Keynesian equilibrium: Aggregate expenditure = Real GDP.

and $AE=AE_a=7600$. Then it proceeds at a slope equal to the MRR of 0.6 until $AE=Y=19{,}000$ at point **e**, which is the equilibrium level of real GDP.

The equilibrium level of real GDP can also be determined using the equation for aggregate expenditure. As we saw earlier, the equation for aggregate expenditure is $AE=AE_a+MRR(Y)$. In equilibrium, $AE=Y$. So, substituting Y for AE, we get $Y=AE_a+MRR(Y)$. Simplifying, $Y(1-MRR)=AE_a$. Therefore, the equilibrium level of real GDP is

$$Y = \frac{AE_a}{(1-MRR)} = AE_a \times \text{Multiplier}.$$

In Figure 12.5, $Y = 7600 \times \dfrac{1}{(1-0.6)} = 7600 \times 2.5 = \$19{,}000$ billion.

Point **e** is the equilibrium level of real GDP because the economy tends to adjust until it reaches that point. To the left of point **e**, $AE>Y$, inventories are decreasing, so businesses increase production and real GDP increases as a result. To the right of point **e**, $AE<Y$, inventories are increasing, so businesses decrease production and real GDP falls.

Note that as we saw in the previous chapter, equilibrium real GDP can occur above or below potential real GDP. Once we know equilibrium real GDP and potential real GDP, we can determine whether the economy is experiencing a recessionary gap or an inflationary gap or whether the economy is at normal capacity.

We can also plot out injections and leakages associated with the aggregate expenditure model. Figure 12.6 plots out the injections, $I+G+X$, and the leakages, $S+T+IM$, from the table in Figure 12.3. Injections in this model are all autonomous—they do not vary with real GDP (national income)—so injections are fixed at $7400 and the slope of the injections curve is 0. Leakages vary with income, because savings, taxes, and imports all increase as real GDP increases. This is why the leakages curve has a positive slope. In fact, the slope of the leakages curve is 0.4, which is equal to $(1-0.6)=1-MRR$.

In Figure 12.6 on the next page, the leakages and injections curves intersect at equilibrium when real GDP is $19,000 billion, which corresponds to the equilibrium in Figure 12.5 when $Y=AE$.

Now that we have demonstrated how the aggregate expenditure curve is constructed and how equilibrium is determined, we need to discuss the factors that cause the aggregate expenditure curve to shift.

12.3 SHIFTS IN THE AGGREGATE EXPENDITURE CURVE

As we saw above, a movement along the aggregate expenditure curve is caused by a change in real GDP (Y). When real GDP increases, consumption increases due to the marginal propensity to consume and import purchases increase because of

MACROECONOMIC MODELS

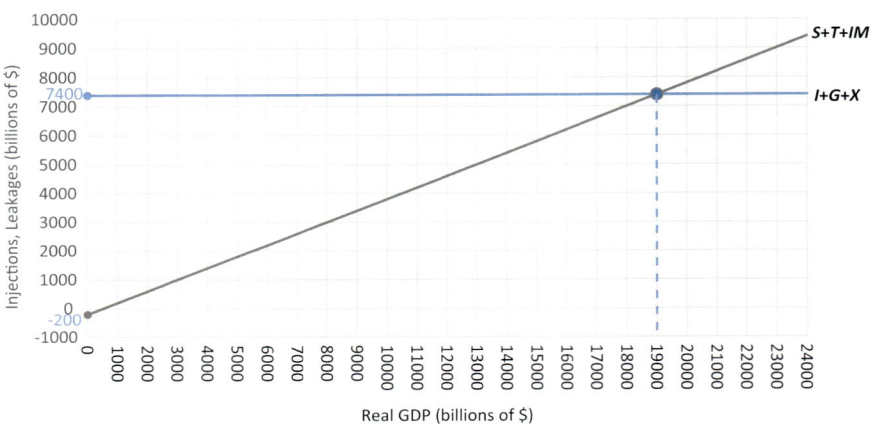

FIGURE 12.6 Injections ($I+G+X$) and leakages ($S+T+IM$).

the marginal propensity to import, moving us along the aggregate expenditure curve.

In general, shifts in the aggregate expenditure curve are caused by autonomous changes in all of the factors that shift the aggregate demand curve that we studied in the previous chapter. However, there are two major exceptions: (1) Changes in national income (real GDP) cause a movement along the AE curve and a shift in the aggregate demand curve and (2) changes in prices (the GDP deflator) in situations where prices affect macroeconomic variables cause a shift in the AE curve and a movement along the AD curve. Autonomous changes in C, I, G, X, or IM cause **parallel** shifts in AE, as we will see below.

Autonomous changes in consumption (C_a) are caused by shifts in wealth, consumers' expectations, lump sum tax changes (that do not depend on income), demographic factors such as the age of the population, and prices (the GDP deflator's effect on consumer wealth). Autonomous changes in investment are driven by changes in business sales forecasts, interest rates, expectations about profitability, businesses' need for productive capacity, new technology opportunities, investment taxes or tax credits, and prices (the GDP deflator's effect on interest rates). All government spending changes are considered autonomous (G_a). Lastly, autonomous changes in net exports ($X_a - IM_a$) are caused by fluctuations in foreign income, relative goods prices, exchange rates, tariff rates, and prices (the GDP deflator's effect on relative goods prices).

A shift in the **slope** of the AE curve is a result of changes in the marginal responding rate and any of its components. This includes the marginal propensity to consume, the tax rate, the marginal propensity to import, and, possibly, the marginal propensity to invest and the marginal propensity for government purchases if these factors vary with real GDP (e.g., if these factors are not autonomous).

Figure 12.7 lists all 22 of the factors that cause a shift in the aggregate expenditure curve.

Figure 12.8 (page 300) shows how an autonomous change in aggregate expenditure affects the AE curve and the equilibrium level of real GDP. Suppose

The factors that cause autonomous changes in the components of AE, and thereby shift the AE curve.

Autonomous Consumption (C_a)	Autonomous Government Spending (G_a)
1. **Wealth** (stocks, bonds, real estate values)	13. **Government decisions**
2. **Expectations** (consumer confidence)	Autonomous Net Exports ($X_a - IM_a$)
3. **Income taxes** (lump sum tax changes)	14. **Foreign income** (directly affects exports)
4. **Demographic factors** (age structure)	15. **Relative goods prices** (foreign vs. domestic goods prices)
5. **Prices** (effect of inflation on consumer purchases)	16. **Exchange rates** (effect on goods prices)
Autonomous Investment (I_a)	17. **Tariffs** (raise or lower prices of foreign or domestic goods)
6. **Sales expectations** (business forecasts)	18. **Prices** (inflation raises prices of domestic goods)
7. **Interest rates** (cost of financing investments)	Changes in the slope of AE
8. **Expectations about profitability** (output, input prices)	19. **Marginal Propensity to Consume** (MPC)
9. **Need for productive capacity** (fully or under-utilized)	20. **Marginal Propensity to Import** (MPM)
10. **Technology** (new opportunities)	21. **Marginal Propensity to Invest** (MPI)
11. **Taxes on investment** (or investment tax credits)	22. **Marginal Propensity for Government Purchases** (MPGP)
12. **Prices** (effect on borrowing costs)	

FIGURE 12.7 The determinants of shifts in the aggregate expenditure curve.

that the economy starts out in equilibrium at point **a** with an autonomous expenditure level of $7600 billion (the first point on AE_0), a slope of 0.6 (the MRR), and an equilibrium real GDP of $19,000 billion. Now suppose that there is an autonomous increase in expenditure of +$1600, which shifts the AE curve up by exactly that amount to AE_1. This could have been caused by an autonomous increase in consumption, investment, government spending, or net exports.

Notice that the new equilibrium, where $AE_1 = Y$, occurs at point **b** at a new real GDP of $23,000 billion. A $1600 billion increase in autonomous aggregate expenditure caused a $4000 billion increase in real GDP because of the multiplier. Recall from the previous chapter that the multiplier determines how many times each $1 of spending gets respent, which then determines the total increase in real GDP. In this example, the multiplier is

$$\text{Multiplier} = \frac{1}{1-\text{MRR}} = \frac{1}{1-0.6} = \frac{1}{0.4} = 2.5.$$

Each $1 increase in spending causes real GDP to change by $2.5, because when people spend money it becomes someone else's income and they spend a portion of it (equal to the MRR), which becomes someone else's income, and so on. Thus, a $1600 billion increase in autonomous aggregate expenditure causes an increase in real GDP of $1600 billion×2.5=$4000 billion.

Now suppose that, starting at point **a**, autonomous aggregate expenditure decreases by $2000 billion. This causes a decrease in real GDP of $2000 billion×2.5=$5000 billion. Real GDP decreases from $19,000 billion to $14,000 billion, and the equilibrium point moves from point **a** to point **c**.

We can also use the equation of the aggregate expenditure curve to determine the equilibrium level of real GDP. Originally, $Y_0 = \frac{AE_a}{(1-\text{MRR})} = \frac{7600}{(0.4)}$ = $19,000 billion. Now that autonomous expenditure has decreased to $5600 billion, $Y_2 = \frac{AE_a}{(1-\text{MRR})} = \frac{5600}{(0.4)} = \$14,000 \text{ billion}$.

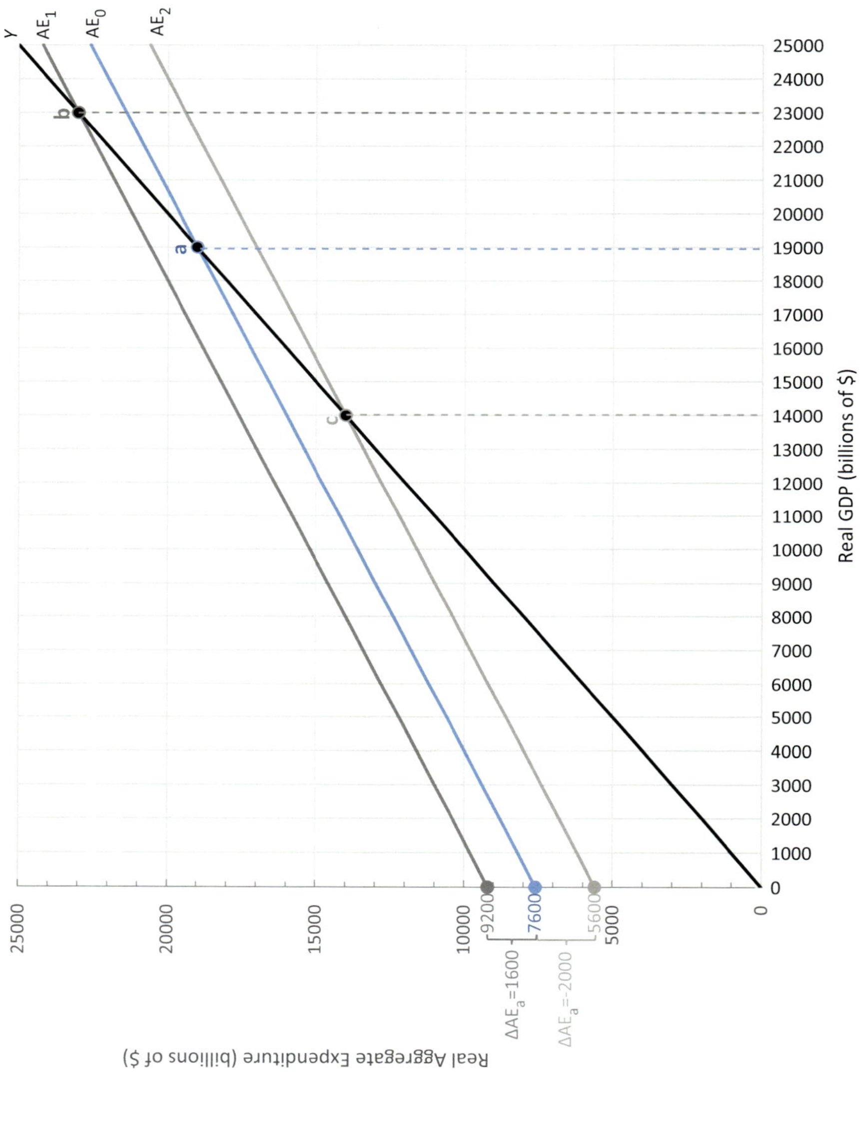

300 MACROECONOMIC MODELS

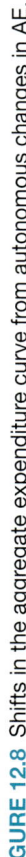

FIGURE 12.8 Shifts in the aggregate expenditure curve from autonomous changes in AE.

Now let's examine changes in the slope of the AE curve in more detail.

When one of the components of the marginal respending rate (MRR) changes, the AE curve changes in slope but autonomous expenditure does not change. Because MRR=MPC(1−t)−MPM, any increase in MPC, decrease in t, or decrease in MPM will increase MRR and increase the slope of the AE curve. Any decrease in MPC, increase in t, or increase in MPM will decrease MRR and reduce the slope of the AE curve.

In Figure 12.9, the original aggregate expenditure curve is AE_0, which starts out when autonomous aggregate expenditure is 8000 and has a slope of 0.6. Mathematically, $AE_0 = 8000 + (0.6)Y$. The equilibrium level of real GDP in Figure 12.9 with aggregate expenditure curve AE_0 is $20,000 billion at point **a** where $AE_0 = Y$.

Now suppose that the marginal respending rate increases to 0.75, due to an increase in the marginal propensity to consume, a decrease in the tax rate, or a decrease in the marginal propensity to import. The aggregate expenditure curve shifts to AE_1, which starts out at 8000 and proceeds at a slope equal to 0.75: $AE_1 = 8000 + (0.75)Y$. The new equilibrium, where $AE_1 = Y$, is at $32,000 billion at point **b**.

Or, suppose that the marginal respending rate decreases to 0.5 due to a decrease in the marginal propensity to consume, an increase in the tax rate, or an increase in the marginal propensity to import. The aggregate expenditure curve would shift to

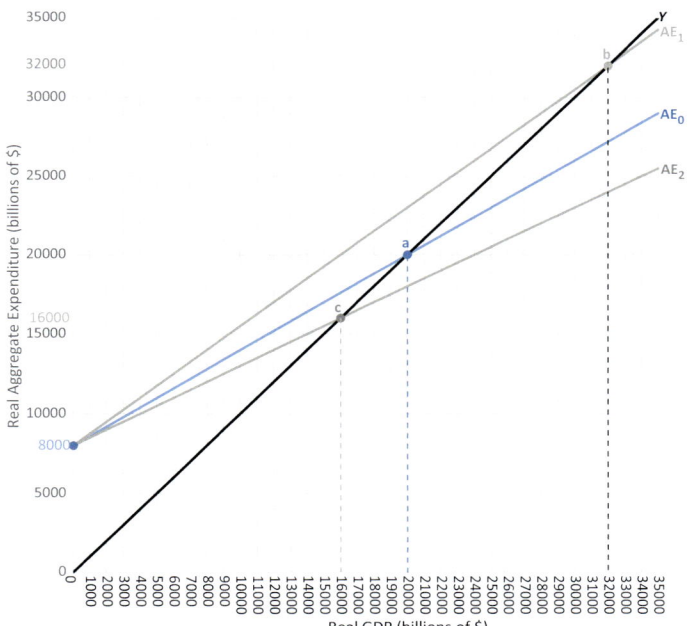

FIGURE 12.9 Shifts in the aggregate expenditure curve from a change in MRR.

AE_2, where $AE_2 = 8000 + (0.5)Y$. Equilibrium for this aggregate expenditure curve would be where $AE_2 = Y$, at $16,000 billion at point **c**.

The aggregate expenditure curve can also be used to determine whether the economy is experiencing an inflationary or a recessionary gap and what policies might work to close the gap. Therefore, if the model is accurate, it can be extremely useful to policymakers.

12.4 AGGREGATE EXPENDITURE AND RECESSIONARY AND INFLATIONARY GAPS

A recessionary gap is the amount that equilibrium real GDP is below potential real GDP (the economy's normal capacity). An inflationary gap is the amount that equilibrium real GDP is above potential real GDP.

In Figure 12.10, potential real GDP is $20,000 billion. The economy is initially in equilibrium at point **a** where $AE_1 = Y$, so equilibrium real GDP is equal to potential real GDP (Y_p). $AE_1 = 8000 + (0.6)Y$. With an MRR of 0.6, the multiplier is equal to 2.5.

Now suppose that there is an autonomous decrease in consumption of $2000 billion, which causes the aggregate expenditure curve to shift down from AE_1 to AE_2. This causes real GDP to decrease by $2.5 \times 2000 = 5000$ billion, so the

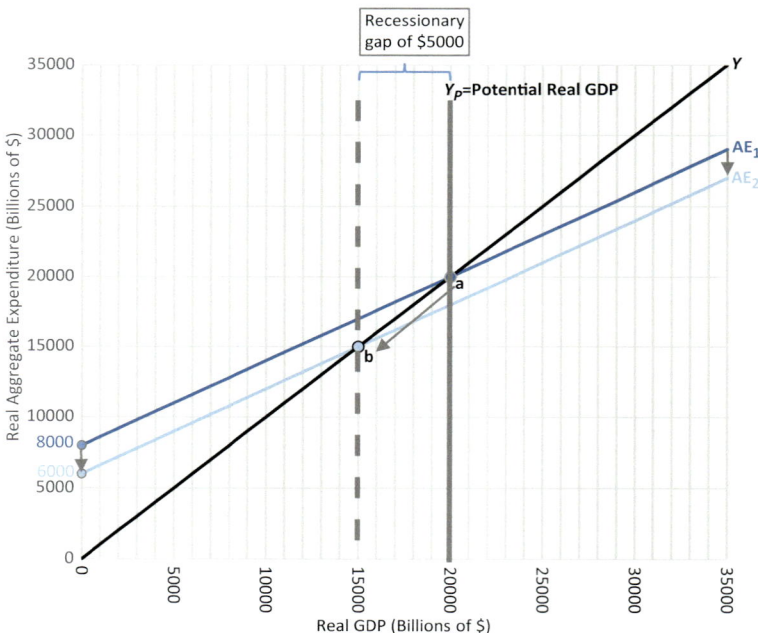

FIGURE 12.10 A recessionary gap (equilibrium real GDP < potential real GDP).

new equilibrium real GDP at point **b** is $15,000 billion. Now, the economy is experiencing a recessionary gap of $5000 billion, which is the difference between equilibrium real GDP and potential real GDP.

Recall that, in a recession, economists who adhere to the classical model believe that wages and input prices will fall, reducing business costs, causing firms to produce and supply more goods and services, which increases incomes and moves the economy back to potential real GDP. In the Keynesian model, wages and input prices are sticky and do not fall quickly, if at all. Furthermore, if wages and input prices do fall, this erodes consumers' purchasing power and undermines some businesses' profitability, factors that serve to keep the economy in a recession indefinitely.

Modern policymakers adhere to the Keynesian model. Therefore, they would advocate taking steps to eliminate the recessionary gap. This would require increasing autonomous expenditure by $2000 billion to achieve a $5000 billion increase in real GDP (after the multiplier effect is incorporated). The government could increase government spending directly by $2000 billion. They could reduce interest rates and hope that consumers and investors would increase autonomous consumption and autonomous investment. Or they could give consumers a tax cut to stimulate consumption. Note, however, that the tax cut would have to be much larger than $2000 to achieve an increase in consumption of that amount because consumers save some proportion of any disposable income they receive. Recall that for tax cuts, $\Delta C = \text{MPC}(\Delta T)$. If we want to achieve a change in autonomous consumption of $2000, and if the MPC is 0.9, then we can solve for ΔT:

$$\Delta C = 2000 = 0.9(\Delta T); \Delta T = \frac{2000}{0.9} = \$2222.22.$$

It takes a $2222.22 decrease in taxes to achieve a $2000 increase in consumption when the MPC is 0.9.

Note that we are talking about a lump sum tax cut, rather than a change in the tax *rate*. A lump sum tax cut is where the government gives citizens a lump sum of money but does not change the tax rate they pay on income. For example, in 2020, the U.S. government gave most citizens a lump sum payment of $1200 to try to stimulate consumer spending in the midst of the COVID-19 recession. Unfortunately, much of that money was saved due to consumer pessimism, which caused a decline in the MPC. A change in the tax rate changes the MRR, which changes the slope of the aggregate expenditure curve. A decrease in the tax rate from 20% to 10% would have achieved a similar impact, but a tax cut of that magnitude would need to be reversed the next time the economy began to boom or it would fuel inflation. Therefore, it is much simpler to enact a straightforward, lump sum tax cut for stabilization policy than it is to make changes to tax rates.

The aggregate expenditure model can also depict the economy experiencing an inflationary gap. Figure 12.11 shows the economy initially in equilibrium at point **a** where $AE_1 = Y$, so equilibrium real GDP is equal to potential real GDP

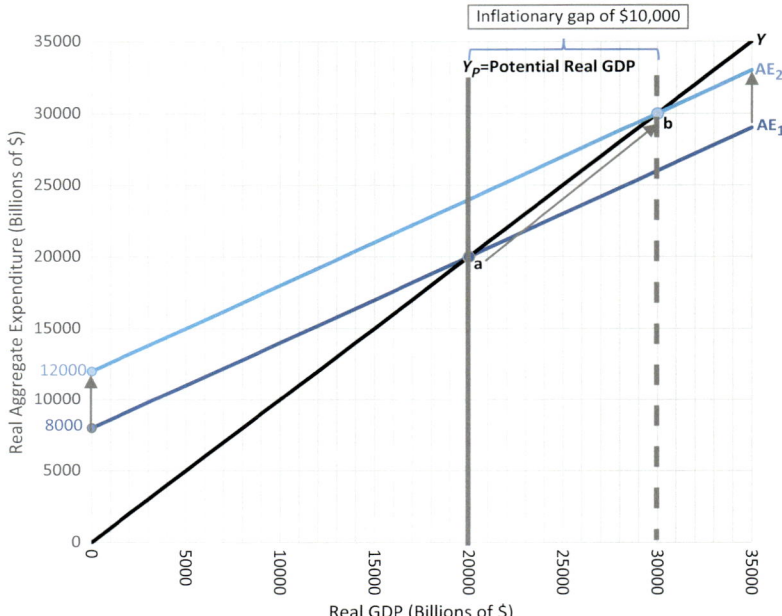

FIGURE 12.11 An inflationary gap (equilibrium real GDP > potential real GDP).

(Y_p). Now suppose there is a huge increase in government spending of $4000 billion to fight a major war. This causes the aggregate expenditure curve to shift to AE_2, which causes equilibrium real GDP to increase to $30,000 billion, which can be seen at point **b**. There is now an inflationary gap of $10,000 billion.

To avoid inflation, the government will need to cut other areas of spending, raise interest rates to curb business investment and consumption, or increase taxes (by $11,111 billion if the MPC is 0.9) in order to shift the aggregate expenditure curve back to AE_1.

Now that we have described how the aggregate expenditure curve works, it is time to discuss the relationship between aggregate expenditure and aggregate demand and the debates economists have over which model is most useful.

12.5 THE AGGREGATE EXPENDITURE CURVE AND THE AGGREGATE DEMAND CURVE

The aggregate expenditure curve and the aggregate demand curve have identical components, but they serve different purposes. The aggregate demand curve shows the total level of spending *at each price level*. The aggregate expenditure curve shows the total level of spending *at each level of national income*. Thus, the aggregate demand model focuses on the relationship between prices and aggregate spending, whereas the aggregate expenditure model focuses on the relationship between income and aggregate spending.

In the mainstream aggregate demand model, an increase in prices causes aggregate demand spending to decline for three reasons:

1. The real balance effect: Higher prices reduce consumer wealth, causing them to spend less.
2. The real interest rate effect: Higher prices cause real interest rates to rise, which causes consumers and investors to purchase less consumption and investment goods.
3. The foreign trade effect: Higher priced domestic goods cause exports to decline and imports to increase, thereby reducing net exports.

Figure 12.12 shows the impact of higher prices on both aggregate demand (AD) and aggregate expenditure according to the mainstream model. According to the AD curve, if prices increase from P_1 to P_2, then the aggregate quantity demanded declines from Q_1 to Q_2 due to decreases in consumption, investment, and net exports. In the aggregate expenditure model, the increase in prices would cause autonomous decreases in consumption, investment, and net exports, which cause the AE curve to *shift* from AE_1 to AE_2, causing real GDP to decrease from Q_1 to Q_2. Similarly, if prices increase again from P_2 to P_3, aggregate quantity demanded decreases from Q_2 to Q_3 in the aggregate demand graph. The aggregate expenditure curve decreases again from AE_2 to AE_3 in the aggregate expenditure graph. Therefore, *a movement along the aggregate demand curve from an increase in prices causes a shift in the aggregate expenditure curve.*

Political economists generally believe that prices have a very minor impact on aggregate expenditure most of the time. As we saw in the previous chapter,

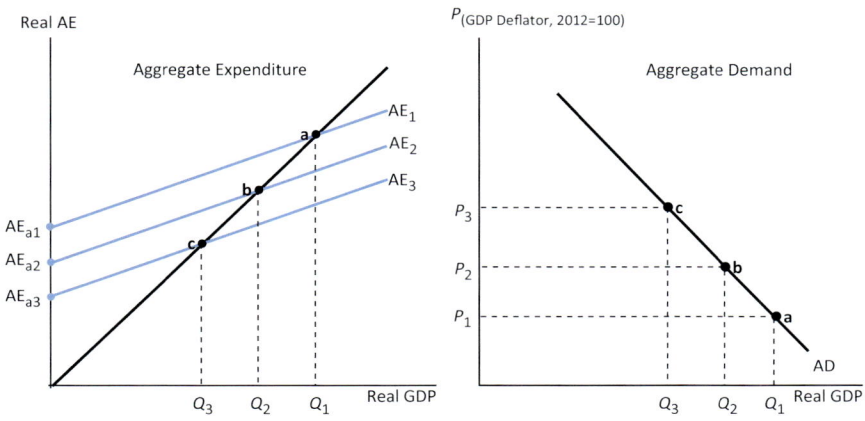

FIGURE 12.12 The correspondence between aggregate expenditure and aggregate demand.

research by political economists indicates that the real balance effect, foreign trade effect, and real interest rate effect are usually very small or even nonexistent. If prices have no effect on spending, we would have an AD curve that is vertical, and there would not be shifts in AE when prices change.

Furthermore, political economists argue that demand factors tend to drive supply responses: When consumers demand more products, suppliers increase their supply and vice versa. The aggregate supply curve is only relevant when a supply shock occurs.

Therefore, instead of utilizing a model that focuses on the impact of prices, political economists prefer to focus on the factors that drive aggregate spending, which they see as the driving force in the macroeconomy. Thus, the aggregate expenditure model forms the core of the political economy approach. Mainstream economists, on the other hand, give prices and aggregate supply a large role in their models of the macroeconomy.

12.6 CONCLUSION

This chapter laid out the Keynesian model of aggregate expenditure and income. The aggregate expenditure model begins with the consumption function. Consumption increases as disposable income increases: Consumers spend a percentage of each increase in income on consumption purchases. That percentage is called the marginal propensity to consume. The remainder of consumers' disposable incomes is saved. Because taxes affect disposable income, they also affect consumption. Lump sum taxes affect autonomous levels of consumption, whereas tax rates (%) affect the marginal propensity to consume. As a general rule, consumption purchases are driven by income, consumers' marginal propensity to consume (or save), and the tax rate.

The aggregate expenditure model consists of consumption, investment, government spending, and net exports: $AE = C + I + G + (X - IM)$. AE contains autonomous expenditure, which involves variables that *do not* change as income changes, including autonomous consumption, autonomous investment, autonomous government spending, and autonomous exports. AE also includes induced expenditure, which involves variables that *do* vary as income changes, including induced consumption (determined via the MPC and the tax rate) and induced imports (determined by the marginal propensity to import). Thus, AE is equal to autonomous expenditure plus induced expenditure, which can be written as

$$AE = AE_a + MRR(Y).$$

The equilibrium level of aggregate expenditure can be found where real aggregate expenditure is equal to real GDP (national income): $AE = Y$. Whenever $AE > Y$, business inventories fall, causing production to increase, which causes real GDP (Y) to increase until equilibrium is reached. Whenever $AE < Y$, businesses' inventories increase, and they cut production and thereby reduce real GDP (Y) until equilibrium is reached.

When AE = Y, injections are equal to leakages, meaning that investment plus government spending plus exports are equal to savings plus taxes plus imports. On a graph, the equilibrium level of aggregate expenditure and income is found where the AE curve intersects the Y (45°) curve.

The AE curve experiences a parallel shift whenever one of its autonomous components changes. Using the multiplier, the change in real GDP will be equal to the change in autonomous expenditure multiplied by the multiplier: $\Delta Y = \Delta AE_a \times \dfrac{1}{(1-MRR)}.$

The AE curve experiences a change in slope whenever the marginal propensity to consume, tax rate, or marginal propensity to import change, causing a change in the MRR. The equilibrium level of real GDP can be found by multiplying autonomous expenditure by the multiplier: $Y_e = AE_a \times$ Multiplier. When the MRR increases, the multiplier increases, which will also increase equilibrium Y. When the MRR decreases, the multiplier decreases, which will decrease equilibrium Y.

Equilibrium real GDP can occur above or below potential real GDP, which means the economy can experience an inflationary gap or a recessionary gap. Policymakers can close an inflationary gap or a recessionary gap by engaging in fiscal and/or monetary policy, subjects we will study extensively in the next two chapters.

Lastly, mainstream economists tend to treat the aggregate expenditure curve as part of aggregate demand and focus on aggregate demand and supply as the key model for understanding the macroeconomy. Political economists tend to treat the aggregate expenditure curve as the key to macroeconomic understanding, and they view the aggregate demand and supply model as only useful in specialized circumstances, such as when a supply shock occurs.

In addition to debating which model is most useful, mainstream and political economists vigorously debate the extent to which fiscal policy and monetary policy should be used to stabilize the macroeconomy. It is to these subjects that we turn next.

QUESTIONS FOR REVIEW

1. Use Figure 12.13 on the next page to answer the following questions.
    a. What is the tax rate?
    b. What is autonomous consumption?
    c. What is the marginal propensity to consume?
    d. What is savings when $Y = 4000$ and $Y = 6000$?
    e. If the tax rate increased to 50%, what would consumption be when $Y = 1000$?

MACROECONOMIC MODELS

Y	DI	C
0	0	600
1000	750	1200
2000	1500	1800
3000	2250	2400
4000	3000	3000
5000	3750	3600
6000	4500	4200

FIGURE 12.13 Y, DI, and C.

2. Use Figure 12.14 to answer the questions below. In this case, $t=0.25$, MPC $=0.8$, investment is autonomous, government spending is autonomous, exports are autonomous and equal to 200, and the MPM is 0.1.
   a. Complete the table.
   b. Determine the equilibrium level of Y and AE.
   c. What is the equation for the aggregate expenditure curve in this example?
   d. If there is an autonomous increase in investment of $500 billion, what would the new equilibrium level of Y and AE be?

Y = GDP	T	DI	C	S	I	G	X − IM	AE
0			400		600	800	200	
1000								
2000								
3000								
4000								
5000								
6000								

FIGURE 12.14 Table of AE and its components for problem 2.

3. Use Figure 12.15 to answer the questions below.
   a. What is the equilibrium level of real GDP in Figure 12.15?
   b. What is the marginal respending rate in Figure 12.15? What is the equation for AE_1?
   c. Why is it impossible for $12,000 billion to be the equilibrium level of real GDP with aggregate expenditure curve AE_1? Explain briefly.
   d. Suppose there is a decrease in autonomous investment of $1000 billion. What will the new equilibrium level of real GDP (Y_2) be? Explain, and show your work.
   e. Suppose that the marginal respending rate for aggregate expenditure curve AE_1 changes to 0.5. What will the new equilibrium level of real GDP (Y_3) be? Explain and show your work.

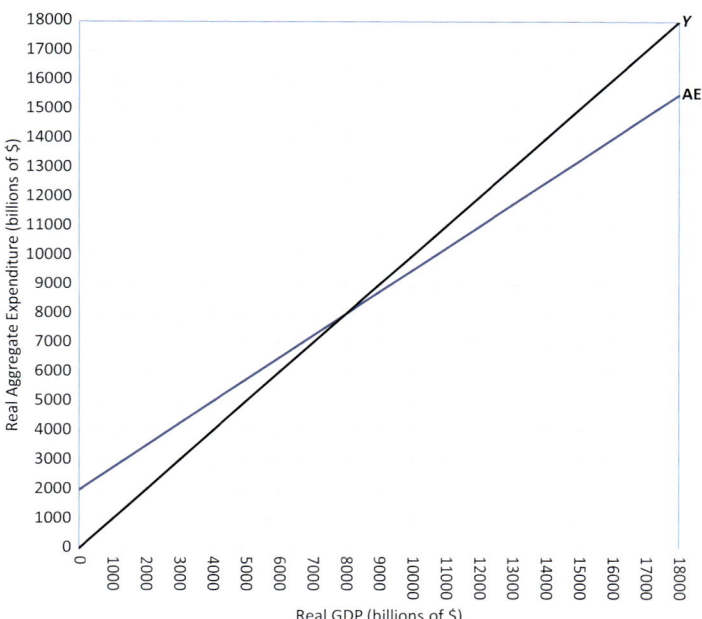

FIGURE 12.15 Graph of AE and Y for problems 3 and 5.

f. Copy the graph above. On your graph, show the new aggregate expenditure curve that results in part D when there is an autonomous decrease in investment of $1000 billion. Also show the new aggregate expenditure curve that results in part E when the marginal respending rate changes to 0.5.

4. Which of the following will cause the slope of the aggregate expenditure curve to decrease? Select one or more of the following, and explain your answer briefly.
   a. A decrease in autonomous consumption expenditures.
   b. A decrease in the marginal propensity to consume.
   c. A decrease in the tax rate.
   d. A decrease in the marginal propensity to import.
5. Suppose that potential real GDP (Y_p) in Figure 12.15 is $12,000 billion and that the current aggregate expenditure curve is AE_1.
   a. How large is the inflationary or recessionary gap?
   b. How much would the government need to change government spending to move the economy from its current equilibrium on AE_1 to Y_p?
   c. Assuming that the MPC is 0.95, how much would the government need to change lump sum taxes to move the economy from its current equilibrium on AE_1 to Y_p?

6. Using Figure 12.12 (which connects AE to AD), explain what impact a decrease in prices would have on aggregate demand and aggregate expenditure according to mainstream economists. How would political economists respond to this analysis?

NOTE

1 The general form for the equation of the consumption function is the following: Consumption at any level of Y, C_Y, can be found using autonomous and induced consumption: $C_Y = C_a + (MPC)\Delta DI$. $\Delta DI = DI_Y - DI_0$. In addition, $DI_0 = 0$ in these models. When $Y = 0$, DI is also 0. Therefore, $\Delta DI = DI_Y$. Therefore, as long as $DI_0 = 0$, $C_Y = C_a + (MPC)DI_Y$.

PART V
Stabilization policy

Recurring economic crises are one of the features of modern capitalist economic systems. Every 8 to 12 years, the U.S. economy enters a major crisis that requires government response to stabilize the situation. Sometimes these crises are driven by financial factors. Sometimes they are a result of austerity policies in a particularly fragile economic environment. Sometimes they are the result of shocks from factors external to the domestic economy, such as the oil price shocks of the 1970s or the COVID-19 pandemic shock of 2020. Failure to act would likely turn recessions into depressions, as we learned in the 1930s, so the government must take action to stabilize the economy when crises occur.

In Chapter 13, we study one possible method for dealing with an economic crisis: Fiscal policy. Fiscal policy involves using government spending and taxation to affect the economy. One of the major debates in modern economics and politics is about how (and whether) governments should utilize fiscal policy. According to the New Keynesian approach, utilizing fiscal policy to stabilize the economy can improve on market outcomes. Critics from the right (laissez-faire economists), however, argue that the government should do less, and critics from the left (political economists) argue that the government should do much more. In addition, how the government should approach the issue of the national debt and budget deficits is an important and controversial topic. Laissez-faire economists often advocate a balanced budget, whereas political economists and supply-side economists argue that running deficits improves economic growth if the money is spent properly. The New Keynesian position falls in the middle: Deficits should be run during recessions, the government should run surpluses during booms, and small deficits to fuel long-term economic growth are acceptable when the economy is at capacity. Interestingly, the fact that large deficits did not have negative consequences in the last four decades is causing economists to reconsider their objections to deficit spending.

DOI: 10.4324/9780429399350-17

Chapter 14 takes up money, banking, and the financial sector, illustrating how financial markets work in theory and practice. Every citizen needs to understand the importance of money, banking, and financial markets to a modern economy. This chapter introduces the mainstream economics view of the money market, the banking sector, and the financial sector. It also introduces students to basic financial instruments (stocks and bonds) and other important issues relevant to personal finance. The chapter also introduces the political economy model of financial markets and the role of banks in creating money. Also discussed is the rise of the finance, insurance, and real estate (FIRE) sector and the increasing financialization of modern economies.

Chapter 15 discusses monetary policy options that central banks can implement to stabilize economies. The appropriate role for monetary policy is another area where there is significant disagreement among economists. The mainstream, Keynesian view is that monetary policy should be used to stabilize the economy. In a crisis, the central bank should lower interest rates and, in the case of a liquidity trap, implement quantitative easing. This should help to avoid a potentially ruinous deflation. In a boom, monetary policy should be used to slow down the economy to prevent a bust or to engineer a soft landing. Laissez-faire economists want less intervention on money markets, whereas political economists, and especially modern monetary theory adherents, want more intervention.

Chapter 16 takes up economic crises in more detail, including the Great Depression, the financial crisis of 2007–2008, and the COVID-19 recession. One of the great problems in economics is how to avoid a financial crisis, closely followed by the problem of how to end a financial crisis once it occurs. This chapter describes mainstream views of the causes of economic crises, as well as those of laissez-faire and political economists. Particular attention is paid to the ideas of Hyman Minsky on financial fragility and modern Marxist economists studying economic crises.

13 Fiscal policy, debt, and deficits

Fiscal activism vs. austerity and the macroeconomic role of government

In 2019, the global economy was in fragile condition. A decade after the financial crisis of 2007–2008 and Great Recession of 2008–2009, the macroeconomy once again was unstable. Some of this was driven by a corporate debt bubble that threatened to burst. Some instability was a product of geopolitical instability, including uncertainty related to Brexit (the United Kingdom leaving the European Union [E.U.], which destabilized European markets) and the U.S.–China trade war sparked by President Trump's tariffs on Chinese imports. Many economists predicted a recession in 2020 as investors signaled deep pessimism about the future.

Into this uncertain macroeconomic environment came the COVID-19 pandemic. Beginning in Wuhan, China, the COVID-19 virus spread rapidly around the world, resulting in more than 14 million cases and 600,000 deaths by the end of July 2020. To stop the spread, most governments shut down economies and issued stay-at-home orders, and many businesses closed stores and offices. The result was a devastating global recession, which the International Monetary Fund projected would be the worst recession since the Great Depression. Unemployment in the United States spiked to 14.7%, and stock markets dropped initially by 30%.

It was in this environment that the U.S. government embarked in the most dramatic stimulus program in its history. Between March and June 2020, the U.S. government spent $2791 billion, 13% of U.S. gross domestic product (GDP),[1] on tax cuts, unemployment benefits, business bailouts, health care, and other emergency fiscal measures. Meanwhile, the U.S. central bank, the Fed, engaged in about $4000 billion of monetary stimulus, lowering interest rates to 0%, buying assets from banks and corporations, and flooding banks and asset markets with money.

The U.S. government felt comfortable engaging in its largest stimulus program ever in part because the stimulus package enacted in 2009, which was also large by historical standards, was quite effective in reducing the depth of the Great Recession. In addition, the dire predictions of deficit hawks that large deficits

DOI: 10.4324/9780429399350-18

would generate inflation and harm financial markets did not come true after the 2009 recession.

The 2020 stimulus had the immediate impact of propping up asset markets, as stocks rebounded to near their values before the pandemic hit. However, unemployment rates stayed stubbornly high at first, sparking debates over whether or not additional stimulus was warranted. Some economists were worried about government deficits increasing even further if new stimulus programs were enacted. Others argued that deficits were a minor problem in the face of a devastatingly deep recession. This debate over fiscal activism (stimulus) or austerity is one of the most important ones in modern macroeconomics, and it is the subject of this chapter.

The chapter begins by laying out the landscape of modern U.S. government spending and taxation policy, detailing what the U.S. government prioritizes. We compare U.S. priorities with those of other developed countries. Next, we describe automatic stabilizers and discretionary policies that governments can use to combat economic instability, especially recessions. Utilizing the aggregate demand and aggregate supply model, we show how discretionary fiscal policy affects aggregate demand and GDP, as well as how it can close recessionary or inflationary gaps.

We then turn to the debate over the role of government in the macroeconomy and the debate over fiscal activism vs. austerity regarding fiscal policy. This debate revolves in important ways around U.S. government budget deficits and whether or not deficit spending creates problems and is something to be avoided or whether deficit spending fosters prosperity and is to be embraced. Laissez-faire advocates prefer austerity, New Keynesian economists advocate deficits in recessions to stimulate aggregate demand and benefit the poor, supply-siders are fine with deficits as long as the money goes to corporate interests, and political economists advocate deficit spending if it benefits workers, families, and communities and if it fosters growth and productivity. We then take up examples of how fiscal policy was used to combat the Great Recession of 2008–2009 and the COVID-19 recession of 2020.

13.0 CHAPTER 13 LEARNING GOALS

After reading this chapter you should be able to:

- Describe the major fiscal priorities of the U.S. government and compare and contrast those priorities with the approaches of other governments in developed countries.

- Explain the use of automatic stabilizers and discretionary fiscal policy to stabilize the economy.

- Use the aggregate demand–aggregate supply model to analyze the impact of changes in government spending and lump sum taxes on aggregate demand, real GDP, and prices.

- Critically evaluate the arguments of laissez-faire, supply-side, New Keynesian, and political economists on the size and role of government and the use of fiscal policy in recessions.

- Analyze the arguments of economists regarding the appropriate size of government deficits and debt.

- Describe and evaluate the effectiveness of the fiscal policies used in the Great Recession and the COVID-19 recession to stabilize the economy.

13.1 THE SIZE AND ROLE OF GOVERNMENT IN THE MACROECONOMY

Fiscal policy is **the use of government spending or taxation to improve economic outcomes.** Fiscal policy can be **used to address macroeconomic market failures such as recessions, unemployment, or price instability and to improve the rate of economic growth**.

The size and role of government expanded dramatically in developed countries after the Great Depression of the 1930s, marking the rise and maturation of the mixed capitalist economic system. Once governments embraced the idea that market failures could be solved, government programs in numerous areas proliferated. The major categories of government spending in the modern era are (1) public and quasi-public goods, (2) social spending, and (3) government administration.

Public and quasi-public goods include health, education, defense, policing, fire protection, infrastructure, research and development funding, basic scientific research, industrial support, and other core government functions that provide goods that markets do not supply effectively. **Social spending** includes support for children, families, the elderly, and the incapacitated, along with spending on health programs for the poor, active labor market programs to develop workers' skills, unemployment benefits, and housing subsidies. Social spending involves creating a safety net for those who cannot gain sufficient subsistence within the market system. **Social spending that involves the transfer of income from the government to individuals or businesses, such as welfare payments or direct business subsidies**, is called a transfer payment. **Government administration** involves spending on the justice system and all regulatory bodies. Performing market facilitation and regulation requires highly skilled, well-paid government officials with substantial expertise in specialized areas, along with buildings, labs, and other support structures.

The degree of spending and intervention in all three of these areas varies widely based on each country's philosophy. Market-dominated economies generally are less regulated and spend less on social programs, public goods, and government administration. Social market economies involve more regulations and administration, as well as more generous spending on social programs and public goods. State-dominated economies vary depending on the governing philosophy of the group dominating the state political infrastructure. China's Communist Party spends extensively on public goods, especially infrastructure, while providing a less generous safety net. Some areas of life in China are strictly regulated, especially labor markets, whereas environmental rules are lax. Cuba spends extensively on safety nets and public goods, but rules governing business operations are very strict.

Figure 13.1 shows the major categories of U.S. federal government spending, which amounted to $4.4 trillion in 2019. The priorities are an interesting indication of the unique aspects of the U.S. economic system. First, as with many countries, the United States provides income stabilization for those who fall on hard times. This helps individuals, families, and communities, while also supporting aggregate demand in recessions. Social Security, which is the national U.S. pension program, is the largest source of government transfer payments, and income security, which includes unemployment insurance, welfare programs, and food assistance, also is significant. Most people do not understand the U.S. Social Security system, so it is worth taking a minute to explain why it was created and how it works.

Category of Federal Government Spending	Billions of $	% of Budget
Social Security	1,044.4	23.5%
National Defense	686.0	15.4%
Medicare	651.0	14.6%
Health	584.8	13.1%
Income Security	514.8	11.6%
Net Interest	375.2	8.4%
Veterans Benefits and Services	199.8	4.5%
Education, Training, Employment, and Social Services	136.8	3.1%
Transportation	97.1	2.2%
Administration of Justice	65.7	1.5%
International Affairs	52.7	1.2%
Agriculture	38.3	0.9%
Natural Resources and Environment	37.8	0.9%
General Science, Space, and Technology	32.4	0.7%
Community and Regional Development	26.9	0.6%
General Government	23.4	0.5%
Energy	5.0	0.1%
Commerce and Housing Credit	-25.7	-0.6%
Undistributed Offsetting Receipts	-98.2	-2.2%
Total, Federal Outlays	4,448.3	100.0%

FIGURE 13.1 Table of U.S. federal government spending, 2019.

Case study: The importance and future of the U.S. Social Security program

Without a pension, once a person can no longer work, they would have no income and would have to depend on their savings or the assistance of others. Prior to the establishment of Social Security in the United States, it was common for the elderly who had worked in low-wage jobs and who had no surviving family members to be destitute. Social Security was started as a pay-as-you-go system during the Great Depression when the elderly were the poorest segment of the U.S. population. It was decided that existing workers and employers would pay a percentage of their wages and salaries directly to retirees as a national pension system. When you work, a portion of your wages is taken out to pay Social Security benefits to a current retiree. When you retire, other workers will have money taken out of their paychecks to pay you. Your Social Security benefits are determined by your salary, with higher earning workers receiving higher payouts, although there is a cap on both Social Security taxes and Social Security benefits.

Due to the fact that future Social Security payments depend on future workers' contributions to the program, Social Security is affected by demographics. The post–World War II baby boom lasted until 1964, creating a large number of productive people. As this group retires in ever-larger numbers, and as baby boomers live longer lives, there are fewer workers to replace them, because modern families have fewer children. Therefore, in the near future there will be fewer workers paying into the Social Security system while more people than ever before are drawing Social Security benefits. Beginning around 2034, the U.S. Social Security system will start running deficits. Unless the government decides to alter the structure of the program, Social Security recipients will receive reduced Social Security payments of about 79% of the level of benefits they are entitled to receive.

Some changes that would resolve the problems with Social Security include delaying the age at which people can start collecting Social Security benefits, allowing more immigrants into the United States to provide a larger workforce to support retirees, reducing Social Security benefits, or increasing Social Security taxes. None of those solutions is politically popular, so it is unclear the direction in which the government will go.

The United States is a major outlier internationally in terms of its spending on national defense. Direct national defense spending in 2019 was $686 billion, more than 15% of the federal government budget. When veterans' benefits and services are added, the total is almost $900 billion, which is 20% of the federal budget. The other big-ticket item in the federal budget is spending on health care. Medicare for the elderly and various other health programs, including Medicaid for the poor, add up to about 28% of the federal government budget. The United States spends more per capita on health care than every country in the world, despite having poor health outcomes for such a rich country.[2] Notice that the other parts of the federal budget are relatively small in comparison to spending on health, defense, and income security.

State and local governments in the United States have different priorities. Figure 13.2 shows that state and local governments are responsible for education, local infrastructure, and local services. Rather than having a national system for education and health, most of the decisions regarding these services are made at the state or local level.

Except during periods of war, the U.S. government only constituted 1.2% to 3.5% of GDP from 1800 to 1930. After that, the U.S. government grew substantially with the move from a laissez-faire economy to a mixed economy with a small safety net. From 1930 to 1941, the U.S. government grew from 3.6% of GDP to 10.5% under President Roosevelt. Roosevelt's New Deal programs included substantial fiscal stimulus and the creation of programs such as Social Security and unemployment insurance. With World War II, the subsequent Cold War with the U.S.S.R., and regional conflicts in Korea, Vietnam, Iraq, and Afghanistan, the United States maintained a permanently increased military after 1941. Meanwhile, social programs, infrastructure spending, health and education services, and government regulatory agencies expanded.

Figure 13.3 shows that the U.S. government grew substantially in size and influence relative to GDP until 1976, when it reached 32% of GDP. Since 1976, the size of the U.S. government as a percentage of GDP has stayed about the same, increasing during recessions and decreasing with booms but averaging 31.9% of the economy.

Categories of U.S. state and local government spending	Billions of $	%
State and local government spending, 2017		
Education	1010	27.6%
Public welfare (welfare, hospitals, health)	678	18.5%
Transportation (highways, airports, ports)	318	8.7%
Public safety (police, fire)	260	7.1%
Environment, parks, sewage, and housing	248	6.8%
Utility expenditure (electric, water)	232	6.3%
All other (interest, administration, etc.)	913	24.9%
Total state and local spending	3660	100.0%

FIGURE 13.2 Table showing U.S. state and local government spending, 2017.

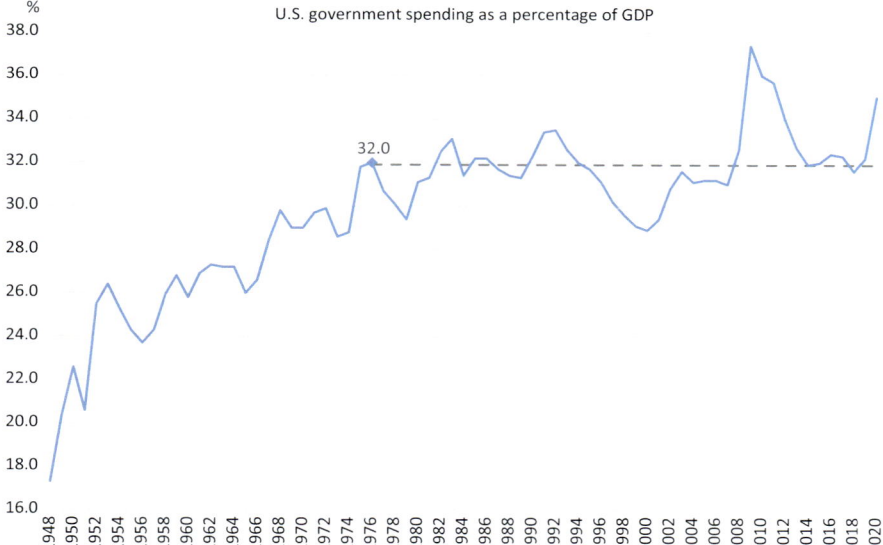

FIGURE 13.3 Total U.S. government spending as a percentage of GDP, 1948–2020 (Q1).

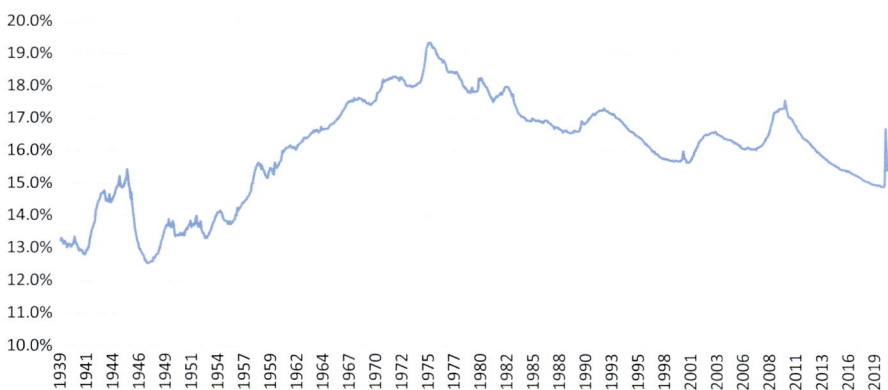

FIGURE 13.4 U.S. government employment as a percentage of total employment, 1939–2020.

Similarly, Figure 13.4 shows that the number of government employees in the United States increased as the mixed economy was being developed. Since the mid-1970s, however, U.S. government employment decreased as a percentage of total employment. In May 2020, federal, state, and local government bodies in the United States employed 21.2 million people, which was 15.4% of the U.S. workforce.

Figure 13.5 compares the size of government as a percentage of GDP in the United States to other developed countries.[3] European social democracies have

Country	Government spending, % of GDP
France	56.13
Belgium	52.38
Denmark	51.41
Sweden	49.88
Norway	48.69
Italy	48.58
Austria	48.49
Germany	43.87
Netherlands	42.16
Spain	41.34
Canada	41.32
United Kingdom	40.84
Japan	38.74
United States	37.95
Australia	36.71
Switzerland	34.15
South Korea	32.44
India	27.29
Mexico	26.34
Ireland	25.74

FIGURE 13.5 Table of general government expenditures as a percentage of GDP, 2018.

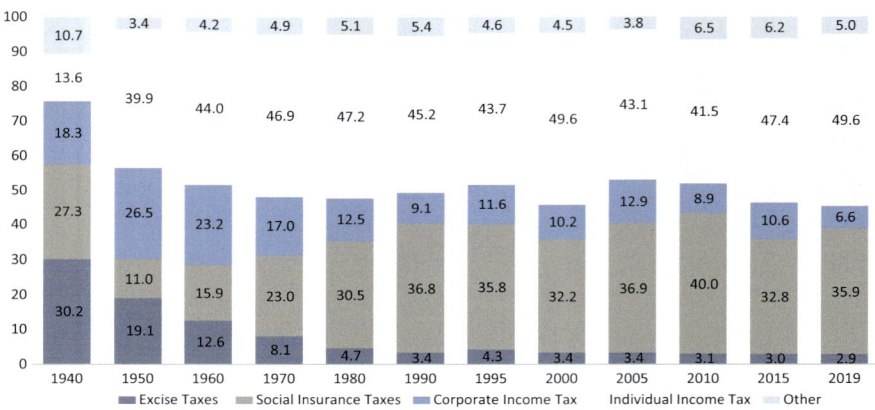

FIGURE 13.6 Sources of tax revenue as a percentage of total U.S. government revenue, 1940–2019.

much larger government sectors, primarily due to large safety nets, active labor market programs, public health care and health insurance systems, and greater spending on public goods.

Governments must also decide how to pay for their expenditures. This includes decisions on who or what to tax and how much deficit spending (and borrowing) to engage in. Figure 13.6 shows the major sources of tax revenue for the U.S. government from 1940 to 2019. Excise taxes on goods used to be a major source of income, but they are insignificant in the modern United States. Corporate taxes have also declined significantly as a source of funds, from 26.5% in 1950 to 6.6% in 2019. Much of the recent decline in corporate taxes is a result of the influence of supply-side economists on economic policy. Meanwhile, taxes on individuals—both social insurance taxes (social security and unemployment insurance) and individual income taxes—increased dramatically.

Another key issue is how the tax burden is shared. Most countries have a progressive tax system, in which the rich pay a larger percentage of their income in taxes than the poor. A progressive tax code reflects a philosophy that the people who have benefited from an economic system and who are more able to pay should shoulder a greater share of the tax burden and that inequality and poverty are significant market failures that need to be corrected via some measure of redistribution. The United States is a major exception here. As Emmanuel Saez and Gabriel Zucman demonstrated in their important 2019 book *The Triumph of Injustice*, the United States has a flat tax burden where the poor pay about the same percentage of their income in taxes as the rich. Figure 13.7 on the next page shows the tax rates payed by each percentile (*P*) of the U.S. population. The average tax rate in the United States is 28%. The poorest 10% of the population pay a 25.6% tax rate, which is, astoundingly, a higher tax rate than that paid by billionaires. The richest 400 families in the United States pay only a 23% tax rate once all of their tax dodges (such as offshore accounts and accounting tricks) and special tax rates (such as very low taxes on capital gains) are taken into account. This disparity prompted multi-billionaire Warren Buffett to note the inherent unfairness of a tax code whereby he was paying a lower percentage tax rate than his hard-working secretary!

The poorest 50% of the population is hit especially hard by sales taxes and payroll taxes, which are quite regressive, meaning that the poor pay a higher percentage of their income on these than the rich. Income taxes are progressive, in that income tax rates increase as income increases, except for the top 0.01%. Here, a quirk of the U.S. tax code comes into play: Most of the super-rich get their income from capital gains—profits from buying and selling assets such as stocks, bonds, and real estate. Capital gains are taxed at a much lower rate than income, so the super-rich who have the most capital gains pay less in income taxes than the upper middle class does. Corporate and property taxes are only slightly progressive, and the estate tax is very small, leaving the U.S. tax code flat for the most part and regressive at the top.

The U.S. tax code has changed dramatically in the last 60 years. In 1960, the super-rich paid a 56.3% tax rate, an amount 145% higher than they paid in 2018. Meanwhile, in 1960, the bottom 50% of taxpayers paid a tax rate of 21.6%, 12% lower than the 24.2% average tax rate they paid in 2018. Under the influence of supply-side economics, tax rates on corporations and the rich were lowered dramatically, tax evasion was tolerated, and tax rates on the working class were increased. Unfortunately, as we saw earlier, supply-side policies did not improve economic growth.

Putting the material in this section together, we can observe the following characteristics of U.S. fiscal policy. First, the U.S. government plays a significant role in the economy, but that role is much smaller than the role played by governments in most other developed countries. The United States spends less on public goods and safety nets, while also taxing the wealthy less than other countries. Interestingly, the United States often does more in one arena of economic policy—the utilization of discretionary fiscal policy.

322 STABILIZATION POLICY

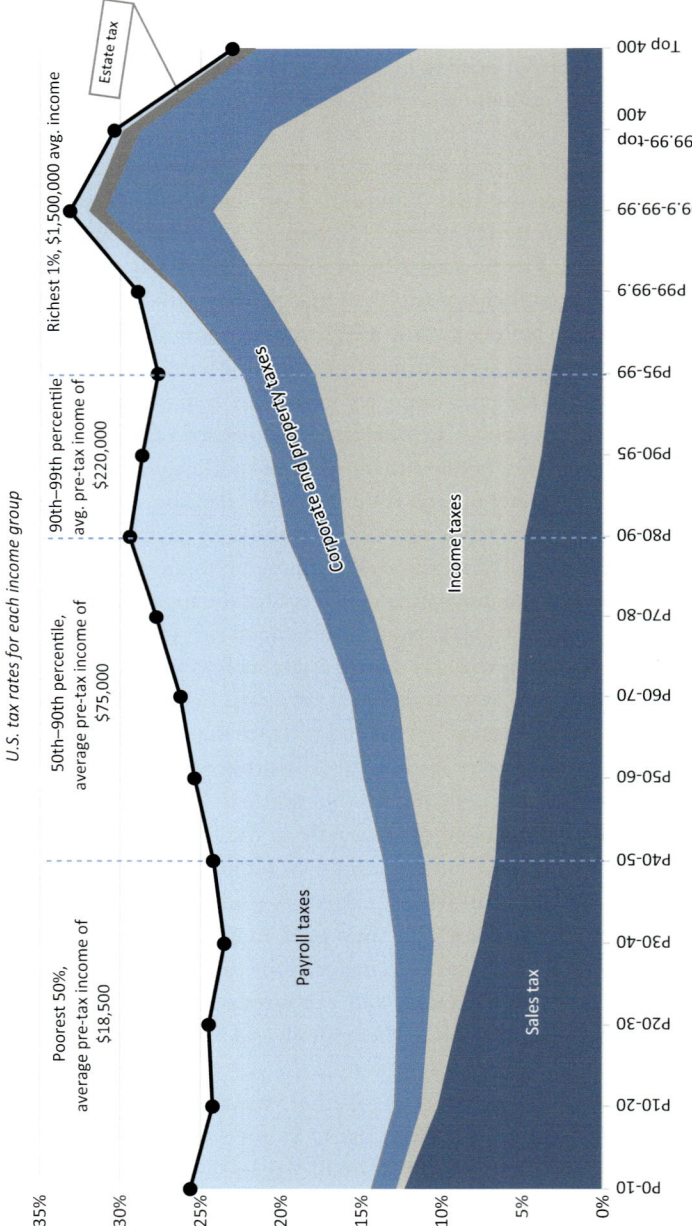

FIGURE 13.7 U.S. average tax rates by income group in 2018 (% of pretax income).

13.2 AUTOMATIC STABILIZERS AND DISCRETIONARY FISCAL POLICY TO CORRECT INSTABILITY

One of the major roles for fiscal policy is to stabilize the economy. The government has three fiscal policy tools at its disposal to stabilize the macroeconomy: Government spending, tax policy, and automatic stabilizers. **Automatic stabilizers** are **programs that automatically increase spending or reduce taxes in recessions and do the opposite when the economy is overheated**. One of the main benefits of automatic stabilizers is that they do not require political action—the programs are set up to function automatically for any citizen who falls upon hard times.

Automatic stabilizers are a key aspect of the safety net in most countries, and they include unemployment insurance, along with programs to help the poor such as welfare, food assistance, housing assistance, and government-provided health care. Whenever an economy hits a recession, governments automatically pay out increased assistance to the increasing numbers of the unemployed and the poor, increasing aggregate demand in the process. When the economy booms, spending on these programs declines. A progressive tax code also serves as an automatic stabilizer, reducing taxes when people have lower incomes in recessions and increasing taxes when incomes increase during booms.

Some governments utilize automatic stabilizers extensively because they are so effective in combating recessions quickly. Figure 13.8 shows that the Netherlands

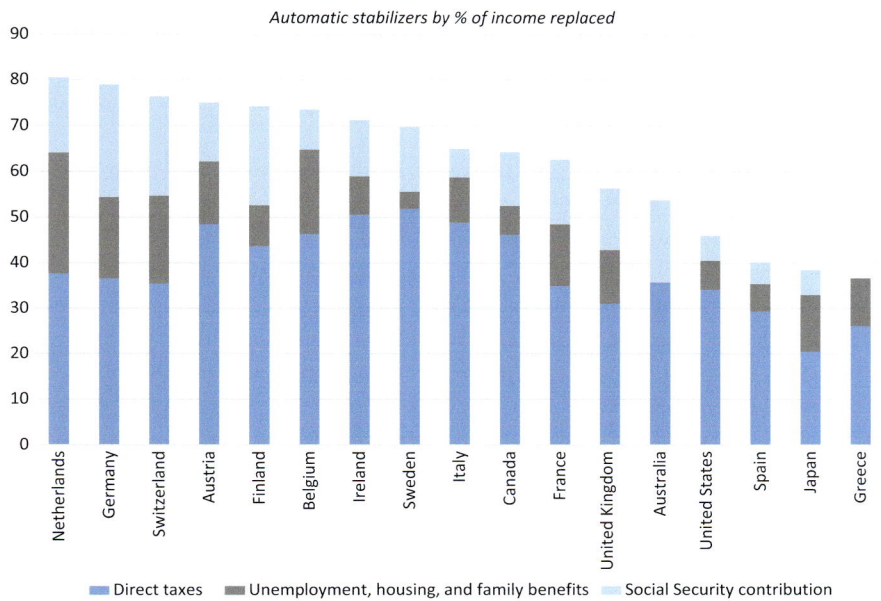

FIGURE 13.8 Automatic stabilization of shocks to household income by country, 2019.

offsets 80.5% of any shocks that people experience in a recession via automatic stabilizers.[4] The United States, on the other hand, offsets only 46.1% of shocks with automatic stabilizers due to the lack of a progressive tax code and the very small U.S. safety net (featuring relatively low levels of unemployment, housing, and family benefits).

An intriguing automatic stabilizer was the Swedish policy that allowed corporations to invest tax free in recessions in the 1950s and 1960s. As a result, whenever Sweden entered a recession, there was an increase in business investment by companies that were in stable condition and that wanted to benefit from paying no corporate taxes on the money they used to invest. The tax savings was significant enough to generate additional private sector investment in Sweden at a time when private companies in other countries were cutting their investments. This example demonstrates that governments can be creative with the design of automatic stabilizers.

Even the most generous of automatic stabilizers do not replace all of the income lost in a recession. Therefore, governments need to take additional action. **Discretionary fiscal policy** is **fiscal policy that is "at the discretion" of government officials**, meaning that **government officials must take additional actions in order for such policy to take effect**. **Expansionary fiscal policy** refers to **increases in government spending or reductions in taxes that stimulate aggregate demand**. **Contractionary fiscal policy**, also called **austerity**, refers to **cuts in government spending and increases in taxes that reduce aggregate demand**.

Discretionary fiscal policy is always slower to impact the macroeconomy than automatic stabilizers. In the United States, it takes time for congress and the president to agree on what action to take. Then, the policy takes time to be implemented and even longer to have an impact. Nonetheless, discretionary fiscal policy is considered by many economists to be the most effective tool in combating a major recession.

For example, economists estimate that infrastructure spending has the largest multiplier of any type of government spending. Spending on schools, technology, and transportation systems, including roads, bridges, trains, and airports, creates jobs directly in the construction industry, usually one of the hardest-hit sectors in recessions. Such spending also makes private sector operations more efficient, reducing transit time and improving productivity. In addition, government infrastructure spending spills over into private sector investment as businesses see new opportunities. Better education, technology, and skilled workers can be a major attraction to business investment. For example, every time new train lines, roads, or airports are built, new communities and businesses spring up around the transportation hubs. Discretionary fiscal policy directly stimulates aggregate demand and can eliminate a recessionary gap.

13.3 FISCAL POLICY AND THE AGGREGATE DEMAND AND AGGREGATE SUPPLY MODEL

One of the major tasks of government is to enact the appropriate discretionary fiscal to stabilize the economy. Figure 13.9 on the next page shows the economy in a recession at point **a** with a real GDP at $18,000 billion and a price index of 101. The recessionary gap is $2000 billion—the difference between real GDP at point **a** and potential real GDP. In order to increase real GDP by $2000 billion, the government will have to enact policies that cause aggregate demand to shift by $3000 billion, from AD_1 to AD_2, moving the economy from point **a** to point **b**. That will create inflationary pressures, causing the economy to move along the aggregate demand curve from point **b** to point **c** as inflation occurs.

The government can estimate the amount of government spending or tax cuts necessary to increase AD by $3000 billion using the multiplier. Recall that the multiplier can be computed using the marginal respending rate (MRR). Suppose that the MRR is 0.5. Using the formula for the multiplier

$$\text{Multiplier} = \frac{1}{1-\text{MRR}} = \frac{1}{1-0.5} = 2.$$

Therefore, an increase in government spending of $1500 billion would cause the AD curve to shift by $1500b \times 2 = \$3000b$, moving the economy to potential real GDP. If the government spent enough money on various projects, such as building roads, bridges, schools, high-speed internet, and other infrastructure, it could eliminate the recessionary gap.

The government could also cut taxes in order to increase AD, but taxes always have a smaller impact on AD than government spending because some percentage of tax cuts is saved. In 2020 when the government sent checks for $1200 to most taxpayers to combat the COVID-19 recession, 30% of taxpayers reported that they planned to save the money instead of spending it. This information indicates that the marginal propensity to consume (MPC) in 2020 was 0.70. The MPC often drops in bad recessions because people are pessimistic about the future, causing them to save more and spend less. We can compute the change in consumption from a tax cut as follows: $\Delta C = -(\Delta T \times \text{MPC})$.[5] If we use the same multiplier of 2, then the economy needs an increase in consumption spending of $1500 to shift the AD curve by $3000 to eliminate the recessionary gap. To increase consumption by $1500, with an MPC of 0.7, we would need a tax cut of $2143 billion:

$$\Delta C = -(\Delta T \times MPC); \quad 1500 = -(\Delta T \times 0.7); \quad \frac{1500}{0.7} = -\Delta T; \Delta T = -2143.$$

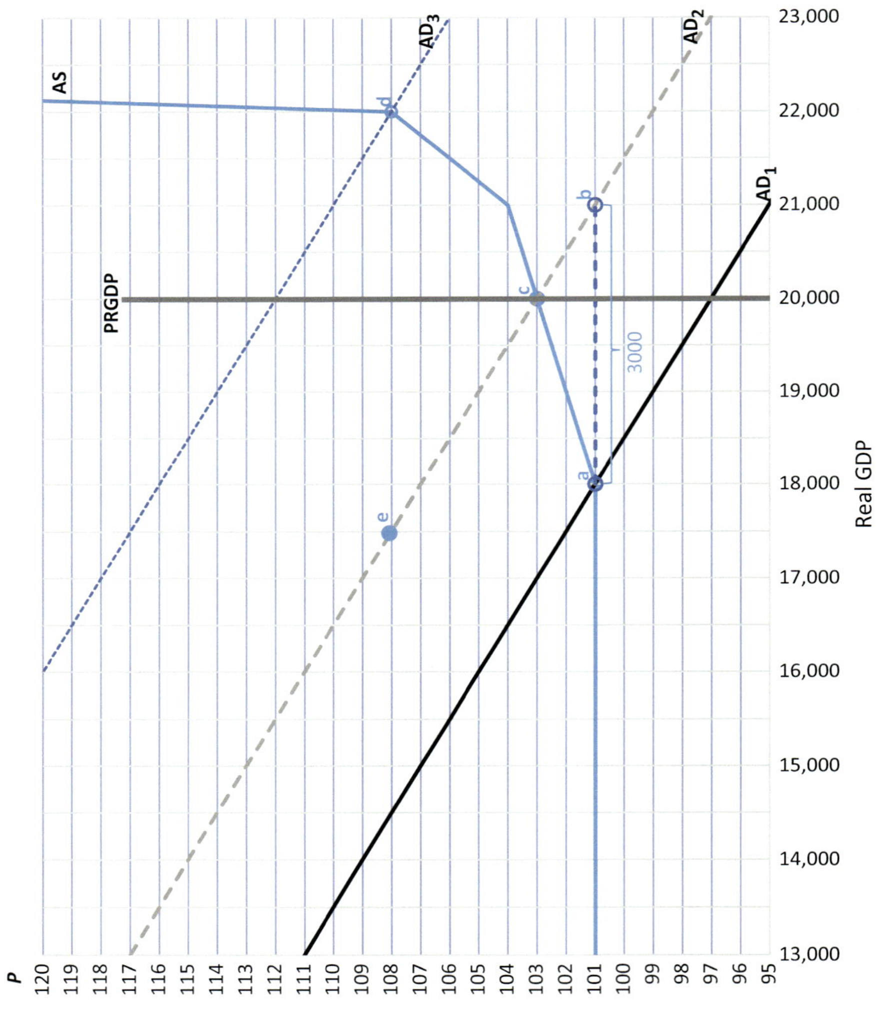

326 STABILIZATION POLICY

FIGURE 13.9 Fixing a recessionary or inflationary gap with fiscal policy.

A tax cut of $2143 billion causes consumers to spend 70% of that amount, given that the MPC is 0.7, which is $1500, while the remaining 30% is saved. In this example, the tax cut has to be 43% larger in absolute value than the spending increase to achieve the same impact on aggregate demand and real GDP.

The **tax multiplier** is **used to compute the impact of a lump sum change in taxes on aggregate demand**:

$$\text{Tax multipler} = -(\text{Multiplier}) \times (\text{Marginal propensity to consume}) = -\frac{\text{MPC}}{1-\text{MRR}}.$$

In the above example, with an MPC of 0.7 and a multiplier of 2, the tax multiplier would be 1.4. A tax cut of $2143 billion would cause a change in aggregate demand of $2143 × 1.4 = $3000 billion.

Note that economists do not know the precise position of the economy at any moment, but they still attempt to estimate the position of the economy relative to potential real GDP and the amount of government intervention necessary to move the economy there. This can give us substantial insight into the appropriate amount of spending needed in a recession. Economics is an inexact social science, but it can still give us good estimates of what policies to enact and how effective they are likely to be.

Suppose that the economy is overheated and the government expects an asset bubble or an inflationary episode such as a wage–price spiral to form. In this case, the government can reduce government spending or increase taxes. Such policies, known as austerity, would cause the AD curve to decrease. As before, spending cuts would have a larger impact than tax increases. Also, if the economy was in the steep part of the AS curve, the shift in AD would have to be larger than the amount of the inflationary gap to move the economy back to potential real GDP.

For example, suppose the economy is in equilibrium at point **d** in Figure 13.9, at a real GDP of 22,000 and a price index of 108 where AD_3 intersects AS. There is an inflationary gap of $2000 billion, but the AD curve will need to shift by $4500, the horizontal distance between AD_3 and AD_2 (the distance from point **d** to point **e**), to move the economy's equilibrium from point **d** to point **c** at potential real GDP. If we use an MRR of 0.5 and a multiplier of 2, government spending would need to decrease by $2250 billion to shift the AD curve by $4500 billion. With an MPC of 0.7 and a tax multiplier of 1.4, a tax increase of $\frac{2250}{0.7}$ = $3214 billion would be needed to decrease AD by $4500 billion.

Interestingly, the government can also stimulate the economy by increasing spending and increasing taxes at the same time. If the government increases spending by $1000 billion and increases taxes by $1000 billion, aggregate demand will increase by (1 − MPC) × (The change in government spending). Aggregate demand will increase by $1000 billion because of the change in government spending but decrease by $700 billion (−MPC×∆T) from the increase in taxes, resulting in a net initial increase in AD of $300 billion and a total increase in AD of $600 billion once the multiplier is incorporated. In this case, the **balanced budget multiplier** would be equal to **the multiplier minus the tax multiplier**:

Balanced budget multiplier = Multiplier − Tax multiplier = 2 − 1.4 = 0.6.

Therefore, the government can actually increase aggregate demand and real GDP by increasing government spending and increasing taxes by the same amount. The downside is that there will be a decrease in household savings as a result of the tax increase, which might impact financial markets, something we will study in the next chapter.

13.4 THE DEBATE OVER FISCAL POLICY

Now that you have a good understanding of the major areas of government spending and the major contours of fiscal policy, we next turn to debates over (1) the size and role of government in the macroeconomy and (2) the extent to which the government should use fiscal policy to stabilize the macroeconomy. There are four major perspectives on fiscal policy. Laissez-faire economists prefer a minimal role for government, and they usually oppose extensive fiscal stabilization policies. Supply-side economists prefer a small role for government regulation, though they are willing to use fiscal policy on behalf of corporate interests. New Keynesian economists see a substantial role for government regulation and stabilization policy. Political economists see the necessity for a large role for government in regulation, stabilization, and guidance of the macroeconomy.

Laissez-faire economists generally believe in a very limited role for government in the macroeconomy. They prefer few regulations and limits to the size and scope government regulatory bodies, limited spending on public and quasi-public goods, and very constrained safety nets. In fact, laissez-faire economists have argued against providing unemployment insurance or safety nets because, in their view, such programs interfere with incentives for people to work. Public goods should be provided by the private sector whenever possible.

It is worth noting that research on unemployment indicates the vast majority of people want to work and prefer a job over accepting unemployment benefits. However, if the only option is unsatisfying work at low wages, some people might choose to collect unemployment benefits. Laissez-faire economists argue that workers should accept whatever options are available, whereas political economists argue that the state should ensure that workers have better choices.

Laissez-faire economists do not believe in undertaking significant government efforts to stabilize the economy. There are several reasons for this. **First**, they believe that **policy lags** render government intervention too ineffective. There is a **recognition lag**, where policymakers do not realize there is a problem until it is already too late. There is a **legislative lag** while politicians debate the best policy and negotiate with those who disagree. There is an **implementation lag**, where it can take months for the government policy to actually take effect. Implementation lags are especially problematic for fiscal policy because it takes so long for spending programs to get up and running. Then, there is a **reaction lag** where it can take additional months or even a year for policies to have their full impact on the economy. Laissez-faire economists see these lags as debilitating. New Keynesian economists acknowledge the existence of lags but believe the government can still implement effective policy given good forecasting and the fact that recessions are followed by periods of slow growth that still require expansionary fiscal policy.

Second, laissez-faire economists believe that **markets are generally self-adjusting and efficient**, so fiscal intervention is usually unnecessary. Cyclical unemployment is dismissed as a product of the unwillingness of workers to accept lower wages: In theory, according to laissez-faire theorists, if workers would accept lower wages, they would be hired immediately by businesses, eliminating unemployment. Unemployment, from this perspective, is voluntary rather than a product of the macroeconomic environment. Like classical economists, modern laissez-faire economists see the macroeconomy as self-adjusting, returning to normal capacity without government intervention.

Third, following the ideas of Friedrich Hayek, laissez-faire advocates tend to believe that **recessions serve a useful purpose** in weeding out inefficient firms. If recessions do happen, they are not necessarily a bad thing.

Given their criticisms of government intervention, laissez-faire advocates do not want stabilization policies to be enacted. With respect to fiscal policy, many laissez-faire advocates want to require a **balanced government budget** each year and refrain from interfering in the economy except for providing basic public goods. Each time the economy in the United States hits a recession and budget deficits increase due to declines in tax revenues and increases in spending on automatic stabilizers, some laissez-faire politician will argue that the government should balance its budget even in a recession by implementing austerity policies. However, as we will see below, austerity policies tend to devastate fragile economies.

Conservative, **supply-side** economists tend to agree with laissez-faire economists on the benefits of deregulation and reducing the size of government agencies. In addition, they often advocate reductions in spending on social welfare programs for the poor, which also aligns with the laissez-faire approach. The differences can be found regarding policies toward tariffs, deficits, subsidies, and taxes. Laissez-faire economists prefer unregulated trade with negligible tariff rates, whereas many supply-side economists, especially those in the Trump administration, advocated protecting U.S. businesses with tariffs on foreign competitors. Laissez-faire economists prefer balanced budgets, whereas U.S. presidents pursuing supply-side policies, including Ronald Reagan, George H.W. Bush, George W. Bush, and Donald Trump, all ran up huge budget deficits while giving generous tax cuts, tax shelters, and subsidies to the wealthy and to corporations.

During the coronavirus recession of 2020, President Trump's supply-side advisors advocated expansionary fiscal policy, including tax cuts for businesses and wealthy business owners, as well as increased government spending on infrastructure. They advocated expansionary monetary policy as well, encouraging the Fed to slash interest rates and to engage in significant quantitative easing. These policies are somewhat consistent with Keynesian economics, except that the focus of fiscal policy is on corporations and owners rather than workers and the poor.

New Keynesian economists believe that a larger degree of government intervention is necessary for the smooth operation of a capitalist economic system. The market needs oversight in many areas, including food, health, environment, and labor markets. In addition, markets require key support structures to make them work, including infrastructure; a smoothly functioning legal system; a well-educated, well-trained, and well-paid workforce; a stable banking system; support for innovation in the form of patent law and public scientific research; a national health system to prepare for pandemics; and much, much more.

Usually, the most effective way to regulate and support markets is via the creation of a government agency to oversee markets in areas where market failures exist. U.S. government administrative bodies include the Offices of Management and Budget, National Intelligence, and Trade; the Departments of Agriculture, Commerce, Defense, Education, Energy, Health and Human Services, Housing and Urban Development, Interior (parks, fish, mining, land), Justice, Labor, State (diplomacy), Transportation, Treasury, and Veterans Affairs; and a host of additional agencies including the Central Intelligence Agency, NASA, and the Post Office. Each of these areas was deemed important enough for congress and the president to create an agency to regulate and support activity in a key area.

New Keynesians believe that one of the most important jobs for government is stabilization policy. The economy is fundamentally unstable and can stay in a recession indefinitely. Therefore, from this perspective the government *must* intervene to restore business and consumer confidence in recessions. This is best achieved via the stimulation of aggregate demand, rather than aggregate supply, which is an area of disagreement with supply-side economists. To New Keynesians, recessions can cause significant long-term damage without government intervention.

Workers thrown onto unemployment for several years in a deep recession will lag behind other workers in skills and experience and may never catch up to their peers who stay employed. Strong, viable businesses may go bankrupt due to temporarily terrible conditions, even though they are quite profitable under normal circumstances. General Motors, the largest U.S. automaker, declared bankruptcy in 2009 in the depths of the Great Recession. Without a government bailout they likely would have closed permanently. Instead, the government helped GM stay open. GM quickly returned to profitability after the recession, repaid the government, and earned record profits in 2015. Therefore, the government can play a significant role in safeguarding a country's private sector base in a severe recession, preserving companies that are in trouble but that will be fine once the recession ends. Protecting profitable companies with a bright future will improve the country's economic growth performance, because those companies will grow rapidly once the economy leaves the recession.

Note, however, that the government probably should not support dying industries. Companies that are in trouble during the economic boom before a recession are likely destined for bankruptcy in the long term. Bailing such companies out during a recession would not save them. Failing companies would still need bailouts after the recession. For example, during the COVID-19 recession of 2020, J.C. Penney, Neiman Marcus, J. Crew, Pier 1, and numerous other retailers declared bankruptcy—but these companies had struggled for years as shoppers shifted from traditional retail shopping to e-commerce. Bailing out these companies would likely end up being a long-term bailout, which could end up costing the government large sums of money in perpetuity. Long-term bailouts lead to the **soft budget constraint problem**, where **the government continually bails out an industry that cannot become competitive in markets**. Without a limit on government bailouts—a budget constraint—companies do not need to become competitive to survive. Governments that offer companies continual bailouts can quickly find themselves in a budgetary nightmare, where they are spending large sums subsidizing companies with no future. The United Kingdom did this in the 1970s when it bailed out steel, coal, and other declining industries. Thus, it can be important for the government to be targeted and selective with bailouts or to impose strict time limits for government support. Nonetheless, keeping companies with bright futures afloat remains a key element of effective stabilization policies.

Political economists prefer a larger degree of government intervention in all aspects of the economy. They see market failures as endemic to capitalism; therefore, markets only work with a substantial degree of government regulation and oversight. Oversight requires independently funded government agencies that have the power to regulate and even to direct markets. Most social market economies (SMEs) utilizing the political economy approach have a ministry of industry or a similar planning body that coordinates investment, conducts research into new technologies, and promotes industrial development in key growth industries. SMEs also usually have active labor market policies that train and funnel workers directly into new industries. From the political economy perspective, good governance is a source of competitive advantage that can stimulate industrial development more effectively than the private sector alone.

Similarly, political economists want the government to go much further than other approaches when it comes to stabilization policy. Given that the government has the power to end recessions via discretionary fiscal policy and stabilization policy, it should do so. The main problem in recessions is a lack of sufficient aggregate demand, as investors and consumers curtail their spending. The best way to end recessions is by spending a large amount of money, especially on infrastructure and putting people to work directly. Infrastructure spending improves the efficiency of the economy, stimulating additional rounds of investment, and it employs construction workers, who are among the first to be laid off in recessions as housing starts falter and as businesses cancel construction projects. Because unemployment spikes in recessions, putting people directly to work ensures that they have an income. Instead of paying unemployment benefits to people who are not working, the government can pay people to do productive jobs in their communities. There are plenty of things that need to be done in every community, after all.

A dramatic expansion of fiscal spending requires the government to engage in significant deficit spending, borrowing money to finance expansionary fiscal policy in recessions. Government debt and deficits is another controversial topic in economics.

13.5 THE SIZE OF GOVERNMENT DEBT AND DEFICITS

Figure 13.10 shows the annual U.S. federal budget deficit or surplus from 1970 through 2020.[6] The budget deficit or surplus is computed by taking all government spending (G) and subtracting net tax revenue (T):

$$\text{Budget deficit} = G - T.$$

Prior to 1970, the U.S. government ran very small deficits in recessions. Budget deficits during recessions are called **cyclical deficits**, because they **occur as a result of recessions during the business cycle**. The government sometimes ran

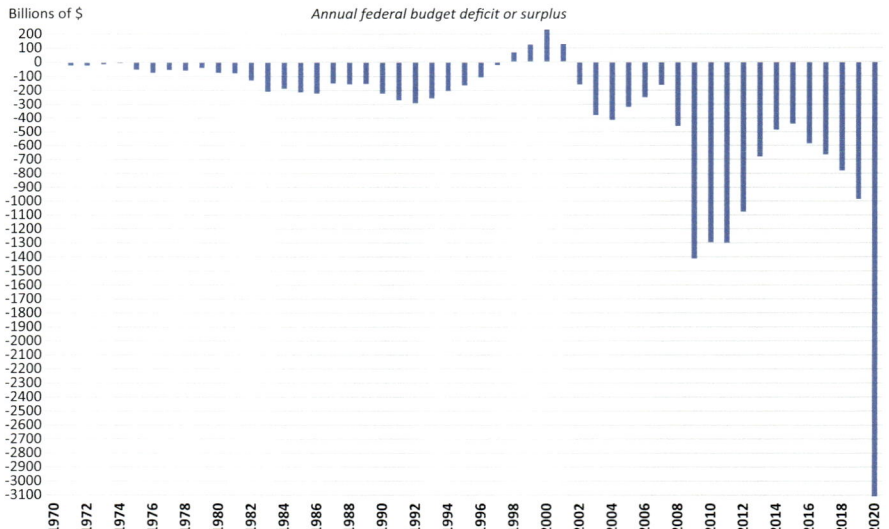

FIGURE 13.10 Federal budget deficit or surplus, 1970–2020.

small surpluses when the economy was booming prior to 1970. This is a reflection of moderate, Keynesian economic policy.

The U.S. government began running **structural deficits**, **the portion of the government deficit that exists even when the economy is at its normal capacity**, in the 1980s with the advent of supply-side economics. The boom of the 1990s and political gridlock caused a brief period of surpluses, but the return of supply-side policies in the 2000s under George W. Bush once again led to structural deficits. The Great Recession of 2007–2009 and the slow growth in subsequent years caused massive cyclical deficits, on top of existing structural deficits. Annual deficits fell from 2010 to 2016 as the economy grew under President Obama. President Trump, elected in 2016, returned to supply-side policies, and deficits increased significantly even though the economy was growing. The COVID-19 recession of 2020 was met with a massive increase in government spending (which we explain in more detail below), causing the annual budget deficit to reach record levels.

Figure 13.11 shows the total accumulated national debt of the U.S. government, which is computed by adding up all of the annual deficits.[7] The debt seems to be increasing exponentially, so it is easy to think that the United States may soon be overwhelmed by its debts. That is not likely to be the case, however, because GDP also increased dramatically during this period.

Economists are less concerned with the total level of debt than they are with the level of debt relative to GDP. This is because a high level of debt is not problematic if it is also accompanied by a high GDP.

We can explain this using the analogy of loans for home purchases. When people need a mortgage to buy a home, the bank cares much less about the buyer's total level of debt than they do the buyer's debt relative to their income. A home buyer with a high level of income will have little trouble paying off similarly high levels of debt. It is only when a buyer's debts are very high relative to income that

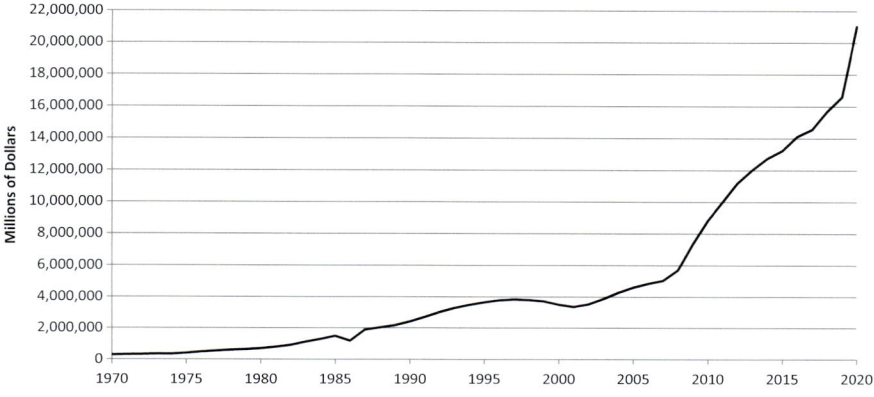

FIGURE 13.11 Total U.S. national debt held by the public, 1970–2020.

a bank would be worried about getting paid back. Research indicates households that exceed a debt/income ratio of more than 43% will have trouble paying back their mortgage. A higher income means a lower debt/income ratio and a higher likelihood of repayment. Similarly, a high level of debt is easy to pay back for a country with a high GDP. Total U.S. debt reached $23.2 trillion in the first quarter of 2020, but U.S. GDP was also very high at $21.5 trillion.

Figure 13.12 shows the U.S. public debt as a percentage of GDP—the debt-to-GDP ratio—from 1970 to 2020.[8] The increase in debt as a percentage of GDP is much gentler than the increase in total debt. Nevertheless, the steady increase in the debt/GDP ratio worries some economists.

Figure 13.13 shows that though the U.S. national debt as a percentage of GDP is quite high, it is not as high as the debt/GDP ratio in Japan, Greece, and Italy,

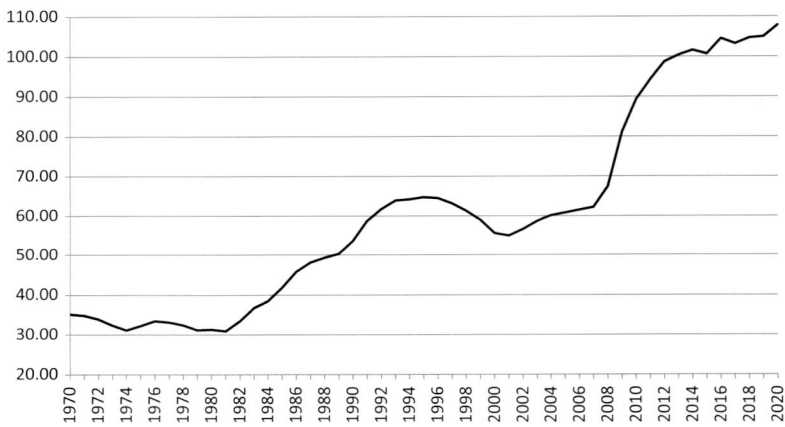

FIGURE 13.12 U.S. public debt as a percentage of GDP, 1970–2020.

Country	Debt as a % of GDP
Japan	237.5
Greece	174.2
Italy	133.4
United States	106.7
Belgium	99.6
France	99.2
Spain	96.0
Brazil	90.4
Canada	88.0
United Kingdom	85.7
South Africa	57.8
Germany	56.9
South Korea	40.5
Switzerland	39.5
Sweden	37.2
Norway	36.8
Denmark	33.6

FIGURE 13.13 Table showing national debt as a percentage of GDP, various developed countries, 2020.

countries that experienced significant economic crises in recent years. Interestingly, the U.S. focus on military spending and tax cuts for businesses and the wealthy ends up generating much larger deficits than most social market economies that spend significant amounts on social welfare programs. Ironically, although the Nordic countries Sweden, Norway, and Denmark are considered to have some of the most generous social welfare programs in the world, they also have the lowest debt ratios of developed countries.

After discussing government deficits and debt, next we need to consider the extent to which government debt is problematic. As is so often the case, economists disagree on this topic.

13.6 THE DEBATE OVER GOVERNMENT DEFICITS AND DEBT

The major opponents of deficit spending are laissez-faire economists, who oppose government intervention unless there are exceptional circumstances. Laissez-faire economists generally oppose running annual budget deficits and accumulating increasing levels of government debt. They believe deficits increase the likelihood of inflation and cause higher interest rates, which can crowd out (reduce) private sector investment and reduce economic growth. They see deficits placing a burden on future generations.

New Keynesian economists argue that any problems created by cyclical deficits that occur during recessions are minor and are more than offset by the benefits of deficit spending. Government spending, tax cuts, and interest rate cuts will stimulate aggregate demand and help to eliminate any recessionary gap, thereby contributing to economic growth. Inflation and high interest rates are almost never a problem in recessions; rather, the major recessionary problems are deflation and pessimism about future sales, both of which can be improved by expansionary fiscal policy financed by borrowing. However, New Keynesian economists are not usually in favor of structural deficits.

Supply-siders do not see deficits as a problem as long as they are created by policies that stimulate aggregate supply. Tax cuts can provide increased incentives to work, save, and invest, which should increase economic growth if the money is invested in productive new business ventures. In theory, tax cuts may pay for themselves in the long run if they stimulate enough growth.

Political economists also do not see deficits as problems, as long as deficits are generated by policies that improve the well-being of workers, stimulate aggregate demand, and enhance long-term growth prospects. Deficits that enhance productivity and create new industries are a good thing. Political economists advocate spending on education, health care, infrastructure, research and development, public transportation, technology, and a green new deal to create jobs in sustainable energy and other environmental areas. To political economists, unless spending results in clear signs of macroeconomic problems, such as inflation and high interest rates, a country should not worry about deficits. Deficit spending should continue until unemployment and underemployment are eliminated.

Below, we go through some specific areas of disagreement, starting with the most important area of debate—whether deficits cause the crowding out or crowding in of private sector investment.

1. **Crowding out vs. crowding in of private sector investment**

    According to laissez-faire economists, increases in government deficits increase the demand for money, which can cause interest rates to increase. This may result in the government borrowing money that could have been used by the private sector, causing a decline in private sector investment. Because laissez-faire economists prefer private sector investment to public sector investment, this is seen in a very negative light.

    New Keynesian economists note that crowding out has not been a significant problem for decades in the United States, and it is never a significant problem in recessions when private sector investment is very low. As long as the government injects sufficient liquidity (supplies of money) into the banking system, crowding out does not seem to occur in recessions. In general, the problem in recessions is too much savings and too little investment. According to the Keynesian **paradox of thrift**, **when consumers save more, this reduces aggregate demand, which in turn reduces GDP, which then reduces savings**. Increased saving results in less economic activity, which decreases incomes and savings. This is especially problematic in recessions: When consumers and investors save more and spend less, savings piles up in banks. Interest rates fall, but consumers and investors do not want to borrow money due to pessimism about the future. In this environment, there is plenty of savings to go around, and no crowding out of private sector investment will occur. Even in financial crises with a large number of bank failures, the central bank can increase the money supply to ensure that there is always enough money in banks for lending. Therefore, with appropriate policies, there is no reason to expect crowding out in recessions.

    Furthermore, good government policy actually *crowds in* private sector investment. By improving macroeconomic conditions, government spending can encourage the private sector to invest. This is especially likely if the government spends money on infrastructure, technology development, or other programs that enhance the efficiency of the private sector, thereby providing opportunities for profitable private sector investment.

    Supply-side economists are also unconcerned with deficits, in recessions or expansions, if they improve the conditions for suppliers. This usually means corporate tax cuts or decreases in taxes for the wealthy who form or invest in companies. Supply-siders hope that the tax cuts will generate sufficient economic growth in the future to offset the initial deficits the tax cuts create.

Political economists are unconcerned with deficits under most conditions, especially if the money is used to stimulate aggregate demand. Political economists agree with Keynes that stimulus money should go to the unemployed and the poor, who suffer the most and who will increase their spending the most when given money. The resulting increase in aggregate demand should help to crowd in investment. Additional government investments in infrastructure, education, training, basic scientific research, technology, and other growth-generating activities will also help to stimulate growth and crowd in private sector investment.

2. **Budget deficits may contribute to trade deficits and international indebtedness**

In general, mainstream economists argue that any country consuming more than it produces must by definition run a trade deficit. Recall the leakages and injections equation from Keynes:

$$I + G + X = S + T + IM$$

$$(IM - X) = (I - S) + (G - T).$$

This equation implies that the trade deficit, the amount of exports (X) that is less than imports (IM), is a product of low national savings by households, businesses, and government. Trade deficits occur when savings (S) is less than investment (I) and when government spending (G) is less than net taxes (T). Figure 13.14 shows U.S. net national savings since 1950. U.S. households saved 10% to 13% of their incomes from 1950 to 1984. However, after 1984, the personal savings rate averaged 7%. At the same time, government savings became significantly negative due to recurring budget deficits. The result is a net national savings rate that declined to 2% in 2019, a number that is extraordinarily low by international standards. In comparison, the net national savings rate in France is 5%, Germany's is 11%, Sweden's is 12%, Norway's is 18%, and China's is 25%.

Trade deficits can be a problem, because when a country spends more than its income, it accrues debts to its trading partners in the amount of the trade deficit. If the United States produces $20 trillion worth of goods and services, it also generates $20 trillion in income in the process. However, if the United States consumes $21 trillion worth of goods when it produces $20 trillion worth of goods, then it has a trade deficit of $1 trillion. Furthermore, the United States owes domestic citizens and other countries $1 trillion for the extra goods it purchased, which it must pay for by borrowing money.

Most economists do not see the money a country owes to its own citizens as a drain on the economy, because payments to a country's own citizens increase the home country's income and stimulate its economy. However, the external debt—the money a country owes to foreign countries—is usually seen as a

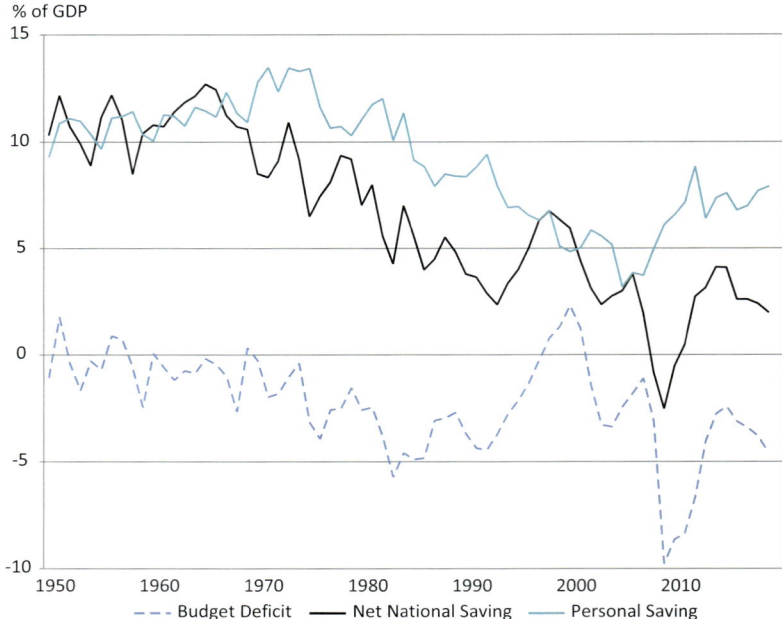

FIGURE 13.14 U.S. net national saving, personal saving, and budget deficit as a percentage of GDP (1950–2019). Source: FRED.

Country	U.S. Treasury Debt Held (billions)
Japan	$ 1119.52
China	1107.54
United Kingdom	325.03
Brazil	304.03
Ireland	273.64
Luxembourg	239.57
Switzerland	230.14
Cayman Islands	222.23
Hong Kong	214.42
Belgium	198.25
Taiwan	178.89
Saudi Arabia	176.72

FIGURE 13.15 U.S. Treasury debt held by other countries in 2019.

drain on the economy, because those payments flow out of the country. In the mid-1980s, 11.5% of U.S. government debt was held by foreign governments, corporations, and citizens. By 2019, 39% of U.S. government debt was held by foreign countries. Figure 13.15 shows the countries that hold the largest amounts of U.S. government Treasury debt. The United States has a large trade deficit with most of these countries.

When the U.S. government makes payments to foreign countries, those payments are a leakage from the U.S. economy that can reduce U.S. GDP if the money is not returned to the United States. We will study the issue of trade deficits and foreign exchange flows in more detail later when we take up international financial issues.

Laissez-faire economists see unregulated trade as a great benefit to consumers everywhere. Trade deficits indicate large benefits accruing to home country consumers, who get lots of inexpensive foreign goods and a higher standard of living. They also believe that trade deficits will be naturally corrected by an exchange rate devaluation as the United States floods the world with dollars, although this has not proven to be the case. Prior to President Trump, most supply-side politicians in the United States adhered to the laissez-faire position. Trump saw trade deficits as a threat to the United States and imposed tariffs on China and other trading partners to reduce trade deficits.

Political economists from the modern monetary theory (MMT) perspective also see little problem with trade deficits. Bill Mitchell argues that when a foreign country runs a trade surplus, it is depriving its citizens of the use of their own resources, goods, and services, selling these items to the country with the trade deficit in exchange for assets. The trade surplus country has a lower standard of living and the trade deficit country a higher one as a result.

Other political economists, however, argue that trade deficits undermine jobs and wages in countries that run trade deficits, making workers worse off. Similarly, John Maynard Keynes believed in the regulation of international trade to reduce or eliminate trade imbalances, which he saw as destabilizing. However, many New Keynesian economists view unregulated trade more favorably, agreeing largely with laissez-faire economists that trade deficits are a minor problem and that they will eventually correct themselves. As you can see, economists' perspectives regarding budget deficits and trade deficits do not fall neatly into clear patterns.

3. **Budget deficits can be inflationary**

    Laissez-faire economists argue that increases in spending, and the increases in the money supply that tend to accompany expansionary fiscal policy, will inevitably lead to inflation. However, empirical evidence indicates otherwise, according to other economists. Vast increases in government spending and the money supply did not generate inflation in any recessionary period in the United States, so most economists discount this argument.

4. **Large deficits, especially during booms, can cause the government to lose the ability to use expansionary fiscal policy when needed and represent a burden on the macroeconomy**

    Due to worries about budget deficits becoming a drain on the economy, politicians are often unwilling to back additional spending when deficits are high. In the depths of the financial crisis and Great Recession of 2007–2009, conservative U.S. congressional representatives refused to engage in additional expansionary fiscal policy due to worries about budget deficits, which had increased to record levels. However, New Keynesian and political economists argued that additional spending would shorten the length of the recession and improve the strength of the recovery.

This leads us to the central question: Are large budget deficits and a growing national debt a bad thing? To laissez-faire economists, the answer is invariably yes: Deficits reduce private sector growth and mortgage a country's economic future. Many New Keynesian economists agree, arguing that deficits in recessions are fine but they should be offset by surpluses during expansions to balance the budget over the course of the business cycle. However, political economists disagree, arguing that deficits are central to economic growth.

13.6.1 Is the deficit a myth?

One of the most interesting and important arguments in favor of deficit spending was made by Stephanie Kelton, a leading MMT economist, in her 2020 book, *The Deficit Myth*.[9] Most economists argue that the total amount of government spending is limited by the amount of tax revenues. Modern monetary theory instead asserts that a sovereign country that conducts transactions in its own currency backed by the state (fiat currency) can run up unlimited deficits as long as it has sufficient resources (labor, capital, and natural resources). Therefore, **there is no limit to federal spending. The government can create money out of thin air by printing it or transferring it to banks or people with a single keystroke.** The federal government can never run out of money, and the only thing stopping it from spending is political support and the upper limit of resource capacity. There should never be crowding out, because as soon as money is in short supply, the government can simply print/create more of it. The government controls the rate of interest and can set it wherever it wishes.

The philosophy Kelton is articulating here is called **functional finance**, based on the ideas of Abba Lerner, which proposes that **governments should decide how much to spend and tax based on the impact of these policies on prosperity for all, not based on how large the deficit is. Deficits are largely unimportant in sovereign nations that control their own currency.**

According to MMT, **inflation, not a budget deficit, is the sign of government overspending**. If an economy is operating close to full employment and there is no more capacity for output, then additional spending could cause inflationary pressures. But, unless a country is actively experiencing inflation, it can safely continue to increase government spending and promote greater prosperity.

In addition, when a government pays out more money than it receives, the nongovernment sector experiences a surplus. **Government deficits directly enrich the private sector.** On the other hand, government surpluses take money out of the private sector, reducing economic activity.

Critics of MMT argue that it is never clear where the limits to economic capacity are, nor can we assume that government spending will necessarily be useful and productive. If government money is funneled into financial markets, it could create destructive bubbles. Too much circulation of a currency might also cause people and corporations to be less willing to accept it, which could undermine the goals of expansionary fiscal policy and cause a currency crisis. Despite these criticisms, the argument that the government should spend money on useful programs until problems materialize remains compelling to many political economists. Interestingly, although most economists do not accept the MMT approach, there has been a remarkable movement toward acceptance of large government deficits in recent years, indicating the increasing influence of the MMT approach. We see this in the fiscal policy approaches to the Great Recession and the COVID-19 recession.

13.7 FISCAL POLICY IN ACTION: FIGHTING THE GREAT RECESSION AND THE COVID-19 RECESSION

After the financial crisis of 2007, the U.S. economy plunged into the Great Recession of 2008–2009. Economists estimated that aggregate demand fell by $1200 billion as the stock market plunged and consumers and investors curtailed their spending. Although some laissez-faire economists opposed enacting expansionary fiscal policy, the vast majority of economists advocated a very large fiscal stimulus due to the severity of the recession.

In response to the recession, one of the first acts of the Obama administration was to pass the American Recovery and Reinvestment Act (ARRA) of February 2009. ARRA included $288 billion in tax cuts for households and businesses, especially for the poor; $224 billion for extended unemployment benefits, education, training, and health care; $105 billion for infrastructure spending; and $175 billion on other types of job-creating spending. At the time, this was the largest fiscal stimulus ever passed by the U.S. government.

Although it is hard to be precise, the Congressional Budget Office[10] estimated that ARRA had the following impact:

- Increased real GDP by 1.7% to 9.2%
- Reduced unemployment by 1.1% to 4.8%
- Increased full-time employment-years by 2.1 million to 11.6 million.

If we take the average of the low and high estimates for the economic impact, which is a reasonable approach, ARRA has a very positive impact on the U.S. economy, increasing real GDP by about 5.5% and reducing unemployment by about 3%. However, the economic recovery after the Great Recession was sluggish, which seems to indicate that the stimulus was not large enough to eliminate the recessionary gap. Nevertheless, the U.S. stimulus was much more effective in restarting economic growth than the austerity policies pursued in the E.U.

The Great Recession provided a dramatic contrast between the Keynesian expansionary fiscal policies implemented in the United States and the laissez-faire austerity policies implemented in the euro area of the E.U. The U.S. Great Recession was deep and lasted about a year and a half. As noted above, expansionary fiscal policy improved economic growth and the U.S. economy grew steadily but slowly after 2009. The euro area of the E.U. also experienced a deep recession in 2008–2009, recovered briefly, and then entered a second recession beginning in 2011 that lasted an additional two years.

The reason for the double-dip recession in the E.U. stemmed largely from the austerity policies its policymakers adopted. After a small initial stimulus in 2009, E.U. policymakers insisted that countries that were hard hit by the financial crisis, including Greece and Spain, slash government spending and raise taxes to reduce their budget deficits. Laissez-faire economists recommending this policy hoped that reductions in government deficits would improve business confidence, reduce crowding-out, and stimulate business investment. However, just the opposite occurred. Decreases in government spending and higher taxes in fragile EU economies caused consumer spending and business investment to plummet. Unemployment in Greece and Spain reached 29% and 27%, respectively.

From 2008 to 2015, the U.S. economy grew by an annual average of 1.36%, while the euro area of the E.U. experienced an average annual growth rate of only 0.26%. The euro area was almost completely stagnant for seven years thanks to their policy choices. To New Keynesian economist Paul Krugman, laissez-faire economists who thought austerity would improve business confidence and investment in recessions were engaging in magical thinking, believing in the "confidence fairy." Unfortunately, like the tooth fairy, the confidence fairy proved to be a myth.[11]

The contrasting experiences of the United States and the E.U. in the Great Recession helped to convince most economists and policymakers that fiscal and monetary stimulus policies were crucial in addressing a major recession. Both the United States and the E.U. took more dramatic steps in the next recession.

When the economy plunged into the even deeper COVID-19 recession in 2020, President Trump and the U.S. Congress were willing to enact a much larger stimulus. In late March 2020, the U.S. government passed the $2 trillion Coronavirus Aid, Relief, and Economic Security (CARES) Act. Reflecting the supply-side focus of the Trump administration, the biggest benefits went to large corporations, followed by small businesses, as shown in Figure 13.16. Households were given cash directly, as were the unemployed, but little direct government spending or job creation took place.

The result of the fiscal stimulus plus a huge monetary stimulus from the Fed was a dramatic resurgence of the stock market. The Standard and Poor's 500 index of the 500 largest U.S. companies had dropped from 3386.15 on February 19, 2020, to 2237.40 on March 23. After the stimulus, the stock market rebounded to almost the same level, reaching 3215.60 on July 16. In previous recessions, it usually took stock markets years to rebound.

FISCAL POLICY, DEBT, AND DEFICITS

CARES Act Spending Category	Amount (billions)
Subsidies and tax cuts for large corporations	$500
Small business loans and grants	$377
State and local government funding for COVID-19 response, other programs	$340
Cash payments to households	$300
Extra unemployment payments	$260
Public health spending on hospitals, other areas	$154
Student loan and other loan forgiveness	$44
Safety net support (food)	$26
National security spending	$17

FIGURE 13.16 CARES Act of 2020 major spending categories.

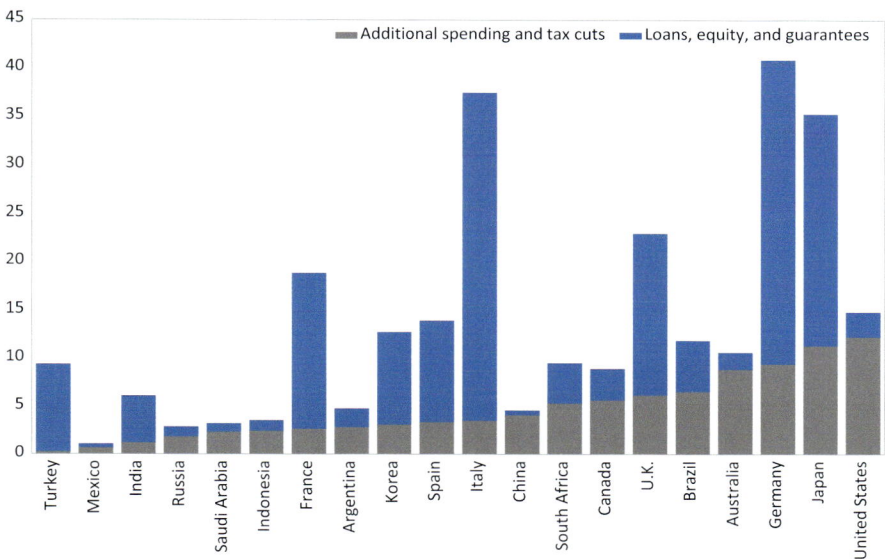

FIGURE 13.17 Fiscal (grey) and monetary (blue) responses to the COVID-19 recession as a percentage of GDP.

However, the stimulus had a much smaller impact on unemployment at first. The unemployment rate increased from 3.5% in February 2020 to 14.7% in April at the start of the recession. By June 2020, the unemployment rate dropped thanks to the stimulus but only to 11.1%. Fortunately, an additional $3 trillion of stimulus under the Biden administration in early 2021, along with reductions in COVID-19 cases due to a massive vaccination effort, resulted in a booming economy, causing the unemployment rate to drop to 3.6% by May 2022. Unfortunately, the boom was accompanied by surging inflation of over 8%, driven partly by a higher demand for goods as well as by disruptions to energy supplies from the Russia–Ukraine war and continued coronavirus disruptions to the supply of goods from China.

Figure 13.17 shows that the United States initially allocated more money as a percentage of GDP than other developed countries on spending and tax cuts but less in total stimulus than some countries. Germany and Denmark spent most of their stimulus funds on keeping workers employed.

Fiscal policy remains somewhat controversial, although it appears that a modern consensus in favor of expansionary fiscal policy has re-emerged in the wake of the Great Recession. It will be interesting to see whether this consensus continues.

13.8 CONCLUSION

The role of government in the United States increased steadily from the Great Depression until the 1970s, after which it stabilized at an average of 31.9% of the economy. The major areas of government spending are the purchase of public and quasi-public goods, social spending, and government administration. The U.S. government plays a significant role in the economy, but it spends less on public goods and safety nets than most other developed countries. The United States also taxes the wealthy much less than other countries and has a relatively flat tax structure instead of a progressive one. Other developed countries have progressive tax structures where the rich pay a larger percentage of their income in taxes than the poor.

Governments can use automatic stabilizers and discretionary fiscal policy to stabilize economies. In recessions, increases in government spending and decreases in taxes increase aggregate demand, and if they are large enough, they can eliminate any recessionary gap and return the economy to potential real GDP. In an overheated economy, the government can decrease spending or increase taxes to eliminate any inflationary gap.

Economists often disagree on the utilization of fiscal policy. Laissez-faire economists generally oppose the use of fiscal policy in recessions, arguing that markets quickly correct themselves and that crowding-out, policy lags, and other problems render fiscal policy ineffective. They often advocate austerity and oppose increasing government deficits. New Keynesian economists strongly advocate the use of fiscal policy in recessions, seeing it as the best way to stabilize the economy and arguing that government spending tends to crowd in private sector investment. They are comfortable with deficit spending in recessions. Supply-side economists advocate the use of tax cuts for corporations and the wealthy to stimulate aggregate supply and are not concerned with deficit spending. Political economists advocate strategic government spending to benefit workers and to generate growth. Deficit spending in service of these goals is encouraged.

The steady growth of the U.S. federal debt and growing budget deficits even in non-recession years indicate an increasing acceptance of debt by U.S. politicians. Most economists are troubled by the increasing debt levels, but political economists from the modern monetary theory perspective argue that deficit spending is not problematic as long as the economy is below full capacity.

Expansionary fiscal policy was used to combat the Great Recession of 2008 and the COVID-19 recession of 2020. In the Great Recession, expansionary fiscal policy in the United States proved to be much more effective than austerity policy in the euro area in stabilizing the macroeconomy. The E.U., United States, and other developed countries engaged in record fiscal stimulus in 2020, causing an explosion in national debts. Time will tell whether these stimulus policies were effective or whether the debts will prove to be debilitating.

QUESTIONS FOR REVIEW

1. Describe the priorities that emerge from the role and size of the U.S. government. What does the United States prioritize? How do U.S. priorities differ from those in other developed countries?
2. Explain the difference between automatic stabilizers and discretionary fiscal policy. Give examples in your answer.
3. Use Figure 13.18 to answer the following questions. Suppose the economy is currently in equilibrium where AD_1 intersects AS.
   a. What is the amount of the recessionary or inflationary gap?
   b. If the marginal respending rate (MRR) is 0.6, how much will the government need to change spending to move the economy to a new equilibrium at potential real GDP?
   c. If the marginal propensity to consumer is 0.8, how large of a lump sum tax change would be needed to move the economy to a new equilibrium at potential real GDP?

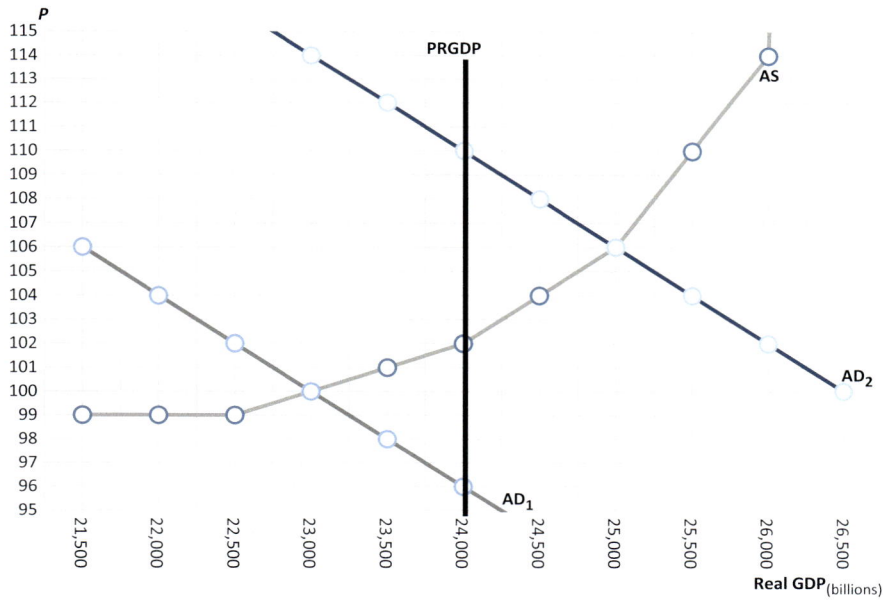

FIGURE 13.18 Aggregate demand and supply problem.

4. Use Figure 13.18 to answer the following questions. Suppose the economy is currently in equilibrium where AD_2 intersects AS.
   a. What is the amount of the recessionary or inflationary gap?
   b. If the marginal respending rate is 0.8, how much will the government need to change spending to move the economy to a new equilibrium at potential real GDP?
   c. If the marginal propensity to consume is 0.95, how large of a lump sum tax change would be needed to move the economy to a new equilibrium at potential real GDP?
5. Compare and contrast the different perspectives of economists on fiscal policy. Which perspective do you find most convincing? Why?
6. Describe what has happened to U.S. budget deficits and the national debt of the federal government over the last 50 years.
7. Critically evaluate the different perspectives of economists on government budget deficits and debt. What are the main areas of disagreement? How do you think the government should approach the issue of deficit spending? Explain, and support your answer.
8. Explain Stephanie Kelton's argument that the government should not worry about large government budget deficits except under certain conditions. What are some criticisms of this approach?
9. Describe the fiscal policies used to stabilize the economies of the United States and the euro area during the Great Recession of 2008. Were the policies effective? Why or why not? How did developed countries change their policies to combat the COVID-19 recession of 2020?

NOTES

1. 2019 U.S. GDP was used for this calculation.
2. See Geoffrey Schneider, *Economic Principles and Problems* (London: Routledge, 2022), ch. 21 for more details. Most health economists attribute high U.S. costs and poor health outcomes to the emphasis on private sector health care, and the inefficiencies in private health care markets. The United States pays far more for prescription drugs and basic medical services than any other country.
3. Source: OECDStat.
4. Source: OECD, *OECD Economic Outlook,* Vol. 2019, no. 2. https://www.oecd-ilibrary.org/sites/f21b05be-en/index.html?itemId=/content/component/f21b05be-en, accessed August 6, 2021.
5. Note that for simplicity we are assuming here that the tax change is a "lump sum" change and does not vary with income, and we are assuming the marginal propensity to import is 0 when it comes to the impact of lump sum tax cuts.
6. The 2020 deficit figure was estimated by the Congressional Budget Office in June 2020. Changes in government policies or tax collection after this date are not reflected in this estimate.
7. Source: FRED, Federal Reserve Economic Data.

8 Ibid.

9 My thanks to Spandan Marasini, who wrote the initial draft of this section.

10 Congressional Budget Office, "Estimated Impact of the American Recovery and Reinvestment Act on Employment and Economic Output in 2014," February 2015. https://www.cbo.gov/sites/default/files/114th-congress-2015-2016/reports/49958-ARRA.pdf, accessed August 6, 2021.

11 Paul Krugman, "Myths of Austerity," *New York Times,* July 1, 2010. https://www.nytimes.com/2010/07/02/opinion/02krugman.html?ref=paulkrugman, accessed August 6, 2021.

14 Money, banking, and the financial sector

How money markets make the world go around

In modern capitalist economies, money seems to be the most important priority. Many individuals and businesses spend their entire existence trying to accumulate as much money as possible. Ironically, money has no intrinsic value: It is only worth the paper it is printed on or the electronic credit in your account. But money is important because people believe in its enduring value, and they are willing to part with goods, services, labor, property, and assets in exchange for money.

Money started out as a simple social construct—as a registry of debts or as a commodity such as a unit of wheat to keep track of who owed what to whom. However, the modern monetary system is much more complicated. Money is now mostly a system of electronic debits and credits, and printed money is becoming less and less important. Banks and financial markets that control much of a country's money loom ever larger in importance, so much so that they often influence economic policy to be more favorable to money markets than to workers and manufacturers. Thus, money is about claims on resources, but it is also about economic and political power.

This chapter takes up money, banking, and the financial sector, illustrating how money markets and financial markets work in theory and practice. Given their importance, every citizen needs to understand the role of money, banking, and financial markets in modern economies.

This chapter begins by discussing the history of money and its role in the modern world. Next, we take up the banking sector and how banks create money. Subsequently, we introduce the mainstream economics and political economy models of the money market. Next, we take up financial markets, including stocks, bonds, and real estate. Financialization, a term used to describe the rise and increasing dominance of the finance, insurance, and real estate (FIRE) sector, is then discussed.

DOI: 10.4324/9780429399350-19

MONEY, BANKING, AND THE FINANCIAL SECTOR

14.0 CHAPTER 14 LEARNING GOALS

After reading this chapter, you should be able to:

- Describe the history of money and the role it has played in various economies.

- Differentiate between commodity money and fiat money and explain why economists believe that fiat money is better for economic stability.

- Explain how banks work and how they can create money via the **money (deposit) multiplier**.

- Use the mainstream and political economy models of the money market to determine how changes in key variables will affect the money supply and the interest rate.

- Compare and contrast the mainstream economics and political economy models of the money market and explain the debate over whether money is exogenously or endogenously determined.

- Describe the role that financial markets, especially stock markets, play in the economy.

- Critically analyze the concept of financialization and whether or not financialization presents a significant problem in modern economies.

14.1 DEFINING MONEY—IT'S NOT WHAT YOU THINK

To many people, money is the central focus of their existence due to its importance in modern capitalism. Having money means you can buy the necessities of life. If you successfully accumulate money, you are an important person with power and influence. It often seems that money is the central driver of the modern world—that "money makes the world go around."

This is ironic given that some economists do not see money as particularly important. Many laissez-faire economists argue that money has no significant impact on the "real" economy, affecting only prices. In economic terminology, laissez-faire economists argue that money is "neutral," having no positive or negative impact on the real economy. Other economists disagree, arguing that money has a very important impact on real economic variables. And, as we will see, a poorly managed monetary system is a recipe for disaster.

In the modern economy, **money** is **a unit of account, which may also be a physical item such as a printed piece of paper, that is accepted as payment** for taxes, debts, and goods and services. Money can also be issued as credit (loaned out). Historically, money has taken on two main forms, as **an account of debits and credits in a ledger and as a medium of exchange for trading**.

Anthropological research has established that most exchanges in ancient human societies were gifts, with an understanding that at some point there was likely to be a reciprocal gift. You would share what you had with other community members, with the understanding that you would be "paid back" in the future when you needed something. Ancient societies featured strong bonds of community, including reciprocity and redistribution, because larger, more united groups had a greater likelihood of success in the challenging environment facing hunter-gatherer societies. The fact that exchanges took the form of gifts (redistribution) and reciprocity meant that money was unnecessary, so it did not exist in the modern sense.

According to anthropologist David Graeber, the earliest form of money probably happened when "I owe you one," became "I owe you one unit of something."[1] There is evidence that units of wheat were the first units of account—in essence the first form of money. In ancient Babylonia, the mina was the unit of account, and it was equal to 10,800 grains of wheat.[2] Thus, the earliest forms of economic exchange seem to have taken the form of loans and an early form of debt bondage. Debts were kept track of on "tally sticks," such as the one displayed in Figure 14.1.[3] Eventually, debts denoted on tally sticks were replaced with loans of money, along with the idea of interest payments or some other form of return on loans.

The development of **commodity money**, where **gold, silver, or other precious commodities are used as the primary unit of account**, accompanied the rise of private property and the development of a government (state) that needed to engage in taxation to support itself. Figure 14.1 shows ancient Chinese metal coins, carved with official characters to make them harder to duplicate and counterfeit.

Many different commodities have served as money in human societies. Livestock, grains, salt, peppercorns, cocoa beans, tea, precious metals, rare cowrie shells, decorated belts, large carved stones, and beaver pelts have all served as

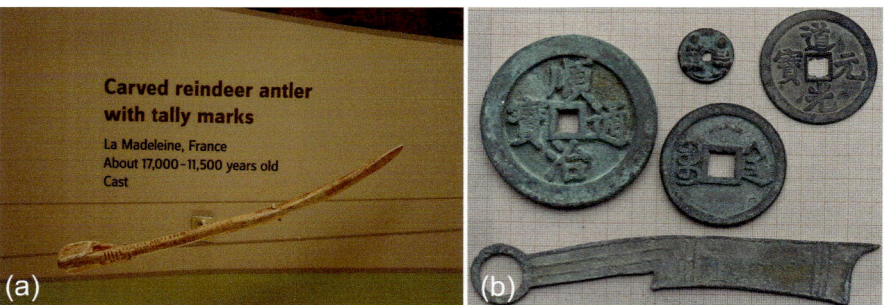

FIGURE 14.1 An ancient French tally stick (left) and ancient Chinese coins (right).

commodity money in particular times and places. Even in the modern world we occasionally see commodities serving as money. In prisons, cigarettes sometimes serve as a form of currency. In Russia in the late 1990s when the Russian ruble lost all of its value, people started to use cases of vodka as currency. In the isolated regions of Columbia where cocaine is produced, coca paste is often accepted as payment.

In general, commodity monies have two important things in common: They are scarce, but they are not impossibly rare. If leaves on trees were money, then everyone would have vast amounts and the money would not be able to maintain its value. If money was something impossibly rare, there would not be enough of it to facilitate debt payments and exchange.

Commodity money is useful because it makes exchanges much more efficient. Without money, exchanges have to be done via barter, with both people trying to trade something they have for something they want. Barter, however, is very inefficient: If either party does not want what the other person is trading, then no exchange will take place. That is, there has to be a "coincidence of wants" in order for barter to take place. Barter is also made difficult by the lack of common prices. For barter to work, there has to be a common understanding of the worth of each commodity in terms of all other commodities.

Money simplifies this process immensely. Each person can sell what they have for money to a person who wants it. Then, they can use that money to buy what they want. In addition, the prices of all items can be expressed in terms of money, so it is easy to establish relative prices for all goods and services. Money facilitates commerce by serving as a medium of exchange.

In theory, commodity money has intrinsic value, in that the commodity being used as money—often gold or silver—is useful and pretty. Human beings have long valued shiny things like gold, silver, and diamonds. However, commodity money's primary source of value is that the state requires its citizens to use it and people have to pay taxes and debts in commodity money. This is why the move from commodity money to fiat money occurred without significant problems.

Fiat money is **money that is established as legal tender by government fiat**, which is an official government decree. In the modern world, fiat money is **paper money or electronic accounts that have value because the state declares that they do and because people need the fiat money to pay their taxes and debts and to engage in economic activities in a particular society.**

Fiat (paper) money originated in China in the 11th century. Initially, the paper money could be exchanged for a certain amount of silk, silver, or gold, linking the paper money to a commodity. By the 13th century, the link between paper money and commodities had been severed. Unfortunately, excessive spending by the Chinese government in the face of commodity shortages resulted in hyperinflation and an economic collapse. This episode highlights the fact that *one of the main roles for government in a fiat money system is to preserve the value of its currency and to avoid price instability.* Fiat money only has value as long as people believe it does. Fiat money must be useful for paying taxes and debts and for purchasing goods and services or it loses its value.

Officially, the U.S. dollar was on the "gold standard" for much of its history. A government whose currency is on the gold standard promises that each unit of currency (such as one dollar) can be exchanged for a certain amount of gold. The gold standard was important early in U.S. history in giving people confidence in the value of the dollar. Currencies only work to facilitate exchange, including government purchases, if they are widely accepted.

The U.S. partially abandoned the gold standard in 1933 when financial panics during the Great Depression caused people to withdraw their money from banks and to hoard gold. President Roosevelt and congress stopped allowing dollars to be exchanged for gold so they could shore up the nation's money supply. Nonetheless, the U.S. officially maintained an exchange rate of one ounce of gold equal to $35 until 1971, when President Nixon completely abandoned the gold standard to stop foreign countries with large dollar holdings from buying up U.S. gold reserves. Since then, the U.S. dollar has been exclusively a fiat currency. Other countries quickly followed and the gold standard became a relic of history.

The abandonment of commodity money and the gold standard relates to the fundamental problem with commodity money: Fluctuations in the value of gold (or whatever commodity is being used as the basis for money) cause instability in the macroeconomy, with severe fluctuations in prices and output. The equation of exchange illustrates how this can play out.

According to the **equation of exchange**:

$$\text{Money supply}(M1) \times \text{Velocity}(V) = \text{Price level}(P) \times \text{Real GDP}.$$

Recall that velocity is the number of times a dollar changes hands in a year.

Now consider what it would mean for an economy utilizing a commodity like gold as its currency. A fixed money supply implies that there can be no growth in real GDP. Thus, economic growth is at the mercy of supplies of gold. The only choice a country would have if it wanted to stimulate growth would be to put less gold into each coin (called "debasing" the currency), thereby increasing *M1* enough to facilitate economic growth.

Another way to think about this is as follows: If more goods are produced (higher real GDP), the only way consumers can purchase more goods is if they have more money. If more goods are produced while the amount of money available to consumers stays the same, then some goods will not be purchased, potentially causing a glut, deflation, and a serious downturn. Therefore, having too little money presents a major constraint on macroeconomic growth.

Having too much money can also be problematic. When the United States used gold coins as money, every time there was a large influx of gold, if there was not a similar increase in the production of goods, the economy would experience significantly higher prices. Using the equation of exchange above, if M1 increases substantially, and if velocity and real GDP are stable, then the result will be an increase in *P* equal to the increase in M1.

When the United States used the gold standard, it experienced dramatic bouts of inflation and deflation, more regular economic crises, and lower levels of economic growth. With fiat money, the central bank is able to increase the money supply when needed to facilitate growth and prevent deflation, and it can decrease the money supply to reduce inflationary pressures when needed. Thus, fiat money improved economic stability and performance markedly. As one example, during the financial crisis of 2007–2008, a time of huge upheaval and deflationary pressures, the U.S. central bank (the Fed) was able to dramatically increase the money supply to offset the crisis. Although the huge increase in the money supply scared many politicians and commentators, who predicted rampant inflation, that did not occur. Instead, deflationary pressures subsided and real GDP growth was restored, stabilizing the economy. Economic research shows that there was *23 times* less variance in prices during the financial crisis with fiat money and activist Fed policy than there was under the gold standard from 1919 to 1933.[4] Thus, fiat money plus sound macroeconomic policy fosters stability and growth much better than the gold standard did. As we will see in the next chapter, managing the money supply in a manner that fosters economic growth while maintaining price stability is the major job of central bank officials.

Interestingly, in the modern economy, very few people handle paper money. Money is mostly a unit of account, transferred electronically between employers and employees, consumers and businesses, business and the government, and so on. This is why in the modern economy, money is defined as a "unit of account" that facilitates transactions of all types.

14.2 THE USES AND MEASUREMENT OF MONEY

In all economic systems, money is a crucial tool of the government. Money is issued by the government to purchase what it needs to function. Taxes are levied by the government to create a demand for money so that its citizens must use the currency to pay taxes. Once accepted as a medium of exchange, money becomes the primary unit for economic transactions.

The main purposes of money are as follows:

1. Money is a **unit of account**, which is used to express the value of items and the amount of debts.
2. Money is a **medium of exchange**, which is used in transactions. Money eliminates the need for barter and thereby increases the efficiency of the economy.
3. Money is a **store of value**. It is a financial asset that, if saved, can be used in the future to make purchases. Money can also be loaned out so others can

make purchases for a fee (an interest payment). Also, money is extremely "liquid," in that it can easily be used to buy goods or to purchase financial assets.

Note that money can only serve as a unit of account for debts and as a store of value if its value will be relatively stable over time. If people expect a currency to be worthless in the future, they will not hold it as an asset, nor will they be willing to loan money to someone with the expectation of future payments.

In general, money must have a stable supply and be difficult to counterfeit. If money will be used for physical spending in a store or a market, it must also be easy to carry and durable.

Interestingly, so-called cryptocurrencies like Bitcoin have some but not all of the characteristics of fiat money. Cryptocurrencies can be created (mined) in limited amounts via powerful computers. They have deep, complex encryption that prevents simple duplication. Therefore, Bitcoin is supplied by market participants, although the supply is limited to preserve the value of a Bitcoin. Enough people accept Bitcoin that it can serve as a medium of exchange and as a unit of account for short-term transactions. Where Bitcoin encounters problems is with respect to stability of value over time.

National currencies always have value as long as the governments issuing them have the ability to tax. You will always need to have some of the government-issued currency to pay your taxes. The value of Bitcoin, however, would fall to nothing as soon as people lost faith in it. Bitcoin is not a government currency, and no one can make you use it. Thus, the value of a Bitcoin depends entirely on the faith of those who hold it. The dramatic fluctuations in the price of a Bitcoin demonstrate the fundamental instability of a nongovernmental form of money.

The first Bitcoin exchange was created in 2010. In its first year, the value of a Bitcoin increased by 900% in five days. Later in the year, it fell by 94%. Even after becoming more established, the value fluctuated dramatically. In the mid-2010s, the value of a Bitcoin sometimes changed by as much as 30% in one day and 500% in three weeks. National currencies are much more stable as long as they are well managed.

Some people continue to use Bitcoin because it bypasses government and no record is kept of Bitcoin transactions, making it very good for illegal transactions. Bitcoin's success prompted numerous imitators, and many Wall Street banks started to become involved in the cryptocurrency market. In November 2021, cryptocurrencies reached $3 trillion in value, before dropping to $1.2 trillion in May of 2022 as investors fled high-risk crypto for the safety of bonds after the Fed increased interest rates.

In modern economic systems, we use different measures of the amount of money in the economy based on different definitions of liquidity. **Liquidity** in financial economics refers to **the ease with which an asset can be converted into cash**. Therefore, cash money is the most liquid asset because it is already cash.

Economists also consider checking accounts, traveler's checks, demand deposits, and other types of accounts that consumers can spend immediately as the same as cash.

The **money supply**, M1, also called the money stock, is equal to **cash held by the public and near-cash accounts** (checkable deposits). These liquid assets are spent the most frequently.

M2 is equal to M1 plus short-term accounts that can be easily converted into cash, usually with one simple step. M2 includes savings accounts, money market accounts, mutual funds, and other fairly liquid assets that can be converted into cash by making a transfer in an online account or going to the bank.

M3 is equal to M2 plus large certificates of deposit and savings accounts as well as business savings. Because banks only keep a small amount of cash as reserves, large withdrawals from M3 will often take several days, which means that large deposits are the least liquid form of money in banks.

The amount of money in the economy—M1 and M2—is a crucial variable in determining how much money will be spent by consumers. Therefore, it is tracked very carefully by economists. One of the major jobs of the central bank is to manage M1 and M2 such that there is enough money for purchases and for economic growth but not too much money so that inflation is generated.

Figure 14.2 shows the amount of money (M1 and M2) in the U.S. economy on March 2 and July 13, 2020. The Fed increased the money supply dramatically during this period to combat the COVID-19 recession, something we will take up later in more detail.

Although the government establishes a country's currency, banks have a tremendous influence over the total amount of money in an economy. Banks perform a useful service in a capitalist economy, but they can also contribute to instability if not properly regulated.

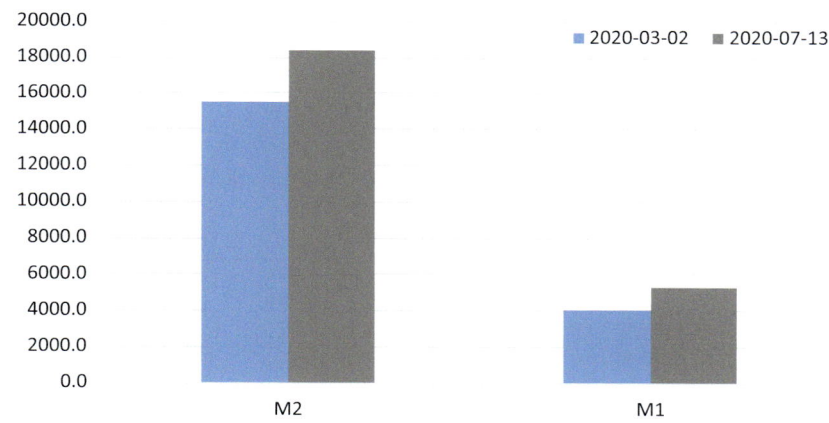

FIGURE 14.2 M1 and M2 (billions of $).

14.3 BANKS, THE BANKING SYSTEM, AND THE MONEY MULTIPLIER

Banks make profits by loaning out money to people, businesses, and institutions and charging those borrowers interest on their loans. The money that banks loan out comes from bank owners as well as depositors. Thus, banks are called **financial intermediaries** because they match savers with borrowers: They take in deposits from savers and they use those deposits to make loans to borrowers. Bank profits depend on the difference between the interest banks receive from borrowers and the interest banks pay to depositors.

We can see these two sides of a bank in Figure 14.3(a), which shows a bank T-account. A T-account is a classic accounting device to display a balance sheet for an organization with the assets on one side and the liabilities on the other. On the liability side, banks owe money to their depositors and to the bank owners. On the asset side, the bank keeps reserves, which are **cash or deposits at the central bank** that can be transferred to any depositor who needs to withdraw money. The other bank assets are the loans, stocks, bonds, other securities, and properties that generate income for the bank.

To make the most money possible, banks prefer to keep as little money as possible on hand as cash. More loans or purchases of stocks and bonds result in more profits. Therefore, banks only keep enough money on hand to cover what depositors need, or a larger amount if required by law.

The banking **required reserve ratio (RRR)** is **the percentage of deposits that banks are required by law to hold as reserves**. In order to qualify for federal banking insurance in the United States, banks must agree to abide by the RRR.

Historically in the United States, the required reserve ratio on checking accounts has been 10%, whereas the RRR for savings accounts and other deposits is much lower because these accounts are used less frequently for spending. In Figure 14.3(b), if a bank customer deposits $100,000 in their checking account, the bank's liabilities have increase by $100,000. With an RRR of 10%, the bank will keep $10,000 of the checking account deposit in reserves, as required by law, and loan the rest out ($90,000) to increase their profits.

The fact that banks do not keep most of their deposits in cash means that there can be a "run on the bank" if a large number of depositors try to withdraw

Assets	Liabilities
Reserves	Checkable Deposits
Loans	Savings and Time Deposits
Stocks, Bonds, Securities	Owner Equity
Property	

(a)

Assets		Liabilities
Reserves $10,000		$100,000
Loans	$90,000	

(b)

FIGURE 14.3 (a) Table of a bank T-account and (b) Table of the effect of a deposit on reserves.

a lot of money at the same time. This situation is depicted memorably in the classic Christmas film *It's a Wonderful Life*, when panicked depositors came into their community bank to withdraw money at the same time. The protagonist, George Bailey, responds,

> You're thinking of this place all wrong. As if I had the money back in a safe. The money's not here. Your money's in Joe's house … right next to yours. And in the Kennedy house, and Mrs. Macklin's house, and a hundred others. Why, you're lending them the money to build, and then, they're going to pay it back to you as best they can.

Bank runs tend to occur when people lose faith in a bank or the banking system. During the Great Depression, banks failed one after another as people lost confidence in banks. Even healthy banks experienced bank runs. This is why the government established the Federal Deposit Insurance Corporation, the Federal Savings and Loan Insurance Corporation, and other banking insurance programs. The government guarantees that it will replace the money in your accounts if the bank loses it. This way, depositors can always have faith that their money will be safe, even if the bank fails.

Meanwhile, the government regularly inspects the books of federally insured banks to make sure they are not engaging in overly risky behavior. This helps to ensure the stability of the financial system. As we will see later, deregulation of banking in the 1980s and 1990s set the stage for two speculative real estate bubbles and the financial crisis of 2007–2008.

Banks also have a dramatic impact on the economy because of how they create money. Deposit creation occurs as banks take in and loan out money. The **money multiplier**, also called the deposit multiplier, is **the amount of money that banks create with each dollar of reserves**. The money multiplier works much like the spending multiplier we studied earlier.

If we start with an initial $100,000 deposit and a required reserve ratio (RRR) of 10%, as we saw above, the bank will loan out $90,000 and keep $10,000 in required reserves. As long as economic conditions are favorable, banks tend to loan out all of their excess reserves, because this is how they make money.

Now suppose that $90,000 is loaned to a home buyer, who writes a check to the homeowner for that amount. The homeowner deposits the check in the checking account at their bank, giving that bank $90,000 in reserves. This bank will keep $9,000 in required reserves and loan out the $81,000 in excess reserves. That $81,000 loan gets spent on something else, perhaps a sports car, which is deposited in the car dealership's bank. The car dealership's bank now has $81,000 in reserves. It will keep $8100 in required reserves and make $72,900 in new loans. And so on.

The total amount of deposits created is equal to $100,000 + 90,000 + 81,000 + 72,900 + ….

This can be rewritten as $100,000 \times (1+0.9+0.9^2+0.9^3+\ldots)$. This infinite series has a solution in the following form:

$$\Delta \text{Deposits} = \Delta M1 = (\$100,000) \times \frac{1}{(1-0.9)}$$

$$= (\$100,000) \times \frac{1}{0.1} = \$100,000 \times 10$$

$$= \$1,000,000.$$

In this case, the money multiplier is 10. Each $1 increase in deposits ends up creating $10 in total deposits, as the same money is lent and re-lent multiple times by multiple banks.

From this equation, we can also see that the equation for the money multiplier is

$$\text{Money multiplier} = \frac{1}{\text{Required reserve ratio}(\text{RRR})}.$$

The money multiplier will be smaller if banks hold excess reserves or if people hold cash instead of depositing money. Holding excess reserves means that a bank is not lending out money that it is legally allowed to lend and is therefore willingly sacrificing profits. Banks only hold excess reserves if the likelihood of default is so high that it is better to hold cash and give up on earning interest than it is to make a risky loan. *The money multiplier will be larger if banks can easily borrow reserves to loan out money whenever they see a good opportunity.* Due to the dramatic effect of banks on the money supply, they can be a significant source of instability.

In 2020, the U.S. Fed reduced reserve requirements to zero and began adjusting interest rates and banks' reserves by altering the **interest on reserve balances (IORB)**, which is **the interest rate the Fed pays banks on reserves deposited at the Fed**. With no reserve requirement, the money multiplier now has no limit. But the Fed can incentivize banks to hold reserves by increasing the IORB, which therefore has a similar effect as increasing the reserve requirement.

Like any business, banks exist to make the maximum amount of money possible. They do this by paying depositors as little interest as possible on their deposits, and they try to charge borrowers as much interest as possible on loans while minimizing the risk of default. Higher risk loans will come with higher interest rates, as well as a higher risk of default. If the banking market is sufficiently competitive, depositors and borrowers will get fair interest rates, but if banks have monopoly power, banks are able to extract monopoly profits.

To reduce the risk of making loans, banks demand **collateral** from borrowers. **Collateral is something pledged by a borrower to provide security for repayment of a loan. Collateral is forfeited to the bank if the borrower**

defaults on the loan. For most bank loans, the bank is entitled to keep the home or business if the homeowner or business owner defaults on their loan. The bank can then sell the home or business to recoup their losses.

Banks have a financial incentive to loan out as much money as possible, but the more banks loan out, the riskier their financial situation is. This is because banks are loaning money to increasingly risky borrowers as they expand their lending. In addition, bank loan defaults tend to come in clumps when economic conditions deteriorate. If large numbers of borrowers default at the same time, banks can end up without enough cash to meet the needs of depositors, who want to write checks to pay bills and get cash when they need it. This is why **one of the main roles of the central bank is as a lender of last resort**, to lend money to banks when they run short of cash.

Once banks have substantial losses greater than or equal to the ownership stake of the bank owners, banks have an incentive to undertake risky loans to try to recoup their losses. Often, bank owners' stake in the bank is as little as 3%, and the rest of the money belongs to depositors. If bank losses exceed 3% and bank owners have lost all of their own investment, they are gambling entirely with other people's money, so they have less incentive to be prudent with their loans. In many instances, we find that failing banks make increasingly risky loans to try to recoup losses. This is another reason why government regulation of banking is so important.

There are many different types of banks in the modern world. **Retail** banks, **savings and loan** banks, and **credit unions** take in deposits and make loans to individuals and small businesses. **Commercial** banks deal primarily with businesses. **Private** banks offer traditional banking services as well as financial investment services and trust and estate planning for wealthy individuals. **Investment** banks handle large corporate investments, including underwriting and issuing securities (stocks and bonds); supporting mergers and acquisitions; creating, selling, and insuring derivatives; and investing directly in all types of domestic and international asset markets. The **central** bank oversees the banking system and manipulates the money supply and interest rates via monetary policies.

Banks are regulated carefully due to their substantial impact on the economy. In the United States, the Glass-Steagall Act of 1933 separated the banking sector into traditional banking, where banks take in deposits and make loans to families and businesses, and investment banking, where banks make riskier, more speculative investments. The idea was to insulate insured, safe banks from high-risk banks that were not insured by the government. However, beginning in the 1980s, banking regulations were relaxed, and investment banks were allowed to merge with retail banks and savings and loans. Unfortunately, this corresponded with more regular banking crises, as we will see later.

One of the most important aspects of money is its relationship to interest rates. Interest rates are a major determinant of the amount of business investment and consumer spending that occur. The amount of items purchased using borrowed money is so vast that credit markets loom large in macroeconomic analysis. To understand the relationship between money and interest rates, economists developed various models of the money market.

14.4 THE MAINSTREAM ECONOMICS MODEL OF THE MONEY MARKET

The mainstream model of the money market depicted in Figure 14.4 shows a supply and demand curve for money (M1). M1 includes cash and checkable deposits, and it is the money that households and businesses use to make most of their purchases. The first important thing to note about this graph is that the price of money—the price of holding cash—is the interest rate. If you keep your money as cash instead of depositing it in an interest-bearing account in a bank or buying a bond, you are losing the return that you could make on your money, which is the going rate of interest. In essence, the interest rate is the opportunity cost of holding cash.

People demand money—that is, they desire to hold cash—for three reasons, which are listed below.

1. **Transactions demand**. The **transactions demand for money** is **the amount of cash or checkable deposits that individuals need to keep available to make purchases (transactions)**. If interest rates are high, people will keep as little cash as possible and instead put their money into bonds or interest-bearing money market accounts. If interest rates are low, they will keep more of their money in cash or checkable deposits for convenience.
2. **Precautionary demand**. The **precautionary demand for money** is **the amount of cash or checkable deposits that people keep as a**

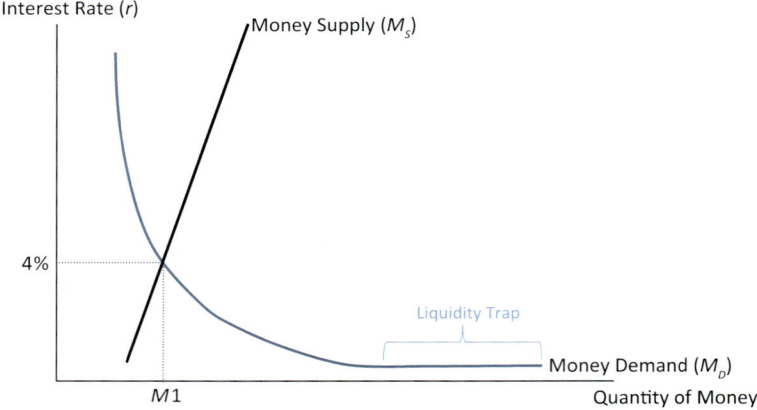

FIGURE 14.4 The mainstream model of the money market.

contingency to meet unexpected expenses. When people are worried about keeping their job, they often keep a larger amount of cash on hand. However, higher interest rates encourage people to hold less cash and to place more money into interest-bearing accounts and securities.
3. **Speculative demand**. The **speculative demand for money** reflects **the amount of cash or checkable deposits that people want to hold as a safe asset to maximize returns on all of their assets**. Investors nearly always hold a certain amount of their portfolio as cash because it is safe and because having cash allows them to very quickly take advantage of any opportunities that arise.

In general, the money demand curve is downward-sloping because people want to hold less cash and more interest-bearing securities and accounts when interest rates are high. When interest rates are low, there is very little return on interest-bearing assets, so people tend to hold more cash. Thus, an increase in the interest rate causes a decrease in the quantity of money demanded, and a decrease in the interest rate causes an increase in the quantity of money demanded.

Notice that the money demand curve becomes flat when interest rates approach 0%. The flat part of the demand curve for money is called a **liquidity trap**, which **occurs when people believe that interest rates can fall no further and can only increase**. When a liquidity trap occurs, no matter how much the central bank increases the money supply, interest rates will stay the same and **people will hold all new money as cash because they believe interest rates will increase in the near future**. No one will buy a government bond at a low interest rate and lock themselves into a low rate of return if they expect the interest rate to increase very soon. The existence of a liquidity trap indicates that there are limits to how effective monetary policy that increases the money supply can be in stimulating the economy.

The **determinants of the demand for money**, the factors that *shift* the money demand curve, are the following:

1. **Income** (real GDP): Higher incomes result in people spending more money, which increases the demand for money in order to engage in more transactions.
2. **Price level**: The higher the price level, the more money (cash) people need to buy goods and services, increasing the demand for money.
3. **Expectations**: When investors expect the price of stocks to crash, they will sell their stocks and hold their assets as cash until the crash occurs or their expectations change. This increases the demand for money.
4. **Preferences**: If people are risk averse, they tend to hold more money as cash and to place less money in riskier assets like stocks. If they have a high level of risk tolerance, they will hold less cash and invest more of their money in riskier assets. If people prefer to use credit cards for purchases, they have a lower demand for cash.

STABILIZATION POLICY

5. **Asset transfer costs**: Moving money out of stocks, bonds, and some money market accounts comes with a fee, and sometimes those fees can be significant. If fees are low, investors can keep their money in stocks or bonds and sell those assets whenever they need cash. If fees are high, investors will tend to keep more money in cash to avoid the costs associated with transactions.
6. **Changes in regulations**: The government can affect the amount of money that people want to hold as cash via regulations. For example, in 1980, the U.S. government allowed banks to start paying interest on checking accounts, which made it more attractive to keep money in checkable deposit accounts, increasing the demand for money.

Suppose there is an economic boom that dramatically increases incomes. We would expect a significant increase in money demand because people need more cash to make more purchases. This would cause the money demand curve to increase (shift up and to the right), causing interest rates to increase, as depicted in Figure 14.5(a).

In mainstream economics, the money supply is determined by the amount of money the central bank prints and distributes electronically and by the money multiplier. The money supply curve is straight up and down (vertical). This model assumes that banks loan out all excess reserves and that banks cannot borrow reserves when they want them. The money supply curve would be upward-sloping if banks hold excess reserves when interest rates are low and no good loan opportunities are available, whereas banks increase lending as interest rates rise and loans become more profitable.

Shifts in the money supply curve (the *determinants* of money supply) occur due to changes in the behavior of the central bank. The money supply curve would increase (shift to the right), as it does in Figure 14.5(b), if the central bank decides to increase the money supply by printing money, purchasing bonds or other assets, or crediting banks' accounts. The money supply curve would decrease if the central

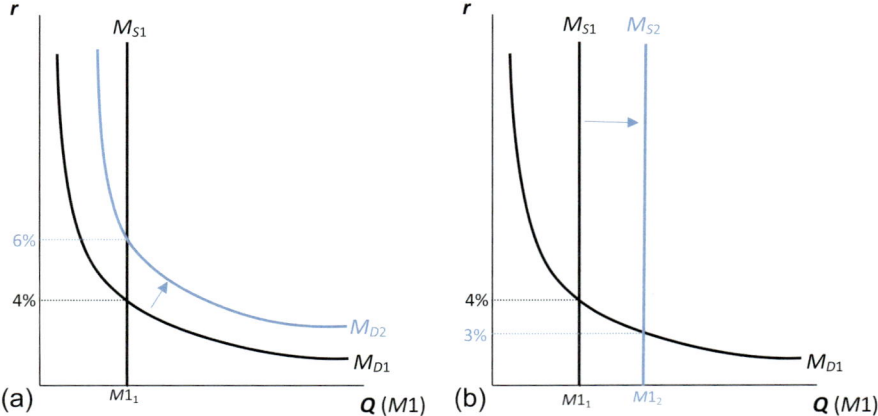

FIGURE 14.5 (a) An increase in money demand and (b) An increase in money supply.

bank decided to take in money from banks by selling government bonds or if it printed less money than usual.

As we will see in the next section, political economists have a very different model of the money market. Political economists argue that banks rely intensively on borrowing reserves to create new loan opportunities, which means that the money market is driven in a fundamental way by private bank money creation.[5]

14.5 POLITICAL ECONOMISTS ON ENDOGENOUS MONEY

In mainstream economics, it is typically assumed that banks do not hold excess reserves, and the money supply is typically depicted as a vertical line that is controlled entirely by the central bank (the Fed in the United States). The money supply from this view is *exogenous*, determined (externally) by the Fed and unaffected by the internal dynamics of banks and the economic system. The Fed changes the interest rate by increasing or decreasing the money supply (M1) in a very controlled fashion by changing the quantity of banks' excess reserves, precisely determining the amount of money in the economy. If the Fed wants banks to loan out more money, they purchase bonds and other securities from the public, the public gets more money in their bank accounts, banks have excess reserves, and banks reduce interest rates to encourage more people to borrow these excess reserves. Banks then loan out those excess reserves to increase profits.

An open market sale would do the opposite. If the Fed undertakes an open market sale in the mainstream model of the money market, it sells bonds to the public, taking money out of the banking system in exchange for government bonds and increasing the interest rate. *In this model, the central bank determines the money supply and money demand curve determines the rate of interest.*

Research by political economists shows that, in general, the money supply is *not* controlled with precision by the central bank. Instead, they see an **endogenous money supply**, which means that **the money supply is determined by economic variables *within* the economic system, especially real GDP, expected business sales, business investment, consumer confidence, and consumer spending**. What we see is that banks and the Fed generally respond to increases in the demand for money from borrowers by supplying more money.

For example, banks extend large amounts of credit to numerous businesses, and especially to the largest corporations. These lines of credit are negotiated ahead of time, so that any time a corporation needs money, for whatever purpose, it can access funds. This is similar to a consumer who has a credit card with a prearranged credit limit that allows them to *borrow funds at any time* to finance purchases.

Most important, large loans from banks to corporations take place *whether or not the bank has excess reserves*. If a corporation needs to borrow money, it writes a check (or debits its account) and the bank automatically extends the corporation a new loan to cover that check. If the bank does not have enough excess reserves to cover the new loan, as is often the case, it simply borrows the money from other banks (or other financial institutions), paying the federal funds rate of interest, which is the interest rate banks charge each other for lending reserves. If enough banks do this simultaneously, the federal funds rate may rise. However, the Fed, which usually seeks to maintain the federal funds rate at a targeted level, will then increase the supply of money to keep the federal funds rate at its target. Thus—and this is the key insight—**the money supply tends to increase whenever borrowers, as a group, demand more money to finance their purchases of investment and consumer goods.** *Banks create the money that borrowers need by crediting borrowers' accounts and borrowing any necessary reserves.* In this analysis of the money market, **the central bank sets the interest rate, and the demand for money determines the amount of money supplied**, as depicted in Figure 14.6.

Banks do this because it is how they make money. Why turn down a borrower with good credit who wants to borrow more money when all the bank needs to do is borrow a portion of the loan to cover the reserve requirements? If real GDP is expanding and there are good investment opportunities, banks will gladly create money to loan to creditworthy borrowers.

Banks also become creative in circumventing reserve requirements when it is profitable to do so. If the Fed is trying to slow down the economy by tightening credit and raising interest rates, banks can create new financial instruments that are not subject to the same level of regulation and thereby create additional funds for lending. During the housing bubble of 2006–2008, banks created new mortgage instruments, called collateralized mortgage obligations (CMOs), where they loaned money to sub-prime (bad credit) borrowers who wanted to buy homes. Banks then bundled those mortgages into large packages of loans and sold those loan packages

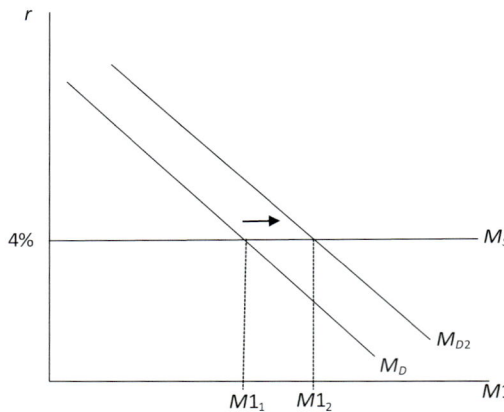

FIGURE 14.6 The political economy model of an increase in the money supply (M1).

as CMOs to banks, investors, and insurance companies, leaving CMO-creating banks with large sums of newly created money. CMOs were not subject to reserve requirements, so the amount of loans banks could create was *virtually unlimited*.

Note that the central bank still has considerable power even in the political economy model. The central bank can regulate the demand for credit by raising interest rates to slow down the economy or by lowering interest rates to stimulate it. These efforts are of necessity imprecise because, as we have seen, business investment is erratic and driven by expectations of future sales and profits. If businesses expect bad days ahead, decreases in interest rates usually have a negligible impact on investment. If the economy is booming and opportunities abound, slightly higher interest rates are unlikely to deter investors.

The political economy model of the money market also implies that the equation of exchange is wrong about several things. First, M1 is not determined by the Fed; it is determined by banks' lending opportunities. Second, inflation usually stems from rapid increases in real GDP, not increases in M1.

Another important implication is that banks are pro-cyclical accelerators. They loan out ever-increasing amounts of money when the economy is booming, dramatically expanding the money supply in response to increased borrowing requests. But, when the bottom falls out, banks curtail lending, so banks exacerbate busts by ceasing money creation. The fact that the banking system inherently destabilizes the economic system, fueling both booms and busts, is why political economists generally favor increased regulation of banks. This is very different from the view of financial markets promoted by laissez-faire economists, in which banks and financial markets are seen as so efficient and competitive that no regulations are necessary.

14.5.1 A hybrid model of the money market

If we take the insight from the mainstream model that the Fed can manipulate the money supply to some degree and add to that the political economy insight that the supply of money is endogenous but that increases in the demand for money can result in increases in interest rates, we get the graph in Figure 14.7 (next page). The Fed sets the interest rate based on their goals for the economy (stimulus, contraction, or stability). The money demand curve shifts based on business and consumer demand for funds, which is driven by expectations and the macroeconomic environment. Large shifts in the demand for money can cause interest rate changes. The Fed can shift the money supply, but it is not clear how large an impact that will have on business investment or consumer purchases unless they take dramatic action.

Now that we have explored the banking sector and the money market, the other key component of the financial sector is asset markets. The markets for stocks, bonds, and real estate are one of the most important components of the economy, and yet they are largely disconnected from the well-being of many workers and families.

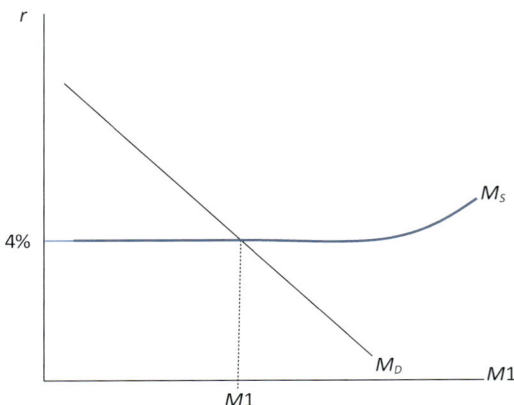

FIGURE 14.7 A hybrid model of the money market.

14.6 ASSET MARKETS: STOCKS, BONDS, AND REAL ESTATE

There are six main types of assets: **Cash** or checkable deposits, **stocks** (equities), **bonds** (fixed income assets), **derivatives**, **insurance**, and **real estate**. Stocks, bonds, derivatives, and other financial instruments bought and sold by financial investors are called *securities*. Purchasing securities or real estate involves a higher risk than keeping your money in cash, but returns tend to be higher on average the more risk you are willing to take, except when securities markets crash, of course. Thus, securities markets feature high-risk, high-reward options.

Securities markets are regulated by the Securities and Exchange Commission. There are extensive rules prohibiting insider trading (buying or selling stocks because you have special knowledge about a transaction or company that is not available to the public) and limiting other types of harmful behavior.

It is very important to distinguish financial investment in securities, sometimes called financial capital, from investment purchases, which are business purchases of machinery, equipment, and other capital goods. Financial capital is invested in financial markets, where it has an indirect impact on aggregate demand by impacting consumer and investor behavior. Business investment purchases are a direct and important component of aggregate demand. For most economic analysis, investment purchases are much more important than financial investment.

Stocks are **an ownership share in a company that entitles the owner to a share of the company's earnings**. **Earnings are realized either through a higher stock price as a company becomes more profitable or by dividend payments to stockholders.** Stock shares for a company come into being during an initial public offering (IPO), where a company offers the opportunity for investors to buy shares of the company. IPOs serve the purpose of cashing out the founders of the company and/or raising new funds so the company can expand. After the IPO, investors buy or sell shares of previously issued stocks.

The prices of previously issued stocks tend to reflect financial investors' expectations regarding future profitability. For example, for many years Tesla and Amazon featured soaring stock prices even though they were not yet profitable, because investors had faith in their business models. Stock prices tend to fluctuate dramatically but typically have a higher average rate of return than bonds.

Corporate **bonds** are loans from the person who buys the bond to the corporation that issues the bond. Bonds pay a fixed rate of return (similar to a rate of interest) on the date that the bond matures. Bonds come with various levels of risk and various maturity dates. If an investor does not want to hold a bond until it matures, they can sell it before the maturity date.

The price of a previously issued bond is inversely related to interest rates. For example, if a corporate bond is issued guaranteeing a 5% return but interest rates fall to 3%, the corporate bond will increase in value because it is paying a higher return than other types of interest-bearing financial instruments.

Bond values are much more stable than stock prices, and they come with a guaranteed return. Therefore, on average, bonds are lower risk and they pay a lower rate of return than stocks.

A *derivative* is **a contract between two or more economic actors where the value of the derivative is based on particular financial assets and the conditions under which those assets are exchanged**. A futures contract for wheat is a form of derivative where one party would agree to sell a certain amount of wheat to another party on a certain date in the future for a certain price. Derivatives are essentially bets and hedges.

For example, suppose the current price of a bushel of wheat is $5 per bushel but you think the price of wheat will fall to $4 per bushel in the future because there will be a bumper crop this year. To make money, you can create a derivative contract to sell 1 million bushels of wheat in the future at $5 per bushel when the next crop comes in. If you are correct and the price of wheat has fallen to $4 per bushel by the time your contract comes due, you can buy 1 million bushels of wheat for $4 per bushel in wheat markets and sell wheat to the business that agreed to pay $5 per bushel via the futures contract, thereby making $1 million. Note, however, that if you are wrong and the price of wheat increased to $6 per bushel, you would lose $1 million. Meanwhile, the person willing to buy wheat in the future at $5 per bushel might want to enter into this contract as a hedge against risk. For example, King Arthur Baking Company needs wheat to make its flour. Not knowing what the price of wheat will be in the future presents a large risk for their business. But, if they lock in the price of wheat at $5 per bushel, then no matter what happens to the wheat market, they know they will get the wheat they need at a price that is acceptable to them.

Derivatives are the riskiest form of financial assets. They involve making bets on futures markets that are inherently uncertain and variable.

Insurance involves **the purchase of a hedge against risk or an untimely event, where the insurer collects premium payments and provides compensation for a specified loss**. Therefore, insurance is also a financial bet. When a company sells you life insurance, they are making a bet that the premiums you pay for insurance coverage and the returns that the insurance company receives on those premiums will be greater than the payout from the insurance company when you die. Insurance companies invest heavily in stocks, bonds, and derivatives to achieve the highest return possible, so they can fall victim to the booms and busts of asset markets.

Real estate investments involve **the purchase, rental, and sale of all types of property, including land and buildings**. Real estate markets can be stable for years, but they also sometimes fluctuate wildly with interest rates and recessions. They are like any other asset in that they have an underlying value, a rate of return, and their value can fluctuate dramatically depending on market conditions.

Stocks are the most visible and important securities, so it is worth spending a little time discussing how stock markets work and what drives them. First, stocks fluctuate dramatically on a daily basis. Every day in stock markets, huge amounts of money change hands as financial investors make bets on whether or not stocks are going to go up in the short run or in the long run. Many short-run fluctuations are driven by program trading, where computer programs analyze market trends and make trades buying or selling stocks based on those trends. Value investors like Warren Buffett focus instead on the long term, investing in companies that have the best prospects for future growth.

Stocks are very hard to predict because they do not follow a systematic model. Economic analysis indicates that stock prices follow a **random walk**, such that it is virtually impossible to predict their movements. Nonetheless, there are certain metrics that can give us a general idea of whether stocks are priced correctly.

One of the best ways to determine whether stock prices are overvalued or undervalued is to look at the price–earnings (P/E) ratio, which compares a company's stock price (P) to the company's earnings (profits) per share (E):

$$\frac{P}{E} = \frac{\text{Share price}}{\text{Earnings per share}}.$$

In general, a stock with a higher *P/E* ratio than other stocks is expensive—it has a relatively high price and a relatively low level of profits. A low *P/E* ratio indicates a relatively inexpensive stock that may be a good buy. If a stock's price is $100 a share and its earnings per share are $5, its *P/E* ratio is 20, and it would take 20 years for an investor to get a return that was equal in value to their stock purchase.

However, there are additional complexities that go into evaluating a *P/E* ratio. A company that is growing rapidly may have a high *P/E* ratio based on investors' expectations of future profits rather than the current level of earnings. For public and whose stocks are publicly traded on stock markets. Generally speaking, stock markets are not a good reflection of the performance of the economy as a whole. When workers are less powerful and wages are low, this can support corporate profitability and lead to high stock prices. From March 20 to July 20, 2020, in the midst of the COVID-19 pandemic of 2020, the S&P 500 stock market index increased by 46.4% while unemployment stayed stubbornly high at over 11%. Conditions for workers and communities were miserable. But the Fed injected trillions of dollars into financial markets, and interest rates were at historic lows, so money poured into stock markets and stock prices rose dramatically even as the rest of the country was suffering.

The fact that the interests of financial markets—Wall Street—are often diametrically opposed to the interests of workers and communities—Main Street—is particularly troubling given the extent to which financial markets have become an increasingly dominant force in global economies. This phenomenon has been labeled "financialization" by political economist Gerald Epstein.[7]

14.7 FINANCIALIZATION

Financialization refers to **the increasingly dominant role of financial motives, financial markets, financial actors, and financial institutions in the operation of the domestic and international economies**. The financial sector includes financial, insurance, and real estate (FIRE) markets. FIRE grew significantly in value, profits, and political power over the last five decades.

The process of financialization of the global economy began in the 1970s. Manufacturing in developed countries stagnated during this decade, so investors' money flowed increasingly into the profitable FIRE sector. The rise of FIRE was further driven by the neoliberal (laissez-faire plus supply-side) economic philosophy that swept the globe beginning with Margaret Thatcher in England in 1979 and Ronald Reagan in the United States in 1980. Neoliberal policymakers attacked unions while pushing for deregulation of financial markets, laissez-faire trade policies, tax cuts for the wealthy and for corporations, and reductions in the size of the state (austerity).

From 1969 to 2019, the FIRE sector increased in size from 14% of U.S. GDP to 21%. Over the same period, the share of corporate profits belonging to the FIRE sector increased almost twofold to 26.4%, indicating that the FIRE sector receives a disproportionately larger share of profits.

Significant income and capital gains tax cuts incentivized the nation's top earners to invest in securities, flooding financial markets with money. Maximizing shareholder value became the mantra of corporations, resulting in waves of mergers and corporate takeovers, accompanied by layoffs for workers. Financial innovations, such as the creation of complex derivatives and other forms of securitization, offered new opportunities for speculative investments. As FIRE profits surged, workers' wages stagnated and the number of jobs in manufacturing industries continued to decline.

The FIRE sector's increased size and power gave them the ability to get politicians to adopt increasingly favorable policies toward the FIRE sector. Policies liberalizing international financial flows and facilitating the use of tax havens allowed investors to move their money anywhere in the world where returns were the highest and taxes the lowest. In the United States, burgeoning trade deficits and manufacturing job losses were largely ignored in favor of policies to encourage a strong dollar and an emphasis on unregulated trade and financial flows. These policies undermined manufacturing but were extremely profitable for the FIRE sector.

The speculative core of the FIRE sector, however, led to increasingly common financial crises. These included the savings and loan crisis and Latin American debt crisis of the 1980s, the Asian financial crisis of the late 1990s, the internet stock crash of 2000, and the real estate bubble and financial crisis of 2007–2008. Demonstrating the power of the FIRE sector, U.S. investment banks were bailed out during the financial crisis to the tune of more than $700 billion, while many workers lost their homes and ended up destitute and desperate. The U.S. government's willingness to bail out Wall Street while it let Main Street suffer sparked the Occupy Wall Street movement and led to an increasing number of young people rejecting the U.S. economic model.

The coronavirus pandemic exposed additional weaknesses of the neoliberal model and its emphasis on the FIRE sector. The underfunding of public health systems left many countries unable to cope with the pandemic. In the United States, however, Wall Street continued to receive the bulk of bailouts, while workers, communities, hospitals, and public health systems continued to struggle. Thus, in 2020, the FIRE sector seemed to be as dominant as ever in the United States.

Political economists are very critical of financialization, arguing that it has reshaped the world in favor of financial corporations and against workers. Political economists advocate policies to rein in the FIRE sector, taxing financial transactions and the wealthy, re-imposing capital controls to limit global speculative behavior and tax havens, and enacting policies that benefit workers and communities and protect them from the destabilizing tendencies of the FIRE sector.

Laissez-faire and supply-side economists, who were the architects of the neoliberal policies that fostered the rise of the FIRE sector, continue to see financial markets as dynamic and essential to modern capitalism and deregulation as a benefit to economic growth. The growth of the FIRE sector is, from this perspective, a natural result of markets pursuing efficiency and the maximum possible economic growth.

New Keynesian economists strive for a middle path, with increased regulation of the FIRE sector that will preserve its essential characteristics while reining in its excesses. After the financial crisis, New Keynesian economists advocated significant regulations on banking and derivatives markets, while proposing that the core of the FIRE sector be left unchanged. We will explore these debates further in the next two chapters.

14.8 CONCLUSION

Money, banking, and financial markets are very important in modern economic systems. How they work is often unclear to most people, so this chapter attempted to describe the essential features of money, banking, and financial markets.

Money is a unit of account that forms a crucial component of modern economic systems. Money is created by governments so they can provision themselves. Money gives governments the ability to tax their citizens in their own currency and to spend money on the goods and services the government needs in order to function. A nation that has a sovereign currency controls the supply of its own money.

Modern economies use fiat money, rather than commodity money or the gold standard, so that the government has greater control over the money supply. This allows the government to increase the supply of money to foster economic growth or in the case of a banking crisis.

Banks make money making loans to borrowers and charging interest on those loans. The money for bank loans comes from depositors or from borrowed reserves. Banks create money via the money multiplier, whereby the same deposit is loaned out again and again by one bank after another, albeit in ever-decreasing amounts.

Mainstream economists use a model of the money market to try to anticipate the factors that will cause interest rates to rise or fall. In the mainstream, New Keynesian model, the money supply curve is vertical and determined by the central bank, so the money supply is viewed as exogenous—determined by factors external to the economy (the central bank decision-making process). The money demand curve is downward-sloping and becomes flat as it nears 0% interest to reflect a liquidity trap. A liquidity trap occurs when interest rates cannot fall further and investors prefer to hold cash rather than to invest in low-return bonds or risky stocks. In a liquidity trap situation, monetary stimulus is usually ineffective.

In the political economy model of the money market, the money supply curve is flat, with interest rates set by the central bank. The money demand curve is steep. The quantity of money in the economy is determined by the demand curve for money, because banks can always borrow reserves if people want to borrow and spend more money than usual. This makes the money supply endogenous—determined by the level of economic activity and the demand for loanable funds.

In addition to banks, securities markets for stocks, bonds, and derivatives and real estate markets play an important role in the economic system. The finance, insurance, and real estate (FIRE) sector comes with higher levels of risk but pays a higher level of return in exchange for that risk. Stock markets form regular bubbles that burst, often dragging the rest of the economy into a recession when that happens. The Shiller CAPE index in one good measure of when a stock market is in a bubble situation.

The FIRE sector became increasingly dominant over the last 50 years with the advent of neoliberal policies—a process called financialization. Political economists see financialization as problematic because it involves society's resources being increasingly captured by the wealthy individuals and corporations that control the FIRE sector. Laissez-faire and supply-side economists prefer the deregulatory, low-tax environment that gave rise to financialization. New Keynesian economists prefer more regulation of the FIRE sector than laissez-faire economists but less than the amount advocated by political economists. The next two chapters explore financial regulation and financial crises in more detail.

QUESTIONS FOR REVIEW

1. Explain why the gold standard and commodity money fell out of fashion and why modern economists prefer fiat money.
2. Why will a government-issued form of money always be safer to hold than a cryptocurrency such as Bitcoin?
3. How is the money multiplier related to the required reserve ratio? Explain briefly. What factors would cause the money multiplier to be larger? What factors would cause the money multiplier to be smaller?
4. Explain why banks rarely hold excess reserves. What might prompt a bank to hold excess reserves?
5. Why do economists consider the interest rate to be the opportunity cost of holding your money as cash?
6. Explain the slope of the money demand curve in the mainstream model of the money market. Why is it downward-sloping? Why does it get flatter as interest rates approach 0%?
7. How would each of the following factors affect the money market according to mainstream economists?
    a. A major recession causes real GDP to fall significantly.
    b. Inflation occurs due to an increase in oil and other energy prices.
    c. Investors expect a major economic boom.
    d. The central bank decreases the amount of money in circulation.
8. What are the main differences between the mainstream model of the money market and the political economy model of the money market? Why does it matter if the money supply is exogenous or endogenous?
9. According to the political economy theory of endogenous money, which of the following are true (select one or more options)?
    a. The Fed determines the money supply.
    b. The Fed sets the rate of interest.
    c. Money demand determines the rate of interest.
    d. Banks create money by making new loans and later finding the reserves they need.
    e. Banks can only create money out of excess reserves.

f. The money supply is determined by the demand for money from businesses and households.
g. The money supply is determined by the Fed.
h. Banks need to be carefully regulated.
i. Financial markets are so efficient that banks do not need to be regulated.

10. In your own words, define the term "financialization." Why do political economists see financialization as a problem? Why do laissez-faire and supply-side economists disagree?

NOTES

1 David Graeber, *Debt: The First 5000 Years* (Brooklyn, NY: Melville House), 2021.
2 L. Randall Wray, "Introduction to an Alternative History of Money." Levy Economics Institute of Bard College, Working Paper No. 717, May 2012. http://www.levyinstitute.org/publications/introduction-to-an-alternative-history-of-money, accessed August 6, 2021.
3 Source: Wikimedia commons, public domain files. See: https://commons.wikimedia.org/wiki/File:Carved_reindeer_antler_with_tally_marks_(4697848661).jpg and https://commons.wikimedia.org/wiki/File:Chinese_cash_coins_b.jpg.
4 See Matthew Obrien, "Why the Gold Standard Is the World's Worst Economic Idea, in 2 Charts," *The Atlantic* (August 26, 2012).
5 This section draws heavily on James K. Galbraith and William Darity Jr., *Macroeconomics* (Delft, the Netherlands: VSSD, 2005), as well as various works by L. Randall Wray.
6 Source: Robert Shiller, "Online Data Robert Shiller," http://www.econ.yale.edu/~shiller/data.htm, accessed January 31, 2021. The S&P 500 is considered to be a very good indicator of the stock values of the largest corporations in the United States.
7 Spandan Marasini did some of the research and writing for section 14.7.

15 Monetary policy

The role of central banks in stabilizing economies and regulating financial markets

When the economy falls apart, the first place people turn is to central banks, institutions that can use monetary policy quickly to try to stabilize the economy. Central bankers are the first responders in an economic crisis, able to take dramatic action as soon as an economy experiences a crisis. However, as we will see, the ability of central banks to stabilize an economy in a major crisis is limited, so monetary policy often must be combined with fiscal policy.

The appropriate role for monetary policy is an area of significant debate and disagreement among economists. The mainstream, New Keynesian view is that the central bank can and should use monetary policy to stabilize the economy. In a recession, the central bank should increase the money supply, lower interest rates, and, in the case of a liquidity trap, implement quantitative easing. This should help to avoid a potentially ruinous deflation and to jump-start economic growth. In an overheated economy, monetary policy should be used to slow down the economy to prevent a bust and to engineer a soft landing.

Laissez-faire economists want less government intervention in money markets. They see central bank intervention as destructive, especially given policy lags, and prefer to have the establishment of a monetary rule whereby the government allows the money supply to grow at a fixed rate each year.

Political economists, and especially modern monetary theory (MMT) adherents, want more central bank intervention and regulation. They argue that the central bank should increase the money supply until there are clear, definite signs of inflation. They are much more concerned with unemployment than inflation, so they encourage the use of monetary stimulus to foster growth and reduce unemployment until the economy reaches its maximum capacity.

Supply-side economists see low interest rates as a policy with clear benefits for suppliers. In recent years they agreed with political economists that substantial monetary stimulus was warranted to encourage economic growth even when the economy was booming.

DOI: 10.4324/9780429399350-20

The regulatory landscape in an economy is also important. Some economies, like the United States and the United Kingdom, feature freewheeling financial markets with few restrictions in which investment banks and other financial entities are free to create new financial instruments and engage in risky speculation. Other economies, such as China, feature a very constrained financial system featuring significant state control. As is usually the case, social democracies fall in between the market-dominated approach and the state-dominated approach, offering financial markets that are more contained than those in the United States but much freer than those in China.

This chapter begins by describing how the regulation of the banking sector and financial markets has evolved in the United States. Next, the chapter lays out the five policy tools that the Fed can use to change the money supply and interest rates. Fed policy changes have an impact on aggregate demand, aggregate supply, and real gross domestic product (GDP), although, as we will see, the impact of contractionary monetary policy is much greater than the impact of expansionary monetary policy. The chapter concludes by taking up two controversial areas of monetary policy: The debate over the nonaccelerating inflation rate of unemployment theory and the debate over the connection between expansion of the money supply and inflation.

15.0 CHAPTER 15 LEARNING GOALS

After reading this chapter, you should be able to:

- Describe the regulatory landscape of U.S. banking and financial markets.
- List, explain, and analyze the impact of the U.S. Federal Reserve Bank policy tools.
- Use graphs of the money market and aggregate demand and aggregate supply to analyze the impact of different monetary policies.
- Explain the theory and debate over the nonaccelerating inflation rate of unemployment.
- Summarize and critically evaluate the views of laissez-faire, New Keynesian, supply-side, and political economists on expansionary monetary policy and its relationship with inflation.

15.1 THE REGULATORY LANDSCAPE OF U.S. FINANCIAL MARKETS

The central bank of a country is one of the most important economic institutions. It is often said that, after the head of state, the head of the central bank is the next most important government official in terms of their impact on the economy.

The U.S. banking system evolved in fits and starts after independence from England in 1776. There were several attempts at creating a central bank, but these ended in failure, often because the central bank was undermined by state banks. From 1837 to 1863, bank charters were easy to obtain and many private banks were created, issuing their own currency (bank notes) backed by gold and silver. Reserve requirements and interest rates for state banks were set by state governments. However, regular banking panics led to the National Banking Acts of 1863 and 1864, which established a national currency backed by gold and authorized a newly created Department of the Treasury to regulate nationally chartered banks.

Throughout the 1800s, the gold standard continued to cause destabilizing fluctuations in the economy, slowing growth when too little gold was available but fueling inflation when new discoveries of deposits or new technologies to improve extraction increased the supply of gold. During the late 1800s and early 1900s, the banking industry consolidated under the influence of a few huge investment banks, led by J.P. Morgan and Company. These banks controlled a majority of the nation's wealth, and they were able to use their power to gain control over the major industries of the era, leading to even more consolidation of wealth.

Outraged by the dominance and exploitation of a handful of wealthy bank owners and industrialists, the regular banking panics, and the open corruption of politicians of the era, the members of the Progressive Movement organized in resistance and demanded substantive change. The Federal Reserve Act of 1913 established a new, national central bank that would manage the currency and that could serve as the lender of last resort during a banking liquidity crisis. The first U.S. dollar was printed in 1914. The Federal Reserve Act also established the Federal Reserve banking system to regulate banks in each region of the United States.

Political pressure also resulted in the ratification of the 16th Amendment to the U.S. Constitution in 1913 allowing the income tax. This was important in creating demand for dollars. All citizens now needed U.S. dollars to pay their taxes, so the dollar replaced bank notes and gold as the standard currency. The passage of the Clayton Antitrust Act of 1914 reduced the power of heavily concentrated industries, fostering competition in banking, steel, and other key industries.

The Federal Reserve system was refined significantly during the Great Depression, allowing the Fed to engage in emergency support of banking and establishing the deposit insurance system to restore depositors' faith in banks. To reduce the negative impact of speculative behavior on the banking system, the Glass–Steagall Act separated commercial (safe) banking from (risky) investment banking. Commercial banking was insured by the government, whereas investment banking was not.

After World War II, the Bretton Woods system of international monetary management was established. The system included the creation of the International Monetary Fund (IMF) and the World Bank to promote stability in countries that face a crisis but do not have the resources to cope with the crises themselves. Bretton Woods also established a foreign exchange convertibility system whereby all currencies would be convertible into U.S. dollars, and the dollar became the world's reserve currency. As we will see later, serving as the world's reserve currency has meant that people, firms, and governments around the world like to hold dollars, which has increased the value of the dollar in foreign exchange markets above levels where it would normally trade. This is one of the factors contributing to chronic U.S. trade deficits.

With the advent of neoliberal economic philosophy and policy in the United States beginning around 1980 under President Reagan, the banking sector in the United States was deregulated to a significant degree. Instead of being restricted to small business loans and home mortgages, savings and loan banks were allowed to merge with commercial banks and to make loans for speculative purposes. To increase their profits, savings and loans engaged in real estate speculation and loaned money to governments in developing countries that paid high interest rates. However, many real estate investments collapsed, and several large Latin American governments were unable to make their debt payments. Following the first wave of banking regulation in the United States, more than 23% of savings and loan banks failed, and they had to be bailed out by the government to prevent a wider shock to the economy.

In 1999 the Glass-Steagall Act was repealed, and investment banks were allowed to gain control over commercial banks and savings and loans. A huge wave of mergers and acquisitions ensued, as Wall Street firms snapped up smaller banks to expand their opportunities. This set the stage for the massive real estate and derivative speculation of the 2000s, which culminated in the financial crisis of 2007–2008 and that required another government bailout. We will study the financial crisis in more detail in the next chapter.

A modicum of regulation was reinstated with the Dodd-Frank Wall Street Reform and Consumer Protection Act of 2010. Dodd-Frank increased Fed oversight of banks and required large banks to demonstrate that they were behaving responsibly and not in a manner that was likely to require future bailouts. However, much of Dodd-Frank was repealed under the Trump administration's return to neoliberal policies, which left the U.S. banking system in a relatively deregulated state as of 2020. It will be interesting to see whether the latest round of deregulation follows the same pattern and contributes to another bout of speculation, bank failures, and bailouts. The main overseer of the banking system in the United States is the Fed.

The Federal Reserve Bank or "Fed" is the central bank of the United States. It is an independent institution that does not have to answer directly to politicians. The chair of the Fed and the members of the Federal Reserve Bank Board of Governors are nominated by the president and approved by the senate. Once approved, the Fed can act with complete autonomy, although it may sometimes react to pressure from government officials or businesses. This structure is designed to give the Fed the ability to resist political pressure and to act as it sees fit with respect to monetary policy.

Central bank independence can prevent bad economic policies from being enacted for political ends. For example, politicians who are in power prefer to have example, in 2020, Amazon's *P/E* ratio was 144, when the average *P/E* ratio for most companies was around 20. But this does not necessarily mean that Amazon's stock was overvalued. In 2020 Amazon's sales were exploding during the COVID-19 pandemic and investors expected large future profits as Amazon's dominance of retail sales increased. Due to the limitations of *P/E* as a measure of the value of stocks, investors also look at dividend yields, price-to-book value ratios, and price-to-sales ratios to get a comprehensive picture of how a firm's stock is doing.

Economist Robert Shiller, who successfully predicted the internet stock crash of 2000 and the housing crash of 2007, constructed a variation of the *P/E* ratio called the cyclically adjusted-price-to-earnings (CAPE) ratio to determine whether an asset market is overvalued, undervalued, or accurately valued. Because earnings fluctuate widely with the business cycle, CAPE takes the average of ten years of earnings (E10) and adjusts them for inflation. Current stock prices divided by average real earnings over the last decade gives us an indication of whether stocks are generally overvalued or undervalued compared to historical averages.

Figure 14.8 shows the Shiller CAPE from 1881 to 2020 for the S&P 500, which is a stock market index measuring the value of 500 large, important, and representative publicly traded U.S. companies.[6] Historically, whenever the CAPE index gets over 20 it has been as sign that returns over the next 20 years will decline. CAPEs over 30 usually are followed by steep drops.

Stock markets tend to reflect the profitability and growth prospects of publicly traded companies—those companies that have issued stock for sale to the general

FIGURE 14.8 Shiller CAPE price/*E*10 ratio, 1881–2020.

the central bank keep interest rates low in order to stimulate growth and fuel their re-election prospects. President Trump frequently called on the Fed to lower interest rates when the economy was booming in 2018 and 2019. The Fed, however, was worried about inflationary pressures at the time and resisted Trump's calls for lower interest rates.

Central banks in most developed countries are independent from political influence, including the European Central Bank, the Bank of England, and the Bank of Japan. In these countries, it is not uncommon for central banks to undertake actions that politicians dislike. However, in other countries, including China, Russia, and a host of developing countries, the central bank is controlled directly or indirectly by government officials. In these countries, central bank actions are an extension of the state's goals and priorities and the political interests of those in power.

In the modern era, central banks are tasked with crucial, but potentially conflicting, macroeconomic goals: Minimizing unemployment and promoting economic growth while preserving price stability. Federal Law established the **U.S. Fed's goals** as **maximum employment, stable prices, and moderate long-term interest rates**. The European Central Bank, on the other hand, is only tasked with maintaining stable prices. The issue of the appropriate focus of the central bank in terms of employment and inflation is complex and controversial, as we will see later.

Next, we turn to the tools the Fed has at its disposal to affect the economy. Understanding *how* the central bank does its work will help you anticipate how changes in central bank policy will affect interest rates, financial markets, and you!

15.2 THE FED'S FIVE POLICY TOOLS

The U.S. Fed has five policy tools that it can use to affect interest rates. (Other central banks have a similar toolbox.) These policy tools are open market operations, changes to the discount rate, changes to the federal funds rate, changing the required reserve ratio or the interest rates on banks' excess reserves, and quantitative easing or tightening. We explain each of these tools below.

1. **Open market operations** involve **the purchase or sale of government securities (bonds)**.

    An **open market purchase** is a **central bank (Fed) purchase of government bonds from the public**. The Fed offers to buy bonds for slightly above market value, which makes individuals want to sell more bonds than they usually would. When individuals accept the Fed's offer, the Fed takes in people's bonds and credits their accounts with cash. Thus, *the impact of an open market purchase is to increase the amount of money people have in their bank accounts.* As people's accounts increase in size, banks experience an increase in excess reserves that they can lend out. Therefore, the money supply increases by the amount of the Fed purchases of bonds multiplied by the money multiplier. According to the mainstream economics model of the money market, an increase in the money supply causes interest rates to fall, and this will lead to increases in business investment purchases and consumer durable goods purchases, increasing aggregate demand and stimulating the economy.

An open market sale does the opposite. An **open market sale** is **a central bank (Fed) sale of government bonds to the public**. The Fed offers buyers an attractive rate of return, usually slightly above the going rate of return, to encourage people to buy bonds. Once the sale is accepted, the Fed gives the public bonds but takes money from the accounts of the public as payment for the bonds. This leaves the public with more bonds but less cash. *The impact of an open market sale is therefore to decrease the amount of money people have in their bank accounts.* This decreases banks' reserves, decreasing the money supply, causing interest rates to increase and spurring reductions in business investment and consumer durable goods purchases. The reduction in investment and consumer spending would, in turn, decrease aggregate demand and slow the economy.

2. The **discount rate** (also called the primary credit rate) is **the rate of interest the Fed charges banks to borrow reserves**.

   Recall that the Fed is the lender of last resort. Banks who want to lend out more money can always borrow reserves from the Fed, but they have to pay the Fed interest on what they borrow. If the Fed wants to increase the money supply, it can lower the discount rate. This means banks can borrow reserves more cheaply, which means it is more profitable for banks to make loans. To decrease the money supply, the Fed can raise the discount rate. This discourages bank lending by making it more expensive for banks to obtain the reserves they need to make loans.

3. The **federal funds rate** is **the rate of interest banks charge each other on extremely short-term loans (often overnight), and it is controlled indirectly by the Fed**.

   Though the Fed does not set this interest rate, the Fed manipulates it via open market operations. By increasing the amount of money in banks via open market purchases, the Fed can drive down the federal funds rate. Open market sales will reduce the amount of money in banks and increase the federal funds rate. The federal funds rate is very important because it is a key determinant of whether or not it is profitable for banks to borrow to create new loans.

   Figure 15.1 shows the effective federal funds rate and the discount rate from 2004 to 2020. The Fed sets a target interest rate range for the federal funds rate, and then it engages in open market purchases or sales of bonds until it achieves the "effective" federal funds rate within the range it is targeting. The Fed sets the discount rate about 1% higher than the federal funds rate. The **prime interest rate** is **the rate of interest private banks charge**

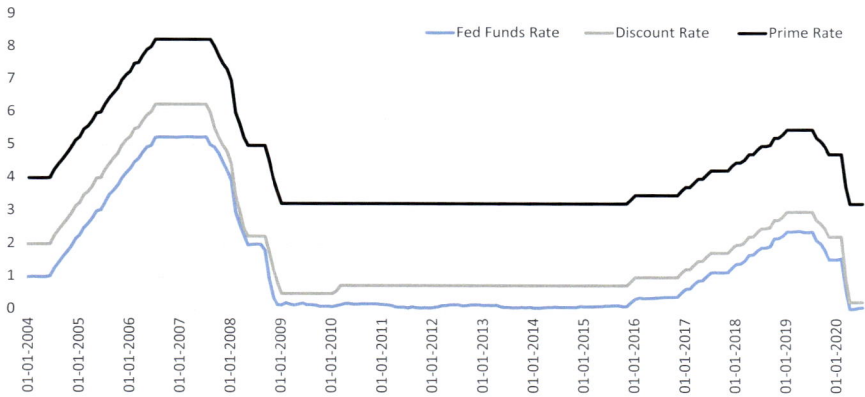

FIGURE 15.1 Effective federal funds rate and primary credit (discount) rate (%), 2004–2020.

their best customers—the biggest corporations with the most collateral and the most secure financial situation. The prime rate of interest clearly moves with the federal funds rate, averaging 3.09% higher since 2004. Thus, it is clear that *the Fed is the primary force determining interest rates in the U.S. economy.*

Figure 15.1 shows the Fed engaging in contractionary monetary policy from 2004 to 2006 and from 2016 to 2019, when it raised the federal funds rate and the discount rate when the economy was overheated to slow down the economy. From 2007 to 2009 and in 2020, the Fed lowered the federal funds rate and the discount rate significantly to stimulate the economy in the face of serious recessions.

4. Changing the **required reserve ratio** or the **interest rate on reserve balances (IORB)** also has a dramatic influence on bank reserves, the money supply and interest rates.

    Decreasing the required reserve ratio allows banks to loan out more of their reserves and increases the size of the money multiplier. To stimulate borrowing in the COVID-19 recession of 2020, the Fed lowered the reserve requirement to 0%, allowing banks to loan out a lot more money if they wanted to. Increasing the required reserve ratio reduces the amount banks can loan out and reduces the size of the money multiplier, decreasing the money supply.

    The Fed can also manipulate banks' reserves by **changing the interest rate the Fed pays to banks who hold excess reserves (the IORB)**. If the Fed wants banks to hold fewer excess reserves, it can reduce the interest rate it pays. If the Fed wants banks to hold more excess reserves, it can increase the interest rate it pays on banks' excess reserves.

5. The Fed's fifth policy tool is a relatively new one, quantitative easing or tightening. **Quantitative easing (QE)** occurs **when the Fed purchases bonds or other assets from banks and businesses**.

QE was used for the first time in the U.S. after the financial crisis of 2007–2008. The Fed makes these purchases with new money that is injected into the banking system at a time when banks would normally be saddled with bad loans that would require banks to scale back on lending and devote resources to covering losses. New money then swells the size of the bank reserves in the economy equal to the quantity of assets purchased. Banks take the new money and buy assets to replace the ones they sold to the central bank. This leads to an increase in stock prices and lowered interest rates, which in turn may help to boost businesses' investment purchases. Buying "toxic" assets can be extremely helpful to troubled banks given that banks could not sell such assets on the open market because there is no demand for them.

Figure 15.2 shows that the Fed began to conduct significant quantitative easing in late 2008, buying more than $1 trillion in assets. As the financial crisis deepened, the Fed continued with its QE asset purchases, until it accumulated $4.5 trillion by 2014.

The opposite of quantitative easing is **quantitative tightening**, which occurs **when the Fed sells bonds and assets from its portfolio back to investors**. Figure 15.2 shows that the Fed began selling some of the assets it had accumulated, also called "unwinding," in 2018.

Statistical evidence from the Fed indicates that the QE asset purchases after the financial crisis probably reduced the U.S. unemployment rate by 1.5% and increased real GDP by 3%. Bank of England economists estimate that the first €200 billion QE purchases caused a 3% cut in the interest rate and raised Britain's real GDP by 2%.

There are also some potential dangers from QE. Pushing interest rates to 0% could make it hard to rein in inflation in the future. Low interest rates could prompt the government to borrow too much and investors to take on risky investments. However, economists worry more about deflation and low levels of investment than inflation and excessive borrowing in an economic crisis.

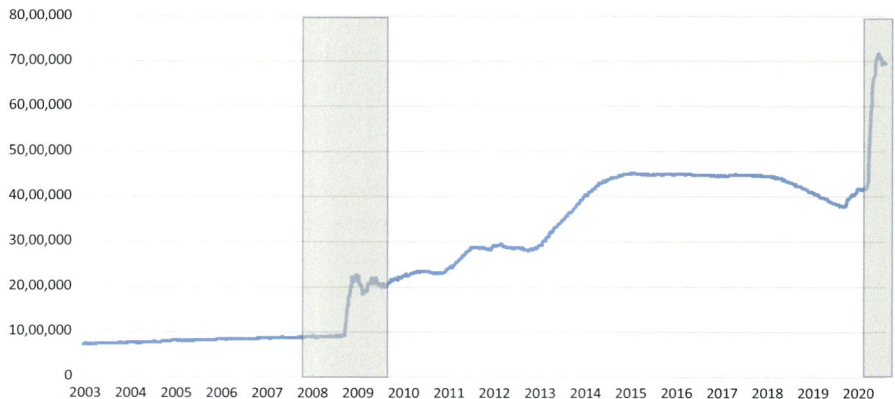

FIGURE 15.2 Total assets held by the Fed (millions of $), 2003–2020.

Furthermore, *QE is the only major policy option that the Fed can use if the economy is in a liquidity trap.* Recall that in a liquidity trap, interest rates have fallen to near 0%, and investors hold cash instead of buying bonds or putting their money in interest-bearing accounts because the return is too low to justify tying their money up. Additional increases in the money supply have no effect on the economy: Interest rates cannot drop further, and investors and consumers are too pessimistic to spend money. With increases in the money supply ineffective, the only expansionary monetary policy option that can work is quantitative easing. Fed purchases of assets, especially toxic ones, cause asset prices to increase, restoring confidence in asset markets and the broader economy.

When the COVID-19 recession hit in 2020, the Fed embarked on a significant monetary stimulus using QE, purchasing more than $3 trillion from banks and other financial intermediaries.

Many of the QE purchases amount to bailouts of banks for bad decisions they made. As we will see later, banks made a lot of very bad, very risky investments in the sub-prime housing market in the 2000s, which sparked the financial crisis. Despite the fact that banks exercised bad judgment, the Fed felt compelled to bail out the banking sector to prevent the financial collapse from spiraling into a full-on depression. Although this move was probably necessary from a macroeconomic standpoint, it did not sit well with workers who lost jobs in the Great Recession but who did not benefit from a massive bailout. When bank executives went ahead and awarded themselves huge bonuses in the midst of the Fed bailout, it sparked an outcry that culminated in the Occupy Wall Street movement in 2011.

Next, we go into how Fed policy works in theory using the mainstream model of the money market and the aggregate demand and aggregate supply model developed earlier. However, as we will discuss later, the reality is often different from the theory when it comes to monetary policy.

15.3 USING MODELS TO ANALYZE HOW MONETARY POLICY AFFECTS THE ECONOMY

Figures 15.3(a) and 15.3(b) (next page) depict the mainstream model of the money market and the aggregate demand and aggregate supply model, respectively. Point **a** in Figure 15.3(b) shows the economy deep in a recession, with a $3 trillion recessionary gap. To eliminate the recession, the Fed needs to enact policies that will cause the aggregate demand curve to shift from AD_1 to AD_2, which is a $4 trillion difference measuring horizontally along the price line. If the marginal respending rate is 0.5, which would make the multiplier equal to $\frac{1}{(1-0.5)} = 2$, the Fed needs to enact policies that will cause an initial increase in aggregate demand of $2 trillion,

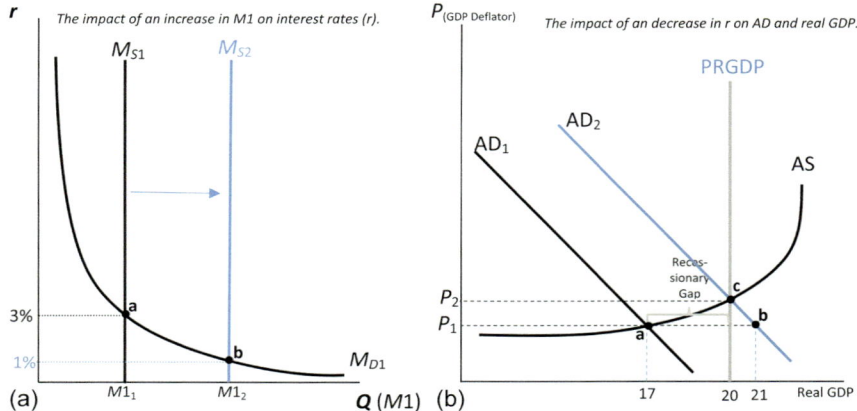

FIGURE 15.3 (a) An increase in money supply and (b) The goal of expansionary monetary policy.

which will cause a total change in aggregate demand of $4 trillion after the multiplier effect plays out.

The Fed uses its key policy tools to control the money supply and interest rates. To increase the money supply and reduce interest rates, the Fed can conduct an open market purchase of bonds, reduce the discount rate and the target federal funds rate, reduce reserve requirements or the interest on reserve balances, and engage in quantitative easing. If the Fed does enough of this, it can lower interest rates significantly. In Figure 15.3(a), the Fed increases the money supply from M_{S1} to M_{S2}, which causes interest rates to decrease from 3% to 1%.

This significant decrease in interest rates will cause businesses to increase their investment purchases and consumers to increase their durable goods purchases, increasing aggregate demand. Lowering interest rates significantly also makes it more profitable for financial investors to put their money into the stock market, because the return on money market accounts and bonds is so low. Therefore, the decrease in interest rates would also improve stock market values. If the Fed undertakes enough monetary stimulus, it might be able to increase aggregate demand by the amount that is needed.

Unfortunately, the real world does not always respond in the hoped-for manner. Monetary policy tends to have limited effectiveness in recessions. Since the Great Depression, economists have known that monetary policy can easily pull back the economy via contractionary monetary policy, but using monetary policy to cause the economy to expand in a recession is like "**pushing on a string**."

There are a number of reasons why expansionary monetary policy is often ineffective in recessions. First, liquidity traps occur when the Fed lowers interest rates to near 0%. After that point, further increases in the money supply have no effect on interest rates or aggregate demand. Second, consumer confidence plummets in recessions due to layoffs and wage freezes. Consumer spending declines and consumer saving increases. Increasing the money supply in such an environment does not tend to encourage additional consumer spending. Third, business confidence also declines in recessions, which reduces business investment purchases. Few businesses want to expand the size of their operations when sales are falling, even if interest rates are low. Thus, *there is often very little change in aggregate demand from expansionary monetary policies in deep recessions.*

This is why truly effective stabilization policy in recessions involves a combination of expansionary fiscal policy *and* expansionary monetary policy. If the Fed makes sure interest rates are as low as possible, and if the government increases spending on infrastructure and other items that stimulate job growth and business expansion, then consumers and businesses may start to spend again. This is known as "priming the pump."

Monetary policy is effective at slowing the economy. If the central bank raises interest rates high enough, it will strangle business investment purchases and consumer durable goods purchases, decreasing aggregate demand. The Fed played a significant role in the recessions of 1982, 1990, 2000, and 2007 by engaging in contractionary monetary policy, raising interest rates, and decreasing the money supply. The Fed always hopes to effect a "soft landing," where aggregate demand decreases slightly and returns to potential real GDP, where the economy settles. However, once an economy experiences a decline in aggregate demand, the layoffs and financial market declines that follow tend to undermine consumer and investor confidence. This sparks additional rounds of decreased spending and sends the economy into a recession.

We now know the different types of policies the Fed can use to affect the money supply, interest rates, aggregate demand, and real GDP. However, choosing which policy to apply and how large the stimulus or contraction should be is a complicated decision that is driven by the theoretical framework being used by policymakers. As is so often the case, economists do not agree on the best theoretical approach to monetary policy.

15.4 THE DEBATE OVER THE NAIRU THEORY

In Chapter 10 we discussed the concept of the natural rate of unemployment. This idea was related to the Phillips curve, which posited an inverse relationship between inflation and unemployment. In the United States in the 1960s there seemed to be a clear, inverse relationship.

Drawing on this information, Milton Friedman and a group of laissez-fare economists developed the **nonaccelerating inflation rate of unemployment (NAIRU) theory**. According to the NAIRU theory, **when the unemployment rate falls below the natural rate of unemployment** (the normal rate of unemployment when the economy is not in a recession), **inflation is expected to increase and perhaps to accelerate** (increase at an increasing rate). Once inflation got started, the theory was that it would accelerate because of a wage-price spiral and changing inflationary expectations. When inflation occurred, workers would demand higher wages to maintain their purchasing power, and businesses would raise prices because they expected costs to increase. This would cause another round of inflation and another round of wage demands and price increases. In essence, the rate of unemployment that prevents inflation, the NAIRU, is the natural rate of unemployment. Similarly, **when the unemployment rate goes above the natural rate of unemployment, inflation is expected to fall**.

Economists estimate that the natural rate of unemployment ranged between 4.5% and 6% in the United States in recent decades. The NAIRU theory was used by laissez-faire economists to argue against the utilization of government spending to stimulate the economy, arguing that it would eventually result in inflation. Furthermore, whenever the unemployment rate dropped below 6%, economists subscribing to the NAIRU theory would argue in favor of contractionary monetary policy to eliminate inflationary pressures.

However, in the last three decades, there has been no clear relationship between inflation and unemployment in the United States. During the 1990s, 2000s, and 2010s, booms resulted in unemployment rates significantly below the natural rate of unemployment, and yet there was no significant increase in inflation during these episodes. When inflation increased to over 8% in 2022, price increases were attributed partially to a low unemployment rate of 3.6% but also to supply disruptions from the coronavirus pandemic and price gouging by corporations in uncompetitive markets. Thus, most New Keynesian economists are skeptical that the government must adhere strictly to the natural rate of unemployment idea.

Nonetheless, most New Keynesian economists believe there is some level of unemployment that would trigger inflation, so the underlying core idea of the NAIRU theory is still widely believed. As Paul Krugman argued,

> A market economy … requires that a certain number of people who want to work be unable to find jobs so that their example will discipline the wage demands of those who are already employed. Even liberal economists like myself grudgingly accept the conclusion that a responsible Fed must sometimes raise interest rates in order to limit the number of jobs and maintain a suitably high rate of unemployment.[1]

The debate is over how low the level of unemployment would need to drop before generating inflation. In 2019 the U.S. unemployment rate dropped to 3.5% without significant inflation. The natural rate of unemployment may have fallen dramatically as globalization and the decline of unions undermined the ability of workers to demand higher wages and the ability of firms to raise prices.

The idea that we need to maintain a high rate of unemployment to contain prices is unacceptable to political economists. The NAIRU theory has been deeply destructive and as well as inaccurate from this perspective. As Stephanie Kelton wrote,

> This underlying faith in the idea that there's some inescapable constraint on the economy's employment potential ... caused the Fed to systematically underestimate the extent to which the unemployment rate could safely fall. This misreading drove the Fed to raise interest rates in the hope of choking off a further drop in unemployment, essentially aiming to deny millions of underemployed and unemployed people access to jobs on the belief that the NAIRU limit had already been reached.[2]

Many countries have reduced the unemployment rate to below 2% without facing inflationary pressures. Wage and price controls can be used to limit inflation to get the unemployment rate even lower without generating inflationary pressures. Thus, there is no reason that a government cannot pursue true full employment, where everyone who wants to work has a job.

From the political economy perspective, the government should continue to create jobs, spend money, and increase the money supply until inflation actually occurs, rather than decreasing the money supply just because we think that inflation might happen. Thus, instead of the current practice of maintaining a relatively high rate of unemployment to keep inflation low, *political economists want to reduce unemployment until there are concrete signs of inflation*. Political economists see the NAIRU theory as beneficial to employers because it maintains a level of unemployment that keeps wages low and profits high, but this comes at a direct cost to workers.

Most central banks follow the NAIRU/New Keynesian approach, raising interest rates if the unemployment rate drops significantly below the natural rate of unemployment. When the unemployment rate in the United States dropped below 5% in 2015, the Fed began nudging up interest rates, and it increased them steadily for the next four years as the unemployment rate fell further. Subsequently, the Fed lowered interest rates as fragile conditions emerged in 2019, and the Fed decreased interest rates to 0% when the COVID-19 recession hit in 2020. When the unemployment rate dropped to 3.6% and inflation surged in 2022, the Fed increased interest rates.

Another related area of debate is regarding the relationship between monetary policy and inflation. Here again, the theoretical background adopted by the Fed chair will drive their selection of policies.

15.5 THE DEBATE OVER EXPANSIONARY MONETARY POLICY AND INFLATION: HAWKS, DOVES, AND OWLS

There are three major perspectives on how the Fed should manage the money supply to deal with recessions. Economists from the **laissez-faire** perspective do not want the Fed to engage in activist management of the money supply. They tend to be aggressive "**hawks**" on inflation, opposing dramatic efforts to stimulate the economy in recessions due to worries about inflation and advocating austerity to control inflationary pressures. **"Doves"** are **New Keynesian** economists and many **supply-side** economists who support extensive monetary stimulus policies in recessions, including quantitative easing. However, there are limits to how far doves want to go with monetary stimulus. Lastly, **political economists**, especially modern monetary theory economists, want even more extensive stimulus policies. They advocate increasing monetary stimulus significantly while carefully monitoring the economy for signs of inflation, which involves a more detailed and complex macroeconomic management approach. Here, you might think of an **"owl,"** keenly observing the situation and adjusting if it sees signs of trouble. We go into each group in more detail below.

Inflation hawks are opposed to significant monetary stimulus in recessions due to worries about inflation. The hawk moniker is intended to signify a very aggressive stance with respect to fighting inflation. The group most against central bank monetary stimulus is the strand of laissez-faire economics called monetarism, founded by Milton Friedman. As with other laissez-faire strands, monetarists believe in the efficiency and self-adjusting properties of unregulated markets and oppose government intervention utilizing monetary policy. Therefore, laissez-faire advocates do not want stabilization policies to be enacted by the central bank.

In addition to subscribing to the NAIRU theory (see above), Friedman opposed expansionary fiscal policy in recessions because he thought private sector investment would be crowded out. (See the debate on this topic in chapter 13 on fiscal policy.) He also opposed expansionary monetary policy in recessions because of **policy lags**. To Friedman, the central bank takes time to realize there is a recession, and then it must meet to decide on a policy. Once the central bank implements a policy, it takes the policy time to affect the economy. Friedman's research showed that it could take up to 18 months for monetary policy to affect the economy. By then, the recession might already be over.

Instead, in the realm of monetary policy, Milton Friedman argued for a **monetary rule**, whereby the Fed would set money supply growth just above the expected rate of growth in real GDP. If real GDP was expected to grow by 2%, the money supply would be allowed to grow by 3%. This would allow enough increase in the money supply for economic growth to occur but not enough to generate significant inflation. Recall the equation of exchange:

$$M1 \times \text{Velocity} = P \times \text{Real GDP}.$$

The second component of Friedman's analysis was the **quantity theory of money**: **If we assume that velocity is constant, that real GDP cannot be influenced by M1, and that money can influence prices but not vice versa**, **then** Friedman's famous dictum that **inflation is always caused by too much money** will hold.

For example, if velocity is fixed, a 3% increase in M1 with a 2% rate of growth in real GDP would keep inflation to 1%. However, if the Fed engages in significant monetary stimulus, allowing the money supply to grow by 10%, then with 2% real GDP growth this action would generate 8% inflation.

The monetary rule Friedman proposed would prevent the Fed from actively intervening to stabilize the economy. With this approach, the Fed would be more concerned with fighting inflation—a hawkish approach—than with reducing the unemployment that accompanied a recession.

History has not been kind to the laissez-faire, hawkish approach to monetary policy. As we saw in Chapter 10, there is no systematic correlation between the money supply (M1) and inflation as predicted by the quantity theory of money. As we saw in Chapter 13, austerity policies in Europe, which included less monetary stimulus than in the United States, slowed economic growth in the European Union relative to the United States. Thus, central bankers in most countries, even those with conservative political leanings, have dismissed the most strident views of inflation hawks. Instead of targeting the money supply, as Friedman advocated, *central banks now target the interest rate* and worry about maintaining enough growth in recessions.

Most mainstream economists from the **New Keynesian** perspective qualify as inflation **doves**, in that they are comfortable with substantial monetary stimulus in recessions. They are more concerned with generating employment and avoiding deflation than they are with inflation when the economy enters a downturn.

New Keynesians point out that M1 is only one influence on nominal GDP, and other factors are far more important. Factors influencing business investment and consumer confidence are particularly crucial in a recession. Increasing the money supply, lowering interest rates to 0%, and purchasing toxic assets can all play a role in propping up financial markets and improving business and consumer confidence. Therefore, the monetarist assumption that M1 cannot affect real GDP is incorrect.

Furthermore, the crowding out of private investment from government borrowing is a non-problem in recessions when firms are not investing anyway. Instead, government borrowing and investment can crowd in private sector investment.

The assumption that velocity, V, is constant is also inaccurate. As Figure 15.4 shows, the velocity of money changes significantly with the business cycle. The velocity of M1 fell in every recession (2000–2001, 2007–2009, 2020), and in the worst recessions it fell sharply. From January 1 to April 1, 2020, velocity fell by 27%! This means the Fed had to increase M1 significantly just to offset declines in velocity, and the Fed needed to increase M1 by more than 27% for it to have any expansionary impact. In such a situation, a monetary rule would have been a disaster, resulting in massive declines in prices and real GDP.

Figure 15.4 also shows that the velocity of money increased during the boom from 2004 to 2007. This is one of the reasons the Fed felt the need to increase interest rates during this period to reduce inflationary pressures. New Keynesians worry about economic growth and increases in M1 or velocity generating inflation during expansions, so they often advocate contractionary monetary policy at such times.

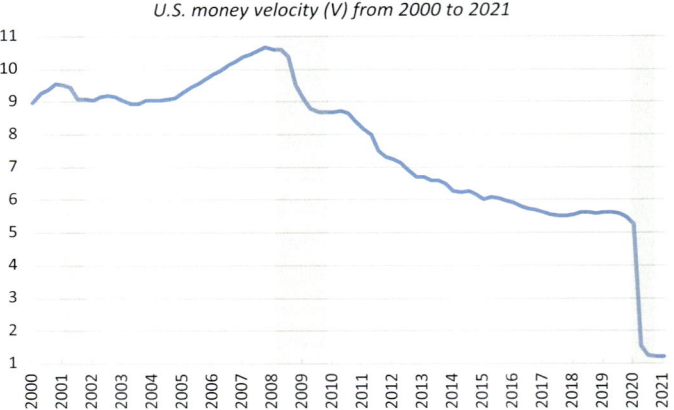

FIGURE 15.4 Velocity of money in the United States, 2000–2021.

Most modern central bankers subscribe to the New Keynesian approach. In recessions, they are dovish on inflation, willing to increase M1 to reduce unemployment and not worrying about inflationary pressures. In a boom, New Keynesians believe the money supply should be reduced and interest rates should be increased to reduce inflationary pressures. Thus, *the core New Keynesian approach is that effective monetary policy can and should be used to stabilize an economic system.*

Political economists want to go much further than New Keynesians in stimulating the economy. They are more dovish than the New Keynesian doves, in that they view unemployment as the most important macroeconomic problem and inflation as a relatively minor and quite controllable problem. Political economists note that capitalist economies almost always operate with insufficient aggregate demand, which means there is almost always too much unemployment. Only once in the last century—during World War II—was there true full employment in the United States such that everyone who wanted to work was able to find a job. In all other periods, there has been room for more monetary and fiscal stimulus.

Rather than relying on the NAIRU theory and the quantity theory of money, many political economists advocate an approach originated by Abba Lerner called **functional finance**. With the functional finance approach, **central banks and governments make decisions based on achieving explicit macroeconomic goals, including stabilizing the business cycle, achieving true full employment, fostering economic growth, and maintaining price stability**. From this perspective, the government should engage in deficit spending, fund job creation, and increase the money supply to foster growth and unemployment until there is actual evidence of inflation.

Note that to achieve full employment without inflation, the government would need to monitor the macroeconomy carefully to make sure it does not exceed its "speed limit," which is the where the economy grows so quickly that inflation accelerates. Resource and labor markets need to be carefully monitored for signs of shortages that might result in inflationary pressures. Thus, the political economy approach involves a greater level of government intervention and macroeconomic monitoring, with the goal of stimulating aggregate demand and achieving true full employment that is well below the NAIRU.

President Trump and his supply-side economic advisors sided with political economists in advocating significant monetary stimulus when the economy was booming in 2018–2019. They agreed with New Keynesians and political economists that monetary stimulus was necessary in the COVID-19 recession of 2020. Cutting businesses' borrowing costs is consistent with the supply-side focus on reducing businesses' costs and stimulating financial markets to improve the business investment climate. The Fed continued engaging in monetary stimulus in 2021 under President Biden, but the Biden Fed eventually engaged in contractionary policy in 2022 when the economy boomed and inflation topped 8%.

With regard to monetary policy, we see some predictable positioning, with laissez-faire economists advocating no government intervention, New Keynesian economists preferring some government intervention, and political economists arguing for extensive government intervention. Interestingly, supply-siders, who often side with laissez-faire economists, differ in the realm of monetary policy, where they side more with political economists due to their desire to stimulate financial markets.

15.6 CONCLUSION

This chapter began by describing how the U.S. government regulated banks and financial markets during its history. The banking sector was constantly shifting and quite unsteady for the first 160 years. The establishment of a central bank and national currency during the Civil War did not end that instability. The gold standard, regular banking panics, and the massive consolidation of banking in the hands of the robber barons exacerbated the problems with the unstable and unequal financial system. Banking regulation began in the early 1900s and increased dramatically during the Great Depression, after which the system became more stable. However, the deregulation of banking beginning in the 1980s set the stage for another round of financial market instability for the next four decades.

In the modern United States, the Fed has five central bank policy tools it can use to stabilize the economy: Open market operations, the federal funds rate, the discount rate, reserve requirements, and quantitative easing or tightening. The Fed can decrease the money supply and increase interest rates in booms to slow the economy as it tries to engineer a soft landing. The Fed can increase the money supply and decrease interest rates in recessions to stimulate aggregate demand. However, Fed policy is much more effective in slowing the economy than stimulating it.

Fed policy choices can be controversial. Laissez-faire economists subscribe to the nonaccelerating inflation rate of unemployment (NAIRU) theory, arguing that low unemployment will cause accelerating inflation and so the Fed should maintain tight monetary policy. New Keynesian economists worry more about unemployment than inflation, so they advocate somewhat more expansionary monetary policy. Political economists see unemployment as the most important macroeconomic problem, so they advocate significant monetary expansion until virtually all unemployment is eliminated.

There are similar disagreements regarding the relationship between the money supply and inflation. Laissez-faire economists argue that the Fed should not increase the money supply in recessions because it will cause inflation without improving growth. New Keynesian economists disagree with this argument, given that deflation, not inflation, is the big risk in recessions and that increases in the money supply can, if paired with expansionary fiscal policy, stimulate aggregate demand. Political economists advocate even more dramatic monetary policy expansion until actual signs of inflation actually emerge.

Central bankers have more economic power and influence than most heads of state. That is why these debates over monetary policy are so crucial. The decisions on monetary policy loom particularly large during economic crises, as we will see in the next chapter.

QUESTIONS FOR REVIEW

1. How has the regulation of banks and financial markets changed over the course of U.S. history?
2. List the Fed's monetary policy tools. Explain how the Fed could use each policy tool to reduce the money supply and increase interest rates.
3. What happens to banks, the money supply, and interest rates if the Fed engages in an open market purchase?
4. What is quantitative easing, and how can it help to stimulate the economy?
5. Figure 15.5 shows the economy in an overheated state at point **a**.
   a. How large is the inflationary gap?
   b. What policies can the Fed use to cause a decrease in aggregate demand? Explain.

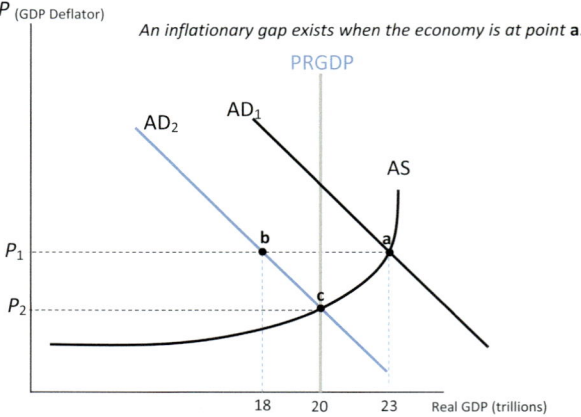

FIGURE 15.5 An inflationary gap at point **a** and its elimination.

c. If the marginal respending rate is 0.8, how large of a decrease in investment and consumption would it take to move the economy back to potential real GDP (PRGDP)?
6. In your own words, define the NAIRU theory. Explain the different perspectives on NAIRU.
7. Explain the perspectives of hawks, doves, and owls on expansionary monetary policy and its relationship to inflation. Which perspective do you find most compelling? Why?
8. You have just been appointed the new chair of the Federal Reserve Bank. The president wants your immediate input on (a) how best to regulate banks and financial markets and (b) the best monetary policy to use given the current state of the economy. Write an essay in which you take up these key issues. Refer to specific macroeconomic schools of thought in your essay and the ideas you find most compelling in understanding banking and monetary policy.

NOTES

1 Paul Krugman, "The Way We Live Now," *New York Times*, May 23, 1999, section 6, p. 24.
2 Stephanie Kelton, *The Deficit Myth: Modern Monetary Theory and the Birth of the People's Economy* (New York: Public Affairs, 2020).

16 Crises, financial and otherwise

On the causes and consequences of economic crises and how they can be averted

What causes an economic crisis? To some economists, recessions are one of the great mysteries in economics, caused by unpredictable shocks that are external to the system. From this perspective, crises are virtually impossible to predict.

Other economists have made their living predicting crises. Keynes was certainly very good at it, as was Hyman Minksy. Their insights give us ideas for what the underlying causes of crises might be.

Keynes focused on investment volatility as the driving force behind recessions. Political economists extend this analysis to include all factors that can cause a profit squeeze toward the end of a boom. After the oil shocks of the 1970s, economists added supply shocks to the list of factors that could cause recessions. Minsky and political economists analyzed the role that asset bubbles could play in driving the business cycle. Meanwhile, laissez-faire economists focused on monetary and productivity shocks, misperceptions, and government errors as factors likely to create recessions. Taken together, these approaches provide insights into the factors that might lead to the next recession. We can also learn a lot from analyzing history.

The dot-com recession of 2000–2001 and the Great Recession of 2007–2009 were both driven by asset bubbles in which speculators invested in risky assets that eventually crashed, dragging the rest of the economy with them. Indeed, asset bubbles have increased in importance as a driver of crises in recent decades as financial markets have been deregulated. The COVID-19 recession of 2020, on the other hand, was caused by a pandemic that forced economies to shut down to contain the virus, simultaneously eroding supply and demand.

The degree of fiscal and monetary stimulus enacted by governments has increased dramatically in each of the last three recessions, helping to alleviate the worst problems created by the recessions but failing to lift the economies into full recovery quickly. Thus, macroeconomic management of the business cycle remains a complex and inexact science about which there is much disagreement.

DOI: 10.4324/9780429399350-21

We begin the chapter by reviewing the classic analysis of recessions pioneered by John Maynard Keynes.

16.0 CHAPTER 16 LEARNING GOALS

After reading this chapter, you should be able to:

- List and explain the different factors economists have identified that can result in a recession.

- Compare and contrast the different explanations of the business cycle put forth by Keynesian, political, and laissez-faire economists.

- Identify and describe the characteristics of the last three U.S. recessions.

- Critically evaluate the ideas of economists regarding recessions and their applicability to the last three U.S. recessions.

Economists have put forth a variety of explanations regarding the causes of recessions. We go through the most important ones below. The major factors that have caused recessions include (1) investment volatility, (2) a profits squeeze, (3) supply shocks, and (4) asset bubbles. As we go through these different factors, we will also outline the different economic perspectives on the causes of crises. We begin with Keynes, who significantly advanced our understanding of the business cycle through his studies of investment volatility.

16.1 CYCLICAL INVESTMENT VOLATILITY (KEYNES)

Some of the best analysis of the causes of recessions comes from John Maynard Keynes and the modern economists who center their analysis on Keynesian ideas. This includes New Keynesians as well as political economists who focus on the role of aggregate demand and the volatility of business investment purchases as a major driver of many recessions.

In Keynesian analysis, there is a natural cycle of business investment given the uncertainty of profitability. According to Keynes, businesses' investment purchases, in which they buy capital goods in order to expand the size of their operations, is the most volatile component of gross domestic product (GDP) and is the component most likely to drive changes in the business cycle. As political economist John Harvey observed, in every U.S. business cycle since 1950 save one, [businesses] physical investment [purchases] rapidly decelerated at the end of the expansion and then collapsed to bring on recession (the exception being the 1960s, when the data are affected by the fact that government spending on the Vietnam War and the War on Poverty propped up the economy longer than the market would have done by itself). On average, construction of new capacity rose at nearly 16% (adjusted for inflation) in every year of expansions but the last, when it dropped to 6.6%. Over the recessions, it "grew" at −13.5% per year. There is no other economic variable that is more tightly associated with the business cycle than this, nor is there one whose variability is more dramatic.[1]

Thus, we see a dramatic decline in the rate of business investment purchases just before a recession and then a crash after the recession begins. Real GDP growth parallels changes in business investment purchases, declining from 5.6% to 3.5% after the initial decline in investment and dropping to −1.2% during recessions.

The Keynesian recession story starts in the ashes of a recession. After several years of slow growth and declining investment, opportunities begin to emerge. New technologies, new products, and new markets offer promising potential profits, encouraging businesses to expand and sparking an increase in business investment purchases of capital goods. This creates jobs and income, which spurs an increase in consumer spending, which creates additional opportunities for profitable investment. The boom boosts consumer and investor confidence, which causes additional rounds of spending on consumer durables and business capital goods.

After several years of expansion, however, consumers have all of the durable goods they need, and the most promising investment opportunities are gone. Now all that is left are riskier investments. Profit rates inevitably decline in the late stages of the business cycle from these forces. The decline in investment that usually accompanies the decline in profit rates sows the seeds of the recession. Demand for construction workers, materials, and numerous other sectors declines as businesses stop expanding, and this reduces income and employment. Now households do not have enough income to buy everything that is produced, and gluts of goods start to emerge.

As the economy becomes fragile late in the expansion, all it takes is a nudge to push the economy into a recession. The precipitating event could be a steep increase in interest rates by the Fed, a plunge in the stock market as investors lose confidence, or many other factors. Whatever sparks the crash, once business and consumer confidence is undermined, there will be dramatic declines in business investment and consumer durable goods purchases, pushing the economy into a recession. After a period of declining growth and then slow growth, which can be minimized with enough government stimulus, the cycle begins anew.

Note that declines in investment can be caused by numerous factors. They can be driven by the normal dynamics of the business cycle, as described above.

Investment may also decline due to rapid and large increases to interest rates, such as those that occurred in the United States in 1980 and 1990. This would be characterized as an aggregate **demand shock**—**a decrease in aggregate demand from something other than the normal, cyclical investment patterns**. Indeed, according to political economists, any factors that reduce profit rates in most businesses will cause a decline in business investment purchases and nudge the economy toward a recession.

16.2 PROFIT SQUEEZE (POLITICAL ECONOMISTS)

A theory similar to the Keynesian approach is the political economy approach grounded in Marxian and post-Keynesian ideas that focus on the **profit rate** as the major driver of the business cycle. The **profit rate** is equal to **the total amount of profit accrued by a firm divided by the total capital invested by the firm**:

$$\text{Profit rate} = \frac{\text{Total profits}}{\text{Total (physical) capital investment}}.$$

As noted above, early in the business cycle, firms' investment purchases of capital goods tend to be very profitable. They are investing in productive new technologies and expanding into profitable new areas. This profitability draws in even more new investment as businesses see opportunities expanding. Also, the profits that are generated as the boom gets started become available to be invested, providing a further stimulus to investment.

Eventually, however, the profit rate starts to decline later in the business cycle, and that stifles investment. A declining profit rate makes firms more reluctant to make investment purchases, and it gives firms less money with which to make those purchases. So far, the story is similar to the Keynesian one. What political economists add are some additional reasons why the profit rate may decline.

The profit rate can decline due to a number of factors. One reason is (1) **underconsumption**. If businesses have expanded their capacity significantly but if consumers scale back on their goods purchases, as they tend to do in booms after they have purchased all of the durable goods they need, then the profit rate falls.

A second reason the rate of profit can decline during a boom is a (2) **wage squeeze**. As the economy grows and unemployment falls, workers are able to demand higher wages. This increases businesses' costs and reduces their profit rate.

The third reason is the (3) **increasing difficulty in squeezing profit out of a business with ever-larger amounts of capital**.[2] As the business cycle progresses, capital investments tend to become less and less productive as increasingly marginal projects get funded. Once capital investment purchases boost productivity by a smaller amount than they increase costs, there will be a decline in the profit rate.

Empirical work by Tom Weisskopf indicates that the most important reason for the decline in the profit rate in business cycles prior to 1970 was the wage squeeze. When unions were powerful and the U.S. economy was a manufacturing powerhouse, workers received significant real wage increases during booms, which undermined profit rates and fostered conditions for a recession. However, as the decline of unions, globalization, and neoliberal government policies reduced the power of workers to demand wage increases, the factors driving the decline in the profit rate at the end of the business cycle changed.

Instead of wage increases undermining profits, Erdogan Bakir shows that other factors became more important in undermining businesses' profit rates late in U.S. business cycles after 1970.[3] The major factors undermining profits were (4) higher domestic prices and the deterioration in U.S. terms of trade, (5) declining productivity from increasing bureaucratization of businesses, and (6) financialization.

In the global, neoliberal era, the output prices U.S. corporations can charge are kept low by global competition, while the costs of food, rent, health care, and other goods purchased by U.S. workers keep increasing. Even though real wages are stagnant, the cost of workers relative to the price of output is increasing, undermining the profit rate. In essence, U.S. businesses experience higher costs (higher nominal wages) toward the end of boom periods, but the higher costs are due to increases in health care, food, and housing prices, not from higher wages.

In addition, U.S. corporations expanded the size of management relative to the number of productive workers since the 1970s. U.S. firms are now significantly more bureaucratic on average than overseas firms, and this costly bureaucratic structure increases businesses' costs of production and reduces productivity and profits. Lastly, the additional interest and dividend payments that firms have to make as the financial sector has increased its dominance also erode the profit rate.

Figure 16.1 shows how useful the profit rate analysis of political economists can be. Bakir's work demonstrates that late in every economic expansion and immediately prior to every recession, there is a sharp drop in the profit rate. This analysis can be used to predict when recessions occur as long as future business cycles follow similar patterns.

Figure 16.1 also shows a steady decline in businesses' capital investment purchases since the 1970s, which is a significant factor driving slower growth of real GDP in the United States in recent decades.

So far, we have focused on demand factors, and especially business investment purchases, as the major driver of crises. However, supply factors can also play a role.

16.3 SUPPLY SHOCKS

Supply shock recessions are caused by factors that cause aggregate supply to decrease. The most important modern examples of supply shocks are the recession of 1973–1975 and the double-dip recession of 1980–1982, both of which were

CRISES, FINANCIAL AND OTHERWISE 399

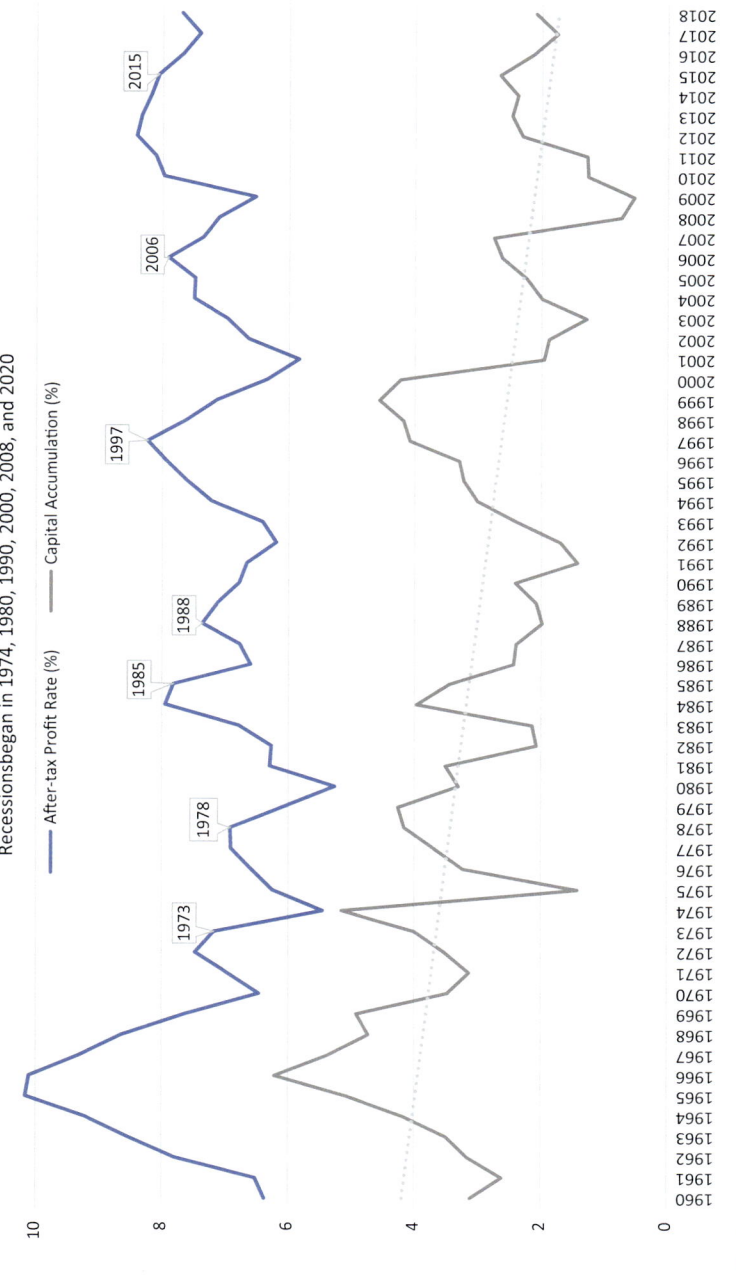

FIGURE 16.1 Profit rate and capital accumulation (Bakir), 1960–2018.

driven by significantly higher oil prices. The price of oil quadrupled in 1973, raising costs for all businesses, and particularly those that used a lot of energy. This was accompanied by a significant stock market crash, as high oil prices undermined profitability for numerous businesses.

Figure 16.2 shows the economic impact of a supply shock using the aggregate demand and aggregate supply model. The increase in oil prices causes the profitability of virtually all non-oil businesses to decline. Businesses have to raise prices and cut costs to survive, resulting in mass layoffs. The result is one of the worst macroeconomic outcomes possible: Stagflation, which is the simultaneous occurrence of stagnation (a recession) and inflation.

Whereas demand shocks can be corrected by expansionary fiscal and monetary policy to stimulate aggregate demand, supply shocks are more difficult to solve. Increases in aggregate demand can eliminate the recessionary gap and move the economy back to potential real GDP (PRGDP). However, even more inflation may result from this expansion. Reducing aggregate demand via contractionary policies would eliminate inflation, but it would push the economy deeper into the recession.

In 1979, Fed chair Paul Volcker raised interest rates to 20% to eliminate inflationary pressures. His efforts were successful in eliminating inflation but at the devastating cost of a major recession.

The supply shocks of the 1970s spurred economists to analyze the supply side of the economy in more detail and prompted the development of supply-side economics as an attempt to solve supply shocks. In theory, the best cure for a supply shock that caused a decrease in aggregate supply would be policies that could cause an increase in aggregate supply. Therefore, President Reagan focused on tax cuts for corporations and the wealthy, along with the deregulation of trade, the environment, labor markets, and other aspects of the economy. Unfortunately, Reagan's supply-side policies did not stimulate business investment enough to generate a significant improvement in economic growth. Stimulating the supply side

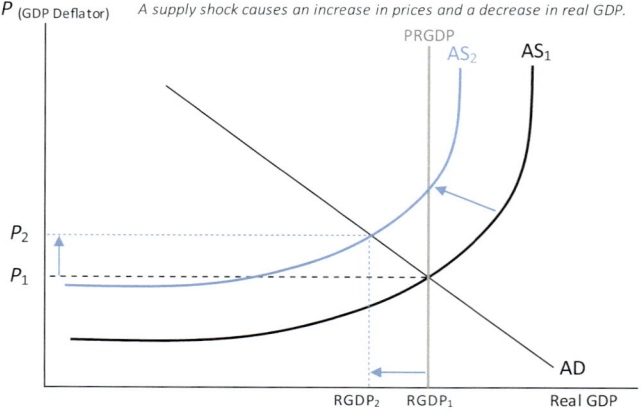

FIGURE 16.2 Stagflation from a supply shock.

of the economy remains a difficult goal to achieve. We will return to this topic in the chapter on economic growth later in the book.

Whereas supply shocks dominated economic conversations in the 1970s and 1980s, asset price bubbles were a major issue in the 1990s and 2000s. Some of the most perceptive observations on asset bubbles come from political economist Hyman Minsky.

16.4 ASSET BUBBLES AND MINSKY'S FINANCIAL INSTABILITY HYPOTHESIS[4]

Perhaps no factor looms so large in recent recessions as the ability of asset bubbles to drag the economy into a recession when they burst. Asset bubbles occur when financial markets make huge bets on assets that prove, in retrospect, to be overvalued. Such behavior prompted John Maynard Keynes to remark, "When the capital development of a country becomes a by-product of the activities of a casino, the job is likely to be ill-done."

In modern capitalism, finance has become a major force affecting the entire global economy. Thus, any analysis that ignores the role of finance is bound to be fundamentally flawed. In mainstream economics, it is typical to ignore the financial sector, assuming that it simply links borrowers with lenders without impacting the rest of the economy. Mainstream economists typically assume markets are stable, assets are always priced correctly (the efficient market hypothesis), investors rationally balance risks and rewards (the capital asset pricing model), and any deviations from this situation are small or temporary. That approach is difficult to support given the recent financial crisis and the increasing occurrence of asset bubbles.

One of the most useful analyses of the role of finance in modern capitalism comes from Hyman Minsky in the form of his **financial instability hypothesis**. Building on the foundation of the Keynesian business cycle, Minsky adds the role of psychology in financial investments to help us understand why financial markets are prone to recurring crises and why stability breeds excess, which is, in turn, destabilizing.

One of Minsky's major insights is that in financial markets "stability is destabilizing."[5] Rather than tending toward a stable equilibrium, stability breeds excessive risk taking. As investors gain confidence that the good times will never end, as they did in the booms of the 1990s and early 2000s, they engage in increasingly risky investments. The spectacular booms in asset markets are followed by equally spectacular busts. In the modern economy, *the financial sector tends to* **exacerbate** *the trends in the goods and services sector*, amplifying the business cycle. To understand exactly how this takes place, we need to understand the **Minsky cycle**.

16.4.1 The Minsky cycle

As Keynes noted, in the typical business cycle, after one to two years in a recession followed by another two to three years of slow growth, new business opportunities start to arise. Firms identify new products that could be sold, new markets they can exploit, new technologies that can reduce costs, and so on. Meanwhile, consumer confidence starts to improve along with job growth. Thus, after several years in which very little investment takes place, firms begin to invest again, expanding purchases of plants and equipment and increasing their productive capacity. This causes incomes to increase and unemployment to fall, starting the economic expansion.

What Minsky adds to this story is the role of financial institutions in the boom. The increase in business investment must be financed somehow. In order to finance billions of dollars in new investments, firms borrow from banks.

16.4.1.1 Phase 1: Stable finance (the "hedge finance" phase)

The investments early in a boom are usually fairly safe. Businesses invest in sound opportunities with a high expected return. They are confident that the increases in revenues from their investments can easily pay off the interest and the principal that they borrowed from banks.

Minsky calls this safest stage of the cycle "hedge finance." Investments are "hedged" in that they are very safe and unlikely to experience financial losses. (This has nothing to do with hedge funds, which are often very risky.) Expected revenues from investments exceed payments on interest and the principal, so the risk of default is very low. Both businesses and banks are in a stable situation. But, as noted above, stability breeds instability. Success leads to excess which leads to a crash.

16.4.1.2 Phase 2: Risky finance (the "speculative finance" phase)

As the boom gathers speed, business confidence improves, and this has a major consequence: Firms are now willing to take on much more risk. Once all of the best investment opportunities are taken, firms must increasingly look for higher risk investments. High levels of confidence encourage businesses to borrow even more money to finance these higher risk investments. In the process, they take on even more debt, committing larger and larger portions of their expected revenues to debt service.

This phase of the Minksy cycle is termed the "speculative" phase. As businesses borrow more and more money for riskier and riskier investments, the expected revenue from the investments will reach a point where it covers the interest payments but not the principal. Thus, the only way businesses can pay off their debt is if the investment ends up being unexpectedly successful and revenues increase. But, until they experience a revenue increase, businesses will have to keep refinancing their loans whenever they come due. They will make the interest payments on the loan, but they will not pay any principal. This phase of the cycle is called "speculative finance" because businesses are speculating that their investments will eventually result in an increase in revenues sufficient to pay off their debts.

Meanwhile, banks, assuming that the boom will continue and that businesses will have no problem paying off their debts, are quite comfortable making riskier loans that require less collateral. Collateral is security that is provided for repayment of a loan, which is forfeited in the event of a default. For example, a business financing an expansion of their operations would have to put up as collateral their existing business assets in order to secure bank financing. That way, if the investment fails and the firm cannot pay the bank, the bank can seize the assets of the business as compensation. Normally, a bank would not loan to a business without significant collateral, but when confidence is high, banks tend to relax their rules regarding collateral. In addition, normally, banks would require borrowers to pay off the interest and some of the principal of the loan. This, too, is relaxed when confidence is high.

Banks, flush with cash because of the boom (savings and business profits are pouring into bank accounts), also start to create new financial products and to work to circumvent rules and regulations in order to take advantage of new opportunities. Hence, we get bank speculation to go along with the business speculation already underway.

As the economy booms, the government tends to take in larger amounts of tax revenues and reduces spending on unemployment and social programs (austerity). This happens at the same time that the central bank (Federal Reserve) raises interest rates. Austerity and higher interest rates combine to slow the economy somewhat and increase the risk of default on speculative investments. The good times also prompt calls for deregulation, because all is well in financial markets. When financial markets have seemingly exhausted the less risky investments, they clamor for deregulation to be able to invent new financial instruments, as savings and loan banks did in the 1980s (leading to the savings and loan crisis of the late 1980s) or as investment banks did in the late 1990s and early 2000s (leading to the financial crisis of 2007–2009). This combination of deregulation, fiscal and monetary tightening, and riskier investment opportunities moves the economy from a stable structure to a fragile financial situation.[6]

16.4.1.3 Phase 3: The Ponzi finance phase and the crash

As the bubble reaches a fever pitch and confidence improves even more, businesses increase investment further in the riskiest ventures and take on debt they cannot afford, relying on the hope that the investments will be more successful than they appear. Businesses take on so much debt that they cannot make the principal or the interest payments, which means that they must borrow more and more money just to make the interest payments on their debts. Their debts continue to mount until the hoped-for increase in revenue from the investment happens.

This is called the "Ponzi" phase of the cycle because businesses are borrowing money that they cannot pay back given existing conditions. Their only hope of paying back their loans is if their investments generate substantial new revenues.

This is very similar to a Ponzi scheme, such as that perpetrated by Bernie Madoff, where an unscrupulous investment manager takes in money from investors but, rather than investing it, squanders it. His only hope of paying off the original investors is if new investors also entrust him with their money, at which point the Ponzi scheme operator uses the money from the new investors to pay dividends to the original investors. The Ponzi scheme can only continue as long as new investors continue to give new money to the Ponzi investment manager so he can continue to pay off his other investors. Once new investments dry up, the whole Ponzi scheme will collapse.

Similarly, in the Ponzi phase of the business cycle, businesses are borrowing money that they cannot possibly pay back unless their risky investment is actually successful in generating new revenues. While they wait for the hoped-for increase in revenues, they must continue to receive financing from banks to cover their principal and interest payments. There is an inherent instability in such a situation.

Businesses in this phase of the cycle will not default as long as banks continue to loan them increasing amounts of money. However, once the economy becomes this fragile, numerous factors can derail the boom. Multiple defaults can occur if (1) revenue flows from investments turn out to be lower than expected, (2) interest rates increase,[7] (3) banks get scared and curtail lending, or (4) a prominent firm or bank defaults on payments and scares investors or lenders.

Once businesses, investors, or banks are spooked, we have reached the "Minsky moment," and the financial bubble collapses rapidly. As everyone tries to unload risky assets, their prices plummet, and bankruptcies and defaults ensue. The risky investments collapse. Firms lay off workers and income and employment fall, reducing consumer spending and making the situation even more dire. The economy spirals into recession, and only a significant injection of money into financial markets by the central bank (such as the Fed) and a large increase in government spending by the government can stop the crash.

16.4.2 The super-Minsky cycle

There is also a trend in financial markets where the likelihood of a severe financial crash increases over a period of several decades. If the regular recessions and crashes are mild, there will be increasing calls for deregulation over time. For example, financial markets were deregulated substantially in the 1990s and early 2000s after two decades of relatively stable growth. The more financial markets are deregulated, the riskier the behavior can be. This will tend to increase the severity of the crash as deregulation proceeds, resulting in a major crash such as the Great Depression of the 1930s or the Great Recession of 2007–2009. Of course, in the wake of a major crash, calls for new regulations emerge and safeguards are put back into place. This stabilizes the system and reduces the severity of the next several recessions. That is, until the lessons have been forgotten and renewed calls for deregulation are heeded, setting up the next major crash.

As numerous publications and economists from both mainstream and political economy perspectives have noted, Minsky's financial instability hypothesis is very important in understanding the modern business cycle. Minsky left us with a number of key ideas that we can use to anticipate and possibly to avoid future crises:

- Stability is destabilizing: Stability encourages excessive risk-taking, which leads to fragility and crisis.
- Over the long term (several decades), stability is destabilizing partly because it encourages deregulation of financial markets, which encourages a larger speculative boom and much deeper bust.
- Over the typical ten-year business cycle, stability is destabilizing because of the manner in which improvements in confidence encourage businesses and banks to engage in increasingly risky behavior.
- In the first "stable" or "hedge" phase of the business cycle, firms make sound investments and banks make sound loans that should be successful and that have a low probability of default.
- In the second "risky" or "speculative" phase, as the economy grows and confidence improves, firms take on more debt and make increasingly risky investments while banks create new, riskier financial securities. The probability of defaults increases.
- In the third "Ponzi" phase, rapid growth and appreciating asset values cause the boom to reach a fever pitch as firms and banks make even riskier investments, and the probability of defaults becomes very high.
- At some point, when it becomes clear that the risky investments will not generate the necessary returns, the economy reaches a "Minsky moment"—panic selling ensues, and the market crashes. The financial market crash causes reduced investment and consumer spending, unemployment increases, and the economy falls into a recession.

If we take Minsky's analysis to heart, then financial markets, and markets in general, must always be regulated to prevent Ponzi-like behaviors. Only then can we avoid the worst excesses of financial markets and the deep recessions that follow a financial market collapse.

Political economists and New Keynesian economists study crises and how they work. Most laissez-faire economists tend to assume that recessions will be short-lived and focus instead on long-term characteristics of macroeconomic markets. Nonetheless, laissez-faire economists developed some ideas on what might cause a recession, which are taken up in the next section.

16.5 LAISSEZ-FAIRE ECONOMISTS' THEORIES OF THE BUSINESS CYCLE

Building on Milton Friedman's research, **monetarist theories of the business cycle** **credit monetary factors with driving fluctuations in real GDP**. Some of Friedman's most important research showed that one of the major causes of the

Great Depression was the huge decrease in the money supply that occurred as one bank after another failed. Using Friedman's quantity theory of money,

$$M1 \times V = P \times \text{Real GDP},$$

a large decrease in M1 can cause deflation (a decrease in P) and a large decrease in real GDP.

In the modern era, most central banks have learned this key lesson: The central bank must act as the lender of last resort and must ensure that banks and financial markets have sufficient liquidity in a crisis. This is why the Fed injected trillions of dollars into the economy in 2008 and in 2020. Friedman thought that monetary stimulus might be enough to stop a recession, so he did not advocate additional fiscal stimulus. However, as we saw in the chapter on fiscal policy, countries that combined monetary and fiscal stimulus fared much better in response to the Great Recession than those that did not use both.

Laissez-faire economists also developed **real business cycle theory**, which **attributes recessions to productivity shocks caused by changes in technology and the legal and regulatory environment**. A major innovation in one sector, such as the development of the internet, can cause huge disruptions in other sectors, such as retail shopping. Also, a major shift in government, such as the switch in Russia from communism to capitalism, can undermine existing productive institutions and cause a crisis. Although it is certainly true that productivity shocks can cause recessions, this does not explain the regularity with which recessions occur.

Laissez-faire economists are also less concerned with recessions than other economists because of their belief in the flexibility of markets. For example, laissez-faire economists often argue that recessions are a result of workers demanding wages that are too high. From this perspective, if workers would reduce their reservation wage—the lowest wage rate that they will accept—in recessions, they would all find work. This **market misunderstanding theory** **attributes the cause of a recession to misperceptions by workers or other economic actors**.

The **political business cycle theory** argues that **business cycles can result from policies of politicians to improve their re-election chances**. There are definite indications that political behavior can contribute to business cycles. Republican Senate majority leader Mitch McConnell stymied efforts by the Democratic Obama administration to engage in fiscal stimulus after the Great Recession, but he supported large stimulus packages under Republican President Trump. Thus, it is always important to include political considerations in economic analysis of the business cycle given the importance of political decisions on fiscal policy.

Laissez-faire economists often highlight the political business cycle because it reinforces their belief that government intervention is usually self-serving and inefficient. This contrasts with the other theoretical approaches that emphasize the need for effective government intervention to fix recessions and, possibly, to alter economic conditions such that recessions are less likely.

Now that we have studied economists' theories regarding the factors that drive the business cycle, we turn to case studies of recent recessions. This will help you understand the unique dynamics that drive each business cycle, as well as the patterns that emerge.

16.6 THE RECESSION OF 2001: INTERNET/TECH OVERINVESTMENT AND STOCK BUBBLE

After the 1990 recession, the U.S. economy began to grow rapidly. Much of this growth was driven by the so-called new economy, which included businesses in the information technology sector such as fiber-optic cables, personal and business computers, and the development of the internet. Computer ownership in the United States more than doubled during this decade as computers changed from a luxury to a necessity. Internet use exploded. As investors began to see the internet as the next big thing, investment in the tech sector also exploded.

Herd behavior is **the tendency of human beings to emulate the behavior of others**. Emulation, where people copy others with the goal of doing as well as they are, is a pattern found in much human behavior. Veblen identified pecuniary emulation, where people imitate the tastes and fashions of the classes above them and strive to fit in, as one of the major forces shaping human behavior. Similarly, in financial markets, investors emulate others to make sure they are not missing out on the next big thing. FOMO, fear of missing out, is a major driver in financial markets. Once a handful of big investors decided that the internet was the next big thing, huge numbers of investors followed suit, to the point of incredible irrationality.

A few new internet companies showed incredible promise, such as Netscape and the other first internet browsers. They were quickly followed by dozens of "dot-com" companies, so-named because of the .com end on their website address. The dot-coms ended up with huge stock valuations, even though most of them had never made a profit and some of them had never even sold a product!

Tech stocks at the time were concentrated in the NASDAQ Composite Stock Index because they were too small and new to be listed on the larger stock indexes. Figure 16.3 on the next page shows that from 1995 to 2000, the NASDAQ Composite index increased 400%, reaching a price/earnings ratio of 200, which is more than ten times the price/earnings ratio that is considered to be dangerously high.

This situation is what economists call an **asset bubble**, which occurs **when a particular asset, such as stocks or property, increases in price rapidly and irrationally in a relatively short period of time** (less than ten years). An asset value is irrational when its price is wildly out of line with traditional asset valuation measures, such as the price/earnings ratio for stocks.

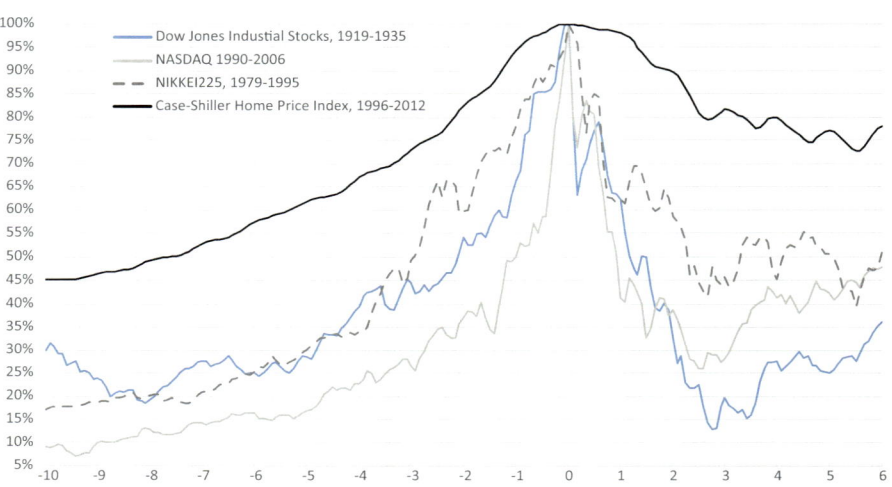

FIGURE 16.3 Asset bubbles (% of peak value).

In 2000, a series of events undermined confidence in the tech sector. The Fed increased interest rates, which raised the costs of borrowing. Japan entered a recession, spooking investors that a global recession was coming. U.S. judge T. P. Jackson ruled that Microsoft was engaged in monopolistic practices and should be broken up (a ruling later softened on appeal), which reduced confidence in the tech sector's big players. And investors and business publications began questioning the value of tech stocks.

As a result, the tech bubble burst. Over the next two years, tech stocks lost 75% of their value. As you can see in Figure 16.3, compared with other asset bubbles, the NASDAQ bubble had the steepest increase and steepest initial crash in modern history. This crash was more extreme than the stock market bubble and crash that preceded the Great Depression and the crash of the Japanese Nikkei stock index in 1989.

One might think that after one asset bubble, investors would not be so quick to jump into another one. Unfortunately, the dot-com bubble was followed by an even more devastating crash, this time in the housing market in 2007.

16.7 THE GREAT RECESSION OF 2007–2009: THE SUB-PRIME MORTGAGE BUBBLE

The story of the financial crisis and Great Recession begins in the ashes of the dot-com crash. With the recession of 2001, the Fed lowered interest rates significantly to 1% and kept interest rates there through 2004. This provided lots of inexpensive money for banks to loan out.

Meanwhile, housing prices were increasing rapidly, as shown in Figure 16.3 with the Case-Shiller Home Price Index. Cheap money and booming home prices meant that a lot of money could be earned in real estate speculation, so investors began to move money into real estate markets, pushing up home prices even faster. Meanwhile, homeowners saw booming house prices as evidence of newfound wealth, so many households borrowed heavily against their increased home values to buy goods. Unfortunately, the increase in household debt also meant a greater risk of default, as we will see later.

Banks, flush with cash and able to obtain more cash for almost no cost, began to look for new people to whom they could loan money. Once all of the creditworthy borrowers had taken out mortgages to purchase homes, banks and mortgage companies turned to high-risk borrowers: Real estate speculators and sub-prime borrowers. To entice borrowers, banks set up high-risk loans with a low two-year "teaser" rate around 4%, often with no down payment but with interest rates set to balloon to as much as 27% after two years.

Real estate speculators saw the rapidly rising housing prices as an opportunity to make a lot of money fast. They borrowed huge amounts of money from banks and bought houses in areas where home prices were increasing rapidly. The speculators assumed that home values would continue to rise, which would allow them to flip the house (resell it) within two years, before the high interest rates on their loans kicked in. The percentage of houses sold to speculators increased from 20% in 2000 to 35% in 2007.

Sub-prime borrowers are **people who are likely to have difficulty making loan payments on time and have a high risk of default**. Normally banks would be reluctant to loan money to sub-prime borrowers due to the high likelihood of default. However, two factors reduced their concerns. First, the historically steady increase in home prices, along with the recent boom in real estate markets, provided them with a false sense of security that home loans were not very risky. Historically, home loans have much lower rates of default than other loans, and with increasing house prices, banks could recoup their mortgage losses by foreclosing on and selling any homes where borrowers stopped paying.

With financial markets awash with cash and interest rates low, retirement funds and other institutional investors were looking for higher returns wherever they could find them. To satisfy this demand, banks began engaging in the process of **securitization** of mortgages, bundling mortgages together and selling them as particular kinds of derivatives called a collateralized mortgage obligations (CMOs) and collateralized debt obligations (CDOs).

A **collateralized mortgage obligation**, also called a mortgage-backed security, is **a derivative consisting of a bundle of many home mortgages, which is sold to investors who expect to get a return on their CMO purchase but who also assume the risk of default associated with the mortgages**. In essence, a CMO is a financial security that investors can purchase whose underlying value is derived from the expected mortgage interest and principal payments, subject to the risk of default. Individual CMOs packaged loans valued at over $100 million, and investors could buy into many different levels of each CMO. The highest level, or "tranche," had a lower expected return but the least default risk, and the lowest tranche had the highest expected return and the highest default risk. Most CMOs contained four or five different tranches, and they were sold primarily to institutional investors such as insurance companies and banks.

Figure 16.4 shows the explosion of CMOs from 2002 to 2007, where they went from $0 per year to $126 trillion! Subprime loans increased from 8% of mortgages in 2004 to 20% in 2006, and the ratio was much higher in places where home prices were rising fastest, which is also where real estate speculation was at its highest.

A **collateralized debt obligation** is **a derivative consisting of a bundle of various forms of debt instruments, such as mortgages, auto loans, student loans, credit card debt, and so on**. In the 2000s, CDOs often contained several CMOs along with other kinds of debt, making them extremely complex bundles of bundles of loans that were hard for investors to assess accurately. CMOs and CDOs are similar, because they are both **a security that is backed by a pool of debt**, so they are often lumped together under the label of **collateralized loan obligations (CLOs)**.

Because they knew CLOs could be risky, investment banks used another type of derivative called a credit default swap (CDS) to reduce their risk exposure. A **credit default swap** is **a derivative in which one investor pays to swap their credit risk on a CMO or CDO with another investor. The purchaser of a CDS pays a fee to the CDS issuer. In exchange, if the CMO or CDO defaults, the CDS issuer pays the purchaser of the CDS.**

CDSs were at the heart of the financial crisis. An investor could buy a risky CMO, but if they bought a CDS as insurance, they were taking on no significant risk themselves. This meant they had no financial incentive to care about how risky the CMO might be. Meanwhile, CDS issuers were happy to issue CDSs because they thought the risk of default on mortgages would continue to be low, as it had been historically. And most CLOs were given the highest possible ratings by the agencies that were supposed to accurately assess their risks.

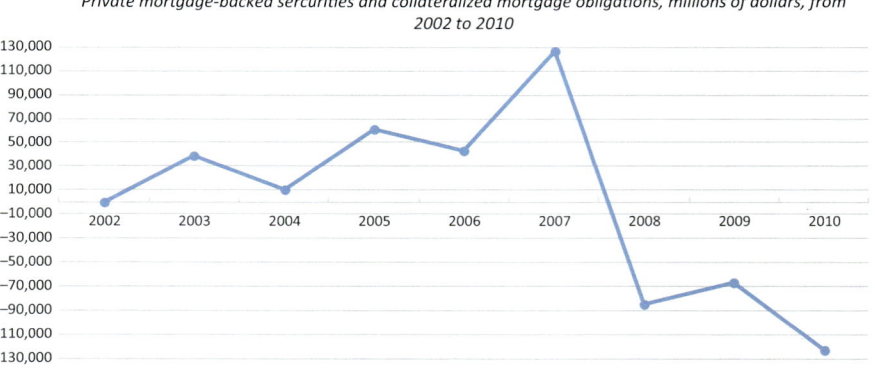

FIGURE 16.4 Flow of private MBSs and CMOs.

Here is where another incentive problem comes into play. Ratings agencies in the United States are private firms that are paid by large investment banks to rate securities in an objective fashion. Ratings can range from "D" to "AAA." However, ratings agencies make the bulk of their money by rating the most complex derivatives, and investment banks issuing the derivatives like to pick the ratings agency that issues the most favorable ratings. Therefore, ratings agencies have a direct financial incentive to give investment banks higher ratings on their derivatives than is warranted. Leading up to the financial crisis, this is exactly what happened. Ratings agencies like Moody's, Standard & Poor's, and Fitch gave sub-prime CMOs and CDOs AAA ratings, even though there was an extremely high likelihood of default. From 2004 to 2006, CMOs and CDOs looked like a sure thing to investors: They paid high interest rates and they came with the highest possible rating, which seemed to indicate that they were secure.

Now we can add another layer to the story, excessive leveraging, which is a problem in most financial crises. **Leveraging** refers to **the use of debt to purchase an asset, with the hope that the profit from the asset purchase will exceed the borrowing cost**. Buying an asset with borrowed money is doubly risky. There is a risk to the asset purchaser that the asset may not pay off. And there is a risk to the bank loaning money, because if the asset purchase does not pay off, the purchaser may default on the loan used to make the purchase.

Derivatives were not regulated by the Fed prior to 2010, and they had no reserve requirement. When a bank makes a "bet" by purchasing a CMO—betting that they will get a good return on their purchase—the CMO is an asset. Then the bank can go to another lender and say, "We need to borrow money for another investment; here is a CMO as collateral in case we default on the loan." Then they can use the money they borrow to buy another CMO, which is now another asset in their portfolio, which they can borrow against to by another CMO. Banks were making bets, funded by other bets, funded by still more bets. The analogy is a house of cards, because the bank has accumulated a mountain of debt but it has very little equity, and if it loses its equity, the bank will default on its loans.

The assets-to-equity ratio is a measure of how many assets a bank has relative to the amount of equity the owners have in the bank. In 2003, the huge investment banks Morgan Stanley, Lehman Brothers, Bear Stearns, Merrill Lynch, and Goldman Sachs had an asset/equity ratio of about 19 to 1. By 2007 the ratio had increased to over 32 to 1.

As if investment in high-risk CLOs was not enough, banks started engaging in highly unethical CDS speculation. As we saw above, CDSs started out as insurance in case the CLO defaulted. Now, however, Wall Street firms started purchasing CDS policies on CLOs that they did not own themselves. Goldman Sachs, Deutsche Bank, Morgan Stanley, and other big investment banks sold sub-prime mortgages packaged as CLOs to investors, and they purchased credit default swaps sold by a third party, often AIG insurance, to bet that the CLOs they sold were going to default. In essence, *in a classic example of* **moral hazard**, *investment banks* *sold CLOs they knew were likely to fail and then used CDSs to place bets that the CLOs would fail.*

Eventually, the house of cards started to collapse. U.S. home prices began to decline steeply in 2006 as the Fed increased interest rates to more than 5%, which undermined new home sales, and as the two-year "teaser" rates on sub-prime loans started to increase. Overbuilding also contributed. By 2008, home prices had fallen by more than 20%.

Mortgage default rates increased dramatically, as did foreclosure rates. Many speculators and homeowners simply walked away from their mortgages, because they owed more money on their house than it was now worth. The sub-prime market collapsed, so the trillions of dollars in CLOs based on those subprime mortgages lost almost all of their value. Investment banks that invested heavily in CLOs—and this was most of the big banks—began to collapse. Companies that sold credit default swaps taking the default risk from the CLOs were liable for huge payouts, and they also collapsed. Banks were so intertwined that when one failed, the other banks who had investments in the failing bank also were at risk of failure.

Banks were now so short of liquidity due to their huge losses that many stopped loaning out money. Lehman Brothers went bankrupt, and Merrill Lynch was on the verge of failure until it was purchased by Bank of America. Goldman Sachs and Morgan Stanley were forced to get emergency loans from the Fed. Ninety banks failed from late 2007 to mid-2009.

Consumers, seeing the value of their homes decline dramatically, cut back on consumption spending. The rest of the economy followed the housing and banking sectors into the crash. Stock prices decreased by 40% in 2008. The result was the worst recession since the Great Depression.

Putting all of this together, we can list the following factors as crucial drivers in the financial crisis:

- Deregulation of the banking sector that allowed federally insured banks to combine risky investment banking (derivatives) with mortgage banking.
- An abundance of cheap money searching for a higher return.
- Moral hazard, herding, and a lack of ethics, as mortgage companies increasingly pursued sub-prime and real estate speculation loans, only to convert these loans to CMOs and CDOs that they sold at inflated values.
- The rise of housing speculation and sub-prime lending driving a bubble in the housing market.
- Improper standards and incentives in the ratings industry, which benefited financially from giving high ratings to unsafe derivatives.
- Moral hazard, herding, and a lack of ethics driving investment banks to sell high-risk CLOs and then bet against them.
- Over-leveraging of investment banks, as they made bets on top of bets in risky markets.

The crisis was so dire that the government responded quickly and dramatically with a massive bailout of financial markets. The Fed pushed interest rates to near 0% and injected liquidity into the banking system, loaning trillions of dollars to banks that needed funds. They bailed out huge banks and insurers that were considered too big to fail. They purchased $700 billion in stock and toxic assets from troubled banks as part of the Troubled Asset Relief Program (TARP) of 2008. The government bailed out failing companies including General Motors and Chrysler, whose car sales had dried up. In one of the most controversial steps, the Fed engaged in quantitative easing over and beyond TARP, buying securities of all types in financial markets to prop up asset values and to stabilize the financial sector.

In terms of fiscal policy, the Obama administration spent almost $800 million on the American Recovery and Reinvestment Act (ARRA), which was passed in February 2009. This included a mix of tax cuts, extended unemployment benefits, and about $300 billion in direct spending on infrastructure and other job-creating activities. At the time, New Keynesian economists noted that this would not be enough to end a recession as deep as this one, and they were correct. The economy struggled with slow growth until 2015, when U.S. real GDP growth per capita finally exceeded 2%.

To address the problems with the banking system, the U.S. government passed the Dodd-Frank Wall Street Reform and Consumer Protection Act of 2010. This act imposed stricter regulation on banking and extended basic banking regulations to other parts of the financial sector, including derivatives markets. The Act empowered government regulators to identify threats to financial stability, such as when banks become too big and too dominant, and it established the Consumer Financial Protection Bureau to protect investors from fraudulent behavior in asset markets. To address the manipulations of Goldman-Sachs and other investment banks, the Dodd-Frank act instituted a basic regulation: Financial advisors must act in the client's interest and cannot recommend assets to clients that are known to be likely to fail without full disclosure of information. Writing in 2017, Federal Reserve Chair Janet Yellen observed that Dodd-Frank "substantially boosted resilience without unduly limiting credit availability or economic growth."

However, parts of Dodd-Frank caused investment banks much angst, especially the rule that they had to act in their client's interests, which they saw as too difficult to interpret and apply. This and other parts of Dodd-Frank were repealed by the Trump administration as part of its move to deregulate industries.

The dramatic fiscal and monetary stimulus enacted by the U.S. government was successful in forestalling another depression, and the new regulations stabilized the financial sector, but these efforts were not enough to stimulate a return to robust economic growth for several years. Interestingly, the large deficits the government ran from 2008 through 2019, ranging from $440 billion to $1410 billion, did not result in high interest rates or inflation. This gave government officials more confidence in running large deficits when the COVID-19 recession hit in 2020.

16.8 THE INVERTED YIELD CURVE AND THE COVID-19 RECESSION OF 2020

In addition to signs of a bubble, one of the other signs of an impending recession is an inverted yield curve. The **yield curve** is **the difference between interest rates on short-term bonds and interest rates on long-term bonds**. In general, long-term bonds pay a higher interest rate because you are tying your money up for a longer period of time and your money is subject to more inflation risk. If you purchase a ten-year bond paying 2% interest and the inflation rate surges to 5% before your bond matures, you will lose a lot of money in real terms. As a result, bond buyers usually need to be paid a premium to put their money into long-term bonds.

However, every so often the yield curve *inverts*, such that interest rates on short-term bonds are higher than interest rates on long-term bonds. The factors behind an inverted yield curve include the following: (1) Investors expect slow growth and low inflation, so they are willing to buy a bond promising a steady but low long-term return, and (2) investors expect the Fed to keep cutting short-term interest rates to stimulate the economy, so they wait to purchase short-term bonds and the return on short-term bonds falls as a result.

In essence, an inverted yield curve is a sign that large numbers of investors expect a recession and, as we have studied, when businesses expect a recession, this tends to cause behaviors that cause a recession. Furthermore, *every recession in the United States since 1955 was preceded by an inverted yield curve*. As Figure 16.5 shows, the United States experienced an inverted yield curve, with interest rates on ten-year treasury bonds lower than interest rates on two-year treasury bonds, just before the advent of recessions of 1990, 2000, and 2007. Interestingly, the yield

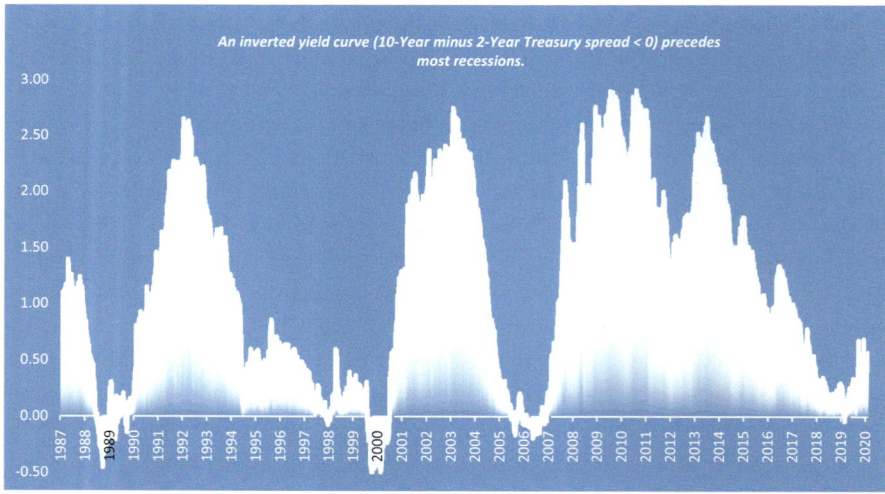

FIGURE 16.5 Ten-year minus two-year Treasury spread, 1987–2020.

curve also inverted briefly in 2019, leading many economists to predict a recession in 2020 even before the COVID-19 pandemic hit. The economy was clearly in a fragile state when the pandemic forced economies into lockdowns and caused a massive, sharp recession.

In the second quarter of 2020, the U.S. economy shrank by 9.5% (an annual rate of 32.9%) and the Eurozone economy shrank by 12.1%, the steepest declines since the creation of modern economic statistics in the 1950s. This was a product first and foremost of the shutdown to control the pandemic, as governments forced businesses to close and workers to stay home to contain the novel coronavirus that causes the deadly COVID-19 disease.

The shutdown also led to declines in consumer spending, especially on travel, entertainment, and restaurant purchases, and declines in business investment as expected sales plummeted. There were also disruptions in supply chains, as manufacturers had trouble getting parts from places hard hit by the virus and as global trade slowed.

The United States, the European Union, and most other developed countries engaged in massive fiscal and monetary stimulus to combat the recession (see the chapters on fiscal and monetary policy for details). In the United States, tax cuts, bailouts, and quantitative easing were extremely effective in returning the stock market to its previous levels. The stock market dropped more than 30% from February 20 to March 23, 2020, but it recovered all the ground it lost by August 19, 2020, thanks to the trillions of dollars injected into financial markets.

However, unemployment rates remained extremely high for most of 2020. More important, the fractured U.S. public health system and the ineffective response of the Trump administration meant that the rate of infections soared in the United States well after most other developed countries contained it. As U.S. colleges attempted to reopen in the fall of 2020, one college after another had to close their campuses and move to remote instruction due to virus outbreaks. Meanwhile, European universities where the virus was more contained were able to stay open thanks to extensive testing, quarantine, and contact-tracing infrastructure managed by the national government.

By mid-2022, it was apparent that the largest stimulus in U.S. history had been successful in quickening the end of the COVID-19 recession. The unemployment rate dropped from 15% in April 2020 to 3.6% in May 2022. However, additional waves of infections continued to pose a threat and to disrupt global supply chains of goods.

16.9 CONCLUSION

Recessions are difficult to predict with precision, but patterns do emerge that help us anticipate when recessions are likely to occur. John Maynard Keynes focused on the cyclical patterns in business investment purchases. After a recession and a period of slow economic growth, new technologies, products, and markets emerge that offer the promise of above-normal profits, enticing businesses to expand into new areas. The increase in business investment purchases creates jobs and raises incomes, sparking expansions in consumer spending and starting a boom. After several years of a booming economy, the promising investment opportunities have all been taken and consumers have purchased the houses and cars they need, so a decline in investment and consumption tends to occur. The economy becomes fragile and is nudged into a recessionary spiral by an event that causes businesses and consumers to lose confidence and dramatically curtail spending.

Political economists broaden Keynesian analysis to include additional factors that can cause the profit rate to fall during a boom. Underconsumption can lead to a glut of goods and declining profits. A wage squeeze can occur as workers demand higher wages during a boom. It can become increasingly difficult for businesses to squeeze profit out of ever-larger amounts of capital. Higher domestic prices cause higher nominal wages, a factor that undermines profits. Declining productivity from increasing bureaucratization can raise costs and lower productivity. And the increasing dominance of the financial sector can extract revenues out of other sectors, reducing profit rates of non-financial corporations.

Laissez-faire economists attribute recessions to exogenous shocks or market misunderstandings. Monetarist theories of the business cycle credit monetary factors with driving fluctuations in real GDP. Real business cycle theory attributes recessions to productivity shocks caused by changes in technology and the legal and regulatory environment. Market misunderstanding theory attributes the cause of a recession to misperceptions by workers or other economic actors. And political business cycle theory notes that business cycles can result from policies of politicians to improve their re-election chances.

When we examine the last three recessions, we see the importance of asset bubbles in driving the boom–bust cycle. In the 1990s, tech stocks increased in value by 400%, even though tech companies where not very profitable. In the 2000s, home prices increased by more than 100% and sub-prime mortgages increased dramatically, even though many of the people buying homes had poor credit and were unlikely to be able to pay off their mortgages. In both cases, the asset markets crashed once investors realized their folly. When asset markets crashed, this spooked investors and consumers, caused bank failures, and resulted in a full-fledged recession.

In addition to the home price bubble, the financial crisis of 2007–2008 was driven by the creation of opaque derivatives called collateralized loan obligations that disguised the amount of risk they contained, especially when they were given AAA ratings by self-interested ratings agencies. Frustration with financial shenanigans led to the passage of the Dodd-Frank Act in 2010, which imposed stricter financial market regulations to prevent such events from reoccurring. However, much of Dodd-Frank was repealed during the Trump administration's push to deregulate markets.

The COVID-19 recession marked a different type of downturn, driven by a public health crisis and the necessity to close businesses and to require people to work from home to contain the pandemic. Record-breaking stimulus efforts caused financial markets to rebound. Unemployment proved much more difficult to address as numerous businesses shuttered in the difficult conditions, taking more than a year to recover. Countries with robust public health systems fared much better than those without, demonstrating the importance of systematic health care in protecting a country's citizens and economy in a globalized world where viruses spread rapidly.

Interestingly, the forces driving recessions seem to be shifting in the modern United States. Asset bubbles, trade flows and relative prices, and global disease transmission now loom large. The clear policy response to minimize these destructive forces would be greater regulation of financial markets, stabilization of trade flows and wages for workers, and investment in public health systems. However, vested interests make such public policy decisions difficult.

QUESTIONS FOR REVIEW

1. Explain the Keynesian idea that the patterns in business investment purchases drive the business cycle.
2. According to political economists, what are the major factors that can reduce the profit rate and lead to a recession? Explain each one briefly.
3. Using Figure 16.2 on page 400, explain why a supply shock presents a difficult conundrum for policymakers, forcing them to choose between fighting inflation and fighting unemployment. How are supply-side policies designed to resolve this conundrum?
4. Explain the key ideas in Minsky's financial instability hypothesis in your own words. In your answer, describe each phase of the business cycle carefully.
5. Describe the different laissez-faire theories of the business cycle. What are the main differences between laissez-faire approaches to recessions and those of new Keynesian and political economists?
6. What is an asset bubble? How does this concept help us understand the recessions of 2000–2001 and 2007–2009?
7. What is a CLO (collateralized loan obligation)? What is a CDS (credit default swap)? Explain briefly in your own words. How did these derivatives feature in the financial crisis of 2007–2008?
8. What are the essential features of the financial crisis of 2007–2008? Who was primarily to blame? How did economic theory promoting deregulation contribute to the financial crisis? Given the major causes of the financial crisis,

how do you think the government should approach regulating financial markets in the modern era?
9. What is an inverted yield curve? Why do many economists see this as a precursor to a recession?

NOTES

1 John T. Harvey, "Why do Recessions Happen? A Practical Guide to the Business Cycle," *Forbes*, April 18, 2011. https://www.forbes.com/sites/johntharvey/2011/04/18/why-do-recessions-happen-a-practical-guide-to-the-business-cycle/#762aa0407100

2 Marx used the term the "organic composition of capital" to refer to the ratio of labor expenditure to capital investment purchases. As businesses invest more and more in capital, they will experience a decline in the profit rate if the productivity increases from the new capital are not greater than the increase in costs from the capital purchase.

3 Erdogan Bakir, "Capital Accumulation, Profitability, and Crisis: Neoliberalism in the United States," *Review of Radical Political Economics* 47, no. 3 (2015): 389–411.

4 The author would like to thank Janet Knoedler and Erdogan Bakir for their feedback on this section. Any errors are, of course, my own.

5 L. Randall Wray, *Why Minsky Matters* (Princeton, NJ: Princeton University Press, 2016), 15.

6 Ibid.

7 Higher interest rates mean that firms have to borrow even more money to keep financing their risky investments and the return from the investments has to been even higher in order to stave off losses.

PART VI

Growth and global interconnectedness

The modern global economy features a wide variety of economic systems, some of which are growing quickly and some of which are growing slowly or not at all. China and South Korea, two of the economies that grew most rapidly in recent decades, used a state-led approach to innovation and growth, with the government directing resources into strategically important areas. Other rapidly growing economies, such as India and Ireland, used a more market-based approach. However, state-led and market-focused economies elsewhere are not experiencing the same level of economic growth as these successful economies.

Chapter 17 explores theories and policies related to the sources of economic growth. Economic growth is one of the most complex and least understood topics in economics. If there were a simple formula for economies to implement in order to achieve rapid economic growth and the prosperity that accompanies it, all countries would adhere to this formula. In actuality, there are many different methods for achieving rapid economic growth. Some successful approaches to growth are largely state directed, whereas others take a more laissez-faire, market-oriented approach. This chapter lays out the approaches to economic growth taken by economists from the New Keynesian, laissez-faire, and political economy perspectives. The chapter then discusses the growth approaches and experiences of real-world economies in the modern era and whether or not economic growth can be achieved in a sustainable way to preserve the environment.

Chapter 18 takes up another set of issues related to economic growth—international trade and protectionism. Laissez-faire economists advocate unregulated (free) trade based on the theory of comparative advantage, which posits that unregulated trade increases productivity and efficiency and results in a higher standard of living (and rate of growth) for people in countries that pursue unregulated trade. New Keynesian economists prefer trade with modest regulation. Political economists believe that trade should be managed carefully and that key industries should be protected in order to stimulate domestic economic development. The debate over whether or not to pursue unregulated or regulated trade is an ongoing and important one in economics, underlying debates over trade agreements and economic integration (such as the European Union). Trade also has a major impact on macroeconomic flows of money and resources. In addition, trade can be a major driver of economic growth for globally competitive, export-oriented economies, or it can result in deindustrialization and stagnation.

Chapter 19 on international finance and financial flows begins with economic theories regarding the market for foreign exchange. We examine how the supply and demand for foreign exchange affect exchange rates. Exchange rates in turn affect the prices of domestic and foreign goods, so exchange rates play an important role in determining which industries are successful in a particular country. Countries can choose fixed or flexible exchange rate systems, which can cause very different outcomes. Next, we turn to a discussion of the balance of payments, trade deficits, and trade surpluses. Trade deficits are an important and controversial topic in U.S. economics and politics. Financial flows, which are a product of trade flows and other factors, can be managed by the government or allowed to flow freely. This is related to the issue of exchange rate instability, a significant problem of developing countries that can result in currency crises. The chapter concludes with a discussion of fiscal and monetary policy in an open economy.

The book ends with Chapter 20 on economic development, a topic that economists have wrestled with since Adam Smith attempted to ascertain the nature and causes of the wealth of nations in 1776. In the last 50 years, some countries, such as South Korea, Botswana, and China, have succeeded in escaping desperate poverty, building a better life for a majority of their populations. However, many other countries in the developing world remain mired in poverty, with little sign of progress. This chapter reviews the development experiences of a variety of low-income and middle-income countries in recent decades. We also take up the different theories that economists utilize to analyze economic development.

17 The sources of economic growth

Economic growth is one of the most important goals for an economic system. Governments across the world prioritize economic growth because if it occurs, the standard of living of a country's population improves. In general, people with a higher material standard of living are happier and healthier.

Despite the prioritization of growth, it can be quite difficult to achieve sustained economic growth over a long period of time. The drivers of economic growth are complex and not well understood. As evidence of this, despite the fact that almost all countries pursue strategies to stimulate economic growth, the growth rates of countries vary widely. In the last two decades, China, India, and Vietnam experienced per capita gross domestic product (GDP) growth rates of more than 5% per year, whereas Japan, the European Union (E.U.), and the United States experienced annual per capita GDP growth of about 1%. If there were a clear set of policies to stimulate rapid economic growth, then all countries would be able to achieve it simply by adopting those policies, but clearly that is not the case.

The reality is that there are many different ways to achieve sustained economic growth, from the state-directed approach of China and South Korea to the more laissez-faire approach of India and Ireland. Furthermore, governments that try to emulate the policies of countries that are growing rapidly are often unsuccessful despite adopting similar approaches.

There are also complexities surrounding the relationship between growth and sustainability. Historically, economic growth has been associated with environmental destruction. However, with the potentially devastating consequences of climate change, a key question emerges: How can economies continue to grow while also preserving the environment? Some countries, such as Germany, are incorporating sustainability into their approach to economic growth with great success. Growth in Germany has been accompanied by improvements in their environmental record in recent decades. Other countries, such as China, have adopted a

DOI: 10.4324/9780429399350-23

very resource-intensive approach to generating growth, which means that Chinese growth has come at the expense of the environment.

The complexities of economic growth are reflected in the wide varieties of views on the topic seen in the economics profession. This chapter features both mainstream and alternative views regarding the major forces that drive economic growth. Mainstream, New Keynesian theories tend to stress the growth of factors of production (capital and labor), technological progress, and certain key institutions (property rights, rule of law, stability). Supply-side economists focus on private sector incentives, preferring to minimize government intervention and maximize private sector flexibility. Political economists highlight the role of a wider range of institutions on growth, especially the role of government as a facilitator and engine of growth, the importance of aggregate demand and the profit rate, and the need for labor market arrangements that foster equality, productivity, and innovation.

The chapter begins by discussing the importance of economic growth in determining the standard of living of people within an economic system, along with some of the variations in growth experiences around the world. We then turn to the mainstream, New Keynesian model of economic growth, which focuses on the role of capital goods, improvements in technology, and human capital as key drivers of growth. Utilizing these ideas, mainstream economists advocate policies to increase savings and investment, stimulate innovation, and improve education and training. In contrast, supply-side (laissez-faire) economists take a different approach to growth, arguing that deregulation along with tax cuts for the wealthy, corporations, and workers will be most effective in stimulating growth. Next, we turn to the ideas of political economists, who see the effectiveness of the state as the main driver of growth along with the overall macroeconomic environment.

The chapter concludes by discussing growth and sustainability, as economists try to determine how modern economic systems can continue to grow without creating excessive environmental devastation. Effective policies that stimulate the development of green technologies and industries while phasing out dirty ones could allow modern economies to grow sustainably. Establishing such a system is one of the major issues of our times.

17.0 CHAPTER 17 LEARNING GOALS

After reading this chapter you should be able to:

- Explain how exponential growth affects the standard of living of various countries.

- Describe, compare, and evaluate the New Keynesian, supply-side, and political economy models of economic growth and the policies each group advocates to stimulate growth.

- Discuss the various perspectives on growth and sustainability and determine what you think would be the best approach to resolve the seeming contradictions between growth and environmental preservation.

We begin by taking up the importance of economic growth in determining a nation's standard of living, along with some of growth experiences of countries around the globe.

17.1 THE IMPORTANCE OF ECONOMIC GROWTH

To classical economists such as Adam Smith and Karl Marx, economic growth and the distribution of income were the most important topics of study. Economic growth determined a country's standard of living, which was seen as the major determinant of well-being, and the distribution of income determined whether or not most of the population was benefiting from economic growth. Growth still occupies an important place in modern economics and remains the top economic priority for most countries.

Growth is an exponential process, which means that its impact grows larger and larger with time. In a typical year in the United States, real per capita GDP grows by about 2%, so output is 102% as large as output the previous year. This is a result of an increase in the number of businesses, productivity from business investment in additional capital goods, better technology that increases productivity even further, an increase in the quantity of laborers, and better skills and knowledge that increase labor productivity. Next year, even more businesses will form, more capital goods will be purchased, new technologies will be invented, and new skills and knowledge will be created, increasing real per capita GDP by another 2%. In essence, *machines, factories, and businesses can create additional machines, factories, and businesses*. Now real per capita GDP is 2% higher than 102%, or 104.04% of the amount two years ago. The following year, real per capita GDP will be 106.12% of the original level. Then 108.24%. Then 110.4%. And so on. Notice that because growth builds on growth exponentially, real GDP per capita goes up slightly faster than the 2% rate of growth.

Due to the fact that growth is an exponential process, over time, small differences in growth lead to large differences in a country's standard of living, as measured by per capita GDP. A simple way to observe these differences is with the **rule of 70**, **a mathematical formula that estimates how many years it takes for a variable growing at an exponential rate to double**.

$$\text{Number of years for a variable to double}\,(t) = \frac{70}{\text{Annual \% growth rate of the variable}\,(g)}.$$

To give an example of the impact of different rates of economic growth, from 1960 to 2018, the average annual rate of growth in U.S. per capita GDP was 2%: $t = 70/2 = 35$. This meant that U.S. income doubled every 35 years. However, since 2000, annual growth in U.S. per capita GDP has been closer to 1%, which means it will take 70 years for our income to double if this lower growth rate persists. From 1980 to 2018, China experienced an annual rate of growth in per capita GDP of 8.5%, which meant that incomes in China doubled every 8.2 years $\left(t = 70/8.5 = 8.2\right)$! As a result, a Chinese worker earning $1000 in 1980 would see their income double five times in 41 years to reach $32,000 in 2021.

We can solve for the increase in the worker's income as follows. The worker's income starts at $1000, doubles once to $2000, doubles a second time to $4000, doubles a third time to $8000, doubles a fourth time to $16,000, and doubles a fifth time to $32,000. Mathematically, we can use the following formula:

$$\text{New income} = \left(\text{Original income}\right) \times 2^{(\text{number of doublings})}.$$

In this example, the new income is $1000 \times 2^5 = \$32,000$. Thus, the rate of growth determines how quickly incomes increase.

Rapid economic growth has transformed poor countries into rich countries. Poor economic growth has constrained citizens in other countries to poverty for the long term. Figure 17.1 shows the large countries that have grown the most quickly in recent decades, with China, South Korea, Vietnam, and India leading the way. Most developed countries are clustered in the middle, close to the world average, with Ireland and Norway above average and Italy and Switzerland below average. Toward the bottom is Nigeria, with growth averaging only 0.54%, Iran experiencing no growth, and Saudi Arabia experiencing negative growth with the decline in oil prices, its major export, in recent years.

According to the **convergence hypothesis** put forth by Clark Kerr and some other mainstream economists, **the productivity growth rates (and growth in per capita real GDP) of poor countries should tend to be higher than for rich countries, because poor countries can imitate and learn from the experiences of rich countries**. If this occurs, then all economies should eventually converge to the same level of per capita income. However, Figure 17.1 shows us a much more uneven pattern. China, South Korea, Vietnam, and other countries with the most rapid economic growth rates are converging with rich countries. However, Brazil, Kenya, Mexico, and Nigeria, among others, are actually falling further and further behind. Thus, one of the major trends in recent decades has been the amazing success of some developing countries while most developing countries are still mired in poverty. In the next section, we explore some of the reasons for these widely disparate growth experiences and the theories economists developed to explain economic growth patterns.

THE SOURCES OF ECONOMIC GROWTH 425

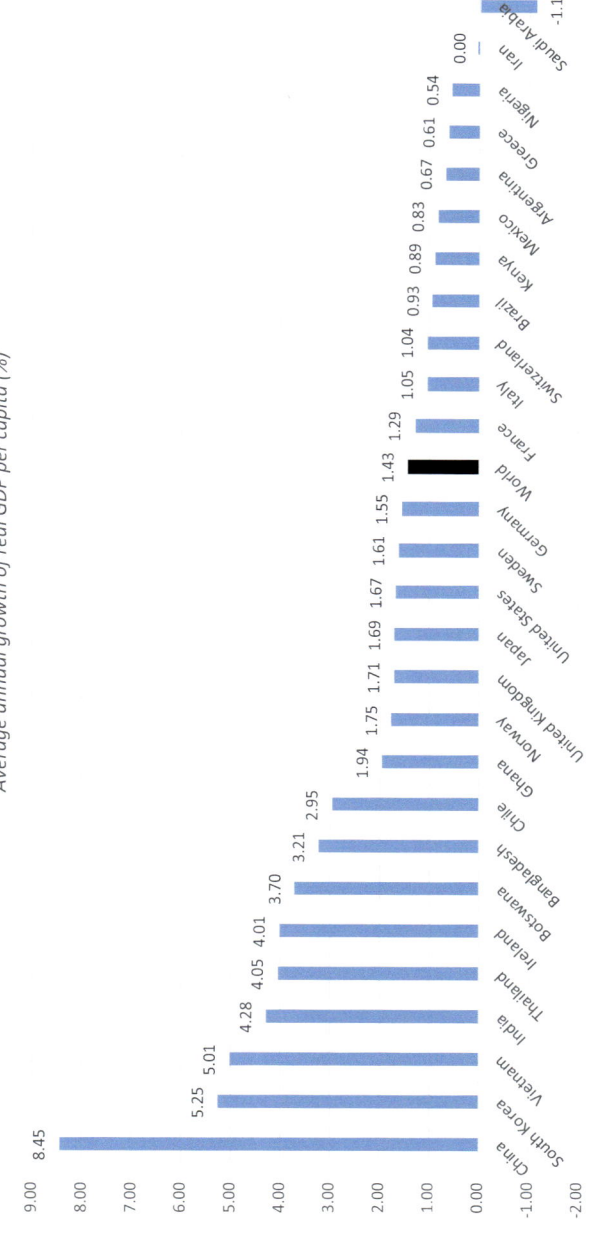

FIGURE 17.1 Average annual growth of real GDP per capita, 1980–2019.

17.2 THE MAINSTREAM, NEW KEYNESIAN APPROACH TO ECONOMIC GROWTH

To mainstream New Keynesian economists, **economic growth** is **the long-term, sustained increase in the economy's capacity (potential real GDP)**. Sustained economic growth from the mainstream perspective is driven by improvements in labor productivity—when each laborer can produce a greater quantity of goods and services.

The **three sources of improvements in labor productivity**, which are the primary drivers of economic growth from this perspective, are (1) **increases in physical capital goods**, (2) **improvements in technology** (the quality of capital goods), and (3) **the quality of laborers** (often referred to as human capital). Mainstream economists estimate that improvements in technology have the greatest impact on economic growth.

The mainstream model of economic growth can be expressed by the following equations:

$$Y = AF(K, L) \tag{1}$$

$$\frac{\Delta Y}{Y} = \frac{\Delta A}{A} + \alpha_K \frac{\Delta K}{K} + \alpha_L \frac{\Delta L}{L} \tag{2}$$

In these equations, Y is real GDP and ΔY is the change in real GDP, so $\Delta Y/Y$ is the growth rate in real GDP. A is total factor productivity, which is a measure of technology, and ΔA is the change in total factor productivity, so $\Delta A/A$ is the contribution of technology to economic growth. K is the country's existing physical capital stock, and ΔK is the change in the country's capital stock (business investment purchases of plants and equipment). α_K is capital's share of total income, which is usually 30% (0.30) in the United States. Therefore, $\alpha_K \frac{\Delta K}{K}$ represents capital's contribution to economic growth. L is the size and quality (human capital) of the country's labor force, and ΔL is the change in the size and quality of the labor force. α_L is labor's share of total income, which is usually 70% (0.70) in the United States. Thus, $\alpha_L \frac{\Delta L}{L}$ is labor's contribution to economic growth. Therefore, equation (1) tells us that real GDP depends on technology and the stocks of capital and labor. Equation (2) tells us that growth in real GDP is a function of changes in (a) technology, (b) the capital stock, and (c) the quality and quantity of labor. These factors and their contribution to productivity and economic growth are explored below, starting with what happens when there is an increase in the capital stock.

17.2.1 Increase in the capital stock

Mainstream economists use a production function (the total product of labor) to show the relationship between labor and output. Figure 17.2 shows the total product

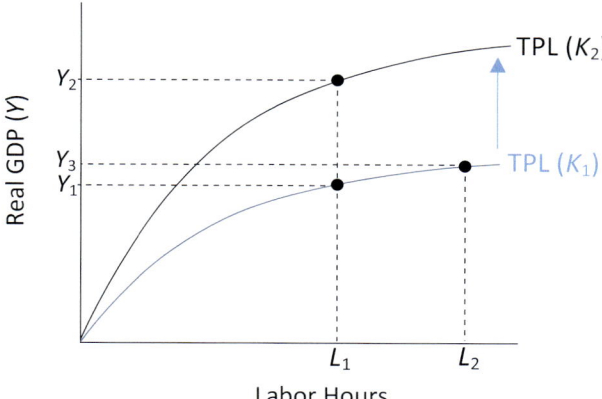

FIGURE 17.2 Change in a country's production function from an increase in capital $(K_2 > K_1)$.

of labor curve for two different levels of capital goods, a smaller level K_1 and a larger level K_2. With a given amount of labor, L_1, the amount of output varies directly with the amount and quality of capital goods. With a smaller amount of capital, K_1, the economy produces an output (real GDP) of Y_1. When economic actors invest in additional capital goods, such that $K_2 > K_1$, output increases from Y_1 to Y_2.

There is a direct, positive relationship between the amount of capital goods and the productivity of laborers. If workers have more capital or better capital to work with, they are more productive during each hour they work, and therefore output will increase for each amount of labor hours. Or, to be more precise, *for a given level of technology and number of labor hours, labor productivity tends to increase as the capital stock increases.* As a classic example, a lumberjack with a chainsaw can cut down eight times as many trees in the same amount of time as a lumberjack with an axe—an 800% increase in productivity per labor hour.

An increase in the quantity of labor hours from L_1 to L_2 (holding capital constant), perhaps from an increase in immigration or an increase in the working-age population, would move the economy along the production function, causing real GDP to increase from Y_1 to Y_3. Note that productivity per labor hour does not increase, but total production of goods and services does increase because there are more laborers performing more work. This analysis assumes that there are additional jobs for the new laborers to do.

17.2.2 Improvements in technology

Mainstream economists estimate that as much as 60% to 80% of economic growth is a result of technological change. The impact of an improvement in technology is similar to the impact of an increase in the capital stock: *With better technology, workers can produce more output per hour of labor.* This would shift the production function in Figure 17.2 up in the same way that an increase in the capital stock would.

17.2.3 Improvements in the quality of labor (human capital)

One of the key drivers of productivity is the level of education and training of laborers. This is sometimes called "human capital" to capture the idea that the value of human labor increases with the amount of education and training they receive. Economic research indicates that improvements in human capital are more important than increases in physical capital in increasing growth. German manufacturing firms, which produce many of the highest value manufactured goods in the world (everything from BMW, Mercedes, Audi, and VW cars to Kuka industrial robots to Sennheiser and Bosch electronics), invest between $25,000 and $200,000 in training for each worker in addition to the education and training provided by the government. They see this training as essential in the production of the highest quality goods. An improvement in human capital would also shift the production function in Figure 17.2 up in the same manner as an increase in the capital stock or an improvement in technology. After an increase in human capital, production of goods and services would be higher for each labor hour worked.

17.3 NEW KEYNESIAN POLICIES TO STIMULATE ECONOMIC GROWTH

Given the mainstream, New Keynesian view that economic growth is driven by improvements in labor productivity and increases in labor productivity are driven by improvements in the capital stock, technology, or human capital, New Keynesian policies to encourage economic growth focus on these three areas. The most important policies from this perspective are (1) policies to stimulate savings and investment, including a stable political system with secure property rights; (2) policies to stimulate technology development; and (3) efforts to improve education and training.

17.3.1 Policies to increase the capital stock by stimulating savings and investment

Investment purchases of physical capital result in a larger capital stock, which increases productivity and economic growth. Recall that physical capital includes **plants** (factories, office buildings, other physical structures) and **equipment** (computers, software, robots, internet infrastructure, and so on). Policies that stimulate investment in plants and equipment tend to increase economic growth. However, sparking increases in investment purchases of physical capital goods is extremely difficult given the unpredictability of investment. As John Maynard Keynes pointed out, investment is extremely risky and uncertain, so it requires just the right conditions.

We can utilize the major determinants of investment from previous chapters to come up with policies that might stimulate additional amounts of business investment purchases. First, the largest determinant of business investment is expectations of future sales. Therefore, **policies that lead to sustained growth in the demand** for businesses' products will stimulate investment, because businesses will have confidence that their investment will see a return. Possible policy options include **stabilization policies** in recessions to stimulate growth and **policies to increase wages and incomes**, especially of workers who spend most of their incomes. In the United States in the 1950s and 1960s, government support of unions and U.S. manufacturing dominance created a virtuous circle, where higher wages sparked an increase in consumer purchases that caused businesses to increase investment in the size of their operations, which then caused additional job creation and even higher wages.

More controversial, a country might **protect domestic markets** from foreign competition to give domestic companies a larger market share. However, such policies may not be successful if trading partners respond with similar protective efforts, as is often the case.

Policies to **reduce real interest rates** can also lead to increases in investment purchases if the macroeconomic conditions are right. If businesses have good investment opportunities and if interest rates are low, the conditions for an increase in investment are good. But as we know from decades of research, when economic prospects are poor, lowering interest rates tends to have little or no impact on investment purchases.

Investment tax credits or other **tax policies that increase the profitability of investing** may increase investment. These can include investment tax credits, subsidies for key inputs such as imported technology to reduce the costs of investing, and subsidized loans. Some economists advocate policies to increase savings so banks have more money to loan out. However, as we know from Keynes, more savings means less consumption spending, which can erode aggregate demand and the investment climate. Thus, economists tend to disagree on whether or not prioritizing savings is a good idea.

Many economists also advocate **making an economy open to foreign direct investment (FDI)** in order to stimulate investment purchases in the domestic economy. In theory, foreign direct investment, which is purchases of domestic companies and capital goods by foreign companies and investors, can increase a country's capital stock directly. Even though FDI capital is controlled by foreign owners, it will increase productivity and jobs in the domestic economy. New Keynesian economists tend to encourage developing economies with low savings rates to try to attract foreign direct investment as a means to improve economic growth. For example, a study by Bellak et al. indicated that lowering taxes, improving labor productivity, providing infrastructure, increasing research and development funding, and lowering labor costs tend to increase foreign direct investment.[1] China is credited with attracting substantial FDI via all of these policies. Note, however, that China insisted that all foreign investors have a local partner and utilize the latest technology, which guaranteed that Chinese firms would gain the latest technical knowledge and experience in order to become globally competitive. Other countries that do not have China's clout are often at the mercy of foreign investors, which can lead to a "sweatshop model" of foreign direct investment based on low wages and exploitative working conditions. The sweatshop model is not generally associated with significant, long-term growth because it does not stimulate domestic aggregate demand, local knowledge, or local technology in a significant way, and the country owning the sweatshops reaps the lion's share of the benefits.

Another crucial variable is the **stability of the political climate**. Investment is highly risky, so it thrives in an environment that fosters stability. Political stability is very important. Countries where regular coup attempts happen or where elections are frequently disputed experience instability, which tends to reduce investment. Countries that have a stable government with a cohesive set of laws and rules that are applied systematically and fairly provide a stable basis for firms to invest. New Keynesian economists also emphasize the role of stable **property rights** in fostering investment. Businesses that are secure that they will be able to reap the benefits from their investments, and not have them stolen, will tend to invest more. Corrupt governments where insiders regularly seize private businesses, such as Russia in the 2000s, have the effect of stifling investment.

17.3.2 Policies to stimulate technological innovation

Improvements in technology allow firms to get more output from the same amount of labor or to keep output the same while employing fewer laborers. Either way, technological development can improve the profit rate for businesses. However, technological development is uncertain. A firm can invest huge sums on new technology only to have it flounder. For example, the Google+ social media platform intended as an alternative to Facebook or Samsung's fragile Galaxy Fold folding smart phone both involved substantial investments in new technologies that did not pay off. Or a new technology can lead to huge profits if successful—for example, Google's internet search engine or Apple's iPhone.

One of the major roles for governments is to structure a nation's economy in such a way that technological development is encouraged. Given that New Keynesian economists credit technology with the primary role in driving economic growth, innovation policy should be one of the most important priorities for a government striving to stimulate growth.

One of the most direct and effective ways to promote innovation is to increase funding for **research and development (R&D)**, which involves **activities designed to result in scientific breakthroughs, the design and introduction of new products, or improve existing products or manufacturing processes**. Government funding for scientific research at universities and government research labs, often called "basic" science, can lead to transformational breakthroughs. For example, the internet was created by university researchers with funding from the U.S. military. In general, due to the uncertainty and long time frame involved in scientific breakthroughs, corporations rarely devote significant amounts to such endeavors. This is why government funding is so crucial and why governments are the primary source of funding for the basic scientific research that results in major innovations.

However, the private sector is good at using scientific breakthroughs to design and introduce new products or new manufacturing techniques. Corporations turned the internet, originally designed for sharing information between researchers, into a vehicle for ecommerce, social media, coordinating supply chains, and much more. The government can encourage private sector spending on research and development by offering tax breaks to reduce the cost of spending on private sector R&D. But there is no substitute for government funding for scientific research at universities and government research centers, which generates regular scientific breakthroughs that spill over into the private sector, creating new products, industries, and jobs in the process. As another example, *every* new drug developed and approved in the United States from 2010 to 2016 was based at least in part on research from the National Institutes of Health. This research involved more than $100 billion in funding, more than 90% of which was considered "basic" scientific research.[2]

Due to the importance of R&D and a skilled workforce, **increasing access to higher education and improving its quality**, especially in technology-related fields in science, technology, and engineering, can be a good way to foster technological innovation. One of the reasons the United States is the leader in many tech industries is its impressive university system, generally seen as the best in the world.

Given the importance of innovation for economic growth, researchers have tried to identify the best ways to stimulate innovation. Authors of the Global Innovation Index, constructed by researchers at Cornell University, INSEAD,[3] and the United Nations, determined that the following elements have a direct impact on innovation: Political stability, government effectiveness, regulatory quality, rule of law, ease of starting or closing a business, education, research and development, information and communication technologies, infrastructure, ecological sustainability, market sophistication, number of knowledge workers, innovation linkages (between universities, governments, and businesses), knowledge absorption and creation, and creative outputs.[4] Based on these measures, the top ten countries in the Global Innovation Index rankings for 2020 are displayed in Figure 17.3 (next page).

Switzerland leads the way (as it has for the last ten years) with an economic system that features extremely skilled, well-trained, and knowledgeable workers; high research and development expenditures; advanced universities that collaborate effectively with industries; science and technology clusters; efficient, noncorrupt government; strong sustainability; and an infrastructure that may be the world's most efficient. Sweden, ranked second for many years, features a similar set of

Global Innovation Index Rankings for 2020		
Rank	Economy	Score
1	Switzerland	66.1
2	Sweden	62.5
3	United States	60.6
4	United Kingdom	59.8
5	Netherlands	58.8
6	Denmark	57.5
7	Finland	57.0
8	Singapore	56.6
9	Germany	56.5
10	South Korea	56.1

FIGURE 17.3 Table showing the Global Innovation Index rankings, 2020.

characteristics, along with some of the most sophisticated government–university–industry partnerships in existence, as we discuss below. Interestingly, the United States, ranking third, has some similarities, especially its top quality universities, science and technology clusters, and innovative private sector. The United States has some unique strengths, such as its entrepreneurial climate, creative sector, and incentives for revolutionary innovation, but it also has some notable weaknesses, including uneven government quality and poor performance with respect to sustainability.

It often surprises people that an emphasis on sustainability is a contributor to innovation. However, the world is increasingly demanding sustainable products. Those companies that can produce sustainably have a huge advantage in the modern marketplace, making sustainability a key ingredient in successful innovation.

People often do not expect a vibrant creative sector, including art, literature, music, cinema, and theater, to be an essential contributor to innovation. Creative thinking is where new ideas come from, which directly fosters innovation, so countries featuring strong creativity tend to be very innovative. This is why U.S. employers regularly rank creativity as one of the top abilities they are looking for in job applicants.

Interestingly, only one of the countries atop the Global Innovation Index, South Korea at number ten, ranks in the top ten for per capita economic growth (shown in Figure 17.1 on page 425). Thus, there is much more to economic growth than fostering innovation, as we will discuss below.

17.3.3 Policies to improve education quality and access, training, and skills

In addition to its contributions to innovation, human capital is crucial to economic growth in other ways. More educated and better trained workers are more productive and earn higher incomes, which stimulates aggregate demand at the same time as it improves the functioning of firms. Economists estimate that education is more important than investment in stimulating economic growth.

Figure 17.4 shows educational spending as a percentage of GDP in various OECD countries. Norway spends the most, at 6.6% of GDP, and Ireland spends the least, at 3.4% of GDP. Notice that the Anglo-Saxon economies—the United Kingdom and its former colonies such as the United States, Ireland, and Australia—spend less on public education and more on private education than other countries.

The Nordic countries, whose educational systems are rated the most effective in terms of student learning and overall access, feature high levels of public spending and very little private spending. This is largely because they have decided that quality education is a human right and that the economy benefits from everyone receiving a first-rate education. Even poor children in these economic systems get a quality education and a (free) college education.

The United States usually ranks below the OECD average in math, science, and reading skills, primarily due to the extreme inequality of the U.S. educational system. In the United States, where property taxes tend to determine how much money each school district has, rich towns have excellent schools and poor towns have poor schools.

Education in only one component of human capital. Training and skill development are another key component. Note that although Germany spends

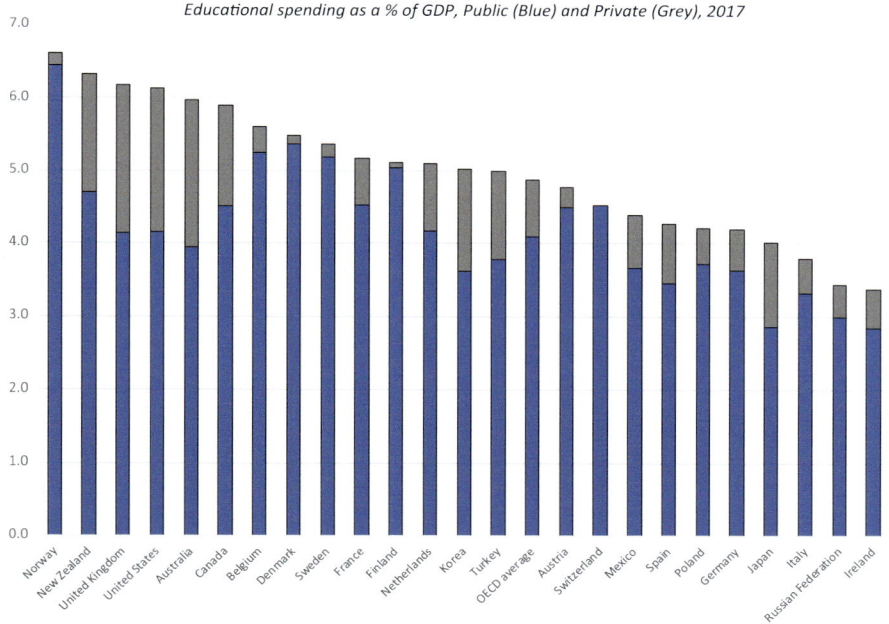

FIGURE 17.4 Educational spending as a percentage of GDP, various countries.

a below-average amount on education, they spend an above-average amount on training and skills, which is a major reason their manufacturing firms are so productive and their manufactured goods of such high quality. U.S. spending on worker training is among the lowest of developed countries, whereas the social market economies of Europe spend the most.

Now that we have examined the mainstream approach to economic growth, we need to consider other perspectives. First, we discuss the laissez-faire, supply-side approach to economic growth. Then, we take up the political economy approach.

17.4 THE SUPPLY-SIDE (LAISSEZ-FAIRE) APPROACH TO ECONOMIC GROWTH

As we saw earlier, supply-side economists prefer a laissez-faire approach to the economy. Government interventions from this perspective are confined primarily to assisting corporations (suppliers) and the wealthy (investors), so that they create jobs and wealth that trickle down to average people.

More specifically, supply-side economists have the following theories regarding growth:

1. Economic growth is determined primarily by aggregate supply rather than aggregate demand (supply creates demand according to supply-side theories), so the conditions impacting firms are paramount.
2. As with mainstream economists, supply-siders believe that the major drivers of growth are increases in investment purchases (capital), technological change, and increases in the number and productivity of laborers. However, they believe that different factors drive changes in these variables.
3. Incentives for saving and investment are the primary determinants of economic growth. The major factors affecting savings and investment are policies that determine their after-tax returns. According to the supply-side approach, tax cuts for the wealthy, reductions in capital gains taxes, and tax cuts for businesses are the preferred policies to increase savings and investment and thereby stimulate growth.
4. Labor supply can be increased via tax policy as well by reducing the marginal tax rates that workers pay. In theory, this gives workers an incentive to work more, increasing labor supply and, in turn, promoting productivity and growth.
5. Deregulation of businesses can facilitate investment and growth and should be pursued vigorously.

President Trump used these ideas to argue that his 2017 tax cuts for U.S. corporations and the wealthy would provide "rocket fuel" for the economy, generating jobs and growth in the process. However, a comprehensive 2020 study by David

Hope and Julian Limberg of Kings College London examined 18 advanced countries over 50 years and found that major tax cuts for the rich increase inequality but have no significant effect on economic growth or unemployment.[5] Their research compared countries that passed laws for major tax cuts in a given year with those that did not. The impact of tax cuts over the next five years included permanent increases in inequality but no increase in growth or employment relative to countries that did not implement tax cuts for the rich.

There is some evidence that tax cuts for laborers can increase labor supply slightly, especially for adults who are the second earner in a family. However, the impacts on labor supply are very small, and there is no measurable increase in economic growth as a result.

Although the latest economic research has not been kind to supply-side theories, these ideas continue to be important in the United States and some countries where conservative politicians still subscribe to these views. In other countries such as the social democracies of Europe, political economy theories have held much more influence. We turn to these ideas next.

17.5 THE POLITICAL ECONOMY APPROACH TO ECONOMIC GROWTH

Political economists agree with much of the mainstream, New Keynesian approach to economic growth, but they have a few disagreements. In particular, they argue that a much broader set of factors determine the rate of economic growth and that the government is the most important determinant of the growth rate, followed by aggregate demand.

First, political economists see the **government, its quality, and the economic system it establishes with its policies** as the most important factors in determining the level of innovation and growth. In Maria Mazzucato's book *The Entrepreneurial State*, she points out that governments do much more than support basic scientific research. In addition to basic science, governments fund areas along the entire innovation chain, including applied research, early stage financing for high-risk endeavors, infrastructure support, education and training support, and much more. As one example from the United States, Apple received money from the Small Business Investment Corporation and then developed the smart phone based on technologies that were almost all developed through government funding and projects, including the internet, GPS, touchscreens, and voice activation.

Some governments partner directly with the private sector in collaborative projects designed to stimulate innovation and job creation. Perhaps the most sophisticated example of this is the **triple helix approach to innovation** utilized by Sweden and the other Nordic countries, in which **government, universities, and industry interact as partners to generate ideas, invent and spread technologies, and develop industries and communities**. Governments establish the partnerships, fund the research, and build the infrastructure for the developing industry. Universities conduct the scientific research that leads to breakthroughs and train workers and managers in the best techniques for the new product or industry. And the private sector designs and introduces new products and processes based on the scientific breakthroughs, utilizing the infrastructure, training, and new ideas. This approach is credited with stimulating the biotechnology industry and the information and communications technology industry in Sweden, which is now among the leaders in these sectors in the E.U. Twenty percent of new private sector products in Sweden can be tied directly to research partnerships with universities, and the impact of the triple helix model is felt more broadly in the development of technology clusters featuring universities, multiple firms, workers, and government support tailored to a particular industry.

Interestingly, countries that have grown the most rapidly over the last 50 years have all used what economists call a **developmental state**, where **the government undertakes macroeconomic planning and policies to stimulate industrial development in strategic sectors**. Japan, China, and South Korea have been particularly effective with this approach. China has some unique advantages as the world's largest country with a vast potential market, which made it easier for China to attract foreign investment and technology under favorable conditions. Therefore, South Korea's economic performance as the country with the second most rapid growth of per capita GDP may be more impressive.

The South Korean developmental state featured the following key characteristics:

- **Land reform**. South Korea seized vast estates from absentee Japanese landowners and redistributed the land to independent family proprietors, firmly establishing property rights, incentives for productivity, and a strong agricultural base from which to grow.
- **Industrial policy and planning**. The South Korean government identified industries in which the country could succeed, spent money on R&D to identify the best technologies for those industries, subsidized local conglomerates to enter those industries, and invested massively in infrastructure (postal service, telecom, rails, air, and ports), education, and training to give those industries a competitive advantage.
- **Protectionism and monitorable performance standards**. Using the infant industry approach, South Korea protected the new industries from foreign competition with tariffs until they could be internationally competitive. The government also subsidized key inputs to keep their costs low. However, firms receiving protection were required to increase domestic investment and employment, R&D spending, and exports. The strong export orientation forced firms to become internationally competitive quickly or be faced with the withdrawal of government support. Once firms were competitive, subsidies could be reduced or eliminated, and funding could shift to new areas.

- **Sequential industrialization**. South Korea began by producing simple manufactured goods that fit with their existing skills and resources, including grain production, energy, and textiles. As their manufacturing experience, skills, and technology improved, they shifted to steel, electronics, and machinery and then to cars and shipbuilding. More recently, they dramatically increased R&D spending, developed an advanced technology sector, and increased efforts to spur creative thinking and creative industries to fuel new ideas and innovations.

The results were impressive. In 1960, South Korea was one of the poorest countries in the world. By 2020, South Korea was a wealthy country, with a higher GDP per capita the most E.U. countries. South Korea's per capita rate of economic growth has averaged 5.25% for the last four decades, and its products are admired around the world, including Hyundai and Kia cars, Samsung and LG phones, TVs and appliances, and K-Pop.

Thus, from a political economy perspective, the effectiveness of government, including planning and execution of economic development programs, is paramount in driving economic growth. The impact of government on innovation and growth is based on far more than support for basic science and the establishment of stable property rights.

Second, political economists stress the **importance of aggregate demand** to investment and growth. Without the expectation of future sales and profits, businesses will not invest in new capital or spend on R&D to develop new technology. Future sales depend on having sufficient aggregate demand. Aggregate demand depends most significantly on the income and willingness to spend of the population as a whole. This is one of the reasons why infant industry protection can stimulate investment and growth—it ensures that a new industry will have a protected market with sufficient demand for its products. The key is to make sure the protection eventually is removed or reduced, as South Korea did, so that firms become internationally competitive rather than serving as a perpetual drain on the economy.

From the political economy perspective, economic growth can be driven by higher wages, in direct contradiction to the supply-side argument. Higher wages increase aggregate demand, causing businesses to increase production. Businesses produce at a higher rate of capacity when demand is high and may even start to run out of excess capacity if the surge in demand is large enough. The combination of **higher profits** from increased sales and running out of production capacity (**higher capacity utilization**) stimulates new investment and growth. This helps us to understand why the most rapid and sustained period of economic growth in the United States in the last century was during the 1950s and 1960s, when U.S. real wages also increased rapidly.

Correspondingly, one of the reasons for the slowing of growth in the United States and in other developed countries in recent decades is the significant increase in **inequality** and its impact on aggregate demand. Because rich people spend a smaller percentage of their income than the middle class and the poor, the redistribution of income from the poorest 80% to the richest 1% results in a decline in aggregate demand, which undermines expected sales and profits for most businesses.

Some economies try to circumvent insufficient domestic demand by orienting their economies toward exports. This is true of Germany, China, South Korea, and Japan, all of which established policies to promote exports. Export-oriented policies include low-cost government loans, subsidies, protection from foreign competition as new industries are being established (infant industry protection), and policies to keep labor costs low.

The degree of inequality is also important in determining whether the benefits of economic growth are broadly shared. Economic growth that is only experienced by the richest portion of a country's population, as has been the case in the United States in recent decades, does not improve the lives of most of the population. This defeats the primary purpose of economic growth, which is to improve the lives of a country's residents.

The third major determinant of investment and growth from a political economy perspective is the **profit rate**. Businesses cannot invest unless they have a sufficient rate of profit over and above their costs of production. But they also need a reason to invest their profits, instead of just sitting on them. In 2019, Apple kept more than $200 billion in cash because they did not have good opportunities for investment that would have a good expected return. Apple also did not face stiff enough competition that they felt compelled to put that money toward R&D. Thus, investment requires a sufficient profit rate along with enough competition, demand, and stability to encourage firms to invest. In general, a country can expect a high level of investment if it is able to establish a stable or increasing level of aggregate demand, sufficiently competitive markets, and a macroeconomic environment in which corporations can earn adequate profits.

This highlights the extent to which **incentives for firms** to invest are a key determinant of the rate of investment. After the supply-side Trump tax cuts in 2017, most firms used their windfall for stock buybacks, which increased the value of their stock but had no impact on the amount of investment in capital goods. As noted above, there was no uptick in economic growth as a result of the tax cuts. On the other hand, South Korea's insistence that corporations use tax breaks or subsidies for investment in R&D activities meant that government funds were channeled directly into productive corporate activities.

Another interesting focus in political economic analysis is on **the use of society's surplus** and whether the surplus is invested productively in capital goods or spent wastefully on consumer goods. Under feudalism, most of the surplus generated by society was spent on churches, castles, riches for nobles, and other consumption goods rather than on capital goods that could have increased productivity and growth. The result was a stagnant society.

We still see this distinction today. In many dictatorships, government officials use the country's surplus to fund luxurious living for themselves rather than investing in new productive capacity or human capital. Turkey's president Recep Tayyip Erdogan built himself a presidential palace with 1150 rooms and opulent furnishings at a cost of more than $1 billion. Imagine how many productive businesses could have been funded and how many educations paid for had that money been spent on productive activities.

In contrast, economic systems that promote investment in physical and human capital tend to experience more rapid economic growth. The governments of China and South Korea channel society's surplus funds directly to investments that will enhance economic growth. In the United States, tax cuts for corporations and the wealthy in 2017 did not stimulate investment because there was no requirement that the funds be used in a particular way.

Another key factor in political economy is the importance of incentives in the workplace to give workers reasons to be productive. Worker productivity is directly tied to the intensity with which workers apply themselves during work, which is driven by **labor market incentives**. In coercive, exploitative systems—the "stick approach"—workers are more likely to have a hostile attitude toward their employer and to shirk work whenever possible. In more cooperative systems where workers are involved in decision making and rewarded for their productivity—the "carrot approach"—workers tend to enjoy their work and to enthusiastically embrace efforts to increase productivity.

Germany, Japan, and South Korea are famous for their labor productivity, which is tied to worker involvement in key decisions about how work is done, incentives for workers to come up with ideas to improve the efficiency of their work, and relatively cooperative labor–management relations that foster shared interests and identity. Unions often play a positive role in establishing these types of employment relations in particular industries. Germany led the world in labor productivity in 2017 due to their combination of worker incentives and training, along with their cutting-edge technology.

Related factors that affect worker productivity include health care, childcare, and other forms of family support. Better medical coverage makes workers healthier and more productive. Free or subsidized childcare makes it easier for people to work and makes it less likely that they will need to miss work. Generous family leave programs encourage parents, and especially women, to stay in the workforce after they start a family, increasing the country's labor force participation rate and its productivity over the long term.

Taken together, the political economy approach to growth focuses much more on the role of the state and the overall environment affecting innovation and investment. Furthermore, political economists emphasize the importance of aggregate demand and the profit rate in determining investment and growth. As a result, political economists support much more extensive government intervention to increase the rate of growth, whereas laissez-faire, supply-side economists support less government intervention and New Keynesian economists pursue a middle path. Another area in which political economists see the need for extensive government intervention surrounds the topic of growth and sustainability.

17.6 GROWTH AND SUSTAINABILITY

Increasing alarm at environmental devastation and climate change in recent decades has resulted in a new emphasis on sustainable growth in the modern world. As we know, without adjustments in how we structure our economic systems, it is likely that we will not be able to continue to experience the same amount of economic growth that we have in the past.

Until very recently, economists tended to emphasize economic growth above all other economic goals. One of the reasons environmental issues were ignored was due to an idea called the environmental Kuznets curve, which theorized that **as countries grow and became wealthier, they can afford to pay more attention to the environment, developing technologies, regulations, and clean production methods that reduce their environmental impact**. According to this theory, **environmental destruction should increase during the first step of industrialization, then level off, and then decline as a country's standard of living increases**.

Figure 17.5 shows an environmental Kuznets curve for the United States, plotting tons of carbon dioxide emissions per capita against real GDP per capita. We can see the inverted U shape that the environmental Kuznets theory predicts, but

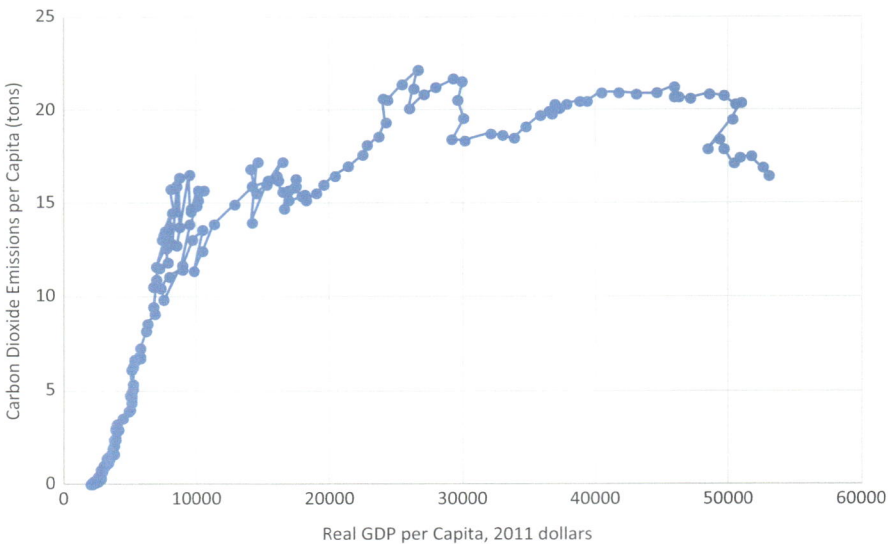

FIGURE 17.5 The U.S. environmental Kuznets curve for CO_2, 1800–2016.

the drop in CO_2 emissions has not been dramatic considering how wealthy the United States has become. If other countries follow the same pattern, then we will not get rich enough fast enough to stave off disastrous climate change.

Figure 17.6 on the next page plots carbon dioxide emissions in tons per capita and real GDP per capita for every country in the world in 2019. Instead of an inverted U shape, we see a general upward trend, indicating that as countries get wealthier, they emit more CO_2. It appears that the environmental Kuznets curve does not accurately explain the connection between growth and environmental destruction.

Instead, we see the influence of sustainability policies on a country's environmental impact. Countries well below the trend line, such as Norway, Singapore, Sweden, Switzerland, and Costa Rica, actively pursue sustainability via government policies. They are able to achieve a much smaller impact on the environment at the same income level as other countries.

Countries above the trend line pay little attention to the environmental impact of their economies. Examples include Kuwait, Saudi Arabia, the United States, Russia, and South Africa. These countries all rely heavily on fossil fuels, including the dirtiest ones, such as coal and oil, and do little to promote renewable energy use and carbon sequestration. Given that global efforts to date have not been very effective in reducing environmental destruction, there could be devastating consequences in the near future that will impact economic growth.

Climate change and other forms of environmental degradation are eroding the productive capacity of numerous industries. Therefore, countries that prioritize unsustainable growth now will pay the price of devastating economic declines in the future. In *Limits to Growth*, systems analysts Meadows, Randers, and Meadows observe that "an exponentially growing economy depletes resources, emits wastes, and diverts land from the production of renewable resources."[6] Eventually, sometime later this century, the exhaustion of nonrenewable resources like oil and the reductions in food and renewable resource production from ocean acidification, climate change, soil loss, and pollution will lead to reductions in productivity, declines in real GDP per capita, decreases in human well-being, and possibly even mass starvation. Only immediate and dramatic efforts to establish a sustainable economic system can prevent this eventuality according to their forecasts, which have proven disturbingly accurate to date.

Given the fact that growth to date has been associated with greater environmental destruction, some economists, such as Nicholas Georgescu-Roegen and E.F. Schumacher, advocate zero growth or even **degrowth**. Unless people reduce their consumption of products, resources, and energy, and without a reframing of society's orientation away from unlimited economic growth, these economists see little hope for the planet. Schumacher, in his famous book *Small Is Beautiful*, argues that material wealth is hollow and unfulfilling and we can actually achieve greater happiness and well-being by focusing on meaningful work, deep human relationships, and living in harmony with nature, while reducing our consumption of material goods and our ecological footprint.

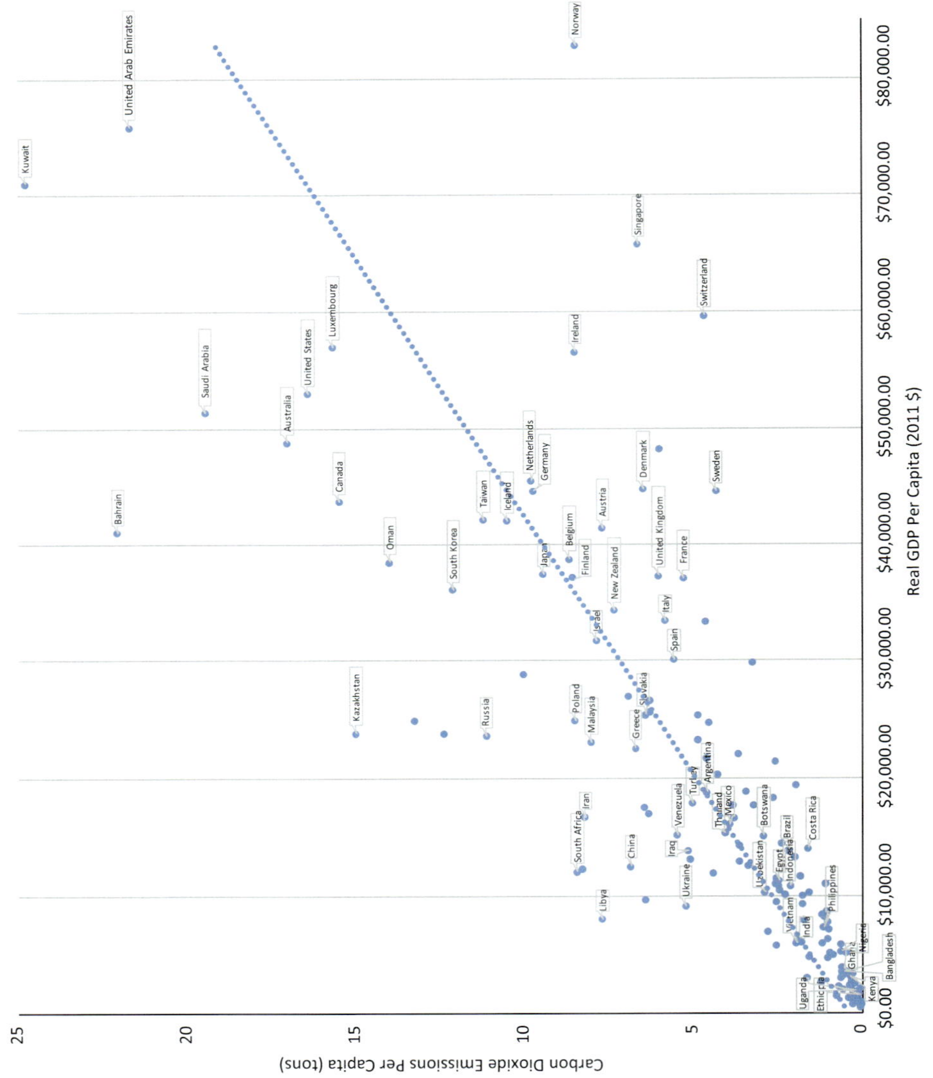

FIGURE 17.6 Real GDP per capita and CO_2 emissions per capita, 2019.

As an alternative to degrowth, most political economists push for **sustainable growth**. As noted earlier, evidence indicates that most environmental regulations do not reduce economic growth and, if done effectively, environmental policy can actually increase growth. In order to increase economic growth, environmental regulations need to be structured to promote investment in new technologies, which can then lead to lower costs and the development of new products. Germany's investments in green technology and Costa Rica's investments in eco-tourism and geo-thermal energy have fueled economic growth. This is the reason why many political economists believe that governments should enact targeted policies that improve sustainability and promote growth at the same time.

17.7 POLICIES TO PROMOTE SUSTAINABLE GROWTH

Most people desire a higher standard of living, but we also need to preserve our environment if we want to be able to maintain our standard of living in the future. Therefore, a key question for modern economic systems is to identify the best policies to generate sustainable growth. Some of the best ideas are described below.

Incentivize pollution reductions via taxes or tradable emissions permits. One of the best ways to move away from pollution-generating activities is to tax them or make them costly. The vast majority of economists support a carbon tax to impose a cost on any activity that generates carbon dioxide, which is the main driver of global climate change. Or governments can establish markets for pollution rights via tradable emissions permits, which similarly incentivizes economic actors to pollute less. (See chapter 20 in Schneider, *Microeconomic Principles and Problems*, for more details.) Also, governments should reduce subsidies for environmentally destructive activities, such as U.S. subsidies for oil exploration. So far, countries that have implemented these programs have not experienced declines in economic growth and have experienced some of the largest reductions in pollution.

Similarly, industrial agriculture contributes significantly to climate change and should be discouraged, whereas regenerative grazing and sustainable agriculture, which sequester carbon and generate healthier food, should be subsidized. Suburbanization and production that results in deforestation must be curtailed, and tree planting and measures to preserve valuable natural areas such as the Amazon rain forest must be established. Fossil fuel–based cars and airplanes need to be phased out and replaced with public transportation and electric vehicles that utilize sustainably generated electricity. Recycling and composting can be required to disincentivize and reduce waste.

Incentivize or directly engage in investment in sustainable practices and alternatives. The key to sustainable growth is the development of new technologies that reduce pollution and resource use while improving productivity. Governments can conduct extensive research and development on such initiatives and subsidize research at universities and business research labs. Governments can also establish industrial clusters with the appropriate infrastructure, education, and private sector partners to develop new processes and products utilizing the green technologies they develop.

The right set of policies could lead to a complete reorientation of an economic system from unsustainable growth to sustainable growth. Indeed, this is the whole premise of the "Green New Deal" proposed in various countries, which seeks to create jobs in new, sustainable industries at a faster rate than jobs in dirty industries are destroyed. Unfortunately, even though evidence indicates that these policies are likely to work, they are opposed vigorously by the vested interests that would be harmed by this change toward environmental preservation. Fossil fuel producers, dirty industries, and producers of goods that harm ecological sustainability all oppose the Green New Deal, and their political clout makes such changes difficult to implement. It will be interesting to see whether the groundswell of support for sustainable practices is strong enough to overcome the inertia created by the opposition of unsustainable industries toward sustainable growth.

17.8 CONCLUSION

We began this chapter by discussing how economic growth is a major determinant of the standard of living of people within a country. Some countries such as China, South Korea, and Vietnam are growing quickly using a state-led approach. Other countries, including India and Ireland, have been successful in recent decades with a more market-oriented approach. Using the rule of 70, we can determine that these rapidly growing countries are seeing a doubling in their GDP per capita every 8 to 17 years. But other countries utilizing state-led approaches (such as Brazil) and market-led approaches (such as Mexico and Kenya) have been much less successful. Therefore, a country's broad approach to generating growth is not enough to explain divergences in growth rates.

To attempt to explain growth patterns, the New Keynesian model of economic growth focuses on the role of capital goods, improvements in technology, and human capital. New Keynesian economists advocate policies to increase savings and investment, stimulate private sector innovation, and improve education and training to stimulate growth.

Supply-side economists believe that public sector intervention reduces growth and prefer deregulation of the economic system as well as tax cuts for the wealthy and corporations—a trickle-down approach. In contrast, political economists argue that the effectiveness of the state is the main contributor to economic growth. In addition, political economists view the overall macroeconomic environment, and especially the maintenance of adequate aggregate demand to spur investment, as crucial.

Lastly, we discussed how economic systems need to adjust their approach to engineer more environmentally sustainable growth. Countries need to implement policies that encourage R&D activities and investment in green technologies and sustainable industries to replace dirty ones. This could result in growth that is not as environmentally destructive as has historically been the case. With the looming problems associated with climate change and other environmental choke points, creating economies that feature sustainable growth is an urgent priority.

QUESTIONS FOR REVIEW

1. Vietnam's real GDP per capita has been growing by 5% per year, while Switzerland's has been growing at 1% per year. Using the *rule of 70* and assuming that these growth rates stay the same, if Vietnam's real GDP per capita is currently $3000 and Switzerland's real GDP per capita is $90,000, what will each country's real GDP per capita be in 70 years? What will each country's real GDP per capita be 140 years?
2. Explain the convergence hypothesis in your own words. Does evidence indicate that the convergence hypothesis accurately explains growth patterns?
3. Using the graph in Figure 17.7, show what will happen to the U.S. economy if (a) there is a major breakthrough in robotics that improves productivity and (b) the number of workers in the United States declines significantly due to immigration restrictions.

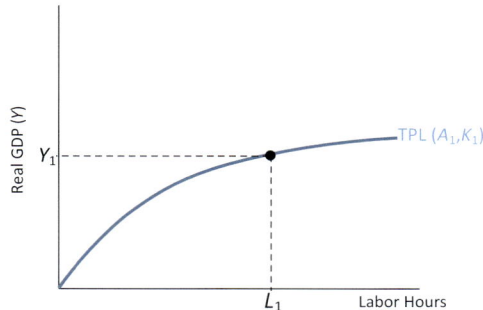

FIGURE 17.7 Production function for the United States.

4. According to the New Keynesian approach, what are the major factors that contribute to economic growth? What policies do New Keynesian economists advocate in order to stimulate growth? Which of these policies do you find most compelling? Why?
5. What are the key elements of the supply-side approach to economic growth?

6. What are the key elements of the political economy approach to economic growth?
7. Compare and contrast the approaches to innovation and growth taken by (a) New Keynesian economists, (b) supply-side economists, and (c) political economists. Which approach do you find most compelling? Explain and support your answer.
8. Explain the environmental Kuznets curve. Does the evidence support this theory? Why or why not?
9. Suppose that you are appointed the chair of the U.S. president's council of economic advisors, and you are asked to suggest a set of policies to promote economic growth while preserving sustainability. What policies would you prioritize and why?

NOTES

1 C. Bellak, M. Leibrecht, and R. Stehrer, "Policies to Attract Foreign Direct Investment: An Industry-Level Analysis," OECD Global Forum on International Investment VII, 2008, https://www.oecd.org/investment/globalforum/40301081.pdf

2 See E.G. Cleary, J.M. Beierlein, N.S. Khanuja, et al., "Contribution of NIH Funding to New Drug Approvals 2010–2016," *Proceedings of the National Academic of Sciences (PNAS)*, 155, no. 10 (2018): 2329–2334, https://www.pnas.org/content/115/10/2329.

3 INSEAD is the Institut Européen d'Administration des Affaires.

4 See Global Innovation Index, "Global Innovation Index 2020," https://www.globalinnovationindex.org/, accessed August 7, 2021.

5 See David Hope and Julian Limberg, "Footing the COVID-19 Bill: The Economic Case for Tax Hike on Wealth," *The Conversation*, https://theconversation.com/footing-the-covid-19-bill-economic-case-for-tax-hike-on-wealthy-151945, accessed August 7, 2021.

6 Donella Meadows, Jorgen Randers, and Dennis Meadows, *Limits to Growth: The 30-Year Update* (White River Junction, VT: Chelsea Green Publishing, 2012), 147.

International trade and integration

How unregulated trade, protectionism, and trade agreements affect economies

The global integration of economic systems completely restructured modern economies over the last 50 years. Economies went from being relatively isolated in the first half of the 20th century to extremely integrated by the 2020s. The impact of global integration was complex, with some people and some countries benefiting significantly while others lost ground.

Globalization, and the international trade that drives it, dramatically reshaped many countries and communities. Developed countries saw their manufacturing industries and blue-collar wages decline, while their tech and service sectors boomed. Global manufacturing shifted to China, South Korea, India, Taiwan, and other newly industrialized economies, although some developed countries like Germany and Japan were able to maintain their high-end manufacturing. Some developing countries caught up with the wealthy nations of the world, but others fell further behind and became increasingly marginalized.

During the globalization era, the United States pursued unregulated ("free") trade policies for the most part. This approach changed somewhat under the Trump administration. In early 2021 it was not yet clear whether President Biden would reverse Trump's protectionism or return to the unregulated trade approach that dominated from 1980 to 2017.

Most other developed countries opened up their markets to trade and foreign investment somewhat but continued to pursue neo-mercantilist trade policies intended to give advantages to key domestic industries. Europe became much more integrated internally with the creation of the European Union (E.U.), at the same time that they maintained protections against countries elsewhere. The United States integrated to a lesser degree with the Mexican and Canadian economies under the North American Free Trade Agreement (NAFTA). As a result, by the 2020s, the global trading system was a hodgepodge of trading blocs and trade agreements with a wide variety of provisions.

DOI: 10.4324/9780429399350-24

At its heart, the debate over trade policy and globalization is a debate about economic theory. The arguments for unregulated trade are based on the theory of comparative advantage, developed two centuries ago by economist David Ricardo. According to this theory, trade makes everyone better off, increasing global efficiency and raising average standards of living. One of the key questions confronting modern policymakers is whether or not this theory still applies. Most mainstream, New Keynesian economists believe that it does. For example, Gregory Mankiw stated, "*Economists* view the United States as an ongoing experiment that confirms the benefits of free trade."[1] However, Mankiw glosses over the many problems that trade has created in communities in the United States, as evidenced by the widespread opposition to free trade policies in large swaths of the country.

Unlike mainstream economists, political economists find unregulated trade to be problematic on many levels. Although Mankiw and most mainstream economists prefer unregulated ("free") trade, some liberal mainstream economists and most political economists argue that protecting specific industries with tariffs can be useful in fostering economic growth, especially in the case of new, "infant" industries. Tariffs and other forms of protection can have a dramatic effect on the fortunes of particular industries. A sound set of policies to manage trade can lead to more robust economic development and better outcomes for most people, according to the political economy view.

This chapter begins by discussing why countries trade. We then outline the theory of comparative advantage, which underlies the reasoning for mainstream economists' support of unregulated trade. We go on to discuss the limitations of this theory as it applies to the modern world. Subsequently, the chapter takes up issues of protectionism and tariff and non-tariff barriers that countries use to protect particular industries. The chapter then turns to current trade patterns, political economy approaches to trade, and economic integration via international trade agreements such as NAFTA and the European economic union.

18.0 CHAPTER 18 LEARNING GOALS

After reading this chapter, you should be able to:

- Explain the theory of comparative advantage in words and using a graph.

- Use production possibilities curves to determine comparative advantage and to construct consumption possibilities curves.

- List and analyze the assumptions behind the comparative advantage model.

- Explain the arguments for and against protectionism.

- Describe U.S. trade patterns and analyze political economy theories that attempt to explain these trade patterns.

- Evaluate the costs and benefits of economic integration via trade agreements versus a managed trade approach.

We begin with the cornerstone belief of economists who advocate unregulated trade, the theory of comparative advantage.

18.1 TRADE AND THE THEORY OF COMPARATIVE ADVANTAGE

Human beings have traded goods and services for thousands of years. There is sometimes a social goal in such exchanges. Trading goods with another community or country can build ties and relationships, which can reduce the likelihood of conflict.

But the primary reason for trade is for people in one geographical location (the importer) to obtain goods that are unavailable to them from another geographical area that has the desired goods (the exporter). For trade to occur, it must be mutually beneficial: Both parties must be willing to make the exchange. Thus, in theory, trade makes both parties better off. The exporter benefits financially from selling more goods, and the importer benefits from obtaining goods that they could not have obtained without trade.

Economists often go even further in extolling the virtues of unregulated trade. If every country specializes in the production of the goods that it can produce best (highest quality for the lowest cost) and then exports those products to the rest of the world, while importing the products that it is least effective at producing, the entire world will see a higher standard of living. In theory, with unregulated trade, goods will be produced and exported from locations where it is most efficient to do so. However, as we will see later, this rosy depiction of unregulated trade does not capture many of the modern realities.

Economists developed the theory of comparative advantage to explain the benefits of specialization and trade in more detail. The basic principle of the theory of **comparative advantage** is that **a country should produce and specialize in those goods that it can produce for a lower opportunity cost than its trading partners**. In other words, a country should produce what it is *relatively* best at producing.

For example, suppose that the United States can produce both computers and textiles more efficiently than Mexico but, due to a lack of technology and skilled labor, computers have a much higher *opportunity cost* in Mexico. This means that

Mexico would have to give up the production of a huge proportion of its other goods in order to be able to produce small amounts of computers.

Meanwhile, textiles have a very low opportunity cost in Mexico. Despite the fact that textile production is less efficient in Mexico than it is in the United States, the plentiful supply of inexpensive labor means that Mexico can produce textiles for a very low opportunity cost. Increasing the production of textiles will result in very little loss in the production of other goods.

In the United States, producing textiles has a very high opportunity cost—it takes away resources that could be used in the production of other high-value goods, such as computers. So it is **relatively** cheaper to produce textiles in terms of computers in Mexico. In other words, the resources used to produce textiles in Mexico are more abundant and relatively less expensive than in the United States.

In theory, the United States benefits from trade with Mexico because, by **specializing** in the production of computers and exporting them to Mexico in exchange for textiles, the United States can gain more computers and textiles than it could possibly produce by itself. Mexican consumers are willing to give up a lot of textiles for each computer because they are so expensive (they have a high opportunity cost) in Mexico before trade occurs.

18.1.1 A graphical illustration of comparative advantage

To illustrate the theory of comparative advantage, economists use production possibilities curves and consumption possibilities curves. Recall that **a production possibilities curve (PPC) shows all combinations of two goods that a country can produce given its existing resources and technology**. For simplicity, we will assume that resources are not specialized, so opportunity costs stay constant along the production possibilities curve, making the PPC a straight line.

Suppose that, using a certain amount of resources, the United States can produce either 10 units (tons) of textiles or 40 units (thousands) of computers. Meanwhile, with the **same** amount of resources, Mexico can produce either 5 tons of textiles or 10 units of computers (in thousands). These production possibilities curves are illustrated in Figure 18.1.

In this example, the United States has an **absolute advantage** in both goods, meaning that **the United States can produce more of both goods with the same amount of resources than Mexico**. But the United States does not have a *comparative* advantage in the production of both goods.

If we use T for textiles (in tons) and C for computers (in thousands), then in the United States, $10T = 40C$. U.S. resources can produce either $10T$ or $40C$, so these amounts are equal in terms of the amount of resources they require. Dividing both sides by 10, we get $1T = 4C$. This means that the opportunity cost of 1 unit of textiles ($1T$) is equal to 4 units of computers ($4C$). Each time the United States produces 1 unit of textiles, it is using resources that instead could have produced four units of computers. Similarly, if we take our original equation $10T = 40C$

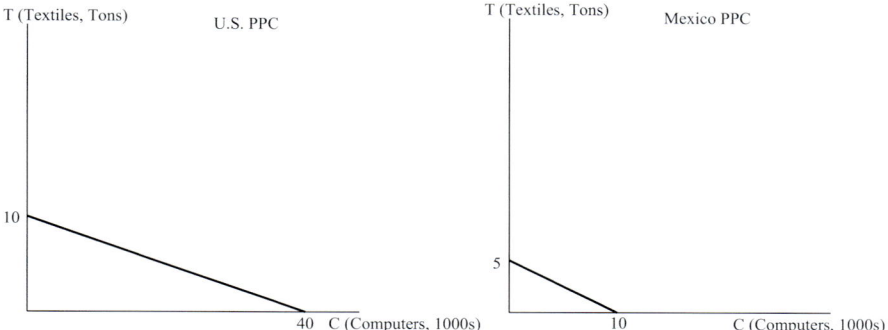

FIGURE 18.1 Production possibilities curves for the United States and Mexico.

and divide both sides by 40, we get $1C = \frac{1}{4}T$. Each time one unit of computers is produced, the United States is sacrificing the production of ¼ of a unit of textiles.

In Mexico, using the PPC in Figure 18.1, we can see that $5T = 10C$. Mexico can produce either 5 units of textiles or 10 units of computers with its existing resources. Dividing both sides of the equation by 5, we can rewrite that equation as $1T = 2C$. Therefore, in Mexico, the opportunity cost of producing one unit of textiles is 2 units of computers. Similarly, $1C = \frac{1}{2}T$ in Mexico.

Putting these results together, each unit of textiles "costs" 2 computers in Mexico ($1T = 2C$), whereas in the United States each unit of textiles "costs" 4 computers ($1T = 4C$). Mexico has a **comparative advantage** in the production of textiles, because *Mexico can produce textiles for a lower opportunity cost*.

But in Mexico, $1C = \frac{1}{2}T$, whereas in the United States, $1C = \frac{1}{4}T$. Thus, the United States has a comparative advantage in computer production because the United States can produce computers for a lower opportunity cost:

$$\left(\frac{1}{4}T_{US}\right) < \left(\frac{1}{2}T_{Mexico}\right).$$

According to mainstream economists, in order to increase efficiency, the United States should specialize in what it produces most efficiently (computers) and trade them to Mexico for what they produce most efficiently (textiles).

When countries trade, the opportunity costs in each country adjust and end up in between the original opportunity costs that existed in each country before trade occurred. Before trade, computers would have been very expensive in Mexico and textiles would have been very expensive in the United States due to opportunity costs. After trade, computers will become cheaper in Mexico thanks to U.S. computer exports and textiles will become cheaper in the United States thanks to Mexican textile exports. For example, suppose that after trading, the opportunity costs in the United States and Mexico settled on a ratio of $1T = 3C$, in between the opportunity costs in each country that existed before trade. This is known as the **international terms of trade**, which are **the opportunity costs at which goods will trade internationally**.

At the international terms of trade of $1T = 3C$, both Mexico and the United States can be better off by specializing in the good in which they have a comparative advantage and trading for the other good. (Note: In comparative advantage problems, you will be given the international terms of trade.) Now, both countries can exchange $1T$ for $3C$. Note also that both countries can exchange $1C$ for $\frac{1}{3}T$ given the international terms of trade $\left(1C = \frac{1}{3}T\right)$.

The gains from trade are illustrated in the graph in Figure 18.2 showing production possibilities curves and the **consumption possibilities curves** that result after trade. A **consumption possibilities curve (CPC)** shows all combinations of two goods that can be consumed by a country after specialization and trade. The CPC is constructed by starting at the point where the country specializes entirely in the good in which they have a comparative advantage. The other endpoint of the CPC is found by determining how much of the other good the country could get if it traded *all* of the specialized goods it produces to the other country at the international terms of trade.

In Figure 18.2, the U.S. PPC runs from $10T$ to $40C$. But with trade, the United States should specialize and produce only computers, $40C$. If the United States decides to export all $40C$, then using the international terms of trade of $1C = \frac{1}{3}T$, the United States will get in exchange $40C = 40 \times \frac{1}{3}T = 13.3T$. (You multiply both sides of the international terms of trade by the number of units of computers the United States can produce.) Thus, the U.S. consumption possibilities curve is the straight line between $40C$ and $13.3T$ in Figure 18.2.

If the United States were originally consuming at point **A** on its PPC, it can now consume **more of both goods** after trade at point **B** on its CPC.

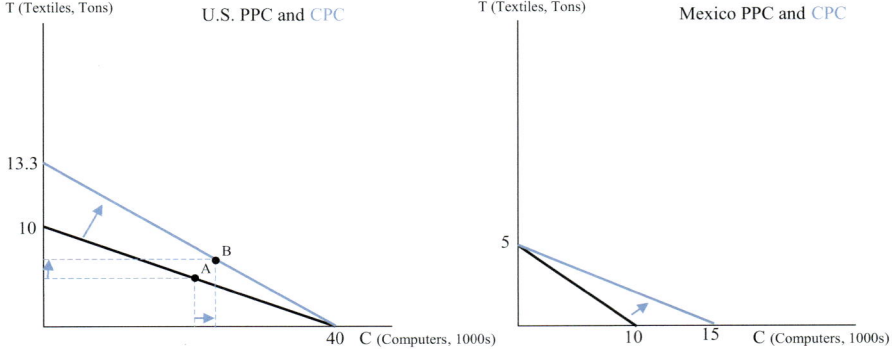

FIGURE 18.2 Consumption possibilities curves for the United States and Mexico.

Mexico's CPC starts at $5T$ and extends to $15C$, because $1T = 3C$ at the international terms of trade, which means that $5T = 15C$. Mexico also can consume more of both goods than it did before (unless it only desired to consume textiles).

Both countries can now consume more of both goods along their consumption possibilities curves by specializing in the production of the good in which they have a comparative advantage and trading this good to their trading partner. Specialization and trade increase efficiency, and trade makes both countries better off.

According to the theory of comparative advantage, unregulated trade will result in maximum global productivity and increased standards of living. Each country specializes in what it is relatively best at producing, which increases productivity and makes people in all trading countries better off. As one concrete example, economists Robert Lawrence and Lawrence Edwards estimated that trade with China increased the standard of living of U.S. citizens by $250 a year in 2008. However, as we will see below, political economists find that this analysis misses key aspects of modern trade.

18.2 PROBLEMS WITH THE THEORY OF COMPARATIVE ADVANTAGE

The first problem with the theory of comparative advantage is that unregulated trade tends to benefit countries that have an advantage in lucrative industries more than countries that do not. David Ricardo promoted unregulated trade in England in the 1800s when such policies were clearly advantageous to England. England was the first country in the world to industrialize, so they had an advantage over other countries in most manufactured goods. Unregulated trade allowed their industries to dominate potential competitors, helping them to maintain their status as the leading industrial power.

This is why other countries such as the United States and continental Europe protected their industries to give their companies time and space to develop and to become globally competitive. To date, no large country has successfully developed its economy via unregulated trade.

In addition, the theory of comparative advantage is often wrong when it comes to explaining global trade patterns. For much of the 20th century, countries in Africa, South America, and southeast Asia tended to specialize in producing raw materials, whereas the United States and European countries tended to specialize in producing manufactured goods, which seems to be explained by the theory of comparative advantage. Africa, South America, and Southeast Asia have abundant natural resources, so they specialize in producing these goods and export them to developed countries. The United States and Europe have advanced technology and skilled labor, so they specialize in exporting financial services and manufactured goods.

However, this trade pattern ignores the role of colonialism in destroying manufacturing in developing countries and supporting manufacturing in Europe. For example, England destroyed India's cutting-edge textile industry and forced India to grow cotton for British textile manufacturers during the colonial era. England's industrial dominance was a product of imperial strategy, not a result of greater efficiency.

Furthermore, developed countries like the United States and in Europe import *and* export manufactured goods from each other, as we will see below. These countries simultaneously have comparative advantages and disadvantages in the same product categories. The United States *imports and exports* cars, computers, smart phones, and many other products. It is not at all clear which country has a comparative advantage in these product categories.

The reasons behind the failures of the theory of comparative advantage to explain modern trade patterns have to do with the unrealistic assumptions upon which it is based. If these assumptions do not hold, then there is no reason to expect trade to improve everyone's welfare as the theory predicts. Political economists offer the following critique of the assumptions behind the theory of comparative advantage.

18.2.1 Assumption 1: Factors of production (labor and capital) are mobile internally but not externally

In Ricardo's era, it was uncommon for firms to move their operations outside of their home country. But in the modern world, multinational corporations can move their factories almost anywhere in the world. Companies move operations to where labor is cheaper or environmental regulations are lighter, which leads to lower costs and more profits.

As a result, it has become less meaningful to talk about a *country* having a comparative advantage—the real source of advantage may be the resources, technology, and skills controlled by a particular *company*. Political economists argue that **comparative advantage of countries has been replaced by the competitive advantage of companies**. As a result, the flow of capital around the globe in search of lower costs can lead to changes in a country's comparative advantages. The United States once had a significant comparative advantage in automobiles. Now, a significant amount of U.S. car manufacturing is done in Mexico. The Apple iPhone is a U.S.-designed product, but it is assembled in China from parts made all over the globe.

Apple's supply chain used parts sources all over the globe to make the iPhone 6, as identified in the list below:

- Accelerometer: Bosch in Germany, Invensense in the United States
- Audio chipsets and codec: Cirrus Logic in the United States (outsourced for manufacturing)
- Baseband processor: Qualcomm in the United States (outsourced for manufacturing)
- Batteries: Samsung in South Korea, Huizhou Desay Battery in China
- Cameras: Sony in Japan; OmniVision in the United States produces the front-facing FaceTime camera chip but subcontracts to TMSC (in Taiwan) for manufacturing

- Chipsets and processors: Samsung in South Korea and TSMC in Taiwan, alongside partner GlobalFoundries in the United States
- Controller chips: PMC Sierra and Broadcom Corp in the United States (outsourced for manufacturing)
- Display: Japan Display and Sharp in Japan, LG Display in South Korea
- DRAM: TSMC in Taiwan, SK Hynix in South Korea
- eCompass: Alps Electric in Japan
- Fingerprint sensor authentication: Authentec makes it in China but outsources it to Taiwan for manufacturing
- Flash memory: Toshiba in Japan and Samsung in South Korea
- Gyroscope: STMicroelectronics in France and Italy
- Inductor coils (audio): TDK in Japan
- Main chassis assembly: Foxconn and Pegatron in China
- Mixed-signal chips (such as NFC): NXP in the Netherlands
- Plastic constructions (for the iPhone 5c): Hi-P and Green Point in Singapore
- Radio-frequency modules: Win Semiconductors (module manufacturers Avago and RF Micro Devices) in Taiwan, Avago technologies and TriQuint Semiconductor in the United States, Qualcomm in the United States for LTE connectivity
- Screen and glass (for the display): Corning (Gorilla Glass) in the United States, GT Advanced Technologies produces the sapphire crystals in the screens
- Semiconductors: Texas Instruments, Fairchild, and Maxim Integrated in the United States
- Touch ID sensor: TSMC and Xintec in Taiwan
- Touchscreen controller: Broadcom in the United States (outsourced for manufacturing)
- Transmitter and amplification modules: Skyworks and Qorvo in the United States (outsourced for manufacturing).

The software and design for the iPhone is developed in the United States, but the assembly and most parts production take place in China at Foxconn and other large Chinese firms. Apple may move some assembly to India in the near future due to cost savings available there.[2] Thus, even though the iPhone was invented in the United States and Apple is a U.S. company, it is hard to say that the United States has a comparative advantage in smart phones. That advantage lies with Apple, and its supply chain located all over the globe, and especially in China.

18.2.2 Assumption 2: Technology is fixed and does not change over time

The theory of comparative advantage is static and assumes that a country will maintain a comparative advantage in the same types of products over time. However, technological changes can alter export patterns. As technology is assimilated and disseminated, other countries may end up exporting goods that were originally invented and exported by a different country, so the pattern of comparative advantage can change dramatically. For example, the United States invented the television, but it produces very few televisions today. Production has moved to other locations, such as Taiwan, South Korea, and China, where costs are lower and technology is better.

Countries can use technological assimilation and development to capture industries. For example, when South Korea was starting to produce cars, they protected their market against imported cars using tariffs until their car companies were globally competitive. By imitating and improving technology, they were able to become efficient. Only then did South Korea lower trade barriers and begin engaging in less regulated trade. As we saw in the previous chapter, this is known as **infant industry protection**, where a country protects firms when they are starting out so that they can gain a foothold in an established industry. Today, South Korean car companies Hyundai and Kia are internationally competitive and have a steadily increasing share of the global automobile market.

There are also spillover benefits from creating clusters of industries, such as Silicon Valley in California, Research Triangle Park in North Carolina, and the Special Economic Zone in Shenzhen, China. Creating industrial clusters spurs innovation and technological development, and it can create jobs in high-wage sectors of the economy. Governments can play a role in stimulating industrial clusters through infrastructure, education, and subsidies, which can have a large payoff if a cluster becomes a dynamic source of innovation and growth. Technological development thus becomes a key reason why comparative advantage can shift. And technological development can be manipulated via government policies to protect infant industries, attract foreign investment, and promote innovation.

18.2.3 Assumption 3: Productive resources are fully employed and move quickly and easily between industries

The theory of comparative advantage assumes that resources—labor and capital—will flow quickly and easily from the sector *without* a comparative disadvantage into the sector *with* the comparative advantage. Resources should flow out of dying industries and into growing industries. The real world seldom works this way, unfortunately. The United States used to have a comparative advantage in manufacturing steel. In recent years, it lost the comparative advantage in steel but gained a comparative advantage in software and technology. However, the U.S. rust belt still features decrepit steel plants in run-down towns and cities such as Detroit, Youngstown, and Allentown. Workers and resources in these locations were not able to find new jobs and purposes in new industries. Instead, these regions feature chronically underemployed workers and unused resources. Former steel workers do not have the skills required by the new industries, nor can they afford the kind of retraining they would need to be successful in a new industry.

In addition, the theory of comparative advantage assumes that all countries are producing at full capacity—that is, they are on their production possibilities curve. However, as noted in earlier chapters, economies are rarely at full employment. This means that countries need to expand the production of goods to reach full capacity, which implies that countries can reduce unemployment by producing more goods domestically rather than importing goods from other countries.

Furthermore, as Keynes demonstrated, demand creates supply; therefore, employment and income are driven first and foremost by demand factors (the autonomous level of spending). Unregulated trade has the impact of reducing employment and income in less competitive countries as demand for their products declines and increasing incomes in more competitive countries as demand for their products increases.

To political economists, this is a strong argument in favor of protectionism. Indeed, the need to create or preserve jobs has been used to justify protectionism in the United States from Alexander Hamilton in 1790 to Donald Trump in 2020. This is why most countries today pursue neo-mercantilist policies in which they subsidize exports and put up barriers to imports, including tariff and non-tariff barriers.

18.2.4 Assumption 4: Trade benefits everyone

Economists who believe in the theory of comparative advantage argue that the benefits from trade are widespread, increasing the standard of living of citizens. However, this ignores the fact that the distribution of the benefits from trade is extremely uneven. The workers and owners of firms in exporting industries see a higher demand for their products, increasing incomes and benefiting the communities in which they are located. Workers and owners of firms in industries losing out to imports end up with lower incomes and their communities fall on hard times.

Furthermore, trade has increased the incomes of skilled workers and business executives, while reducing the incomes of blue collar workers in developed countries. Because most people are blue-collar workers, trade has reduced wages for most workers in developed countries. Thus, trade has contributed directly to inequality.

18.2.5 Assumption 5: Trade is free and fair

As trade disputes show, trade is often unfair. Chinese firms have been accused of stealing the technology and intellectual property of U.S. firms, undermining the U.S. comparative advantages in key tech sectors. In Japan, collaborative business arrangements make it extremely difficult for foreign firms to compete in some sectors, such as the car market, which has the effect of reducing imports. In addition, countries should not be able to gain an advantage in trade by repressing laborers or ignoring environmental problems. If countries can gain an advantage via a race to the bottom by paying lower wages and reducing environmental regulations, this undermines the notion that trade makes all people better off and that trade is fair.

18.2.6 Assumption 6: Interdependence created by trade is not a problem

With specialization and trade, countries produce a smaller range of products. However, less developed countries (LDCs) that specialize in primary products such as coffee or cocoa are vulnerable to price fluctuations and can experience a deterioration in their terms of trade over time (the prices of their exports fall while their imports increase in price). Countries actually need diversified exports to provide a stable export sector to generate funds to pay for imported goods. Specializing in a narrow range of goods can foster instability. Countries may also wish to protect key sectors for national defense reasons, so they do not have to depend on key imported goods in the event of a major conflict.

One of the implications of the interdependence issue is that all industries are not equal. Some industries, especially those that come with high-wage jobs and linkages to many other industries, are better for economic growth than others. A country may want to protect high-linkage, high-wage industries to preserve good quality jobs and maintain export diversification.

18.2.7 Assumption 7: Exchange rates adjust to equalize trade flows so exports equal imports

In theory, a country that runs chronic trade deficits will experience an outflow of currency, causing its currency to depreciate. The depreciation of the currency, in turn, causes exports to become more competitive and imports to become more expensive, which should eliminate any trade deficit. (Trade surpluses should be eliminated by an identical process in reverse.) However, in reality, many countries run chronic trade deficits or trade surpluses. This topic is taken up in more detail in the chapter covering international financial flows. For current purposes, the important issue is that countries are affected differently by trade flows. Countries like the United States that run chronic trade deficits benefit from inexpensive imported goods, but they lose industries and jobs to foreign countries. Countries like China and Germany that run chronic trade surpluses experience more job growth, but their consumers receive fewer benefits from trade.

In conclusion, we see that trade provides broad, general benefits in the form of lower prices and better quality goods. It does seem to be the case that trade has increased the standard of living of people *on average*.

However, it is not the case that trade benefits everyone. There are clear winners and losers from trade. If a country worked to make sure that those harmed by trade received some of the benefits, then it might be possible to argue that trade would indeed make everyone better off. But without substantial trade adjustment assistance, many workers, firms, and communities have strong reasons to oppose unregulated trade. The differential impact of trade is one of the reasons many countries turn to protectionism.

18.3 PROTECTIONISM: USING TARIFF AND NON-TARIFF BARRIERS TO PROTECT INDUSTRIES

The main policies a country can use to protect specific industries are tariffs and quotas. A **tariff** is **a tax on imported goods**. An **import quota** is **a limit on the quantity of a good that can be imported**. Other policies a country can use to protect industries include subsidies and laws or regulations that prevent or impede trade.

There are a number of reasons why a country may want to protect some of its industries:

1. **Infant industry protection**. As noted above, one of the strongest reasons to protect an industry is to foster economic development. New industries usually need protection until they gain the size and experience necessary to compete at the international level.
2. **Strategic industry protection**. Certain industries may be deemed so essential to a country's interests that they cannot be entrusted to production in foreign locations. Typically, industries associated with national defense fall within this category. The United States has protected its steel, electronics, and metalworking industries for national defense reasons. Similarly, certain industries are essential for clusters of economic development. The U.S. technology industry is centered in Silicon Valley outside of San Francisco, where Google, Apple, Xerox, Intel, IBM, Adobe, and many other companies are clustered. There are substantial spillover benefits to industrial clusters: Inventions in one company are picked up and utilized by another company and vice versa. For this reason, the U.S. government protected Intel from foreign competition during a period in which foreign microchips were threatening its business. This allowed for continuing, fruitful collaborations between Intel and other U.S.-based computer companies such as Apple and Dell. Some countries also choose to protect industries that employ large numbers of people.
3. **Strategic trade policy**. When other countries are engaging in unfair trade practices, tariffs are one of the best options a country can use to force foreign countries to change their trade practices. For example, in 2018 the Trump administration argued that China was pursuing unfair trade practices by stealing U.S. intellectual property, requiring U.S. firms to invest in China in order to sell goods there, and unfairly subsidizing the manufacturing of steel, aluminum, and other products. President Trump imposed tariffs on Chinese goods to try to force them to reduce their trade barriers and buy more U.S. goods. Similarly, tariffs can be used to reduce imports by countries that face chronic trade deficits (when exports exceed imports).

4. **Raise revenue**. In many developing countries with large informal economies, it is difficult to raise tax revenues. Incomes are low, and many transactions occur in cash, which makes them untraceable and difficult to tax. But imported goods are tracked carefully and come through specific international shipping outlets, such as ports or airports. This makes taxes on imported goods one of the easiest ways for governments to raise revenue.

Note that protectionism may not help a particular industry if the foreign country retaliates. As soon as President Trump imposed tariffs on Chinese goods in 2018, the Chinese government imposed tariffs on U.S. goods in response. Thus, protecting particular industries may only be effective for a country if no retaliation occurs.

Tariffs have the effect of increasing the price and reducing the quantity of an imported good purchased in the country that imposes the tariff. Figure 18.3 shows the impact of a 100% tariff on a foreign good. The market is initially in equilibrium at a price of $12 and a quantity of 7000. Then, the government imposes a 100% tariff on the product, which has the effect of doubling the price at which each quantity can be sold. If the firm exporting the product sells it for $5, the government adds a tariff of $1.00 \times 5 = \$5$, so the new price with the 100% tariff is $10. If the firm's product sells for $10, the tariff is $10, and the new price with the tariff becomes $20. The new supply curve $S(1 + \text{tariff}) = 2S$ is twice as steep as the original supply curve S. The new equilibrium that results is at a price of $20 and a quantity of 5000. The tariff has the effect of increasing the equilibrium price and reducing the equilibrium quantity sold.

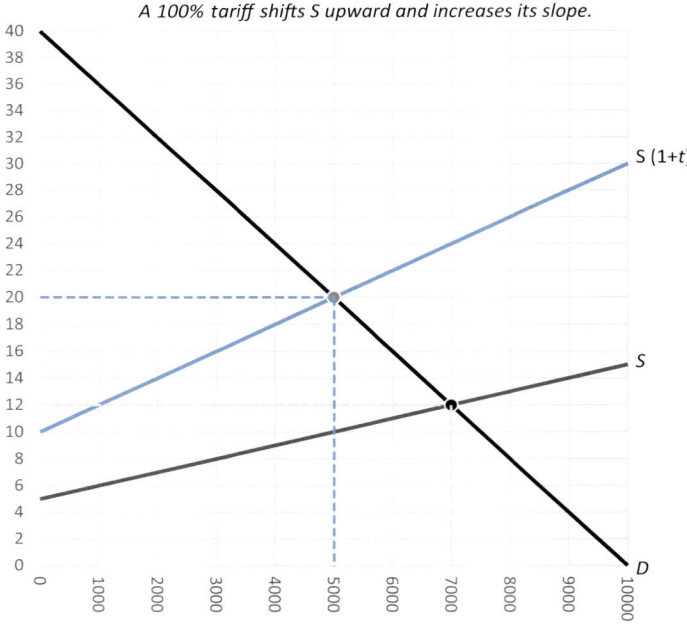

FIGURE 18.3 The effect of a 100% tariff.

This is very bad for the foreign seller of the product. Not only do they sell a smaller quantity but they make a lot less money than they used to. They supply 5000 units of their product at a price of $10, and then the government adds another $10 to that in the form of the 100% tariff, making the price to consumers $20. In the tariff graph, the original supply curve reflects the money going to the seller, and the new supply curve adds in the cost of the tariff. The government would take $10 × 5000 = $50,000 in tariff revenue.

The government could achieve a similar result by imposing a quota. Suppose the government instituted a quota, or a maximum limit, of 5000 units on exports of the product depicted in Figure 18.3. The new supply curve would become a vertical line at $Q=5000$, which would result in an equilibrium at $Q=5000$ and $P=\$20$, achieving the same result as the tariff. The only difference is that the quota does not raise revenue for the government, whereas the tariff does.

Occasionally, governments resort to other forms of non-tariff barriers in trade. For example, countries can establish very strict rules about importing goods or they can restrict the types of products they allow to be imported. Many European countries ban genetically modified organism (GMO) food crops due to concerns about health and the environment associated with the pesticides and herbicides that are sprayed on GMO crops. This prevents genetically modified crops grown in the United States from being exported to Europe.

In general, tariff and non-tariff barriers protect specific domestic industries from foreign competition, thereby improving their profitability. We can see the impact of tariffs directly in the changes of trade patterns.

18.4 U.S. TRADE PATTERNS

Figure 18.4 shows the top U.S. trading partners in 2017.[3] Note the large trade deficits (imports greater than exports) with China, Mexico, Japan, Germany, and South Korea. The only top trading partners with which the United States has a trade surplus are the United Kingdom and Brazil. As we will see in the next

Rank	Country	U.S. Exports to Partner, 2017	U.S. Imports from Partner, 2017	U.S. Exports to Partner, 2019	U.S. Imports from Partner, 2019	Total Trade with U.S. 2019	% of Total U.S. Trade, 2019
1	Mexico	243	314	256.4	358.1	614.5	14.80%
2	Canada	282.4	300	292.7	319.7	612.4	14.80%
3	China	130.4	505.6	106.6	452.2	558.9	13.50%
4	Japan	67.7	136.5	74.7	143.6	218.3	5.30%
5	Germany	53.5	117.7	60.3	127.5	187.8	4.50%
6	South Korea	48.3	71.2	56.9	77.5	134.4	3.20%
7	United Kingdom	56.3	53.1	69.2	63.2	132.3	3.20%
8	France	33.6	48.9	37.8	57.4	95.2	2.30%
9	India	25.7	48.6	34.4	57.7	92.1	2.20%
10	Taiwan	25.8	42.5	31.2	54.3	85.5	2.10%
11	Netherlands	42.2	17.7	51.2	29.8	81	2.00%
12	Italy	18.3	50	23.8	57.2	80.9	2.00%
13	Vietnam	8.1	46.5	10.9	66.7	77.6	1.90%
14	Brazil	37.1	29.4	43.1	30.9	73.9	1.80%
15	Ireland	10.7	48.8	9	61.8	70.8	1.70%

FIGURE 18.4 Table showing the top U.S. trading partners, 2017 and 2019.

chapter, mainstream economists link U.S. trade deficits to the low U.S. savings rate and an extremely strong currency.

China dropped from our top trading partner in 2017 to third place in 2019. This happened after a major trade dispute between the United States and China, in which both countries imposed significant, wide-reaching tariffs on the other. As a result, U.S. imports from China declined by $53 billion and U.S. exports to China declined by $24 billion in 2019.

According to the theory of comparative advantage, the United States should specialize in the goods in which it has a comparative advantage and import the goods in which it does not. It is instructive to look at the categories of products that form the largest U.S. exports and imports. Figure 18.5 shows the top ten categories of exports and imports for the United States in 2019. Interestingly, for the most part, the United States both exports and imports the same product categories. The United States exports and imports computers, oil, vehicles, electrical machinery and equipment, medical equipment, plastics, precious metals, pharmaceuticals, and organic chemicals. In these goods categories, no clear pattern of comparative advantage emerges.

The only seemingly clear areas of comparative advantage are in the categories of aircraft and spacecraft, which U.S. industry dominates, and furniture, which our trading partners dominate. Thus, in the modern era, it is misleading to assume that a country has a comparative advantage in an entire product category. Instead, we see competitive companies in the United States and competitive companies in other countries within the same product category. For example, the United States exports cars made by Ford, Chevrolet, Chrysler, and Tesla, and it imports cars made by Toyota, Honda, Hyundai, Mercedes, VW, BMW, and some others.

The patterns that emerge from the trading data on the United States and other developed countries indicate that countries tend to trade the most with other countries that (1) are geographically close, (2) have similar tastes and preferences, (3) have similar resource endowments and technologies, and (4) are open to trade. In essence, developed countries tend to trade the most with other developed countries that are similar to them.

Countries do get some goods from countries with different resource endowments, as predicted by the theory of comparative advantage. The United States

U.S. Top Exports (and Import Rank)	Volume (billions)	% of Exports	U.S. Top Imports	Volume (billions)	% of Imports
1. Machinery including computers (1)	$206	12.5%	1. Machinery including computers	$379	14.8%
2. Mineral fuels including oil (4)	$200	12.1%	2. Electrical machinery, equipment	$352	13.7%
3. Electrical machinery, equipment (2)	$173	10.5%	3. Vehicles	$310	12.1%
4. Aircraft, spacecraft	$136	8.3%	4. Mineral fuels including oil v	$210	8.2%
5. Vehicles (3)	$133	8.1%	5. Pharmaceuticals	$128	5.0%
6. Optical, technical, medical apparatus (6)	$91	5.5%	6. Optical, technical, medical apparatus	$97	3.8%
7. Plastics, plastic articles (8)	$65	3.9%	7. Furniture, bedding, lighting, signs, prefab bldgs.	$67	2.6%
8. Gems, precious metals (9)	$60	3.6%	8. Plastics, plastic articles	$61	2.4%
9. Pharmaceuticals (5)	$54	3.3%	9. Gems, precious metals	$58	2.3%
10. Organic chemicals (10)	$39	2.4%	10. Organic chemicals	$55	2.1%

FIGURE 18.5 Table of largest value export and import products for the United States, 2019.

imports clothing, which requires labor-intensive production, from Bangladesh, China, India, and other countries where labor is cheap and plentiful. The United States imports cocoa, coffee, and tropical fruits from countries with climates that can easily produce such goods. The United States exports high-technology goods and airplanes because of its technological edge in those products. However, the goods that the United States either exports or imports make up a small portion of U.S. trade.

So, if resource endowments that determine comparative advantage are not the major influence over what goods and services a country exports, what is? Political economists focus on absolute advantage, comparative institutional advantage, and other factors to explain international competitiveness.

18.5 POLITICAL ECONOMY VIEWS ON TRADE AND COMPETITIVENESS

The theory of comparative advantage argues that specialization and trade derive from a country's abundant resources. If a country has lots of good agricultural land, it will specialize in agricultural products. If a country has abundant skilled labor and advanced technology, it will specialize in tech goods. However, as noted above, trade patterns do not support the theory of comparative advantage much of the time because countries both import and export the same categories of goods. Given the problematic assumptions behind the theory of comparative advantage and the observed trade patterns in the modern world, political economists developed a different set of principles regarding trade.

Political economists argue that firms, not countries, are the appropriate level of analysis for trade flows. In addition, firms in competitive markets must produce goods for a lower costs than their competitors if there are no significant quality differences. This means that (1) **to political economists, absolute advantage is usually more important than comparative advantage in determining trade flows. International trade occurs between firms, not countries, and firms operating in competitive global markets must have the lowest prices, and therefore the lowest costs, to be successful.**

The need for firms to have the lowest costs possible also helps us to understand globalization and the shift of global manufacturing to low-cost locations. When Apple began to worry about how much more the iPhone cost than the smart phones made by Samsung, they started to outsource more of their production to China. This is why it does not matter that U.S. engineers designed and created the iPhone and that production was initially based primarily in the United States. To political economists, the United States does not have a comparative advantage in smart phones—Apple has an absolute advantage in smart phones.

Political economists also note the extent to which (2) **unregulated trade policies tend to undermine workers**. Although the theory of comparative advantage implies that workers will be better off with trade, experiencing a higher standard of living and shifting out of declining sectors into growing ones, the reality has been much different. During the neoliberal era of deregulated trade and globalization, U.S. labor's share of national income declined from 65% in 1970 to 60% in 2019. Similar declines occurred in other developed countries. Even in developing countries, the threat that employers can move wherever labor is cheapest is used as a threat to keep wages low and workers compliant. With the steady erosion in workers' well-being during the era of "free" trade, the theory of comparative advantage appears to be more of an ideological argument in favor of multinational firms and against the majority of workers than an accurate descriptor of real-world trade patterns.

Therefore, political economics advocates policies to prevent trade from becoming a race to the bottom, where firms seek out the most vulnerable workers and the most lax environmental standards to reduce their costs and gain a competitive advantage. **Corrective tariffs** can be applied to countries or regions that exploit laborers or that do not adhere to the same environmental standards. This evens the playing field and ensures that domestic companies do not have to face unfair competition.

Political economists also argue that (3) **unregulated trade can undermine effective aggregate demand**, reducing employment and incomes. Political economic research indicates that demand factors are usually more important than supply factors in driving production, employment, and growth. To the extent that unregulated trade undermines aggregate demand by driving down wages and bankrupting uncompetitive businesses, it will have a detrimental impact. After their pursuit of unregulated trade policies, the United States and the United Kingdom developed rust belts featuring empty, rusting factories and impoverished cities, but new industries did not develop to replace the dying ones in these locations. To political economists, **managed trade policies** to stimulate exports and limit trade deficits are better for the majority of workers than unregulated trade, which tends to benefit multinational corporations.

Political economists also argue that trade patterns between countries can be exploitative. Throughout most of the last century, less developed countries were constrained to producing primary products such as agricultural goods and minerals. Unfortunately, the real prices of primary products have fallen in recent years, indicating that primary product exporters are getting less money for their products than they used to. The primary reason for this is the difference in income elasticity between manufactured goods and high-end services on the one side and primary products on the other. As economies get richer, their expenditure on high-end goods and services increases relative to their expenditure on primary products. Over time, this means the demand for high-end manufactured goods and services outstrips the demand for primary products, and the relative prices of manufactured goods will increase relative to the prices of primary products.

This highlights the extent to which (4) trade patterns result in **unequal exchange**, where **resources are systematically transferred by global trade flows from developing countries that produce primary products to developed countries**. When we consider the fact that the former colonial powers, especially England, Spain, Portugal, the Netherlands, and Belgium, systematically dismantled manufacturing in their colonies and set up the colonies to supply them with primary products, the persistence of the resulting trade patterns is deeply troubling. Only a small number of former colonies have been able to escape the trap of primary product specialization to engineer the structural transformation of the economy toward higher value manufactured goods.

Nevertheless, the fact that some countries have been able to transform their economies via a developmental state, as discussed in chapter 17 on economic growth, indicates that (5) *the right set of policies can be beneficial in creating the appropriate environment for manufacturing*. This is the essential insight behind the theory of comparative institutional advantage as developed by political economists.

The **theory of comparative institutional advantage** posits that **trade patterns are driven by particular combinations of institutions (government policies and support, infrastructure, labor skills and training, education systems, communities, industrial clusters, and innovation systems) that create advantages for specific types of production in particular places, attracting economic actors to locate production in certain geographical locations**. One of the most important implications of the theory of comparative institutional advantage is that governments can guide and shape trade patterns by altering local institutions and incentives. This was the strategy pursued by the developmental states and triple helix models we studied in the previous chapter.

According to the theory of comparative institutional advantage, trade and industrial development are driven largely by state policies. Economic growth and development are stimulated by fostering the best possible institutional environment for growing industries. This includes the provision of infrastructure, efforts to develop technology via R&D spending or foreign direct investment (with local partners), education and training, protectionism or other measures to ensure a sufficient demand for products, provision of subsidized financing, and more. China, South Korea, and Japan have been particularly adept with this approach.

Interestingly, supply-side economists also emphasize the institutional environment facing businesses, although they advocate a very different set of policies. Supply-side economists focus primarily on business profits, arguing that the government should work to give domestic companies advantages and disadvantage foreign competition, usually via tariffs. This was the approach taken during the Trump administration in the United States from 2017 to 2020. However, without the other types of support noted above, this approach had limited impact in rejuvenating U.S. manufacturing.

Despite these criticisms of unregulated trade and the theory of comparative advantage, in recent decades, countries moved increasingly toward free trade. Most of these changes occurred as a result of international trade agreements to reduce tariffs. These efforts to integrate global economies have caused major changes in the world and a recent backlash against globalization.

18.6 GLOBAL INTEGRATION AND RESISTANCE TO GLOBALIZATION

During the Great Depression and World War II, global trade collapsed and countries retreated from international entanglements. With the end of World War II, the United States emerged as the globally dominant power and began pushing unregulated trade and a greater degree of international cooperation. Partly this effort was to bring countries together to avoid future conflicts, and partly it was intended to open up new markets to dominant U.S. manufacturers.

The effort at global economic integration began with the General Agreement on Tariffs and Trade (GATT) of 1947, which reduced tariffs and promoted trade among countries signing the agreement. At the same time, the World Bank and the International Monetary Fund were established to assist struggling economies and to promote market-based development in the developing world, in part as a counter to the Soviet Union's influence. GATT was followed by the creation of the World Trade Organization (WTO) in 1995 to further reduce tariffs and facilitate trade between nations. The creation of the WTO, along with the fall of the Soviet Union in 1990, ushered in the era of neoliberalism in which the entire world became enmeshed in a global system of international trade that was less regulated and less protectionist than any previous era. The neoliberal era was very good for some regions, countries, and individuals and very bad for others.

GATT and the WTO established rules for countries that joined their organizations with respect to tariffs, intellectual property, regulation of foreign corporations, and other aspects of international exchange. Multinational corporations played a key role in shaping WTO policies, which resulted in rules that are very favorable to corporations and less favorable to workers and other interests. The result has been very good for multinational corporations, which can now move easily to most countries that are WTO members and be confident that there will be little interference with their operations. Few countries felt like they could stay out of the WTO because the world's largest consumer markets, especially the United States and the E.U., would not be as accessible otherwise.

However, the WTO is deeply controversial, in part due to the way in which they have impeded the ability of countries to institute modest regulations that affect foreign companies. Companies with a complaint against any regulation or trade policy of a country can lodge a complaint with the WTO. In its findings, the WTO tends to be more sympathetic to companies than to regulators. For example, Japan passed a law prohibiting the importation of apples sprayed with toxic pesticides and Europe tried to ban hormone-treated beef due to the potentially negative impact on health. In both cases, the WTO ruled that these laws were unfair restrictions of international trade, and countries were not allowed to impose these restrictions that were intended to protect the health of their populations.

At the same time that the WTO was expanding, countries were forming trading blocs in which they eliminated tariffs with particular trading partners, usually those in close geographic proximity. According to the World Bank, average global tariff rates fell steadily from around 10% in 1990 to about 2% in 2015, thanks largely to the WTO and to trade agreements that eliminated tariffs among trading bloc members. By the 2010s, international trade was less regulated than it has ever been.

There are four major types of trading bloc agreements:

1. A **free trade area** reduces or eliminates tariffs between member countries. The result of a free trade area is increased trade with groups members but reduced trade with the rest of the world.
2. A **customs union** creates common external tariffs (customs) on non-member countries, while reducing or eliminating tariffs between member countries. Countries in a customs union behave like a single country with respect to trade.
3. **Common markets** go even further, allowing capital and labor mobility between countries in the bloc, along with lower (or no) internal tariffs and common external tariffs. Workers and firms can move freely within member countries.
4. An **economic union** involves central economic coordination and a common currency, along with capital and labor mobility, low or no internal tariffs, and common external tariffs. An economic union functions like a single-country economy in most respects.

18.6.1 The European Union

The European Economic Community was created in 1957 to open up European economies to each other and to bring about a degree of economic integration between member states. This was followed by the European Union, which began as a common market and in 1999 became an economic union with the adoption of a common European currency, the euro. By this point, European economies were closely integrated.

Tariffs between E.U. countries were completely eliminated, and the E.U. maintained common tariffs on goods from other countries. Companies could move any part of their operations to other E.U. countries, and workers could move freely between countries to find work. In these respects, the E.U. economy operates like that of a single country, although individual member states still retain much autonomy in other arenas. The E.U. government is therefore more of a body to regulate competing interests than a central government.

Most economic studies indicate that joining the E.U. had substantial benefits for almost all member states (except for Greece, as we will see later). The share of trade between member countries increased substantially, and it decreased with the rest of the world. Companies were able to become more competitive, and workers could seek out new opportunities. Meanwhile, generous safety nets and social programs ensured that no one was excessively disadvantaged by changes caused by the economic integration. Campos et al. found that joining the E.U. increased a country's per capita economic growth by about 0.67% per year for most countries and by more than double that for Ireland and a few other countries.[4]

Some interesting collaborations between countries resulted in the formation of new industries and research institutes that would not have been possible without economic integration. For example, Airbus, a European multinational aerospace corporation with significant operations in France, Germany, Spain, and the United Kingdom, was founded in 1970 and became the world's largest airplane manufacturer in 2019. The European Organization for Nuclear Research built the Large Hadron Collider, the world's largest machine, to develop scientific breakthroughs in science.

However, the organization of the E.U. had some significant flaws that meant that it was ill-equipped to deal with economic crises, especially the financial crisis of 2008 to 2010. One of the main problems was that the E.U. had no mechanism to deal with member states experiencing a major economic shock related to trade deficits.

As one of the least developed countries in the E.U., Greece regularly ran trade deficits with countries like Germany because it imported expensive German manufactured goods like cars and electronics and exported lower value goods like tourist services. When Greece was an independent country, it could devalue its currency, the drachma, to increase the prices of imported goods and decrease the prices of its exports, improving the competitiveness of its export products and reducing its trade deficits. This would stem the outflow of money and stabilize the economy.

After Greece joined the E.U. and adopted the euro, it could no longer devalue its currency to stay competitive. Greece's outflows of money accelerated, and by the time of the financial crisis of 2008, Greece could no longer pay its debts. However, instead of bailing out a struggling member state, like the U.S. government does when one of its 50 states falls on hard times, the E.U. insisted on austerity policies (higher taxes and cuts to government spending) to reduce Greece's debts. As is always the case, austerity reduced Greece's gross domestic product (GDP) and increased unemployment, making the situation even worse. Thanks to these shortsighted policies, Greece entered a depression that lasted from 2008 to 2016, and even in 2019 after growth had returned, the unemployment rate remained above 17%. The E.U. had no mechanism to deal with a macroeconomic crisis of one of its member states, demonstrating that a currency union without macroeconomic policy coordination and stabilization was a poor structure.

The E.U. also failed to anticipate the impact of adding impoverished Eastern European countries to the bloc and the hostility that immigrant workers would face as they moved to different countries within the E.U. In 2004 the E.U. added eight Eastern European countries from the former Soviet Union Bloc, including Poland, Hungary, and Czechia. In 2007 Bulgaria and Romania were added. These were poor countries relative to the rest of Europe, and their economies were still struggling after the conversion from centralized, state communism to capitalism. Once they joined the E.U. and people were able to move freely, workers left Eastern Europe in droves seeking better jobs and pay in other countries, especially England, which was growing more quickly than the rest of the E.U. at the time.

The share of foreign-born residents soared in England to 13.4% of the population. Eastern Europeans filled low-wage service jobs and put a strain on public services. British workers saw this as a major threat to their well-being and started backing initiatives to get the United Kingdom to leave the E.U.—**Brexit**. However, British banks and manufacturers, which depended on selling to E.U. markets, opposed Brexit, fearing the loss of a huge portion of their business. After a bitter and divisive campaign filled with disinformation, the United Kingdom voted narrowly to leave the E.U. Brexit took place on January 31, 2020, marking the first departure from the E.U. Only time will tell whether the E.U. fractures further in the face of ongoing challenges.

18.6.2 The North American Free Trade Agreement

As Europe became increasingly integrated, the United States felt the need to expand its access to nearby markets and resources, which it achieved with the North American Free Trade Agreement and the subsequent revision labeled the U.S.-Mexico-Canada Agreement (USMCA). NAFTA took effect in 1994, immediately eliminating tariffs on more than half of industrial products. By 2009, tariffs on all industrial and agricultural products traded between the three countries were completely eliminated. The goal was to create a North American supply chain, adding cheap Mexican labor and Canadian natural resources and skilled labor to U.S. manufacturing prowess. It was also hoped that the agreement would make U.S. and Canadian companies more competitive, boost Mexico's GDP, and reduce the number of Mexican migrants as a result.

Trade between the three countries increased sharply after NAFTA was implemented, increasing from $290 billion in 1993 to $1100 billion in 2016, an increase of 279%. The U.S. stock of foreign direct investment in Mexico increased from $15 billion to $100 billion during the same time frame. Economists estimate that NAFTA had no significant impact on U.S. GDP, leaving it essentially unchanged from its normal growth trajectory. There were some benefits for North American consumers as the prices of some products dropped.

However, the impact on many workers was quite negative. Economist Robert Scott estimates that 683,000 U.S. jobs were lost from 1993 to 2010.[5] U.S. manufacturers did move to Mexico as predicted, but wages in Mexico stayed very low. According to Luis Villanueva, the Mexican "sectors that produce for the export market are sectors that pay among the lowest wages within the manufacturing sector."⁶ The Mexican maquiladoras—factories along the U.S. border producing for export—are infamous for low wages, unsafe working conditions, and lax environmental standards. Meanwhile almost 2 million Mexican corn farmers were put out of work when they could not compete with heavily subsidized U.S. corn, leading to an explosion of Mexican immigration to the United States. This was, of course, the opposite of what NAFTA hoped to achieve.

The USMCA agreement tweaked NAFTA slightly, establishing new rules of origin that required 75% of automobiles to originate in member countries to qualify for no tariffs (an increase from 62.5%) and rules requiring 40% of each vehicle to come from factories paying at least $16 per hour (e.g., U.S. and Canadian factories). In most other regards, the trade agreement was largely unchanged.

The NAFTA/USMCA experience illustrates some of the classic lessons of unregulated trade. Consumers tend to benefit somewhat, paying lower prices for goods. Producers and workers in competitive industries benefit, seeing higher demand for their products, more jobs, and higher profits. Producers and workers in uncompetitive industries experience significant harm, as businesses close, jobs are eliminated, and communities that depend on the income from these jobs experience economic decline. Workers tend to lose bargaining power, and many experience lower wages as they are forced to compete with low-wage workers from other countries.

As another indication of the problems that trade agreements can create for workers, U.S. job losses were even higher after China joined the WTO and qualified for lower tariffs. Daron Acemoglu et al. estimated that import competition from China eliminated more than 2 million U.S. jobs from 1999 to 2011.[7]

As we can see from the information above, after World War II, most countries in the world reduced tariffs, increased trade, and formed a series of trading blocs that reduced protectionism and increased the economic integration of particular regions of the world. Between WTO rulings hostile to labor, health, and the environment and the steady erosion of jobs and wages in developed countries as manufacturing moved to China, India, South Korea, Mexico, and other less expensive locations, globalization led to increasing dissatisfaction with unregulated trade.

18.6.3 Resistance to neoliberal globalization

Throughout the period during which trade was liberalized (deregulated) and economies were increasingly opened to international competition, there was resistance from workers and communities threatened by globalization. Each time the WTO meets there are mass protests by labor unions and activists who see unregulated trade as a fundamental threat to people, communities, and the global environment. Donald Trump was elected in the United States in 2016 in part due to his pledge to renegotiate NAFTA and prevent U.S. jobs from moving to China. During his presidency, Trump began many trade wars with other countries, raising tariffs to try to increase U.S. jobs. His efforts were often canceled out, however, by retaliatory foreign tariffs on U.S. goods. Boris Johnson was elected U.K. prime minister on his Brexit platform to end the U.K.'s participation in the E.U., which he successfully delivered.

Interestingly, even though tariffs were reduced in recent decades, most countries still utilize some form of strategic trade policy to protect and promote key domestic industries. In cases where the use of tariffs is limited by trade agreements, countries use subsidies and non-tariff barriers to protect and assist industries. These countries are adopting more of a managed trade approach drawing on the ideas of political economists instead of the laissez-faire approach promoted by the WTO and the theory of comparative advantage.

To a large degree, modern economists appear to be repeating the debates of the great economists of earlier eras. Adam Smith and David Ricardo argued in favor of unregulated trade to improve people's standard of living, whereas Karl Marx maintained that international trade fosters a race to the bottom that results in labor exploitation and environmental devastation. Keynes, of course, falls somewhere in the middle, arguing in favor of trade as long as it is regulated carefully to ensure that everyone benefits.

18.7 CONCLUSION

Most mainstream, New Keynesian economists are staunch believers in unregulated (free) trade. This belief is grounded in the theory of comparative advantage, which posits that if all countries engage in unregulated trade, they will end up specializing in goods that they are relatively best at producing. If every country specializes in this manner, global productivity will improve and everyone will experience a higher standard of living. Countries specialize in those goods that reflect their endowments of resources (land, labor, capital, and natural resources). Some government policies may be necessary to assist those harmed by trade but, in general, unregulated trade is viewed as the best policy.

However, the United States does not tend to trade the most with countries that have different resource endowments. Instead, the largest trading partners of the United States are nearby, open to trade, have similar tastes and preferences, and have similar resource endowments and technologies. This has important implications for trade theory and policy.

Political economists are skeptical of the theory of comparative advantage. Instead, they focus on the winners and losers from unregulated trade, noting that workers and manufacturing communities in developed countries have paid a steep price for globalization. Global multinational corporations have been the main beneficiaries because they are able to scour the globe to find new markets and the lowest possible costs of production. Political economists prefer to manage trade to protect key industries and to ensure that workers and communities are shielded from the destructive side of global trade. They also argue that comparative advantage in key industries can be gained via the right set of policies.

Trade policy and economic integration can be deeply controversial. The United States pursued unregulated trade beginning in the 1970s and later through the vehicles of NAFTA and the WTO, believing that these policies and trade agreements were broadly beneficial. But the election of Donald Trump in 2016 ushered in a new era of protectionism that indicated a shift in approach. Similarly, the E.U. pursued economic integration and less regulated trade until very recently, when its stability was shattered by the financial crisis and the collapse of the Greek economy. Subsequently, the mass movement of Eastern Europeans to the United Kingdom spawned Brexit and further E.U. disintegration. It will be interesting to see whether the pro-trade arguments of mainstream economists hold sway or whether the United States and the E.U. continue to move toward a more protectionist stance in the future.

The debate over trade policy reflects the deep divisions between mainstream economists and political economists. Laissez-faire economists for the most part put their faith in markets and the ability of private actors to innovate and yield outcomes that tend to benefit society. Unregulated trade is the ultimate expression of a market-oriented philosophy in that corporations determine what goods are produced, how they are made, and *where* they are made. New Keynesian economists generally prefer unregulated trade, but there must be adequate trade adjustment assistance, retraining, reeducation, community redevelopment, and other measures to ensure that trade benefits everyone.

Political economists distrust markets to make those decisions without government oversight, worrying about ethical lapses (worker and environmental exploitation) by corporations as well as the destruction of communities as industries move abroad. Political economists advocate the use of industrial policies such as the triple helix to construct a comparative institutional advantage in key industries to create jobs and increase incomes in the domestic economy.

As always, it is left to the reader to determine which perspective you find most compelling.

QUESTIONS FOR REVIEW

1. (a) Explain the theory of comparative advantage and why most mainstream economists believe that unregulated trade increases the welfare of citizens on average. (b) List and briefly explain the main problems with the theory of comparative advantage.
2. Protectionism has long been utilized as a tool for economic development.
    a. What are the major **policies** used in protectionism?
    b. What are the main **arguments** for protectionism?
    c. What are the main **costs** generated by protectionism?
3. The **theory of comparative advantage** demonstrates that, in theory, *all* countries can benefit through specialization and trade.

a. The graphs in Figure 18.6 show production possibilities curves for the United States and Kuwait, using an identical amount of resources for one month. Copy the graphs onto a sheet of paper. Determine which country has a comparative advantage in oil and which in rocket launchers using the PPCs. **Show your work.**

b. **Draw consumption possibilities curves** on your graphs. Assume that the international terms of trade are 1 rocket launcher for 2 units of oil (1RL=2O).

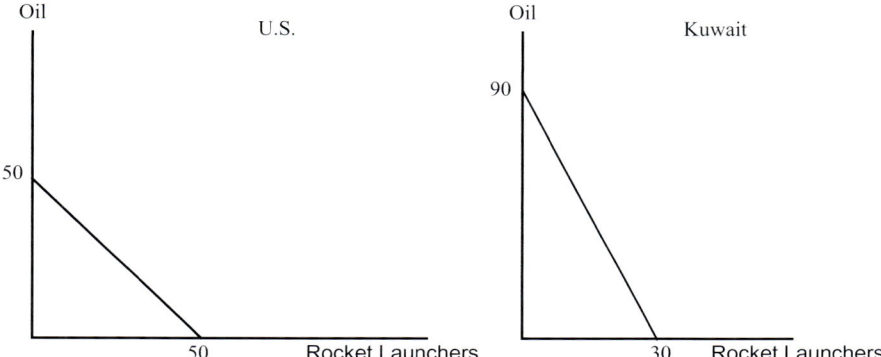

FIGURE 18.6 PPCs for the United States and Kuwait.

4. The graphs in Figure 18.7 show production possibilities curves for the United States and Japan, using an identical amount of resources for one day. Determine which country has a comparative advantage in beef and which in automobiles using the PPCs. Show your work. Copy the graphs onto a sheet of paper. Draw consumption possibilities curves on your graphs. Assume that the international terms of trade are 1 automobile for 3 units of beef (1A=3B).

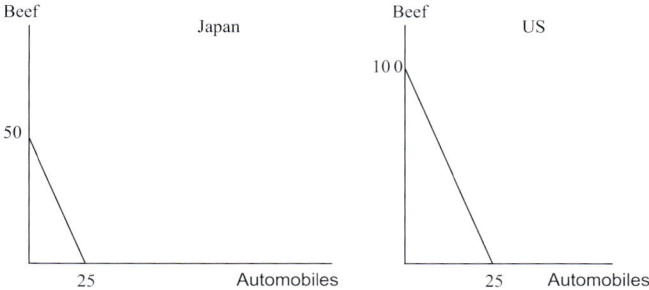

FIGURE 18.7 PPCs for Japan and the United States.

5. In 2018, the Trump administration imposed 25% tariffs on imports of steel into the United States. Using a graph, show how that tariff would affect the

equilibrium price and quantity of imported steel. Assume that the initial price of steel is $2000 per ton. What impact would these tariffs have on U.S. steel makers? What impact would the steel tariffs have on U.S. car companies that use a lot of steel to manufacture cars?
6. Describe U.S. trade patterns. Compare these trade patterns with the predictions of the theory of comparative advantage and political economy trade theories regarding the products that countries should specialize in producing and export. Which ideas do you find most accurately capture the realities of U.S. trade patterns? Explain, and support your answer.
7. Describe the experiences of the E.U. and the United States with economic integration via trade agreements. What are the benefits of economic integration? What are the costs? Do you think the United States should continue to pursue the economic integration of North America? Why or why not?
8. Write an essay in which you assess the strongest arguments in favor of unregulated trade and the strongest arguments in favor of protectionism. Determine what approach you think your country should utilize when it comes to trade and exchange rates, and support your arguments with examples from the text and from other sources.

NOTES

1 Gregory Mankiw, *Principles of Economics* (Boston: Cengage, 2015), 188.
2 See Christopher Minasians, "Where Are Apple Products Made?" September 18, 2017, https://www.macworld.co.uk/feature/apple/where-are-apple-products-made-3633832/, accessed April 1, 2018.
3 Source: U.S. Census Bureau, "Foreign Trade," www.census.gov/foreign-trade, accessed February 2, 2021.
4 Nauro Campos, Fabrizio Coricelli, and Luigi Moretti, "The Eye, the Needle and the Camel: Rich Countries Can Benefit from EU Membership" (VOX, CEPR Policy Portal, 2016), https://voxeu.org/article/how-rich-nations-benefit-eu-membership.
5 See Robert Scott's work for the Economic Policy Institute, summarized at https://www.epi.org/blog/and-if-you-believe-this-ive-got-a-great-deal-to-sell-you-the-economic-impacts-of-the-revised-nafta-usmca-agreement/, accessed January 24, 2021.
6 Luis Villanueva, "Are Manufacturing Workers Benefiting from Trade? The Case of Mexico's Manufacturing Sector," *International Journal of Development Issues* 16, no. 1 (2017): 25–42.
7 Daron Acemoglu, David Autor, David Dorn, et al., "Import Competition and the Great U.S. Employment Sag of the 2000s," *Journal of Labor Economics* 34, no. 1 (2016).

International finance and open economy macroeconomics

Exchange rates, financial flows, and the balance of payments

International finance is a complex and important topic. Exchange rates can fluctuate widely, causing large swings in the prices of imports and exports. Billions of dollars can be made or lost very quickly in foreign exchange markets. International flows of money can fuel economic growth or cause an economic system to crash. This instability sometimes prompts governments to attempt to fix exchange rates in place and to regulate financial flows, although problems can result from such efforts.

This chapter begins with the market for foreign exchange and how the supply and demand for foreign currency affect exchange rates. Exchange rates in turn affect the prices of domestic and foreign goods, so exchange rates play an important role in determining which industries are successful in a particular country. In general, the exchange rate for a particular currency is determined by the supply and demand for that currency. Exchange rates change when people shift the amount of foreign goods or investments that they want, which in turn affects the relative prices of goods and assets. By affecting the relative prices of goods in different countries, exchange rates are an important factor in determining the demand for domestic and foreign goods, which can have a large influence on the success or failure of particular industries.

Next, we turn to the balance of payments and how international flows of money impact the economy. Inflows of money into an economy result from selling exports to other countries or from foreign investment in domestic assets. Outflows of money occur due to buying imports or from corporations and individuals investing in overseas assets. Because the balance of payments is an accounting identity, the inflows and outflows of money in the balance of payments must be equal. However, analysis of the balance of payments also makes it clear that when countries experience a trade deficit (imports greater than exports), they also end up with a financial account surplus (inflows of foreign capital greater than outflows of domestic capital). Trade deficits therefore result in greater foreign ownership of domestic assets. Most laissez-faire and New Keynesian economists see no significant problem with trade deficits, whereas political economists argue that trade deficits are likely to eliminate jobs and reduce growth.

Some countries allow market forces to dictate exchange rates, whereas other countries adjust currency flows to achieve a fixed exchange rate in order to try to achieve greater stability. Similarly, some countries allow international financial capital to flow in and out freely. Other countries strictly limit international financial flows. The variation in approach depends on a country's tolerance for the instability that can come from rapid swings in exchange rates and international investment flows and the country's willingness to utilize government intervention to achieve greater stability.

19.0 CHAPTER 19 LEARNING GOALS

After reading this chapter, you should be able to:

- Use a supply and demand graph of the foreign exchange market to analyze how particular events will affect exchange rates, exports, and imports.
- Describe the components of the balance of payments and explain how trade deficits and surpluses relate to financial account surpluses and deficits.
- Critically evaluate the arguments for and against trade deficits.
- Compare and contrast the different types of exchange rate regimes.
- Assess the arguments for and against regulating the flows of international capital.

We begin with the mainstream economic model of the market for foreign exchange.

19.1 EXCHANGE RATES AND THE FOREIGN EXCHANGE MARKET

An **exchange rate** refers to **the amount of one currency that exchanges for another** in a foreign exchange market. For example, in 2008, one U.S. dollar ($) exchanged for half of a British pound (£): $1 = £0.5. This also meant that one British pound was equal to two U.S. dollars: £1 = $2.

Then, from 2009 to 2021, the dollar appreciated—increased in value—relative to the pound. In 2021, one U.S. dollar exchanged for 0.75 pounds ($1 = £0.75). If we divide both sides by 0.75, we find that £1 = $\$\frac{1}{0.75}$ = $1.33. Therefore, the British pound depreciated—decreased in value—relative to the U.S. dollar.

A currency **appreciates** when the currency's value increases relative to a foreign currency. A currency **depreciates** when its value decreases relative to a foreign currency. Because exchange rates measure the value of one currency in terms of another currency, *whenever the domestic (home country) currency appreciates against a foreign currency, the foreign currency depreciates against the domestic currency and vice versa.*

In the mainstream economics model of the foreign exchange market, the value of a country's currency—the exchange rate of one currency with respect to another—is determined by the forces of supply and demand in the **foreign exchange market**. The foreign exchange market is where all buyers and sellers of a currency interact. Actors in foreign exchange markets include central banks, private banks, companies, investment firms, brokers, investors, and individuals.

In a foreign exchange market, the price of a currency is the exchange rate, which is the amount of a foreign currency that one unit of the domestic currency can purchase. On the quantity axis, the equilibrium quantity is the total amount of domestic currency exchanged for the foreign currency. The supply of the domestic currency comes from domestic country banks, businesses, investors, and consumers who want to exchange domestic country currency for foreign currency, usually so they can purchase foreign country goods or invest in foreign country assets. Basically, anyone who wants foreign goods or assets must supply their domestic currency in exchange for foreign currency at some point to buy the foreign goods or assets. The demand for domestic currency comes from foreign country banks, businesses, investors, and individuals who want domestic country goods or assets. The exchange rate determines the prices of domestic country goods and assets relative to the prices of foreign goods and assets.

Figure 19.1(a) on the next page shows a graph of the foreign exchange market for U.S. dollars relative to the British (U.K.) pound. The price of the dollar is the amount of foreign currency one dollar will buy—in this case, 0.5 pounds (£). The **supply curve** reflects U.S. citizens, banks, and businesses that are exchanging dollars for pounds. They are supplying (selling) U.S. dollars and demanding (purchasing) British pounds, because they want something British and you can only buy British items with British pounds. Typically, the supply curve of dollars is U.S. actors that want to buy British goods, travel in the United Kingdom, or buy British stocks and bonds.

The **demand curve** in the foreign exchange market for the dollar consists of U.K. citizens, banks, and businesses that are exchanging pounds for dollars. They are demanding dollars, which they purchase by supplying pounds. U.K. actors want U.S. dollars because they need dollars in order to buy U.S. goods, stocks, or bonds or to travel in the United States.

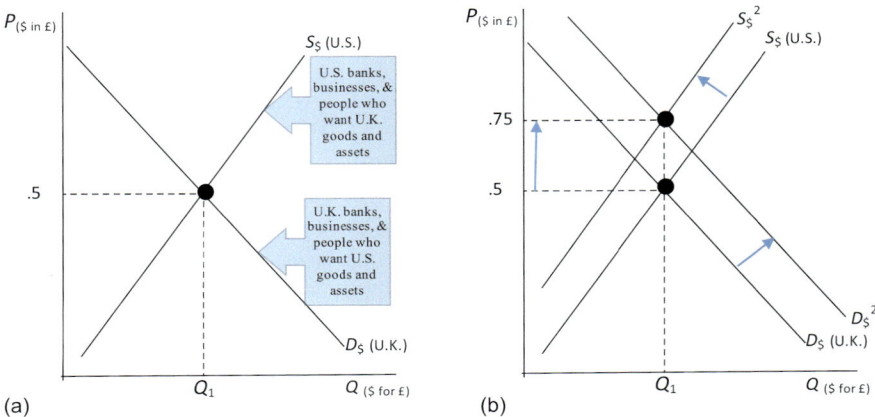

FIGURE 19.1 (a) The foreign exchange market for U.S. dollars and (b) U.S. assets become more attractive.

The demand curve for a currency slopes downward because as a currency increases in value (appreciates), home country goods and assets get more expensive and foreign citizens reduce their quantity demanded. The supply curve slopes upward because as a currency appreciates in value, foreign goods and assets get cheaper, so home country citizens supply more home currency to obtain more foreign currency, which they use to buy more foreign goods and assets.

As with all supply and demand graphs, a change in the exchange rate (the price of the dollar) causes a movement along the supply and demand curves. Shifts in supply and demand curves are caused by changes in the fundamental determinants of the location of the curves. (Recall the supply and demand model in earlier chapters.)

Figure 19.1(b) shows what happened to the foreign exchange market for U.S. dollars from 2007 to 2021. After the financial crisis hit in 2008, investors flocked to U.S. Treasury bonds, which are often considered the world's safest asset. Also, the U.S. economy recovered more quickly than the U.K. economy from the financial crisis, making it a more attractive investment location. And in 2016 when the U.K. decided to exit from the European Union (Brexit), investors feared that the British economy would face some major economic problems. For all of these reasons, U.S. investors decided to reduce their purchases of U.K. stocks and bonds from 2007 to 2021, reducing the supply of dollars (they did not need as many British pounds as usual because they were not investing as much in the U.K. economy). The supply of U.S. dollars decreases from S_s to S_s^2. Meanwhile, U.K. investors purchased more U.S. stocks and bonds than usual because the United States was a safer place to invest, increasing the demand for dollars. The demand for dollars increased from D_s to D_s^2. The result was a significant appreciation of the U.S. dollar, which was matched by an equally severe depreciation of the British pound.

As a general rule, whenever the domestic country (in this case the United States) changes its behavior, the supply curve of the domestic currency shifts. Whenever the foreign country (in this case the United Kingdom) changes its behavior, the demand curve for the domestic currency shifts. Notice that foreign exchange markets often feature double shifts, with both supply and demand curves shifting in opposite directions, because events often affect consumers or investors in both countries.

In the modern economy, international financial flows are so large, exceeding $1 trillion per day, that they have a major impact on currency values. In most cases, when an economy's expected economic performance is strong, there is a strong demand for that country's currency as investors seek out that country's assets. Therefore, *currencies tend to appreciate in countries with strong expected growth.*

19.2 THE DETERMINANTS OF SHIFTS IN SUPPLY AND DEMAND IN FOREIGN EXCHANGE MARKETS

The same rules that apply to regular supply and demand models apply to foreign exchange markets. A change in the price (exchange rate) causes a movement along the supply and demand curves. A change in one of the determinants of demand shifts the demand curve. A change in one of the determinants of supply shifts the supply curve.

19.2.1 Determinants of demand

The location of the demand curve in the mainstream foreign exchange market model is determined by the following factors:

1. **Government demand for its own currency.** Governments can purchase their own currency using gold or reserves of foreign currencies that they keep on hand.
2. **Changes in foreign incomes**. If foreign incomes increase, they will want more domestic country exports, which will cause them to increase their demand for domestic country currency.
3. **Changes in foreign tastes and preferences for domestic goods and investments**. If citizens' tastes in the foreign country change so that they want more domestic country products, their demand for domestic currency increases.
4. **Changes in relative interest rates**. If interest rates increase in the domestic country relative to the foreign country, foreign investors who seek out high interest rates (the highest return) for their money will demand more domestic country currency so they can buy more domestic interest-bearing bonds.

5. **Changes in relative prices of goods**. If goods prices decrease in the domestic country relative to the foreign country, consumers in the foreign country will want more domestic country goods, increasing the demand for domestic currency.

Decreases in the demand for a nation's currency would be a result of decreased government purchases of the nation's own currency, decreases in foreign incomes, foreign tastes changing so they demand less domestic country goods, a decrease in relative interest rates, or an increase in domestic country goods prices.

Most of the factors affecting the demand curve for a currency are a product of changes in foreign country behavior. In general, any factor that causes foreign citizens to want more goods or assets (stocks or interest-bearing bonds) from the domestic country will cause an increase in the demand for the domestic country's currency, shifting the demand curve up and the right. Any factor causing foreign citizens to want less of the domestic country's goods or assets would cause a decrease in the demand curve.

19.2.2 Determinants of supply

The location of the supply curve in the mainstream foreign exchange market model is determined by the following factors:

1. **Changes in the government's supply of its own currency**. Governments can supply more of their own currency, using it to purchase foreign currencies.
2. **Changes in domestic country incomes**. When home country consumers have more money, they will buy more goods, and some of those goods will come from foreign countries. To buy more foreign goods, they must increase the supply of home country currency in exchange for foreign currency.
3. **Changes in home country tastes and preferences for foreign country goods and investments**. If home country consumers prefer more foreign country goods than they used to, more home country currency will be supplied to purchase more foreign goods.
4. **Changes in relative interest rates**. If interest rates decrease in the home country relative to the foreign country, home country investors who seek out high interest rates for their money will invest *more* money abroad, buying more foreign interest-bearing bonds and increasing their supply of home country currency.
5. **Changes in relative prices of goods**. If goods prices increase in the home country relative to the foreign country, consumers in the home country will want more foreign country goods, increasing the supply of home country currency.

A decrease in the supply of a currency would result from a decrease in government supply of its own currency, a decrease in home country incomes, reduced home country preferences for foreign goods or investments, higher relative home country interest rates, or lower relative home country prices.

Notice that changes in relative interest rates and changes in relative prices appear in *both* the demand and the supply list of determinants in exchange markets. These factors cause **double shifts**.

Now let's consider some examples. To get you used to applying this model to any country, we will use Japan and the euro area as the two sides of the foreign exchange market. In the foreign exchange market for the Japanese yen, Japanese banks, consumers, and investors are the ones supplying yen in exchange for euros. Japan is the domestic (home) economy. The amount of yen Japanese actors supply depends on how many European goods and assets they want. Meanwhile, the demand for yen comes from European banks, consumers, and investors who want Japanese goods and assets. The amount of yen they demand (which is also the amount of euros they supply) depends on how many Japanese goods and assets Europeans want.

Figure 19.2(a) shows what happens to the foreign exchange market for Japanese yen (¥) when incomes in the euro (€) area increase. When European consumers have more income, they buy more products, and some of the products they buy will be Japanese. When the demand for Japanese exported goods increases, European importers must pay for those goods in Japanese yen, so the demand for yen increases, shifting up and to the right and moving the equilibrium from point **A** to point **B**. The result is an appreciation of the yen, whose exchange rate value increases from €0.008 to €0.009. The quantity of yen exchanged for euros increases from Q_1 to Q_2.

In Figure 19.2(b), we see what happens to the exchange rate value of the Japanese yen when interest rates in the euro area increase. A very important thing to understand in foreign exchange markets is that **international money tends to**

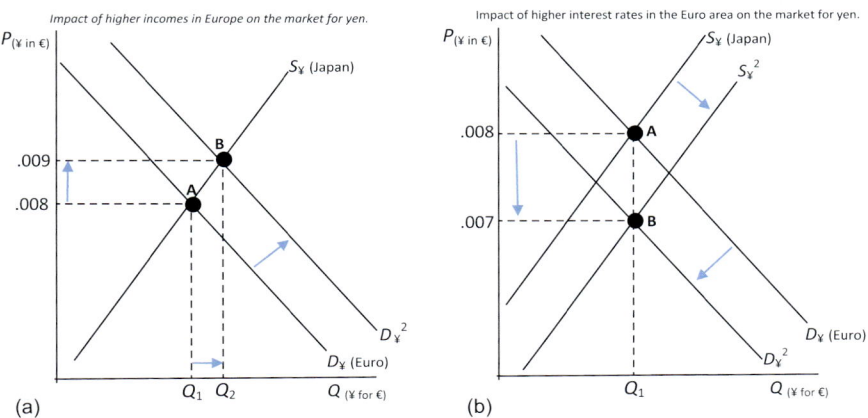

FIGURE 19.2 (a) Increase in incomes in Europe and (b) Interest rates in euro area increase.

flow wherever interest rates are higher. At any given time, there are a lot of international investors looking to put their money in bonds that pay a high interest rate, so any country that has higher interest rates relative to other countries will see an inflow of foreign money.

In this example, interest rates in the euro area increase. This causes a double shift in the foreign exchange market. Japanese investors want to move some of their money to Europe to take advantage of the higher interest rates there, so there is an **increase in the supply of yen**. Japanese investors exchange yen for euros so they can buy European bonds and other interest-bearing securities. Meanwhile, European investors who usually invest some of their money in Japanese bonds decide to invest less than usual in Japan, preferring to invest their money in European bonds that come with new higher interest rates. Therefore, the **demand for Japanese yen decreases** as euro area investors exchange fewer euros for yen. This increase in supply and decrease in demand for yen causes the value of the yen to depreciate from €0.008 to €0.007.

Now let's go through some additional examples to make sure you understand how foreign exchange markets work.

Suppose that the prices of Japanese goods decline relative to the prices of European goods. What would happen to the foreign exchange market for the Japanese yen? Japanese consumers who usually buy European goods would buy less than usual, because Japanese goods are now relatively cheaper. The supply of yen would decrease. European consumers would buy more Japanese goods than usual because they are relatively less expensive, increasing the demand for yen. The result would be a decrease in supply and an increase in demand for yen, both of which would cause the yen to appreciate (increase in value relative to the euro).

Now suppose that the central bank of Japan wants to give a boost to Japanese exports. To do so, they supply more Japanese yen, which they use to buy up euros. This increase in the supply of yen causes the value of the yen to fall. The yen depreciates relative to the euro. How does this help Japanese exports?

Suppose that a Toyota Prius, made in Japan, normally sells for ¥2,500,000. If the exchange rate is ¥1 = €0.008, then €1 = ¥$\frac{1}{0.008}$ = ¥125 That means a Prius selling for ¥2,500,000 will sell for €$\frac{2,500,000}{125}$ = €20,000.[1]

Now suppose that the yen depreciates due to the Japanese central bank's actions, falling to ¥1 = €0.00666. This means that €1 = ¥$\frac{1}{0.00666}$ = ¥150. The Prius, which still sells for ¥2,500,000 in Japan, now costs €$\frac{2500000}{150}$ = €16,667. The Japanese central bank action reduced the price of the Prius, and of all Japanese export goods, significantly, which will help Japanese exporters sell more goods in Europe. Exchange rates can have a major impact on a country's imports and exports as well as their financial markets.

Political economists view exchange rate markets as extremely speculative in nature. The vast majority of currency market trades involve speculation rather than exchanges related to international trade or investment. This makes exchange markets subject to extreme fluctuations and speculative bubbles that can be destabilizing (and that are hard to model). Hence, as we will see later, many political economists advocate the regulation of exchange markets to improve stability.

19.3 EXCHANGE RATES, TRADE, AND MARKETS FOR GOODS AND SERVICES

Exchange rates directly affect the prices of imports and exports as well as the value of assets. Therefore, exchange rates impact goods markets and financial markets significantly, and they affect aggregate demand and aggregate supply.

The following are the key principles regarding how exchange rates affect other markets:

- Depreciation of a home country's currency makes foreign goods more expensive for home country consumers (reducing imports) and makes home country goods cheaper for foreign consumers (increasing exports). When a currency depreciates, each unit of that currency buys fewer foreign goods than it used to, making them more expensive. The decreases in imports and increases in exports increase aggregate demand. Imported inputs become more expensive, however, so aggregate supply decreases slightly, with the degree of the shift depending on the percentage of a country's inputs that are imported.
- Depreciation of a home country's currency makes its money worth less relative to foreign money, which reduces the value of home country assets. This can hurt home country financial institutions, especially banks.
- Appreciation of a home country's currency makes its goods more expensive relative to the prices of foreign products, reducing exports and increasing imports. This has the effect of decreasing aggregate demand. Aggregate supply increases slightly with a currency appreciation because foreign inputs become less expensive.
- Appreciation of a home country's currency makes its money worth more relative to foreign currencies, which increases the value of home country assets.

Because of the impact on exports, currency devaluation has been a frequent tool used by countries to promote export industries. The 2015 World Economic Outlook published by the International Monetary Fund (IMF) found that a 10% devaluation of a nation's currency can boost exports by an average 1.5% of gross domestic product (GDP).[2] Thus, currency devaluation can provide a significant boost to economic growth.

There are some potential problems with devaluing a nation's currency to promote growth, however. First, devaluation tends to increase prices and harm consumers. Devaluation makes all foreign goods prices higher, because the home country currency buys less than it used to. Imported inputs get more expensive, raising the costs of production. The increase in the prices of imported goods also allows domestic firms to raise their prices. In addition, devaluation reduces the value of a country's financial assets. Assets in foreign countries become relatively more expensive. Thus, devaluing a currency has some substantial benefits, along with some costs.

China has regularly been accused of maintaining an artificially low exchange rate in order to promote exports. After the financial crisis hit in 2009, numerous countries engaged in competitive devaluations of their currencies to try to promote exports. Of course, if countries simultaneously attempt to devalue their currencies, there will be no impact on exchange rates or exports. For example, if the Japanese government supplies more yen to buy euros but the European government supplies more euros to buy yen, their actions cancel each other out. However, countries that did not devalue their currency in 2009 saw reduced exports to countries that did devalue their currency.

The impact of exchange rates on trade and financial flows is one of the major factors driving changes in a country's balance of payments. It is to this topic that we turn next.

19.4 INTERNATIONAL FINANCE AND THE BALANCE OF PAYMENTS

International finance involves the flows of goods and services, income, assets, and other forms of financial capital between countries. These flows can have a large influence on economic outcomes, so it is important to understand how they work.

The **balance of payments** measures **all of the transactions in which the currency of one nation is exchanged for the currency of another nation during a particular period of time** (usually one year). Mostly, currency exchanges occur because of trade (exports or imports) or because of purchases of another country's assets (financial investments). The balance of payments is an accounting identity tracking these flows, and all of the inflows of money—the credits—must balance all of the outflows of money—the debits. This is displayed in Figure 19.3.

Within the balance of payments, the major issues economists focus on are the following:

- The current account deficit or surplus, which is driven primarily by any trade deficit (the amount imports exceed exports) or surplus (the amount exports exceed imports).
- The financial account surplus (the amount foreign purchases of home country assets exceed home country purchases of foreign country assets) or deficit.

Because credits (inflows) always balance debits (outflows), *any current account deficit is always matched by a financial account surplus, and any current account surplus is always matched by a financial account deficit.*

Home Country Balance of Payments Credits Any inflow of money from a foreign country	Home Country Balance of Payments Debits Any outflow of money to a foreign country
Current Account	**Current Account**
Incoming money from **exports** of home country goods and services	Outgoing money to pay for **imports** of foreign country goods and services
Investment and salary income earned by home country citizens in foreign countries	**Investment and salary income** earned by foreign country citizens in the home country
Foreign aid (unilateral transfers) given from foreign countries to the home country	**Foreign aid** (unilateral transfers) given from the home country to foreign countries
Financial Account	**Financial Account**
Foreign purchases of home country assets (stocks, bonds, property, and other assets)	**Home country purchases of foreign country assets** (stocks, bonds, property, etc.)
Money from the **sale of foreign assets** (stocks, bonds, property, and other foreign assets) by the home country	Money from the **sale of home country assets** (stocks, bonds, property, and other assets) by the foreign country
Incoming transfers of assets (migrants' remittances, fund and asset transfers)	**Outgoing transfers** of assets (migrants' remittances, fund and asset transfers)
Capital Account: debt forgiveness and other capital and nonfinancial transfers to foreign citizens	**Capital Account**: debt forgiveness and other capital and nonfinancial transfers to home country citizens

FIGURE 19.3 Table showing the two sides of the balance of payments.

Categories of the U.S. Current Account, in millions of dollars.	2017	2018
Exports of goods and services and income receipts (credits)	$ 3,433,239	$ 3,701,694
Exports of goods and services	2,351,072	2,500,756
Goods	1,553,383	**1,672,331**
Services	797,690	828,425
Primary income receipts (investment income, compensation)	928,118	1,060,362
Secondary income (current transfer) receipts	154,049	140,576
Imports of goods and services and income payments (debits)	3,882,380	4,190,166
Imports of goods and services	2,903,349	3,122,862
Goods	2,360,878	**2,563,651**
Services	542,471	559,211
Primary income payments (investment income, compensation)	706,386	816,066
Secondary income (current transfer) payments	272,645	251,237
Capital transfer receipts and other credits	24,788	9,418
Capital transfer payments and other debits	42	10
Current account deficit	**-424,395**	**-479,064**

FIGURE 19.4 U.S. current account.

19.4.1 Trade deficits and the current account

Figure 19.4 displays the U.S. current account for 2017 and 2018. Notice in particular that in 2018 U.S. exports of goods were $1,672 billion and U.S. imports of goods were $2,563 billion, which means that in 2018 the United States experienced a trade deficit in goods of $891 billion. This was offset somewhat by a trade surplus in services. This left the United States with a current account deficit of $479 billion in 2018. That money flowed out of the United States to foreign countries.

Figure 19.5 (next page) shows the countries with which the United States experienced its largest trade deficits in 2019. The trade deficits with China are particularly large, followed by those with Mexico, Japan, Germany, Vietnam, and Ireland.

Country	U.S. Exports to Trading Partner	U.S. Imports from Trading Partner	U.S. Trade Deficit
China	106.6	452.2	345.6
Mexico	256.4	358.1	101.7
Japan	74.7	143.6	68.9
Germany	60.3	127.5	67.2
Vietnam	10.9	66.7	55.8
Ireland	9.0	61.8	52.8
Italy	23.8	57.2	33.4
Canada	292.7	319.7	27
India	34.4	57.7	23.3
Taiwan	31.2	54.3	23.1
South Korea	56.9	77.5	20.6
France	37.8	57.4	19.6

FIGURE 19.5 Largest U.S. trade deficits, 2019.

Categories of the U.S. Financial Account, in millions of dollars	2017	2018
Net U.S. acquisition of financial assets excluding financial derivatives	$ 1,182,749	$ 301,618
Net U.S. incurrence of liabilities excluding financial derivatives	1,537,683	800,913
Financial derivatives other than reserves, net transactions	23,074	-20,261
Financial Account Surplus	331,860	519,556
Statistical discrepancy	92,536	-40,492
Current account deficit	-424,395	-479,064

FIGURE 19.6 U.S. financial account.

Figure 19.6 shows the U.S. financial account and capital account in 2017 and 2018. The financial account includes all financial flows into and out of a country. The U.S. financial outflow is primarily the purchase of capital assets outside the United States by the U.S. government, institutions, citizens, or businesses. Meanwhile, the U.S. financial inflow is the purchase of U.S. capital assets by foreign governments, institutions, citizens, or businesses. The difference is the statistical discrepancy, which has to do with the amounts of money that vanish each year, held as cash for a variety of reasons (some of them illegal).

Notice that the financial account surplus is very close to the amount of current account deficit. This has an important implication: *A nation with a trade deficit is also experiencing foreign purchases of domestic assets.* A nation with a trade surplus is acquiring foreign assets. The capital account includes various other transfers of assets and is so small for the United States that it has a negligible impact on the balance of payments.

When we compare the current account deficit for the United States with the financial and capital account surpluses, we see the mirror image graph depicted in Figure 19.7. The larger the current account deficit, the larger the financial account surplus.

Normally, mainstream economists expect exchange rates to adjust when a nation has a large trade deficit. Trade deficits cause a large outflow of a country's currency. By flooding the international market with its currency, a country causes its currency to depreciate. The depreciation in currency causes home country goods to become cheaper, which boosts exports and reduces imports, thereby

INTERNATIONAL FINANCE AND OPEN ECONOMY 487

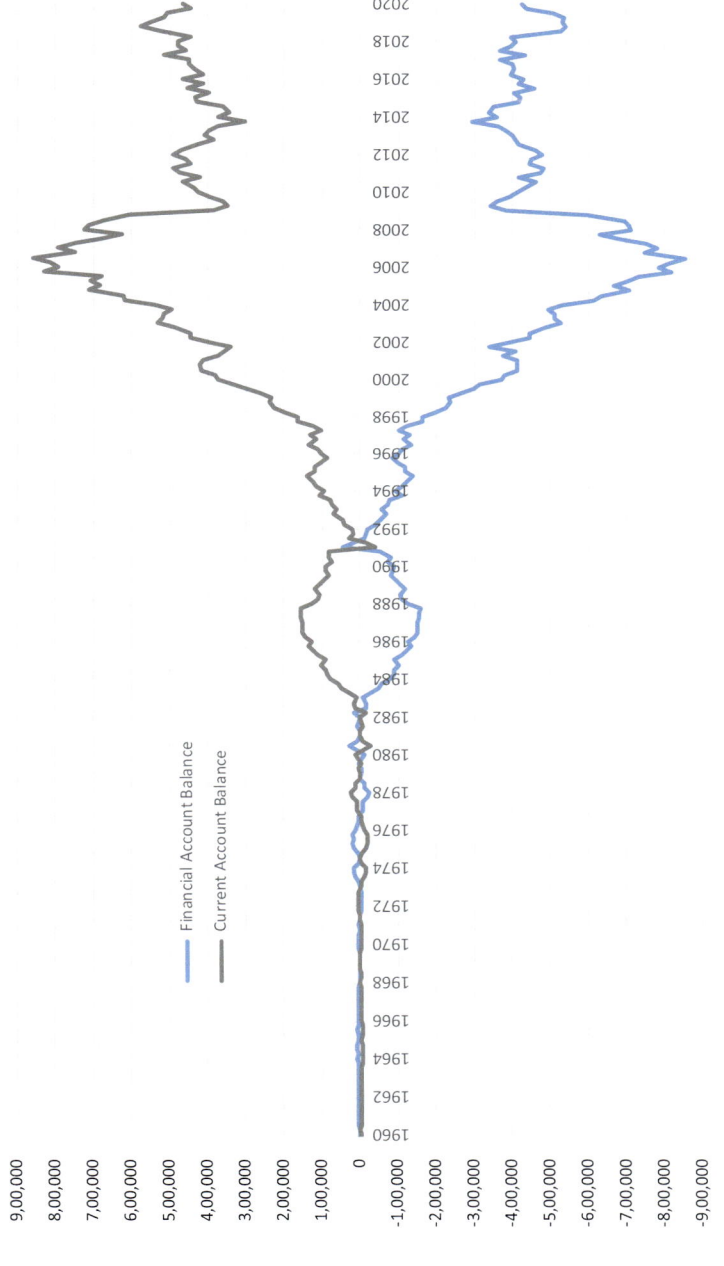

FIGURE 19.7 U.S. financial account and current account, 1960–2020 (millions of $).

eliminating the trade deficit. Trade surpluses would have the opposite effect. Thus, according to mainstream economic theory, trade deficits and surpluses should automatically be eliminated by adjustments in exchange rates.

However, political economists point out that in the modern era, chronic trade deficits and surpluses are the norm for many countries. Furthermore, these imbalances can lead to some significant problems, even though there are benefits to consumers from the "extra" imports.

The root cause of trade deficits can be determined by analyzing the key GDP accounting identities behind the balance of payments that were described earlier in the book.

$$GDP = C + S + T = C + I + G + X - IM$$

$$S + T + IM = I + G + X$$

$$(S - I) + (T - G) = (X - IM).$$

Therefore, trade deficits ($X - IM$) are a product of the amount savings is less than investment ($S < I$) and the amount taxes are less than government spending ($T < G$; budget deficits).

19.5 THE CAUSES OF U.S. TRADE DEFICITS

There are three major causes of U.S. trade deficits that economists from various perspectives have identified: (1) Low U.S. national savings, (2) high savings rates in several countries that are important U.S. trading partners, and (3) high demand for U.S. assets.

1. **Low U.S. national savings.** The U.S. government runs chronic budget deficits, and U.S. consumers save very little compared with consumers in the rest of the world. Mainstream economists therefore identify *low U.S. national savings as the major source of the U.S. trade deficit*. Any country that consumes more than it produces is by definition consuming more than its income, so it *must* run a trade deficit. The extra goods being consumed must be produced by a foreign country. Therefore, if the United States wants to eliminate the trade deficit, it would need to save more and consume less, and the government would need to balance its budget. This would be quite painful, involving major decreases to aggregate demand and possibly a recession.

    Whereas mainstream economists focus on low national savings as the primary culprit, political economists focus on a different set of issues. Political economists argue that that major source of U.S. trade deficits is the surge of foreign investments in U.S. assets, which takes the form of foreign purchases of U.S. stocks, bonds, property, companies, and other assets. This is a product of high foreign savings, the status of the U.S. dollar as the world's reserve currency that central banks and investors prefer to hold, and active efforts by foreign central banks and foreign investors to purchase U.S. assets. High demand for U.S. assets increases the demand for the dollar, causing the dollar to appreciate and U.S. exports to increase in price.

2. **High foreign savings.** Many trading partners of the United States have extremely high rates of savings and low levels of consumption. As a result, these high-savings countries end up producing more goods than they purchase, resulting in a trade surplus in their country. This is especially true of Japan, South Korea, China, and Germany. Figure 19.8 shows that the savings rates in these countries, especially China, are much higher than the savings rate in the United States.[3]

   Sometimes high savings rates can be attributed to culture: Citizens of some countries have always had high rates of savings. However, high savings rates and low levels of consumption are also a product of specific economic policies. For example, (a) some countries actively suppress wages. In China and Germany, the state actively pursues low wage policies. This limits the amount of goods their consumers purchase, leading to low levels of consumption and high savings rates. Another factor is (b) the subsidization of exports, something that China, Japan, South Korea, and Germany all engage in. Subsidizing exports takes domestic money that could have been spent on consumption and uses it instead for production. In addition, (c) high domestic taxes on the consumption of goods and services, such as Germany's 19% value-added tax, reduce domestic consumption. Trading partners that systematically suppress consumer demand while subsidizing production tend to run trade surpluses, which generate large inflows of foreign (U.S.) currency into their countries.

3. **High demand for U.S. assets and currency.** Financial markets in the United States are viewed as a uniquely profitable investment environment, with little regulation and generous government bailouts if things get bad.

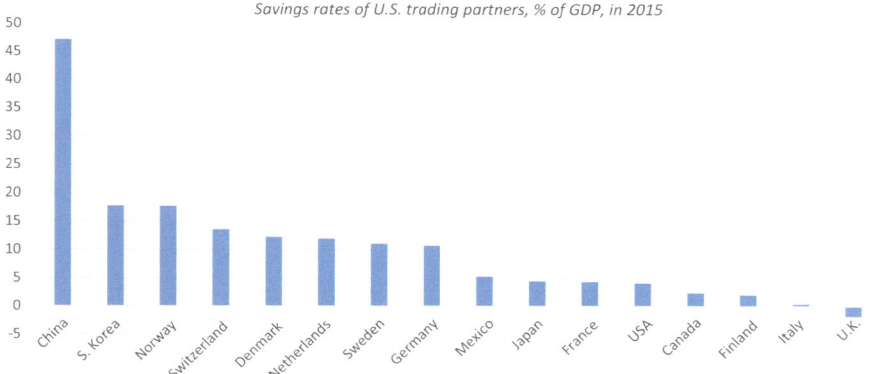

FIGURE 19.8 Savings rates of U.S. trading partners.

U.S. government bonds are viewed as one of the world's safest assets. As a result, investors all of over the world have a high demand for U.S. assets.

Similarly, the U.S. dollar was set up after World War II as the world's reserve currency in order to make international transactions easier. The dollar continues to serve this role, with more than 90% of foreign exchange transactions involving the dollar and more than 60% of international reserves held in dollars. In essence, the dollar is used around the world in transactions that have little or nothing to do with the U.S. economy. Consequently, there is generally more demand for the dollar than for other currencies, which causes the dollar to appreciate in value above its normal level, contributing to trade deficits.

Outsized financial flows into the United States are exacerbated when the countries that run trade surpluses with the United States take the dollars they earned on exports and invest those sums in U.S. asset markets. This provides an additional factor that keeps the U.S. dollar overvalued, while providing an outlet for the surplus of funds generated in trade surplus countries. The high demand for U.S. assets, coming from foreign savings, foreign asset demand, and foreign trade surplus revenues, increases the demand for the U.S. dollar, causing the dollar to appreciate in value and making U.S. goods more expensive, thereby reducing exports and contributing directly to the trade deficit.

Note that, regardless of the primary reason for trade deficit (low U.S. national savings, high savings in trading partner economies, or high demand for U.S. assets), the consequences are the same: *A country with chronic trade deficits will experience increasing levels of foreign ownership of domestic assets as long as these relationships persist.* Some economists see this as a major problem, whereas others do not.

19.6 THE CONSEQUENCES AND THE DEBATE OVER TRADE DEFICITS

There are a number of different perspectives on trade deficits. Most political economists find trade deficits problematic because they can reduce employment in the United States, hurting U.S. workers. Supply-side economists argue that foreign countries unfairly advantage their own firms and disadvantage U.S. firms, which is bad for U.S. industrial development. Laissez-faire economists believe that trade deficits are primarily a product of too much government spending, which they would like to rein in via austerity policies. Most mainstream New Keynesian economists, however, see trade deficits as a relatively harmless phenomenon that enhances the U.S. standard of living without significant costs. These perspectives are described in more detail below.

Critics of U.S. trade deficits include U.S. labor leaders, political economists, and liberal mainstream economists who argue that *foreign countries are hurting U.S.*

employment via their manipulative trade practices. Note that this problem occurs under very specific circumstances.

By engineering their economies to increase production while holding consumption levels steady, trade surplus countries can increase their own employment levels at the expense of employment in countries running trade deficits. Production in trade surplus countries outstrips domestic consumption, and the excess supply is sold to foreign country consumers. At the same time, when the United States exports less than it imports, aggregate demand is lower than it would have been otherwise (recall that aggregate demand includes net exports, $X-IM$).

If the inflow of foreign money from the trade deficit stimulates new investment, then aggregate demand (and U.S. income and employment) will be maintained, and the trade deficit will not harm U.S. employment. However, in recent years in the United States there has been an overabundance of money in financial markets, which means that *the addition of foreign funds is not being invested productively*. Therefore, *any country with excess liquidity in financial markets that exports less than it imports will see lower levels of aggregate demand, lower GDP, and fewer jobs*. Unfortunately, this has been the U.S. experience in recent years, meaning that *the United States is directly experiencing economic costs (lower employment and GDP) from the trade deficit*.[4] From the perspective of political economists and some liberal mainstream economists, U.S. workers should be protected from subsidized foreign competition to prevent these negative outcomes.

It is worth pointing out that although the trade deficit may be costing U.S. workers jobs, it is very good for U.S. financial markets. The flood of international money keeps interest rates low, and the flood of foreign purchases of U.S. assets increases the value of the U.S. stock market and other U.S. assets. Some investors, like Warren Buffet, worry that the United States will be "colonized by purchase" of assets by foreign countries, steadily losing control of its assets.[5] Other investors argue that the infusion of foreign investment provides liquidity and opportunities that lead to job and income creation.

President Trump, and the supply-side economists who supported him, made U.S. trade deficits a major political issue. Trump engaged in trade wars with China and numerous other countries, imposing tariffs on their goods and threatening to keep those tariffs in place until the trade surplus countries started purchasing more U.S. exports. These countries then retaliated by imposing tariffs on U.S. goods. Trump succeeded in reducing the U.S. trade deficit slightly but at a huge cost to numerous U.S. businesses that experienced higher costs from tariffs on inputs and declining export sales.

Laissez-faire advocates like Martin Feldstein argue that the U.S. trade deficit is primarily a result of too much government spending. Laissez-faire economists would like to resolve the issue by dramatically reducing the amount of government spending.

However, the majority of mainstream, New Keynesian economists see the trade deficit as mostly harmless. First and foremost, U.S. trade deficits indicate that

U.S. consumers have a higher standard of living, consuming more goods than they could afford without having access to surplus goods from trading partners. In addition, foreign investment increases U.S. asset values and allows the United States to maintain a high level of domestic investment. The increased payments to foreign owners have not, as yet, proved to be a problem. This led conservative mainstream economist Gregory Mankiw to argue, "Whether a trade deficit represents a problem depends on whether our spending is prudent or profligate."[6] As long as businesses are investing money wisely and consumers are not spending beyond their means, trade deficits are not a problem from this perspective. According to the standard mainstream economic models, rational, well-informed consumer and investor behavior ensures that trade deficits are not problematic.

In contrast, most political economists dispute that injections of foreign capital are being invested productively given low levels of business investment (in capital goods) in the United States in recent decades. Furthermore, consumer debt levels are extremely high, calling into question the rationality of the spending behavior of the modern U.S. consumer. And, as noted above, political economic research notes the negative impact of trade deficits on U.S. aggregate demand and employment.

We have focused on the U.S. experience in this section. Other countries, however, experience balance of payments issues very differently. Developing countries cannot run persistent current account deficits like those of the United States because international investors usually are not willing to purchase large quantities of developing country assets. Running current account deficits can cause a developing country to experience rapid currency depreciation, inflation, and unemployment. In this sense, developing countries are often balance-of-payments constrained, in that they are forced to balance international inflows and outflows.

Given that trade deficits or surpluses depend in part on exchange rates, countries can affect their trade balance by manipulating their exchange rate. Alternatively, they can allow market forces to determine their exchange rate. The decision to manage a country's exchange rate or let it "float" is discussed in the next section.

19.7 FIXED VS. FLOATING EXCHANGE RATE REGIMES

One of the major issues that each government must decide when it comes to international finance is whether or not it will allow its currency to float freely based on the forces of supply and demand or whether it wants to try to maintain a fixed exchange rate to build more stability into the economic system. Each option comes with its benefits and potential problems.

In general, there are three major types of exchange rate regimes: Freely floating, managed float, or fixed. A **floating exchange rate regime** is when **the government does not regulate the exchange rate, allowing its country's** currency to fluctuate with market forces. This can lead to widespread fluctuations in a nation's currency. Figure 19.9 shows the fluctuations in the price of one euro in U.S. dollars from 2016 to 2021. These are two relatively stable currencies, but it is common for the exchange rate to fluctuate by 15% to 20% in a single year. For businesses that depend on importing and exporting, this introduces a significant amount of variability into their operations.

Countries sometimes turn to fixed exchange rates to facilitate exchange with particular trading partners, such as countries within the euro region, or to stabilize an economic system and give confidence to investors that their money will retain its value. Foreign exchange risk is one of the biggest hurdles facing an international investor or trader. If you invest in a country and its currency crashes, your money will lose a large share of its value. For example, if you invested in Venezuela's major industry, oil and gas, at the beginning of 2020, by the end of 2020 your investment would have lost 70% of its value due to the dramatic depreciation of Venezuela's currency. Investors can purchase futures contracts that allow them to lock in a particular exchange rate, but such contracts can be expensive, especially when a country is unstable.

A **fixed exchange rate regime** exists **when the government of a country pegs (fixes) the value of its currency relative to another currency**. Given the constant fluctuations in the supply and demand for a country's currency, a fixed exchange rate can only be maintained through vigilant efforts by a country's central bank. In reality, fixed exchange rates fluctuate slightly around the official rate.

There are numerous examples of fixed exchange rates. Before European Union (E.U.) members adopted the euro, they pegged their currencies to the German Deutsche Mark to make the currency conversion possible. Rather than adopt the euro, Denmark pegs its currency to the euro so that it can trade easily with other E.U. countries. In addition, Denmark can adjust its currency if it experiences a crisis, something that Greece was unable to do once it adopted the euro as its currency.

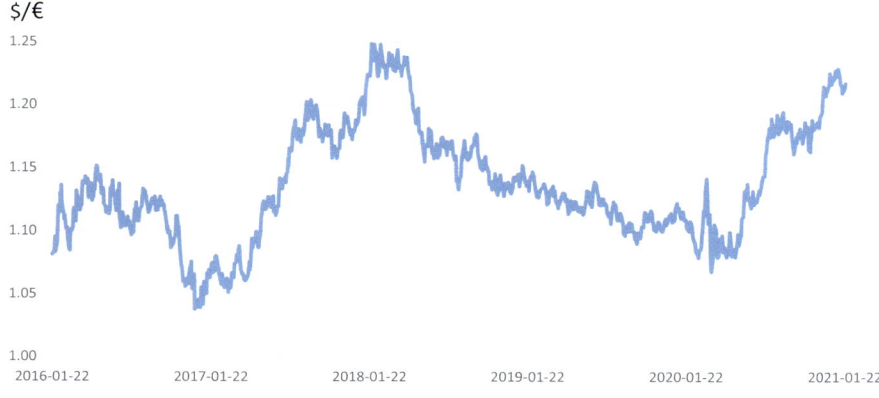

FIGURE 19.9 U.S. dollars per euro, 2016–2021.

Small countries also sometimes peg their currencies to an established one to reduce fluctuations and stabilize the economy. Panama and Cuba peg their currencies to the U.S. dollar.

Governments have three main tools they can use to alter the supply or the demand for their currency in order to maintain its value: (1) Purchase or sell its own currency, (2) restrict access to international exchange, or (3) change interest rates.

Suppose that Japan wants to peg its currency to the euro at €1 = ¥100 (¥1 = €0.010) to facilitate trade with Europe, thereby making exporters and importers in Japan and Europe secure in the knowledge that investments and exchanges will garner a reliable return. The government of Japan will need to manipulate the demand or supply of their currency to keep the exchange rate with the euro steady.

Figure 19.10(a) shows the yen originally in equilibrium at point **A** at an exchange rate of ¥1 = €0.009, below the target the government set. The

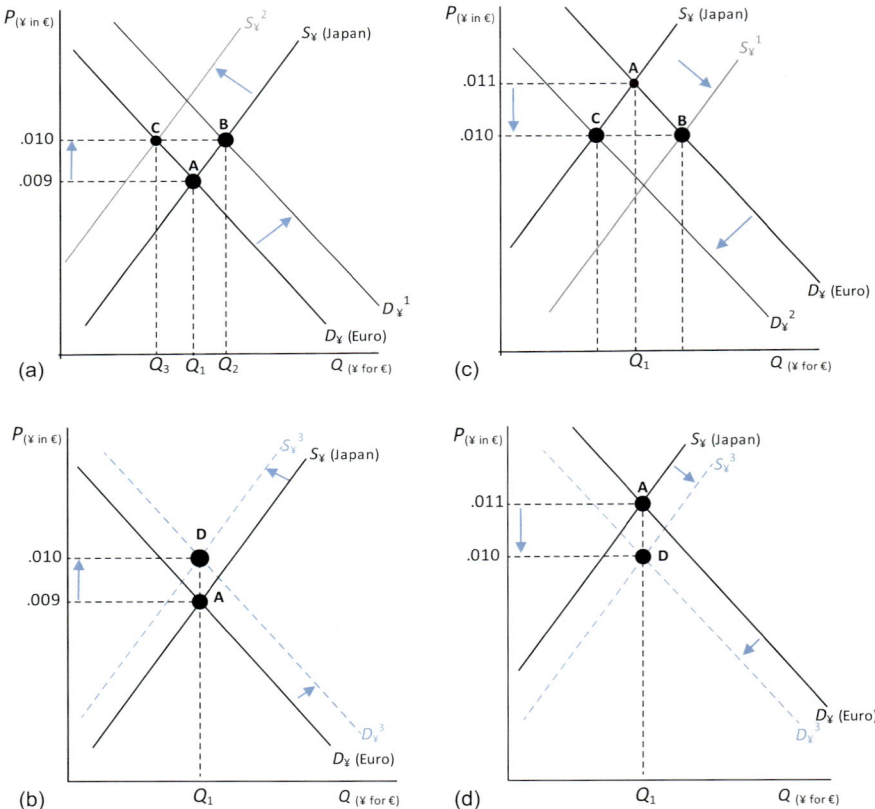

FIGURE 19.10 (a) Actions to increase the value of the yen, (b) Increase in interest rates in Japan, (c) Actions to decrease the value of the yen, and (d) Decrease in interest rates in Japan.

government has three choices to increase the value of the yen, all of which involve decreasing the supply and/or increasing the demand for yen.

1. The government can increase the demand for yen by **buying its own currency** (yen) utilizing gold or foreign exchange reserves it has accumulated. This will increase the demand for yen from $D_¥$ to $D_¥^2$, moving the market to a new equilibrium at point **B** and increasing the value of the yen back to its target of ¥1 = €0.010. In order to buy more of its own currency, governments must accumulate gold or the currencies of their trading partners. This action is only possible until the government runs out of its precious metal and foreign exchange reserves.
2. The government can reduce the supply of yen by instituting **foreign exchange controls** such as instituting a licensing system that strictly limits the amount of foreign exchange that individuals and firms can purchase. The result is that fewer domestic entities are able to supply their currency in exchange for a foreign currency, reducing the supply of yen. The shifts the supply curve of yen in Figure 19.10(a) from $S_¥$ to $S_¥^2$, causing the value of the yen to increase back to its target of €0.010. Many developing countries install limits on purchases of foreign currencies to keep financial capital from leaving the country.
3. The government can **increase interest rates** to draw money into the country. As shown in Figure 19.10(b), higher interest rates in Japan will decrease the supply of yen from $S_¥$ to $S_¥^3$ as Japanese investors keep more of their money in Japanese interest-bearing securities. Meanwhile, the demand for yen will increase from $D_¥$ to $D_¥^3$ as foreign investors also seek out Japanese interest-bearing securities. The result is an appreciation of the yen from €0.009 to €0.010. Note that although higher interest rates do help to raise the value of a country's currency, there will be some negative consequences due to the impact of higher interest rates on domestic consumption and investment.

Maintaining a strong currency makes it easier for a country to accumulate foreign assets and purchase foreign goods, although it makes a country's exports more expensive.

If a country's currency is above its target exchange rate, the government will have to take actions that would reduce demand and/or increase supply of its currency. Figure 19.10(c) shows Japan in equilibrium at point **A** with an overvalued currency of ¥1 = €0.011. The government has three choices to cause the yen to depreciate.

1. The government can **increase the supply of its own currency** (yen) and use it to buy the foreign currency (euros). This increases the supply of yen from $S_¥$ to $S_¥^1$, causing the value of the yen to depreciate to the target of ¥1 = €0.010 at point **B**. Because governments can create unlimited amounts of their own currency, there are no limits on the amount of this a government

can undertake. However, too much supply of a currency could cause its value to drop too much, which would lead to inflationary pressures and eventually could result in people refusing to accept a currency. Therefore, governments use this option judiciously.

2. The government can **impose foreign exchange controls on the amount of domestic currency that foreign investors can purchase**. This reduces the demand for the domestic currency (yen), shifting the demand curve from $D_¥$ to $D_¥^2$ and causing the value of the yen to depreciate from 0.11 to 0.10 at point **C**. Countries that want to limit foreign control over domestic markets often impose this type of foreign exchange control.

3. The government can **decrease interest rates**, which will cause domestic investors to supply more yen in order to purchase more euro-denominated bonds that pay higher interest rates. The supply of yen shifts from $S_¥$ to $S_¥^3$ in Figure 19.10(d). Similarly, European investors will decrease their demand for yen, as they buy fewer Japanese bonds than normal due to lower interest rates in Japan. The demand for yen shifts from $D_¥$ to $D_¥^3$. The new equilibrium at point **D** in Figure 19.10(d) has returned the yen to its pegged rate of 0.010 euros.

Many countries maintain their currencies at an artificially low exchange rate to promote exports. However, this hurts consumers by increasing the prices of imported goods and it hurts investors by reducing the value of domestic currency.

Countries who find the fluctuations in floating exchange rate regimes too destabilizing but see the fixing of exchange rates as overly restrictive can opt for a middle ground. A **managed float exchange rate regime** is **when the government establishes a target zone for its currency, and intervenes whenever its currency leaves the target zone**. Thus, a currency would be allowed to appreciate or depreciate somewhat, but the government would step in to intervene if the changes in the currency's value were too dramatic.

According to the IMF, in 2013, 82 countries used a managed float exchange rate regime, 25 countries used a fixed regime, and 65 countries used a floating regime. So most countries manage their currencies in some manner, although many of the world's largest economies, including the United States and the E.U., allow their exchange rates to float.

Laissez-faire and New Keynesian economists tend to prefer floating exchange rates due to their faith in markets. Political economists often prefer managed float or fixed exchange rate systems due to their emphasis on stability, although there are some notable dissenters who think that floating exchange rates allow for more expansionary fiscal policies.

One of the main sources of instability in many economies, especially smaller ones, is the impact of large flows of international capital. Therefore, another issue for governments is whether or not to manage flows of financial capital.

19.8 UNREGULATED VS. MANAGED FINANCIAL CAPITAL FLOWS

In the modern world, international "hot" money flows rapidly around the globe seeking the highest return and the next big thing. A small economy can find itself devastated by withdrawals of financial capital or buoyed by inflows. And international financial flows can switch directions very quickly depending on the whims of investors. This makes the management of international financial flows a major issue for most countries, and especially for small ones. The Asian financial crisis of 1997 shows the difficulties that can result from large swings in financial flows.

In the 1980s and early 1990s, international investors poured money into rapidly growing Asian economies, including South Korea, Thailand, Hong Kong, Malaysia, and the Philippines. High interest rates and rapid growth in these countries attracted a spike in international investment, which in turn caused a huge increase in asset prices, especially stocks and real estate prices. These Asian countries borrowed extensively from Western investors to finance economic expansion. So much money was available that companies began to invest in very risky endeavors. At the same time, many of these countries were running current account deficits, driven at least in part by their financial account surpluses, and they were trying to maintain a fixed exchange rate.

By the mid-1990s, economic growth picked up in the United States and Europe driven by the tech boom. As these developed countries grew, their central banks increased interest rates to rein in inflation. The combination of rapid growth and high interest rates in the United States and Europe drew international financial investors back to developed countries, and they began pulling their money out of their Asian investments. Meanwhile, Chinese competition began to displace other competitors in Asia.

Investors pulled money out of their non-Chinese Asian investments en masse, causing real estate prices and stock prices to crash. As investors sold Asian currencies, the currencies also began to depreciate rapidly, forcing governments trying to maintain fixed currencies to raise domestic interest rates and buy up their own currency using their foreign exchange reserves. But the governments ran out of foreign exchange reserves quickly given the volume of money being withdrawn from their countries, and the high interest rates they established were devastating to their domestic economies. Countries were forced to abandon their fixed exchange rates and allow their currencies to float, at which point currency values plummeted. After the devaluation, companies that borrowed extensively from Western banks could not meet their payment obligations. The Thai baht devalued from 25 baht per dollar to almost 50 baht per dollar, losing half its value. This meant that the amount of payments of Thai debts to U.S. banks doubled within a few months.

One after another, Asian economies crashed. The IMF and the World Bank had to step in to bail out the countries to prevent an even worse disaster.

The Asian financial crisis had disturbing similarities to the Latin American debt crisis of the 1980s and the Mexican peso crisis of 1994–1995. In each case, international "hot" money flooded into smaller, developing economies to take advantage of good returns, leading to a speculative asset bubble and unsustainable borrowing. Then, when the international money was withdrawn, the result was devastating crashes and significant suffering. The frequency of these speculative bubbles has led to calls in many countries for regulation of international financial flows.

International capital controls are **rules or laws that restrict the movement of inflows and/or outflows of financial capital**. There are two main types of international capital controls: (1) Direct controls where the government imposes limits on capital flows and (2) taxes or other incentives that increase the cost of shifting capital internationally. Many developing countries restrict outflows of international investment to prevent the types of panics that sparked the Asian financial crisis. International capital controls are extremely useful to countries attempting to maintain a fixed exchange rate system, because it prevents destabilizing outflows of currency. And capital controls can be helpful to countries trying to promote economic development because they prevent foreign investors from flooding in and driving up exchange rates and asset values.

Laissez-faire economists argue that restricting international financial flows introduces distortions into markets that will lead to inefficiencies in the allocation of capital, pushing it into less productive uses. New Keynesian economists prefer a middle ground, imposing capital controls in emergency situations but allowing market forces to work most of the time.

19.9 CONCLUSION

This chapter began by examining how markets for foreign exchange work. Currencies tend to appreciate in value when a country offers higher rates of return or when a country's assets are viewed as a good investment due to strong economic prospects. Currencies also tend to appreciate when a country's inflation is low, because global consumers snap up low-priced goods. Currencies tend to depreciate when a country's rates of return are low or when a country's goods prices are relatively high.

Some countries actively maintain a depreciated currency in order to promote exports. There is some evidence that this policy can stimulate economic growth by boosting exports. However, this aggressive posture can spark trade wars, such as the one between the United States and China in 2018. Trade wars can end up hurting both countries as exports plummet and goods prices increase.

The balance of payments catalogs all international flows of money. It yields one very important insight: Current account deficits are matched by financial account surpluses. Normally, according to mainstream economic theory, exchange rate fluctuations would tend to eliminate any trade deficits or surpluses. However, in the modern world we see the perpetuation of trade deficits in some countries like the United States and the perpetuation of trade surpluses from some countries such as China, Germany, Japan, and South Korea. Political economists attribute these chronic imbalances to the importance of asset flows and their role in altering currency values.

U.S. trade deficits are a hotly debated topic among economists. Trade deficits tend to hurt U.S. workers and businesses, who lose out to foreign competition, but they benefit U.S. consumers, who get cheap foreign goods, and U.S. investors, who experience higher asset values. Foreign consumers in trade surplus countries are harmed in the process, because they are not able to purchase as many consumer goods as they would otherwise. Foreign workers and firms benefit from the expanded levels of production they experience with trade surpluses.

Political economists and supply-side economists tend to oppose trade deficits due to their negative impact on U.S. workers and firms. Laissez-faire economists oppose trade deficits because they are emblematic of too much government spending. On the other hand, most mainstream, New Keynesian economists believe that trade deficits are a boon for consumers and do not have significant economic costs because foreign investment is, in theory, used productively for job-creating activities.

The chapter also took up fixed, flexible, and managed exchange rate regimes. Fixed exchange rates promote stability but can be hard to maintain in the face of international financial flows. Flexible exchange rates require no government intervention, but they can be very unstable. Most countries use a managed float regime to give exchange rates a degree of stability without being overly restrictive.

Lastly, international financial flows can be destabilizing to an economy, as was the case with the Asian financial crisis of 1997. International "hot" money can flood into a booming small economy, causing an asset price bubble and an exchange rate appreciation. Both of these events can destabilize a developing economy and result in a subsequent crash. As a result, some countries use capital controls to limit the degree of fluctuation in international financial flows.

QUESTIONS FOR REVIEW

1. For each question below, draw a graph of the foreign exchange market for U.S. dollars in British pounds, and show how each of the following events will affect the price of the dollar and the quantity of dollars exchanged for British pounds. Explain your answer briefly.
    a. Incomes in the United Kingdom decrease.
    b. Interest rates in the United States decrease.
    c. The prices of U.S. goods decrease.

2. Suppose that U.S. interest rates rise relative to those in Europe. What effect will this have on the value of the U.S. dollar relative to the euro?
3. Suppose that the European Central Bank decides to sell euros in order to buy dollars. What effect will this have on the value of the euro relative to the U.S. dollar? Explain using a graph of the foreign exchange market for euros.
4. Describe the relationship between current account deficits and financial account surpluses.
5. Under what circumstances will a trade deficit lead to reductions in employment? Explain carefully.
6. Who benefits the most from a trade deficit? Who is harmed the most by a trade deficit?
7. Describe the major perspectives on why trade deficits are problematic. Also explain why many economists do not consider trade deficits to be a problem.
8. Suppose that the U.S. dollar is pegged to the euro at a rate of $1 = €1. Suppose also that the value of the dollar falls to $1 = €0.8. What policies can the U.S. government implement to return the value of the dollar to its pegged (fixed) rate of $1 = €1?
9. Explain the causes of the Asian financial crisis. How might capital controls prevent such a crisis from happening in the future?

NOTES

1 We are assuming that there are no tariffs or transportation costs in this example.
2 International Monetary Fund, "Adjusting to Lower Commodity Prices," *World Economic Outlook*, September 2015, https://www.imf.org/en/Publications/WEO/Issues/2016/12/31/Adjusting-to-Lower-Commodity-Prices, accessed February 2, 2021.
3 Source: OECD Stat.
4 Paul Krugman, "Trade Deficits: These Times Are Different," *New York Times*, March 28, 2016.
5 Warren E. Buffett, "America's Growing Trade Deficit Is Selling the Nation Out from under Us," *Fortune*, November 10 (2003), p. 106.
6 Gregory Mankiw, "Surprising Truths about Trade Deficits," *New York Times*, October 5, 2018, https://www.nytimes.com/2018/10/05/business/surprising-truths-about-trade-deficits.html.

20 Economic development

The barriers facing less developed countries and how they can be overcome[1]

Ever since Adam Smith, economists have attempted to determine the factors that foster economic development and determine the "wealth of nations." Economists typically divide economic systems into three main categories of development: High-income, developed economies that have industrialized, middle-income countries that undertake some basic manufacturing, and less developed (or underdeveloped) countries whose economies have yet to industrialize. **Less developed countries (LDCs)** are **low-income, low human development countries that face substantial structural impediments to economic development and are highly vulnerable to economic and environmental shocks**.

To most economists, the number and magnitude of the problems of less developed countries merit special attention. According to UNICEF, the United Nations International Children's Emergency Fund, almost a billion people suffer from malnutrition, even though the world produces enough food for everyone to have enough to eat. More than 2 billion people do not have access to clean water or adequate sanitation facilities. The World Bank[2] estimates that 690 million people live in extreme poverty, which they define as living on less than $1.90 per day. (Try to imagine what it would be like to survive on that amount.) More than 40% of the population in sub-Saharan Africa lives in extreme poverty. Women and children are particularly impacted by extreme poverty due to patriarchal cultures and unequal economic regimes that persist in many less developed countries.

Even though much progress has been made regarding poverty and deprivation in many poor countries, there is still much more to be done. This chapter offers a brief description of some of the reasons that economists have identified for why some countries are less developed than others. It also discusses what economic development means and the possible policies that might help to improve the lives of poor people in less developed countries. Economic development includes economic growth as well as more broadly defined human development. Furthermore, an economic system needs to feature broad-based development that benefits everyone,

DOI: 10.4324/9780429399350-26

not just a handful of elites. The chapter also reviews some of the most important debates economists have had regarding the most appropriate policies to stimulate economic and human development.

20.0 CHAPTER 20 LEARNING GOALS

After reading this chapter you should be able to:

- Define human and economic development.
- Discuss how geography, colonialism, slavery, and path dependency impact economic development.
- Describe, compare, and contrast structuralist-instutionalist and laissez-faire theories regarding development.
- Critically evaluate the major issues surrounding foreign aid, gender, culture, and development that economists have wrestled with in recent years.
- Analyze the unique problems facing LDCs and develop your own ideas regarding the policies that could be used to improve their level of human development.

We begin by discussing a surprisingly complex question.

20.1 WHAT IS "DEVELOPMENT"?

To early economists, economic development referred primarily to economic growth, and economic growth was driven primarily by industrialization. Thus, the focus was on the factors that can cause an agrarian country to become industrialized. As we saw in the chapter on economic growth, mainstream, New Keynesian economists focused on the need for countries to increase investment in physical capital goods, improve their technology, and increase human capital.

The measures economists typically used to track development were income per capita and economic growth. However, a country that is very unequal can have a very high income per capita and high levels of growth, even while a majority of the population benefits little from that growth. Therefore, economic development using standard measures of growth and per capita income is not the same as the human development of the whole population.

In the modern era, economists have broadened the definition of development significantly. The broader definition of development is captured by the United Nations Human Development Index (HDI), which includes three key categories:

(1) Long and healthy life, (2) knowledge, and (3) a decent standard of living. The concept of *human* development focuses on the ability of people to reach their full potential and to live productive and creative lives. The HDI for selected countries is displayed in Figure 20.1.

One of the most famous development economists, Amartya Sen, argued that "the success of a society is to be evaluated primarily by the substantive freedoms that members of that society enjoy."[3] Sen uses the positive definition of freedom—the ability to have opportunities and to control one's life—which is also known as the "capabilities" approach to development. True development, to Sen, must include access to education and health care, political and civil rights, economic opportunities, a decent income, and safety and security. These are all key ingredients that allow people to reach their full potential (develop their capabilities) and live a good life. Sen sees five key freedoms as essential to human development in that they advance the capabilities of a person: (1) Political freedoms, (2) economic facilities, (3) social opportunities, (4) transparency guarantees, and (5) protective security.[4]

Figure 20.1 on the next page shows that income and human development are not always synonymous.[5] In 2019, Equatorial Guinea had a gross national income (GNI) of almost $14,000 per capita, making it a middle-income country. However, most of the country's income was captured by the country's dictator, Teodoro Obiang Nguema Mbasogo, and his cronies. Meanwhile, the typical person in Equatorial Guinea lives in desperate poverty, experiences relatively poor health outcomes, has one of the lowest life expectancies in the world at 58.7 years, and has limited access to education and opportunity.

At the opposite end, Cuba had a GNI per capita of $8,621 in 2019, but their life expectancy was 78.8 years and their mean years of schooling exceeded all but the wealthiest of countries. In essence, Cuban citizens have a high level of human development despite having a modest national income per capita, whereas Equatorial Guineans have a low level of human development despite a high level of national income per capita.

Column 8 of Figure 20.1, GNI per capita rank minus HDI rank, shows this contrast between per capita national income and human development. Countries that are very unequal, in which most people have a lower level of human development than we would expect for a country with their income level, have negative numbers in column 8. This category of countries includes Equatorial Guinea as well as the United States, another country with a high average income but in which many citizens confront poverty, poor health, a lack of access to quality education, and limited employment opportunities. Countries where health, knowledge, and education outstrip income have positive numbers in column 8, such as Sweden, the United Kingdom, and Cuba.

Nonetheless, it is also the case that most high-income countries also feature high levels of human development. Therefore, the next key question is: Why are some countries rich with high levels of human development while others are poor

HDI Rank	Country	Human Development Index (HDI) (value)	Life Expectancy at Birth (years)	Expected Years of Schooling	Mean Years of Schooling	Gross National Income (GNI) per Capita (2017 PPP $)	GNI per Capita Rank Minus HDI Rank
VERY HIGH HUMAN DEVELOPMENT							
1	Norway	0.957	82.4	18.1	12.9	66,494	7
2	Ireland	0.955	82.3	18.7	12.7	68,371	4
6	Germany	0.947	81.3	17.0	14.2	55,314	11
7	Sweden	0.945	82.8	19.5	12.5	54,508	12
10	Denmark	0.940	80.9	18.9	12.6	58,662	2
13	United Kingdom	0.932	81.3	17.5	13.2	46,071	13
17	United States	0.926	78.9	16.3	13.4	63,826	-7
19	Japan	0.919	84.6	15.2	12.9	42,932	9
23	South Korea	0.916	83.0	16.5	12.2	43,044	4
26	France	0.901	82.7	15.6	11.5	47,173	-1
31	United Arab Emirates	0.890	78.0	14.3	12.1	67,462	-24
35	Poland	0.880	78.7	16.3	12.5	31,623	8
40	Saudi Arabia	0.854	75.1	16.1	10.2	47,495	-16
46	Argentina	0.845	76.7	17.7	10.9	21,190	16
52	Russian Federation	0.824	72.6	15.0	12.2	26,157	2
54	Turkey	0.820	77.7	16.6	8.1	27,701	-4
62	Costa Rica	0.810	80.3	15.7	8.7	18,486	6
62	Malaysia	0.810	76.2	13.7	10.4	27,534	-11
66	Mauritius	0.804	75.0	15.1	9.5	25,266	-10
HIGH HUMAN DEVELOPMENT							
70	Cuba	0.783	78.8	14.3	11.8	8,621	45
70	Iran	0.783	76.7	14.8	10.3	12,447	26
74	Mexico	0.779	75.1	14.8	8.8	19,160	-8
74	Ukraine	0.779	72.1	15.1	11.4	13,216	19
79	Thailand	0.777	77.2	15.0	7.9	17,781	-10
84	Brazil	0.765	75.9	15.4	8.0	14,263	1
85	China	0.761	76.9	14.0	8.1	16,057	-11
100	Botswana	0.735	69.6	12.8	9.6	16,437	-27
101	Jamaica	0.734	74.5	13.1	9.7	9,319	13
107	Indonesia	0.718	71.7	13.6	8.2	11,459	-4
113	Venezuela	0.711	72.1	12.8	10.3	7,045	11
114	South Africa	0.709	64.1	13.8	10.2	12,129	-14
116	Egypt	0.707	72.0	13.3	7.4	11,466	-14
117	Vietnam	0.704	75.4	12.7	8.3	7,433	3
MEDIUM HUMAN DEVELOPMENT							
123	Iraq	0.674	70.6	11.3	7.3	10,801	-16
128	Nicaragua	0.660	74.5	12.3	6.9	5,284	6
131	India	0.645	69.7	12.2	6.5	6,681	-5
133	Bangladesh	0.632	72.6	11.6	6.2	4,976	7
138	Ghana	0.611	64.1	11.5	7.3	5,269	-3
143	Kenya	0.601	66.7	11.3	6.6	4,244	5
145	Equatorial Guinea	0.592	58.7	9.7	5.9	13,944	-57
150	Zimbabwe	0.571	61.5	11.0	8.5	2,666	14
154	Pakistan	0.557	67.3	8.3	5.2	5,005	-15
LOW HUMAN DEVELOPMENT							
159	Uganda	0.544	63.4	11.4	6.2	2,123	15
161	Nigeria	0.539	54.7	10.0	6.7	4,910	-19
162	Côte d'Ivoire	0.538	57.8	10.0	5.3	5,069	-25
163	Tanzania	0.529	65.5	8.1	6.1	2,600	2
168	Senegal	0.512	67.9	8.6	3.2	3,309	-11
169	Afghanistan	0.511	64.8	10.2	3.9	2,229	0
170	Haiti	0.510	64.0	9.7	5.6	1,709	7
170	Sudan	0.510	65.3	7.9	3.8	3,829	-18
173	Ethiopia	0.485	66.6	8.8	2.9	2,207	-3
175	Congo (Dem. Republic)	0.480	60.7	9.7	6.8	1,063	11
179	Yemen	0.470	66.1	8.8	3.2	1,594	2
181	Mozambique	0.456	60.9	10.0	3.5	1,250	3
182	Burkina Faso	0.452	61.6	9.3	1.6	2,133	-9
182	Sierra Leone	0.452	54.7	10.2	3.7	1,668	-4
185	South Sudan	0.433	57.9	5.3	4.8	2,003	-10
187	Chad	0.398	54.2	7.3	2.5	1,555	-5
188	Central African Republic	0.397	53.3	7.6	4.3	993	0
189	Niger	0.394	62.4	6.5	2.1	1,201	-4

FIGURE 20.1 Table of the Human Development Index (HDI), select countries, 2019.

with low levels of human development? Economists have a wide variety of economic theories to explain this phenomenon, as we will see below.

A careful perusal of Figure 20.1 yields several important insights that begin to address the issue of why some countries are rich and others poor. The poorest countries in the world, and those with the lowest level of human development, are located primarily in sub-Saharan Africa. The next poorest region is South Asia.

ECONOMIC DEVELOPMENT

Region	Human Development Index (HDI) (value)	Life Expectancy at Birth (years)	Expected Years of Schooling	Mean Years of Schooling	Gross National Income (GNI) per Capita (2017 PPP $)
Very high human development	0.898	79.6	16.3	12.2	44,566
Developing regions					
Eastern Europe and Central Asia	0.791	74.4	14.7	10.4	17,939
Latin America and the Caribbean	0.766	75.6	14.6	8.7	14,812
East Asia and the Pacific	0.747	75.4	13.6	8.1	14,710
Arab States	0.705	72.1	12.1	7.3	14,869
South Asia	0.641	69.9	11.7	6.5	6,532
Sub-Saharan Africa	0.547	61.5	10.1	5.8	3,686

FIGURE 20.2 Table showing the human development of various regions of the world in 2019.

Figure 20.2 shows that the human development levels of the highest income countries, which include countries in Western Europe, the United States, some oil-rich countries, and other countries that have successfully industrialized, vastly exceed the human development levels of less developed regions, especially sub-Saharan Africa and South Asia.[6]

Interestingly, most regions of the world had income levels that were almost equal until the era of colonialism and slavery began.[7] After that point, we see a dramatic divergence in economic development experiences. Therefore, it is important to wrestle with the impact of geography and the legacies of colonialism and slavery.

20.2 GEOGRAPHY, COLONIALISM, SLAVERY, AND PATH DEPENDENCY

Due to an abundance of good luck, the crops most suitable to agriculture and the animals best suited to domestication were prevalent in the fertile crescent. That is why the earliest agriculture-based empires developed in this region, which is centered around the Nile, Tigris, and Euphrates rivers and next to the Mediterranean Sea.

From the fertile crescent, farming spread to nearby areas with similar climates, especially Europe. As a consequence of the abundance of food, Europe experienced the most rapid population growth, the most extensive development of cities, the most resistance to disease (a necessity in highly populated cities), and the most sophisticated development of military technology. Or, to use the words of Jared Diamond, Europe developed guns, germs, and steel that allowed it to dominate the rest of the world.[8] Meanwhile, agriculture was much more difficult in Africa's tropical climate, and few African animals could be domesticated.

This example shows us a crucial aspect of economic development: *Geography is one of the most important determinants of a country's economic opportunities*. New crops and technologies spread quickly to nearby countries. When one country is growing quickly, this stimulates the economies of its neighbors, which can sell increasing quantities of goods to the growing country. On the other hand, countries that are isolated or that are surrounded by other countries that are poor and that have low technological capacity will have fewer opportunities to develop.

We still see the impacts of the colonial era today. *Almost all of the poorest countries in the modern world were once colonies of European powers.* England, Spain, Portugal, France, the Netherlands, Italy, Germany, and Belgium used their technological advantages in weapons and ships to scour the world for slaves, forced laborers, precious metals, and raw materials. The colonial powers set up **institutions**—legal and economic systems, belief systems (including religious institutions), land ownership structures, and industrial structures—that enriched themselves while impoverishing the vast majority of their colonial populations. The economies of colonies were structured to provide cheap labor and raw materials to their colonial overlords, and colonies were prevented from competing with the manufacturing industries of the colonial power.

From the 1500s until the mid-to-late 1900s, European colonizers dominated most of the developing world. At its peak, the British empire was the largest empire in history, controlling 25% of the world's land surface with colonies in North America, Australia, Africa, and Asia.

The impacts of colonialism were particularly hard on Africa. From 1600 to 1900, 12 million Africans were enslaved and 36 million killed.[9] African democratic traditions were undermined because the colonizing powers preferred authoritarian governmental structures to dominate colonial populations. Infrastructure, including ports, roads, and rail lines, was installed to facilitate the extraction of resources from the interior and to funnel those resources to the coast for export to Europe. However, internal trade between colonies was discouraged or prohibited, limiting the size of colonial markets. Manufacturing industries located in colonies were dismantled so that the colonizers could sell high-value home country manufactured goods at high prices to their colonies. Raw materials production in colonies was developed under brutally exploitative labor conditions so that colonial powers could obtain inputs for their industries at the lowest cost possible. Similar processes occurred in Latin America and South Asia, as the colonial powers drained their colonies of labor, money, and resources. As a consequence of colonial domination, colonies grew much more slowly than sovereign nations.[10]

Unfortunately, *the poor growth performance of former colonies continued long after they achieved independence*, indicating a concept know as path dependence. **Path dependence** refers to **the dependence of economic outcomes on the structure of previous outcomes and institutions**. *History matters* significantly in determining a nation's economic trajectory, because a country's political and economic institutions are developed under particular historical circumstances, and these institutions play a fundamental role in shaping the options and incentives available to economic actors. In addition, institutions tend to change very slowly over time.

Colonies began to gain their independence after World War II, beginning with Ghana in 1957 and ending with the democratic elections marking the end of apartheid in South Africa in 1994. Many of the struggles for independence involved violent conflicts, as many of the colonizing powers resisted the notion that colonies should govern themselves. In repressive colonial regimes, it was not uncommon for leaders of colonial independence movements to go from jail to becoming president of a newly independent country.

Unfortunately, even after independence former colonies faced an ongoing struggle to develop. As Acemoglu, Johnson, and Robinson observed, "In the Congo or the Gold Coast, [colonizers] set up extractive states with the intention of transferring resources rapidly to the metropole. These institutions were detrimental to investment and economic progress. ... [T]hese early institutions persisted to the present" because modern elites have no incentive to make changes.[11] In a number of cases, leaders of newly independent former colonies were only too happy to slip into the role of the colonizer, extracting resources and enriching themselves in the process.

Consider some of the following examples. General Ibrahim Babangida amassed $23 billion when he ruled Nigeria, Jose Eduardo dos Santos amassed $20 billion as president of Angola, and Mobutu Sese Seko accumulated $5 billion as president of Zaire. These are desperately poor countries, so the vast fortunes of the dictators were amassed without regard for the human development of the populace. The process of the enrichment of political leaders in former colonies continues today in many countries that were not able to restructure their institutions to be broader and more inclusive.

Large corporations seem only too willing to assist corrupt leaders in pillaging developing countries' resources. Exxon Mobil and Marathon Oil have both helped "President" Mbasogo of Equatorial Guinea plunder that country's resources, just as Shell Oil assisted Babangida in Nigeria. The De Beers diamond conglomerate and other South African business interests helped various members of the governing African National Congress party to enrich themselves after South Africa became a democracy in 1994. Thus, in many less developed countries, we see a form of **neocolonialism** where **a country's rulers ally themselves with Western corporations to maintain the status quo and preserve the extractive institutions and relations that were established under colonialism**. Former colonies are left exporting a few primary products that are extracted by multinational corporations (MNCs). The MNCs keep a majority of the profits, which they send back to their home countries, further limiting economic activity in the former colonies.

Some countries were able to escape the clutches of extractive neocolonial institutions to build vibrant, inclusive economies. And yet all developing countries face structural barriers to development that are difficult to overcome. Understanding the barriers to development and the policies that might circumvent those barriers forms the core of the structural–institutional approach to economic development.

20.3 STRUCTURAL-INSTITUTIONAL ANALYSIS OF ECONOMIC DEVELOPMENT

The structural-institutional approach to economic development focuses on the structures and institutions of the global economy that present barriers for economic development and how they might be overcome. Most early development economists and contemporary political economists adopt such an approach. Some of the key topics taken up within this approach include the following:

- How the global trade system is structured to benefit wealthy countries at the expense of poor countries by maintaining the trade patterns that emerged under colonialism
- The unique culture and institutions that facilitate and inhibit development in each country or region
- How gender roles and ethnic groupings impact development
- Structures that allow the existing elites in many LDCs work to prevent changes that would threaten their privileged status, often at the expense of development
- The extent to which there is a common national interest versus conflicting narrow interests dominating the government
- The characteristics of the domestic educational system and the technological capabilities of workers and firms
- The structure of businesses, and especially if most people are engaged in work in the formal sector or the informal sector (featuring small-scale enterprises in which work is done for cash and is not taxed or regulated by the government)
- The extent to which the government is able to design and support a robust plan for economic development that removes barriers and develops the country's labor skills, capital markets, technological capacity, financial infrastructure, and enterprises.

One of the key issues in the above list is the global trade system and how existing trade patterns present severe challenges for LDCs.

As we noted in Chapter 18, most modern mainstream economists argue that all economies should specialize in the production and export of goods in which they have a comparative advantage. However, due to colonialism, most LDCs were prevented from developing their manufacturing industries and were forced to specialize in primary products. According to economists from the structural-institutional perspective, the tendency to specialize in primary products such as coffee, cocoa, copper, and other agricultural and natural resource-based products is one of the most important structural problems facing LDCs.

If primary products became increasingly valuable over time, it might not be problematic for a country to specialize in their production. Unfortunately, that has not been the case. Raul Prebisch and Hans Singer were the first to document **the long-term tendency of primary product prices to fall relative to the prices**

of manufactured goods, a phenomenon that is called the **Prebisch-Singer thesis**. There are a number of reasons why this happens.

As incomes increase over time, people tend to spend a little more on food and clothing, and they use a slightly larger amount of raw materials. These goods have a low income elasticity of demand: Demand for primary products increases only slightly as income increases. But people tend to purchase much larger quantities of advanced manufactured goods and complex services as they get richer. They spend a lot more on smart phones, computers, and cars, and they also demand more financial services, health care, higher education, and leisure activities. Therefore, advanced manufactured goods and complex services have a high income elasticity of demand, unlike most primary products and simple manufactured goods. Figure 20.3 shows economists' estimates for a variety of income elasticities. Note that food and clothing have the lowest income elasticities, whereas automobiles and leisure activities have the highest.

As a result, as the global economy grows and people become wealthier, there is an increasing demand for complex services and advanced manufactured goods and a stagnant or decreasing demand for most primary products.

Therefore, less developed countries that export primary products and simple manufactured goods tend to experience declining terms of trade: The prices of the goods they export decline relative to the prices of the goods they import. As their export products get less and less valuable, less developed countries experience lower levels of income from exports while they must devote increasing amounts of money to purchasing imports. This can result in increasingly large LDC trade deficits with developed countries, resulting in increasing indebtedness of LDCs.

As Figure 20.4 on the next page shows, the prices of essential food commodities fell dramatically from 1900 to 2015, by an average of 63.5%.[12] Thus, any country exporting food commodities made much less money in the modern era than used to be the case.

Commodities are also subject to dramatic fluctuations in quantities and prices due to abrupt changes in supply from extreme weather (droughts, floods, climate changes, or bumper crops in good years). Similarly, the prices of minerals and petroleum products fluctuate wildly based on new discoveries (locating of new

High Income Elasticity Goods and Services	Income Elasticity	Low Income Elasticity Goods and Services	Income Elasticity
Movies in theaters	3.4	Housing	0.7
Foreign travel	3.1	Tobacco, fruits, vegetables	0.6
Automobiles and trucks	3.0	Gas, furniture, beef	0.5
Vacations	1.9	Clothing	0.3
Jewelry, watches, health care	1.6	Electricity, food, pork	0.2
Education, leisure	1.5	Margarine	-0.2
Books, restaurant meals	1.4	Public transportation, rice, flour	-0.4
Computers	1.2		

FIGURE 20.3 Table showing goods and services with high and low income elasticities.

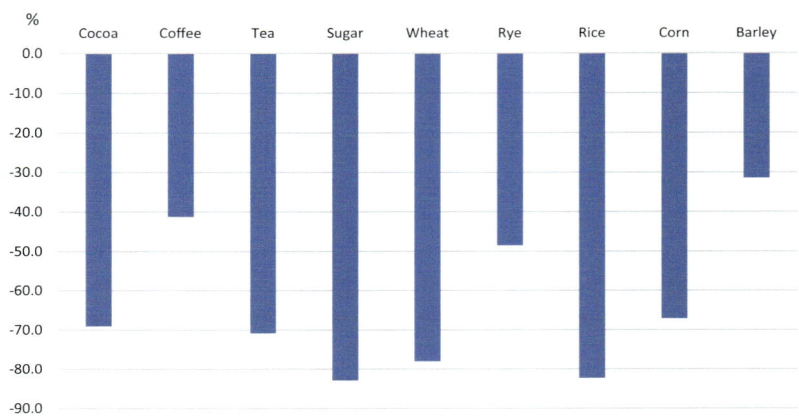

FIGURE 20.4 Percentage change in commodity prices from 1900 to 2015.

deposits), the development of synthetic substitutes, and swings in demand due to busts or booms. Volatility of export prices can be devastating to less developed countries. An economy that depends on commodity exports can swing from a boom to a bust in just a few months. As we have studied, instability harms business investment and tends to reduce the rate of economic growth.

To combat the declining terms of trade and the resulting instability, Prebisch argued that less developed countries needed to engineer a structural transformation of their economy by creating the conditions for industrialization. Instead of relying on their comparative advantage in primary products, LDCs should enact policies to stimulate manufacturing. Furthermore, given the disadvantages that less developed countries faced due to limited technology and skills, infant industries would need to be protected from foreign competition until they could compete internationally.

This strategy, known as the **infant industry promotion strategy**, proved to be very effective in some countries but difficult for other countries to implement effectively. As we saw earlier in Chapter 17 on economic growth, some countries, including South Korea and China, were incredibly successful with protecting infant industries and systematically developing skills, technologies, and industrial capacity until their economies were no longer poor. Their efficient state sectors successfully incentivized domestic businesses to become globally competitive and to continuously invest in new industrial development projects. These countries selected industries in which they could develop a competitive advantage based on existing skills, resources, and infrastructure, augmented by substantial government support and financing. In both South Korea and China, we see the importance of a strong, organized, and efficient state, coupled with a unified national interest that allows the state, private sector, and workers to unite behind a shared approach to development.

This is termed a **developmental state**, as we saw in Chapter 17, where the government undertakes macroeconomic planning and policies to stimulate industrial development in strategic sectors. The point is to reorient an LDC economy toward new, dynamic, high-value sectors by creating the perfect set of institutions to stimulate advanced, export-oriented industries. The requisite institutions include strong educational systems, substantial financial support, tariff protections, state planning, and incentives for companies to innovate and become internationally competitive. The fact that the governments of China, South Korea, and other newly industrialized Asian countries made support for industries conditional on achieving success in international markets is a testament to how important the incentive structure is in creating viable, competitive industries. MIT economist Alice Amsden referred to this as a "performance-based allocation" system: Firms would only receive state support if they were successful in international markets.[13]

South Korea and China were also successful in developing industries with substantial linkages to other sectors of the economy. When industrial linkages exist, expansion in one sector fosters increased development of other sectors. For example, the textile (cloth manufacturing) sector has **backward linkages** to **industries that supply the sector with inputs (the sector's supply chain)**. Backward linkages for the textile sector include cotton, wool, sewing machines, thread manufacturing, and loom manufacturing. A sector also has **forward linkages** to **industries at subsequent stages of production that use the finished product in their production process**. Forward linkages for textiles are clothing manufacturing and any other industry that uses manufactured cloth, including car seat production, tent production, and so on. A sophisticated economic development plan can utilize backward and forward linkages to develop products up and down the supply chain, building industrial partnerships and stimulating multiple industries simultaneously.

The more advanced and complex the products that are exported, the more linkages exist and the more additional industries are stimulated. Commodities with the most linkages include machinery, metals, and chemicals. These products utilize many inputs and are used in the production of many other final products. Commodities with the least linkages are agricultural commodities and petroleum.

The clear implication is that economic development requires the steady augmenting of a country's **industrial capabilities**, so that LDCs can move away from commodities with few linages that sell for low prices into commodities that sell for higher prices and that stimulate additional industrial development via multiple linkages.[14] Therefore, **strategy switching**—constantly adjusting an economic development plan to take advantage of new, more advanced, industrial opportunities—is another crucial component of successful state-led development.

The existence of self-reinforcing economic development reflects **positive externalities** that stem from the industrialization process, which the famous development economist Gunnar Myrdal termed "spread effects." In addition to stimulating industries with linkages, industrialization causes businesses to become familiar with technologies, global supply chains, banking systems, and export markets that can foster additional opportunities. These positive spread effects can help to overcome the "backwash effects" that work to keep LDCs poor and focused only on primary products. In this manner, creating the right institutional structure can lead to self-sustaining economic development.

Although Japan, China, and South Korea were very successful with infant industry protection and steadily advancing industrial production, other countries were less consistently successful. Brazil unsuccessfully tried to develop its computer industry in the 1970s and 1980s behind protective tariffs. They were hampered by technological deficiencies, inefficient private sector firms, the lack of a local supply chain, and ineffective government intervention. On the other hand, protectionism helped Brazil to develop less complex industries such as small airplane manufacturing, automobile assembly, and ethanol production. Brazil, South Africa, and other middle-income countries can get caught in a **middle-income trap**, in which **a country successfully develops some basic manufacturing but is unable to move into more advanced, higher value-added production**. Challenges facing middle-income countries include maintaining macroeconomic stability, promoting a sustained process of productive diversification and technological change, creating efficient and sustainable infrastructures, building an efficient institutional framework within a more cohesive society, and gaining access to protected markets of developed countries.[15] It has proven to be very difficult for most middle-income countries to move beyond basic industrialization and into the highest echelon of economic development.

Other countries were not even able to move from the low-income to the middle-income category. Countries that had no significant manufacturing capability when they became independent from their colonizers usually opted to use the state to undertake the initial industrialization effort. They lacked the local business experience, entrepreneurs, and technological capacity for business formation to occur on its own, so they formed state-owned enterprises (SOEs) to begin the industrialization process. In cases where the state was inefficient and corrupt and where low levels of education and technology resulted in poor productivity, the combination of protectionism and inefficiency meant that many SOE industries were never able to become efficient enough to compete internationally.

Unfortunately, inefficient, uncompetitive SOEs needed perpetual protection and government support to survive, becoming a drain on many LDC economies. But LDCs were reluctant to allow uncompetitive SOEs go bankrupt for fear of losing their small manufacturing sector and the jobs that accompanied it. This resulted in the **soft budget constraint problem**, in which a government continually bails out an industry that cannot become competitive in markets. The SOE has no incentive to become efficient, because it can count on perpetual government bailouts.

From 1950 to 1980, most LDCs implemented infant industry protections, coupled with state-directed and state-subsidized development programs. Some of these programs were successful and others were not. LDCs also spent a lot of money on infrastructure and education, which had been neglected under colonialism. In addition, most newly independent countries were somewhat unstable politically, so they spent a lot on the military. Military expenditures also spiked as a result of cold war conflicts between the United States and the U.S.S.R. in numerous LDCs.

LDCs with corrupt governments and ineffective development programs experienced particularly large government budget deficits. The oil price shocks of the 1970s, when oil prices spiked in 1974 and again in 1980, caused the prices of imports for non-oil-exporting countries to increase dramatically relative to the prices of their exports. These LDCs were forced to borrow extensively to import the oil they needed for energy. LDC debts mounted steadily during this period, culminating in the LDC debt crisis of the 1980s.

Heavily indebted LDCs faced a crisis when banks stopped lending to them due to their ballooning debts. They had no choice but to go to the World Bank and the International Monetary Fund (IMF) for assistance. These international financial organizations serve as lenders of last resort for developing countries that cannot borrow from commercial lenders.

In the 1980s, the World Bank and the IMF were run by economists who insisted on a laissez-faire approach to economic development, leading to significant changes in the policies utilized in heavily indebted LDCs. These laissez-faire economists argued that new policies were needed and that the infant industry protections and state-led development efforts advocated by structural-institutional economists had been a mistake.

20.4 STRUCTURAL ADJUSTMENT AND THE LAISSEZ-FAIRE APPROACH TO DEVELOPMENT

Heavily indebted poor countries cannot borrow money easily. Wealthy countries are able to issue bonds, print money, or create deposits in emergencies to sustain their spending. But investors do not want to buy the debt of poor countries with large trade deficits. Therefore, issuing bonds (an open market sale) in a crisis is not effective. Unfortunately, the other monetary policy alternative in a debt crisis, increasing the money supply via printing money or creating electronic deposits, can lead to rapid inflation if local output is stagnant due to the crisis. Many LDCs were subject to hyperinflation when they printed large amounts of money while the economy stagnated after the oil price shocks. Brazil's rate of inflation went as high as 82.4% *per month* during its hyperinflationary period, which lasted from 1985 to 1994. Bolivia's rate of inflation in 1985 was more than 20,000%.

The only option for heavily indebted LDCs facing a downturn is to ask for emergency loans from the World Bank and the IMF. However, the World Bank and the IMF impose strict conditions on LDC borrowers with the goal of reforming their economic systems to be more economically sustainable. In the 1980s and 1990s, when the World Bank and the IMF were staffed by economists with a laissez-faire ideology, the conditions imposed on LDC borrowers were particularly harsh in character.

Specifically, the World Bank and IMF insisted on a market-dominated, laissez-faire policy regime called **structural adjustment**. Structural adjustment involved the following key components: (1) Austerity (including large cuts in government spending and increases in tax revenues), (2) privatization of SOEs (selling SOEs to private investors), (3) market-oriented domestic reforms such as deregulations of markets, (4) reduction or elimination of protective tariffs, and (5) opening up of banking and capital markets to free mobility of funds and foreign investment. In other words, they insisted on an extreme laissez-faire approach to economic development despite the fact that there had never been a case of a less developed country succeeding in this way. Indeed, the most successful economies in the world since 1950 have all used state-led development policies.

The economists at the World Bank and the IMF had a reasonable theoretical argument, however. Countries that were heavily indebted had been pursuing state-led development without success, which left the countries with inefficient, uncompetitive SOEs and high levels of debt. Scaling back government spending, reducing tariffs, and encouraging competition would, in theory, improve the efficiency and competitiveness of LDC markets. Opening up financial markets to foreign investment could stimulate investment in viable new industries.

Unfortunately, the results of structural adjustment programs were in most cases disastrous. For example, the most valuable SOEs were sold to local elites at below-market prices. As a consequence, SOEs stayed under the control of the same vested interests and continued to operate in LDC markets that were not competitive. This proved to be even worse for local consumers. Once all pretense of government control was eliminated, the former SOE firms were free to exploit their monopoly status to reap huge profits by raising prices and reducing quality, all at the expense of the local population.

Austerity policies involved slashing government spending on important programs such as infrastructure, health, poverty alleviation, education, and other areas essential to economic development. Poverty and hunger increased dramatically. In some cases, corrupt governments would lay off useful government workers (teachers, nurses, doctors, and construction workers) while continuing to pay their cronies who did no actual work. As we studied earlier, in the best of circumstances, austerity policies tend to have negative impacts on growth by reducing aggregate demand and threatening the stability of the business climate. In LDCs, austerity policies were doubly devastating, reducing aggregate demand *and* eliminating productivity-improving programs such as education, health, and infrastructure.

Eliminating trade barriers also proved to be problematic. Many LDC companies were not able to compete internationally without some protection from foreign competition. The result of reducing tariffs was significant deindustrialization in LDCs. In South Africa, manufacturing declined by almost 50% after tariffs were eliminated.[16]

The World Bank and IMF argued that new industries would develop due to increased foreign investment once markets were liberalized. However, the instability caused by structural adjustment and the structural deficiencies in LDCs (low productivity due to poor education and infrastructure) meant that LDCs were not attractive locations for foreign investment. As a result of austerity and tariff reductions, South Africa's unemployment rate exploded, increasing from 4.4% in 1994 to 27% in 2003, an increase of 614%.

Liberalization of capital flows also created problems. Once investors could easily move their money into and out of LDC banks and financial markets, financial instability in LDCs increased. If an LDC seemed shaky, money would pour out of the country to safer havens. Companies also moved their corporate headquarters abroad and began keeping profits there. For example, Anglo American PLC, the parent company of the De Beers mining conglomerate, moved their headquarters from South Africa to England once financial controls in South Africa were eliminated.[17]

Rapid outflows of money in LDCs without foreign exchange controls frequently cause their currencies to devalue significantly, increasing the prices of essential imports such as food, oil, and technological inputs for manufacturers. Ever since capital markets were liberalized, most African countries have experienced significant net outflows of funds as local and international investors move their money to safe havens in developed countries such as Switzerland. The financial outflows reduce the amount of money available for investment in new industrial ventures in the LDCs. Eventually, instability and capital flight prompted some countries to reinstitute capital markets controls and regulations, rejecting the recommendations of the IMF and World Bank.

Ultimately, structural adjustment policies were a failure almost everywhere they were tried. Latin American and sub-Saharan African LDCs that had structural adjustment imposed on them by the IMF and World Bank experienced deindustrialization, stagnant growth, increased poverty, and decreases in health outcomes. It took more than two decades for these countries to recover.[18]

Meanwhile, most Asian countries that were not subjected to structural adjustment programs and that continued to pursue state-led development experienced significant success. Many heterodox and New Keynesian economists consider the structural adjustment era of the 1980s and 1990s to be one of the great policy debacles in economics in the modern era.[19]

20.5 FOREIGN AID, CULTURE, AND DEVELOPMENT EFFORTS SINCE 2000

As the World Bank and the IMF pursued structural adjustment policies in the 1980s and 1990s, large amounts of foreign aid poured into LDCs, and especially sub-Saharan Africa, the poorest region of the world. However, the foreign aid did not seem to be working given that economic growth in aid-receiving regions was lower than that in other regions in the world during this period. People began to question the whole idea of foreign aid and the policies of aid agencies.

Foreign aid rarely comes without strings attached. Countries that give aid to LDCs often insist that the aid recipient purchase goods from them. The United States gives military aid to LDCs and then requires that it be used for purchases of U.S. military goods. This does little to stimulate economic development in the LDC, however. Large amounts of aid funds go to staff at aid agencies who receive high salaries and benefits. Many of the smartest people in LDCs are drawn out of the government or the private sector to work in aid agencies, draining the local economy of some of its most talented people.

Foreign aid is also criticized for fostering corruption. Countries with corrupt dictators are regular recipients of foreign aid, which helps to keep them in power. The World Bank, IMF, and United States have all sent aid to Equatorial Guinea at some point, despite the corruption of its dictator.

Frustration with the ineffectiveness of structural adjustment policies and foreign aid led to a rethinking of development aid in general. In September 2000, the United Nations published a list of Millennium Development Goals designed to refocus the international community directly on issues that improve human well-being. The millennium development goals are as follows:

1. Eradicate extreme poverty and hunger.
2. Achieve universal primary education.
3. Promote gender equality and empower women.
4. Reduce child mortality.
5. Improve maternal health.
6. Combat HIV/AIDS, malaria, and other diseases.
7. Ensure environmental sustainability.
8. Develop a global partnership for development.

The focus is clearly on the health, well-being, and opportunities available to the very poorest people in the poorest countries.

The increased emphasis on issues related to gender stem from research demonstrating the importance of improvements in the opportunities for women in stimulating economic development and improving human development measures. Development projects can have a negative impact on women and families if they are not structured carefully.

For example, the World Bank established numerous programs in Africa that were designed to improve property rights in regions where land was allocated via traditional, informal kinship relations. Under traditional kinship property systems, tribal chiefs allocate land to community members based on local customs and traditions. No one owns the land in the sense that there is no official title to the land and it cannot be bought and sold. The land is farmed by those with traditional rights to it, and very often by women. Women traditionally have grown about 70% of the food and produced about 60% of the agricultural goods in Africa, largely within traditional kinship systems.[20]

The World Bank thought that it would be a good idea for African countries to adopt Western-style property rights, where one person owns the land and it can be bought and sold to the highest bidder. In theory, this would result in land being allocated to the most productive farmer. However, when legal titles to land were being awarded under World Bank programs, men grabbed most of the land due to their inside connections to governments and aid agencies, even though many of the men granted legal property rights had never farmed before. This approach left many of the most productive farmers—the women—with no access to land and no way to feed their families and caused agricultural production to fall in many regions.[21]

On the other hand, development projects that improve women's opportunities have been very successful. Women are the major providers of food and funds for children's education in LDCs, but women have historically been denied access to the formal economy and especially to the financial system. Therefore, allocating additional resources to women has a direct, positive impact on families and on overall productivity by improving the capabilities of an underutilized portion of the labor force. In addition, when women have more opportunities, they tend to have fewer children, reducing population growth, a major problem confronting poor LDCs.

It is worth noting that in desperately poor families, one's security in old age depends on having enough able-bodied children to support you once you can no longer work. Children are a source of labor and income once they are old enough to work, and they are a source of financial security for their parents later in life. Given high infant mortality rates and the lack of pensions for the poor in LDCs, poor families generally have a direct incentive to have as many children as possible. However, providing economic opportunities to people, and especially to women, reduces their need to have children.

High population can reduce economic development. When a country's population is growing rapidly, it must devote ever-increasing amounts of resources just to providing food and shelter for its people. This leaves fewer resources (less surplus) to invest in growth-enhancing investments. This is another reason why improving women's opportunities is good for a country's economic development.

Along with gender roles, other aspects of a country's **culture** can significantly impact economic development. Some economists argue that a country's cultural beliefs play a substantial role in how effectively the economy embraces new opportunities and challenges. According to Acemoglu et al., "Some societies may have values that encourage investment, hard work, and the adoption of new technologies, while others may nurture superstition and suspicion of new technologies and discourage hard work."[22] However, this statement veers dangerously close to the arguments made by colonizers that their societies were better and more civilized than those of their colonies because of their culture.

A more complex analysis of culture and the development process would note that culture does, indeed, shape how people behave and how the development process unfolds. But no one culture is inherently superior, and no set of cultural characteristics is inherently prone to economic success. In Asian countries with strong Confucian cultures, such as Japan, China, and South Korea, respect for authority and elders is an essential cultural value. These countries benefited from state-centered development efforts building on this cultural value system. Leaders felt an obligation to care for their people. Businesses and workers felt an obligation to go along with the state development plans as long as the plans were successful. Respect for authority and an efficient government acting in the national interest can be a dynamic combination.

In cooperative cultures, such as the Nordic countries of Northern Europe, state-centered development efforts were also effective. The triple helix model in which universities, businesses, and the government cooperated in developing new industries was remarkably successful in Sweden, for example. Cooperation can also foster economic development in regions that are culturally predisposed to such efforts.

Anglo-Saxon cultures (the United Kingdom and the colonies in which the British settled) feature individualistic attitudes and less tendency toward cooperation and deference to authority. In such countries, market-dominated development efforts were generally effective with only a modest level of government protection and intervention.

The lesson seems to be that each country must find its own path to economic development success, building on its unique culture and the opportunities that are available to it. The insistence of U.S. and U.K. economists on market-based approaches to development may be more of a reflection of the cultural biases of Anglo-Saxon economists than a reflection of the actual development experiences of successful, high-income countries.

Another change in the last few decades has been a reconsideration of austerity programs. In response to the ongoing debt burdens of LDCs, the World Bank and IMF created funds to help heavily indebted poor countries pay off their debts. If countries enact sound policies, as defined by the World Bank and the IMF, they can qualify for debt relief. This has been a boon to some LDCs.

Building on research on the role of culture and institutions in development, the World Bank and the IMF recently began focusing more on the institutions that facilitate development and on the importance of effective governance. In this sense, there has been some convergence in thinking about economic development, although the World Bank and IMF still prefer market-dominated approaches to state-led efforts when designing policy programs to stimulate economic development in LDCs.

Since 2000, the World Bank has been investing in and studying the effectiveness of development programs via **randomized controlled trials (RCTs)**, in which **experiments are conducted on the behavior of economic actors** (people!) in poor countries to determine which economic policies and programs are most effective. For example, ever since the formation of the Grameen Bank in Bangladesh by Muhammad Yunus, economists have been fascinated with the notion of using social entrepreneurship and microfinance to solve problems in poor communities. The Grameen Bank makes microloans to poor women at subsidized interest rates and has been famous for stimulating economic activity and improving lives. The World Bank undertook a large-scale RCT to determine the effectiveness of such programs.

Social entrepreneurship involves **citizens working voluntarily and creatively to solve a society's problems**. A social entrepreneur tries to achieve success in the *social* realm, rather than focusing strictly on profit in the way traditional entrepreneurs do. The Grameen Bank microlending programs are one of the best-known forms of social entrepreneurship, because their goal is to improve society rather than to maximize profits. Microlending works as follows.

Donors provide funds to the Grameen Bank and agree to forgo interest payments on the money. They are trying to achieve a social improvement by donating money to a worthy cause. The Grameen Bank then uses the donated money to provide loans to poor families. Specifically, the bank identifies groups of *five* prospective borrowers from a community who have a strong social bond with each other. Often the borrowers are poor women who are traditionally denied access to credit and who are well integrated into the community. *Two* of the five prospective borrowers receive a microloan in the first stage. If the two borrowers repay the principal and a small interest payment (enough to cover the administrative costs of the program) over a one-year period, then the other members of the group become eligible for a loan. If they repay their loans, then another round of microlending can occur. The funds can be lent out over and over again as long as the loans are repaid. This structure leads to substantial peer pressure on borrowers to use the loans for something productive and then to repay the loans, creating a collective responsibility for repaying each other. The Grameen Bank model thus encourages donors to make a difference by offering loans at subsidized interest rates (social entrepreneurship), and poor women use those loans to create businesses and otherwise improve their lives and the lives of their family members.

A series of six RCTs were conducted in countries in various parts of the world to determine the effectiveness of microlending. Some groups of borrowers were given access to credit and others were not. The results indicated that microlending resulted in "some evidence … that expanded access to credit increases business activity."[23] Microlending appears to have a small, positive impact on the lives of participants. It has failed to foster large-scale economic development, however.

Some economists worry about the ethics of RCTs: Is it ethical to conduct experiments on poor people, even if the experiment has the potential to improve the efficacy of economic policy? Furthermore, though microlending does seem to result in a small increase in business development and a small increase in incomes, it has not resulted in significant improvements in the lives of the poor in the way that an effective developmental state can. Would it be better for LDCs to concentrate their limited resources on larger-scale government development programs rather than on small-scale efforts such as microlending?

The World Bank and the IMF increasingly acknowledge the role that institutions play in development. In keeping with their focus on market-led development, they tend to design aid programs that focus on institutions such as property rights, the legal system, and the enforcement of contracts, which are essential to the effective functioning of markets.[24] However, property rights and contracts are easily subverted in countries with corrupt governments, highlighting the importance of democratic governance and a robust civil society.

This puts donors in a difficult spot. Funneling aid to countries with corrupt regimes can help to keep existing elites in power. But cutting off support to these regimes could harm millions of desperately poor people. This is one of the many dilemmas confronting economists who study economic development.

20.6 CONCLUSION

As with many subjects in economics, economic development is a complex topic about which economists disagree. Even determining the goals of economic development is difficult and controversial. Traditionally, economists have focused on economic growth and per capita income to measure a country's degree of economic development. More recently, economists have turned to human development and especially the freedoms and opportunities available to the majority of people as a better metric of success.

Historically, a number of factors impacted why some countries are rich and others are poor. Geography played a large role, determining why European countries developed first and why they were able to colonize most of the globe. Colonialism and slavery deprived colonies of the chance to develop, reducing most of them to an impoverished, unindustrialized state.

Even after independence from their colonial power, most colonies were unable to achieve rapid economic development. Too often, postcolonial governments partnered with multinational corporations to enrich themselves while maintaining colonial patterns of exploitation (neocolonialism).

The structural-institutional approach to economic development focuses on the factors that make it difficult for poor countries to develop. For example, the colonial trade patterns that consigned colonies to producing and exporting primary products proved to be increasingly detrimental as primary product prices fell over the last century. Creating the right institutional conditions for industrialization proved to be the best way for less developed countries to escape poverty. This required infant industry protectionism, investments in education and infrastructure, subsidized financing, and a system that incentivized firms to increase exports and become internationally competitive. Japan, South Korea, China, and other newly industrialized East Asian countries used this approach successfully.

However, many countries in other regions were unable to industrialize successfully behind protective tariffs. Other countries were able to develop basic industries but were unable to make inroads into advanced industries, falling into the middle-income trap.

With the LDC debt crisis of the 1980s, the World Bank and the IMF imposed structural adjustment programs on heavily indebted LDCs, forcing them to adopt an extreme laissez-faire development plan. The results were overwhelmingly negative, with countries experiencing more than two decades of stagnation.

In more recent years, international organizations have focused on improving the effectiveness of foreign aid via randomized controlled trials. They have also paid increased attention to the impact gender roles and culture have on development. Improving the opportunities for women has substantial benefits for LDCs.

QUESTIONS FOR REVIEW

1. Describe the various measures of economic and human development that economists have used. Which measure do you find most compelling? Why?
2. Explain why having a high income does not always result in a country having a high level of human development. Given the examples in the book, is per capita income, economic growth, or human development a better measure of a country's economic development?
3. What role has geography played in the economic development of various regions in the world?
4. How did colonialism and slavery impact the economic development of colonial regions and the economies of the colonizers?
5. Explain the concept of neocolonialism and how it helps us to understand the ongoing development challenges facing former colonies.
6. Describe the structural-institutional approach to economic development. What are the strengths and limitations of this approach?
7. Describe the laissez-faire approach to development and the impact of laissez-faire policies, especially structural adjustment, on developing countries.
8. Compare and contrast the structural-institutional and laissez-faire approaches to economic development. Which approach do you find most compelling? Support your answer with examples.
9. Explain what a randomized controlled trial (RCT) is and why economists use them. Do you think it is ethical to use such trials? Why or why not?
10. Muhammed Yunus once argued that we do not need governments to solve society's problems. We can rely on social entrepreneurship. Given what you have studied, what are the strengths and weaknesses of this argument?

11. Suppose that you are appointed the chief economist for a less developed country. Using the material from this chapter and from Chapter 17 on economic growth, what approach to human development would you take? How might your approach need to be adjusted depending on the unique characteristics of different countries?

NOTES

1 The author would like to thank James Cypher, Matias Vernengo and Shahram Azhar for their helpful ideas and comments as the chapter was being conceptualized.
2 The World Bank is an international financial institution that provides loans and grants to governments of low- and middle-income countries in financial distress, usually accompanied by conditions that require the recipient governments to enact market-based policy reforms.
3 Amartya Sen, *Development as Freedom* (New York: A.A. Knopf, 1999), 18.
4 Ibid., p. 10.
5 Source: United Nations Development Programme (UNDP), *Human Development Report 2020*, http://hdr.undp.org/en/2020-report, accessed August 11, 2021.
6 Ibid.
7 See Berhanu Nega and Geoffrey Schneider, "Africa Rising? Short-Term Growth vs. Deep Institutional Concerns," *Forum for Social Economics* 45 (2016): 283–308. doi:10.1080/07360932.2016.1200108.
8 Jared Diamond, *Guns, Germs and Steel: The Fates of Human Societies* (New York: Norton, 1999).
9 James M. Cypher, *The Process of Economic Development*, 5th ed. (New York: Routledge, 2021), ch. 3.
10 Ibid.
11 Daron Acemoglu, Simon Johnson, and James A. Robinson. "The Colonial Origins of Comparative Development: An Empirical Investigation," *American Economic Review* 91, no. 5 (2001): 1369–1401.
12 Source: Our World in Data, "Real Commodity Price Index of Food Products," https://ourworldindata.org/grapher/real-commodity-price-index-food-products?time=1915.2015&country=~OWID_WRL, accessed August 2, 2021.
13 Cypher, supra note 5, ch. 10.
14 Jesus Felipe, Utsav Kumar, and Arnelyn Abdon, "How Rich Countries Became Rich and Why Poor Countries Remain Poor: It's the Economic Structure ... Duh!" *Japan and the World Economy* 29 (2014): 46–58.
15 Jose Antonio Alonso and Jose Antonio Ocampo, *Trapped in the Middle? Development Challenges of Middle-Income Countries* (Oxford: Oxford University Press, 2020).
16 Geoffrey Schneider, "The Post-Apartheid Development Debacle in South Africa," *Journal of Economic Issues* 52, no. 2 (2018): 306–322.
17 Ibid.
18 United Nations, Department of Economic and Social Affairs, *World Economic and Social Survey*, 2017, https://www.un-ilibrary.org/content/books/9789210605984/read, accessed August 11, 2021.

19 This section draws on the following sources: Geoffrey Schneider, "An Institutionalist Assessment of Structural Adjustment Programs in Africa," *Journal of Economic Issues* 33, no. 2 (1999): 325–334; Geoffrey Schneider and Berhanu Nega, "Limits of the New Institutional Economics Approach to African Development," *Journal of Economic Issues* 50, no. 2 (2016): 435-443.

20 Michael Barratt Brown, *Africa's Choices* (London: Routledge, 1999).

21 Schneider and Nega, supra note 18.

22 Daron Acemoglu, David Laibson, and John List, *Economics* (Boston: Pearson, 2015), 515.

23 Abhijit Banerjee, Dean Karlan, and Jonathan Zinman, "Six Randomized Evaluations of Microcredit: Introduction and Further Steps," *American Economic Journal: Applied Economics* 7, no. 1 (2015): 12.

24 Schneider and Nega, supra note 18.

Glossary of key terms and concepts

Absolute advantage: when a country can produce more of a good with the same amount of resources as another country.

Aggregate demand (AD): the sum of the demands for all goods and services by all economic actors, including households, businesses, banks, and government agencies, at various price levels. $AD = C + I + G + X - Im$.

Aggregate expenditure curve: the total level of real spending, including consumption, investment, government spending, and net exports, at each level of real GDP.

Aggregate supply (AS): the total quantity of output supplied by all producers at various price levels. $AS = Income = GDP = C + S + T$.

Appreciation: when a currency's value increases relative to a foreign currency.

Asset bubble: when a particular asset, such as stocks or property, increases in price rapidly and irrationally in a relatively short period of time.

Austerity: a government policy to reduce or eliminate social programs like food stamps, unemployment insurance, and education, in order to balance the government budget.

Automatic stabilizers: programs that automatically increase spending or reduce taxes in recessions and do the opposite when the economy is overheated.

Autonomous consumption (Ca): the level of consumption that does not depend on disposable income.

Backward linkages: linkages to industries that supply inputs to an industry (an industry's supply chain).

Balance of payments: all of the transactions in which the currency of one nation is exchanged for the currency of another nation during a particular period of time.

Balanced budget multiplier: the multiplier when government spending increases by the same amount that taxes decrease. It is equal to the multiplier minus the tax multiplier.

Business cycle: the pattern of booms and busts created by economic fluctuations in market capitalist economies.

Business inventories: the value of unsold goods held by retailers, wholesalers, and manufacturers.

Capital goods: the machinery, equipment, buildings, and productive resources (other than labor) used to produce goods and services.

Capitalism: An economic system in which the capital goods and other productive resources (land, natural resources) are privately owned and are bought and sold in markets based on the pursuit of profits.

Ceteris paribus assumption: all other relevant factors do not change.

Choice: when consumers, producers, and governments select from among the limited options that are available to them due to scarcity.

Class: a group of people that has a specific relationship with the production process (e.g., capitalists, workers, slaves, lords).

Collateral: something pledged by a borrower to provide security for repayment of a loan. Collateral is forfeited to the bank if the borrower defaults on the loan.

Collateralized debt obligation (CDO): a derivative consisting of a bundle of various forms of debt instruments, such as mortgages, auto loans, student loans, credit card debt, and so on.

Collateralized loan obligations (CLOs): a security that is backed by a pool of debt.

Collateralized mortgage obligation (CMO) (mortgage-backed security): a derivative consisting of a bundle of many home mortgages, which is sold to investors who expect to get a return on their CMO purchase but who also assume the risk of default associated with the mortgages.

Commodity money: when gold, silver, or other precious commodities are used as the primary unit of account. Example: the gold standard.

Communism: an economic system in which the government controls society's productive resources and makes the major economic decisions. Each person works according to their abilities and is paid according to their needs.

Comparative advantage (theory of): a country should produce and specialize in those goods that it can produce for a lower opportunity cost than its trading partners.

Comparative institutional advantage (theory of): trade patterns are driven by particular combinations of institutions (government policies and support, infrastructure, labor skills and training, education systems, communities, industrial clusters, and innovation systems) that create advantages for specific types of production in particular places, attracting economic actors to locate production in certain geographical locations.

Complementary good: a product that consumers tend to purchase along with another good; when the price of one good increases and consumers buy less of it, there will also be a decrease in the demand for any complementary goods.

Conspicuous consumption: the practice of consumers purchasing and using goods for the purposes of displaying their status and importance to others.

Consumer goods: goods that are purchased and used by consumers but that do not contribute to future productivity.

Consumption possibilities curve (CPC): shows all combinations of two goods that can be consumed by a country after specialization and trade. The CPC is constructed by starting at the point where the country specializes entirely in the good in which they have a comparative advantage. The other end point of the CPC is found by figuring out how much of the other good the country could get if it traded all of the specialized goods it produces to the other country at the international terms of trade.

Contractionary fiscal policy (austerity): cuts in government spending and increases in taxes that reduce aggregate demand.

Convergence hypothesis: the productivity growth rates of poor countries should tend to be higher than those for rich countries, because poor countries can imitate the experiences of rich countries. All economies should eventually converge to the same level of per capita income.

Creative destruction: the process by which businesses are forced to invent constantly to stay one step ahead of the competition and where creative, new industries inevitably destroy and replace older ones.

Credit default swap (CDS): a derivative in which one investor pays to swap their credit risk on a CMO or CDO with another investor. The purchaser of a CDS pays a fee to the CDS issuer. In exchange, if the CMO or CDO defaults, the CDS issuer pays the purchaser of the CDS.

Cyclical deficits: deficits that occur as a result of recessions during the business cycle.

Cyclical unemployment: unemployment caused by the decreased demand for labor in a recession

Deflation: a decrease in the average level of prices in an economy.

Demand curve: a curve that shows the quantity of a good buyers would like to purchase at each price within a particular period of time.

Demand shock: a decrease in aggregate demand from something other than the normal, cyclical investment patterns.

Democratic socialism: an economic system where the most important resources of society are controlled democratically by all citizens, including workers, who usually have little say in how market capitalist economies are run.

Depreciation: when a currency's value decreases relative to a foreign currency.

Derivative: a financial security whose value is derived from an underlying asset or group of assets. Derivatives involve a contract between two or more economic actors, and the value of the derivative varies with the fluctuations in the value of the asset(s) underlying the derivative.

Determinants of demand: the six factors that determine the location of the demand curve and whether or not it shifts to the left or to the right. The determinants of demand are (1) disposable income and wealth, (2) tastes and preferences, (3) the prices of substitute and complementary goods, (4) the number and size of buyers, (5) buyers' expectations about the future, and (6) the availability and cost of consumer credit.

Determinants of supply: the five factors that determine the location of the supply curve and whether or not it shifts to the left or to the right. The determinants of supply are (1) the cost, productivity, and availability of inputs; (2) the technology available to make the product; (3) sellers' expectations about the future; (4) changes in the profitability of other markets the seller can supply; and (5) the number and size of sellers.

Developmental state: the government undertakes macroeconomic planning and policies to stimulate industrial development in strategic sectors.

Dialectics: a method of analysis focusing on contradictions and the struggle of opposing forces.

Diminishing returns (law of): as more units of a variable input (such as labor) are added to a fixed amount of other inputs (such as capital), the marginal productivity of the variable input will eventually decrease (after all specialized tasks are filled).

Discount rate (primary credit rate): the rate of interest the Fed charges banks to borrow reserves.

Discretionary fiscal policy: fiscal policy that is "at the discretion" of government officials. Government officials must take additional actions in order for such policy to take effect.

Disposable income (DI): the income people have to spend after the government has taken out taxes (after tax income). $DI = C + S$.

Double movement: Polanyi's term for the push for the development of markets by businesses (first mercantilists and then capitalists), which was met by a counter movement by workers and communities to regulate markets.

Economic growth: the long-term, sustained increase in the economy's capacity (potential real GDP), driven by improvements in labor productivity.

Economic model: a theoretical, simplified construct designed to focus on a key set of economic relationships.

Economies of scale: the decrease in average total cost a firm experiences as it produces a larger quantity, due to increases in productivity (increasing returns to scale) or cost advantages from being larger. The sources of economies of scale include technology, specialized skills, bulk purchasing, financial benefits, and marketing advantages.

Efficiency (productive): in mainstream economics, a situation in which all resources are employed as productively as possible.

Efficient market hypothesis: financial markets always incorporate all available information and function in an efficient manner, so asset prices (the prices of stocks, bonds, and derivatives) are always accurate and cannot form irrational bubbles.

Endogenous money supply: the money supply is determined by economic variables within the economic system, especially real GDP, expected business sales, business investment, consumer confidence, and consumer spending.

Environmental Kuznets curve: a theory that as countries grow and became wealthier, they can afford to pay more attention to the environment, developing technologies, regulations, and clean production methods that reduce their environmental impact. Environmental destruction should increase during the first step of industrialization, then level off, and then decline as a country's standard of living increases.

Equation of exchange: Money supply (M1) $\times$ Velocity (V) = Price level $(P) \times$ Real GDP.

Exchange rate: amount of one currency that exchanges for another.

Expansionary fiscal policy: increases in government spending or reductions in taxes that stimulate aggregate demand.

Federal funds rate: the rate of interest banks charge each other on extremely short-term loans (often overnight), and it is controlled indirectly by the Fed.

Fiat money: money that is established as legal tender by government fiat (an official government decree); paper money or electronic accounts that have value because the state declares that they do and because people need the fiat money to pay their taxes and debts and to engage in economic activities in a particular society.

Financialization: the increasingly dominant role that financial motives, markets, actors, and institutions play in global economies.

Fiscal policy: the use of government spending or taxation to improve economic outcomes. Fiscal policy can be used to address macroeconomic market failures such as recessions, unemployment, or price instability and to improve the rate of economic growth.

Fixed exchange rate regime: when the government of a country pegs (fixes) the value of its currency relative to another currency.

Floating exchange rate regime: when a government does not regulate the exchange rate, allowing its country's currency to fluctuate with market forces.

Forward linkages: linkages to industries at subsequent stages of production that use the finished product in their production process.
Frictional unemployment: unemployment resulting from normal turnover in the labor market.
Functional finance: governments should decide how much to spend and tax based on the impact of these policies on prosperity for all, not based on how large the deficit is. Deficits are largely unimportant in sovereign nations that control their own currency.
GDP deflator: the ratio of prices in the particular year to prices in the base year.
Genuine progress indicator (GPI): a monetary measure of economic welfare that accounts for benefits and costs experienced by a particular population from investment, production, trade, and consumption of goods and services.
Government: provides the institutions that develop and implement policies for the state.
Gross national product (GNP): the total market value of goods and services produced by a country's citizens and companies during one year, which is equal to gross domestic product plus the net income from foreign investments.
Hegemony: when a particular group exerts undue influence within a society.
Herd behavior: the tendency of human beings to emulate the behavior of others.
Historical materialism: Marx's approach to the study of economics, focusing on the class conflicts and technological changes that provoke changes in the material conditions of society over time.
Human capital: the skills, dexterity, knowledge, habits, and creativity that improve productivity.
Hyperinflation: rapidly accelerating inflation that is out of control.
Import quota: a limit on the quantity of a good that can be imported.
Induced consumption: consumption induced by changes in income, found by multiplying the MPC by disposable income.
Industrial policy: a strategic initiative coordinated by the government to create favorable conditions for a particular industry.
Infant industry promotion strategy: a country protects and subsidizes a new industry until it can be globally competitive.
Inferior goods: goods that consumers want to buy less of as their income or wealth increases or more of as their income and wealth decreases.
Inflation rate: the percentage increase in the average level of prices, such as the Consumer Price Index for urban consumers.
Inflationary gap: the amount that real GDP is above potential real GDP.
Inputs: the factors of production—labor, capital, land, and natural resources—used to produce goods and services.
Institutional economics: the study of the institutions that shape an economy, how the economy and those institutions evolve, and how human beings are shaped by culture and institutions and seek status and power within those structures.
Institutions: the organizations, social structures, rules, and habits that structure human interactions and the economy.
Insurance: the purchase of a hedge against risk or an untimely event, where the insurer collects premium payments and provides compensation for a specified loss.
Interest on reserve balances (IORB): the interest rate the Fed pays banks on reserves deposited at the Fed.
International capital controls: rules or laws that restrict the movement of inflows and/or outflows of financial capital.

International terms of trade: the opportunity cost at which goods will trade internationally.

Intersectionality: the interconnectedness of various social stratifications, especially class, race, and gender, along with sexual orientation, age, and disability, in creating overlapping and interdependent systems of power and discrimination.

Labor force: a measure of all people available for work, including all people working and all people who are unemployed and are actively seeking work.

Labor force participation rate: the percentage of the population working, self-employed, or unemployed divided by the number of people of working age who are eligible to work in a country.

Labor union: an organization of workers formed to promote its members' interests with respect to wages, job security, benefits, and working conditions.

Law of demand: other things being equal, the quantity of a good demanded is inversely related to its price. When price increases, quantity demanded decreases. When price decreases, quantity demanded increases.

Law of diminishing marginal utility: as a person consumes more and more of one product, while holding consumption of other products constant, that person experiences a decline in the additional (marginal) utility from each additional unit of that product consumed.

Law of increasing opportunity cost: if resources are specialized and if all resources are being used efficiently, then as more and more of one good is produced, the opportunity cost of producing each additional unit of that good will increase.

Law of supply: other things being equal, the quantity of a good supplied is directly related to its price. When price increases, quantity supplied increases. When price decreases, quantity supplied decreases.

Less developed countries (LDCs): low-income, low human development countries that face substantial structural impediments to economic development and are highly vulnerable to economic and environmental shocks.

Leveraging: the use of debt to purchase an asset, with the hope that the profit from the asset purchase will exceed the borrowing cost.

Limited liability corporations: joint stock companies in which the activities and property of the firm are separated from the private property of the firm's owners, the stockholders. Owners do not assume liability for the firm's debts—all they can lose is the amount they invested in the firm, limiting their liabilities.

Liquidity: in financial economics, the ease with which an asset can be converted into cash.

Liquidity trap: when people believe that interest rates can fall no further and can only increase, so people hold all new money as cash because they believe interest rates will increase soon.

Long run: in microeconomics, the period of time in which all inputs are variable and can be adjusted. Suppliers can build entirely new plants, install new technology and equipment, and increase their productive capacity in the long run. In macroeconomics, the period in which variables adjust to their long run equilibrium.

Long-run aggregate supply: the economy at "full employment," when the economy is producing at its maximum normal capacity given existing resources and technology.

Macroeconomic problems created by wage and price deflation: declines in wages undermine aggregate demand and declines in prices undermine business profitability, both of which harm the economy in particular ways.

Macroeconomics: the study of the aggregate forces that shape national economies.
Mainstream economics (ME): the study of how society manages its scarce resources to satisfy individuals' unlimited wants.
Managed float exchange rate regime: when the government establishes a target zone for its currency and intervenes whenever its currency leaves the target zone.
Marginal cost (MC): the increase in cost from producing another unit of a good. $MC = (\Delta TVC/\Delta Q)$.
Marginal propensity to consume (MPC): the change in consumption (ΔC) that results from a change in disposable (after-tax) income (ΔDI). $MPC = \Delta C/\Delta DI$.
Marginal propensity to import (MPM): the increase in imports that results from an increase in disposable income.
Marginal respending rate (MRR): the additional spending that is generated from a change in income. MRR depends on the marginal propensity to consume, the net tax rate (t), and the marginal propensity to import (MPM): $MRR = MPC(1-t) - MPM$.
Marginal revenue (MR): the addition to total revenue from selling an additional unit of output. $MR = \Delta TR/\Delta Q$.
Market: an institution that organizes and facilitates transactions between buyers and sellers.
Market-dominated economies (MDEs): economic systems in which the primary economic decisions are made by private actors (businesses, individuals) in the market. Governments and social values play a secondary role.
Market failure: when market outcomes are either inefficient, destructive, or counter to the public interest.
Market misunderstanding theory: the cause of a recession is misperceptions by workers or other economic actors.
Market-supporting institutions: the set of institutions that must exist in order for markets to function effectively; these include property rights, laws to facilitate the aggregation of capital, trust, contract laws, competition, a lack of coercion, and physical, market, and financial infrastructure to lower transactions costs.
Markets always clear: the neoclassical theory that supply always equals demand in all markets, so the invisible hand of the market always allocates resources efficiently.
Markup pricing: when a firm sets price by adding a markup to their average total (accounting) costs of production. That markup may be above, below, or equal to a normal profit depending on market conditions and the firm's strategic goals.
Microeconomics: the study of distinct economic actors, such as consumers, workers, and firms, and how they interact in the economic system.
Middle class: small business owners, managers, and professionals who have some control over their working lives and who often supervise others but who do not have control over a significant amount of resources or workers and who must usually answer to the ruling class.
Middle-income trap: a country successfully develops some basic manufacturing but is unable to move into more advanced, higher value-added production.
Mixed market capitalism: an economic system in which private sector firms and individuals produce goods and services for markets for profits and a public sector established by the government regulates those markets and provides public goods such as schools, roads, airports, health care, and other goods and services that are usually provided inadequately by private markets.

Monetarist theories of the business cycle: monetary factors with driving fluctuations in real GDP.

Money: a unit of account, which may also be a physical item such as a printed piece of paper, that is accepted as payment for taxes, debts, and goods and services. Money can be issued as credit (loaned out). Money takes two main forms, as an account of debits and credits in a ledger and as a medium of exchange for trading.

Money (deposit) multiplier: the amount of money that banks create with each dollar of reserves. Money multiplier = 1/(required reserve ratio (RRR)).

Money supply (M1) (money stock): cash held by the public and near-cash accounts (checkable deposits).

Monopoly: the least competitive market structure with only one firm present and no close substitutes (a unique product). Monopolies are maintained by prohibitive barriers to entry, and their control over the market gives them complete control over prices.

Monopoly power: the ability of large firms to control prices.

Monopsony: when there is only one buyer of a product or resource.

Moral hazard: in a principal-agent problem, when agents act in their own best interests and when those interests are contrary to the interests of their principals.

Multiplier: a responding process whereby a dollar in spending becomes income for someone else, which they then spend, which becomes additional income, and so on, so that a dollar of spending is respent multiple times. Multiplier = 1/(1 − MRR).

Natural rate of unemployment: the normal rate of unemployment when the economy is not in a recession (full employment).

Necessary product: the resources necessary for a community's survival, including food, shelter, and the replacement of tools and materials used up in production.

Neoclassical economics: the study of how rational actors in competitive markets determine incomes and the prices and quantities of goods and services through the interaction of supply and demand.

Neocolonialism: when a country's rulers ally themselves with Western corporations to maintain the status quo and preserve the extractive institutions and relations that were established under colonialism.

Neoliberalism: contemporary ideas grounded in the classic, laissez-faire liberalism of Adam Smith. Market-oriented policy prescriptions include reducing trade barriers, deregulating financial markets, austerity (especially reductions in spending on the welfare state), deregulation, reduced taxation on the rich, and the privatization of government assets and functions.

Nominal GDP: the value of all final goods and services produced in a particular place at current prices (the total revenue of a country or region).

Nonaccelerating inflation rate of unemployment (NAIRU) theory: when the unemployment rate falls below the natural rate of unemployment, inflation is expected to increase and perhaps to accelerate.

Normal goods: goods that consumers want to buy more of when their income or wealth increases and that they want to buy less of when their income or wealth decreases.

Okun's law: a 1% increase in the rate of unemployment is associated with a 2% decrease in the growth of real GDP.

Opportunity cost: what is given up when a choice is made to allocate resources in a particular way.

Paradox of thrift: when consumers save more, this reduces aggregate demand, which in turn reduces GDP, which then reduces savings.

Path dependence: the dependence of economic outcomes on the structure of previous outcomes and institutions.

Pecuniary emulation: when people from the lower classes imitate the culture, habits, and spending of the upper classes to achieve status for themselves.

Phillips curve: a theory positing an inverse relationship between inflation and unemployment based on the impact of booms and busts on businesses' costs of production.

Pluralistic economics: a social science whose practitioners, from a variety of distinct schools of thought, study economies, how they grow and change, and the how they produce and distribute the goods societies need and want.

Plutocracy: a situation in which the group that dominates the economic system is made up of the wealthiest members of society.

Political business cycle theory: business cycles can result from policies of politicians to improve their reelection chances.

Potential real GDP: the output of goods and services that would be produced if the economy were utilizing all of its productive resources, including all of its employable workers and all of its capital stock.

Prebisch-Singer thesis: the long-term tendency of primary product prices to fall relative to manufactured goods.

Precautionary demand for money: the amount of cash or checkable deposits that people keep as a contingency to meet unexpected expenses.

Prime interest rate: the rate of interest private banks charge their best customers—the biggest corporations with the most collateral and the most secure financial situation.

Production possibilities curve (PPC): a model that shows all combinations of two goods that can be produced, holding the amount of resources and the level of technology fixed.

Profit rate: the total amount of profit accrued by a firm divided by the total capital invested by the firm.

Progressive political economics (PPE): the study of social provisioning—the economic processes that provide the goods and services required by society to meet the needs of its members.

Property rights: when a productive resource such as land or a slave belongs to a particular person or group instead of to society as a whole.

Public good: a good that is nonexcludable and nonrivalrous. Public goods are available to everyone equally, whether or not they pay.

Quantitative easing (QE): when the Fed purchases bonds or other assets from banks and businesses.

Quantitative tightening: when the Fed sells bonds and assets from its portfolio back to investors.

Quantity demanded: the amount of a good or service that buyers are willing to purchase at each price in a particular time period.

Quantity supplied: the amount of a good or service that sellers are willing to offer for sale at each price in a particular time period.

Quantity theory of money: a theory that the quantity of money in circulation (M1) is directly proportional to the price level of goods and services. $MV = PQ$. Assumes velocity is constant and real GDP cannot be influenced by the money supply.

Quasi-public goods: goods or services that have some but not all of the characteristics of public goods. Examples include the provision of health care and education to individuals, where society as a whole reaps substantial external benefits and where competition is inefficient or wasteful.

Radical political economics (RPE): the study of power relations in society, especially conflicts over the allocation of a society's resources by various social classes and how those conflicts cause society to evolve.

Randomized controlled trials (RCTs): experiments are conducted on people to determine which economic policies and programs are most effective.

Real business cycle theory: recessions are due to productivity shocks caused by changes in technology and the legal and regulatory environment.

Real estate investments: the purchase, rental, and sale of all types of property, including land and buildings.

Real gross domestic product (real GDP): the total output of goods and services produced within an area in a given time period, corrected for changes in prices so that real GDP only measures actual changes in the amounts of goods and services produced.

Real gross domestic product per capita: real GDP divided by the number of people in a country.

Real wage rate: the existing wage rate at current prices, called the nominal wage rate, divided by the price level. This gives us the wage rate in constant dollars, called the real wage rate.

Recession: a generalized slowdown of economic activity where reductions in production result in an increase in unemployment. A decline in production (real GDP) for six months or more (at least two quarters) is considered to be a recession.

Recessionary gap: the amount that real GDP is below potential real GDP.

Required reserve ratio (RRR): the percentage of deposits that banks are required by law to hold as reserves.

Research and development (R&D): activities designed to result in scientific breakthroughs, design and introduce new products, or improve existing products or manufacturing processes.

Reserves (bank): cash or deposits at the central bank.

Rule of 70: a formula that estimates how many years it takes for a variable growing at an exponential rate to double. The number of years for a variable to double = 70/(annual % growth rate of the variable).

Say's law: supply creates its own demand, and savings is always equal to investment.

Scarcity: when a society's seemingly unlimited desire for goods and services exceeds the resources available to produce and provide those goods and services.

Seasonal unemployment: unemployment that results from changes in the seasonal demand for labor.

Short run: the period of time in which the supplier cannot adjust the size of operations (their capacity). The supplier's capital stock (buildings, machinery, and equipment) is fixed. Suppliers are only able to adjust their variable inputs in the short run, especially the amount of labor they hire.

Social entrepreneurship: citizens working voluntarily and creatively to solve a society's problems.

Social market economies (SMEs): economic systems in which social values take a leading role in directing the economy, usually through the actions of a government which manages the economy in accordance with social values.

Socialist economic system: an economic system in which the means of production and distribution are either owned or regulated by society.
Soft budget constraint problem: when a government continually bails out an industry that cannot become competitive in markets.
Specialization of labor: particular tasks are performed by specific individuals, rather than everyone performing all tasks.
Specialization of resources: when some resources cannot be easily adapted from one use to another.
Speculative demand for money: the amount of cash or checkable deposits that people want to hold as a safe asset to maximize returns on all of their assets.
Stabilization policy: increasing government spending, reducing taxes, and reducing interest rates in recessions, while doing the opposite when the economy is growing too quickly.
Stagflation: when stagnation (declining production and worker layoffs) and inflation occur at the same time.
State-dominated economies (SDEs): economic systems in which the government is the main economic actor in most major industries or economic decisions, owning or controlling most of the economy.
Status-seeking: the human propensity to try to achieve the highest social status possible, as defined by the particular culture of the community.
Sticky wages and prices: in a recession, wages and prices do not fall fast enough to encourage businesses to hire more workers and consumers to buy more goods.
Stocks: an ownership share in a company, which entitles the owner to a share of the company's earnings. Earnings are realized either through a higher stock price as a company becomes more profitable or by dividend payments to stockholders.
Structural deficits: the portion of the government deficit that exists even when the economy is at its normal capacity.
Structural unemployment: unemployment resulting from the permanent displacement of workers due to automation, globalization, shifting demand for products, and other forces that eliminate the need for certain skills in the workplace.
Substitute good: a product that consumers are willing to purchase instead of another good; when the price of one good increases, many consumers will switch to buying the substitute good, increasing the demand for the substitute.
Supply curve: a curve that shows the quantity of a good sellers will offer for sale at each price within a particular period of time.
Supply-side economics: the belief that the primary determinant of economic growth is the profitability of suppliers, including corporations and wealthy business owners. The best way to achieve profitability is therefore to eliminate regulations and to reduce taxes on corporations and the wealthy.
Surplus product: the amount that is produced over and above what is needed for the community's survival (the necessary product).
Surplus value: the amount of value produced by workers over and above the cost of their wages (including benefits).
Sustainability: the ability of an economic system to sustain itself over time by meeting its current needs without compromising its future. Sustainability has three primary dimensions: environmental, social, and financial.
Tariff: a tax on imported goods.
Tax multiplier: a measure used to compute the impact of a lump sum change in taxes on aggregate demand. Tax multiplier = $MPC/(1 - MRR)$.

Technology: the tools, skills, and scientific knowledge that society develops in the use of resources to produce goods and services.

Theory of demand: in mainstream economics, consumers' willingness to pay for a product (demand) depends on the benefit (marginal utility) they expect to get from consuming the product, the price of the product, disposable income and wealth, tastes and preferences, the prices of substitute and complementary goods, the number and size of buyers, expectations about the future, and the availability and cost of consumer credit.

Theory of supply: in mainstream economics, a seller's willingness to offer a product for sale (supply) in a perfectly competitive market depends on the price they expect to get from selling the product, the cost, productivity and availability of inputs, the technology available to make the product, sellers' expectations about the future, changes in the profitability of other markets the seller can supply, and the number and size of suppliers.

Traditional economy: an economy in which resources are allocated based on communal patterns of reciprocity and redistribution and in which tasks are allocated and knowledge and skills preserved through established social relationships.

Transaction: an agreement between economic agents—buyers and sellers—to exchange goods, services, or assets.

Transactions costs: the costs incurred when engaging in a transaction, including transportation costs, information costs that are incurred when actors identify and evaluate different opportunities, and bargaining, monitoring, and enforcement costs.

Transactions demand for money: the amount of cash or checkable deposits that individuals need to keep available to make purchases (transactions).

Transfer payment: social spending that involves the transfer of income from the government to individuals or businesses, such as welfare payments or direct business subsidies.

Triple helix approach to innovation: government, universities, and industry interact as partners to generate ideas, invent and spread technologies, and develop industries and communities.

Unemployment rate: the number of people actively seeking work but without a job divided by the labor force.

Unequal exchange: when resources are systematically transferred by global trade flows from developing countries that produce primary products to developed countries.

Unregulated market capitalism (laissez-faire): an economic system in which the main productive resources of society—the labor, land, machinery, equipment, and natural resources—are owned by private individuals, who use those resources to produce goods and services that are bought and sold in markets for profits.

Utility: the amount of satisfaction a person gains from consuming a product.

Velocity: the number of times a unit of currency ($) changes hands in a year.

Vested interests: the group dominating society, whose goal is usually to preserve the status quo that they benefit from.

Volatility of investment: the Keynesian theory that business purchases of capital goods (investment) depend primarily on expected future profits, which is driven largely by expected sales, and expectations can vary dramatically.

Wealth: the value of the assets held by individuals and households.

Working class: those who must sell their labor to others in order to survive in a capitalist system.

Yield curve: the difference between interest rates on short-term bonds and interest rates on long-term bonds.

Index

Pages numbers in *italic* indicate a figure on the corresponding page.

absolute advantage 463
ACA *see* Affordable Care Act
Acemoglu, Daron 124
active labor market policies 132–133, 241
AD *see* aggregate demand
AD curve *see* aggregate demand curve
Addie Card 71, *71*
advertising 7, 11, 86, 90, 172
AE curve *see* aggregate expenditure curve
affirmative action laws 116
Affordable Care Act 117–118, 129
Africa 52, 54, 79, 149, 184, 453, 506, 516–517
African Americans 84–85, 116
aggregate demand 104, 106, 111, 177–178, 181, 185, 197, 200, 209, 211–213, 226–227, 229, 234, 240, 242, 247, 260, 304–305, 316, 324–328, 330–331, 335–337, 341, 366, 380, 383–385, 391, 397, 400, 429, 433–435, 437–439, 444, 464, 483, 488, 491–492; components of 263–264; decline in 104, 247; definition of 263; impact of increase in 266; importance of 437; inequality impact on 438; and multiplier 273–275
aggregate demand and aggregate supply (AD–AS) model 260–261, 281, 283, 383, *384*; for economy 262–263, *263*; limitations of 280–283
aggregate demand curve 260–261, 264–266, 268, 273–274, 281, 282–284, 298, 304–305, 305–306, 325, 327, 383; real-world 264; slope of *263*, 264, 281–282
aggregate demand curve shifts 264, 266, 273; with change in exchange rates 270; with change in wages 270; with consumption changes 266; with government spending changes 266; with investment changes 266–267; with multiplier 273–275; price index changes with 264, 265, 266
aggregate economics 175
aggregate expenditure: autonomous 293, 299, 301; components of 292–293, 296; equilibrium level of 306
aggregate expenditure curve 294, 296–305, 298–299, 301, 305
aggregate expenditure-income model 260, 287
aggregate expenditure model 291–294, *292*, 296–297, 303, 305–307; and aggregate demand curve 304–306, *305*; business inventories 294–295; components of 292; consumption in 292–293; equation for 294; inflationary gap 303–304, *304*; investment and government spending 293; MRR 293–294; net exports 293; recessionary gap *302*, 302–303; shifts in 297–302, *300*, *301*; total taxes in 292
aggregate supply 197, 260, 264, 306, 330, 335, 398, 400, 434, 483
aggregate supply curve 261, 263–266, 269, 273–274, 277–278, 282–284, 306; on prices and real GDP 269, *269*; slope of 265, *265*, 282

aggregate supply curve shifts 264, 265; with change in exchange rates 270; with change in wages 270; determinants of *268*, 269, *269*; toward equilibrium price index 262
aggregation of capital 149
agriculture 46–47, 54, 64, 73, 111, 316, 330, 505; agricultural markets 110; agricultural price supports 110; agricultural technology 51; impact on economic system 73–74; productivity 73–74; as protected sector 64
Airbus 468
alienation 80
Amazon 91, 147, 234, 367; consumer shopping behavior on 11–12; strengths of 11–12
American Recovery and Reinvestment Act (ARRA) of 2009 341–342, 413
Anglo-Saxon cultures 518
anti-Semitism 51
antitrust laws 79
Apple 79, 91, 171, 435, 438, 454–455, 459, 463, 466
Argentina 241
Aristotle 41
AS *see* aggregate supply
AS curve *see* aggregate supply curve
Asian financial crisis of 1997 371, 497–498, 497–500
assembly line 92
asset bubbles 195, 327, 394–395, 401, 407–408, 416
asset markets 178, 314, 365–366, 366–370, 368–369, 383, 401, 413, 416, 490; bonds 367; derivative 367; insurance 368; real estate investments 368; stocks 366–368
asset(s) 148, 160–161, 191, 213, 248, 266, 339, 348, 354, 356, 361–362, 366–368, 381–383, 394, 401, 403–404, 411, 413, 475, 477–478, 480–481, 488–491; domestic 486, 490; fixed income 366; foreign 485–486, 495; values 195, 248, 253–254, 405, 407, 413, 483, 492, 498–499
asset transfer costs 362
asset transfers 485–486
Assyrians 49
austerity policy 7, 107, 130, 186, 251, 254, 311, 314, 324, 327, 329, 342, 370, 389, 403, 468, 490, 514–515; balancing government budget 5, 6; definition of 4; in euro area of E.U. 342; justification for 4
Australia 17, 18, 125–126, 134, 220, 225, 320, 323, 343, 433, 506
Austrian economics 22, 242
authority of feudal lord 50
automatic stabilizers 314, 323–324, 329, 344
autonomous consumption 291–292, 296, 299, 303
autonomous expenditure 299, 301, 306

B-2 stealth bombers, opportunity cost of U.S. spending on 24, 35–36
Babangida, Ibrahim 507
"backwash effects" 512
Bakir, Erdogan 398
balanced budget multiplier 327–328
balance of payments 475; definition of 484; major issues of 484; two sides of *485*
bank accounts 363, 379–380, 403
banking insurance programs 356, 357
banking sector 83, 108, 312, 348, 359, 365, 378, 383, 391, 412
banking system 6, 63, 93, 106–108, 111, 117, 150, 151, 197, 201, 211, 229, 312, 336, 348, 356–357, 359, 363, 365, 371–372, 377–378, 382, 391, 413, 511, 514; bailout of 117; deregulation of 357, 378; financial crisis of 2008 117; regulation of 376–378; regulations of 107–108, 359, 378, 391; required reserve ratio (RRR) 356, 367
bank owners, ownership stake of 359
bankruptcy 94, 104, 192, 199, 330–331, 404
banks 372; collateral 358–359; derivative investments 191–192; failures of 108, 190, 192; financial incentive to loan out 359; as financial intermediaries 356; functions of 355; impact on economy 357; loans to corporations 363–364; money multiplier 357–358; mortgages to "sub-prime" borrowers 192; nominal interest rates hike by 249; profits of 356; reserve requirements circumvented by 364; reserves 356; "run on the bank" 356–357; T-account 356, *356*; types of 359
barter 250, 351, 353
behavior: human 86–87, 96, 259, 407; investor 103, 278, 366, 492

INDEX   539

Better Life Index 126, 218–221, 225–227
Biden, Joseph 118, 192
Bitcoin 354
BLI *see* Better Life Index
Bodin, Jean 252
bonds 178, 191, 248, 266, 299, 312, 321, 348, 354, 356, 359–360, 362–363, 365–368, 372, 379–380, 382, 384, 414, 477–478, 482, 485, 488, 513
borrowers 248–249
Botswana 184
brand reputation and trust 150
Brazil 220, 239, 334, 338, 343, 424, 444, 461, 504, 512
Bretton Woods system of international monetary management 377
Brexit 313, 469, 478
British economy 254, 478
British Empire: culture and values of 125; profiting from mercantilism 53–54
budget 1, 4–6, 11, 107, 153, 243, 316, 318, 329–330, 340, 488
budget deficits 5, 6, 107, 111, 186, 200–201, 311, 329, 332, *332*, 337–342, 488, 513
bullionism 53
bureaucracy 3, 137
Bureau of Labor Statistics 238
Bush, George H. W. 187
Bush, George W. 117, 191, 329
business confidence 103, 106, 242, 342, 385, 402
business cycle 1, 14, 97, 102–103, 112, 120, 175, 177, 193–198, *196*, 200–201, 234, 275, 332, 340, 369, 389–390, 394–398, 401, 404–407, 416; definition of 177; laissez-faire approach to 196–197; laissez-faire economists' theories of 405–407; New Keynesian approach to 193, 195, 197; political economy approach to 197; prices and wages 193, 196; profit rate in 397; real GDP and potential real GDP 193, 195, *195*; strong growth and recessions 193, 195–196; supply-side approach to 197; unemployment rates 193, 196, *196*; *see also* Minsky cycle
business environments, women's fashions in 88
business expectations 103

business investment 14, 63, 103, 108, 111, 181, 183, 186, 191, 200, 247–249, 267, 277–278, 280, 304, 324, 342, 359, 363, 365, 366, 380, 385, 389, 396–398, 400, 402, 415, 416, 426, 429, 492; incentives for firms for 438; policies stimulating 428–430; recession impact on 63–54, 63–64
busyness as high status 89
buyers: expectations about future 164; number and size impact on demand 163–164

calamities and real GDP 217
Calvinism 52
Canada 125–126, 134, 187, 220, 225, 320, 323, 334, 343, 461, 486, 489
Cannan, Edwin 100
capital 31, 54, 59, 65, 77, 79, 100, 147, 149, 153, 168, 214, 222, 251, 269, 281, 321, 340, 397, 416, 426–427, 434, 454, 456, 467, 471, 485, 498; accumulation 75, 399; aggregation 147, 149; investment purchases 397–398
capital gains 321
capital goods 22, 30–32, 47, 54, 75, 102–103, 209, 366, 396–397, 426–427, 429, 438, 492; growth in PPC from 31–32, *32*; profits invested in 75; purchases of 64, 100, 260
capitalism 1, 3, 16, 41–43, 44, 53–55, 59–60, 63, 94–95, 109, 114–115, 120, 130, 136–138, 144, 183, 198, 331, 406, 469; bottom produced by 78–79; capital accumulation in 75; "creative destruction" of 114; definition of 54; dehumanizing effect of 79–80; economic crises 81; factors changing structure of 82–83; lack of bargaining power 70; markets in 147; modern 48, 68, 77, 79–80, 149, 171, 371, 401; primary focus of 55; regulated 17, 56, 80, 82, 118; rise of 55; spread of 69–70; uneasy beginnings of 54; unregulated 68, 76, 82, 199; workers' conditions under 70–72, 95; *see also* commodification
Capitalism, Socialism and Democracy (Schumpeter) 114
capitalist businesses, productive aspect of 89

capitalist manufacturing 52
capitalist system 1, 15, 56–60, 74, 80–81, 118, 152, 181, 200; competition 57–58, 75; education 60; egalitarian system 60; equal distribution of income 58; government regulation 59–60; mixed market 136; productivity 57; profit motive 58; property rights in 148; reducing regulations on imports and exports 59; self-interest 58–59; social class in 74–75; specialization of labor 57; and workers, exploitative relationship between 73–76
"capital–labor accord" era: GDP growth during 115–116; increase in incomes during 116; middle-class lifestyle in 115
capital markets 180, 210, 508, 514–515
capital stock 165, 195, 212, 426–428; policies to increase 428–430; production function and 426–427
captive markets 55
carbon dioxide emissions per capita 198; and real GDP per capita 441, *442*; U.S. environmental Kuznets curve for 440, *441*
Card, David 13
CARES Act of 2020 *see* Coronavirus Aid, Relief, and Economic Security Act of 2020
Carnegie, Andrew 83
car suppliers, supply curve for *169*, 169–170
Case-Shiller Home Price Index 408
cash money 354
Castro, Fidel 138
Catholic Church 51
CDOs *see* collateralized debt obligations
CDS *see* credit default swap
CDSs *see* credit default swap
central banks 187, 196, 249, 254–255, 312–313, 336, 353, 355–356, 359, 361–363, 364, 365, 375, 382, 385, 388–391, 403–404, 406, 477, 482, 489, 493, 497; attempts at creating 377; autonomy of 379; benefits of independent 378–379; functional finance approach of 390; high interest rates by 249–250; importance of 376; macroeconomic goals of 379; money supply control by 363; power in political economy model 365, 375; roles of 359, 375
centralization of control 137

central planning 112–115, 137–139; bureaucracy and 138; of China 139, 189; and dictatorship 113, 138; production inefficiencies 114; of Soviet Union 114, 137
ceteris paribus assumption 25
chicken processing firms, availability of laborers for 168
child labor "reforms" in England 71
China 18, *18*, 31–32, 34, 79, 118, 120, 122–123, 127, 144, 182, 184, 189–190, 192, 201, 234, 239, 313, 316, 337–339, 343, 351, 420–421, 424, 429–430, 436, 438, 444, 447, 453–456, 458–459, 461–463, 465, 470, 484–486, 489, 491, 504, 510–512, 518; Chinese coins *350*; economic growth of 31, 140, 189–190; environmental record of 140; Pew Research Global Attitudes survey of 140–141; SEZs and foreign investment in 140, 189; state-dominated economy of 139–141; transition toward market socialist economy 139–141
Choice 22–23
Christian hostility, towards European Jews 51
Christmas, commodification of 80
circular flow model of macroeconomy 62, *62*, 100–102, *101*, 209–211, *210*, 226–227, 264, 271; expenditure side of 209, 226; income side of 209, 211, 226
civic engagement 219
Civilian Conservation Corp 110
civil liberties 128
civil rights movement 116
Civil Works Administration 110
class 47; conflicts 73–74; mobility 85; structure 48, 74, 84; system of society 34
Clayton Antitrust Act of 1914 377
climate change 129, 198, 218, 223, 421, 440–441, 443, 509
Clinton, Bill 117, 187–188
CLOs *see* collateralized loan obligations
CMOs *see* collateralized mortgage obligations
Cobb, John 221
Coca-Cola 90
collaborative business arrangements 457
collateral 358–359
collateralized debt obligations 409–410, 409–411

collateralized loan obligations 410, 416
collateralized mortgage obligation 192, 364, 409
collateralized mortgage obligations 192, 364–365, 409–411
collective bargaining 110
college education, opportunity cost of 23
colonial empires 53–54, 74, 506–507
command communism 112
commercial banking 377
commercial banks 359
commodification: of Christmas 80; of holidays and societal events 80; of labor 79–80; of love 80; of public services 80–81
commodity money *350*, 350–352
common markets 467
communism 18, 41, 77, 81, 82, 137–138
Communist Manifesto, The (Marx and Engels) 72, 73, 77, 79
Communist Party 316
communist uprisings 137
communities 219
comparative advantage, theory of 64, 462; assumptions behind 454–458; basic principle of 449–450; development of 448; graphical illustration of 450–453, *451*, *452*; problems with 453–458
comparative institutional advantage, theory of 465
competition 41, 151; income regulation by 58; influence on efficiency and growth 57–58; from international firms 188–189, 201; Marx's views on 78–79; and mercantilist policies 56; moral sentiments and 58; profit motive in 58; as race to bottom 78; Smith's views on 78; system of justice and 58; winners and losers in 79
competitive advantage of companies 454
competitive capitalism *see* capitalism
competitive companies 462
competitive labor market 61
competitive markets 58–59, 147, 152, 154–157, 164–165, 282, 438, 463
competitiveness 463–466
complementary goods 162–163
concentration of capital 79
Confucian cultures 518
conservative economists 9

conspicuous consumption 33, 95; culture influence on 89; definition of 88, 89; goods 88
conspicuous leisure 88, 95
consumer behavior 1, 11–12; from mainstream economy perspective 10; from political economy perspective 11; social factors influencing 11
consumer choices and social status 33–34
consumer confidence 14, 25, 63, 384
consumer credit: availability and cost of 157, 160, 164; card debt 164
consumer demand 113, 181; consumers' tastes and preferences influence on 161–162, *162*; and disposable income, link between *160*, 160–161; model of 10; and prices and quantities of goods, factors affecting 157; in recession 63; and wealth, link between *160*, 160–161
Consumer Financial Protection Bureau 413
consumer goods 11, 22, 28, 30–32, 31, 35, 125, 137, 191, 209, 243, 364, 438
Consumer Price Index 183, 243
Consumer Price Index for urban consumers 183
consumer purchases 209, 247
consumer shopping behavior and Amazon.com: from mainstream economy perspective 11–12; from PPE and RPE perspective 12
consumer spending 14, 25, 180–182, 384–385; decline in 5, 103; decline in recessions 63; and disposable income 288–289; recession impact on 105
consumption: change in 271–272; factors affecting 266; function 288–291, 306; impact of taxes on 291
consumption goods 88, 289, 438
consumption habits 87
consumption possibilities curve 452, *452*
contractionary monetary policy 249–250, 376, 381, 384–386, *385*, 389
contract laws 150
convergence hypothesis 424
cooperation 45, 124, 136, 466, 518
cooperative culture of Nordic countries 130
coordinated market economies *see* social market economies
Corn Laws 64
Coronavirus Aid, Relief, and Economic Security Act of 2020 342–344

corporate reputation and trust 150
corporations 127–128, 454, 464, 466, 507, 520; bank loans to 363–364; MNC 128; power in U.S. system 128
corrective tariffs 464
corruption 516
Corruption Perceptions Index 150
cost advantage 12
cost–benefit analysis 37
cost-push inflation 251
costs of production 104, 168–169, 172, 251, 254, 265, 267, 269–270, 277–280, 284, 398, 438, 484
COVID-19 pandemic 118, 313, 415
COVID-19 pandemic recession of 2020 6, 14, 145, 249, 303, 312, 325, 331, 333, 341–344, 355, 381, 383, 387, 391, 394, 413–415, 417; CARE Act of 2020 342–344; economic systems approach to 242, 253–254; fiscal and monetary responses to 343; impact on oil prices 145; inverted yield curve and 414–415; S&P 500 stock market index 370; stimulating borrowing in 381; U.S. government stimulus program for 313–314, 325, 333, 342–344, 383, 415
CPC *see* consumption possibilities curve
CPI *see* Consumer Price Index
CPIU *see* Consumer Price Index for urban consumers
"crank" economists 4, 7
creative destruction 114
"creative destruction" of capitalism 114
credit default swap 410–412
credit, deflation impact on 247
credit unions 359
crop rotation system 51
crowding out *vs.* crowding in 336
cryptocurrencies 354
Cuba 18, *18*, 138, 316
cultural factors 86
cultural values: and consumption patterns 87–89; market-dominated economies 125; and trust 150
culture: and conspicuous consumption 33–34; dualistic character of 89; effect on customer behavior 12; impact on economic development 517–518; impact on ethical considerations 204; influence on conspicuous consumption 89; influence on economic systems 123;

overt displays of wealth and leisure 87; purchasing patterns shaped by 88; shaping status-seeking 46; status-seeking behaviour and 86–87, 95; traditional economy and 45
currency 498; appreciation and depreciation of 477; devaluation 140, 483; exchange rate of 477; foreign 199, 250, 475, 477–480, 483, 495; maintaining strong 495; pegged to euro 493; tools to alter supply or demand of 494–496; value of 354; *see also* euro; home country's currency; U.S. dollar
current account deficit 484–486, *487*, 492, 498; U.S. 484–486, *487*
customer reviews 12
customs union 467
cyclical deficits 332
cyclical investment volatility 395–397
cyclically adjusted-price-to-earnings (CAPE) ratio 369
cyclical unemployment 234, *235*

Daly, Herman 178, 221
De Beers Corporation 80
debt: deflation impact on 247; economic growth using 199–200; to foreign countries 199; in public and private sector 199; of U.S. government 187; *see also* government debt and deficits
Deepwater Horizon oil spill cleanup effort 217
defense and education, production possibilities curve for: combinations of services in *25*, 25–26, *26*; opportunity cost changes in 27–28; for Russia 28–29; specialization of resources in 27–28
defense spending 2, 31, 36, 187; on B-2 bombers 36; budget of U.S. 318; causes of funding 36; as consumer good 31; of countries 32, *32*; Reagan administration 187
defensive household expenditures and GPI 223
Deficit Myth, The (Stephanie) 340
deficit spending 314
deflation 104–105, 175, 178, 181, 183–184, 229, 243, *244*, 246–248, 253, 256, 278, 279, 312, 335, 352, 375, 382, 389; correcting 248; problems created by 247–248

deindustrialization 116, 118, 131, 135, 232, 420, 515
demand: buyers' expectations affecting 164; change in 160; consumer credit influence on 164; number and size of buyers impacting 163–164; for products 63
demand curve 10, *10*, 157, 260; ceteris paribus assumption 25; expression for 158–159; milk market 170; model of 25, 158; for quantity demanded and market 158–159, *159*; slope of 159
demand curve shifts 159, 172; availability and cost of consumer credit 164; buyers' expectations 164; ceteris paribus conditions of 160; complementary goods 162–163, *163*; disposable income and wealth *160*, 160–161; number of buyers 163–164; size of buyers 164; substitute goods 162–163, *163*; tastes and preferences 161–162, *162*
demand-pull inflation 251
demand shocks 247, 397, 400
democratic rule 128
democratic socialism 8, 17
Deng Xiaoping 139
Denmark 127, 130, 133, 150, 215, 220, 224, 335, 343, 493
deposit multiplier *see* money multiplier
deposits 93, 252, 355–361, 366, 372, 377, 510, 513
derivatives 192, 359; collateralized debt obligation 410; collateralized loan obligations 416; collateralized mortgage obligation 409–410; credit default swap 410; definition of 191, 367; markets 371, 413; rating of 411, *412*; risky investments in 36, 191, 201, 367
deskilling 80
devaluation 140, 483–484, 497
devalued currency approach 251
developmental state 436, 510–511
DI *see* disposable income
dialectics 73
diamond engagement ring 80
Diamond, Jared 48
Dickens, Charles 61
dictatorship 113
discount rate 379–381, 384, 391
discouraged workers 237

discretionary fiscal policy: impact on aggregate demand and GDP 314; recessionary or inflationary gaps 314
disposable income 157, 159–160, 209, 211, 226, 266, 271–272, 288–292, 295, 303, 306; change in 271; and consumer demand, link between *160*, 160–161; and consumer spending 288–289; consumption and savings functions, relationship between 289–291, *290*; increase in 288
disposable personal income *213*, 214
Dodd-Frank Wall Street Reform and Consumer Protection Act of 2010 378, 413
dollar *see* U.S. dollar
domestic and foreign goods, price of 475
Dominos 154, 165–167, *166*
dot-com bubble *see* internet stock bubble
dot-com recession of 2000–2001 394
double-dip recession of 1980–1982 398, 400
double movement 64–65, 71
double shifts 481
DPI *see* disposable personal income
drudgery 80
durable goods purchases 100, 247, 249, 380, 384–385, 396

early human societies 43, 45
Eastern Block 82
Eastern European countries 468–469
Economic agents 146
economic "bads" and real GDP 217
economic booms 7, 31, 77, 139–140, 161, 193, 197, 217, 255, 280–282, 331, 362
Economic Consequences of the Peace, The (Keynes) 101–102
economic crises 9, 187, 199, 229, 242, 247, 256, 281, 311–312, 353, 375, 382, 394, 468; capitalism prone to 81; macroeconomic analysis of 13–15; *see also* Asian financial crisis of 1997; financial crisis of 2007–2008; Great Depression of 1930s; Great Recession of 2008–2009; Mexican peso crisis of 1994–1995
economic debates 4
economic development 501; culture impact on 517–518; definition of 502–503; for early economists 502; geography and 505–506; Human Development Index

503–505, *504*, *505*; impacts of colonial era on 506; measures to track 502; path dependence 506–507; self-reinforcing 511; slavery impact on 506; structural adjustment and laissez-faire approach to 513–515; structural-institutional analysis of 508–513

economic exchange 350

economic growth 31, 52, 178, 181, 182, 444; by capital goods 31–32; causes of 182; of China 31; as exponential process 423; export-oriented policies for 438; formulae for 31; higher wages driving 437; impact of different rates of 424; importance of 423–425; inequality impact on 438; major forces driving 422; of MDEs and SMEs 182; under mercantilism 54; mercantilist policies impact on 56; New Keynesian model of 422, 426–428, 444; New Keynesian policies to stimulate 428–434; political economy approach to 422, 435–440, 444; of poor countries 424; of real GDP per capita 424, *425*; reasons for slowing of 437–438; of SDEs 182; supply-side approach to 422, 434–435, 444; and sustainability, relationship between 421, 422, 440–443; variations 424, *425*; ways to achieve 421

economic instability *119*

economic integration 420, 466–468, 470

"economic man" 10, 11

economic models 36; application of 24–25; assumptions of 25; definition of 24; see also demand curve

economics 11, 36–37; complex nature of 8; definition of 15; as inexact social science 8; kinds of 15, *16*; richness of field of 15; schools of thought in 15, *16*; scientific approach to 12–13

economic systems 7, 43, 175, 182, 218, 501; class antagonisms 73; cultural forces in 33–34; driving force of changes in 73–74; ethical considerations 204; factors shaping 123–124; hegemony of 204; political considerations 204; rules of 7; technology 73–74; variations of 17

economic systems, evolution of 41, 42; agriculture 46–48; authority of lord 48; capitalism 54–55; cities, development of 47; empires 49; feudalism 49–53; government 48; group identity development 47; industrial revolution 54–55; laissez-faire capitalism 55–56; Marx's ideas regarding 69; mercantilism 53–54; peasants of antiquity 48; property rights 47–48; slave economies 48, 49; social class 47–48; surplus product 47; traditional economies 44–46

economic thought 4, 15, 41, 284; schools of 15, *16*, 18

economic union 467

economic well-being, measures of 205; genuine progress indicator 221–224; OECD Better Life index 218–221; World Happiness Index 225

economy: business cycle of 14; challenges associated with study of 8; importance of 7; pluralistic approach to study of 8–9; type of 8

economy car and luxury car, difference between 88

education 60, 219

educational spending, as percentage of GDP *433*, 433–434

education quality and access, policies to improve 432–434

efficiency, in mainstream economics 24

efficient market hypothesis 191

egalitarian culture 131

Egypt 49

Eisenhower, Dwight D. 36

elites and economic systems 124

employer of last resort (ELR) programs 241

employment 13, 26, 71, 77, 78, 104, 116, 131, 132, 136, 178, 188, 219, 230, 231, 234, 237–238, 240, 241, 242, 256, 265, 319, 340, 457; see also full employment

emulation 87–88

enclosure movement 53, 54, 55, 60, 77

endogenous money, political economists on 363–366

Engels, Friedrich 72

England: child labor "reforms" in 71; embracement of Protestantism in 52; industrial revolution in 54–55; infant industry promotion strategy 69–70; seizing common lands in 53; work characteristics in 70–71

Entrepreneurial State, The (Mazzucato) 435

entrepreneurship 133

environment 219
environmental degradation 149, 223
environmental destruction 440–441
environmental Kuznets curve 440–441
environmental sustainability 198
Epstein, Gerald 370
equality, in Nordic countries 133
Equatorial Guinea 148, 503, 507, 516
equilibrium price and quantity 167, 168
Erdogan, Recep Tayyip 439
ethical considerations 33, 204
ethnic differences 85
E.U. *see* European Union
euro 467, 481, 493–494, 496
European Central Bank 379
European Economic Community 467
European Organization for Nuclear Research 468
European Union 118, 130, 135, 196–197, 256, 313, 389, 415, 420, 421, 447, 467–469; austerity policies 130; economy recovery 196–197
evolutionary approach 85–86
exchange: equation of 352; foreign 420, 495; medium of 350–351, 353–354
exchange rates 219, 268, 270, 298–299, 352, 420, 458, 475–479, 482–484, 486, 488, 492–494, 496; adjustment with trade deficit 486; change 475; definition of 476; fixed 492–494, 497; floating 492–493, 496; market forces and 476; principles regarding impact of 483
expansionary monetary policy 111, 193, 248, 253, 330, 376, 384–385, 387, 392; goal in recessions 384, *384*; laissez-faire perspective on 387–388; New Keynesian perspective on 389–390; political economy approach to 388, 390–391; supply-side economists on 388, 391
expected sales 63, 102, 103, 279, 283, 293, 415, 438
expenditure side of circular flow model 209, 226
exports 53–54, 59, 108, 190, 192, 211–212, 226, 263, 268, 281, 284, 293, 299, 337, 436, 438, 452–454, 458–459, 461–464, 468, 470, 475, 482–486, 489–491, 496, 498, 506, 508–509, 513, 520; and import products, U.S. *462*; industries, currency devaluation to boost 483; oriented policies 438; purchases 209
extractive institutions 124
Exxon Mobil 507

Facebook 91
factors of production 454–455
factory inspection 93
factory systems 76
Fama, Eugene 185, 191
fashion trends for women 88
FDI *see* foreign direct investment
Fed *see* U.S. Fed
Federal Deposit Insurance 108
Federal Deposit Insurance Corporation 357
federal funds rate 364, 379–381, 384, 391
Federal Reserve Act of 1913 377
Federal Reserve Bank *see* U.S. Fed
Federal Reserve banking system 377
Federal Reserve Bank of United States 14
Federal Reserve Economic Data 338
Federal Reserve/Federal Reserve Bank *see* U.S. Fed
Federal Savings and Loan Insurance Corporation 357
Fed policy changes: impact on aggregate demand, aggregate supply, and real gross domestic product (GDP) 376
Fertile Crescent, agriculture-based empires of 49
feudalism 42, 49–53, 73, 78–79, 438; agricultural productivity during 73–74; Catholic religion and 51; guildmasters 50; guilds 50–51; hierarchical system of 44; lack of innovation occurred 51; manors in 50; merchants and kings 52; moneylending 51; resource allocation in 50, 52; serf system in 50; specialization of labor in 50; surplus of food 51; urbanization and specialization 51, 74
feudalism, changes undermining: agricultural technology 51; capitalist manufacturing 52; colonization 52; enclosure movement 53; exploration 52; long-distance trade 51–52; market for labor power 53; privatizing common lands 53; shift in ideology and religion 52; specialization 51; urbanization 51
feudal society 51

fiat money 351–354; definition of 351; origin of 351; supply of 352–353; U.S. dollar 352; value of 352
final goods 206
finance 106, 111, 134, 312, 348, 364, 372, 401–403, 497
financial accounts 485–487
financial account surplus 475–476; U.S. 486, *487*
financial assets 14, 353–354, 367, 484, 486
financial capital 197, 366, 484, 495–498
financial capital flows, unregulated *vs.* managed 497–498
financial crisis 5, 7, 13–14, 111, 130, 175, 178, 192, 246, 249, 277, 312–313, 336, 339, 341–342, 353, 357, 371, 378, 382–383, 403, 408, 410–412, 416, 468, 478, 484
financial crisis of 2007–2008 5, 13, 111, 353, 378; causes of 191–192; general equilibrium models of 13–14; housing bubble 14, 192
financial flows, international 371, 458, 479, 497–499
financial infrastructure 151
financial instability hypothesis 401, 404–405
financial, insurance, and real estate (FIRE) markets 312, 348, 370–373
financialization 190, 348, 370–371, 370–374, 398
financial markets 5, 11, 14, 97, 102, 107–110, 112, 117, 130, 147, 175, 186–187, 190–191, 312, 328, 341, 365–366, 368–370, 370–372, 379, 385, 389, 391, 401, 403–407, 413, 415, 482–483, 489, 491, 514–515; bonds 348; deregulation of 117, 187, 190–192, 191, 370, 404, 405; efficient market hypothesis 191; hypercompetitive nature of 191; open 188; real estate 348; regulation of 108, 192, 375, 376; state control 376; stocks 348
financial sustainability 199, 200
Finland 126–127, 130, 134, 220, 225, 323, 432
fiscal activism *vs.* austerity debate 314
fiscal policy 193, 280, 311, 315, 375, 385, 388, 406, 413, 496; AD and AS model 325–328; automatic stabilizers 323–324; discretionary 321, 323–324, 331; expansionary 330; fixing recessionary or inflationary gap with 325–326; government spending 315–320; laissez-faire economists on 328–329; New Keynesian economists on 330–331; political economists on 331–332; supply-side economists on 329–330; tax policy 320–322, 327
fiscal stimulus 318, 341–342, 345, 390, 406
Fitoussi, Jean-Paul 218
fixed exchange rate regime 493–494
flexicurity programs 132–133
floating exchange rate regime 492–493
flow of capital 454
Food Stamps program 116
Ford, Henry 92, 104
foreign aid 485, 515–516
foreign competition 83, 255, 429, 436, 438, 459, 461, 465, 510, 514
foreign currencies 199, 250, 475, 477–480, 483, 495
foreign debts 199
foreign direct investment 465, 469; in China 429–430; stimulating investment purchases 429; "sweatshop model" of 430
foreign exchange controls 495
foreign exchange convertibility system 377
foreign exchange markets 378, 475, 476, 477; mainstream economics model of 477; shifts in demand in 479–480; shifts in supply in 480–483; for U.S. dollars 477–478, *478*
foreign goods 268, 270, 420, 475, 477–478, 480–481, 483, 495
foreign investment 132, 140, 213, 436, 447, 456, 475, 488, 491–492, 514–515
foreign trade effect 264, 281
formal institutions 35
France 18, 32, 72, 87, 126, 134–136, 148, 217, 220, 236, 239, 320, 323, 334, 337, 343, 455, 461, 468, 486, 489, 504, 506
FRED *see* Federal Reserve Economic Data
freedom: definitions of 113; government intervention as threat to 113; Polanyi's views on 113
Free public education 129
free trade 56; and comparative advantage 64; policies of technological leaders 70
free trade area 467
freewheeling financial markets 376

INDEX 547

frictional unemployment 233–234
Friedman, Milton 16, 185, 252, 385, 388–389, 405
full employment 26, 234, *235*, 236, 241, 265, 275, 278, 283, 340, 387, 390–391, 457
functional finance 340, 390
funding 36, 150, 222, 430–431, 436
future sales, expectations of 429

gasoline: increase in market supply of 163; price hike and consumer demand, link between 10
gas prices 162–163
GDP (gross domestic product) 16, 57, 102, 111, 125–126, 135, 175, 177, 206–207, 213, 217, 223–224, 226–227, 232, 243, 245, 264, 271, 276, 290–291, 296, 318–320, 327, 333–334, 336, 338, 343, 370, 421, 433, 468–469, 483, 488–489, 491; per capita in MDEs and SMEs 125, *126*; and unemployment, relationship between 232
GDP deflator 206–207, *208*, 225–226, 245, 267, 269–270, 276, 278, 282, 298, 305, 400
gender 11, 16, 35, 84–85, 116, 148, 151; divisions 85; empowerment 35; equity in Nordic countries 131
gender inequities: in labor force participation rate 240; in property rights 148–149
General Agreement on Tariffs and Trade (GATT) of 1947 128
general equilibrium models 13–14
General Theory of Employment, Interest and Money, The (Keynes) 3, 41
genetically modified organism (GMO) food crops, ban on 461
genuine progress indicator 175, 221; categories of indicators for 222–223; for economic welfare measurement 221–222; *vs.* GDP of OECD countries 224, *224*; of U.S. 223, *224*; variations of 222
geography: and economic development 505–506; influence on economic systems 124
geopolitical instability 313
Georgescu-Roegen, Nicholas 441
German economy 72

German factories 72
Germany 9, 18, 32, 42, 70, 72, 102, 126, 134–136, 149, 179, 182, 220, 225, 239, 242, 320, 323, 337, 343, 421, 432–433, 438–439, 447, 454, 458, 461, 468, 485–486, 489, 504, 506; co-determination of workers 135; education system of 134; hourly compensation in 134, *134*; workers of 134–135
Glass-Steagall Act of 1933 359, 377–378
global climate agreements 198
global economic integration 447, 466–471; GATT and WTO for 466; resistance to 470–471; trading blocs for 467–470
global economy 7, 9, 87, 96, 118, 145, 177, 188, 198, 313, 370, 401, 419, 466, 508–509
Global Innovation Index rankings 431–432, *432*
globalization 68, 77–79, 116, 127–128, 234, 386, 398, 447, 463–464, 466, 470–471
global macroeconomy 178
global manufacturing 447, 463
global trade 7, 193, 415, 466, 471, 508
global trade patterns and comparative advantage 453
GNP (gross national product) 213–214, 226
Goldman Sachs 411–412
gold standard 352–353, 372, 377
goods prices 58, 99, 104, 113, 206, 243, 247, 253–254, 299, 498; declines in 104–105, 181, 247; deflation 104–105; in product markets 151; in rapid growth 254
Google 91
government 56, 344; administration 315, 316, 344; bailouts 330–331, 378, 489, 512; duty of 58–59; innovation and growth determined by 435–436; policies to stimulate industrial development 436; pro-business approach 93; role in reducing transactions costs 151; size and role of 315–322; triple helix approach to innovation 435–436
government budget *see* budget
government debt and deficits 5–6, 107, 117, 197, 200, 314, 333, 335–336, 340–342, 413; debate over 335–340; in recessions 107; size of 332–335; structural deficits 333; U.S. federal budget deficit or surplus 332, *332*; U.S. public debt as

percentage of GDP 333; U.S. public debt held by public 332–333
government disability payments 232
government expenditures: as percentage of GDP 319–320, *320*; sources of tax revenue for 320
government funding 7, 343, 430–431, 435, 438
government-guided development: in Norway 132; in Sweden 131–132
government intervention 8–9, 17–18, 63–64, 98–100, 107, 109, 111–113, 112–115, 117–118, 120, 130, 147, 181, 182, 185, 196, 198–201, 241, 277, 328–330, 335, 388, 391, 406, 434, 439–440; business cycle 112; central planning 112–113; creative destruction 114; freedom 113; laissez-faire approach to 99–100, 328–329; market institutions 114–115; markets and information 113–114; New Keynesian economists on 330; political economists on 331–332; in social market economies 125; to stabilizing markets 114; supply-side economists on 329
government purchases 210–211, 260, 263, 293, 298–299, 352, 480
government-regulated market capitalist economy 42
government regulation 59–60, 185
government sector size 17, *18*
government securities: purchase of 379–380; sale of 380
government spending 5–6, 14, 24, 31, 102, 106–107, 111, 117, 133, 185, 193, 195, 197, 201, 211, 234, 240, 248, 260, 263, 268, 275, 280, 291, 293, 296, 299, 303–304, 319, 323–325, 327–328, 330, 332–333, 335–337, 339–340, 342, 386, 396, 404, 468, 488, 490–491, 514; factors affecting 268; government administration 315; and intervention, degree of 315–316; public and quasi-public goods 315; social spending 315; tax hike and reduction of 5–6; tax revenues below 5; *see also* U.S. federal government spending
government structures 86
government support 128, 188–190, 331, 429, 436, 512
GPI *see* genuine progress indicator

Graeber, David 350
Grameen Bank 519
Grape-Nuts cereal 90
Grapes of Wrath (Steinbeck) 105
Great Depression of 1930s 3, 41–42, 63, 82, 93–94, 101, 103–107, 111, 115, 117–118, 132, 137, 179, 181, 182–183, 192–193, 200, 229, 241, 248, 279, 281, 312–313, 317, 352, 357, 377, 384, 391, 404, 408, 412; deflation 104–105; end of 111; unemployment in 103–104; wage declines 103–104
"Great Leap Forward" 139
Great Recession of 2008–2009 14, 107, 117–118, 144, 175, 192, 197, 232, 238, 253, 281, 330, 333, 339, 341–342, 383, 394, 404, 406, 408, 416–417; American Recovery and Reinvestment Act (ARRA) of 2009 for 341–342, 413; causes of 192; factors as crucial drivers in 408–412; fiscal and monetary stimulus to combat 413; government action to combat 107; high inflation during 253; impact on crude oil demand 144; underemployed laborers in 238
Great Transformation, The (Polanyi) 44, 113
Greece 48, 118, 220, 323, 334, 342, 467–468, 493
"Green New Deal" 444
gross domestic product (GDP) 125
gross national product (GNP) 213, *213*
growth-generating projects, investments in 199–200
guilds 50
Guns, Germs and Steel (Diamond) 48

Haas, Robert 78
Hamilton, Alexander 70, 457
happiness, measures of 175
hard work: ingrained into U.S. culture 127–128; and social status, link between 128
Harvey, John 395–396
Hayek, Friedrich 3, 8, 42, 97, 112–115, 122
HDI *see* Human Development Index
Head Start program 116
health 219
health care 17, 28, 116, 129, 131, 133, 219, 313, 318, 335, 341, 398, 439, 503, 509
heating oil, link between price and demand of 162–163, *163*

"hedge finance" 402
hegemony 204
Henry VIII, King 52
herd behavior 407
hidden unemployment 237, 238
hierarchical class systems 43–44
high school graduate, lifetime earnings of 23
historical change, theory of 72–73
historical materialism 74
history, influence on economic systems 123
Hittites 49
home country's currency: appreciation of 483; depreciation of 483; problems with devaluing 483–484
homelessness 34, 186, 188, 199, 217, 223, 229, 231
homogeneous population 130–131
Hoover, Herbert 94
hourly compensation costs, in manufacturing *134*
household work and real GDP 215, 217
housing bubble of 2006–2008 364
housing markets 14, 117, 383, 408, 412
housing prices 192, 243, 398, 408–409
huge firms, domination of markets by 79, 83
human behavior, culture of leisure class shaping 87–88
human capital 31, 60, 426, 428, 432–433, 439, 444
human development 133, 503–505, 507
Human Development Index 126, 503–505
human economic systems, evolution of 41, 44
human rights, expansion of 131
"Hundred Flowers Campaign" 139
hunter-gatherer societies 73; allocation of resources in 45; characteristics of 44–45; direct democracy in 46; in large group setting 46; social status in 45–46; specialization of tasks in 46; valuing productivity 46
hybrid model of money market 365, *366*
hydraulic fracturing (fracking) techniques 145
hyperinflation 250–251

IBM 170
illegal activities and real GDP 217
illegal immigrant labor, ban on use of 168
IMF *see* International Monetary Fund
immigrant labor of U.S. 127
immigration 92, 127, 269, 317, 427
import purchases 209
import quota 459
impulsive side of customer 12
incentive problem 411
inclusive institutions 124
income 219, 266; aggregate demand and 209; during "capital-labor accord" era 116; for poor and population growth, faulty perceptions of link between 61–62; replacement 240; side of circular flow model 209, 211, 226; and spending, decline in 6; stabilization 316
income inequality: marginal productivity theory of distribution and 99; problem for economy 92–93
income taxes 266, 268, 284, 299, 321–322, 377
Index of Sustainable Economic Welfare *see* genuine progress indicator
India, economic growth of 190
indirect business taxes 214
individualistic cultures 204
induced consumption 291
industrial clusters, spillover benefits from 456, 459
industrialization 124, 223, 440, 510–512, 520
industrial linkages 511
industrial mutation process 114
industrial policies: for economic development 241; and planning 436
industrial revolution 78, 89; in England 54–56; self-sustaining 64–65
industrial sabotage 90
inequality 15, 33–35, 81, 92, 99, 124–126, 129–130, 133, 141, 148, 184, 187, 199, 222, 226, 321, 435, 438, 457; impact on economic growth 438; and poverty, in Nordic countries 133; by unequal property rights 148
infant industry approach 436
infant industry promotion strategy 69–70, 94, 436, 437, 456, 459, 510, 512–513, 520
inferior goods 161
inflation 16, 116–117, 130, 175, 178, 183–187, 195–196, 207, 219, 226–227, 229–230, 236, 243–258, *245*, 247, 277,

289, 299, 304, 325, 335–336, 339–340, 353, 355, 365, 369, 375, 379, 382, 385–393, 396, 400, 413–414, 492, 497, 513; during 1970s 186, 187; during 1980s 187; causes of 251; cost-push 251; demand-pull 251; and money supply, relationship between 252–254, *253*; policies to correct 251; problems created by 248–250; rates 9, 183–184, 196, 243, 246, 248–249, 252, 513; unanticipated 249; and unemployment, relationship between 254–255

inflationary gap 276–277, 297, 302–304, 326–327

inflationary pressures 195, 249, 254, 325, 353, 379, 386–387, 389–390, 400, 496

informal institutions 35

injections 211, 295–296

innovation 45, 49, 51, 58, 60, 79, 97, 114, 118, 129–130, 133, 136, 330, 419, 430–432, 435, 437, 439, 456; elements impacting 431; policies to stimulate 430–432; revolutionary 127–129, 432; sustainability and 432; system, U.S. government 128–129; technological 430–431; triple helix approach to 435–436

input markets 113

input prices 247, 251, 254–255, 265, 268–269, 277–280, 282, 299, 303

institutional analysis of resource allocation 35–36

institutional economics 86

institutionalism 82

interdependence issue 458

interest-bearing accounts 360–361, 383

interest on reserve balances 358

interest rate 14, 63, 100, 103, 106, 111–112, 130, 181, 185, 186, 187, 197, 247–249, 254–257, 266, 267, 268, 279, 293, 298–299, 303–304, 335–336, 340, 360, 367–368, 370, 377, 389–392, 396–397, 403–404, 408–409, 414, 429, 479–482, 491, 494–496; ceilings 249; deflation impact on 247; money relationship with 359–360

interest rate on reserve balances 381

intermediate goods 206, 212

international capital controls 498

international finance 420, 475, 477, 479, 481, 484, 487, 489, 491–493, 495, 497; balance of payments 484–485; trade deficits and current account 485–488

international financial flows 371, 458, 475, 476, 479, 497–499; Asian financial crisis of 1997 497–498; inflows of money 475, 497; Latin American debt crisis of the 1980s 498, 513; outflows of money 475, 497–498

international indebtedness 337

International Monetary Fund 377, 483, 496–497, 513–516, 518, 520, 521

international terms of trade 451–452

international trade 339, 419, 447, 463, 466, 467, 471, 482

internet stock bubble 190–191, 280, 407–408

invention 76, 78, 89, 92, 129, 459; of agriculture 46; driven capitalist economy 55; of machines 57; of robots 169

inventories of goods 262–263

inverted yield curve *414*, 414–415

investment 223; factors affecting 266–267; incentive for 129; purchases 209, 211, 267, 364, 366, 382, 384, 397, 428–429, 434; recession impact on 105; and savings, imbalance between 112; spending 14, 63, 105, 267, 279–280; tax credits 429; in technologies after Civil War 89–90; volatility of 102–103, 105, 181; *see also* business investment

investment banks 108, 238, 251, 359, 371, 376, 377–378, 403, 410–413

investment goods 63, 92, 263–264, 266–267, 284, 305

invisible hand of market, analogy of 59

involuntary part-time employment 237–238

involuntary unemployment 180

IORB *see* interest on reserve balances; interest rate on reserve balances

iPhone 171, 212, 454–455, 463

Iranian Revolution of 1979 and oil prices 117, 186

Ireland 85, 125–126, 134, 220, 225, 239, 320, 323, 338, 419, 421, 424, 433, 444, 461, 468, 485–486, 504

Islamic banks 150

It's a Wonderful Life (film) 357

Jackson, T. P. 408

Japan 18, 32, 115, 117, 120, 126, 134, 136, 149, 181–182, 184, 188–191, 201, 220,

234, 236, 239, 320, 323, 334, 338, 343, 379, 408, 421, 436, 438–439, 447, 454–455, 457, 461, 465–466, 481–482, 485–486, 489, 494–496, 504, 512, 518; corporations 136; culture of 136; interventionist approach of 181; organizational structures of 136; rapid growth of 188–189
"Jim Crow laws," racial segregation by 85
"job guarantee" *See* employer of last resort (ELR) programs
jobs 110, 219; creation 110; search assistance 240
Johnson, Lyndon 116, 182
J.P. Morgan and Company 377

keiretsu 136
Kellogg, manipulative advertising by 91
Kelton, Stephanie 340
Kering 135
Kerr, Clark 424
Keynesian aggregate expenditure–income model 260, 287, 306
Keynesian analysis 200–201; declines in goods prices 104–105, 181; deflation 104–105, 181; multiplier process 105, 181; sticky wages and prices 103–104, 181; volatility of investment 102–103, 105, 181; wage declines 103–104, 181
Keynesian cross *see* Keynesian aggregate expenditure–income model
Keynesian economic policy 112, 117–118, 132, 182, 192, 193
Keynesian economics 111, 175, 184–185, 191, 277, 284, 330, 386, 426
Keynesian model of long-run adjustment: overheated economies 280; recessions 279–280; temporary downturn 278–279
Keynesian paradox of thrift 336
Keynes, John Maynard 8, 14, 41–42, 63, 94–98, 97, 101–102, 101–105, 107, 109, 111–113, 115, 117, 119–122, 181, 200, 242, 247, 275, 278–280, 283, 287, 337, 339, 394–395, 401, 415, 428, 429, 457, 471; on government budgets 107; on government intervention 107; prediction of World War II 101–102; response to wait for long-run equilibrium 94
Keynes, Maynard 3
Klitgaard, Robert 148
Klu Klux Klan, terroristic violence of 85

Krueger, Alan 13
Krugman, Krugman, 342

labor 30–31, 168; and capital 456; changes in seasonal demand for 237; exploitation of 75–77; laws 110; productivity 182, 426–429, 439; supply 434–435
labor force 183, 232–233; characteristics and demographics 236; frictional unemployment of 233; participation rate 183
labor force participation rate 238; gender gaps in 240; for OECD countries 238–240, *239*
labor markets 1, 13, 100, 110, 129, 146, 151, 233, 240, 255, 316, 330, 390, 400; incentives 439; model of 13; policies of Sweden 132–133; prices in 151
labor unions 77, 82, 84–85, 186–187, 236, 245, 470
Laffer, Arthur 185–186
laissez-faire approach 15, 17, 55, 60, 72, 93, 98–99, 101, 105, 107, 113–114, 117, 120, 175, 196–201, 242, 312, 329, 370–371, 388–389, 419, 434, 439, 471, 491, 513
laissez-faire capitalism 15, 55, 60, 73, 80, 82, 191, 198, 200, 253, 311–312, 328–329, 335–336, 339–342, 365, 375, 386, 391, 394–395, 405–406, 419, 490–491, 513; argument for 44; embodiment of 72; fall of 93–94; free trade and comparative advantage 64; *vs.* mercantilism 56; poor laws and 60–62; problems developed under 44; role of government 328–329; Say's laws and 62–64; *See also* capitalist system
laissez-faire-leaning mixed economy 118
land reform 436
large corporations 7, 41
Latin America: debt crisis of 1980s 498; economic growth in 190
law of demand 10, *10*, 157, 159
law of diminishing marginal utility 158
law of supply 165
layoffs 7, 94, 103–104, 229, 234, 247–248, 370, 384–385
LDCs *see* less developed countries
leakages 211
leisure class 82; aspiration to be part of 89; characteristics of 87; human behavior shaped by 87–88

"leisure class" 87–88
lenders 248–249
less developed countries 115, 458, 464, 507–518; challenges for 501, 508; declining terms of trade of 509–510; development efforts 516–520; foreign aid poured into 515–516; infant industry promotion strategy of 512; with large government budget deficits 513; low income elasticities of goods and services of 509; military expenditures 513; Prebisch-Singer thesis and 509; specialized in primary products 508
leveraging 411
liberal economists 15, 17
liberal market economies *see* market-dominated economies
life and community 7
life expectancy 72
life satisfaction 219–220
lifetime earnings 23
lightly regulated capitalism *see* laissez-faire capitalism
limited liability corporation 149
Limits to Growth (Meadows, Randers, and Meadows) 441
liquidity 354–355
liquidity trap 312, 360–361, 372, 375, 383–384
"living wage" 60
local farmers market 151
logical analysis 13
logical deductions 10
long-distance trade 51
long-run adjustment: classical model of 275–278; Keynesian model of 278–280
long-run aggregate supply curve 275, *278*; inflationary gap *276*, 276–277; long-run equilibrium at 276, *276*; recessionary gap 276, *276*
Long-term bailouts 331
Louis XIV, King 87
love, commodification of 80
LRAS curve *see* long-run aggregate supply curve
Lucas, Robert Jr. 185
LVMH 135

Macedonia 49
macroeconomic foundations, for microeconomic behavior 259–260
macroeconomic models 259
macroeconomics 97; complexity of 178; definition of 11, 177; of economic crises 13–15; long-term issue in 178; macroeconomic stability 150; market transactions 150; *vs.* microeconomics 177; short-term issue in 177; and sustainability 198–200
macroeconomic stabilization policy 97, 105–106, 105–107, 127, 130, 132, 175, 177, 181, 197, 234, 240–241, 256, 277, 279, 284, 303, 328, 330–331, 385, 429; for cyclical unemployment 234, 240; facilitating transactions 150; increasing government spending 106; interest rates, reducing 106; stimulating economic growth 107; tax cuts 106; United States 130
macroeconomic theory 200
macroeconomy: approaches to structuring 179; goals of 178
Madison, James 84
mainstream economic models 10, 24, 305, 360, 363, 365, 383, 426
mainstream economics 2, 8–9, 12–14, 16, 18, 22, 24, 33, 35, 43, 86, 151–152, 157, 164, 185, 261, 283, 312, 360, 362–363, 380, 401, 477; changes in prices and quantities 152; choices in 22–23; definition of 8–9; efficiency in 24; methodology 9–10; and political economics, differences between 13–14, 18; scarcity problem in 22; *see also* opportunity costs
mainstream economic theory 31
mainstream economists 1, 8–9, 8–15, 22–24, 28, 33, 35–36, 82, 147, 154, 175, 200, 236, 251, 256, 280, 283, 287, 306, 337, 401, 424, 426–427, 434, 451, 486, 488
making money: donation to political parties for 91; as focus of monopoly capitalism 90; *vs.* making goods 89–92; mergers and acquisitions for 91; by misleading advertising 90, 91; prioritization over good product 90; by reducing competition 90, 91; vested interests for 91–92
Malaysia 141, 188–190, 497, 504
Malthus, Thomas 61
managed float exchange rate regime 496

manipulative advertising, profits via 90
Mankiw, Gregory 448
manors 50
Mantoux, Paul 55
manufactured goods 34, 54, 56, 134, 170, 428, 434, 437, 453–454, 464–465, 468, 506, 509
manufacturing 52–54, 90, 92, 188, 201, 370, 453–455, 459, 465, 469–470, 510, 514; boom and Roaring Twenties 92–93; firms 34, 56, 113, 115, 134, 137, 247, 251, 294, 348, 415, 434, 466, 469, 515; hourly compensation costs in *134*; industries 79, 83, 115, 371, 447, 506, 508; jobs, erosion in 117
Mao Zedong 139
Marathon Oil 507
marginalized workers 237
marginal productivity theory of distribution 99
marginal propensity to consume 271–272, 271–275, 288, 291, 299, 301, 303–304, 306, 325, 327
marginal propensity to import 272–273
marginal propensity to invest 293, 298–299
marginal propensity to save 271, 288
marginal respending rate 272–273, 272–275, 293–294, 296–299, 301–303, 325, 327, 383
market capitalism 8, 16–19, 41, 44, 52, 60, 97, 122
market capitalist economies 17, 58, 97, 152, 171, 177
market-dominated economies 120, 122–124, 126–127, 179, 182, 220, 256, 315–316; countries adopting 125; cultural values reflected by 125; economic decisions in 124; economic indicators of 125–126, *126*; elites and 124; government's role in 124–125; *vs.* social market economies 125–127, *126*; U.S. model of 127–130
market forces 179
market institutions 114–115, 151
market misunderstanding theory 406
market power, for unfair competition 12
market prices 139, 147, 152, 171
market quantity demanded 158
markets 144, 146, 171, 329; in capitalist economies 147; for commodities 152; definition of 146; failures 16, 111–112, 118, 124–125, 130, 175, 178, 199, 226, 229–231, 240–242, 246, 255–256, 321, 330–331; for food 146; informal 147; and information 113–114; infrastructure of 151; for inputs 152; for labor 146; for pizza 154; for stocks 146; types of 146
market supply curve 171
market-supporting institutions 147; competition 151; infrastructure to lower transactions costs 151; lack of coercion 151; laws for aggregation of capital 149; property rights 147–149; trust and contract laws 149–150
market system 17, 52–53, 59, 64–65, 124, 138, 151, 172, 177
market transaction *see* transactions
Marshall, Alfred 101, 157
Marshall Plan 184
Marx, Karl 3, 8, 15–16, 41–42, 63, 65, 95, 122, 137, 471; on class conflict 73; on commodification 79–81; on competition 78–79, 95; on concentration of capital 79; concept of surplus 75–77; concept of surplus value 74–77; on crisis and revolution 81–82; critique of capitalism 68, 72, 74, 95; on globalization 79; gravitated to radical politics 72; on ownership of factories 77; theory of historical change 72–73
material conditions of society 74
mathematical models of economy 10
Mazzucato, Maria 435
MDEs *see* market-dominated economies
ME *see* mainstream economics
median weekly nominal wages 245, *245*
Medicare and Medicaid 116
mercantilism 3, 41–42, 44, 53–56, 58, 60, 73–74, 79; bullionism 53; colonial empires profiting from 53–54; economic growth under 54; economic problems faced by 54, 60; *vs.* laissez-faire capitalism 56; local resistance to 53; problems of 60; Smith's critique to 56; transatlantic slave trade 54; welfare programs 60
mercantilist monopolies 56
mergers and acquisitions 91
Mesopotamia 49
Mexican peso crisis of 1994–1995 498
Mexico 34, 127, 187, 192, 220, 320, 343, 424, 444, 449–452, 454, 461, 469–470, 485–486, 489, 504

microeconomic markets 181
microeconomic models 259
microeconomic phenomena 259
microeconomics 11, 15, 130, 175, 177, 259–260; definition of 11, 177; *vs.* macroeconomics 177
microlending 519
Microsoft 408
middle-class lifestyle 115
Middle East, Fertile Crescent area of 49
middle-income countries, challenges facing 512
middle-income trap 512
military-industrial complex 36
milk prices 170
minimum wage and employment 13
Minksy, Hyman 394
Minsky cycle 401; "hedge finance" phase of 402; "Ponzi" phase and crash of 403–404; "speculative finance" phase of 402–403; *see also* business cycle
Minsky, Hyman 312, 401
Mises, Ludwig von 112, 242
misleading advertising 90, 91
Mitchell, Bill 232
mixed economy of United States 118–120
mixed market capitalism 3, 8, 17, 42, 97; definition of 17; establishment of 115; Hayek's cautions in adopting 97, 142; *See also* New Deal reforms
mixed market capitalist economies 73
mixed market economies 94, 107, 115, 118, 120, 122, 130, 181, 193, 318–319
mixed market–state approach 179
MMT *see* modern monetary theory
mobile devices, opportunity cost of resource devoted to 23
modern capitalism 77, 79; Marx analysis of 68; *see also* commodification
modern economic systems 7, 17, 42, 113, 114, 120, 122, 141, 251, 312, 353, 354, 372, 401, 443, 447, 479; classification of 17; market-dominated economies 120, 122, 124–130; social market economies 120, 122, 125–126; state-dominated economies 124
modern knowledge economy 89
modern macroeconomics 175
modern macroeconomic theory 180
modern monetary theory 312, 339–340, 340–341, 375, 388

Mondragon Cooperative Corporation 148
monetary policy 187, 248, 253, 256, 280, 312, 359, 375, 381, 383–385, 387–389, 391, 400, 415, 420, 513; contractionary 249, 381, 384–386, 389; effectiveness in recessions 384; expansionary 111, 193, 253, 384–385, 387; impact on economy, models to analyze 383–385; of slowing the economy 385
monetary rule 388–389
monetary stimulus 313, 372, 375, 384, 388–389, 391, 394, 406, 413, 415
Money 372
money 6, 14, 23, 32, 36, 41, 50–52, 55, 57, 61–64, 68, 77, 83–84, 91, 93, 99–101, 103, 106, 108, 110–111, 117–118, 120, 126, 130, 132, 135, 147–148, 160–161, 187, 190, 192, 196, 199, 204, 211, 214, 217, 222, 247, 249–250, 252, 254, 259, 264, 266–267, 272, 277, 281, 289–290, 293–294, 296, 299, 303, 311–314, 317, 324–325, 331, 335–337, 339–341, 343, 380–381, 383–384, 387–390, 402–404, 409, 411–412, 414, 420, 429, 433, 435–436, 438–439, 461, 468, 475, 479–480, 482–486, 491–493, 495, 497–499, 506, 509, 512–513, 515, 519; barter 351; borrowing 63, 106–107, 147, 248, 267, 279, 290–291, 332, 336–337, 363, 403–404, 411, 513; commodity 350–351; definition of 349–350; demand 360–366; equation of exchange 352; fiat 351–352; forms of 352; functions of 351; history of 348, 350–352; and liquidity 354–355; nongovernmental form of 354; purposes of 353–354; quantity theory of 252–253, 388–390, 406; relationship to interest rates 359–360; role in modern world 348; standard of living with 57; supply of 352–354; uses and measurement of 353–355; velocity in U.S. 389–390
moneylending 51
money market 312, 360, 363–366, 375, 380, 383; hybrid model of 365, *366*; mainstream economics and political economy models of 348; mainstream economics model of 380; mainstream model of 383, *384*
money market accounts 355, 360, 362, 384

money market, mainstream model of 363; money demand curve 361–362; money supply curve 362; open market sale 363; precautionary demand 360–361; price of holding cash 360; speculative demand 361; supply and demand curve 360, *360*; transactions demand 360

money multiplier 356–358, 357–358, 362, 380–381

money stock *see* money supply

money supply 16, 93, 103, 106–109, 111, 120, 178, 186–187, 193, 234, 240, 247–248, 251–253, 336, 339, 352–353, 355, 380–381, 383–385, 387–392, 406, 513; control by central banks 108–109, 178, 363, 384; economic variables determining 363–364; effect on interest rates 384; Fed policy tools to change 376, 384; and inflation, relationship between 252–254, *253*, 376, 392; open market operations and 379–380; restricted growth of 253

monopolistic companies 41; lack of competition in 58; mercantilist policies and 56; monopolistic conglomerates 68

monopoly capitalism 68, 82, 84, 90–91, 91–92, 96, 115; development of 82–83

monopoly power 83

Morgan, J.P. 83

mortgages 192, 242, 333–334, 340, 364, 409–410, 412, 416

moving assembly line, for 1913 Ford cars 57, *57*

MPC *see* marginal propensity to consume

MPI *see* marginal propensity to invest

MPM *see* marginal propensity to import

MPS *see* marginal propensity to save

MRR *see* marginal responding rate

multinational corporations 79, 127–128, 149, 454, 464, 466, 507, 520

multiplier 105–106, 111, 120, 181, 260–261, 264, 271–275, 278, 280, 283–284, 287, 299, 302, 325, 327–328, 358, 383; and aggregate demand 273–275; effect 271–273; "simple multiplier" 271–272

Myrdal, Gunnar 511

NAFTA *see* North American Free Trade Agreement

NASDAQ Composite Index of technology stocks 191

NASDAQ Composite Stock Index 407

National Banking Acts of 1863 and 1864 377

national consumption 259

national debt of U.S. government 187

national health care system 17

national income 92, 94, 209, 211–214, *213*, 214, 226, 259, 271, 291–294, 297–298, 304, 306, 464, 503

national income measures 211; by aggregate demand 211, *212*; and national product 213, *213*; by type of income 212, *212*; by value added 212, *212*

National Industrial Recovery Act 110

national market system 53–54

natural capital stocks, net depreciation of 223

natural gas, link between price and demand of 162–163, *163*

natural rate of unemployment 256, 385–386; cyclical and 234, *235*; definition of of 234; determinants of 236; high degree of variability of 236; from political economy perspective 236

natural resources 17, 54, 74, 124, 127, 147, 168, 219, 223, 283, 340, 453, 469, 471; influence on economic systems 124; ready access to 127

necessary product 47

necktie as symbol of status 87

negative freedom 113

neoclassical economics and laissez-faire ideology 99–101, 200; marginal productivity theory of distribution 99; Say's law 100–101, *101*; supply and demand 99–100

neoclassical economic theory: decline in prices of goods 104; wages and employment in recession 104

neoclassical theory 180

neocolonialism 507

neoliberalism 116–117, 186, 466

net depreciation of natural capital stocks 223

net exports 260, 268, 270, 287, 291, 293, 295–296, 298–299, 305–306, 491

Netherlands 18, 126, 134, 220, 225, 236, 238–239, 320, 323, 432, 455, 461, 465, 506

net national product (NNP) *213*, 214

net taxes 209

New Deal reforms 107; agricultural price supports 110; banking regulation 108; financial market regulation 108; job creation and labor laws 110; money supply control 108–109; safety net, creation of 109; success of 110–111

"New Deal" reforms 107

New Keynesian approach 15–16, 179, 193, 195, 196–201, 197, 200, 281, 283, 311, 328–330, 335–336, 339–340, 342, 371–373, 375, 388–392, 405, 413, 419, 426, 428–430, 428–434, 435, 440, 491, 496, 515

New Keynesian model of economic growth 422, 426–428; capital stock 426–427; equations for 426; "human capital" improvement 428; technological improvement 427

New Zealand 150

NI *see* national income

Nigeria 507

Nike 78

nominal GDP 206, 225–226, 225–227, 243, 245, 252, 389; by component of aggregate demand 211, *212*; definition of 206; and real GDP 207; for U.S. 206–207, *208*, 211, *212*

nominal interest rates 246, 248–249

nominal wage rate 243, 245, 247–248, 250

nonaccelerating inflation rate of unemployment (NAIRU) theory 385–388, 390–391

nondefensive government expenditures and GPI 222–223

nonmonetary contributions to welfare 222

non-tariff barriers 448, 457, 459, 461, 471

Nordic countries of Europe 130–131, 133, 225–226, 234, 236, 240–241, 433, 435; cooperative cultures of 518; culture and values of 204; educational spending as percentage of GDP 433; job guarantee for workers in 241; labor force participation rate in 238, 240; labor unions in 236; OECD Better Life Index of 220; World Happiness Index rankings of 225, *225*

Nordic flexicurity model 236

Nordic model of social market economies 127, 141, 220; active labor market policies 132–133; cooperative culture 130–139; expansion of human rights 131; gender equity 131; government-guided development 131–132; homogeneous population 130–139; inequality and poverty 133

normal goods: definition of 161; income and wealth impact on demand of *160*, 160–161

North American Free Trade Agreement 187–188, 447, 469–471

Northern European countries 35

Norway 17–18, 126–127, 130, 134, 148, 220–221, 224–225, 236, 239, 320, 334–335, 337, 424, 433, 441, 489, 504; government-guided development in 132; OECD Better Life Index for 220–221, *221*; start-up rates in 133

Obama, Barack Hussein 117, 129, 164, 192, 201, 333, 341, 406, 413

Occupy Wall Street movement 383

OECD (Organisation for Economic Cooperation and Development) 126, 218, 220

OECD Better Life Index 126, *126*, 175, 218–221, 220, 224; in 2019 220, *220*; determinants of 218–219; development of 218; for United States and Norway 220–221, *221*; well-being definition in 220

OECD countries 126, 218, 220, 224, 239; educational spending as percentage of GDP *433*, 433–434; GDP *vs.* GPI *224*; labor force participation rates *239*; UN Human Development rankings 126, *126*

oil crisis 116–117

Oil Fund 132

oil market 144

oil prices 116–117, 144–145, 185, 268, 400, 424, 513; Iranian Revolution of 1979 impact on 186; over last two decades 144–145, *145*; recessions caused by 398, 400; rise in 251, 269, 400; supply and demand factors influencing 144–145, 185

oil supply 144–145

Okun, Arthur 232

Okun's law 232

older workers, unemployment rate of 236

Oliver Twist (Dickens) 61

OPEC *see* Organization of the Petroleum Exporting Countries

open market operations 379–380, 384

open market purchases 379–380, 384
open market sale 363, 380, 513
opportunity costs 2, 31, 33, 35, 37, 215, 360, 449–451, 450–452; analysis of 24; changes with specialization of resources 27–28; of college education 23; concept of 23, 24; of defense spending 32–33; of high school education 23; law of increasing 28–29; of Sony's resources of computer division 23; of spending on B-2 stealth bombers 24, 35–36; without specialized resources 29
optimizing behavior, supply and demand model 153
Organization of the Petroleum Exporting Countries: embargo on selling oil to U.S. 116, 185; role in oil supply 144, 145
overheated economy 107, 195, 251, 256, 276–277, 277–278, 280, 375
Overworked American, The (Schor) 76

paid and unpaid work, time per day devoted to 215, *216*
paper money *see* fiat money
parental leave policies of Nordic countries 131
part-time jobs 238
patent system 129
path dependence 506
patriotism 36
Pax Americana, period of 184
peasants, seizing common lands of 53
pecuniary emulation, Veblenian concept of 87–88
personal consumption 222
personal income *213*, 214
personal relationships 149
Phillips, A.W. 254
Phillips curve 251, 254–255, *255*, 385
physical capital 428
physical infrastructure 151
PI *see* personal income
Pickens, T. Boone 29
pizza companies 154, *154*
pizza, demand curve for: disposable income and wealth impact on *160*, 160–161; quantity demanded and price, link between 157, 158, *158*
Pizza Hut 79, 154, 165–167, *166*
pizzas, supply and demand model of 152, 165–167; assumptions for 154; demand and curve *155*, 155–156, *156*; prices adjustment 155–156, *156*; supply curves 165–166, *166*, 166–167
Plato 41
pluralist economics 9
pluralistic economics 8
plutocracy 204–205
Polanyi, Karl 44, 71, 113, 138
political business cycle theory 406
political climate 430
political economics 1, 9, 13–14, 15, 18, 175, 464
political economists 10–12, 14–15, 18, 33, 35–39, 43, 46, 175, 184, 198–201, 200, 236, 241, 251, 255–256, 260–261, 280–284, 287, 305–306, 328, 331, 335, 337, 339, 341, 363, 365, 371–376, 386–388, 394–395, 397–398, 405, 416, 419, 435, 437, 439–440, 443–444, 453–454, 457, 463–465, 482–483, 488, 490, 492, 496, 508
political economy approach 9, 11, 14, 15, 22, 33, 35, 148, 179, 196, 197, 200, 236, 281, 282–283, 306, 312, 331, 364–365, 387, 390, 397, 404, 419, 434–435, 437–438, 439, 463, 490–491; approach to study resource allocation 35–36; business cycle of economy 14; to economic growth 422, 435–440; of increase in money supply 363–364, *364*; to macroeconomic patterns of business cycle 197
political economy theories 435
"Ponzi" phase and crash 403–404
pooling of financial resources 149
poor, hardships of 61
poor laws: Poor Law Reform Act of 1834 61; Speenhamland system 60–61
population theory of Malthus 61
positive economics 12–13
positive freedom 113
positivism, economic philosophy of 13
postal service 151
Post Foods Company, misleading advertising by 90
potential real GDP 193, 195–196, 265, 275–276, 275–278, 280, 283–286, 297, 302–304, 325, 327, 385, 400, 426
poverty 34, 56, 60, 109, 113, 124, 126, 129–130, 133, 141, 178, 182, 184, 188, 199, 229, 231, 321, 396, 420, 424,

503, 514; in Nordic countries 133; and unemployment 186; in United States 129, 217
poverty alleviation: approaches 56; mercantilist policies impact on 56; Speenhamland system for 60–61
power and control 12
power structures of society 34
PPC *see* production possibilities curve
PPE *see* progressive political economics
PPI *see* Producer Price Index
Prebisch-Singer thesis 509
precautionary demand 360–361
precision manufacturing 134–135
PRGDP *see* potential real GDP
price and quantity demanded, link between: heating oil 163, *163*; natural gas 162, *163*; pizza 157–158, *158*
price and quantity, relationship between: equilibrium point 155, *155*; supply and demand model 155, *155*; in surpluses and shortages 156, *156*; tendencies of firms and consumers 155
price and quantity supplied, link between 165–167, *166*
price–earnings *(P/E)* ratio 368–369
price index 207, 243, 245, 252, 264, 266, 269–270, 325, 327
price instability 229; deflation 229; inflation 229; as market failure 246–251; real interest rate 246; real wages 245, *245*; *see also* deflation; inflation
prices: deflation 104–105; forces causing change in 152; level 243; and resource allocation, link between 152; stability 229, 353, 379, 390; and wages 193, 196
primary credit rate *see* discount rate
primary product prices 508–509
prime interest rate 380–381
"priming the pump" 385
primitive communism 45
private banks 359
private sector debt 199
private sector incentives 241, 242
private sector investment 196, 324, 335–337, 388–389
private sector spending 431
privatizing common lands 53
pro-business legal system 128
pro-cyclical accelerators 365
Producer Price Index 243

production 74
production function 426–428, *427*; capital stock and 426–427; human capital improvement and 428; technological improvement and 427
production inefficiencies 114
production possibilities curve 2, 18, 21, 24–32, 34, 37, 450–452, 457; assumptions behind 26, 29, 34; for capital goods and consumer goods 31–32, *32*; for defense and education *25*, 25–26, *26*; focus of 33; shape of 26–27; for United States and Mexico 450–451, *451*; without specialized resources 29
production possibilities curve shifts: from changes in resources or technology 29–30; from productive resources 30–31
productive activities 34, 212, 214–215, 226, 439
productive capacity 31, 213, 265, 267–268, 298–299, 402, 441
productive resources 18, 30–31, 34, 47, 54, 127, 148, 193, 269, 456–457; capital goods 30; human capital 31; labor 30–31; ready access to 127; underemployment of 34
productive work 87
productivity 31, 46, 48, 53, 57, 59–61, 64, 89, 136, 165, 168, 186, 189, 206, 236, 252, 269, 279, 335, 397–398, 426–429, 434, 436, 439, 441, 453, 517; specialization of labor enhancing 57; Speenhamland system and 60–61; standard of living and 57; technology impact on 168–169; and wealth, link between 57
productivity growth rates 424
product markets 151
profit: capitalists chasing 75; factory owners' efforts to increase 75–76; reinvestment of 75; via manipulative advertising 90
profitability 150, 165, 168, 170, 185–186, 240, 248, 259, 265, 269, 280, 284, 298–299, 303, 330, 367, 369, 397, 429, 461; and aggregate supply curve 265; decline in 104
profit rate 396–399, *397*, 416, 430, 438–439; and capital accumulation 398, *399*; factors causing decline in 397–398
profit squeeze 397–398

progressive political economics 9
progressive political economy 1–2, 9, 12, 15, 18
progressive tax system 321
property rights 47–48, 55, 128, 147–149, 428, 516, 520
property taxes 214, 321, 433
protectionism 128, 419, 436, 448, 457–460, 459–461, 465, 512; infant industry protection 459; non-tariff barriers 461; raise tax revenues 460; retaliation against 460; strategic industry protection 459; strategic trade policy 459; tariffs 460, 460–461
Protestantism 52, 55, 125
Protestant work ethic 127
public and quasi-public goods 315
public goods 17, 48, 60, 128, 222, 225, 316, 320–321, 328
public sector debt 199
public university system 129
public utilities commissions 93
public works projects 110

QD *see* quantity demanded
QE *see* quantitative easing
quality of life 17, 215, 217, 219
quantitative easing 381–382
quantitative tightening 382
quantity demanded 167, 170–171, 281, 305, 478; change in 160; and price, link between 157–159, *158*, *159*
quantity of product: forces causing change in 152; and resource allocation, link between 152
quantity supplied and price, link between 165–167, *166*
quantity theory of money 252

race to bottom 78–79
racial discrimination 84–85, 116
racial distribution of property 148
racial segregation 85
radical (radical political economy) groups 15
radical political economics 1, 9
randomized controlled trials 518–519
ratings agencies 411
raw materials 22, 52–54, 62, 79, 113, 506, 509
RCTs *see* randomized controlled trials

R&D *see* research and development
Reagan, Ronald 3, 112, 117, 187
real balance effect 264, 281
real business cycle theory 406
real estate markets, risky financial securities tied to 14
real estate prices 192, 283, 497
real estate speculation 378, 408–409, 409–410
real GDP 111, 126, 175, 183, 189, 193, 195, 199–200, 206–207, 211, 214–215, 217–218, 221–223, 225–227, *226*, 232, 245, 247, 252, 265–267, 269–271, 273–276, 278, 281, 287, 289, 291–309, 325–328, 352–353, 361, 363–365, 382, 385, 388–389, 398, 400, 405–406, 416, 424, 426–427, 440; aggregate demand as 209; calculation of 206–207; definition of 206; equilibrium level of 296–299, 301; growth 104, 115, 183, 194, 232, 353, 389, 396; as imperfect measure of welfare 218; as indicator of standard of living 206, 209; limitations of 214–218; per capita 119, 125, 183–184, 188–190, *189*, 223–225, 227, 425, 440–441; for U.S. 206–207, *208*; using circular flow model 211
real GPI per capita 223–224
real interest rate 93, 106, 108, 229–230, 243, 246, 248–249, 264, 281, 305–306, 429; effect 264, 281; policies to reduce 429
real wages 104, 229–230, 243, 245, *245*, 247–248, 250, 398, 437
recession 1, 5–6, 11, 14, 63–64, 81, 92–93, 102–107, 110–112, 117–118, 132, 164, 170, 177, 181, 185–187, 191–193, 195–202, 198, 206, 211, 231, 234, 240, 242–243, 247, 249, 251, 253–254, 256, 261–262, 265, 275–277, 279–280, 289, 303, 311, 318, 323–325, 327, 329–332, 335–336, 340–344, 368, 372, 375, 381, 383–385, 387–392, 394–398, 400–401, 404–408, 413–418, 415–417, 429, 488; of 1981–1982 187; of 1990–1991 187; in 1991 117; of 2000–2001 191; in 2008 117–118; asset bubbles and 401; businesses investment in 63; capitalism prone to 81, 120; consumer demand 63; cosumer spending decline in 63; cyclical investment volatility and 395–397; cyclical unemployment in 234, *235*;

decline in incomes 5; definition of 177; due COVID-19 pandemic 118; due to oil crisis of 1970s 116–117; at end of 1970s 186–187; factors causing 394–395; by income inequality 92–93; in Japan 191; laissez-faire approach to 196–197; Minsky cycle and 401–404; New Keynesian approach to 193, 195, 197; panic events sparking 5; political economy approach to 197; profit squeeze and 397–398; recession of 1937–1938 111; recession of 1973–1975 398, 400; strong growth and 193, 195–196; super-Minsky cycle and 404–405; supply shocks and 398–401; supply-side approach to 197; U.S. real GDP decline in 5; way to combat 6
recessionary gap 276, 297, 302–303, 324–325, 335, 342, 383, 400
reciprocity within group 45
redistribution 45
re-education of workers 234, 236
"regulated capitalism" 18
rehabilitative household expenditures and GPI 223
reinvestment of profits 75
Religions 48
remaking of industries 114
required reserve ratio 356, 357, 381
research and development 436–438; government funding for 430–431; private sector spending on 431
reserves 356
resource: endowments 462–463, 471; extraction, economies focused on 124; markets 147; shifts in PPC from changes in 29–30, 30
resource allocation 22, 34–35, 45, 91; culture and conspicuous consumption 33–34; ethical considerations 33; gender empowerment 36; inequality 34–35; institutional analysis of 35–36; mainstream economists on 33; opportunity cost of 37; prices and quantities for 152; in traditional economy 45; underemployment of resources 34
responding process 271
retail banks 359
retail markets 147
retraining and reeducation 234, 236, 241

revolt: by slaves 84; of working class 81
revolution 81–82
revolutionary innovation 128–129
Ricardo, David 64, 180, 448, 453
Road to Serfdom, The (Hayek) 113
Roaring Twenties, rapid growth of 92
robber barons 83–84
Robinson, James A. 124
Robinson, Joan 231
Rockefeller, John D. 83
Roman Empire: rise and fall of 49; slaves in 48
Rome 49
Roosevelt, Franklin Delano 94, 318; 1932 president campaign promises 107; New Deal reforms 107–111; recession of 1937-1938 111
Royal Economic Society 100
RPE *see* radical political economics
RRR *see* required reserve ratio
rule of 70 423
rural industrialization 139
Russian invasion of Ukraine and oil prices 145
Russian Revolution of 1917 137
Russia, PPC of defence and education for 28–29

Saez, Emmanuel 321
safety nets 94, 97, 107, 109, 114, 178, 181, 182, 199, 255, 321, 323–324, 328
sales expectations 266, 267
Samsung 171
savings accounts 248, 355–356
savings and investment: imbalance between 112; policies stimulating 428–430
savings and loan banks 359
savings functions 287, 288–291, 289–291
Say, Jean-Baptiste 62–64, 277
Say's law 62, 180, 200; assumptions of 63; circular flow model of economy 62, *62*, 100–101, *101*; fundamental flaws in 63–64, 103; key theory in 62; popularity in early 1800s 64
Scandinavian countries, SMEs of 127; active labor market policies 132–133; cooperative culture 130–139; expansion of human rights 131; gender equity 131; government-guided development 131–132; homogeneous population 130–139; inequality and poverty 133

scarcity 36; from Marxist perspective 34–35; problem of 22, 33
Schor, Juliet 76
Schumacher, E.F. 149, 441
Schumpeter, Joseph 114
scientific economics 12–13
scientific research 129, 430–431, 436
SDEs *see* state-dominated economies
seasonal unemployment 237
SEC *see* Securities and Exchange Commission
securities 14, 49–50, 59, 62, 113, 133, 217, 231, 356, 358–359, 361, 363, 366, 368, 370, 403, 409–410, 503, 517
Securities and Exchange Commission 108, 366
securities markets 366, 372
Sen, Amartya 218
sequential industrialization 437
serf system 50
serf women, inferior position of 50
SEZs *see* special economic zones
Shiller CAPE price/E10 ratio 369, *369*
Shiller, Robert 369
short run 165
"simple multiplier" 271–272
skilled workers 76, 265, 277, 282, 324, 457
slavery 47–49, 52–54, 73, 84–85, 127, 505–506, 520; justification of 41; *vs.* serf system 50; slave labor 76; slave societies 44
Small Business Investment Corporation 435
Small Is Beautiful (Schumacher) 149, 441
small U.S. firms 41
smartphone market 171
SMEs *see* social market economies
Smith, Adam 3, 8, 41–43, 44, 47, 49, 51, 53, 55–60, 55–61, 63–68, 64–65, 70, 73–74, 78–79, 81–82, 85, 96, 117, 122, 155, 178, 186, 420, 471, 501; on competition 78; critique of mercantilism 56; determinants of wealth 56–57; idealized picture of capitalist system 56–60; laissez-faire capitalism 55–56, 73, 74
social classes 11, 35, 46–47, 74–75, 85, 96
social costs 223
social entrepreneurship 519
socialism 15–16, 81, 94, 109, 114, 136–137, 136–138, 137
socialist economic system 136–137

social market economies 120, 122–127, 130, 134, 136, 182, 184, 256, 316, 331, 335, 434; cultures represented by 125; economic decisions in 125; economic indicators of 125–126, *126*; failures of 141; of France 135–136; of Germany 134–135, 179; government's role in 125; of Japan 136; *vs.* market-dominated economies 125–127, 126; Nordic model of 130–133; social interests in 125
social media, conspicuous displays on 89
Social Security Act 109
Social Security program 97, 108–110, 109, 209, 214, 289, 316–317, 316–318, 320
social spending 315
social status 128; and consumer choices 33–34; criteria for achieving 46; desire to achieve 45; and hard work, link between 128
social sustainability 199
societal values, economic systems shaping 79–80
sodas (soft drinks), demand for 161–162, *162*
SOEs *see* state-owned enterprises
soft budget constraint problem 331
solidarity movement 82
Sony, computer division of 23
South Africa 220, 239–240, 334, 343, 441, 504, 507, 512, 514–515
South Korea 32, 132, 188–190, 201, 320, 420, 424, 432, 436–439, 444, 447, 456, 461, 465, 470, 489, 511–512, 518; car companies of 456; corporations use of tax breaks 438; as developmental state 436–437, 510–511; economic growth of 437; rapid growth of 188, 198
Soviet Union 24, 28, 42, 82, 97, 112, 114, 137, 184, 466
soybean market 170
S&P 500 stock market index 370
Spain 118, 126, 134, 148, 220, 236, 238–239, 320, 323, 342–343, 465, 468, 506
special economic zones 140
specialization and trade 458, 463
specialization of labor 43, 45–46, 49, 51, 57, 64, 79, 452–453, 458, 463; car industry 57; enhancing productivity 57; in feudalism 50
specialization of resources 26; opportunity cost changes with 27–28; Pickens's

proposal of 29; in PPC for defense and education 27–29
speculative demand 361
"speculative finance" 402–403
"spread effects" 511–512
stabilization policy *see* macroeconomic stabilization policy
stable currency 151
stagflation 49, 116, 185–186, 281, 400; of 1970s 116; from supply shock 400, *400*; in United States 185, 186
Stalin, Joseph 82, 137
standard of living 58; economic growth determining 423–425; productivity determining 57
Standard Oil 83
start-up rates, in Norway 133
state capitalism 140–141, 189
state-centered approach 179
state-dominated economies 42, 120, 122–124, 127, 130, 182, 184, 256, 316
state-owned enterprises 512
Statoil 132
status-seeking behaviour 86–87, 95
status-seeking, human beings as 45
Steinbeck, John 105
Stiglitz, Joseph 218
stimulus program for COVID-19 pandemic 313–314
stock market crash of 1929 93, 103, 105
stock markets 5, 93–94, 103, 108, 117, 128, 151, 161, 172, 259, 313, 341–342, 368–370, 372, 384, 396, 415, 491
stock prices 93, 191, 249, 367–368, 370, 382, 412, 497
stocks 93, 164, 178, 191, 214, 219, 254, 266, 280, 299, 312, 321, 356, 359, 361–362, 372, 407–408, 413, 426, 438, 469, 477–478, 480, 485, 488, 497
strategic industry protection 459
strategic trade policy 459
Strauss, Levi 78
structural adjustment policies 513–516
structural deficits 333
structural-institutional approach 507–508
structural unemployment 234, 236, 240–241, 283
sub-prime borrowers 409
sub-prime housing market 117, 383
sub-Saharan Africa 189–190, 501, 504–505, 515

subsidies for poor 60–61
substitute goods 162–163
super-Minsky cycle 404–405
suppliers 12, 100, 117, 136, 147, 152–153, 153–154, 161, 165, 169, 171–172, 185, 260, 306, 336, 375, 434
supply and demand model of commodities markets: assumptions of 152–154; basics of 171; equilibrium price and equilibrium quantity 154–157, *155*, *156*; pizza market 154; *see also* price and quantity, relationship between
supply curve 155, 161, 164–173, 165, 260, 460–461, 477, 479–480, 495; for chicken 168, *169*; equation to express 166–167; model of 165; quantity supplied and price influence on 165–166, *166*; slope of 167
supply curve, factors causing shifts in 167, 172; availability of inputs 168; ceteris paribus conditions of 168; changes in profitability 170; cost of inputs 168; number and size of suppliers 171; productivity of inputs 168; sellers' expectations 170; technology 168–170
supply curve of dollars 477
supply curve shifts 168, 265–266, 268, 284
supply model, aggregate 261, 281, 284, 287, 383, 400
supply shock recessions 249, 306, 394–395, 398, 400–401; economic impact of 400, *400*; factors causing 398; modern examples of 398, 400; supply-side policies to control 400–401
supply-side economics 15, 179, 185–186, 191–192, 193, 197, 199–201, 241, 311, 320–321, 328–330, 333, 336, 371, 375, 388, 400–401, 422, 434–435, 439, 444, 465, 490–491
supply-side tax cuts 117, 187
surplus 47, 51, 104, 107, 156, 171, 311, 333, 340, 488, 492; financial account 475, 484, 486, 497–498; of food 47, 51; of goods 99; product 47
surplus value 74–77; concept of 75; efforts to increase 75–76; as exploitative act 77
survival of individuals 43
sustainability 178, 198, 200–202, 217, 226, 432, 440–441, 443, 445; definition of 198; and economic growth 421, 440–443; environmental 198; financial

199, 200; and macroeconomics 198–200; and real GDP 217–218; social 199
sustainability policies 441
sustainable growth: "Green New Deal" 444; incentivizing pollution reductions for 443; investment in sustainable practices for 443–444
SUV companies, misleading advertising of 91
"sweatshop model" of foreign direct investment 430
Sweden 17–18, 126–127, 130–134, 179, 182, 220, 224–225, 238–239, 320, 323–324, 334, 337, 431–432, 435–436, 441, 503–504, 518; democratic socialism in 17; Global Innovation Index rankings of 431–432; initiative to attract high-wage industries 131–132; Keynesian stabilization policies 132; labor market policies of 132–133; patent filings per resident 132; "triple helix" economic development of 131
Switzerland 70, 126, 134, 148, 220, 225, 238–239, 320, 323, 338, 424, 431–432, 441, 515

T-account 356, *356*
Taiwan 141, 188, 338, 447, 454–456, 461, 486
tally sticks 350, *350*
tariffs 188, 190, 268, 299, 329, 339, 436, 448, 459–461, 460, *460*, 460–461, 465–467, 469–471, 491, 514
tax burden, sharing of 321
tax credits 429
tax cuts 242, 248, 320, 438; impact on aggregate demand 327; for laborers 435; to stimulate hiring 234; for U.S. corporations 186, 434–435
taxes on corporate investment 266, 267
tax multiplier 327
tax rate 16, 133, 187, 289, 291–292, 298–299, 301, 303, 306, 321–322
tax revenues: below government spending 5; reductions in 5, 6; sources for U.S. government 320
Taylor, Frederick 76
tech boom of 1990s 117, 190
technological assimilation and development 456

technological changes: changes in class structures with 74; and production function 427; shifts in PPC from 29–30, *30*
technological innovation, policies to stimulate 430–432
technology 9, 22, 25–26, 29–31, 46, 48–49, 51, 58, 73–74, 82, 86, 89, 134, 140, 153, 165, 168, 189, 252, 267–268, 275, 283, 299, 316, 324, 335, 337, 406, 416, 426–428, 430–431, 435–437, 444, 449–450, 454–457, 462, 465, 471, 505, 510–512; available to make product 168–170; clusters 431–432, 436; definition of 46; development 31, 46, 336, 428; development of 46; and export patterns 455–456; green 443–445; impact on costs of production 168–169; purchases 266, 267; reshaping economic systems 46, 73–74
temporary downturns 277, 278–279
textile (cloth manufacturing) sector 511
Thatcher, Margaret 3, 112, 187
theory of demand 157–159; consumer demand 157; price and quantity demanded, link between 157–158, *158*
Theory of Moral Sentiments, The (Smith) 58
theory of supply 164; price and quantity supplied, link between 165–167, *166*; supply in competitive market 164–165
Theory of the Leisure Class, The (Veblen) 88
Tiananmen Square protests of 1989 140
"tight" or "contractionary" or "hawkish" monetary policy 253
tourism 135
Township and Village Enterprises 139–140
Toyota 136
trade: agreements 420, 466–467, 470–472; benefits from 457; flows 463; free and fair 457; and industrial development 465; interdependence created by 458; international terms of 451–452; patterns 453, 461, 463–465, 508; policy 70, 448, 459, 463–464, 466; political economy views on 463–466; reason for 449; surpluses 53, 339, 420, 458, 461, 485–486, 488–490, 489; unions 81; wars 192, 470, 491, 498
trade deficits 337–339, 371, 378, 420, 458–459, 461–462, 464, 468, 475, 476, 484–486, 488, 490–492, 513; consequences and debate over 490–492;

root cause of 488; *vs.* trade surpluses 488; U.S. *486*, 486–487
trading bloc agreements: European Union 467–469; North American Free Trade Agreement 469–470; types of 467
trading partners 182, 337, 339, 429, 453, 461–462, 486, 488–489, 492, 495
tradition 48; and feudalism 50; role in traditional economy 45
traditional economies 44; allocation of resources in 45; definition of 45; and technologies 46; valuing productivity in 46
traditional kinship property systems 516–517
transactions 149–152, 150, 171, 353, 360–362, 366, 460, 484, 490; contract laws for 150; costs 151; definition of 146; demand 360; of Islamic banks 150; macroeconomic stability 150; supply and demand model 152; trust and 149–150
transatlantic slave trade 54
transfer payments 209, 214, 272, 289
transportation infrastructure 29, 151
Treasury Bills, nominal and real return on 246, *246*
"trickle-down economics" 186
triple helix approach to innovation 435–436
Triumph of Injustice, The (Saez and Gabriel) 321
Tropical Gangsters (Klitgaard) 148
Troubled Asset Relief Program (TARP) of 2008 413
Trump, Donald 118, 192, 329, 339, 379, 457, 470, 491
trust and contract laws 149–150
Turkey 199, 220, 239–240, 343, 504
Turkish lira, devaluation of 199
TVEs *see* Township and Village Enterprises

U.K. economy, radical restructuring of 187
UN *see* United Nations
underconsumption 397
underemployment 223, 236–238, 237–238, 256, 336
unemployed laborers 76
unemployment 1, 62, 64, 76, 94, 99–101, 103–104, 112–113, 117, 125, 132, 175, 177–178, 183, 185–188, 193, 196–197, 226, 229, 245, 247, 249, 251–258, 255–256, 265, 283, 313, 324, 328–330, 336, 342–343, 370, 375, 385–387, 389–392, 397, 402–403, 405, 435, 457, 492; benefits 109, 129, 197, 209, 232, 240–242, 289, 313, 328, 332, 341, 413; cyclical 234, *235*, 240, 255–256, 329; frictional 233–234; and GDP, relationship between 232; hidden 237; impact on community 231; impact on family 231; impact on individual 231; insurance 94, 97, 109–110, 181, 231, 240–241, 256, 316, 318, 320, 323, 328; in laissez-faire systems 230–231; macroeconomic costs of 231–232; as market failure 229, 231; natural rate of 234, *235*, 236, 254–256, 385–387; neoclassical theory for 99–100; policies to reduce 240–242, 256; policy solutions to problem of; seasonal 237; social safety net for mitigating 229; structural 234; and underemployment 237–238
unemployment rate 9, 24, 103, 135, 183, 196, 231–234, 236–238, 237, 240, 242, 254, 256, 314, 343, 382, 385–387, 415, 468; computation of 232; employment insecurity and 237–240; in France 135; official 238; realistic measure of 238; in recessions 234, *235*, 242; in U.S. 231–234, *233*, *235*
unemployment theory, nonaccelerating inflation rate of 376
unionization 115, 128
Union of Soviet Socialist Republics: collapse of 138; economy of 137; system of central planning 114, 137
unions 50, 81, 103, 110, 115, 182, 386, 398, 429, 439
United Nations: Human Development Index *126*, 126–127, 175, 503–505, *504*, *505*; Millennium Development Goals 516; World Happiness Index 225, *225*
United States *see* U.S.
Universal Commercial Code 150
unpaid household work and real GDP 215
unregulated market capitalism 8, 15, 17, 41, 68
unregulated markets 180
unregulated trade 64, 186–189, 329, 339, 371, 419, 453, 457–458, 464–466,

470–472; debate over 448; effective aggregate demand and 464; limitations of 448; mainstream economists' support of 448, 449
unregulated trade policies 463–464
unregulated *vs.* managed financial capital flows 497–498
unsavory behavior, for profit motive 12
"unwinding" *see* quantitative tightening
uprisings against working conditions 72
urbanization 51
U.S. 344; class in 84–85; consumption possibilities curve for 452, *452*; corporate interests, in foreign countries 36; current account *485*; current account deficit 484–486, *487*; decline in real GDP growth of 193, *194*; defense spending 32; educational spending as percentage of GDP 433–434; employment as percentage of total employment 319, *319*; ethnicity in 84–85; financial account surplus 486, *487*; GDP deflator 207, *208*; gender in 84–85; Global Innovation Index rankings of 432; government sector size 17, *18*; industrial revolution 89; infant industry promotion strategies 70; macroeconomic variables 179; manufacturing jobs 188; mixed economy of 118–120, 179; national debt of 187; nominal GDP for 206–207, *208*, 211, *212*; nominal wages and real wages in 245, *245*; OECD Better Life Index for 220–221, *221*; potential real GDP of 193, 195, *195*; poverty rate of 129; production possibilities curve for *25*, 25–26, *26*; race in 84–85; real disposable income and real consumption 288, *289*; real GDP of 5, *5*, 193, 195, *195*, 206–207, *208*; real GDP per capita growth 183; rise of global competitors to 188–190; "rust belt" of 34, 188; social unrest in 184; spending and taxation policy 314; state and local government spending 318; stimulus programs in COVID-19 recession 6, 118, 313–314, 325, 333, 342–344, 383, 415; tax code 321; trading partners *461*, 461–463; unemployment benefits 242; unemployment rate 9, 24, 103, 135, 183, 196, 231–234, 236–238, 240, 242, 254, 343, 382, 385–387, 415, 468; World Happiness Index ranking of 225, *225*; World War II military spending 111; *see also* budget deficits

U.S. Air Force, purchase of B-2 stealth bombers 24, 35–36
U.S. banking system *see* banking system
U.S. Constitution: pro-business legal system 128; ratification of 16th Amendment to 377
U.S. dollar 352; appreciation of 270, *270*; based on "gold standard" 352; creating demand for 377; currencies pegged to 494; exchange rate of 477; fluctuations in price of one euro in *493*; foreign exchange market for 477–478, *478*; strength of 251; as world's reserve currency 377–378
U.S. economic growth 31; from 1948 to 1973 115–116, 182–184; in 1980s 187; during "capital–labor accord" era 115–116; during global capitalism era 116; macroeconomic variables 183, *183*
U.S. economy: from 2008 to 2015 342; amount of money in 355, *355*; economic instability in 118, *119*; growth-stimulating policies 181; income inequality problem for 92–93; in late 1990s 187; manufacturing boom in 92–93; OPEC's embargo impact on 116, 185; recessions experienced by 92; recovery from Great Recession 197; Roaring Twenties of 92; stagflation of 1970s 185, 186; supply-side approach 185–186; supply-side economic policy 185–186, 191; tax cuts for stimulating 186, 187
U.S. Fed 363, 391; autonomy of 378; chair of 378; contractionary monetary policy 381; creation of 93; discount rate 380; federal funds rate 380–381; macroeconomic goals of 379; open market operations 379–380; powers of 186; quantitative easing 381–383, *382*; quantitative tightening 382; required reserve ratio 381; structure of 378
U.S. federal government spending: categories and priorities of 316, *316*; defense spending 318; as percentage of GDP 318, *319*
U.S. financial markets, regulatory landscape of 376–379

U.S. fiscal policy: automatic stabilizers 323–324; characteristics of 321; discretionary 324; tax policy 321–322, *322*; *see also* fiscal policy; U.S. federal government spending
USMCA *see* U.S.-Mexico-Canada Agreement
U.S.-Mexico-Canada Agreement 470–471
U.S. Midwest 188
U.S. military: allocation of resource for B-2 bombers 36; supporting dominant class of corporates 36
U.S. model of market-dominated economies 127–130, 141, 179; early protectionism 128; globalization 128; innovation system 128–129; limited regulations 129; macroeconomic stabilization policy 130; melting pot of immigrants 127–128; multinational corporations 128; pro-business legal system 128; Protestant work ethic 127; ready access to productive resources 127; small welfare state 129
U.S. public debt 111; held by public 332–333; as percentage of GDP 333
U.S.S.R. *see* Union of Soviet Socialist Republics
U.S. Steel 83, 114
U.S. trade deficits: high foreign savings 489, *489*; low U.S. national savings 488–489; U.S. assets and currency demand 489–490
U.S. unemployment rate 24
utility, concept of 157

value added 212, *212*, 214
Veblen, Thorstein 3, 16, 33–34, 41–42, 65, 68–69, 71, 73, 75, 77, 79, 81–83, 82, 85, 91–93, 95–97, 122, 407; on conspicuous consumption 88–89; on culture 86–87; on emulation 87–88; evolutionary approach to economy 85–86, 95; on institutions 86
vested interests 91
Vietnam 141, 182, 189, 318, 421, 424, 461, 485–486, 504
Volcker, Paul 186, 400

wage-price spirals 250, 251
wages 13, 50, 55–56, 61–63, 70–72, 75–77, 81, 90, 98–100, 103–104, 115, 117–118, 134, 139–140, 172, 181, 182, 187, 189, 193, 200–201, 209, 211–212, 214–215, 226, 234, 242, 245, 247–251, 254–255, 259, 264–265, 268, 270, 277–280, 303, 317, 328, 339, 370–371, 387, 398, 406, 429–430, 464, 469–470; declines 103–104, 181; efforts to reduce 76; and employment, link between 13; and incomes, policies to increase 429; mercantilist policies suppressing 56; and price controls 251; and prices in recessions 103–104, 181; in rapid growth 254; shift in AD and AS with changes in 270; and unemployment, link between 76
wage squeeze 397
wage subsidies 60–61
Walmart 11–12, 77, 147, 164
"War on Poverty" 116
Watt, James 56
wealth 266; and consumer demand, link between *160*, 160–161; determinants of 56–57
Wealth of Nations, The (Smith) 56, 59
wealth tax 133, 148
Weisskopf, Tom 398
welfare and unemployment benefits 129
welfare state 112, 129
well-being of human 41, 82, 88, 127, 178, 200, 215, 217–227, 365, 441, 464, 469, 516
western-style property rights 517
white landowners 84
wholesale markets 147
women 35, 46, 50, 71, 76, 83, 85, 88, 116, 131, 149, 215–216, 233, 238, 240, 439, 501, 516–517; in factories 85; fashions 88; and minorities, affirmative action laws for 116; paid and unpaid work of 215; property rights 149; traditional kinship property systems and 517
wool industry 69–70
worker-owned firm 148
workers 5, 8, 13, 16–17, 35, 41, 54–58, 60–62, 90, 92–96, 99–100, 103–106, 109–110, 113, 115–118, 120, 128, 130–136, 138–140, 148–152, 156, 161, 170, 177, 181–182, 185–188, 191, 193, 195, 197–198, 209–210, 212, 215, 217, 231, 233–234, 236–238, 240–242, 245, 247–251, 254–257, 279–280, 284, 317, 328–330, 343, 348, 365, 370–371, 383,

386–387, 397–398, 404, 406, 415–417, 427–429, 434, 436, 439, 456–458, 463–464, 466–472, 490–491, 508, 510, 518; changes to economy for benefit of 93; chronic surplus of 76; control over workplaces 138; deciding to change jobs 233; discouraged 237; factors affecting productivity of 439; forced into retirement 237; hourly compensation costs in manufacturing 134, *134*; marginalized 237; permanent displacement of 234; and property rights 148
workers' conditions 70–72, 95; lack of bargaining power 70; low wages 71–72; and marginal productivity theory of distribution 99; reforms for 71; uprisings prompted by 72; work characteristics 70–71
work hours 65, 68, 76–77, 83, 135, 221
workhouses 61, *61*
work-life balance 126, 204, 218, 220–221, 225
workmanship, instinct of 87
Work Progress Administration 241
Works Progress Administration 110
work week 135
World Bank 149, 377, 466–467, 497, 501, 513–516, 518–521
World Trade Organization 466–467, 470–472
World War I, harsh conditions imposed on Germany after 102
WPA *see* Work Progress Administration
WTO *see* World Trade Organization

Yellen, Janet 413
yen, tools to alter supply or demand of 494–496
yield curve 414
Yugoslavia 138
Yunus, Muhammad 519

Zimbabwe 250, 504
Zucman, Gabriel 321